ASHGATE STUDIES IN MEDIEVAL PHILOSOPHY

Series Editors

John Marenbon, Trinity College, Cambridge, UK
Scott MacDonald, Cornell University, USA
Christopher J. Martin, University of Auckland, New Zealand
Simo Knuuttila, Academy of Finland and the University of Helsinki, Finland

The study of medieval philosophy is flourishing as never before. Historically precise and philosophically informed research is opening up this large but still relatively unknown part of philosophy's past, revealing – in many cases for the first time – the nature of medieval thinkers' arguments and the significance of their philosophical achievements. *Ashgate Studies in Medieval Philosophy* presents some of the best of this new work, both from established figures and younger scholars. Chronologically, the series stretches from *c.*600 to *c.*1500 and forward to the scholastic philosophers of 16th and early 17th-century Spain and Portugal. The series encompasses both the Western Latin tradition, and the Byzantine, Jewish and Islamic traditions. Authors all share a commitment both to historical accuracy and to careful analysis of arguments of a kind which makes them comprehensible to modern readers, especially those with philosophical interests.

THEOLOGY AT PARIS, 1316–1345

Chris Schabel

Chris Schabel presents a detailed analysis of the radical solution given by the Franciscan Peter Auriol to the problem of reconciling divine foreknowledge with the contingency of the future, and of contemporary reactions to it. Auriol's solution appeared to many of his contemporaries to deny God's knowledge of the future altogether, and so it provoked intense and long-lasting controversy; Schabel is the first to examine in detail the philosophical and theological background to Auriol's discussion, and to provide a full analysis of Auriol's own writings on the question and the immediate reactions to them.

This book sheds new light both on one of the central philosophical debates of the Middle Ages, and on theology and philosophy at the University of Paris in the first half of the 14th century, a period of Parisian intellectual life which has been largely neglected until now.

Theology at Paris 1316–1345

Pope Alexander V (Peter of Candia), and Peter Auriol: detail from 15th-century Flemish tapestry "The Franciscan Tree," commissioned by Pope Sixtus IV (Francesco della Rovere), and now in the Tesoro in Assisi.

Theology at Paris, 1316–1345

Peter Auriol and the problem of divine foreknowledge and future contingents

Chris Schabel

Ashgate

Aldershot • Burlington USA • Singapore • Sydney

Published by

Ashgate Publishing Limited
Gower House, Croft Road
Aldershot
Hants GU11 3HR
England

Ashgate Publishing Company
Old Post Road
Brookfield
Vermont 05401–5600
USA

Ashgate website: http://www.ashgate.com

British Library Cataloguing-in-Publication Data
Schabel, Chris.
   Theology at Paris, 1316–1345: Peter Auriol and the Problem
   of Divine Foreknowledge and Future Contingents. – (Ashgate
   Studies in Medieval Philosophy).
   1. Auriol, Peter. 2. Theology–History–Middle Ages,
   600–1500.
   I. Title.
   230'.09023

US Library of Congress Card Number: 00–108822

ISBN 0 7546 0204 4

This book is printed on acid free paper

Printed and bound by Athenaeum Press, Ltd.,
Gateshead, Tyne & Wear.

Contents

Preface

The path that this present study has taken has been as roundabout as the historiographical path, described below in the introduction, that led to the serious lacuna that this book attempts to fill. In the spring of 1989, at the University of Iowa, Katherine Tachau offered a seminar on divine power in the fourteenth century for which students had, among other things, the task of editing or translating relevant texts. Among those chosen were parts of the *Sentences* commentaries of Gregory of Rimini, Andreas of Novocastro, Robert Holcot, and James of Eltville.[1] I edited some questions from John Hiltalingen of Basel, including one on future contingents, in which Hiltalingen mentions no less then eight ways to solve the problem of foreknowledge and future contingents, describing the ideas of a dozen thinkers, mostly fellow Augustinians, from the thirteenth and fourteenth centuries, not including Auriol. Instead, Hiltalingen links Auriol off-handedly to Aristotle in the principal arguments *ad oppositum*, tacitly but erroneously assuming that Auriol denied foreknowledge. I began an edition of book I of Hiltalingen's *Sentences* commentary, but after transcribing about 250 pages I found that Trapp and Marcolino had already begun the project. Had this not been the case, the present study would not exist.[2]

At this point, like Hiltalingen, I took little notice of Auriol, but decided to translate the pertinent questions of Hiltalingen's Augustinian predecessors at Paris Thomas of Strasbourg, Rimini, Alphonsus Vargas of Toledo, and Hugolino of Orvieto, as part of the preparation for my comprehensive examination in medieval philosophy with Scott MacDonald, which took place in the spring of 1991.[3] One thing that struck me almost immediately was that Rimini's (and

---

[1]   Some of the fruits of this seminar have been published. See James Halverson, "Franciscan Theology and Predestinarian Pluralism in Late-Medieval Thought," *Speculum* 70.1 (January 1995), pp. 1–26, and Russell L. Friedman, "Andreas de Novo Castro (fl. 1358) on Divine Omnipotence and the Nature of the Past: I *Sentences*, Distinction Forty-Five, Question Six," CIMAGL 64 (1994), pp. 101–50.

[2]   Nevertheless, I included an edition of Hiltalingen's question on future contingents in my dissertation, "The Quarrel with Auriol: Peter Auriol's Role in the Late-Medieval Debate over Divine Foreknowledge and Future Contingents, 1315–1475" (PhD Dissertation, University of Iowa 1994), pp. 797–807. Marcolino stated, in a letter to me dated 7 August 1991, that he and Trapp had been working on Hiltalingen's *Opera Omnia* (a project Trapp had announced in the 1950s), and at that point the manuscripts had been transcribed and most of the citations had been tracked down. This last task is quite a feat, because no one in the Middle Ages has more citations than Hiltalingen.

[3]   The Rimini translation is the basis for part of *Modality, Order, and Transcendence: Gregory of Rimini on God's Knowledge, Power, and Will. An English Translation of His Lectures on the Sentences, Book I, dist. 35–48*, trans. Russell Friedman and Chris Schabel (New Haven, forthcoming). The Vargas, Orvieto, and Hiltalingen translations will be included in the projected Russell Friedman and Chris Schabel trans, *A Future Contingents Reader. A Late-Medieval Debate in Translation*.

Vargas's to a lesser extent) main opponent in his lengthy treatment of fore-knowledge and future contingents was Peter Auriol. Like Hiltalingen, Rimini gives the reader the impression that Auriol simply denied foreknowledge in denying determinate truth in future contingent propositions, and this squared well with what I knew of the secondary literature. I was not all that interested in what seemed to be a theological dead end.

Therefore, when Professor Tachau offered a seminar on Peter Auriol in the spring of 1991, and several of us 'signed on' with Lauge Nielsen to begin the critical edition of Auriol's theological works, it was natural that I start with Auriol's treatment of future contingents, but I did not expect to find a doctrine remotely like an 'orthodox' position affirming any divine knowledge of the future. I was taken by surprise when I found that Auriol's discussion of propositions was only a small part of a fully articulated system of divine foreknowledge, which most certainly did *not* deny omniscience. It was at this point that I decided to make Peter Auriol's treatment of the subject and its reception the subject of my dissertation. I edited distinctions 38 and 39 of Auriol's *Scriptum in Primum Sententiarum*, and then headed to Cyprus for a stimulating three-semester stint at a secondary school, which left very little time for research. Happily, the University of Iowa awarded me a dissertation fellowship for the 1993–94 academic year.

Collecting materials on the background to Auriol's doctrine was not so difficult, although it will take a few years before we have a clear picture of those from the early fourteenth century who contributed in small but positive ways to Auriol's system. Looking for his impact was another matter. When I discovered that a manuscript that Tachau had found in the Vatican contained previously unedited and even unknown texts by Peter de Rivo, who defended Auriol's opinion during the quarrel at the University of Louvain in the late fifteenth century, I decided to edit those texts and study the quarrel anew. The task now became to link Auriol and Rivo, a task Leon Baudry had already suggested.[4]

I collected all of the treatments of the problem I could find from scholars active in the century and a half between Auriol and Rivo. At first the results were confusing. I discovered that although several Parisian theologians after 1350 discussed Auriol's opinion at some length, at Oxford and Paris in the quarter century after Auriol's lectures on the *Sentences* there just was not that strong a reaction. I therefore concluded prematurely that Rimini spent so much time on Auriol simply because Auriol had not been refuted yet. Up until that point, of works produced in Paris in that period, I had examined the printed editions of Francis of Meyronnes, John Baconthorpe, Peter of Navarre, Gerard of Siena, Thomas of Strasbourg, and Peter of Aquila, and manuscripts of Aufredo Gonteri Brito and, in a very poor microfilm, Michael of Massa. Most of them devoted some but by no means all of their efforts to refuting Auriol. This was quite accidental, however. For one thing, Gonteri read *secundum* Henry of Harclay, who read before Auriol, and therefore should not have been expected

---

⁴   See the Introduction and Epilogue for more details on the quarrel.

to deal with Auriol at length. Moreover, I now think Navarre lectured away from Paris.

Then I went to Italy in the spring of 1994. Looking at manuscripts in the Vatican, Florence, and Bologna I found that Francis of Marchia, Landulph Caracciolo, Michael of Massa, Nicholas Bonet, and the anonymous author of ms. Vienna ÖNB Palat. lat. 1439 focussed almost all of their attention on Auriol, and I later discovered that Gerard Odonis and William of Rubio were also heavily influenced by Auriol. Thus what is true for the field as a whole is true for the individual: if one does not look, one does not find.

I defended the dissertation in August 1994. In the words of a French colleague the work was "un travail colossal," in the value-neutral sense, "qu'il faudra assez vite publier," but in "une forme un peu remanié." Thus the time since then has been spent in correction, revision, and the publication of supporting texts. Progress was rather slow during yet another year at the secondary school level, but since 1995 the University of Cyprus has offered as much support for my research as anyone could ask. With its help, almost all of the 400 pages of preliminary editions and mere transcriptions of texts in volume two of my dissertation, in addition to some others, have been published as critical editions.

Years ago, in my application for some fellowship or other, Professor Tachau, characteristically "seeing the future clearly," had me write that my scholarly vocation was to help investigate and perhaps rediscover the vitality of the University of Paris in the first half of the fourteenth century. I promptly forgot that this was my role, but as it turns out this book is in fact primarily a testimony to an interesting, energetic, and neglected era in Parisian thought.

Such a twisted path has left me in the debt of a great many people, mostly in small ways, but I must single out four individuals and two institutions that I consider *causae sine quibus non* for this book: Russell Friedman; my professors, Katherine Tachau and Scott MacDonald, in the early stages; Lauge Nielsen in the later stages; and the Universities of Iowa and Cyprus. For assistance with some of the texts that have been published, I thank Mario Bertagna, Francesco Del Punta, William Duba, Stephen Dumont, Sten Ebbesen, Jean-François Genest, Zenon Kaluza, Roberto Lambertini, Concetta Luna, Fritz Saaby Pedersen, Paul Vincent Spade, and Giorgio Pini. For checking a manuscript in the Vatican, I thank Kurt Boughan. Robert Andrews, Stephen Brown, Miguel Candel, William Courtenay, Elzbieta Jung-Palczewska, Roberto Plevano, Thomas Prügl, Michael Shank, and Cecilia Trifogli very kindly provided me with microfilms or photocopies of manuscripts. Girard Etzkorn allowed me to use his forthcoming edition of Walter Chatton's *Reportatio in primum* (even though it makes my own edition of Chatton's d. 38 look bad) and his unpublished edition of Chatton's *Quodlibet* (on the condition that I finish it up and publish it!). The following people sent me other materials: Hester Gelber, James Halverson, Maarten Hoenen, John Monfasani, and Marco Rossini. I wish to thank Paul Self for his hospitality. My partner in the study of medieval Cyprus, Nicholas Coureas, connected me with Ashgate and John Smedley. My series

editor, John Marenbon, gave me many valuable comments, especially on philosophical matters, as did an anonymous reader. In the final stages, I relied on
William Duba's comments, proofreading, and computer expertise. Of course,
my colleagues are in no way responsible for whatever problems remain in my
presentation.

The research in the book is based mainly on manuscripts. The following libraries, with great courtesy, gave me direct access to manuscripts: University
of Chicago Library, the Biblioteca Apostolica Vaticana, the Biblioteca Angelica in Rome, the Carmelite Archives in Rome, the Biblioteca nazionale
Marciana in Venice, the Biblioteca Universitaria in Bologna, the library of the
Collegio di Spagna in Bologna, the Biblioteca nazionale centrale in Florence,
the Biblioteca Antoniana in Padua, and the Österreichische Nationalbibliothek
in Vienna. I thank all the libraries mentioned in the Index of Manuscripts for
supplying me with microfilms and/or photocopies of manuscripts or incunab-
ula. The Hill Monastic Manuscript Library, truly an American treasure, gave
me access to microfilms of manuscripts held in libraries in Erfurt, Admont,
Innsbruck, Klosterneuberg, Melk, Pamplona, Tortosa, and Barcelona (Archivo
de la Catedral). The Institut de Recherche et d'Histoire des Textes provided
copies of manuscripts from the Bibliothèques municipales of Dole, Saint-
Omer, and Troyes. The Grabmann Institute in Munich sent photocopies of a
manuscript in Valencia, Biblioteca del Cabildo. I also thank at the University
of Iowa Libraries Chris Africa, Pam Barta, and Joel; the University of Cyprus
Library; and Mary Kite of the University of Missouri Microfilm Service.

All of my family contributed to this effort as well: Alexandra, Brad, Bryan,
Dora, Elizabeth, Frank, and Zeno Schabel.

Nicosia   CHRIS SCHABEL
April 2000

Abbreviations

AHDLMA	*Archives d'histoire doctrinale et littéraire du moyen âge*
BN	Bibliothèque nationale, Biblioteca nazionale
CHLMP	*Cambridge History of Later Medieval Philosophy*, eds. Norman Kretzmann, Anthony Kenny, and Jan Pinborg (Cambridge 1992)
CIMAGL	*Cahiers de l'institut du moyen âge grec et latin*
DSTFM	*Documenti e Studi sulla tradizione filosofica medievale*
DTC	*Dictionnaire de théologie Catholique*
FcS	*Franciscan Studies*
FzS	*Franziskanische Studien*
MPP	*Medievalia philosophica Polonorum*
ÖNB	Wien, Österreichische Nationalbibliothek Palat. lat.
PL	*Patrologiae cursus completus, series Latina*, compiled by J.P. Migne (Paris 1844–64)
RTAM	*Récherches de théologie ancienne et médiévale*
Sent.	*Sententiarum*

Introduction

Western culture has been obsessed with foreknowledge since its beginnings. Already in Homer omens, fate, and the prescient gods play a dominant role, and we can trace this tradition in Western literature through Sophocles to Beowulf to Dante and up to today's authors. Foreshadowing and foreboding are omnipresent even in contemporary popular culture; everywhere we find astrological columns seeking to foresee and foretell the future, and clairvoyants and prognosticators selling their predictions and prophecies even to American presidents. The richness of our vocabulary surrounding precognition is itself an indication of this focus on knowing the future. In an overwhelmingly monotheistic society such as ours, however, this presents a problem.

The problem of divine foreknowledge and future contingents can be put rather simply: how can God know the future without this entailing that the future come about necessarily? More specifically with respect to the main source of contingency, that is, human freedom, how can God know what we shall do in the future, without thereby eliminating our freedom with respect to that same future? That a perfect God should be omniscient and foreknowing was obvious to medieval Christian theologians. It was also usually accepted that God was just and humans free, so that God justly damned those who made poor use of their freedom. These tenets were and are fundamental to Christian doctrine. Reconciling them, however, was a source of disagreement and controversy, and remains so to this day.[1]

The problem also exemplifies the stimulating nature of the study of medieval theology. Medieval theologians had to reconcile many apparent contradictions in order to preserve the tenets of their faith and at the same time satisfy their intellectual demand that their faith be logically coherent. Logic is one tool that medieval thinkers used to solve their theological dilemmas, and it is because of particularly thorny problems that these men further developed logic in the Middle Ages. Even those today who profess to be skeptics philosophically, and who will deny the possibility of attaining any absolutely certain knowledge, can appreciate the efforts of medieval thinkers. Christian scholastics often had the task of taking what was already accepted as 'given' by the

---

[1] Thus there is a huge amount of recent philosophical literature on the problem, usually connected to the medieval or sixteenth-century debate. See for example Calvin Normore, "Divine Omniscience, Omnipotence and Future Contingents: An Overview," in Tamar Rudavsky, ed., *Divine Omniscience and Omnipotence in Medieval Philosophy. Islamic, Jewish, and Christian Perspectives* (Dordrecht 1985), pp. 3–22; the collection of essays *God, Foreknowledge, and Freedom*, ed. John Martin Fischer (Stanford 1989); William Lane Craig, *Divine Foreknowledge and Human Freedom* (Leiden 1991); Linda Trinkaus Zagzebski, *The Dilemma of Freedom and Foreknowledge* (New York–Oxford 1991); and various articles by Richard Gaskin, e.g. "Fatalism, Foreknowledge and the Reality of the Future," *The Modern Schoolman* 71 (Jan. 1994), pp. 83–113.

Bible and Church tradition, and showing how these 'data' fit together logically. On a problem such as the Trinity, whose points of debate were seemingly inexhaustible, theologians used the logical devices which Aristotle and Boethius, primarily, had left them, and which they themselves developed.

The problem of divine foreknowledge and future contingency was as philosophically fruitful as that of the Trinity, and of wider concern. Discussion of the latter problem was confined to Christians, since only they believed in the Trinity. By contrast, divine foreknowledge and future contingents raised some problems for pagan Neo-Platonists, and also Muslims and Jews who, like the Christians, had received revelations in their scripture which led in one way or another to precisely the same problem.[2] This fact emphasizes the ubiquity of the difficulty in Western and Mediterranean society, at least in the Middle Ages. In the West, the thorny issue led to intense discussion concerning, as we shall see, truth, language, propositions, logic, human freedom, reasons for living, and primary principles.

Aristotle treated the logical issues posed by future contingent propositions in his *Peri Hermeneias*, and the problem also worried other pagans in antiquity. The major Christian philosophers of Late Antiquity and the early Middle Ages, such as Augustine, Boethius, and Anselm, had the added element of divine foreknowledge to contend with, and they usually reconciled foreknowledge and future contingency by making some use of the Neo-Platonic notion of God's eternity. Peter Lombard's inclusion of the problem in his *Sentences* assured that theologians lecturing at the new universities, such as Thomas Aquinas and John Duns Scotus, joined in an ongoing conversation and debate on the topic. This debate reached one of its historical peaks in the later Middle Ages, particularly in the first half of the fourteenth century at the Universities of Paris and Oxford.

One of the central figures in this controversy was the Franciscan Peter Auriol. Born in Southern France, near Cahors, in about 1280, he studied in Paris before lecturing on the *Sentences* at the Franciscan *studia* in Bologna and Toulouse from 1312 to 1316. He then went back to lecture on Lombard's text at Paris, the leading medieval university for the study of the most important medieval subject, theology. With the aid of his patron Pope John XXII, Auriol become Master of Theology in 1318, and remained at Paris as regent master until 1320. He rapidly rose in the Franciscan order and the ecclesiastical hierarchy, and Pope John consecrated him archbishop of Aix-en-Provence in 1321. John even lent him money to get him started in his new position. Auriol died soon after, however, probably on 10 January 1322.[3]

---

[2]   See e.g. Richard Sorabji, *Time, Creation, and the Continuum* (Ithaca, NY 1983), on Neo-Platonic ideas, and Rudavsky, ed., *Divine Omniscience*, for several chapters on Islamic and Jewish opinions on the subject in the Middle Ages, showing the universal importance of the issue to peoples of the book.

[3]   Katherine Tachau is preparing a new and more complete biography of Auriol, but for now we shall have to make do with N. Valois, "Pierre Auriol," *Histoire littéraire de la France* XXXIII (Paris 1908), pp. 479–527, and A. Teetaert, "Pierre d'Auriole," DTC XII 2 (Paris 1935),

Although few scholars have recognized it until recently, Auriol left his intellectual mark on most topics in theology,[4] but the problem of foreknowledge and future contingents was one issue to which his name was especially attached for the remainder of the Middle Ages. As we shall see, almost all theologians lecturing at Paris in the quarter century after Auriol's tenure there concentrated their discussion of the problem on Auriol's unique treatment, in which, superficially, Auriol appeared to deny divine foreknowledge altogether, and to overthrow basic logical principles in the process by saying that future contingent propositions are neither true nor false, but rather neutral.

Auriol's solution to the problem was much more complex than a simple denial of truth and falsity in propositions about future contingents, however. In logic, Auriol re-evaluated such terms as 'necessity', 'immutability', and 'contingency', and, following Aristotle, introduced what is somewhat anachronistically described as a 'three-valued logic'. Theologically, he proposed a radical solution to a problem still of interest to philosophers and theologians, involving God's relationship to time and eternity, His attributes, human freedom, and predestination. Many of the lengthy discussions of future contingents in the fourteenth and fifteenth centuries involved Auriol's views — usually their refutation. In 1465 an angry dispute erupted at the University of Louvain over Auriol's position, which led to Pope Sixtus IV's condemnation of Auriol's ideas as expressed by his defender, Peter de Rivo, in 1474. Nevertheless, the fact that Auriol's *Sentences* commentary was printed around 1600 speaks to his continued prominence afterwards. Without Peter Auriol, the problem would have had less urgency for the most important thinkers of the Late Middle Ages, such as Gregory of Rimini.

The philosophical problem has been a popular subject in history and philosophy for some decades, but the story of Peter Auriol's position and role in the Parisian debate over foreknowledge and future contingents has not really been told comprehensively and in any detail until now. Why is there such an

---

cols. 1810–81, modified by Eligius M. Buytaert's introduction to his edition, *Peter Aureoli Scriptum Super Primum Sententiarum*, vol. 1 (St. Bonaventure, NY 1952), pp. vii–xxi.

[4]   Some earlier monographs focussing on Auriol include Raymond Dreiling, *Der Konzeptualismus in der Universalienlehre des Franziskanererzbischofs Petrus Aureoli (Pierre d'Auriole). Nebst biographisch-biblographischer Einleitung* (Münster 1913); Paul Vignaux, *Justification et prédestination au XIVe siècle: Duns Scot, Pierre d'Auriole, Guillaume d'Occam, Grégoire de Rimini* (Paris 1934), especially chapter 2, "Pierre d'Auriole critique de Duns Scot," pp. 43–95, and chapter 3, "Guillaume d'Occam critique de Pierre d'Auriole," pp. 97–140; Rainulf Schmücker, *Propositio per se nota, Gottesbeweis und ihr Verhältnis nach Petrus Aureoli* (Werl in Westfallia 1941); Leo Rosato, *Doctrina de Immaculata B.V.M. Conceptione secundum Petrum Aureoli* (Rome 1959); Werner Dettloff, *Die Entwicklung der Akzeptations-und Verdienstlehre von Duns Scotus bis Luther, mit besonderer Berücksichtigung der Franziskanertheologen* (Münster 1963), especially pp. 22–94; and Severin Rudolf Streuer, *Die theologische Einleitungslehre des Petrus Aureoli. Auf Grund seines Scriptum super Primum Sententiarum und ihre theologiegeschichtliche Einordnung* (Werl in Westfallia 1968). In addition, between 1956 and 1964 no less than eight MA and PhD theses on Auriol were defended, most notably that of Stephen F. Brown, "The Unity of the Concept of Being in Peter Aureoli's 'Scriptum' and 'Commentarium.' With a Critical Edition of the 'Commentarium'," 2 vols. (PhD Dissertation, Université catholique de Louvain 1964). Most recent work has come in the last decade or so; see chapter 3.

important lacuna? It is simply the result of a great series of general and specific accidents in the historiographical tradition. Generally, after a promising start in the works of Pierre Duhem and also Anneliese Maier, for example, the study of the University of Paris in the decades between Auriol and Gregory of Rimini (fl. 1343) has been overshadowed by our investigations of the intellectual achievements at Oxford during the same period. As Katherine Tachau points out, this has had the further result of robbing Auriol of his central role in later-medieval thought.[5] Specifically, historians have placed much more emphasis on the Oxford discussion of foreknowledge and future contingents than on the Parisian debate, so that in this context Auriol's position has been distorted and his significance underestimated.

Unlike some medieval theologians, however, medieval intellectual historians, as a group and as individuals, work neither systematically nor exhaustively. Like the development of some tropical coastline for tourism, the creation of the intellectual history of the Middle Ages has been uneven. The analogy in fact can be taken further: just as one hotel in one bay begets a restaurant, then a miniature golf course, then a disco, and so on in the same locale, a study on one figure in intellectual history begets an edition, a translation, a purely philosophical analysis, etc., of that very figure. While the next bay along the coast may preserve its pristine beaches and cliffs for many decades, regardless of their relative beauty, so also the other scholars, questions, and periods in intellectual history may receive little or no treatment.

Thus Auriol and Paris have received less attention than they should. In the context of future contingents, this story is easy to describe, as is the equally accidental scenario of the origin and development of the present study (see the Preface), which seeks to develop at least one part of that neglected shoreline that is the University of Paris from 1318 to 1343. Already in 1728, Du Plessis d'Argentré published fifty-two columns concerning the now-famous quarrel over future contingents at the University of Louvain in the later fifteenth century — mostly primary sources — but unfortunately they contain only three mentions of Auriol's name. The first accident in the modern historiography surrounding Auriol's opinion came when two articles of documents and commentary concerning the Louvain dispute were published by Paul Frédericq and Jacques Laminne in 1905 and 1906. Despite the fact that the entire quarrel in Louvain between 1465 and 1475 revolved around Peter de Rivo's explicit revival of Peter Auriol's position, in these articles totaling 134 pages only one mention is made of Auriol, and that in a Latin text![6]

---

[5]   See Katherine H. Tachau, *Vision and Certitude in the Age of Ockham: Optics, Epistemology, and the Foundations of Semantics, 1250–1345* (Leiden 1988), p. 315.

[6]   See Charles Du Plessis d'Argentré, *Collectio Judiciorum de Novis Erroribus* vol. 1, part 2 (Paris 1728; reprint Brussels 1963), pp. 258b–284a (Auriol citations on pp. 260b and 271b); Paul Frédericq, "L'hérésie à Louvain vers 1470," *Bulletin de la classe des Lettres et de la classe des Beaux-Arts* (Académie royale de Belgique, Brussels 1905), pp. 11–77 (for the Auriol citation in a document, see p. 51); and Jacques Laminne, "La controverse sur les futurs contingens à l'Université de Louvain au XVe siècle," (*Bulletin*, 1906), pp. 372–438.

Not surprisingly, then, the quarrel was not immediately linked to Auriol or fourteenth-century theology. In 1925, Cardinal Franz Ehrle cited in his book on Peter of Candia's *Sentences* commentary a passage in which Candia says, as in several other contexts, that he will treat the views of Peter Auriol, John of Ripa, and John Duns Scotus on the subject of future contingents. Although Ehrle discussed Peter de Rivo's situation at Louvain in several places, going so far as to publish a document from the quarrel, only once did he link Rivo's name with Auriol's, merely citing the instances in Du Plessis d'Argentré's and Frédericq's texts, without any doctrinal discussion.[7] Clearly Ehrle knew little about Rivo or Auriol on the subject, and in fact led one to believe that there was nothing of interest there, even though Candia himself devoted some 700 lines of text merely to describing Auriol's position.

When Cardinal Ehrle suggested to Hermann Schwamm that the latter do a study of Ripa's treatment of the subject, it only served to obscure Auriol's role even more. In Schwamm's study of Ripa of 1930, he again quoted Candia's statement that he intended to discuss Auriol, Ripa, and Scotus, and later even claimed that "Peter of Candia assigns equal honor only to the opinions of Peter Auriol and of Scotus."[8] Yet he went no further with Auriol in his analysis of Ripa, for unlike previous Parisian theologians, Ripa does not treat Auriol, since Ripa wrote after the initial fervor over Auriol had subsided, and after the proliferation of new sub-issues following the absorption of English trends by Rimini.

Although looking back there are hints that Schwamm knew Auriol's position, these hints would not have helped Schwamm's readers at the time. When in 1934 Schwamm went on to study the reception of Scotus's ideas on the subject, he treated Auriol only in relation to Scotus, citing Auriol's attacks throughout distinctions 38 and 39 of his *Scriptum in Primum Librum Sententiarum*. In his twelve-page treatment of Auriol vs. Scotus, Schwamm devoted only a one-sentence quotation to Auriol's positive position, in this case his view on future contingent propositions. Yet when Schwamm discussed later figures, he betrayed a greater awareness of Auriol's ideas, suggesting for example that Francis of Meyronnes appeared to reject Auriol's view of divine knowledge.[9] These remarks were buried in Schwamm's Scotistic analysis, however, and did very little for the historiographical tradition on Auriol, again obscuring his real significance.

---

[7] See Franz Ehrle, *Der Sentenzenkommentar Peters von Candia, des Pisaner Papstes Alexanders V* (Münster in Westfallia 1925). The passage about Candia and Auriol is on p. 68; the Louvain texts on pp. 297–305; the linking of Rivo to Auriol on p. 136.

[8] Hermann Schwamm, *Magistri Ioannis de Ripa O.F.M. Doctrina de Praescientia Divina* (Rome 1930), p. 160: "Aequalem honorem tribuit Petrus de Candia solummodo sententiae Petri Aureoli et Scoti." Schwamm's quotation of Candia is on p. 152, while Schwamm acknowledges Ehrle's suggestion on p. viii: "Studium commentarii Ioannis de Ripa mihi commendavit Eminentissimus Dominus Card. F. Ehrle..."

[9] For Schwamm's treatment of Auriol's attacks on Scotus, see *Das göttliche Vorherwissen bei Duns Scotus und seinen ersten Anhängern* (Innsbruck 1934), pp. 113–24. He cites Auriol's position on propositions on p. 122, and Meyronnes's rejection of Auriol's 'indistance' notion on p. 153.

It is no wonder that Konstanty Michalski had so much trouble three years later in finding the main defender of the neutrality of future contingent propositions.[10] He knew that Rimini battled against such a position, then he found the same stance attacked by Pierre d'Ailly. Finally he discovered Auriol's name explicitly attached to the opinion in Henry of Langenstein's *Sentences* commentary. He then claimed, probably erroneously, that Thomas Bradwardine's opponent in his *De causa Dei* was also Auriol. At this point Auriol's name in the context of future contingents was expressly and correctly linked with the neutrality of propositions and with a denial of foreknowledge, but *nothing more*. At Oxford, very little was known of Auriol's position except his stance on propositions, and that only dimly. Bradwardine probably did not know Auriol directly, and in any case Bradwardine's description of the opinion does not fit Auriol completely.

Moreover, although Rimini did focus on Auriol's views on propositions and apparent denial of foreknowledge, he ignored other aspects. Thus Peter de Rivo, the main protagonist in the Louvain dispute, would later say that even Rimini had not read all of Auriol's solution. Unfortunately, of all later-fourteenth-century theologians whose works I have inspected, d'Ailly and Langenstein are the ones who follow Rimini most closely, in their case quoting long passages verbatim. No wonder Auriol's view on propositions seemed to later historians to be the *only* element of his treatment of foreknowledge and future contingents. Had they inspected Peter of Candia's writings, or John Capreolus's, or James of Eltville's, or Rivo's, or the works of several Parisian theologians of the 1320s, not to mention Auriol's own works, these historians would have learned otherwise.

Michalski's study was the impetus for Philotheus Boehner's investigation of Ockham and a three-valued logic just eight years later in 1945. In the study, Boehner included editions of most of William of Ockham's texts involving foreknowledge and future contingents, giving his views a somewhat balanced treatment. Boehner concluded, however, that Auriol was the only strong supporter of a three-valued logic in the later Middle Ages, and Boehner included an edition of Auriol's *Scriptum*, book I, distinction 38, article three (based on one of the poorer manuscripts), which is where Auriol treats propositions.[11] There could be little doubt to Boehner's successors that the be all and end all of Auriol's treatment of the entire problem concerned the neutrality of future contingent propositions, and the concomitant denial of divine foreknowledge. This is, for example, Gordon Leff's opinion in his book on Bradwardine, again relying solely on Auriol's distinction 38, article three.[12]

---

[10]   Michalski's adventure is described in his "Le problème de la volonté à Oxford et à Paris au XIVe siècle," *Studia Philosophica* 2 (Lemberg 1937; reprinted in idem, *La philosophie au XIVe siècle: six études* [Frankfurt 1969]), pp. 82–90 (362–70) and texts on pp. 117–19 (397–9).

[11]   See Philotheus Boehner, *The Tractatus de praedestinatione et de praescientia Dei et de futuris contingentibus of William Ockham, Together with a Study of a Three-Valued Logic* (St. Bonaventure, NY 1945). His transcription of Auriol is Appendix IV.

[12]   See Gordon Leff, *Bradwardine and the Pelagians. A Study of His 'De causa Dei' and Its Opponents* (Cambridge 1957), pp. 211–16.

In 1950 Léon Baudry published some 400 pages of philosophical texts surrounding the quarrel over future contingents at Louvain. Here at last was an opportunity to examine Peter Auriol's ideas, if not directly, then at least in some depth. Yet in Baudry's 48–page introduction, he mentioned Auriol on six pages only and, except for a half-page analysis, almost always with reference to Auriol's opinion on neutral propositions. Baudry even suggested that the next goal would be to trace the doctrine of a three-valued logic from Auriol to Rivo.[13] It is obvious from the texts, however, that Rivo knew and followed Auriol's entire doctrine of foreknowledge and future contingents, and that Auriol was his inspiration and source of arguments. We now know, in fact, that Rivo considered his writings collectively to be "A Defense of Lord Peter Auriol's Doctrine in the Matter of Future Contingents."[14]

Independently, Frederick Copleston included a very brief but accurate analysis of Auriol's theory in his giant *History* in 1953, but despite this and Baudry's edition, little new has been done in the past half century either on Auriol's doctrine on foreknowledge or on his Parisian successors' ideas on the subject. Instead, the excitement created by various studies on Ockham and Bradwardine has led to many more investigations of the admittedly interesting Oxford debate. For example, there are now critical editions of questions on future contingents available for at least ten Oxford scholars active between 1315 and 1340, whereas for Paris there are only my own recent editions.[15]

Where there has been interest in Auriol it is usually either indirect via Peter de Rivo or focussed on future contingent propositions or both. Thus Rita Guerlac translated into English Baudry's texts from the Louvain controversy, and Paul Streveler had earlier rendered a small part of that work into English for his dissertation. Rivo plays a role in a dissertation currently in progress, and for the period between Aristotle and the twentieth century the Multiple-

---

[13] Léon Baudry, *La querelle des futurs contingents (Louvain 1465-1475)* (Paris 1950), p. 47. The half-page description of Auriol's stance is on p. 14. Mario Dal Pra employed Baudry's texts soon afterwards in his large "Il tempo e la problematizzazione dell'attualità della verità nel pensiero di Pietro De Rivo," in Antonio Banfi, ed., *La Crisi dell'uso dogmatico della Ragione* (Milan 1953), pp. 33–59, but he only mentioned Auriol twice, in footnotes (p. 40, n. 11, and p. 46, n. 22), the first reference in a list of ten theologians, the second concerning propositions.

[14] See Chris Schabel, "Peter de Rivo and the Quarrel over Future Contingents at Louvain: New Evidence and New Perspectives (Part I)," DSTFM 6 (1995), pp. 363–473, on pp. 366 and 415. This article and Part II, 7 (1996), pp. 369–465, include editions of previously unedited texts by Rivo which more than double what we have from him on the subject. A further important text connected to the Louvain quarrel has been edited by Girard J. Etzkorn, *De Arcanis Dei* (Rome 1997), which Etzkorn assigns to Cardinal Bessarion, although I consider it the work of Georgius Benignus Salviati. In Etzkorn's introduction to the edition (pp. 5–15) there is one mention of Auriol (p. 6, and n. 10), when it is stated that Rivo "allegedly favored" Auriol's position. On this work, the question of authorship, and the Louvain controversy, see the Epilogue below.

[15] For Copleston's analysis see his *A History of Philosophy III: Ockham to Suárez* (Westminster, Maryland 1953), pp. 37-9. The Franciscan Peter of Navarre's *Sentences* commentary on book I has been edited, and may be an exception to the 'no Paris edition' rule. It is not strictly speaking a Parisian commentary, however, since he appears never to have lectured on the *Sentences* there, although he is in the Parisian tradition. Moreover, his work was not edited because of his opinion on future contingents, on which he has little of interest to say. See below, chapter 8. For my editions, see below. For Oxford, see below, chapter 10.

Valued Logic Research Group calls Rivo the primary figure in the history of a three-valued logic.[16] Calvin Normore's chapter, "Future Contingents," in *The Cambridge History of Later Medieval Philosophy*, while being the best summary of the history of the medieval problem, merely highlights Auriol's contribution to the problem of future contingent propositions. Normore and others have continued to emphasize this aspect of Auriol's solution.[17]

Two things should be obvious after all of this: first, it is high time someone did a detailed study of Peter Auriol's discussion of future contingents and divine foreknowledge, and of the reaction to that discussion at Paris down to the time of Gregory of Rimini, a quarter century later. There is even evidence that the preliminary stages of such a study, e.g. Normore's comments and my *Scriptum* edition, are influencing contemporary historical surveys, and Auriol is now seen as a pivotal figure in the history of the problem.[18] The main general treatments of the topic of recent date, however, either skip the entire pe-

---

[16] The Louvain translations are Léon Baudry, *The Quarrel over Future Contingents. Louvain, 1465–1475*, trans. Rita Guerlac (Dordrecht 1989), and Paul Streveler, "The Problem of Future Contingents from Aristotle through the Fifteenth Century, with Particular Emphasis upon Medieval Views" (PhD Dissertation, University of Wisconsin 1970), pp. 74–87 (Rivo) and 106–74 (Fernando of Cordova). Streveler summarized this study in "The Problem of Future Contingents: A Medieval Discussion," *The New Scholasticism* 47.2 (1973), pp. 233–47. In his dissertation, Streveler skips Auriol and goes from Ockham to Rivo. A translation of Rivo's 1465 quodlibetal question is also included, along with texts by Boethius, Anselm, Averroes, Ockham, and Levi ben Gerson, in "Part III: God's Foreknowledge and Free Will" of Andrew B. Schoedinger, ed., *Readings in Medieval Philosophy* (Oxford 1996). Jonathan Evans of the University of Nebraska is currently working on Rivo's ideas. The Multiple-Valued Logic Research Group, based in the GSCIT of Monash University in Australia, does mention Auriol in its web page. Dale Tuggy of Brown University is defending a version of Auriol and Rivo's position in this regard. See his "Indeterminism, Faith and Al Gore" and "Logic without Bivalence: Taking the Leap," both forthcoming.

[17] Normore's brief Auriol discussion is on pp. 369–70 of "Future Contingents," CHLMP, pp. 358–81, but see also his "Petrus Aureoli and His Contemporaries on Future Contingents and the Excluded Middle," *Synthèse* 96 (1993), pp. 83–92. Jos Decorte, "*Sed modum exprimere nescio*. Franciscan Solutions to the Problem of Divine Foreknowledge and Future Contingents," FzS 70 (1988), pp. 123–75, looks at Auriol's opinion on propositions on pp. 151–153. Despite its focus, John Cassidy's "Logic and Determinism: A History of the Problem of Future Contingent Propositions from Aristotle to Ockham" (PhD Dissertation, Bryn Mawr College 1965) does not even treat Auriol's opinion on propositions.

[18] For example, in the recent work edited by John Marenbon, *Medieval Philosophy* (*The Routledge History of Philosophy: Volume III*) (London 1998), in which Stephen F. Brown summarizes Auriol's overall position ("Walter Burley, Peter Aureoli, and Gregory of Rimini", pp. 368–85, on pp. 380–81), Colette Sirat, writing on "Jewish Philosophy" (pp. 65–95), states (p. 89): "The problems of determinism and future contingents which, in Christian scholastic philosophy, had taken a clear form in the work of Peter Aureoli, were raised…" Brown's philosophical introduction ("The Treatise: *De arcanis Dei*") to Etzkorn's edition of Salviati, *De Arcanis Dei* (pp. 16–64; reprinted with Etzkorn's introduction, "A Symposium on God's Knowledge of Future Contingents," from *Miscellanea Francescana* 96 [1996], pp. 561–620), which has a half-dozen passing references to Auriol, does have a brief discussion of his thought on God's relation to eternity (pp. 51–2). Finally, Robert Pasnau's entry, "Aureol, Peter (c. 1280–1322)," in the *Routledge Encyclopedia of Philosophy* I (London 1998), pp. 565a–567a, mentions future contingents as one of four issues where Auriol left a mark.

riod at Paris, as William Lane Craig's work, or limit themselves to a few remarks, as with Maarten Hoenen's book.[19]

Second, the reason that such a study has not been attempted until now has nothing to do with the relative merits of the period in question at Paris. As far as I know, there is no monograph devoted exclusively to theology at Paris from Auriol to Rimini. Although the University of Paris in these decades is included in the "Golden Age of Scholasticism" (1250–1350), we know much less about it than we do about Paris from 1250–1315 or about Oxford from 1315–45. A book surveying the opinions of the main theologians of this period on a single issue would go a long way toward shedding light on theology at Paris between 1316 and 1345.[20] In sum, the fact that the history of the particular theological problem of divine foreknowledge at Paris in these years is mostly the history of the reaction to Auriol explains the title and subtitle of this book.

The book is divided into four unequal parts. Part one concerns the historical and theoretical background to the Parisian debate over divine foreknowledge and future contingents in 1316–45. Chapter one treats the elements of the theories of Aristotle, Augustine, Boethius, Anselm, and Peter Lombard that affected the later-medieval discussion, and introduces the positions of Thomas Aquinas, Henry of Ghent, and John Duns Scotus. The aim of the chapter is to highlight the authoritative passages, explain the technical terminology, and present the basic positions that were common in the early fourteenth century. I do not attempt to fully explicate or justify the opinions of these thinkers on their own terms, something that has been done many time before, but rather I present them as Peter Auriol and his contemporaries saw them. Those with a solid background in the material may wish to skip chapter one. Chapter two, however, provides the immediate historical context in greater detail: the reactions to Scotus, the impact of Durand of St. Pourçain, and most importantly the treatment of Thomas Wylton.

In part two, on Auriol himself, chapters three through six are somewhat small, since they deal in detail with the different aspects of Auriol's theory of divine foreknowledge and future contingents. These chapters are based on my own critical editions of Auriol's works.[21] Chapter three begins with a look at Auriol's life and writings and an attempt to place and date the three versions

---

[19] William Lane Craig, *The Problem of Divine Foreknowledge and Future Contingents from Aristotle to Suarez* (Leiden 1988), ignores Auriol and skips from Ockham to Molina, confining Auriol to a footnote (p. 234, n. 1). Maarten J.F.M. Hoenen, *Marsilius of Inghen: Divine Knowledge in Late Medieval Thought* (Leiden 1993), has only passing references to Parisian theologians between Auriol and Rimini, and Auriol is treated primarily via Rimini.

[20] I have attempted to do this in my "Paris and Oxford between Aureoli and Rimini," in Marenbon, ed., *Medieval Philosophy*, pp. 386–401, and "Parisian Commentaries from Peter Auriol to Gregory of Rimini, and the Problem of Predestination," in Gillian R. Evans, ed., *Commentaries on Peter Lombard's Sentences* (Leiden, forthcoming).

[21] i.e. "Peter Aureol on Divine Foreknowledge and Future Contingents: *Scriptum in Primum Librum Sententiarum*, distinctions 38–39," CIMAGL 65 (1995), pp. 63–212, text on pp. 87–212, and my editions with Lauge Nielsen of the two *Reportatio* versions of distinctions 38–40, which will appear in the first volumes of Auriol's *Opera Theologica*.

of Auriol's *Sentences* commentary where he discusses future contingents. Since all were used by Auriol's successors, each version is of some significance, and Auriol's followers themselves provide clues to their place in Auriol's works. The chapter goes on to explain Auriol's contention that, because immutability is the same as necessity, all of the contemporary positions on the problem except for his own entail the absolute necessity of the future. Auriol rejects the distinction between God's power considered absolutely (*de potentia Dei absoluta*) and as it is actually 'used' in the world (*de potentia Dei ordinata*), because he lays particular stress on divine simplicity. As chapter three explains, instead of *fore*knowledge we must talk about divine knowledge that is neither prior nor present to the future, but rather 'indistant' from the actualities of future contingents, Auriol maintains. Chapter four tries to explicate Auriol's complex stance and its terminology: Deity is the eminent similitude of the actualities of future contingents, abstracting from past, present, and future, representing them indistantly, as completely and more so than It would if It were simultaneously coexisting with the future. Auriol carefully tailors his theory to fit the objections to previous positions. Chapter five outlines what Auriol considers to be a consequence of his theory: propositions about future contingents are neither true nor false, but simply neutral, and because God's knowledge does not precede the future in any way, it does not make such propositions true or false. This was not, contrary to the common historiographical opinion, the foundation of Auriol's position, but it did draw much of the attention of his successors. They focussed on Auriol's statement that "God knows that the Antichrist will come" is false, because "the Antichrist will come" is neither true nor false, and one cannot know such a thing. Auriol has particular trouble explaining prophecy, and ends up espousing a radical theory. Finally, chapter six treats what is a corollary to Auriol's stance. Because for Auriol God is absolutely necessary and immutable, there does not seem much room for contingent activity in the world. Indeed, Auriol leans quite heavily to the "God of the philosophers," unchanging and indifferent to the world, rather than the Judeo-Christian God of revelation Who is active. Auriol does recognize that God operates in the world, however, and so he distinguishes between God's intrinsic will of complacency, equally pleased with whatever occurs, and His extrinsic will of operation, whereby He actually does things, like create the world. To some successors this seemed *ad hoc*, but one has to admire Auriol's intellectual integrity in attempting to tie up his own loose ends.

The third part of the book, chapters seven through nine, concerns the reaction to Auriol at the University of Paris up until the time of Rimini. This era is, relatively speaking, *terra incognita*, and I hope to shed light not only on the specific problem but also on the intellectual currents of the period generally. Necessarily, much of this section is based on manuscript materials, along with a few Early Modern printed editions, but I have critically edited the most significant texts.[22] Chapter seven looks at the Franciscans Landulph Caracciolo and Francis of Meyronnes and their imitators, and Gerard Odonis and Nicolas Bonet, who reject Auriol's intrinsic/extrinsic will division and his theory of indistance, both because they deem those elements of Auriol's stance incoherent and because they wish to emphasize God's relationship with the world that is revealed in Scripture. Bonet even goes on to admit that Auriol may have a point on the neutrality of propositions, but this is after Bonet seems to describe God as less than transcendent. Chapter eight deals with Parisian theologians outside the Franciscan order and continental Franciscans lecturing outside Paris. The Carmelites, Dominicans, and Augustinians of these years, and continental Franciscans outside of Paris, generally display both a lack of originality and a lack of concern over Auriol's position, a fact that suggests much about the nature of the Paris theological faculty. Chapter nine considers a group of theologians who follow the Franciscan Francis of Marchia. Marchia's general importance has not been appreciated, and I hope to demonstrate his impact on medieval thought with an examination of his position on divine foreknowledge. Marchia attacked Auriol's opinion on future contingent propositions and Auriol's claim that absolute necessity followed from foreknowledge. Instead, Marchia developed a distinction between a contingent cause's determination *de inesse*, which allowed for foreknowledge and human activity, and indetermination *de possibili*, which preserved contingency. I explain this distinction at some length, because it was to become the common intellectual property of many thinkers later on. I also treat his followers the Franciscans Aufredo Gonteri Brito, William of Brienne, and William of Rubio, and the Augustinian Michael of Massa, who probably passed Marchia's ideas to and himself influenced Gregory of Rimini.

Part four of the book involves the way Parisian thought in the 1340s is changed by theological and logical developments in England in the 1320s and 1330s, and how Auriol's theory fared after the Black Death. Chapter ten looks at the London and Oxford debate in these decades. I give an overview of the discussion, but with an emphasis on how it relates to Paris, Auriol, and a multi-valent logic. It should not be taken as an effort to paint a balanced or even original portrait of the Oxford discussion, except for Walter Chatton's curious opinion, which betrays a heavy debt to Auriol. The conclusion here is that Oxford and Paris were basically independent of each other in this period, except for Chatton, Adam Wodeham, and perhaps Thomas Bradwardine, but the Oxford debate resulted in interesting developments that would have an impact at Paris after 1340. William of Ockham, Robert Holcot, Chatton,

---

[22]   My editions are as follows: "Aufredo Gonteri Brito *secundum* Henry of Harclay on Divine Foreknowledge and Future Contingents," in Carol Poster and Richard Utz, eds., *Constructions of Time in the Late Middle Ages* (*Disputatio* 2) (Evanston, Illinois 1997), pp. 159–195; "Questions on Future Contingents by Michael of Massa, OESA," *Augustiniana* 48 (1998), pp. 165–229; "Landulphus Caracciolo and a Sequax on Divine Foreknowledge," AHDLMA 66 (1999), pp. 299–343. "Il Determinismo di Francesco di Marchia (Parte I)," *Picenum Seraphicum* 18 n.s. (1999), pp. 57–95, and (Parte II) 19 n.s. (2000), 3–55; and "*Non aliter novit facienda quam facta*. Gerard Odonis's Questions on Divine Foreknowledge," forthcoming.

Wodeham, Richard Fitzralph, Bradwardine, Thomas Buckingham, and others contributed to a stimulating intellectual conversation. Chapter eleven concerns how Auriol's threat fades into the background to a certain extent as the rich Oxford material is introduced into Paris. I begin with Thomas of Strasbourg, OESA, and Peter of Aquila, OFM, theologians from the mid-1330s who seem to have little new to say after the intensity of the 1320s at Paris. With Gregory of Rimini, lecturing 1343–44, we see the full integration of the Parisian and Oxford traditions. Perhaps spurred on by the English heritage, Rimini turns again to a long refutation of Auriol's idea of the neutrality of propositions about future contingents. Alphonsus Vargas of Toledo would again deal with Auriol the following year, but his contemporary John of Mirecourt shows that the focus of attention at Paris was shifting to subissues that originally developed at Oxford. Chapter twelve begins with a description of these subissues in, e.g., Hugolino of Orvieto and John of Ripa, then links the Paris discussion from Auriol to Rimini with the quarrel over future contingents at Louvain, which began in 1465 when Peter de Rivo defended Auriol's position. I try to explain the possible paths which Auriol's ideas took to reach Rivo, including John Wyclif, humanists, followers of Rimini such as Pierre d'Ailly, and conservative defenders of Aquinas and Scotus who saw Auriol as the main threat to their champions. Ultimately the main conduit, besides the manuscripts of Auriol's works themselves, was the very popular *Sentences* commentary of the Franciscan Peter of Candia. Candia, however, although he treated Auriol at great length in a neutral way, was not a follower of Auriol, as some have claimed. The book concludes with an Epilogue describing the Louvain quarrel, in which the participants resurrected the theories of the Parisian theologians Auriol, Marchia, Meyronnes, Bonet, and Rimini from the period from 1316 to 1344, as well as those of Aquinas, Scotus, Pierre d'Ailly, and Peter of Candia. The Louvain dispute and the Epilogue end in Pope Sixtus IV's condemnation of many of Auriol's ideas as Peter de Rivo expressed them.

I must conclude this introduction with a statement of methodology. Except in the case of Peter Auriol, I almost always limit myself to explicit discussions of divine foreknowledge and future contingents, usually contained in distinctions 35 through 40 of book I of commentaries on the *Sentences*, unless directed elsewhere by the citations of the theologians themselves. Information on any particular thinker's view on this problem also lies in questions on creation, on human and angelic knowledge, on prophecy, Christology, God's attributes, predestination and reprobation, grace and merit, and many other places. It would be impossible, however, for me to concern myself with a large number of scholastics, whose works are often solely in manuscript form, and at the same time to sift for possibly relevant bits and pieces of their stance on divine foreknowledge and future contingents from many places in their œuvre. Moreover, this limitation is justified by the practice of the medieval theologians themselves: when they dealt with previous scholastics' views on the issue, they focussed on these explicit passages, believing that unless difficulties were mentioned, the author had not considered them.

One final remark: this book is a work of history, intellectual history, to be sure, but history first and foremost. It is neither a work of philosophy nor theology, and no philosophical or theological idea in this book should be taken as a reflection of my own views. Academic philosophers and theologians may at times be looking for something different. I ask that they accept my historical approach and take what they consider useful. Indeed it is my hope that the texts I have collected and edited and the narrative I have constructed will prove helpful in specialized, analytical studies in their disciplines. My own goal, however, is to tell an interesting story, to show the lines of influence, to demonstrate exactly who were the leaders and who were the followers, to point out details about the people in and practice of theology at Paris, and to keep close to the texts and the terms of the texts, because as an historian I am striving for accuracy and anxious to avoid anachronism.

PART ONE

The Background

Chapter 1

The Roots of the Debate

The Antiqui

Later-medieval solutions to the problem of divine foreknowledge and future contingents were the culmination of the development of ideas surrounding issues that philosophers and theologians had been debating for many centuries. Peter Auriol and other early fourteenth-century scholastics cited with frequency the pertinent texts of these venerable ancients or *antiqui*: Aristotle worried about what would happen if future-tensed propositions had to be either true or false; Augustine and Boethius helped develop and popularize a view of God in eternity that allowed for His immutable knowledge, yet preserved contingency and human free choice; and Boethius and Anselm articulated a modal theory that distinguished between what they considered benign and malignant senses of the necessity that one could tie to God's knowledge of the future. Finally, Peter Lombard influenced later thinkers with the organization of and the doctrine in his *Sentences*, which became the theological textbook of the universities: all theologians in the period of concern in this book had to deal with foreknowledge in distinctions 38 and 39 of book I of their *Sentences* commentaries. The writings of Aristotle, Augustine, Boethius, Anselm and Lombard not only stimulated the basic theories of divine foreknowledge developed in the thirteenth and fourteenth centuries, but they also created a technical theological and philosophical vocabulary that later theologians used to express those theories. For these reasons, some familiarity with their contributions is required.[1]

Aristotle and the Truth of Propositions

Medieval theologians cited various works of Aristotle, the 'Philosopher', in the context of foreknowledge, but chapter nine of *De Interpretatione*, known to

---

    [1]   Hoenen gives brief summaries of the thought of the first four of these figures by way of an introduction (Hoenen, *Marsilius of Inghen*, pp. 159–65), and Bartholomew de la Torre does the same for the last four of the five (B. de la Torre, *Thomas Buckingham and the Contingency of Futures: The Possibility of Human Freedom* [South Bend 1987], pp. 46–58). Conveniently, Richard N. Bosely and Martin Tweedale provide English translations of the treatments of Aristotle, Boethius, and Anselm, as well as Aquinas, Siger of Brabant, Scotus, and Ockham, in *Basic Issues in Medieval Philosophy. Selected Readings Presenting the Interactive Discourses among the Major Figures* (Peterborough, Ontario 1997), pp. 249–307. In addition to the five figures I shall discuss here, Epicurus, Chrysippus, Cicero, Seneca, the Stoic philosophers, Jerome, Origen, and Hugh of St. Victor played minor roles in later discussions.

scholastics by its Greek name, *Peri Hermeneias*, overshadowed all others.² In book I, distinction 38 of innumerable *Sentences* commentaries of the fourteenth century, where scholastics asked something along the lines of "Does God know future contingents?" they first responded rhetorically: "No: there is no determinate truth in future contingents, according to the Philosopher in *Peri Hermeneias*; but God knows only what is true; thus God does not know future contingents."

In chapter four of *Peri Hermeneias*, Aristotle defines 'proposition' as the type of sentence that has truth or falsity, and he thus establishes the Principle of Bivalence — that is, every proposition can and must have one of two 'truth values': it must either be true or false. In the context of their statements on propositional logic, medieval theologians often derived this principle on the basis of a slightly different parallel rule from *Metaphysics IV*, chapter three: "Concerning anything whatever either the affirmation or negation is true," a logical principle so fundamental that they called it the 'First Principle' (*primum principium*). Aristotle sets up a corollary in chapter six of *Peri Hermeneias*, that for every positive proposition there exists its opposite, contradictory, negative proposition and vice-versa. In the Middle Ages this was called the 'Law of Contradictories' (*lex contradictoriarum*), that for each pair of contradictory propositions, for example 'Paris is in France', 'Paris is not in France', exactly one is true and the other false. In the beginning of the famous chapter nine, Aristotle summarizes this rule by saying, in a passage which medieval thinkers often quote directly:

> In the case of *that which is or which has taken place*, propositions, whether positive or negative, must be true or false. Again, in the case of a pair of contradictories, either when the subject is universal and the propositions are of a universal character, or when it is individual, as has been said, one of the two must be true and the other false.³

² Medieval authors typically cited it as book I, chapter 9, although now we consider there to be only one book in *Peri Hermeneias*. Calvin Normore points out that Aristotle also treated the problem in *Metaphysics VI*, chapter 3, but that "[t]he discussion in *Metaphysics VI* was typically understood by medieval writers to be of 'causal' rather than 'logical' determinism" (Normore, "Future Contingents," p. 358, n. 1). There are dozens of modern analyses of Aristotle's views of the problem. For an in-depth discussion of both Aristotle's work and the modern literature on the subject, see Craig, *The Problem of Divine Foreknowledge*, pp. 1–58. There is a certain amount of interpretive controversy regarding *Peri Hermeneias*, a discussion of which I will omit. See also Streveler, "The Problem of Future Contingents from Aristotle," pp. 4–27. Medieval commentaries on *Peri Hermeneias*, often by non-theologians, would be extremely important sources for a history of medieval views of future contingency, but as we are concerned also and specifically with divine foreknowledge, it is to expressly theological contexts that we must turn. See J. Isaac, *Le Peri Hermeneias en occident de Boèce à Saint Thomas* (Paris 1953), for a discussion of such commentaries. There are some more recent works on, including editions of, the commentaries of individual scholastics from a later period, notably Walter Burley (Stephen F. Brown, "Walter Burley's Middle Commentary on Aristotle's *Perihermeneias*," FcS 33 [1973], pp. 42–134), and John Buridan (Johannes Buridanus, *Questiones longe super librum Perihermeneias*, ed. Rita van der Lecq [Nijmegen 1983]).
³ Aristotle, *Peri Hermeneias*, ch. 9: 18a 28–31, quoted from Aristotle, *De Interpretatione*,

As the passage makes clear, Aristotle mentions only propositions about the present and past.

Most fourteenth-century theologians held that Aristotle made an exception for propositions with individual subjects and about the *future*. Aristotle suggests that if those propositional laws applied to future contingent propositions, then everything would take place of necessity, and nothing by our free choice. If the proposition 'Ninevah will fall' were true now, then it appears that Ninevah would necessarily fall. Conversely, if it were false now, then it would be impossible for Ninevah to fall in the future, otherwise the proposition would have been true in the first place. One or the other of a pair of contradictory propositions about the future will be 'verified' by the facts, for Ninevah will either fall or not fall, but if it had been true *beforehand* to say 'Ninevah will fall', then Ninevah's fall was unavoidable. Thus if the Principle of Bivalence is applied to future-tensed propositions of this sort, then there is no real alternative to what comes about. If all things happened of necessity, in a phrase often repeated in the Middle Ages, "There would be no need to deliberate or take trouble" about the future.[4]

Aristotle says these are "awkward results," and the conclusion is impossible, because people know that taking steps and deliberating about the future does indeed affect events, and that those events can either happen or not happen. While most medieval theologians held along with Aristotle that there was no point in deliberating about or denying the existence of something while it exists, and that "everything which is, when it is, necessarily is" (*omne quod est, quando est, necesse est esse*), they also agreed, however, that before things happen, one does not deliberate about them in vain, since not all things happen or will happen of necessity.[5]

What then is the truth-value of statements about future events, such as Aristotle's famous example of the sea battle, which can and can not come about? Scholars have debated this for a long time, and medieval theologians certainly did not agree about the Philosopher's view.[6] Many took him to mean that such propositions are neither true nor false. Of course Aristotle does say

---

in *The Basic Works of Aristotle*, ed. Richard McKeon (New York 1941), p. 45 (italics mine). In chapter 7, Aristotle had given examples of these types of propositions, and set out some rules for them. The affirmative proposition 'every tool is wooden' is universal because 'every' is a universal term, not an individual which would usually be represented by a proper noun, as 'Russell', or with a demonstrative adjective, as 'this tool'. The proper negative contradictory proposition here is 'some tools are not wooden', and one of the two propositions must be true and the other false. It is the same with affirmative and negative propositions about individuals, such as 'Russell is wooden', and 'Russell is not wooden'.

[4]   Aristotle, *Peri Hermeneias*, ch. 9: 18b 31 (*The Basic Works*, p. 47). Of course many modern philosophers would disagree with Aristotle here, and claim that if everything occurs of necessity, so also must we deliberate of necessity.

[5]   Aristotle, *Peri Hermeneias*, ch. 9: 18b 26–19a 22 (*The Basic Works*, pp. 47–8). The statement 'everything which is, when it is, necessarily is' (*omne quod est, quando est, necesse est esse*) becomes an important part of the medieval discussion, beginning with Boethius, and it is for this reason I introduce it here. The necessity involved in this statement is discussed below.

[6]   See Boehner, *The Tractatus*, and later chapters.

that "everything must either be or not be," but many understood that this statement must be taken as a whole, with disjunction 'or' intact. This is why Aristotle continues: "It is not always possible to distinguish and state *determinately* which of these alternatives must necessarily come about."[7] The key word for many medieval theologians is 'determinately', and Aristotle seems to mean that it is not already determined that something will come about, or that something will not come about, and thus the truth or falsity of a proposition about the future has not been determined yet either. A few scholastics held that Aristotle meant to say that propositions about future contingents may be true or false, but not determinately true or false — they are 'indeterminately' true or false. Others claimed that he was only talking about future contingents understood in themselves, not as they are in God's intellect, where such determination obtained. Still others maintained that Aristotle was simply denying that all such propositions have any truth or falsity at all. Instead, they are completely indeterminate with respect to truth and falsity.

Aristotle goes on to say:

> Since propositions correspond with facts, it is evident that when in future events there is a real alternative, and a potentiality in contrary directions, the corresponding affirmation and denial have the same character... it is therefore plain that it is not necessary that of an affirmation and a denial one should be true and the other false. For in the case of that which exists potentially, but not actually, the rule which applies to that which exists actually does not hold good.[8]

Aristotle left the matter at that and did not clarify his position further. In his concern with the necessity or contingency of future events, Aristotle did not consider what fore*knowledge*, especially divine foreknowledge, would have meant as an additional factor. Augustine had no choice.

Augustine, Boethius, and God's Eternity

The influence of Augustine (354–430), Bishop of Hippo, on the theology of the Middle Ages is ubiquitous. In the fourteenth century especially, with theologians' growing interest in historical accuracy, scholars cited the works of Augustine with ever-increasing frequency, more than those of any other Christian theologian.[9] The slight ambiguity of his statements concerning free will and divine foreknowledge provided fuel for several different positions in the

---

[7]   Aristotle, *Peri Hermeneias*, ch. 9: 19a 27–9 (*The Basic Works*, p. 48). One wonders why Aristotle uses the word 'necessarily' in this context.

[8]   Aristotle, *Peri Hermeneias*, ch. 9: 19a 32–19b 4 (*The Basic Works*, p. 48).

[9]   See Damasus Trapp, "Augustinian Theology of the 14th Century: Notes on Editions, Marginalia, Opinions, and Book Lore," *Augustiniana* 6 (1956), pp. 146–274, and for the most prolific of those who cite Augustine, John Hiltalingen of Basel, see Trapp's "Hiltalinger's Augustinian Quotations," *Augustiniana* 4 (1954), pp. 412–49.

later-medieval discussion.[10] As an opening argument against Aristotle, and indeed as a major means of support, later scholastics cited Augustine's remarks against Cicero in *City of God*. Cicero had tried to refute the notions of certain pagan philosophers, some of them Stoics, that humans had a fate or destiny which was already set up in advance. In doing so, Cicero rejected foreknowledge, and he included in his attack astrology, oracles, and any sort of divination. Augustine thought that denying foreknowledge was tantamount to denying God's existence, "for one who is not prescient of all future things is not God."[11] In a pun on Cicero's name, Marcus *Tullius* Cicero, Augustine claimed that astrology was more "tolerable" (*tollerabilis* in some medieval spellings) than the complete denial of any foreknowledge.[12]

Medieval theologians also used his statements about the causal relationship between God's foreknowledge and human action in their principal arguments. Augustine understood that a human 'must' do as God foreknew, but he was not able to explain clearly why this 'having' to do something was compatible with free will. Sometimes he seems merely to say that it is enough that God foreknows we will do something by our free will. Some scholastics accepted this explanation. For Augustine, the connection between foreknowledge and free will is difficult to describe:

> ... a man does not therefore sin because God foreknew that he would sin. Nay, it cannot be doubted but that it is the man himself who sins when he does sin, because He, whose foreknowledge is infallible, foreknew not that fate, or fortune, or something else would sin, but that the man himself would sin, who, if he wills not, sins not. But if he shall not will to sin, even this did God foreknow.[13]

Later theologians disagreed on how to interpret this type of *auctoritas*, or authoritative passage. Since God's knowledge does not change, because God is immutable and perfect, Augustine is compelled to say in *The Trinity*, "He does not, therefore, know all His creatures, both spiritual and corporal, because they are, but they, therefore, are because He knows them."[14] The word 'therefore', coupled with the stress on immutability, seemed to say that fore-

---

[10] For a detailed discussion of Augustine's ideas and a good treatment of the literature, see Craig, *The Problem of Divine Foreknowledge*, pp. 59–78.

[11] Augustinus, *De civitate Dei* V, ch. 9; quoted from idem, *City of God*, trans. Marcus Dods (New York 1950), p. 156.

[12] Augustinus, *De civitate Dei* V, ch. 9 (trans. cit., p. 152).

[13] Augustinus, *De civitate Dei* V, ch. 10 (trans. cit., pp. 157–8). The example of a man's sinning is problematic, because it is, for Augustine, a negative act, the lack of a proper perfection. Nevertheless, this passage serves my present purpose of showing the complexity of his thought.

[14] Augustinus, *De trinitate* XV, ch. 13, no. 22; quoted from idem, *The Trinity*, trans. Stephen McKenna (Washington 1963), p. 152. Other important *auctoritates* are Augustinus, *On Free Will* III, ch. 3, no. 8 (in idem, *Earlier Writings*, trans. J.H.S. Burleigh [Philadelphia 1953], p. 175, slightly modified): "Nothing can happen otherwise than as God has foreknown it," and Augustinus, *The Literal Meaning of Genesis* VI, ch. 17, no. 28 (trans. J. Taylor [New York and Ramsey, N.J. 1982], p. 199): "That which God foreknew was necessarily going to come about."

knowledge causes future things. To this and other like *auctoritates* of Augustine, later theologians opposed an equally enigmatic phrase from Origen appearing on the face of it to say that future things cause foreknowledge.

Of course, later-medieval theologians understood why these passages in Augustine were so ambiguous. Augustine developed a notion of a God outside of time, unchanging, far from the imperfect, ever-changing world of creation, a notion that was difficult to put into words that humans, trapped in time, could understand. Everywhere in fourteenth-century writings one finds quotations from several of Augustine's works where he tries to explain that God does not experience past or future, but everything all at once, simultaneously, in "one eternal, changeless, and ineffable vision."[15] For example, in *De diversis quaestionibus 83*: "For God, nothing is absent, neither the past nor the future, but everything is present to God." Events do not go past God's view; God does not see one thing now, another later, but all at once.

In addition, God's knowledge is as changeless as His essence and substance, and in fact it is the same thing. So in *The Trinity*, Augustine remarks:[16] "God does not know things differently after they happen from before they come about," and: "The foreknowledge that God has of every creature is none other than the divine essence." This notion of God's 'eternal present', for Augustine, preserved simultaneously the idea of a perfect, unchanging, omniscient God, and human free will. Regardless of its possible problems, the argument from eternity would be the basis for most solutions in the High and Late Middle Ages.

Boethius (480–524) elaborated and passed on Augustine's concept of God's atemporal eternity in his most famous work, the dialogue *The Consolation of Philosophy*, and between Augustine and Anselm, Boethius was the most important contributor to the discussion of future contingency and divine foreknowledge in the minds of late medieval thinkers.[17] Book V of *The Consolation*, written with the implicit awareness of both *Peri Hermeneias* and the works of Augustine on the subject, is the most complete theological treatment of the problem of foreknowledge until that time. There, prompted by the question of the character 'Boethius', Philosophia (the feminine personification of philosophy) treats the traditional problem of holding both divine foreknowledge and human free will. First, if God knows beforehand all of our acts, plans, and

---

[15] Augustinus, *De trinitate* XV, ch. 7, no. 13 (trans. cit., p. 468).

[16] See Augustinus, *De trinitate* XV, ch. 13, no. 22, and VII, ch. 1, no. 3. The first passage has an often-cited parallel in *De civitate Dei* X, ch. 12.

[17] The secondary literature on Boethius is extensive. Again, a thorough philosophical discussion, together with a treatment of the literature, can be found in Craig, *The Problem of Divine Foreknowledge*, pp. 79–98. See also Streveler, "The Problem of Future Contingents: A Medieval Discussion," and Norman Kretzmann, "*Nos ipsi principia sumus*: Boethius and the Basis of Contingency," in Rudavsky ed., *Divine Omniscience*, pp. 23–50, which concerns Boethius's *Peri Hermeneias* commentaries. For the role of *De consolatione* in the Middle Ages, see Maarten J.F.M. Hoenen and Lodi Nauta, eds., *Boethius in the Middle Ages. Latin and Vernacular Traditions of the Consolatio Philosophiae* (Leiden 1997), and also Jerome C. Frakes, *The Fate of Fortune in the Early Middle Ages. The Boethian Tradition* (Leiden 1988), for the period up to the tenth century.

wishes, there cannot be free will. If there is free will, then there must be a real possibility for things to occur other than as God has foreknown them, and in that case God does not really have foreknowledge, but only opinion, like our opinion. Boethius declares that this sort of 'knowledge' is no better than Tiresias's, who said "whatever I say will either be or not be."[18] Since this is not the case, and God has true knowledge, things occur of necessity. There is no reason to praise or blame, since people are not in control of their actions; prayer is useless.

For Boethius, the answer lies somewhere in the failure of humans to understand the divine. Boethius's key argument in many ways expands on Augustine's: "Everything which is known is known not according to its own power, but rather according to the capacity of the knower."[19] Philosophia explains that although human reason, as a means for attaining knowledge, can admit knowledge only of things that are fixed and determinate, this need not be the case with a higher means, of which reason cannot conceive. Thus, Philosophia maintains, it is erroneous, albeit understandable, "when human reason supposes that the divine intelligence beholds future events only as reason herself sees them." But whereas reason cannot 'know' contingent future events with certainty:

> ... a certain and definite foreknowledge can behold even those things which have no certain outcome. And this foreknowledge is not mere conjecture but the unrestricted simplicity of (God's) supreme knowledge.[20]

In the final section of *The Consolation*, having pointed to the possibility of knowledge of events whose outcomes are not fixed and determinate, Boethius returns to the task of explaining how events governed by human free will do not come about necessarily. Boethius now develops the notion that God is eternal, and he draws the distinction between the eternal, which is outside of time and unchanging, and the perpetual, which is forever in time and always changing. Never-ending things are continually striving for God's perfection by continually and forever changing, because they cannot match God's immutability and eternity. Therefore, since things are known according to the nature of the knower, God knows all things presently, in His eternal present, as Augustine had suggested. His knowledge "transcends all movement of time and abides in the simplicity of its immediate present. It encompasses the infinite sweep of past and future, and regards all things in its simple comprehension as if they were now taking place." Now since God sees everything as present, Boethius makes the point that God does not really have foreknowledge of anything, but simply knowledge: "For this reason, divine knowledge is

---

[18] Boethius, *De consolatione philosophiae* V, prose 3 (*The Consolation of Philosophy*, trans. Richard Green [Indianapolis 1962], p. 106).

[19] Boethius, *De consolatione philosophiae* V, prose 4 (trans. cit., p. 110).

[20] Boethius, *De consolatione philosophiae* V, prose 5 (trans. cit., p. 114).

called providence, rather than prevision, because it resides above all inferior things and looks out on all things from their summit."[21] This image would be repeated many times by later-medieval theologians.

Boethius and Anselm on Necessity

Although in theological contexts it is to Boethius's *The Consolation of Philosophy*, specifically book V, that most later theologians were drawn, Boethius had also translated and commented on *Peri Hermeneias*, and so besides this early Latin translation, he provided some of the terminology that was used in medieval treatments of future contingents. First, he translated Aristotle's 'opoter etuchen' into '*contingens ad utrumlibet.*' From then on, especially after the thirteenth century, scholars used the phrase '*contingens ad utrumlibet*' to mean that something is able to come about and is able not to come about.[22] Peter Damian later explained the term in this way:

> There are some things that can equally come about and not come about, just as it is for me to ride a horse today, or not to ride; to see a friend or not to see a friend; or for the weather to be calm. Wise men were accustomed to call these things and similar ones of this sort '*ad utrumlibet*', because they are wont equally to occur and not to occur.[23]

Second, Boethius helped develop a theory of another modal term: necessary. Boethius's explanation of Augustine's conception of God's atemporal eternity included the notion that God 'sees' what to us is future as present to Him. This brought Boethius into conflict with Aristotle's contention, mentioned earlier, that "*omne quod est, quando est, necesse est esse,*" because for Aristotle, as Boethius knew, it was impossible to make something that existed in the present not exist in that same present. Thus, in a sense there is a necessity attached to present circumstances, although afterwards in time things can be different. Normally, this necessity presented no problem for Boethius. In modern terms, the *necessitas temporalis* or synchronic necessity of Aristotle's proposition did not take away the diachronic contingency of events. While I am sitting, I 'must' sit by synchronic necessity, since I cannot sit and stand at the same time. At another instant in time, however, I may stand; this is diachronic

---

[21]   Boethius, *De consolatione philosophiae* V, prose 6 (trans. cit., p. 116).

[22]   That is $(\Diamond p) \wedge (\Diamond {\sim} p)$. See Cassidy, "Logic and Determinism," p. 112.

[23]   Petrus Damianus, *De divina omnipotentia* (PL 145, col. 603): "Non nulla sunt, quae videlicet aequaliter possunt evenire, et non evenire: sicut est, me hodie equitare, et non equitare; amicum videre, vel non videre; vel aeram serenam esse. Quae scilicet, et his similia huius sapientes consueverunt ad '*utrumlibet*' appelare; quia solent aeque et contingere, et non contingere," as quoted in Cassidy, "Logic and Determinism," p. 110. *Utrumlibet* is an exceedingly awkward word to translate into English. Norman Kretzmann employed "in either of two ways," meaning that something can be or not be in some way (see Kretzmann, "*Nos ipsi principia sumus,*" pp. 29–30). In this book I will simply use '*ad utrumlibet*' or '*utrumlibet.*'

contingency.[24] The trouble for Boethius was that in God's eternity there is no changing time, but one atemporal, unchanging present. Thus there could be no diachronic contingency, and the 'synchronic' necessity of God's eternity might as well be absolute necessity (*necessitas simplex*), in medieval terminology. Does not therefore God's knowledge of the future impose necessity on it? In *The Consolation of Philosophy*, Boethius says 'no': God imparts no more necessity on the objects of His vision in His eternal present than we do, for example, when we see someone walking down the street. God's vision and our vision do not affect the nature of the object of our vision. If we see the sun rise, this does not affect the necessity — for Boethius — of the sun's rising; the contingency of the man's walking is likewise unaffected by our seeing him. So God's seeing future contingent events does not impose necessity on them.

Does any necessity remain, if it is not imposed on things by God? Philosophia says:

> If you should reply that whatever God foresees as happening cannot help but happen, and whatever must happen is bound by necessity — i f you pin me down to this word 'necessity' — I grant that you state a solid truth, but one which only a profound theologian can grasp.

Some 'necessity' with respect to future events is recognized, but "the same future event," Boethius continues, "is necessary with respect to God's knowledge of it, but free and undetermined if considered in its own nature."[25] Moreover, there are two kinds of necessity, one simple and the other conditional. These types of necessity will be the subject of much discussion later, and they will be given many different names. Boethius's example of simple necessity is the necessity of the proposition 'All men are mortals'. Conditional necessity is that of Aristotle's "*omne quod est, quando est, necesse est esse.*" It is the type of necessity that when we see someone walking, she must be walking. God sees all things which are future to us as present, so all of these things are necessary *on the condition* that God knows them; but considered in themselves, things governed by human free will are absolutely free and contingent.

Boethius's division of necessity into simple and conditional necessity was sufficient to diminish necessity's potential destructiveness for most later theologians, especially at the University of Paris. Still, just as Boethius clarified Augustine's concept of God's atemporal eternity, Anselm adopted and explained more fully Boethius's distinction between different types of necessity, while introducing new terminology.[26] Anselm of Aosta, Bec, and Canter-

---

[24] The various notions of contingency and necessity discussed in this chapter are treated quite clearly in the works of Simo Knuuttila, such as "Time and Modality in Scholasticism," in idem, ed., *Reforging the Great Chain of Being* (Dordrecht 1981), pp. 163–257, and *Modalities in Medieval Philosophy* (London 1993).

[25] Boethius, *De consolatione philosophiae* V, prose 6 (trans. cit., p. 117).

[26] There are several brief treatments of Anselm's position on future contingents. See especially Paul Streveler, "Anselm on Future Contingencies. A Critical Analysis of the Argument of the *De concordia*," *Anselm Studies. An Occasional Journal* 1 (1983), pp. 165–73, and Eileen F. Se-

bury (1033–1109) represents the last important figure before the great recovery of Aristotelian texts beginning in the twelfth century which transformed and initiated rapid change in European Christian thought. He also represents the last of the great 'monastic' thinkers, and after him in the later Middle Ages, the vanguard of intellectual activity was located not in abbeys and priories, but in the towns and cities of a revitalized Europe. Anselm did not actually have much that was new to say about the problem of future contingency and divine foreknowledge, and in his treatise *On the Harmony of God's Foreknowledge, Predestination, and Grace with Free Choice*, Anselm mainly introduced new terminology. Nevertheless, many fourteenth-century theologians, having a choice between Augustine, Boethius, or Anselm to follow, often chose Anselm.

Very early on in this work Anselm makes the strange claim that "it is necessary that something be future without necessity."[27] It is primarily this apparent contradiction in terms that Anselm tries to explain and support in the question. He adds in an often-quoted passage:

> Hence, the foreknowledge from which necessity follows and the freedom of choice from which necessity is absent are here seen (for one who rightly understands it) to be not at all incompatible. For, on the one hand, it is necessary that what is foreknown by God be going to occur; and, on the other hand, God foreknows that something is going to occur without any necessity.[28]

Anselm wishes to show that the necessity that can be attached to our actions is at best a weak one, which does not coerce. Anselm agrees with the statement, "If this thing will occur, of necessity it will occur,"[29] but insists that this is just the necessity by which a tautology must be true. By this necessity, necessarily: the past is past, the present is present, and the future is future. Something could not at once be future and not future, so what is future, must necessarily be future. A future cannot not be future. This type of necessity he calls 'subsequent' or 'accompanying' (*sequens*) necessity. The strong form of necessity is preceding (*precedens*) necessity, and Anselm's example of this is the questionable one 'The sun will rise tomorrow'. Preceding necessity brings it about that the sun rises — it must occur. Subsequent necessity has no force. Every future thing is necessarily future, once you have said that the thing is future.[30] This is no more than saying that every white thing is white. If it is white, it must be white, for it cannot both be white and not white at the same time.

rene, "Anselm's Modal Conceptions," in Knuuttila, ed., *Reforging the Great Chain of Being*, pp. 117–62.

[27] Anselmus, *De concordia praescientiae et praedestinationis et gratiae Dei cum libero arbitrio* I [1], in *S. Anselmi Cantuariensis archiepiscopi opera omnia* II, ed. Franciscus Salesius Schmitt, OSB (Edinburgh 1946); trans. J. Hopkins and H. Richardson, in Bosley and Tweedale, eds., *Basic Issues in Medieval Philosophy*, p. 261b.

[28] Anselmus, *De concordia* I [1] (trans. cit., p. 261b).

[29] Anselmus, *De concordia* I [2] (trans. cit., p. 262a).

[30] Anselmus, *De concordia* I [3] (ed. Schmitt, p. 250, ll. 13–24).

This is not the same as saying that any particular thing will necessarily come about, without the adjective 'future' attached to 'thing' in the first place. No compulsion at all is involved here. When we say that necessarily, God foreknows that a thing is future, subsequent necessity obtains, because 'foreknows' implies 'knows the future', and we are saying the equivalent of 'necessarily, God knows that a future thing is future'.[31] This, of course, is obviously necessary, in the same way that "*omne quod est, quando est, necesse est esse*," by Boethius's conditional necessity, or Anselm's subsequent necessity.

The distinction between the two basic types of necessity required the Augustinian notion of God's atemporal eternity for it to function usefully to save contingency. If God knew with certainty the future as future, before it came about, it was more difficult, but not impossible, to see how free will could be saved. For Anselm, in God's eternal present, "there is nothing past or future, but... all things exist at once without any change."[32] Considered with respect to this present, God knows our free 'future' actions, and they are subject to the weak, subsequent necessity, but considered from our perspective, in time, these actions are completely free of necessity:

> So then, no inconsistency arises if (in accordance with the considerations just presented) we assert of one and the same event that, necessarily, i t is going to occur (simply because it is going to occur), and that it is not compelled to be going to occur by any necessity.[33]

For example, in some way, in God's eternal and immutable present, Anselm is 'always' and immutably writing, but in time his writing is a changing thing; sometimes he writes and sometimes he does not, and in both cases it is dependent on his free will. So from God's perspective, Anselm is necessarily writing by subsequent necessity, but from Anselm's vantage point, there is no necessity and no compulsion.[34]

Anselm's distinction between preceding (or antecedent) necessity and subsequent (or we might say 'relative') necessity, and his application of subsequent necessity to future events seen from God's perspective, was an attractive solution for some later thinkers, although it did not differ that much from Boethius's.[35]

---

[31] Anselmus, *De concordia* I [3] (ed. Schmitt, p. 250, ll. 28–31).

[32] Anselmus, *De concordia* I [4] (trans. cit., p. 264b).

[33] Anselmus, *De concordia* I [4] (trans. cit., pp. 264b–5a).

[34] Anselmus, *De concordia* I [5] (ed. Schmitt, p. 255, ll. 4–11).

[35] It might be mentioned here that Hugh of St. Victor, a transitional figure between Anselm's monasticism and the universities of the thirteenth century, plays a minor role in the fourteenth-century discussion. Hugh is less clear on the subject than Anselm, but perhaps more poetic: "These two ran along together from eternity — what was to be and what was able to be which was not to be." His main emphasis was on the continuing possibility of things to be otherwise, and God's foreknowledge which, from our perspective, anticipates the way things are to turn out. See Hugo de Sancto Victore, *On the Sacraments of the Christian Faith* I, part II, ch. 17 (trans. Roy J. Deferrari [Cambridge, Mass. 1951], pp. 36–7). Hugh's and the opinions of several other twelfth-century thinkers, notably Abelard's, are conveniently summarized in Marcia Colish, *Pe-*

Peter Lombard and the Universities

By about 1100 the basic elements of most later-medieval solutions to the problem of divine foreknowledge and future contingency had been formed, but it took Lombard's *Sentences* as a textbook and the rise of the new universities about 1200 as a forum to ensure that every theologian would come into contact with these fundamental concepts. Peter Lombard (ca. 1095–1160) is a transitional figure in many ways. In his use of composition and division in the context of modal propositions concerning future contingents, for example, Lombard typifies the recovery of Aristotelian logical and scientific texts in the twelfth century. In another way, figures from much later do not simply cite him as an authority to be quoted in support of or in opposition to a position, but they argue with him directly at times, considering him half venerable ancient and half vulnerable peer. This is most likely because of his importance in yet another transition, the transition between the more isolated monastic or cathedral school and the centralized university.

Near the end of the twelfth century the group of schools that had clustered around Paris began to join together when a 'critical mass' of scholars made it a certainty that a large institution there could sustain a teaching staff over time, not depending on one or two masters. This formal institutionalization of learning created a climate in which an organized curriculum could be accepted. A division of the new 'university' into the lower, arts school, and the higher legal, medical, and theological schools gradually came into focus. By the early thirteenth century universities had taken shape in Paris, Oxford, and Bologna, but it was in Paris where theology, the 'queen of the sciences', was most important, and this fact made Paris the most prestigious university in the Late Middle Ages.[36]

Peter Lombard, who became Bishop of Paris, was among several theologians who wrote a '*summa*' of theology, determining the answers to questions on all aspects of things divine. Probably because of his organization and orthodoxy, and certainly because of his location, Lombard's *Sentences*, or 'opinions', was to fill the need for a theological textbook in the new curriculum of the university.[37] To be brief, following Peter Abelard's '*sic et non*' method, which Gratian's *Decretum* also employed in canon law, Lombard asked theological questions and cited authorities both pro (*sic*, or yes) and con (*non*, or no). He then gave answers to the questions, reconciling disagreements between authorities with logical analysis, as had Gratian. Lombard organized his *opus* into four

---

ter Lombard, 2 vols. (Leiden 1994), vol. I, pp. 268–85.

    [36] On the development of the university, see for example Hastings Rashdall, *The Universities of Europe in the Middle Ages*, 3 vols., revised and ed. F.M. Powicke and A.B. Emden (Oxford 1936), and John W. Baldwin's overview, *The Scholastic Culture of the Middle Ages 1000–1300* (Lexington, Mass. 1971).

    [37] The reasons for Lombard's success over others are outlined in Marcia Colish, "Systematic Theology and Theological Renewal in the Twelfth Century," *Journal of Medieval and Renaissance Studies* 18.2 (Fall, 1988), pp. 135–56, and eadem, *Peter Lombard I*, pp. 77–90. The latter book is now the standard work on Lombard.

books, the first dealing with God, the second Creation, the third Christ, and the fourth last things and the Sacraments. When Paris, Oxford, and other later universities eventually made the *Sentences* of Peter Lombard their theological textbook, it meant that Lombard, nicknamed the 'Master of the Sentences', would be immortalized and that every scholar who aspired to become a doctor of theology would have to lecture and comment on the *Sentences* for one or two years. Theology was institutionalized and professionalized.

As all the other books of the *Sentences*, book I, on God, was further subdivided into distinctions, so that distinctions 35 through 48 (the last fourteen) treated God's knowledge, power, and will. Distinctions 38 and 39 involved foreknowledge and future contingents, and this was the forum for the topic throughout the period. Hence every theologian was supposed to lecture on the topic of the reconciliation of divine foreknowledge with the contingency of future events governed by human free will. Many of these lectures were written down, and later revised, constituting our major source of information about the topic in the later Middle Ages.

In distinction 38 Lombard asks the question "is knowledge or foreknowledge the cause of things, or are things the cause of God's knowledge or foreknowledge?"[38] Lombard presents *auctoritates* for possible answers. First he says that knowledge or foreknowledge seems to be the cause of things, for the reason that it is impossible for things to come about if they are not foreknown, and so on. He quotes ambiguous passages from Augustine's *The Trinity* that could lead one to believe that foreknowledge is the cause of things. Lombard says, however, that if God's foreknowledge were the cause of all things, then it would be the cause of evils also, which is "far from the truth." Conversely, things cannot be the cause of God's foreknowledge, because in that case something eternal would have an "alien cause, different from it." No created thing can cause an uncreated thing. Lombard cites a passage of Origen, however, that appears to say that future things are the cause of foreknowledge.[39]

According to Lombard, the answer to the question lies in the correct interpretation of Origen's statement, and that is that future things are only the *'causa sine qua non'* of foreknowledge. Likewise foreknowledge is the *'causa sine qua non'* of future things.[40] In this type of 'causality', one thing is never found

---

[38] Petrus Lombardus, *Sententiae in IV libris distinctae* I, d. 38, c. 1 (vol. 1, ed. Ignatius Brady [Grottaferrata 1971], p. 275, ll. 17–19): "Hic oritur quaestio non dissimulanda, utrum scilicet scientia vel praescientia sit causa rerum, an res sint causa scientiae vel praescientiae Dei." I do not think any really extensive treatment of Lombard's opinions on the subject exists, but see Johannes Schneider, *Die Lehre vom dreieinigen Gott in der Schule des Petrus Lombardus* (Munich 1961), pp. 54–60; Normore, "Future Contingents," pp. 363–364; Marcia Colish, "Peter Lombard and Abelard: The *Opinio Nominalium* and Divine Transcendence," *Vivarium* 30.1 (1992) (pp. 139–56), pp. 150–51; and eadem, *Peter Lombard* I, pp. 285–90.

[39] Lombardus, *I Sent.*, d. 38, c. 1 (ed. Brady, p. 276, l. 10–277, l. 14). It should be obvious to anyone reading Lombard that he makes his own determinations, like most other scholastics, and does not simply repeat what was said earlier by an 'authority' as if that would solve the issue.

[40] Lombardus, *I Sent.*, d. 38, c. 1 (ed. Brady, p. 277, ll. 20–25): "... ita exponentes quod ait Origenes... quod futurum est, scitur a Deo antequam fiat, neque sciretur nisi futurum esset: ut non

to exist without the other: if there are no future things, there is no foreknowledge of them; if there is no foreknowledge of them, there are no future things.
Either element could be considered the 'cause' without which the 'effect' does
not exist. This does not involve efficient causation, in which one part brings
about the other; rather this is similar to a 'sign' (of which Boethius had spoken), one part being merely a 'sign' that the other part obtains also. This type
of 'causation', if one must use the word, seems innocuous to Lombard.

Turning to modal terms involving possibility and necessity, and the question of whether some things are contingent — although he does not use the
term 'contingent' — Lombard analyzes a proposition which he will repeat
several times with variations: 'It can be otherwise than as God foreknew'. The
key to Lombard's analysis, dependent in part on Peter Abelard's treatment, is
an understanding of the logical technique of disambiguating propositions by
reading them in 'compounded' and 'divided' senses.[41] Thus, compound modal
propositions, such as 'I can sit and stand', can be taken in two ways. The
modal term 'can', in the divided sense (or dividedly), is taken to govern both
'sit' and 'stand' separately. Hence, 'I can sit and stand' is true, because 'I can
sit' and 'I can stand' are both true separately. In the composite sense (or
jointly), 'can' governs 'sit and stand' taken together all at once. In this sense
the proposition is false, because one cannot be sitting and standing at the
same time.[42] The objection Lombard wants to refute is this:

(1) God foreknew that this man would read.
(2) It can be that this man does not read.
(3) Therefore it can be otherwise than as God has foreknown.
(4) Therefore God's foreknowledge can be mistaken.[43]

Step (1) affirms divine foreknowledge, and is a simple statement *de inesse*,
about what was the case in reality, i.e. that God knew that the man would
read. Step (2) conserves contingency with the modal 'can', but does not claim
anything about what will or will not be. The main problem lies in the interpretation of step (3), which in the objection seems to have led to the unacceptable
conclusion, step (4). If we take proposition (3) jointly (*coniunctim*) or in the
composite sense (*sensu composito*), then we have to take the modal 'can' as
governing 'be otherwise than as God has foreknown', when it is understood

---

notetur ibi causa, nisi sine qua non fit. Ita etiam dicimus scientiam vel praescientiam Dei non esse
causam eorum quae fiunt, nisi talem, sine qua non fiunt."
    [41] The composite and divided senses of propositions are treated in many places, such as
Norman Kretzmann, "*Sensus Compositus, Sensus Divisus*, and Propositional Attitudes," *Medioevo* 7 (1981), pp. 195–229. For a medieval explanation, see also William Heytesbury, "'The
Compounded and Divided Senses," in Kretzmann and Eleanor Stump, eds. and trans., *Logic and
the Philosophy of Language* (Cambridge 1988), pp. 415–34.
    [42] This is a scope distinction between $(\Diamond p) \wedge (\Diamond \sim p)$ and $\Diamond (p \wedge \sim p)$.
    [43] Lombardus, *I Sent.*, d. 38, c. 2 (ed. Brady, p. 278, l. 27–279, l. 2): "Deus praescivit hunc
lecturum, vel aliquid huiusmodi; sed potest esse ut iste non legat; ergo potest aliter esse quam
Deus praescivit; ergo potest falli Dei praescientia."

that God has in fact foreknown it in some way, as stated in step (1). In this case, it is understood these are both able to obtain in reality simultaneously: being 'otherwise than as God has foreknown' and God's foreknowing. This, however, is false and contradictory, because they are contradictory, incompatible circumstances. Lombard says that taking the proposition jointly implies a condition, such that on the condition that God knows X already, it is impossible that God should know ~X also, given that condition. As Lombard maintains, "If you understand 'It cannot come about otherwise than as God has foreknown' as [claiming that] each cannot be true at the same time [as the other], you understand a truth." So taking the affirmative proposition in step (3) in the composite sense, it is false, because it says that two contradictories are true at the same time.

If on the other hand one takes the proposition disjointedly (*disiunctim*), or in the divided sense (*sensu diviso*), then it is true. In the divided sense, the modal term 'can' governs the two cases separately, so for event X, foreknown by God, 'God foreknows X' is possible and 'X does not occur' is also possible at the same time, and thus 'it is possible for God to foreknow X' is true, and 'it is possible for X not to occur' is true at the same time. But if X will occur, then God foreknows X, and if X will not occur, God does not foreknow X; that is, it is not possible at the same time for God to foreknow X and for X not to occur.[44] When we take proposition three to be true in the divided sense, it does not entail proposition (4) at all. To those who might say that God had to do and know what He did and knew, Lombard simply says that is not true, that God was able to do and know differently. Using the composite and divided senses in this way, and saying such statements are true dividedly, emphasizes absolute divine freedom for Peter Lombard.[45] Thus, having first said that there is no real causal connection between divine foreknowledge and future events, Lombard now uses a logical tool to show how one proposition, which contains both the notion of God's foreknowledge and the possibility of things being otherwise (meaning that these things are contingent), can be considered true. In this way he safeguards both contingency and foreknowledge.

Lombard turns to several related questions in distinction 39 and solves them all in the same way, explicitly or implicitly, by composition and division. First he must state, in the Platonic and Aristotelian traditions, that God is immutable, and that, because His foreknowledge is the same as His knowledge, which is the same as His essence, His foreknowledge is also immutable. If this is the case, God's foreknowledge cannot change, and to the question "whether God's knowledge can increase or decrease," Lombard answers 'No.'[46] He has the same answer for the question whether God can know or foreknow something anew, or in time, because God cannot change His knowledge.[47]

---

[44]   Thus it is wrong to say $\Diamond$(God knows X $\wedge$ ~X) but not to say $\Diamond$God knows X and $\Diamond$~X.
[45]   Lombardus, *I Sent.*, d. 38, c. 2 (ed. Brady, p. 279, ll. 11–28).
[46]   Lombardus, *I Sent.*, d. 39, c. 1 (ed. Brady, p. 280, ll. 2–3; 15–20).
[47]   Lombardus, *I Sent.*, d. 39, c. 2 (ed. Brady, p. 281, ll. 22–4).

This does not mean God cannot know what will never come about, because the proposition 'It is possible for God to know what will never come about', although false in the composite sense, is true in the divided sense. In the composite sense, 'God knows X' and 'X will never come about' cannot be true at the same time, without jeopardizing the certainty of God's knowledge. In the divided sense, however, there is a simultaneous possibility for God to know X and for X never to come about, but there is no possibility for the simultaneous *actuality* of both cases. So 'God can know X' and 'X will never come about' are not contradictory. Moreover, although 'God can know what He does not know', this does not entail that 'God can begin to know what He does not know', for this would mean change. Again, the original proposition, taken in the divided sense, does not entail the second, false one. Similarly God can know more than He knows, but only in the divided sense.[48]

Sine qua non causality, or necessity, and composition and division would play important roles in the discussions of the topic for the next couple of centuries. In addition, one might say that, at least in his discussion of divine foreknowledge and future contingency, Lombard anticipated a tendency prevalent in the latter half of the thirteenth century to emphasize that God can do anything short of a logical contradiction.

The Moderni

Moving from Peter Lombard to theologians active after 1250, one immediately sees that huge changes have occurred in the structure and content of European intellectual activity in the intervening century between the older thinkers, the *antiqui* and the new scholars, the *moderni*. Much of this Lombard himself helped bring about, because a *Sentences* commentary, where one treated questions following Lombard's sequence, had become compulsory. Theologians were now listing many possible arguments in their questions, and, not wishing to leave any answers untouched, giving exhaustive responses to each argument, sometimes regardless of whether those responses clarified the main question. Actual debates with other scholars were beginning to take shape, in some places almost in a different language from that of Lombard, with much more Aristotelian technical terminology. In addition, almost simultaneously with the rise of the university came the creation of the mendicant orders. The new universities had an obvious impact on scholarship, and the Dominicans, Franciscans, Carmelites, and Augustinian Hermits took a keen interest in education. On the one hand they promoted intellectual activity with their system of schools and financial support, but on the other hand they sometimes created a 'team' atmosphere where one group competed against another, or tended to isolate itself. Thus, Dominicans often copied, quoted, argued with, and defended other Dominicans; Franciscans other Franciscans and so on. By the end of the thirteenth century, Dominican and Franciscan positions devel-

---

[48] Lombardus, *I Sent.*, d. 39, c. 2 (ed. Brady, p. 281, l. 25–282, l. 19).

oped, and only the outstanding members of an order had an impact outside that order. Moreover, the 'argument based' *Sentences* commentaries of the 1250s were giving way to 'position-based' works: instead of merely listing arguments, authors focussed on complete positions opposed to their own. The opening principal arguments against their opinions, while not eliminated, were relegated to the background.[49]

By the early fourteenth century, theologians — especially the Parisian Franciscans who dominated there after 1310 — often considered four basic positions in their discussions of divine foreknowledge and future contingents, although these positions were not mutually exclusive. One was based on a distinction between something considered with respect to proximate causes and with respect to the first cause, God. Another elaborated on the notion of God's knowing things in His eternal present. A third was founded on divine Ideas. Finally a fourth theory held that God has knowledge of future contingents via the determinations of the divine will. The first three positions are all found in the works of Thomas Aquinas (ca. 1225–74). While adopting elements from the second and third positions, Henry of Ghent (before 1240–93) developed the last position, that God's foreknowledge was grounded in the determinations of the divine will. John Duns Scotus (1266–1308) would reject the first three theories, and defend and better articulate the last one. Each of these three theologians changed the direction of the debate in fundamental ways. In order to understand the debate at Paris in the first half of the fourteenth century, it is necessary to describe briefly their positions.

Thomas Aquinas

A treatment of Aquinas's ideas on divine foreknowledge for their own sake would take us to many places in his œuvre, and his thoughts on this topic were probably more complex than his medieval critics claimed.[50] For present purposes we shall look at what most early fourteenth-century scholastics took to be Aquinas's position. To theologians of the fourteenth century, unlike twentieth-century thinkers, Aquinas was known almost equally for his two

---

[49]   For an overview of some of these trends as they relate to the genre of the *Sentences* commentary, see Russell Friedman, "The *Sentences* Commentary, 1250–1320," in Evans, ed., *Commentaries on Peter Lombard's Sentences*, forthcoming.

[50]   Not surprisingly, it is easy to find secondary literature on Aquinas's opinion on future contingents. A good place to start is Craig, chapter 4, "Thomas Aquinas," in *The Problem of Divine Foreknowledge*, pp. 99–126. For a more extensive analysis, see Harm J.M.J. Goris, *Free Creatures of an Eternal God: Thomas Aquinas on God's Foreknowledge and Irresistible Will* (Utrecht 1996). Most general summaries of the issue treat Aquinas, but usually these are philosophical analyses dealing with many of Aquinas's texts. A problem with these analyses for the historian is that they often ignore Aquinas's *Sentences* commentary. Julianus Groblicki recognized the importance of this text in his *De scientia Dei futurorum contingentium secundum s. Thomam eiusque primos sequaces* (Krakow 1938), which, *mutatis mutandis*, is obviously an attempt to do for Aquinas and his followers what Schwamm had done for Scotus in *Das göttliche Vorherwissen*. See Hoenen, *Marsilius of Inghen*, pp. 166–75, for a more recent historical discussion of Aquinas's ideas and their immediate reception.

main comprehensive works, his *Sentences* commentary based on his University of Paris lectures of the 1250's, and his later *Summa theologiae*, where he departs from Peter Lombard's ordering of topics. Aquinas became the Dominicans' teaching doctor in 1286, and Dominican students of theology were required to read his *Sentences* commentary in the early fourteenth century; apologists used this work into the fifteenth century.[51] The most important part of Aquinas's discussion in the *Sentences* commentary, for our purposes, is article five of distinction 38, "Whether God's knowledge is of contingents." There Aquinas develops two of the four classic positions of the pre-Auriol period.

(1) The distinction between proximate and first causes: although God is the first cause and He is necessary, this does not mean that things, the effects, are also necessary, since they depend upon proximate causes which may not be necessary: "For when there are many causes in a chain (*ordinatae*), the last effect does not follow the first cause with respect to necessity and contingency, but [it follows] the proximate cause." Aquinas gives examples of some proximate causes, and causes that are not proximate, and he shows that some are necessary and predictable (the sun's rising, eclipses), others less so (the weather), and some contingent (actions depending on free will). In a famous example, the growth of a tree, Aquinas says that although its remote cause is the movement of the sun, which is necessary, its proximate cause is the "generative power" of the plant. Since this generative power can be impeded, the growth of the plant is contingent, even though its remote cause is necessary. Aquinas repeats this distinction and the example in the *Summa theologiae*.[52]

(2) God knows the future as present in His eternity: for certitude about future events, they must be known in themselves, because knowledge of future contingents via their causes is at best conjectural. It is true that future contingents are not determinately true now, as Aquinas recognizes Aristotle to have held,[53] but this is only with respect to our knowledge, to which future things are future. To God, however, Who is in eternity, all times are present, and all things are seen in actuality and have determinate truth. Citing Boethius's dictum that "every cognition is in accordance with the way of the knower,"

[51] See Friedman, "The *Sentences* Commentary, 1250–1320." Aquinas discussed future contingents and divine foreknowledge in other places, notably *De veritate* and *Summa contra gentiles*, but these works were less important in this context for his successors in the fourteenth century.

[52] Thomas Aquinas, *Scriptum super libros Sententiarum* I, d. 38, q. 1, a. 5 (vol. 1, ed. R.P. Mandonnet [Paris 1929], pp. 909–10): "Quandoque enim sunt causae multae ordinatae, effectus ultimus non sequitur causam primam in necessitate et contingentia sed causam proximam..." See *Summa theologiae*, pars I, q. 14, a. 13.

[53] Aquinas, *Scriptum* I, d. 38, q. 1, a. 5 (ed. Mandonnet, p. 907), giving the second objection: "Praeterea, scientia non est nisi verorum. Sed in futuris contingentibus non est alterum determinate verum, ut Philosophus probat I *Periher.*, cap. ult.; ergo..." In his *Peri Hermeneias* commentary from ca. 1270–71, Aquinas agrees with Aristotle that future contingent propositions are not necessarily true or false determinately, but leaves room for some way of speaking about truth in such propositions. See John F. Wippel, "Divine Knowledge, Divine Power and Human Freedom in Thomas Aquinas and Henry of Ghent," in Rudavsky, *Divine Omniscience* (pp. 213–41), pp. 218–20.

Aquinas concludes, "Since therefore God is eternal, it is necessary that His cognition involve the mode of eternity, which is complete being, all at once, without succession."[54] Aquinas explains this eternal present by means of various analogies. The most famous and elegant of these appear in other writings, where he repeats his position. In an often-quoted passage in his *Summa contra gentiles*, Aquinas likens God's eternity to the center of a circle, and time to the circumference. In an equally influential *auctoritas* in the *Summa theologiae*, Aquinas compares God with someone watching people on a road from on high, where the road is the passage of time.[55]

Fourteenth-century theologians often ascribed these two positions to Aquinas explicitly, but in the secondary literature Aquinas has also been linked to a third stance (3), that God knows future contingents via divine Ideas. The opinion holds that there are Ideas in the divine intellect that represent simple things and complex states of affairs in the future, and all the circumstances of time and place. In the case of this theory, however, I have only found one explicit attribution to Aquinas in the works of Parisian theologians from the period with which this book deals. Moreover, in the specific context of future contingents, Aquinas's statements about divine Ideas are not as pronounced as those about the other two positions, and indeed the opinion is more explicit in Aquinas's Franciscan contemporary, Bonaventure, and others endorsed it as well.[56] Peter Auriol himself would describe it in Henry of Ghent's terms. Scotus would refute the position, but given the amorphous nature of its development, his editors could not identify the author of the Ideas opinion.[57] I shall treat divine Ideas more fully while discussing Auriol.

---

[54]   Aquinas, *Scriptum* I, d. 38, q. 1, a. 5 (ed. Mandonnet, pp. 910–11): "Quod qualiter sit, evidenter docet Boethius in fine *De consol.*, lib. V, prosa ult... 'Omnis enim cognitio est secundum modum cognoscentis', ut dictum est. Cum igitur Deus sit aeternus, oportet quod cognitio eius modum aeternitatis habeat, qui est esse totum simul sine successione."

[55]   See Thomas Aquinas, *Summa Contra Gentiles* I, c. 66 (see *Summa Contra Gentiles. Book One: God*, trans. Anton C. Pegis [Notre Dame 1975], p. 219); *Summa theologiae* pars I, q. 14, a. 13 (see *The Basic Writings of Saint Thomas Aquinas* I, trans. Anton C. Pegis [New York 1945], p. 156). As de la Torre notes, to describe how these things are present to God in eternity Aquinas uses the adverbial form 'praesentialiter' in the *Sentences* commentary (p. 911), but the noun 'praesentialitas' in the *Summa theologiae* (I, q. 14, a. 13) (*Thomas Buckingham*, p. 63, n. 63).

[56]   The anonymous author of the commentary in ÖNB 1439 discussed in chapter 7 labels this Aquinas's position: Anon. OFM, *I Sent.*, dd. 38–39, q. 2, a. 2 (ed. Schabel, "Landulphus Caracciolo," p. 341). Cf. Aquinas, *Scriptum* I, d. 38, q. 1, a. 3 (ed. Mandonnet, p. 904): "Sed idea quae est in mente divina, est causa omnis eius quod in re est; unde per ideam non tantum cognoscit naturam rei, sed etiam hanc rem esse in tali tempore, et omnes conditiones quae consequuntur rem vel ex parte materiae vel ex parte formae." Bonaventura, *Commentarius in quattuor libros Sententiarum* I, d. 39, a. 2, q. 3 (*Opera Omnia* I [ed. Grottaferrata 1882], p. 696b): "... Deus omnium ideas habet praesentes et simul, per quas cognoscit res futuras ita certitudinaliter, sicut si essent praesentes..." It is worth noting a recent monograph by Vivian Boland, *Ideas in God According to Saint Thomas Aquinas. Sources and Synthesis* (Leiden 1996), especially pp. 248–70.

[57]   See Johannes Duns Scotus, *Lectura in librum primum Sententiarum*, d. 39, qq. 1–5 (*Joannis Duns Scoti Opera omnia* XVII, eds. Carolus Balic et al. [Vatican City 1973], p. 484) and *Ordinatio in primum librum Sententiarum*, d. 38, pars secunda, et d. 39, qq. 1–5 (*Joannis Duns Scoti Opera Omnia* VI, eds. Carolus Balic et al. [Vatican City 1963], p. 406). Hoenen, *Marsilius of Ing-*

Before passing to Henry of Ghent, the modal theory Aquinas presents in his *Sentences* commentary in this context should be noted, because it was to play a significant role in later discussions. For Aquinas, because God sees all in the eternal present, only the weak 'necessity of the consequence (or inference)' holds, as opposed to the strong 'necessity of the consequent'.[58] In the consequence 'Scott is walking; therefore Scott is moving', 'Scott is walking' is the antecedent and 'Scott is moving' the consequent.[59] In a good consequence, the consequent follows from the antecedent necessarily, so if the antecedent is absolutely necessary, then the consequent would also be necessary absolutely, and this is what Aquinas calls the necessity of the consequent. But if, as in our example, the antecedent, 'Scott is walking', is not necessary absolutely (it is possible for Scott not to be walking), therefore 'Scott is moving' is only necessary on the contingent condition (and this necessity Aquinas also calls conditioned necessity) that Scott is walking. This is the necessity of the consequence: necessarily, if Scott is walking, Scott is moving. As a corollary to this, Aquinas maintains that the proposition 'It is necessary for everything known by God to be', is true '*de dicto*', or in the composite sense, i.e. on the condition that God knows it, but it is false '*de re*', or in the divided sense.[60]

This distinction was the common intellectual heritage of the later-thirteenth century, although it was often expressed in different terms. Bonaventure, for example, spoke of *necessitas simpliciter* vs. *necessitas ex suppositione*, while three decades later his Franciscan confrère Richard of Middleton distinguished between *necessitas causata* and "concomitant necessity." Others used the terms absolute necessity and necessity *secundum quid*, or 'in a certain respect'.[61]

Nevertheless, Aquinas recognizes a further complication, that would resurface many times: God's knowledge is absolutely necessary, and so in the consequence, 'If it has been foreknown by God, then Socrates is running', it seems

---

hen, pp. 171 and 176, thinks that Aquinas is Scotus's source, but Aquinas's words (see previous note) seem to me no closer to Scotus's presentation of the opinion than do Henry's or Richard of Middleton's.

    [58]   Aquinas, *Scriptum* I, d. 38, q. 1, a. 5 (ed. Mandonnet, p. 912).

    [59]   This is really just a syllogism without a major premise, or topic, in this case 'Everything that is walking is moving'.

    [60]   Aquinas, *Scriptum* I, d. 38, q. 1, a. 5 (ed. Mandonnet, p.914).

    [61]   An excellent discussion of many of these terms and their different nuances is in Cassidy, "Logic and Determinism," pp. 135–40. Absolute necessity can be roughly equated with the following: the necessity of the consequent, preceding necessity, antecedent necessity, necessity in the divided sense, simple necessity (something that is *necessarium simpliciter*), caused necessity, and *de re* necessity (necessity attached to a thing in the world). All of these indicate, in this context, a strong necessity prior to and independent of any supposition; something that is necessary in this way cannot be or have been otherwise. On the other hand, conditioned or conditional necessity can be equated approximately with these terms: the necessity of the consequence, subsequent or following necessity, necessity *ex suppositione*, necessity in the composite sense, necessity *secundum quid* (in a certain respect), concomitant necessity, and *de dicto* necessity (necessity attached to assumptions in statements). These necessities correspond to a weak necessity posterior to and dependent upon some assumption about the world; something necessary in this way *can* have been otherwise, given other, possible, circumstances.

that "the antecedent is absolutely necessary, both because every past thing is necessary, and because every eternal thing is absolutely necessary; thus so is Socrates' running..."[62] Aquinas relates that some claim that 'foreknown', although it refers to the past, really depends on the future.[63] This is a response that Bonaventure gave, and Ockham and many others would later agree. Likewise, in the *Summa theologiae* Aquinas reports that some thinkers hold this entire proposition to be contingent: 'God knew this contingent to be future', because it is composed of a necessary proposition ('God knew') and a contingent one. But Aquinas does not accept this, and he objects that since "contingent is used here only as the matter of the proposition, and not as its principal part, hence its contingency or necessity has no reference to the necessity or contingency of the proposition, or to its being true or false." The propositions 'I said a man is an ass' and 'I said Socrates runs' may both be true if I in fact said those things, regardless of whether a man really is an ass or Socrates really does run. Thus whether the object of God's knowledge is in fact contingent has no bearing on the necessity of the past fact that God knew that contingent to be future. Hence the solution based on propositions about the past's having a relationship toward the future fails. This response would be remembered, as would Aquinas's own solution:

> When the antecedent contains anything belonging to an act of the soul the consequent must be taken, not as it is in itself, but as it is in the soul; for the being of a thing in itself is other than the being of a thing in the soul. For example, when I say, 'What the soul understands is immaterial', the meaning is that it is immaterial as it is in the intellect, not as it is in itself. Likewise if I say, 'If God knew anything, it will be', the consequent must be understood as it is subject to the divine knowledge, that is, as it is in its presentiality. And thus it is necessary, as is also the antecedent; 'for everything that is, while it is, must necessarily be'...[64]

As far as the fourteenth century is concerned, Thomas Aquinas and John Duns Scotus provided the common background against which theologians operated. They often recognized, however, that a third figure, who was active in the interim, played a significant role in the development of the background. For this reason Henry of Ghent merits our attention.

---

[62] Aquinas, *Scriptum* I, d. 38, q. 1, a. 5 (ed. Mandonnet, pp. 907–8): "contra, in omni vera conditionali si antecedens est necessarium absolute, et consequens est necessarium absolute... Sed huius conditionalis, 'Socrates currit, si est praescitum a Deo', antecedens est necessarium absolute: tum quia omne praeteritum est necessarium, tum quia omne aeternum est necessarium absolute. Ergo et Socratem currere..."

[63] Aquinas, *Scriptum* I, d. 38, q. 1, a. 5 (ed. Mandonnet, p. 912): "Et si objiciatur, quod est dictum de praeterito, ergo est necessarium; respondent, quod hoc habet instantiam in praeteritis quae dicunt respectum ad futurum; unde cum dicitur hoc fuisse futurum, quamvis sit dictum de praeterito; tamen quia dependet a futuro, non est necessarium."

[64] Aquinas, *Summa theologiae*, pars I, q. 14, a. 3 (*The Basic Writings*, p. 156).

Henry of Ghent

Generally the *Sentences* commentaries of the great secular theologians of the Golden Age of Scholasticism (1250–1350) either have not been identified, as in the case of Henry of Ghent, Godfrey of Fontaines, and Walter Burley, or survive in one or two manuscripts or even mere fragments, as with Henry of Harclay, Thomas Wylton, and Thomas Bradwardine. Because they did not have the institutional backing of the mendicant orders, they instead had to make their reputations after they had become masters of theology, in separate theological treatises such as a *Summa*, or in ordinary or quodlibetal disputations. In a quodlibetal disputation, traditionally held during Advent and Lent, members of the audience asked the supposedly unprepared master a question "about anything at all" (*de quolibet*), and until the written records of such theological exercises died out in the 1320's and 1330's, they constituted an important form of dissemination for the ideas of both secular and regular theologians.[65] Thus for Henry of Ghent (before 1240–93) we rely primarily on a great *Summa* and many quodlibetal questions. Henry's stance on divine foreknowledge is contained in question two of his *Quodlibet* VIII from Paris disputations during Advent in 1284.

Henry's position turns out to be an interesting mixture. I have already mentioned that he endorsed the position based on divine Ideas, and that Peter Auriol, for one, dealt with that position in Henry's terms. He also adopted the theory that God knows the future as present to His eternity, although Henry nuanced his version in response to previous critiques of Aquinas that maintained that eternal presence entailed eternal existence.[66] Henry's version had an impact. Franciscans before Scotus, such as Bonaventure, were not opposed to utilizing eternal presence in their treatments of divine foreknowledge. For example, the influential Richard of Middleton, whose *Sentences* commentary

[65]   On the quodlibetal disputation, see Paul Glorieux, *La littérature quodlibétique de 1260 à 1320*, 2 vols. (Kain, Belgium 1925; Paris 1935), which goes past 1320, and John F. Wippel, "Quodlibetal Questions Chiefly in Theology Faculties," in B. Bazan, idem, G. Fransen, and D. Jacuart, *Les Questions disputées et les questions quodlibétiques dans les facultés de théologie, de droit, et de médecine* (Turnhout 1985), pp. 151–222. After 1330 the *Sentences* commentary becomes more important for seculars such as Richard Fitzralph.

[66]   Brown makes this point in "Walter Burley, Peter Aureoli and Gregory of Rimini," p. 380, and in his introduction to Salviati, *De arcanis Dei*, pp. 51–2. A few years after Aquinas's death in 1274, the Franciscan William de la Mare (ca. 1279) penned a *Correctorium* against the Dominican master, in which he charged that the eternal presence of future events in fact entailed their eternal existence, if not in nature, then at least in God's eternity. This set off a battle over the correct interpretation and defense of Aquinas's opinion, the Dominican Thomas of Sutton (ca. 1290) being one of his supporters (see John F. Wippel, "Thomas of Sutton on Divine Knowledge of Future Contingents [Quodlibet II, qu. 5]," in S. Knuuttila, R. Työrinoja, and S. Ebbesen, eds., *Knowledge and the Sciences in Medieval Philosophy. Proceedings of the Eighth International Congress of Medieval Philosophy* II [Helsinki 1990], pp. 364–72). In addition to Groblicki, *De scientia Dei*, Wippel cites F. Schmitt's study *Die Lehre des hl. Thomas von Aquin vom göttlichen Wissen des Zukünftig Kontingenten bei seinen grossen Kommentatoren* (Nijmegen 1950) for the reception of Aquinas on this issue.

was probably put into its final form in the years just following Henry's *Quodlibet* VIII, supported eternal presence in wording more reminiscent of Henry than of Aquinas.[67] Moreover, later thinkers such as Auriol and Gerard Odonis would borrow Henry's phrase "abstracts from every differentia of time," to describe God's knowledge.[68] Finally, Henry's imagery was important enough that, in the 1320s, one author would attribute the solution based on eternal presence to Henry rather than Aquinas.[69]

The most original and influential element in Henry's contribution to the debate on divine foreknowledge, however, was his assertion that God knows the future primarily because He knows the determinations of His own will. As a few fourteenth-century scholastics were aware, Scotus later adopted this element of Henry's theory as the basis of his own opinion, but he was to reject the other two positions that Henry and many Franciscans had espoused. As in the case of many issues, Henry thus acted as a catalyst for Scotus and the Franciscans, coaxing them toward divine voluntarism.[70]

Although Henry was a secular theologian, he had close intellectual affinities with the Franciscans. One of the important disagreements between the Dominicans and the Franciscans was their differing emphases on the divine intellect and the divine will respectively. One can already discern in the early works of the Dominican Aquinas a tendency to stress the primacy of the divine intellect and, therefore, the necessary nature of God, whereas in the Franciscan Bonaventure's contemporary writings one perceives that the divine will is the more important attribute, and therefore God's freedom is higher. As the thirteenth century drew to a close, the variance between the two main mendicant orders grew, and colored their positions on many issues.[71] The general climate of the latter third of the thirteenth century leaned toward the Franciscan approach and against Aquinas and the Dominicans, and in the year 1277, first at Paris and then at Oxford, authorities condemned numerous articles of which many seemed to restrict God's power. The Condemnations of 1277 are a mere symptom of a wider abhorrence of limitations on God's absolute freedom, and Henry of Ghent was a major figure in this trend.[72]

---

[67] See Richardus de Mediavilla, *Super quatuor libros Sententiarum* I, d. 39, a. 1, a. 1 (ed. Brescia 1591, p. 345a–b). Here Middleton joins in the debate over the interpretation of Aquinas's position, dealing with the objection that "illa non coexistunt quae non existunt..." That Bonaventure also appears to support the eternal presence solution is shown the quotation above, n. 56.

[68] Henricus de Gandavo, *Quaestiones quodlibetales* VIII, q. 2 (vol. 2, ed. Venice 1613, f. 6va): "... nunc eternitatis prout abstrahit ab omni differentia temporis..."

[69] That is, the anonymous author of ÖNB 1439. See Anon. OFM, *I Sent.*, dd. 38–39, q. 2, a. 2 (ed. Schabel, "Landulphus Caracciolo," p. 341).

[70] On the relationship between Henry and Scotus, see recently Stephen D. Dumont, "Henry of Ghent and Duns Scotus,"in Marenbon, ed., *Medieval Philosophy*, pp. 291–328.

[71] See for example Russell L. Friedman, *"In Principio Erat Verbum.* The Incorporation of Philosophical Psychology into Trinitarian Theology, 1250–1325" (PhD Dissertation, University of Iowa 1997), pp. 194–6, which demonstrates how this basic difference affected Franciscan and Dominican theories about the generation of the Son and procession of the Holy Spirit.

[72] The historical literature on the condemnations of 1277 is extensive. See for example

And so Henry claims that unlike humans, whose intellect determines what is to be done and inclines the will toward it, God's will determines what is to be done, and His intellect knows the thing that will be done by knowing the determinations of the divine will. A philosopher, according to Henry, maintains that God does things via the intellect, and of necessity, so that God's intellect is practical. A theologian, on the other hand, must defend God's freedom, and hold that although the divine intellect, via *Ideas*, knows all things and all ways of producing them before the will acts, nevertheless, insofar as they are to be done, it is the will that determines them and the intellect that *quasi* follows.[73]

Henry discusses all three elements of his position at length and more than once, sometimes together in the same sentence, and it is certainly much more complex than has been portrayed here. For present purposes it is enough to know that Scotus would reject Ideas and eternal presence and retain the notion that God knows the future via the determinations of the divine will, and

---

John F. Wippel, "The Condemnations of 1270 and 1277 at Paris," *The Journal of Medieval and Renaissance Studies* 7 (1977), pp. 169–201; Roland Hissette, *Enquête sur les 219 articles condamnés à Paris le 7 mars 1277* (Louvain 1977); and three recent works from the SIEPM conference in Erfurt, August 1997, all in Jan A. Aertsen and Andreas Speer, eds., *Was ist Philosophie im Mittelalter* (Berlin 1998): Alain de Libera, "Philosophie et censure. Remarques sur la crise universitaire de 1270–1277," pp. 71–89, Luca Bianchi, "1277: A Turning Point in Medieval Philosophy?" pp. 90–110, and John Murdoch, "1277 and Late Medieval Natural Philosophy," pp. 111–21. Although it may be true that the condemnations did have an effect on physics and cosmology (see e.g. Edward Grant, "The Condemnation of 1277, God's Absolute Power and Physical Thought in the Late Middle Ages," *Viator* 10 [1979], pp. 211–44), and scholars were certainly aware of the condemnations, whether they changed theology to any significant degree is debatable. As far as future contingents, I agree with Normore ("Future Contingents," p. 376): "The Condemnation of 1277 had clearly established that God's power extended beyond the actual course of nature, but even this had not produced a fundamental change. One still looked to God's causal power for insight into possibility."

[73] See Henricus de Gandavo, *Quodlibet* VIII, q. 2 (ed. Venice, f. 3va–b): "Secundo autem modo scit res sciendo determinationem suae voluntatis. Quia enim et quae determinat voluntas Dei facienda, et hoc modo quo ea determinat, scit intellectus eius ea esse facienda, et sic facienda, et non e converso, ut in hoc voluntas potius sit ratio et causa scientiae et intellectus Dei quam e converso; ut secundum hoc in nobis scientia nostra practica multo magis sit causa rerum operabilium a nobis, inquamtum scilicet intellectus noster determinat operanda priusquam ea determinat voluntas, et cum hoc movet naturaliter et inclinat voluntatem ad sequendum suam determinationem, quam sit scientia divina causa rerum operabilium a Deo, inquantum scilicet secundum praedicta intellectus divinus non determinat operanda, nec sic determinat et inclinat voluntatem divinam, ut non possit proprie dici practicus, sicut intellectus noster. Unde quod eius scientia sit per se causa rerum non potest dicere theologus, qui ponit quod Deus agit res libera voluntate, ita quod posset eas agere et non agere. Sed philosophus, qui ponit quod non agit eas nisi per intellectum et de necessitate, ut iam patebit ex dictis Avicennae. Propter quod philophus etiam potius posset ponere intellectum Dei practicum et ideas [3vb] practicas quam theologus. Unde licet intellectus divina illa quae sunt operanda et similiter modos omnes operandorum a sua voluntate novit quodammodo priusquam voluntas ea determinet esse operanda, et quo ad hoc quodammodo practicus est, et novit illa ideis ut sunt practicae, quae eaedem sunt cum ipsis speculativis, sicut idem est intellectus speculativus et practicus, inquantum tamen operanda sunt non novit nisi quasi praecedente determinatione voluntatis." On this topic, see also Wippel, "Divine Knowledge," pp. 227–8.

this choice had profound repercussions for the entire future of Franciscan theology on this issue. Moreover, it was often Henry's presentation of eternal presence and Ideas that later Franciscans read when dealing with those opinions. More than Henry, however, it was Scotus, a key figure in the probing reanalysis of necessity and possibility that was prevalent in the late thirteenth century, who towers above all others in the period for his influence in the fourteenth and even fifteenth centuries.

John Duns Scotus

Theologians active after the Franciscan John Duns Scotus (ca. 1266–1308) recognized him as an important and profound thinker, and they nicknamed him 'the Subtle Doctor' or, for some Franciscans, simply 'the Doctor'. In later discussions of future contingents and divine foreknowledge, except for those of some Dominicans, his name and ideas are almost always mentioned. Scotus's opinions on the subject are to be found in distinction 39 of his *Sentences* commentaries stemming from lectures at Cambridge, Oxford, and Paris. The *Lectura prima* and the *Ordinatio* (*Opus Oxoniense*), both based on Oxford lectures given before 1300, are the more detailed versions. As these two are very similar, I will simply concentrate on the *Lectura*.[74] There is some question as to whether Scotus was the author of the distinction in the *Ordinatio*, or how close it is to his intentions if a follower put it together from his notes, and thus it is inserted in an appendix in the critical edition. Since later scholastics identify this distinction with Scotus anyway, this worry need not concern us here.[75]

---

[74] This is also what Allan B. Wolter does in "Scotus' Paris Lectures on God's Knowledge of Future Events," in idem, *The Philosophical Theology of John Duns Scotus*, ed. Marilyn McCord Adams (Ithaca, NY 1990), pp. 285–333. The *Ordinatio* material was translated by Wolter in *Duns Scotus, Philosophical Writings* (Edinburgh 1962), again by Martin Tweedale in Bosley and idem, eds., *Basic Issues in Medieval Philosophy*, pp. 284–300, and in part by James J. Walsh in Arthur Hyman and idem, eds., *Philosophy in the Middle Ages. The Christian, Islamic, and Jewish Traditions* (Indianapolis 1973), pp. 632–9. A translation of the *Lectura* forms the basis of A. Vos et al. eds. and trans., *John Duns Scotus: Contingency and Freedom: Lectura I, 39* (Dordrecht 1994), which is a major new secondary study as well. See also Douglas C. Langston, *God's Willing Knowledge. The Influence of Scotus' Analysis of Omniscience* (University Park, Pennsylvania 1986). Hoenen (*Marsilius of Inghen*, pp. 175–84), Craig (the chapter "John Duns Scotus," in *The Problem of Divine Foreknowledge*, pp. 127–45), and de la Torre (*Thomas Buckingham*, pp. 69–81) are brief recent treatments, while Schwamm (*Das göttliche Vorherwissen*) is a still a good historical overview. In the last two decades the number of philosophical treatments had grown tremendously. For example, in E. P. Bos, ed., *John Duns Scotus (1265/6–1308). Renewal of Philosophy* (Amsterdam 1998), of the fourteen collected papers, seven concern in some way what Scotus says on future contingents!

[75] For the chronology, see Charles Balic, "The Life and Works of John Duns Scotus," in eds. J.K. Ryan and B.M. Bonansea, eds., *John Duns Scotus 1265–1965* (Washington D.C. 1965), pp. 1–27, and Dumont, "Henry of Ghent and John Duns Scotus," pp. 293–5, for a summarized update. For a discussion of the authenticity of distinction 39 in the *Ordinatio*, see Wolter, "Scotus' Paris Lectures," and also Stephen D. Dumont, "The Origin of Scotus's Theory of Synchronic Contingency," *The Modern Schoolman* 72 (Jan/March 1995) (pp. 149-67), p. 150, n. 7, which argues for its authenticity. Based solely on a comparison with the *Lectura*, I would certainly agree.

Scholars then and now have recognized Scotus as a pivotal figure in medieval thought, and he altered the path of the debate on future contingents, though perhaps not as much as has been claimed. The first thing Scotus does is attack the three positions found in the work of Aquinas, and numerous Franciscans afterwards would paraphrase Scotus's refutions. Boethius and Aquinas, as we have seen, laid out a theory in which God exists simultaneously with all time. Scotus retorts that the only instant in time that exists is the present one: only *now* exists and can exist. Accordingly, Scotus claims that "nothing is present to eternity except the 'now' of time." Aquinas's analogy of one sitting at the center of a circle fails, because as a radius sweeps out the circumference of the circle, the entire circle does not exist all at once. The circumference, like time, is not static, but in flux, and only the point on the circumference touched by the sweeping radius exists at any one time.[76] This does not mean, however, that Scotus denies that God exists without succession, and that He wills in one eternal 'instant', as we shall see.

Scotus also rejects the position that God knows future contingents via Ideas in the divine mind, giving two particularly forceful arguments. First, because Ideas necessarily represent what they represent, they do not seem suited to representing contingents, in which 'X' or 'not-X' might turn out to be the case. Perhaps Ideas could represent simple terms, such as 'computer', and necessary complexes of terms, such as 'a triangle has three sides', but they could not represent contingent complexes, such as 'this printer will work tomorrow', which we can call X. If God had the Idea of X only, eternally He would know only one part of a contradiction, and there would be no contingency. If He knew both parts, X and ~X, he would know contradictories to be true simultaneously. Second, since Ideas represent both futures that are possible but will not exist, and futures that are possible and will exist, one needs to posit a way to distinguish between what will exist and what will not exist.[77]

Finally, Scotus attacks Aquinas's view that contingency lies in proximate causes. Scotus and Aquinas have fundamentally different starting points in their theories. Although Aquinas considers the first cause, God, to be necessary, he does not think that the chain of natural secondary causes works necessarily. Scotus disagrees completely, and the example of the sun, the plant, and the plant's 'generative power' is opposed to Scotus's view of natural causation, in which the chain of secondary causes cannot originate any contingency:

> ... nothing in the universe is *necessary* without qualification, but only in a certain respect, namely because the secondary causes — insofar as they are considered on their own — have a necessary disposition toward their causes, just as fire considered on its own with respect to heating...[78]

---

[76]   Scotus, *Lectura* I, d. 39, qq. 1–5 (ed. Balic, pp. 507, l. 10–508, l. 6).

[77]   Scotus, *Lectura* I, d. 39, qq. 1–5 (ed. Balic, p. 485, ll. 15–26).

[78]   Scotus, *Lectura* I, d.39, qq.1–5 (ed. Balic, p. 509, ll. 12–19): "... nihil est simpliciter ne-

The main objective of Scotus's discussion is to find how contingency can exist, and how contingents are known. Interestingly, Scotus claims that we have to accept the existence of contingency as obvious, a *per se notum* (something known through itself), because he does not think it can be proven sufficiently through things prior to it or more known, as is required in a proof.[79] For Scotus, contingency, once accepted, cannot lie in secondary causes, on account of the necessity of the chain of causes; therefore contingency must reside in the first cause, if contingency is to exist at all and be passed down to particulars.[80] Most later Franciscans would adopt this stance.

Before explicating fully how contingency arises in God, Scotus explains in what senses humans are free to choose opposite possibilities. In one way we can choose in succession, because we are mutable. For example, 'someone standing can be sitting' is true in the divided sense because a person can choose to change over time from standing in instant A to sitting in instant B. This is the diachronic contingency mentioned above (p. 26). In the composite sense, of course, the proposition is false, because it would imply that her sitting and standing at the same time is possible; this is false because of synchronic necessity.[81]

In a second way, Scotus says, there is a logical potentiality, corresponding to a real potentiality, to will opposites at the same time. Scotus says that in the same instant in which the will wills A, it is able not to will A. As long as there is no repugnance between the terms in the proposition, there remains this logical, formal possibility, which is simply the possibility by which compound modal propositions are true in the divided sense. Propositions such as 'a sitting person can stand', as Lombard had said, are true in the divided sense, because there is no logical, formal repugnance for a person to be standing. In the composite sense, however, there is the relative incompossibility that, assuming this person is sitting, he cannot also be standing at the same time.[82]

What about the corresponding real capacity for opposites? Scotus appears to be aiming at synchronic contingency here. Scotus uses the logical capacity to explain the real one by resorting to atemporal 'instants of nature'.[83] Scotus

cessarium in universo, sed secundum quid tantum, scilicet quia causae secundae — quantum est ex parte earum — habent necessariam habitudinem ad suas causas (sicut ignis ad calefaciendum quantum est ex parte sui)..."

[79] Scotus, *Lectura* I, d. 39, qq. 1–5 (ed. Balic, p. 490, ll. 23–4 and p. 491, ll. 17–18).
[80] Scotus, *Lectura* I, d. 39, qq. 1–5 (ed. Balic, p. 492, ll. 4–12).
[81] Scotus, *Lectura* I, d. 39, qq. 1–5 (ed. Balic, p. 494, ll. 11–20).
[82] Scotus, *Lectura* I, d. 39, qq. 1–5 (ed. Balic, pp. 494, ll. 21–495, l. 24). Boethius, Anselm, Lombard, and Aquinas probably understood there to be a simultaneous capacity for opposites in the way Scotus envisioned. I am inclined to suppose that they would have interpreted "*omne quod est, quando est, necesse est esse*" in a 'Scotistic' sense, given that they applied the rules of composition and division to such propositions as 'God can know what He does not know', since they could not have allowed any succession in God.
[83] Since Simo Knuuttila and Anja Inkeri Lehtinen, "Change and Contradiction: A Fourteenth-Century Controversy," *Synthèse* 40 (1979), pp. 189–207, there has been an explosion in the number of studies devoted to instants of nature, synchronic and diachronic contingency, and the limits of change, much of it having to do with Scotus. Just as there are dozens of studies on

understands there to be a conceptual succession, or logical ordering, in each instant of time — which is itself without succession; these are instants not of time, but of nature. Thus, in a first instant of nature, one is still free, and has a real capacity, to choose one of a pair of opposites. In the second instant of nature the choice is made, and no such real capacity exists. Scotus appeals to this distinction between instants of time and nature because he wants to ground contingency in God, Who only exists in one 'instant' of eternity.[84]

God, then, is immutable, and has no succession. Although He exists perhaps in a different type of eternity for Scotus than for some previous thinkers, it is nevertheless an unchanging one. For Scotus, God exists, wills, and knows in one instant of eternity. In order for God to have freedom then, and in order for contingency to arise from that freedom, He must have the real capacity to will the opposite of what He does will in the eternal instant.[85] Scotus describes the situation carefully, building on Henry of Ghent. Scotus divides God's one instant of atemporal eternity into three or four atemporal instants of nature, or 'signs', in which one instant of nature is in some sense 'prior' to another. In the first instant of nature the divine essence represents to the divine intellect simple terms of propositions, both necessary and contingent.[86] In the second instant, the divine intellect forms all possible propositions, that is every pair of contradictory propositions, but in a neutral way, before they possess truth and falsity, and offers them to His will. In the third instant of nature, the divine will chooses one proposition of each pair of contradictions, and "for that instant for which it wills, [its significate] will be." What happens in this third 'sign' asserts the primacy of God's will, for not until the fourth instant of nature does the divine intellect know the choices of the divine will. Scotus gives two ways for this to happen. The first way appears to be Henry of Ghent's, in that the intellect sees the determination of the will, knows it cannot be impeded, and therefore knows a future thing will be in such and such a temporal instant.

Scotus's view of divine foreknowledge, there are dozens on this issue. A recent broad discussion of Scotus on this and related topics is Michael Sylwanowicz, *Contingent Causality and the Foundations of Duns Scotus' Metaphysics* (Leiden 1996). On instants of nature specifically, see for example Paul Vincent Spade, "Quasi-Aristotelianism," in Norman Kretzmann, ed., *Infinity and Continuity in Ancient and Medieval Thought* (Cornell 1982), pp. 297–307; and Stephen D. Dumont, "Time, Contradiction and Freedom of the Will in the Late Thirteenth Century," DSTFM 3.2 (1992), pp. 561–97.

[84] Dumont has investigated the sources of Scotus's theory of synchronic contingency in "The Origin of Scotus's Theory of Synchronic Contingency," pp. 149–67. Scott MacDonald, in a response, maintains that Scotus promises much here, but fails to deliver. See S. MacDonald, "Synchronic Contingency, Instants of Nature, and Libertarian Freedom: Comments on the 'Background to Scotus's Theory of the Will'," *The Modern Schoolman* 72 (Jan/March 1995), pp. 169–73. I agree with MacDonald that, to the extent that Scotus's theory is supported by good arguments, it is not new, and whatever is new is not well supported.

[85] Scotus, *Lectura* I, d. 39, qq. 1–5 (ed. Balic, p. 497, ll. 20–30).

[86] Not all Scotists will say that in the first instant of nature the essence represents all propositions as neutral to the intellect, and Scotists will disagree on the number of instants of nature involved, positing between three and five.

Although this way was the one followed by almost all Scotists in the four-teenth and fifteenth centuries, and only a couple of figures ascribed it to Henry of Ghent,[87] it introduced a certain degree of 'discursiveness' into God with which Scotus was uncomfortable. Scotus instead says:

> Therefore one can put this another way, and perhaps better, that when the will has determined itself to one side, then that thing has the characteristic (ratio) of being makeable or producible — and the intel-lect sees that proposition not through the fact that it sees the determi-nation of the will, but [rather] His essence is at that point the immedi-ate basis of representing that proposition to the intellect. I am not say-ing that the essence first represents to the divine intellect the terms of that proposition, and from this [represents] the proposition [to the di-vine intellect], just as occurs in our intellect, for in that case the divine intellect would be cheapened; but... just as the divine intellect [read: the divine essence] is immediately the basis of understanding terms for the divine intellect, so also [it is the basis of understanding] the propo-sition.[88]

This is not to say that God's determinate knowledge of the proposition makes that proposition about future contingents as determinately true as those about the past or present. For although in the latter there is determinate truth — even necessary truth — so that it is impossible for them to be false, with re-spect to future contingents God's determinate knowledge is such that allows for enough indetermination that it is still in the power of their cause to do the opposite.[89]

In the whole process of divine willing and knowing there is no time in-volved, no discursive reasoning, only instants of nature. Hence God chooses freely in that one, eternal instant, and has the capacity to choose the opposite of what He chooses in that very instant. This is whence contingency in the world comes. Foreknowledge comes when God's intellect sees in the divine es-

---

[87] Although Henry of Ghent did have a great effect on Scotus, this was not always di-rectly perceived or discussed by later figures debating future contingency. An important excep-tion, to his credit, is Peter Auriol himself, who was well aware of Henry of Ghent's impact, as Schwamm recognized (Das göttliche Vorherwissen, pp. 99–100). Hoenen (Marsilius of Inghen, p. 175) mentions also that Alexander of Alessandria may have known Henry's role.

[88] Scotus, Lectura I, d. 39, qq. 1–5 (ed. Balic, pp. 500, l. 13–501, l. 19): "Ideo potest aliter sic dici, et forte melius, quod quando voluntas determinavit se ad unam partem, tunc illud habet rationem factibilis et producibilis, — et tunc intellectus non per hoc quod videt determinationem voluntatis, videt illam complexionem, sed essentia sua sibi est immediata ratio repraesentandi tunc illam complexionem. Non dico quod essentia primo repraesentat intellectui divino terminos illius complexionis, et ex hoc complexionem (sicut accidit in intellectu nostro), tunc enim intellec-tus divinus vilesceret; sed... intellectus divinus [read 'essentia divina'] sicut immediate est ratio intellectui divino intelligendi terminos, ita et complexionem."

[89] Scotus, Lectura I, d. 39, qq. 1–5 (ed. Balic, pp. 502, l. 18–503, l. 7). The term indetermi-natio is employed in the Ordinatio, where Scotus also says that future contingents have some de-terminate truth in themselves. Cf. Ordinatio I, d. 38, pars 2 and d. 39, qq. 1–5 (ed. Balic, p. 432, ll. 7 and 9).

sence the determinations of the divine will.[90] This position and often the 'first way' were associated with Scotus for the remainder of the Middle Ages.[91] Some theologians, especially outside the Franciscan order, would find Scotus's solution to be in many ways the least satisfactory of all because it appears to deny human free will.[92] Regardless of whether they were correct, Scotus radically redirected the course of the debate, even for his opponents.

---

[90]   Some of the problems of Scotus's theory of divine foreknowledge and future contingents Auriol will attack. I shall note one more: how does the divine will 'know' whether it has chosen a set of compossible true propositions? For example, suppose that the will actualizes "Chris will die at time A" and "Chris will lecture on Scotus at time B (after A)"; how will the divine will know that it must necessarily also actualize one of the infinite number of propositions for times between A and B that say, "Chris will rise from the dead"? If the divine will does know, what is the need for the divine intellect? A possible solution for Scotus would be that the divine intellect must first devise a (perhaps) infinite number of possible histories of the entire world, all logically consistent in themselves. Next, the intellect offers these systems to the will, and finally the will has only one choice to make, although among a perhaps infinite number of options, rather than a perhaps infinite number of choices each with two options. Some of these systems have necessary chains of natural causes, some do not, some have human 'freedom', some do not. The will chooses one system, perhaps for no 'reason', and Scotus would say that it chose a system with necessary natural causes working almost all of the time, miracles occasionally, human free will in some mysterious sense, etc.

[91]   Even here Scotus was probably building on Henry of Ghent. Consider this passage in Henricus de Gandavo, *Quodlibet* VIII, q. 2 (ed. Venice, f. 5rb): "... scit omnia talia sciendo invariabilem essentiam et invariabilem voluntatis determinationem... Quia enim circa instantia temporis determinavit singulis in quibus ea esset facturus et conservaturus, sciendo suam essentiam cum voluntatis suae determinatione invariabili simul et aequali invariabilitate scit futura esse futura cum sunt futura, et non esse futura cum non sunt futura, et esse presentia cum sunt presentia..." Modern commentators appear unaware of this. Cf. Craig, *The Problem of Divine Foreknowledge*, p. 136, and Hoenen, *Marsilius of Inghen*, pp. 175 and 177–8. Perhaps Henry's *Quodlibet* VIII was as confusing for his medieval readers as it is for us, and only a critical edition of the text will help clarify his opinion.

[92]   On this question, see the recent examination and overview of previous literature in Sylwanowicz, *Contingent Causality*, pp. 193–210, and the important analysis of Joachim Ronald Söder, *Kontingenz und Wissen: Die Lehre von den futura contingentia bei Johannes Duns Scotus* (Münster 1998), who also publishes pertinent sections of Scotus's *Reportatio*.

Chapter 2

The Immediate Context

Thomas Aquinas, Henry of Ghent, and John Duns Scotus were the primary figures in the debate over divine foreknowledge and future contingents in the half century before Peter Auriol completed his giant *Scriptum in Primum Librum Sententiarum* in 1316. Aside from Aquinas's distinction between proximate and first causes, in the 1250s Franciscans and Dominicans had been in basic agreement with the theory whose most famous adherent was also Aquinas, that God's knowledge of future contingents somehow involved their presence to God's eternity and divine Ideas. Although there was some debate within the bounds of that agreement, it was still possible for the secular theologian Henry of Ghent to keep both of the those elements in the 1280s, but he added a new notion, that God knows the future via the determinations of the divine will. Around 1300 the Franciscan Scotus effectively split whatever unity there was between the Franciscans and the Dominicans by rejecting Ideas and eternal presence in favor of Henry's new theory, which Scotus articulated much more clearly, adding his distinctive instants of nature account. It is within this context that Peter Auriol would develop a fifth basic theory, and like the other three theologians he changed the direction of the debate for the coming decades in fundamental ways.

In order to understand Auriol's position, it will be necessary to describe his immediate context at the University of Paris in the 1310s.[1] It will be helpful to present the basics of Auriol's opinion first, however, to see how the others anticipate him negatively or positively. Auriol maintained that if there were any metaphysical, logical, or physical determination with respect to future events before they happened, those events would occur of necessity, and there would be no contingency, no free will. Thus God cannot know future events before they happen, otherwise either they would occur necessarily, or God's knowledge would be mistaken. Moreover, Auriol equated immutability and necessity and held to a particularly strong notion of divine simplicity and perfection. He therefore adopted a stance that held that God, in His atemporal eternity, knows all events that are future to us, but not future to Him. God does not know them *before* they happen, because He is temporally *indistant* from them negatively. In Auriol's words, God is the 'eminent similitude' and 'exemplar' of all things, representing them 'indistantly' in His eternity. Along with this, Auriol denied that future-tensed propositions about contingents are true or false. If they were true now, then what they signified would have to come about. In addition, because God's knowledge of such events does not

---

[1] On general dating for this period, I follow Friedman, "The *Sentences* Commentary, 1250–1320."

precede the events temporally, it does not make those propositions true or false. Finally, Auriol wanted to avoid a close connection between God's will and future events, because otherwise, God could know such futures qua future via the determinations of His will, and, according to Auriol, God would be involved causally in sinning, which Auriol found intolerable. Besides, God's intrinsic will was the same as God, atemporal, immutable, and absolutely necessary, and could not for Auriol be the source of activity and hence change. Thus Auriol distinguished between God's intrinsic and extrinsic will. For Auriol, God's intrinsic will 'of complacency', necessary and immutable, is indifferent to things outside Himself, and is equally pleased whether events occur one way or the opposite. To preserve God's activity in the world, however, Auriol resorted to what he called God's active, extrinsic will 'of operation', by which He was involved in creation, for example.

Thus, Auriol's main thrusts are the following: (1) Immutability equals necessity, and if God immutably knows the future before it happens, the future cannot not occur, and thus comes about of necessity; which is false, according to Auriol; (2) therefore God, in His eternity, knows the future not as future, but as present or, more properly, as indistant; (3) future-tensed propositions about contingents are not true or false, and God's knowledge of the future does not make them true or false; (4) there is a distinction between God's intrinsic and extrinsic will.

The Franciscan Reaction to Scotus

Franciscans and Franciscan sympathizers after Scotus generally echoed his attacks on divine Ideas and eternal presence, and adopted the theory based on the determinations of the divine will. In fact, a convenient litmus test for assigning undated Franciscan theological works to this period is whether they react to Scotus and not to Auriol.[2] These theologians usually did not accept

---

[2]   I would date to this period a *Sentences* commentary in Città del Vaticano, Biblioteca Apostolica, Ottob. lat. 360 and Lyon, Bibliothèque de la ville 653, because the author is a Scotist who refutes Aquinas but does not discuss Auriol. Victorin Doucet, *Commentaires sur les Sentences: supplément au répertoire de M. Frédéric Stegmuller* (Florence 1954), p. 112, identifies Ottob. lat. 360 with Lyon 653. In Ottob. lat. 360 (fol. 199v) the author asks "Utrum cum infallibili divina prescientia possint non evenire futura contingentia." On 202r–v, for example, the author discusses and accepts Scotus's four signs, or instants of nature. He treats Aquinas on, e.g., 201v. This commentary displays some similarities to the slightly later work of Peter of Navarre (on whom see below, chapter 8).

Likewise the author of a commentary in Vat. lat. 869 was probably at Paris and comes from the decade after Scotus, unless he is later and very conservative. Stephen Dumont has dated other material in the manuscript to 1312–17, and these dates fit the commentary found on folios 166–89. Questions concerning future contingents in the ms. are as follows: fol. 184ra: "Iuxta distinctionem 38 queritur primo utrum scientia Dei sit causa rerum," fol. 184rb: "Queritur utrum Deus habeat scientiam de futuris contingentibus," and fol. 184vb: "Iuxta distinctionem 39 utrum scientia Dei sit infinitorum," the latter question ending at 185va. All of these appear to be pre-Auriol. For Dumont's discussion of a text in Vat. lat. 869, see Stephen F. Brown and Stephen D. Dumont, "The Univocity of the Concept of Being in the Fourteenth Century: III. An Early Scotist," *Mediaeval Studies* 51 (1989), pp. 19–38, and Brown has also edited the text in the same article.

Scotus's theory in the *second* way he presented it, however, but rather often took it in the first way, that is, the one usually attributed to Henry of Ghent by modern historians. For example, Henry of Harclay, like Henry of Ghent a secular theologian with close connections with Franciscan theology, criticized eternal presence in his Paris *Sentences* commentary from just after 1300, and accepted a non-specific Scotistic stance in favor of the determinations of the divine will. Among the Franciscans, Alexander of Alessandria, in his second redaction of his Parisian *Sentences* commentary (1307–08), rejected both Ideas and 'real' eternal presence in arguing for "Henry of Ghent's" version. This is also the case with John of Bassol, whose *Sentences* commentary is a revision of his lectures at Reims given in 1313. In the early 1310s at Paris, Hugh of Novocastro followed a similar line. William of Alnwick, Scotus's secretary, appears not to have addressed the issue in his *Sentences* commentary of ca. 1314, but in his Bologna *Determinationes* of 1323 he argued expressly against Scotus's second version, because "whatever the divine essence represents, it represents naturally, and what it represents naturally, it represents before the act of the divine will."[3] Auriol himself employed a similar argument against the Subtle Doctor.

By contrast, Robert Cowton, lecturing around 1310 probably somewhere other than Paris, and the author of a *Sentences* commentary attributed to Antonius Andreas († ca. 1335) both adopted a "mixed position" combining the Scotistic determinations of the divine will with a Thomist reliance on eternal presence. As Hoenen points out, this could appear to be a return to Henry of Ghent rather than a mixture of Scotus and Aquinas.[4] Still, despite the fact that it is difficult to find a fully-fledged Scotist on this issue in this period, with the exception of James of Ascoli, it was Scotus's treatment that set the

---

[3] On Harclay see Mark Henninger, "Henry of Harclay's Questions on Divine Prescience and Predestination," FcS 40 (1980), pp. 167–243, for analysis (and later texts), and Schabel, "Aufredo Gonteri Brito *secundum* Henry of Harclay," for Henry's questions from his *Sentences* commentary; on Alexander, see Schwamm, *Das göttliche Vorherwissen*, pp. 132–44, and Marco Rossini, "'Quod coexsistit exsistit': Alessandro di Alessandria e i futuri contingenti," in Leonardo Sileo, ed., *Via Scoti. Methodologica ad mentem Joannis Duns Scoti* II (Rome 1995), pp. 1049–63 (Rossini has been working on the critical edition of this redaction of Alexander's *Sentences* commentary); for Hugh, see Schwamm, *Das göttliche Vorherwissen*, pp. 229–39, and Russell L. Friedman and Chris Schabel, "Hugh of Novocastro's Questions on Divine Foreknowledge and Predestination," forthcoming; for Bassol, see Schwamm, *Das göttliche Vorherwissen*, pp. 206–28; I have inspected Alnwick's *Sentences* commentary in Padova, Biblioteca Antoniana 291, but for his opinion in the *Determinationes*, see Schwamm, *Das göttliche Vorherwissen*, pp. 167–86 (the quote coming from p. 173), and Michael Schmaus's edition of question 12, in "Guilelmi de Alnwick O.F.M. doctrina de medio, quo Deus cognoscit futura contingentia," *Bogoslovni Vestnik* 12 (1932), pp. 201–25 (quotation on p. 214).

[4] Marek Gensler, "Antonius Andreae — the Faithful Pupil? Antonius Andreae's Doctrine of Individuation," MPP 31 (1992), pp. 23–37, redates Antonius's death to between 1333 and 1335, as opposed to Schwamm and Hoenen's ca. 1320, and has doubts the authenticity of the commentary. On 'Antonius' and Cowton, see Schwamm, *Das göttliche Vorherwissen*, pp. 144–51, and Hoenen, *Marsilius of Inghen*, pp. 179–81, also citing Schwamm, *Robert Cowton O.F.M. über das göttliche Vorherwissen* (Innsbruck 1931), which I have not seen.

tone for all Franciscans before Auriol.[5] Indeed, Auriol's own theory was created in conscious opposition to Scotus, as we shall see.

The Dominicans and Durand of St. Pourçain

Despite the apparent weaknesses of Scotus's opinion, direct attacks against him are hard to find before Peter Auriol. Indeed, unlike the Franciscans, the known Dominicans in this period were strangely silent concerning Scotus. Although Franciscans continued to read Dominicans, it appears that the reverse was not always the case, at least on this issue. Instead, Dominicans continued to debate the ideas of Aquinas amongst themselves, in a tradition that had been established by the authors of four *Correctoria corruptorii* written by 1284 against the Franciscan William de la Mare's *Correctorium* of Aquinas. Since after 1286 Aquinas's doctrine was the official teaching of the order, it became a matter of policy to 'correct' friars like James of Metz and Durand of St. Pourçain who supposedly strayed from the Thomist line.[6] The issues discussed were, of course, the proper way of knowing the future via divine Ideas and via the eternal presence of future events in God's eternity, and whether the future could be known through contingent causes.

Auriol was aware of this debate, especially as presented in the *Sentences* commentary of Durand of St. Pourçain, arguably the most important Dominican theologian of the fourteenth century. Auriol does have single brief references to Bonaventure, Richard of Middleton, and Henry of Harclay, but the only later-medieval theologian to play any significant role — at least explicitly — in Auriol's discussion, besides Aquinas, Henry of Ghent, and Scotus, is Durand, who is cited and even quoted twice. Following his fellow Dominican James of Metz (fl. ca. 1300–1303),[7] Durand opts to abandon and refute Aquinas's denial that God can have certitude of future contingents via contingent causes. Expanding on statements from Aquinas' own *Summa contra gentiles*,[8] in a passage that Auriol would quote, Durand maintains that

> Just as a necessary effect follows infallibly from a necessary cause, a contingent effect follows infallibly from an impedible cause that is determined to one side, if the cause is not impeded... Therefore, just as a

---

    [5] Hoenen more or less makes this point in his reevaluation of Scotism, using the example of divine foreknowledge. See Maarten J.F.M. Hoenen, "Scotus and the Scotist School. The Tradition of Scotist Thought in the Medieval and Early Modern Period," in Bos, ed., *John Duns Scotus*, pp. 197–210.

    [6] On the *Correctoria corruptorii* on this issue, see Groblicki, *De scientia Dei*, pp. 90–149. For a survey of the 'correction' literature from William de la Mare to Auriol's time, see Friedman, "The *Sentences* Commentary, 1250–1320."

    [7] See Hoenen, *Marsilius of Inghen*, pp. 168–9.

    [8] See Thomas Aquinas, *Summa contra gentiles* I, q. 67 (*Opera Omnia* XIII, ed. Leonis [Rome 1918], p. 190b, ll. 1–7): "Sicut ex causa necessaria certitudinaliter sequitur effectus, ita ex causa contingenti completa si non impediatur. Sed, cum Deus cognoscat omnia, ut ex supra dictis patet, scit non solum causas contingentium, sed etiam ea quibus possunt impediri. Scit igitur per certitudinem an contingentia sint vel non sint."

necessary effect is foreknown in a necessary cause with certain cognition, in this way, when an impedible cause is known, and all causes that can impede it are known, and in addition those that will impede it and those that will not impede it are known, then it can be known which effect will come about or which one will not come about...[9]

So God knows future contingents via their contingent causes, and by knowing what can and will impede or determine those causes in the future. This is not to say that God knows them directly, however, but rather through the divine essence which represents them to the intellect.[10] Perhaps Scotus influenced him in this modification, but there is no way to be certain.

Another Dominican, Hervaeus Natalis, followed Aquinas on this topic in his own *Sentences* commentary based on Parisian lectures of 1302 and put into final form around 1310.[11] As prior provincial of the Dominicans' French province, a post he held from 1309 to his elevation to minister general in 1318, Hervaeus took issue with the general doctrinal tendencies of James of Metz and Durand. The latter ended up preparing three versions of his *Sentences* commentary in an attempt to maintain his view while staying within Dominican orthodoxy. An analysis of the three versions on the problem of future contingents reveals, however, that the issue was not so much Durand's opinion as his interpretation of Aquinas.[12]

At least three theologians in the years following Durand's Parisian *Sentences* lectures copied large parts of his question on future contingents verbatim. Two of them will be discussed later: the Augustinian Dionysius de Burgo Sancti Sepulchri (1317), and the Dominican Bernard Lombardi (1327). The first theologian to incorporate Durand's material was Peter of Palude, whose Parisian lectures of ca. 1310–12 were put into final form around 1315 or slightly later.[13] In Palude's determination, he points out that, although God

---

[9] Durandus de Sancto Porciano, *In Petri Lombardi Sententias theologicas commentariorum libri IIII*, I, d. 38, q. 3, a. 1 (ed. Venice 1571, f. 104rb, par. 9): "Sicut ex causa necessaria sequitur effectus necessarius infallibiliter, sic ex causa impedibili determinata ad unum, si non sit impedita, sequitur effectus contingens infallibiliter... igitur sicut in causa necessaria praecognoscitur effectus necessarius certa cognitione, sic cognita causa impedibili, et omnibus quae eam impedire possunt, et insuper ea quae eam impedient vel non impedient, certitudinaliter potest cognosci quis effectus eveniet vel non eveniet." On Durand's position, see also M.T. Beonio Brocchieri Fumagalli, *Durando di S. Porziano. Elementi filosofici della terza redazione del "Commento alle Sentenze"* (Florence 1969), pp. 126–32, which to a certain extent treats Durand in isolation from his context.

[10] Durandus, *I Sent.*, d. 38, q. 3, a. 2 (ed. Venice, f. 104vb, par. 18).

[11] See Hervaeus Natalis, *In quatuor libros Sententiarum commentaria* I, d. 36, q. 1 (ed. Paris 1647, pp. 150b–154a).

[12] A similar thing occurred in the context of predestination; see Friedman, "The *Sentences* Commentary, 1250–1320." I thank Russell Friedman for checking Durand's printed version against the first redaction in mss. Paris, BN lat. 12330 and 14454. Durand's changing position will be discussed in Chris Schabel, Irene Balcoyiannopoulou, and Russell L. Friedman, "Peter of Palude and the Parisian Reaction to Durand of St. Pourçain on Future Contingents," *Archivum Fratrum Praedicatorum*, forthcoming, but see the following note.

[13] Palude's commentary predates Durand's third redaction, and on foreknowledge, Palude's copied passage differs from Durand's first (and third) redaction. We can conclude on this basis that Palude used Durand's second version of book I. Since no copies are known to sur-

does know future contingents in their causes, Durand's solution simply begs the question, because the possible impediments and determiners are just as contingent as the effects themselves. Therefore Palude adds that God knows future contingents by knowing Himself as the first contingent cause, who knows His own power and will and knows that nothing can act or even continue to exist without His assistance and conservation. In addition, God also knows future contingents *in se*, not as they are actually present to eternity, but as they are actually represented by or reflected in the divine essence.[14] This, again, may reflect Scotus's influence, but we probably should say that Durand's treatment served to divert Dominican attention away from Scotus and, later, Peter Auriol, although Durand himself, like Aquinas, was a focus of attention for Auriol and others outside the Dominican order.

Thomas Wylton

The only clear attacks on the fundamental elements of Scotus's theory before Peter Auriol come from works by *Thomas Anglicus*, or Thomas of England. What we do not know is how many Thomae Anglici there were or exactly when these attacks were formulated. As we shall see, these questions are of crucial importance because the only significant positive influence on Peter Auriol from the period after Scotus comes from a theologian or theologians named Thomas Anglicus. We have three sources: (1) a Thomas Anglicus authored the *Liber propugnatorius* against Scotus, written between 1311 and 1323; (2) in a question from his Bologna *Determinationes* of 1323, William of Alnwick provides a lengthy description of the attacks on Scotus of a theologian referred to as Thomas Anglicus in the margin of the sole manuscript; (3) we possess a question on foreknowledge and predestination by Thomas Wylton, also known as Thomas Anglicus.

Michael Schmaus tentatively identified the Thomas Anglicus of the *Liber propugnatorius* with an old defender of Aquinas, Thomas Sutton, a Dominican. Schmaus was not certain, and the doubts have increased. Moreover, Thomas Sutton wrote a critique of Robert Cowton in these same years, and a brief comparison of the two works on the subject of foreknowledge revealed significant differences. Therefore it appears doubtful to me that Sutton penned the *Liber propugnatorius*.[15] The Thomas Anglicus of the *Liber propugna-*

---

vive of this version, we can reconstruct it from Palude's text. All three redactions of Durand's question on foreknowledge will be published in Schabel-Balcoyiannopoulou-Friedman, "Peter of Palude."

[14] See Petrus de Palude, *In primum librum Sententiarum*, d. 38, q. 3, a. 3 (ed. Schabel-Balcoyiannopoulou-Friedman, "Peter of Palude").

[15] For the *Liber propugnatorius*, see Michael Schmaus, *Der "Liber propugnatorius" des Thomas Anglicus und die Lehrunterschiede zwischen Thomas von Aquin und Duns Scotus, II Teil: Die Trinitarischen Lehrdifferenzen* (Münster 1930), and on foreknowledge, see Schwamm, *Das göttliche Vorherwissen*, pp 109–12. I inspected the critique against Robert Cowton in Ross. lat. 431. More comparative studies are needed to prove decisively whether Sutton authored the *Liber propugnatorius*.

torius objected to Scotus's position for two main reasons: first, he thought it troublesome, and perhaps begging the question, that on Scotus's account in the first instant of nature the divine intellect did not 'foreknow' the determination of the divine will in a 'later' instant of nature. In fact, Thomas would not grant that there was no actual temporal or quasi-temporal sequence between Scotus's instants of nature. Second, Thomas raised the obvious objection that the divine will cannot be the cause of the contingent decisions of the free human will that result in sin, where the created will and not the divine will determines itself to one side of a contradiction. This was Auriol's main argument against Henry of Ghent and Scotus, and Thomas Anglicus employs wording not unlike Auriol's own.[16] Moreover, this argument is present in Thomas Wylton's work.

The position defended in the *Liber propugnatorius* also resembles Wylton's and Auriol's in some ways. The author emphasizes that a will is free because it can do more than one thing *indifferently*, although when it wills it is then determined toward one. More significantly, Thomas Anglicus draws a distinction between an intrinsic determination of the divine will, from which the effect would necessarily follow, and an extrinsic determination, which allows for contingency and freedom.[17] With respect to Auriol, however, it is difficult to say whether he knew the *Liber propugnatorius* on this issue or even whether the work dates to before 1316, when Auriol finished his *Scriptum* on book one of the *Sentences*.

A similar problem confronts us in the case of the Thomas Anglicus whom Alnwick cites. But here we are at least fairly certain that Alnwick refers to Thomas Wylton, an influential secular theologian who became master of theology at Paris around 1312 and remained regent master until 1320. For one thing, the manuscript containing the marginal reference has other questions against Wylton where the marginalia refer to "Thomas Anglicus de Wilton."[18] Wylton's main argument against Scotus, also found in the *Liber propugnatorius*, is that God cannot foreknow via the determinations of the divine will futures that result from the determinations of the human will, and God certainly can-

---

[16] See Thomas Anglicus, *Liber propugnatorius*, d. 39, q. 2 (ed. Modena 1523, fol. 119rb): "... videretur sufficienter dictum, sic voluntas divina esset causa omnium contingentium quantum ad omnem sui conditionem, et determinaret alteram partem contradictionis cuiuscunque. Sed non est sic, quia certum est quod in creatura intellectuali fiunt contradictiones sive partes contradictionum contingentes culpabiles, quarum voluntas divina non est causa; nec etiam per voluntatem divinam fit determinatio ad unam partem contradictionis vel ad alteram, sed sola voluntas talis creature determinat sibi alteram partem contradictionis, non erit necessarium ipsum ..." Cf. Schwamm, *Das göttliche Vorherwissen*, p. 110. Cf. Petrus Aureoli, *Scriptum* I, d. 38, a. 1 (ed. Schabel, pp. 96–7, ll. 200–11).

[17] See Thomas Anglicus, *Liber propugnatorius*, d. 38 (ed. Modena, fol. 117vb): "Nam per hoc est voluntas libera quod potest indifferenter in plura; sed per hoc quod voluntas vult aliquod singulare operabile non est indifferens ad plura, sed iam determinata est ad unum; ergo etc.," and e.g. d. 39, q. 5 (fol. 121va): "Si causa prima intrinsece est determinata ad causandum talem effectum, talis effectus necessario erit; sed si determinatur extrinsece per causam aliam vel etsi illa causa alia non sit determinata ad talem effectum, non erit necessarium ipsum ..."

[18] For the attribution, see Anneliese Maier, "Wilhelm von Alnwicks Bologneser Quaestionen gegen den Averroismus (1323)," in eadem, *Ausgehendes Mittelalter* I (Rome 1964), pp. 1–40, and Schwamm, *Das göttliche Vorherwissen*, p. 174, n. 19. Schwamm also discusses Wylton's arguments against Scotus as presented by Alnwick, ibidem, pp. 174–5 and 179–82, and the passage in full is in Schmaus, "Guilelmi de Alnwick," pp. 214–16.

not be the cause of sinning. As we shall see, Wylton also posits this argument in his question on foreknowledge and predestination.

Moreover, in the passage from Wylton that Alnwick provides, Wylton's critique of Scotus echoes the positive solution of the *Liber propugnatorius* and, indeed, Peter Auriol's. Wylton maintains that God cannot determine human actions by His unimpedible "efficacious will," because humans would not be responsible for any acts at all. But if He does so by His "permissive will," such a determination cannot be the basis for foreknowledge, because by His permissive will God leaves such things indifferent and indeterminate. In addition, Wylton brings up and refutes a possible defense for Scotus that Auriol deals with in exactly the same way: perhaps God's efficacious will is only the cause of the "positive" element in the act of sinning, and the "deformity" occurs by His permissive will. Wylton rebuts that "whoever wills efficaciously some effect to which he knows a deformity is necessarily attached, wills the deformity as a result."[19]

Since in the period before 1323 I have found these basic arguments only in Auriol and in three works by Thomas Anglicus, two of which are securely attributed to Thomas Wylton, this suggests that Wylton may also be the author of the *Liber propugnatorius*. Moreover, the similarities between Wylton's treatment as William of Alnwick presents it and Auriol's discussion cannot be coincidental. Nevertheless, we cannot be certain about which came first, and in fact it does *not* appear to me that Alnwick's source for Wylton is the same as Wylton's question on foreknowledge and predestination, which we now possess. In the case of the latter, however, there are rather solid grounds for declaring that Wylton's work preceded and influenced Auriol's own.

It is at least certain that Wylton is the "Thomas Anglicus" whom Auriol cites in the *Scriptum*, distinctions 40 and 41, in the context of predestination. Until recently Wylton's thoughts on future contingents were known primarily via the Carmelite John Baconthorpe, writing in the 1320's, who quotes even larger passages from Wylton than does Alnwick. Using Baconthorpe's printed text, Stephen Dumont has identified the very question from Wylton that Baconthorpe uses, "Whether someone predestined can be damned," in ms. Tortosa, Archivo Capitular 88, a question that, as Dumont notes, Xiberta had already identified in ms. Barcelona, Archivo de la Corona de Aragón, Ripoll

---

[19] See Guillelmus de Alnwick, *Determinationes*, q. 12 (ed. Schmaus, pp. 214–15): "... arguit unus doctor modernus [mg.: Thomas Anglicus]... Item secundo probat quod non habeat certam notitiam de actibus humanis futuris et contingentibus ad utrumlibet, quia si determinatio voluntatis divinae concurrat cum voluntate humana ad huiusmodi actum causandum, aut ut est actus voluntatis efficax aut permissivus solum. Si primo modo, sequitur quod nullus actus humanus sit homini imputandus, quia homo contra actum voluntatis divinae efficacem venire non potest. Si secundo modo, cum tali actu stat quod indifferenter una [p. 215] pars eveniat vel alia... Item quarto... Deus non est causa peccati. Si dicatur quod Deus est causa huius actus quantum ad illud quod est positivum in illo, non ratione deformitatis nisi permissive, contra: Quicunque vult efficaciter aliquem effectum cui novit deformitatem necessario esse annexam, vult istam deformitatem ex consequenti, licet non principaliter et primo. Probatio: Aliter numquam peccatum quantum ad deformitatem imputaretur homini. Nam nullus intendit primo ipsam deformitatem, sed aliquod positivum ut delectationem vel utilitatem..." Cf. Aureoli, *Scriptum* I, d. 38, a. 1 (ed. Schabel, pp. 97–8, ll. 212–45).

95. The question does not seem to be from Wylton's *Sentences* commentary, part of which Dumont has also identified, because it contains cross-references to Wylton's *Quodlibet* question 15, from December 1315.[20] This would be our *terminus post quem* for the Wylton question, which might then be from the same quodlibetal debate or from a similar disputation in Lent 1316.

The *terminus ante quem* cannot be later than Lent 1316, because this is the very question that Auriol cites in distinctions 40 and 41 of the *Scriptum*, completed by the summer of 1316 at the latest:

Wylton (ms. Ripoll 95, f. 39va; Tortosa 88, f. 116rb):	Auriol, *Scriptum*, d. 40, a. 4 (ms. Vat. Borghese 329, f. 435va):
Dico distinguendo de possibili: quedam enim est potentia logica que opponitur necessario simpliciter, que solum dependet ex connexione necessaria terminorum, et isto modo est possibilis omnis inherentia cuius predicatum non includitur in subiecto, vel talem connexionem habet cum subiecto quod ratione subiecti, quocumque alio extrinsico circumscripto, possit esse sine eo absque contradictione. Alio modo dicitur aliquid possibile non solum ex causis predictis, sed quia ipsum est possibile nec sue positioni in esse repugnat aliqua causa extrinsica a terminis.	Opinio Thome Anglici: Et idcirco dixerunt alii quod possibile duplex est: quoddam enim est possibile logicum quod opponitur necessario simpliciter, quod quidem necessarium solum dependet ex connexione necessaria terminorum, et isto modo possibilis est omnis inherentia cuius predicatum non clauditur in subiecto... Aliud vero est possibile non solum quia non implicat contradictionem, nec habet repugnantiam ex terminis, ymo nec habet repugnantiam ex aliqua extrinsica causa.

Dating the question to December 1315 or later, and identifying it as a quodlibetal question, is immensely significant for two reasons. First, as will be discussed in the following chapter, there are three versions of Auriol's commentary on book I of the *Sentences*, and all three paraphrase another passage on predestination from Wylton's question. If we have a true *terminus post quem* of December 1315 for this question, then all three redactions of Auriol's commentary date to 1316 or later, and indeed we could connect Auriol's two *reportatio* versions with his Paris period. Second, if Wylton's question is truly one quodlibetal question, i.e. a unit, then we can prove that Auriol also knew Wylton's material on future contingents. In fact Auriol's predestination quotation given above comes from the lines *immediately* following Wylton's treatment of foreknowledge and future contingents. Moreover, since Wylton's solution to the problem reflects Auriol's in important ways, then we could conclude with certainty that Auriol developed his doctrine with Wylton in mind.

---

[20] On Wylton and the identification of this question, see the masterful article by Stephen D. Dumont, "New Questions by Thomas Wylton," DSTFM 9 (1998), pp. 341–79, esp. pp. 359–62. ("Item [14]" on p. 362 must be a typo for "Item [26].") A student of Elzbieta Jung-Palczewska is currently working on a much-needed edition of this question. Dr. Jung-Palczewska has kindly sent me a photocopy of the question in Ripoll 95. For the dating of Wylton's *Quodlibet*, see eadem and Z. Kuksewicz, "The Date of Thomas Wylton's Quodlibet," *Studia Mediewistyczne* 32 (1997), pp. 59–63. On the *Scriptum*'s dating, see below, chapter 3.

The only problem is that the Tortosa manuscript that Dumont describes actually carries an *abbreviation* of the complete text found in Ripoll 95.[21] Almost all of Baconthorpe's question in the printed edition is actually Wylton, and almost all of Wylton's question is quoted by Baconthorpe, so that what appears to be elided in Baconthorpe's text is actually there, although far away, and what Baconthorpe seems to add is in fact in Wylton's question.[22] Indeed, there are two versions of Baconthorpe's commentary on book I, and distinctions 40–41 of the earlier version that survives in ms. British Library, Royal 11 C. VI are virtually another witness to Wylton's complete question in Ripoll 95, nothing added, nothing deleted.[23] Therefore most of the cross-references are not Wylton's at all, but belong to the scribe of the Tortosa manuscript or its tradition, and hence they could have been, and probably were, added well after the question itself was composed. This leaves open the

---

[21] Tortosa 88 omits approximately one quarter of the material in Ripoll 95. Nevertheless, there are numerous errors and at least one *omission per homeoteleuton* in Ripoll 95 (16 words, fol. 37va), where Tortosa 88 (fol. 113vb) and Johannes Baconthorpe, *Super quattuor libros Sententiarum* I, dd. 40-41 (ed. Cremona 1618, p. 386bA–B) carry the text. Ripoll 95 also skips an Augustinian *auctoritas* (fol. 39ra) that is present in Tortosa 88 (fol. 115rb) and Baconthorpe (ed. Cremona, p. 390aB), and the refutation of the argument is *only* in Tortosa 88 (fol. 115va).

[22] That is, the section beginning "Aliter respondet" in Tortosa (Dumont, "New Questions," p. 361) is way back on p. 386bD of the 1618 Cremona edition, but Dumont was misled by the fact that Tortosa not only abbreviates that passage, it omits the next 1.2 columns of what exists in both the Cremona edition and Ripoll 95. The other two full paragraphs quoted from Tortosa on Dumont's p. 361 are similarly summarized. Unfortunately, it was not absolutely clear who is speaking in Baconthorpe's *Sentences* commentary, Wylton or Baconthorpe, and it did not help that the order of the 1618 Cremona edition of Baconthorpe differs from the 1526 Venice edition, or that Baconthorpe's presentation itself is confusing. In brief, pp. 384aC–390bE of the Cremona edition, and ff. 114rb, l. 45–116ra, l. 60 of the Venice edition, are verbatim Wylton, i.e. all of Baconthorpe's d. 40, aa. 1–2, except an interjected paragraph (Cremona, p. 387aA) and the last two paragraphs of a. 2. This corresponds to almost all of Wylton, Ripoll 95, ff. 37rb, ll. 14–33, 37va, l. 3–vb, l. 27; 37vb, l. 47–38rb, l. 5; 38rb, l. 16–39rb, l. 16; and 39rb, l. 52–va, l. 29. It is all in sequence except for the refutations of Baconthorpe's opening arguments for a. 1 (from Ripoll 95, 39ra, l. 38–rb, l. 16), which are placed immediately after the arguments in Cremona (p. 385bA–386aA) but later in Venice (f. 114vb). This means that 80 percent of Baconthorpe's question is actually Wylton, and more than 80 percent of Wylton's material is in Baconthorpe.

The last 2.4 columns of Wylton (Ripoll 95, ff. 39va, l. 30–40ra) concern predestination, the source of Auriol's *Scriptum* paraphrase. It turns out that 100 percent of this is also in Baconthorpe, making up two thirds of the following distinction 41: Ripoll 95, f. 39va, ll. 30–57 = ed. Cremona 394bD–395aB; 39va, l. 57–vb, l. 48 = 392bC–393aD; 39vb, l. 49–40ra, l. 27 = 394aA–bA; 40ra, ll. 27–39 = 394bB–C; 40ra, ll. 40–50 = 395aB–C. Finally, the opening of Wylton's question, 37ra, ll. 43–48 = 392bA–B. It should be stated that Baconthorpe does not cite Wylton anywhere, and in this case he actually adopts Wylton's position (adding some arguments in 393aD–bF).

[23] That is, Royal 11 C VI, ff. 155va–159ra = Ripoll 95, ff. 37ra–40ra. All four witnesses will be needed to establish a good text. There is a marginal reference to Wylton in d. 40 (Royal 11 C VI, fol. 156ra), although not in d. 41, and so it is a good bet that not only do other marginal references to Wylton indicate passages or even whole questions from Wylton, but even parts of Baconthorpe where Wylton is not cited may be Wylton. Here are marginal references to Wylton in Royal 11 C VI, for book I: d. 1, q. 1 (23ra); d. 26, q. 2 (112ra); d. 28, q. 2 (124ra); d. 30 (133va); d. 42 (160vb). For book II: d. 10 (213rb, 214va); d. 19 (244rb). For book III: d. 3 (297ra). On Baconthorpe, see below, chapter 8. In the Wylton quotations that follow I give the foliation of Ripoll 95 and, where applicable, Tortosa 88 and the Cremona edition of Baconthorpe (which is more easily accessible than Royal 11 C VI).

possibility that this question pre-dates the December 1315 *Quodlibet*, and may even be from the *Sentences* commentary from before 1312. Certainly the structure of Wylton's question better suits a quodlibetal discussion, where a master would go off on tangents: although the question is ostensibly about predestination, it turns sharply to foreknowledge first. This would not be necessary in *Sentences* lectures, because foreknowledge is treated just beforehand anyway. Nevertheless there is a marginal note in the Ripoll manuscript that refers to "distinction 38 of the first book," and an internal reference suggests some connection with a *Sentences* commentary.[24] This allows us to hypothesize that the question is somehow an artificial conglomeration of separate material on future contingents and predestination. Thus not only do we not have a solid *terminus post quem* for Auriol's *reportationes*, but we cannot even be certain that Auriol had Wylton's treatment of future contingents before his eyes.

Nevertheless, although Auriol does not mention Wylton explicitly in distinctions 38–39, it is at least likely that Auriol had access to the future contingents section too, especially given the added evidence of the similarities between the opinions of the two theologians. Thus Auriol's own solution may have been influenced, negatively and positively, by Wylton.[25]

---

[24] Ms. Ripoll 95, lower margin of fol. 37rb: "Utrum Deus habeat certam et determinatam scientiam de futuris contingentibus [videtur (?) quod non *add. s.l.*] — articulus secundus. D. 38 primi." Either (1) the future contingents material is actually Wylton's *Sentences* commentary, book I, d. 38, a. 2, or (2) article two of the question in Ripoll 95 is actually distinction 38, or (3) it is just a note refering to like material elsewhere. There is also an internal reference on fol. 39ra: "Per quem modum, questione sequente de ydeis *dicam*," which is different in Tortosa 88 (fol. 115rb): "Per quem modum queras in questione illa qua queritur quomodo Deus cognoscit futura contingentia." This could be a reference to the same question packaged differently. Between Scotus and Auriol it was common to ask in a *Sentences* commentary whether God knows future contingents via ideas right *afterwards*. For example, Hugh of Novocastro's book I, d. 38, q. 2 is "Utrum Deus cognoscat determinate futura contingentia" and q. 3 is "Utrum cognoscat futura contingentia per ydeas." Thus it need not be a reference to Wylton's separate (?) "Questio de ideis" (on which cf. Dumont, "New Questions," pp. 362–6), and in fact the scribe of Tortosa may have made the change in order not to confuse the reader. On seven of the ten notable occasions where Tortosa 88 omits material, usually when Wylton gives opponents' arguments, the scribe refers the reader elsewhere. Three pose few problems: one refers to Scotus (fol. 115ra): "Quere istum processum alibi in Scoto de intellectu et voluntate Dei"; and two refer to (John) Baconthorpe's d. 41, on predestination (116va): "Quere istam opinionem recitatam in Iohanne," and (ibidem): "Queras ibidem." The other four are more complicated (113vb): "Quere in materia de prescientia Dei"; (ibidem): "Quere in questione de eternitate primum argumentum ad questionem"; (ibidem): "Secunda consequentia probatur ibidem in eadem questione, 'hoc fuit semper verum dicere etc.'"; and (114ra): "Et istam rationem cum prioribus quere." Dumont ("New Questions," p. 362) thought the second and third (and we should add the fourth) "are certainly to Wylton's famous *Quodlibet* q. 15 on the eternity of the world." This is probably true, although the material omitted, but included in Ripoll 95 and in Baconthorpe, could easily be contained in a question on whether God knows future contingents because they are present to His eternity. The first reference, to "the material on divine foreknowledge," might seem strange in a question about divine foreknowledge, but Wylton's question in Ripoll 95 and Tortosa 88 really concerns future contingent propositions and the indetermination of the human will, so that *how* God knows future contingents was to be treated elsewhere. The upshot is that I am not absolutely certain that we have references to any quodlibetal questions.

[25] Schwamm (*Das göttliche Vorherwissen*, pp. 124–6) briefly discusses Wylton's ideas on future contingents, as they pertain to Scotus, via the unreliable Baconthorpe edition. Since this edition has many serious errors that severely affect the meaning of the text, I must modify

Wylton's focus is the common problem: "'God knows that X will exist; therefore X will exist'; the antecedent is necessary; therefore [so is] the consequent."[26] He rejects as irrelevant Aquinas's defense that the consequent should be taken as it is in divine knowledge since the antecedent contains something "belonging to an act of the soul." Either "X will exist in the way God foreknows it" is equal to "X will exist absolutely," in which case both propositions are necessary, or the two propositions are not equal, so that one could just as easily say, "This man is dead; therefore a man exists," which is beside the point.[27]

Scotus, on the other hand, claims that the antecedent is determinately and infallibly true, but not necessary. Wylton reports the elements of Scotus's position: (1) contingency is grounded in the divine will, otherwise everything would happen necessarily; (2) there is not only a logical, but also a real capacity for opposites in an instant, and for God in eternity; and (3) there is a different determination in propositions about the future from those about the past and present.[28]

Wylton first attacks the second and third points, what he considers the "foundation" of Scotus's position. Wylton asserts, as would Auriol, that Aristotle demonstrated that *if* there were determinate truth in propositions about the future, then the future would happen necessarily. Moreover, Aristotle proved that there is no real capacity for opposites in an instant, but just a logical one.[29] If one does hold that there is determinate truth in propositions

---

drastically what I wrote about Wylton and Baconthorpe in "The Quarrel with Auriol" (pp. 136–45) and "Paris and Oxford between Aureoli and Rimini," p. 392.

[26] Wylton, *Quaestio de praescientia et de praedestinatione*, a. 2 (Ripoll 95, fol. 37rb; Tortosa 88, fol. 113rb): "Item, sequitur: 'Deus scit hoc fore; ergo hoc erit'; antecedens est necessarium; igitur consequens." Baconthorpe saw the central role the problem played for Wylton, and highlighted it: Baconthorpe, *I Sent.*, d. 40, q. 1 (ed. Cremona, p. 384bC and E): "Utrum divina praescientia tollat nostram libertatem... Ad solutionem huius questionis praemitto considerandum quod tota difficultas materiae de Dei praescientia respectu futurorum contingentium, et materiae de praedestinatione et reprobatione, de non fore consiliandum, nec solicitandum de nostra salute dependet ab hac consequentia: 'Deus scit hoc fore; ergo hoc necessario erit'."

[27] Wylton, ibid. (Ripoll 95, fol. 37va; Tortosa 88, fol. 113va; Baconthorpe, ed. Cremona, p. 386aC –bA): "Quero an iste due propositiones, 'Hoc erit inquantum est prescitum a Deo' et 'Hoc erit absolute', idem significent omnino... Si idem significaverint, cum prima sit necessaria per eos, sequeretur quod secunda esset necessaria, et nihil per consequens contingenter eveniret, ut deducit Philosophus, primo *Peryarmenias*... Si detur aliud... tunc responsio nihil est ad propositum... sic hoc esset bonum argumentum: Iste est homo mortuus; igitur est homo."

[28] Wylton, ibid. (Ripoll 95, ff. 37va–38ra; Tortosa 88, fol. 113vb; Baconthorpe, ed. Cremona, pp. 386bD–387aE). Tortosa omits almost all of this. Baconthorpe omits some arguments in Ripoll 95, f. 37vb, including one on obligations. (Aufredo Gonteri Brito would also leave out obligations material when copying Henry of Harclay's questions.) Baconthorpe does add a paragraph on p. 387aA: "Ex iis (ut mihi videtur)... ergo hoc erit."

[29] Wylton, ibid. (Ripoll 95, fol. 38ra; Tortosa 88, fol. 113vb, most omitted; Baconthorpe, ed. Cremona, p. 387bA–C): "Aristoteles... arguit sic: si verum est dicere, quoniam album vel non album est, necesse est album vel non album esse, sed non intelligit quod necessarium in consequenti dicat veritatem perpetuam consequentis, sed solum impossibilitatem non essendi pro tunc. Patet igitur, secundum intentionem Philosophi, quod quandocumque causa natura precedit effectum, dum modo effectus sit positus in esse, pro instanti pro quo ponitur in esse non potest [non] esse aliqua potentia realis, sed solum logica, que est non repugnantia terminorum. Et ex hoc intendit Philosophus deducere in hiis de futuro quod si esset determinate vera modo 'hoc erit al-

about future contingents, however, then one must also maintain that there is a real capacity for opposites with respect to that future instant, otherwise all would occur of absolute necessity. This Scotus does, but for Wylton, a real capacity for opposites entails that one can deliberate about one's present actions while they are "posited," which Scotus will not accept, according to Wylton.[30] Scotus tried to avoid this difficulty by dividing temporal instants into instants of nature. Wylton cannot see how this resolves the difficulty, because if in the last instant of nature an action is "posited," it must also be posited in the first instant of nature, otherwise something would be both posited and not posited at the same instant of time. Thus there is no real capacity for opposites in an instant.[31]

Turning to God's knowledge, Wylton argues (as would Auriol, although in a *reductio ad absurdum*), that 'God knows that X will exist' is necessary "by necessity absolutely opposed to a real possibility for non-being":

> God knows that this will exist in A; therefore He knew this always, from eternity. And it follows: He always knew this; therefore He was not able not to know it. And consequently it was impossible for Him not to know it. It follows from this: It was necessary for Him to know it from eternity.[32]

Wylton understands that some have tried to resolve the difficulty by admitting that the antecedent, 'God knows that «X will exist»', is determinately true, but claiming that if the consequent, 'X will exist', is also determinately

---

bum', sequeretur quod necesse est ipsum fore album, ex quo deducit quod omnia erunt ex necessiate et nihil ad utrumlibet."

[30]   Wylton, ibid. (Ripoll 95, fol. 38ra; Tortosa 88, fol. 113vb; somewhat different in Baconthorpe, ed. Cremona, p. 387bE): "Igitur qui ponit alteram partem in se determinate veram, et per consequens alteram partem determinatam modo ad essendum pro aliquo futuro <instanti>." Then (also Baconthorpe, ed. Cremona, p. 388aA–B; omitted in Tortosa 88, fol. 114ra): "Quarto sic: quero an in ista, 'Sortes sedet', sit aliqua potentia realis pro instanti pro quo sedet ad non sedendum, vel non. Si non, habetur propositum quod quando sedet necesse est ipsum sedere, ut necesse dicit necessitatem concomitantis et non solum concomitantie, quod ipsi negant. Si dicant quod sic, cum per eos, non obstante quod altera pars de futuro sit determinata in se, quia tamen [38rb] hoc stat possibilitas ut actus non ponatur pro tunc, hoc sufficit ad hoc quod de futuris huiusmodi convenit consiliari. Igitur cum ista possibilitas realis ex natura rei sit in hiis de presenti, sequitur quod de actibus positis de presenti convenit consiliari et negociari, quod ipsi tamen negant."

[31]   Wylton, ibid. (Ripoll 95, fol. 38rb; Tortosa 88, fol. 114ra; not in Baconthorpe): "Quinto sic: quod prioritas nature nihil facit ad hoc quod aliquid possit esse in potentia reali sub opposito eius quod simul in eodem instanti temporis est in esse positum cum ipso, quoniam in uno instanti temporis impossibile est quod aliquid sit in re et non sit. Igitur distinguendo aliquod instans temporis pro quocumque volueris signo nature vel originis, si aliquis actus ponatur esse in ultimo signo, necesse est quod sit in primo, vel in eodem instanti temporis simul esset et non esset."

[32]   Wylton, ibid. (Ripoll 95, fol. 38ra; Tortosa 88, fol. 113vb; some omitted; Baconthorpe, ed. Cremona, p. 387bC–D): "Item, probo quod hec sit necessaria, 'Deus scit hoc fore' necessitate absolute opposita possibili reali ad non essendum. Et arguo sic: Deus scit hoc futurum esse in A, igitur semper ab eterno hoc scivit. Et sequitur: semper hoc scivit, igitur non potuit non scire. Et per consequens impossibile fuit ipsum non scire. Ex quo sequitur: Necessarium fuit ab eterno hoc scire."

true because of the validity of the consequence, it is less determinately true than the antecedent, since it is about the future or contains a future act, and the antecedent is (at least verbally) about the present. Wylton rejects this line of argument, claiming that something that follows from a determinate thing cannot be less determinate. Thus 'X will be' cannot be less determinate than 'God knows that X will be', if it follows from it.[33] Wylton draws an interesting analogy:

> Although in reality there is a possibility for me to be king of France, and similarly there is both an active and passive possibility for me to drown myself in the Seine, because however in the first case the wills of those in whose power it is to make the king of France are determined to the contrary, and similarly in the second case my will is determined to the opposite, I would be considered quite foolish to wonder whether by making some request I could bring about the first result, for I would do nothing. Therefore, since in reality it has been determined what side [of the contradiction] will come about, according to those [Scotists], and much more so than in the case that depends solely on men's free will, given that there were as much determination to one side in futures as they posit, it would be foolish and pointless to take trouble and deliberate about anything.[34]

In short, if the future is determinate in any way, free will is destroyed.

Parallel to this, Wylton denies any notion of 'indeterminate truth', declaring expressly in his *Physics* commentary that "indeterminate truth is not truth speaking simply and absolutely," the type entailed by divine knowledge.[35]

---

[33] Wylton, ibid. (Ripoll 95, fol. 38rb; Tortosa 88, fol. 114ra–b; Baconthorpe, ed. Cremona, p. 388aD–F): "Sed dicetur ad hoc quod hoc est verum ubi propositio de presenti non dependet nec continet in se actum futurum, sed in proposito hec, 'Deus scit A fore', continet actum futurum. Ideo aliter arguo contra hoc [114rb] ... Si detur alia pars, quod hec est magis determinate vera, 'Deus scit hoc fore' quam hec, 'Hoc erit', tunc non sequeretur, 'Deus scit hoc fore; ergo hoc erit', quoniam de magis determinato ad esse non sequitur minus determinatum, sicut nec ex vero necessario sequitur verum contingens, quod est minus verum, cum tamen illam consequentiam concedant."

[34] Wylton, ibid. (Ripoll 95, fol. 38rb; Tortosa 88, fol. 114rb; Baconthorpe, ed. Cremona, pp. 388aE–bA): "Septimo: licet possibilitas sit ex parte rei quod essem rex Francie (Cremona has "Angliae"), similiter possibilitas tam activa quam passiva erit in me ut submergam me in Secana (Cremona has "fluvio"), quia tamen in primo casu voluntas eorum in quorum potestate est facere regem Francie est ita determinata ad contrarium, et similiter in secundo voluntas mea est ita determinata ad oppositum, valde fatuus reputarer si aliquam solicitudinem negociando ponerem circa unum consequendum, nihil enim facerem. Igitur cum sit in re determinata, secundum istos, illa pars que eveniet, et multo magis quam illud quod dependet ex libera voluntate hominum, dato quod esset tanta determinatio futurorum ad alteram partem quantam ipsi ponunt, fatuum esset et frustratorium circa aliquid negotiari vel consiliari, quia ad quamcumque partem consilium detur, idem semper et uniformiter contingeret."

[35] Cecilia Trifogli has kindly sent me a photocopy and provisional transcription of question 11 of Wylton's *Quaestiones super Physicam*, found in MS Cesena, Biblioteca Malatestiana, Plut. VIII sin. 2, fol. 31rb–33rb. The question, "Utrum aliqua eveniant a casu in comparatione ad causalitatem primi principii," involves future contingents to some degree. Cf. Wylton, *Quaestiones super Physicam*, q. 11 (Cesena, fol. 32va): "... nec sequitur 'est nunc verum veritate indeterminata; ergo est nunc verum'; sed est secundum quid et <non> simpliciter, veritas enim in-

Perhaps Wylton is aiming this remark at other Franciscan Scotists, such as Antonius Andreas, who did admit 'indeterminate' truth. Unlike the *Sentences* commentary attributed to Antonius, we are certain that we have his commentary on *Peri Hermeneias*. In that work Antonius seems to be in *agreement* with Aristotle that future-contingent propositions are neither true nor false determinately, but he allows for the possibility of propositions being "indeterminately true."[36] Moreover, Andreas's commentary on the *Ars Vetus* contains verbatim passages from the *Questiones octo in Duos libros Perihermenias, Opus secundum*, which some have attributed to Scotus. The *Opus secundum* also denies that future-contingent propositions are determinately true or false, and allows for their being "indeterminately true;" this is on the basis of different levels of determinations in the causes.[37] Dating for these works is uncertain, but they serve to show that by Auriol's time the truth-value of future-contingent propositions and levels of determination were already being discussed in innovative ways.

Wylton now turns to the other element of Scotus's position: God is the basis of contingency, because secondary causation is necessary. Somewhat as Aquinas did in places, Wylton argues that even though lower things are moved by superior causes, this does not mean things happen necessarily as the effects of those superior causes. He gives an analogy of the plants in a field. Although the sun is a general cause of the growth of crops in a field, nevertheless there remains a considerable amount of contingency. Wylton claims that the general disposition does not explain why one part of the field grows differently from another, why one part is affected by pests more than another (even astrological causes cannot explain this), and why one part is trampled by feet, etc. And especially in the case of the human will, Wylton only admits a certain proneness (*pronitas*) received from superior causes, but no necessity.[38]

---

determinata non est veritas simpliciter loquendo."

[36] For example Antonius Andreas, *In librum Perihermenias*, in *Scriptum in Arte Veteri et in divisionibus Boetii cum questionibus eiusdem* (ed. Venice 1508), 76ra: "Tertium est quod propositio de futuro potest intelligi dupliciter significare aliquid de futuro..." and 76va: "Si autem intelligatur secundo modo... propositio nunc nec erit vera nec falsa, quia nunc est indeterminatum" (Boehner, *The Tractatus*, pp. 79–82, gives lengthier citations). 'Indeterminate' is used at 76va: "Ad tertium dico quod hec: 'te fore album est verum', est distinguenda secundum compositionem et divisionem... Alio modo accipitur in sensu divisionis et non significatur tunc nisi quod 'te verum est fore album', et hec est indeterminate vera sicut est prima."

[37] See Normore, "Petrus Aureoli and His Contemporaries," pp. 84–6.

[38] Wylton, *Quaestio de praescientia et de praedestinatione*, a.2 (Ripoll 95, fol. 38va; Tortosa 88, fol. 114va–b; Baconthorpe, ed. Cremona, p. 388bC–F): "... dato quod est falsum quod Deus immutabiliter et necessario moveret immediate motum et causatum ab eo, nichilominus multa contingenter omni genere contingentie evenirent hic inferius in genere activorum et passivorum. Unde quantumcumque sol, quantum est ex parte sua, produceret flores in hac parte prati, sicut in ista, tamen forte non est eadem dispositio hic et ibi. Et si dicatur quod ista dispositio subditur totaliter virtuti corporum supercelestium, non est verum, quia tunc equaliter produceret vermem et muscam ex una parte terre sicut ex alia, quod non est verum. Item, posito quod hec pars terre sit equaliter disposita ad floritionem sicut alia, adhuc potest impediri floritio per contritionem pedum, et per multas causas particulares contingentes omnino. Et de voluntate humana certum est quod a nullo corpore necessitatur [114vb], nec per se, nec per accidens. Licet autem pronitas

To the extent that this is a description of natural secondary causation it is rather weak and differs from Scotus's (and Auriol's) understanding. But in giving his own solution to the problem, and concentrating on human free will, Wylton puts forth a theory that foreshadows and perhaps influenced Auriol's own. We have already seen hints of this position in William of Alnwick's presentation: Wylton reconciles contingency and divine foreknowledge by distinguishing between two types of divine willing, which correspond to two types of future events. If God wills something by his "efficacious will and good pleasure," as in the case of the creation of the world, it is foolish to bother about it. But if God wills by his permissive will only, which is merely a general cause, humans have their actions in their power, subject only to a kind of general influence. In this way, God indifferently permits humans to choose one part of a contradiction in acting, and this is an important element in both Auriol's theory of foreknowledge and his notion of predestination by "General Election." Of course, for Wylton, whatever we choose and the way we choose it God knows from eternity.[39]

How then does Wylton resolve the problem of the consequent, 'God knows that X will exist; therefore X will necessarily exist'? Citing only Boethius's commentary on *Peri Hermeneias*, Wylton's understanding is that Aristotle denied truth and falsity in future contingent propositions. But Wylton does not seem to be too worried about the prospect that the object of God's knowledge in the antecedent, i.e. 'X will be', is neither true nor false. He is concerned only that it is not false. According to most scholastics, knowledge involves only what is true. If 'X will be' is neither true nor false, then they would consider 'God knows X will be' to be completely false. Not for Wylton, who distinguishes between 'X will be' and 'that X will be is true'. The first is neither true nor false, because what it signifies is indeterminate. The second is false, because it signifies that the indeterminate proposition 'X will be' is true; since 'X will be' is neither true nor false, 'that X will be is true' is determinately false. Hence, as long as 'X will be' is not determinately false, the antecedent, 'God knows X will be', is not false.[40] When it is argued that God's knowledge must

---

quedam sit in voluntate alicuius ex causis superibus, nulla tamen necessitate limitatur ad hanc partem magis quam ad illam."

[39] Wylton, ibid., a. 3 (Ripoll 95, fol. 38vb–39ra; Tortosa 88, fol. 115ra–b; Baconthorpe, ed. Cremona, p. 389bB–D): "Quedam enim vult velle beneplacito et efficaci, sicut productionem mundi, ubi non erat alia causa concurrens effectuum. Aliqua autem non vult velle efficaci, sed solum permissive, et respectu sic productorum voluntas divina est causa activa per generalem influxum tribuens agenti particulari facultatem agenti sic vel sic. Non tamen determinat agens ad aliquam nec efficaciter vult hanc vel illam. Et isto modo voluntas divina est causa actuum nostrorum quantumcumque deformium." And [39ra] "Imaginor sic [115va] quod Deo permittente me agere indifferenter hanc partem contradictionis vel illam (non determinante me magis ad hanc partem quam ad illam) ego eligo alteram partem, eo quod illa pars in esse ponitur vel ponetur. Eius positio ergo in esse et modus ponendi secundum quem ponitur est et fuit nota apud Deum ab eterno." For Auriol's theory of predestination, see below, chapter 6. For Alnwick's presentation of the position, see above, n. 19.

[40] Wylton, ibid., a. 3 (Ripoll 95, fol. 39ra; Tortosa 88, fol. 115va; Baconthorpe, ed. Cremona, p. 385bA–B): "Cum dicit Boethius quod sic dicens mendax est, dico quod hec, 'hoc erit', non significat idem quod hec, 'hoc fore est verum', sed significat quod hoc esse erit verum. Nec iste due sunt eedem, sed prima est causa veritatis secunde, et prima est determinate falsa, et de illa loqui-

be of what is necessary, Wylton replies that this is only in the strict sense of knowledge, a 'habit of a conclusion of a demonstration'. Wylton needs only 'certain awareness' (*certa notitia*).[41] In the *Physics* commentary Wylton has a parallel discussion, bringing up Boethius's on *Peri Hermeneias* and the consequence 'God knows X will be; therefore X will be'.[42] He even goes so far as to say, somewhat as Auriol will, that "Concerning no future contingent does God know that 'that this will be' is true now, because if it were true now, it would not come about as contingent."[43]

Poking holes in Wylton's solution did not prove difficult. Baconthorpe found it amazing that Wylton conceded the necessity of the antecedent, 'God knows X will be', in arguing against Aquinas and Scotus, and then giving his own opinion considered the consequent contingent because of God's permissive will and our free will. Baconthorpe also wondered how, on his reading, Wylton at first rejected Scotus's claim that the antecedent is determinately true, although not necessarily true, then later asserted that it was determinately true.[44] Nevertheless Wylton was an influential theologian. There is little doubt that, like Baconthorpe, Peter Auriol read Wylton's question on divine foreknowledge and future contingents. In his criticism of Scotus's simultaneous real capacity for opposites and instants of nature account, in his distinction between God's active and permissive will, and in his odd attitude toward the truth value of future contingent propositions, one can see very clearly some of the bases for Peter Auriol's solution, although in crude form.

---

tur Boetius. Secunda nec est vera nec falsa, sed erit vera vel falsa. Orationes enim sunt vere quemadmodum et res, ut patet primo *Peryarmenias* in fine, et ideo, quia contingentia futura non sunt modo determinata ad unam partem, ideo propositio asserens se modo esse vera est determinate falsa; sed hec, 'hoc erit', ut significat 'hoc esse erit verum', nec adhuc est vera nec falsa."

[41] Wylton, ibid., a. 3 (Ripoll 95, fol. 39rb; Tortosa 88, fol. 115vb; Baconthorpe, ed. Cremona, p. 385bE): "Ad aliud, cum arguitur quod scientia Dei non potest esse nisi de necessariis, quia scire est eorum que impossibile est aliter se habere, dico quod ipse loquitur de scire maxime proprie dicto, secundum Linconiensem (Grosseteste) quod est habitus conclusionis demonstrationis propter quid. Hic autem accipitur scire pro certa notitia."

[42] Wylton, *Quaestiones super Physicam*, q. 11 (Cesena, fol. 31r–va): "Aliud arguitur ex parte scientie divine: monstrato quocumque effectu, Deus scivit ab eterno hoc evenire, quoniam per Boethium *Super Peryarmenias* [31va] tollere prescientiam contingentium a primo nefas est; sed sequitur 'si Deus scit hunc effectum evenire, ergo eveniet'. Antecedens necessarium; ergo consequens."

[43] Wylton, *Quaestiones super Physicam*, q. 11 (Cesena, fol. 32va): "Et quando arguitur 'antecedens est necessarium; ergo consequens', dico... hic tamen est difficultas ex parte sermonis, an hec 'hoc erit' idem significet quod 'hoc fore est verum', vel possit verificari dupliciter: vel quia hoc fore est verum, vel quia hoc fore erit verum... nam si detur primum, nego antecedens sicut et consequens. De nullo enim contingenti futuro scit Deus quod hoc fore sit nunc verum, quia si nunc esset verum, non foret contingens..."

[44] Baconthorpe, *I Sent.*, d. 40, q. 1, a. 2 (ed. Cremona, p. 390bE–391aA): "Miror de Gilton. Prima quia vult quod hec est necessaria: 'Deus scit hoc fore,' ut patuit supra, ubi arguit contra principalem conclusionem, et tamen concedit quod consequens est contingens, quia solum dependens a sola voluntate permissiva Dei et nostra libera... Secundo miror quod neget quod sit determinate vera, licet non sit necessaria, quia infra in positione sua concedit esse determinate veram."

PART TWO

Peter Auriol's Theory

Chapter 3

Immutability Equals Necessity

Introduction: Auriol's Life and Writings

When Auriol began writing his theological works, there were two basic solutions to the problem of divine foreknowledge and future contingents prevalent in western theology. The first, the position based on eternal presence and, sometimes, divine Ideas, could trace its roots back to Augustine and Boethius, and its most important advocate was the Dominican Thomas Aquinas. The second theory, founded in the determinations of the divine will, was a newer development, initiated by the secular Henry of Ghent and more clearly articulated in Peter Auriol's own lifetime by the Franciscan John Duns Scotus. Auriol attempted to provide a third alternative, and although his opinion failed to attract important followers, it decisively altered the course of the debate for decades and remained a factor until the end of the Middle Ages.

The issue of present concern was not the only one on which Auriol left a distinctive mark. Scholars have long known that Auriol played a critical role in the evolution of the doctrine of the immaculate conception of the Virgin, for example, and that he figured prominently in the discussions concerning the unity of the concept of being, epistemology, universals, grace and merit, and predestination. In the past decade or so, in the wake of the 1988 publication of Katherine Tachau's *Vision and Certitude in the Age of Ockham*, a revival of Auriol studies has led students of intellectual history to return to these issues and to investigate Auriol's place in the debates surrounding other problems.[1]

---

[1] For the earlier studies, see the Introduction, nn. 3–4. Katherine H. Tachau, "The Preparation of a Critical Edition of Pierre Auriol's *Sentences* Lectures," in Alvaro Cacciotii and Barbara Faes de Mottoni, eds., *Editori di Quaracchi 100 anni dopo. Bilancio e prospettive* (Rome 1997), pp. 205–16, could count only 21 studies treating Auriol's thought from 1960 to 1993 (conveniently listed in her n. 5), and in a book entitled *The History of Franciscan Theology*, Kenan Osborne, ed. (St. Bonaventure, NY 1994), Auriol plays virtually no role. By contrast, at least 25 important studies devoted wholly or partly to Auriol have appeared since 1994: Guido Alliney, "Fra Scoto e Ockham: Giovanni di Reading e il dibattito sulla libertà a Oxford (1310–1320)," DSTFM 7 (1996), pp. 243–368 (esp. pp. 269–81); P.J.J.M. Bakker, *La raison et le miracle: les doctrines eucharistiques (c. 1250–c. 1400)* (Nijmegen 1999), esp. pp. 76–86, 239–45, and 381–9; Charles Bolyard, "Knowing *Naturaliter*: Auriol's Propositional Foundations," *Vivarium* 38.1 (2000), pp. 163–76; Stephen F. Brown, "Petrus Aureoli: *De unitate conceptus entis* (*Reportatio Parisiensis in I Sententiarum*, dist. 2, p. 1, qq. 1–3 et p. 2, qq. 1–2)," *Traditio* 50 (1995), pp. 199–248; Alessandro Conti, "Divine Ideas and Exemplar Causality in Auriol," *Vivarium* 38.1 (2000), pp. 99–116; Marino Damiata, "Ockham e Pietro Aureolo," *Studi Francescani* 92 (1995), pp. 71–106; Dallas G. Denery, "The Appearance of Reality: Peter Aureol and the Experience of Perceptual Error," FcS 55 (1998), pp. 27–52; William Duba, "The Immaculate Conception in the Works of Peter Auriol," *Vivarium* 38.1 (2000), pp. 5–34; idem, "Auriol, Aristotle, and Averroes," DSTFM 12 (2001), forthcoming; idem, "Aristotelian Traditions in Franciscan Thought: Matter and Potency According to Scotus and Auriol," in I. Taifacos, ed., *The Origins of European Scholarship*, forth-

There are two difficulties one must confront when attempting to present Auriol's doctrine on any issue. First, Auriol's theological works have not been critically edited, for the most part, let alone translated into modern languages, and in particular his *Sentences* commentary exists in more than one version. Second, all aspects of Auriol's theological system are so interrelated that one does not know where to begin. We will take each of these difficulties in turn.

With respect to the first difficulty, as work proceeds on the critical edition of Auriol's *Opera Omnia*, we shall of course get a much clearer picture of Auriol's academic career and, of particular importance, the chronological relationship between the various redactions of his *Sentences* commentary.[2] The *status quaestionis* is as follows:[3] Peter Auriol was born around 1280, and as a young Franciscan he began his theological studies at Paris soon after 1300, perhaps when Scotus was lecturing there. Auriol's first written work is probably his *Tractatus de paupertate et usu paupere*, perhaps authored in 1311. This tract, addressing the issue of Franciscan poverty, is definitely his first printed

coming; Russell L. Friedman, "*In principio erat Verbum*," chapter 7 "Peter Auriol," pp. 293–340; idem, "Conceiving and Modifying Reality: Some Modist Roots of Peter Auriol's Theory of Concept Formation," in Costantino Marmo, ed., *Vestigia, Imagines, Verba. Semiotics and Logic in Medieval Theological Texts (XIIth-XIVth Century)* (Turnhout 1997), pp. 305–21; idem, "Peter Auriol on Intentions and Essential Predication," in Sten Ebbesen and idem, eds., *Medieval Analyses on Language and Cognition* (Copenhagen 1999), pp. 415–30; idem, "Peter Auriol on Intellectual Cognition of Singulars," *Vivarium* 38.1 (2000), pp. 177–93; Onorato Grassi, "Probabilismo teologico e certezza filosofica: Pietro Aureoli e il dibattito sulla conoscenza nel '300," in Giulio d'Onofrio, ed., *Storia della teologia nel Medioevo III: La teologia delle scuole* (Casale Monferrato 1996), pp. 515–40 (with good pre-1990 bibliography on p. 539); James Halverson, "Franciscan Theology and Predestinarian Pluralism" (1995); idem, *Peter Aureol on Predestination. A Challenge to Late Medieval Thought* (Leiden 1998); Richard A. Lee, "Peter Aureoli as Critic of Aquinas on the Subalternate Character of the Science of Theology," FcS 55 (1998), pp. 121–36; Lauge Olaf Nielsen, "Dictates of Faith versus Dictates of Reason: Peter Auriole on Divine Power, Creation, and Human Rationality," DSTFM 7 (1996), pp. 213–41; idem, "Signification, Likeness, and Causality. The Sacraments as Signs by Divine Imposition in John Duns Scotus, Durand of St. Pourçain, and Peter Auriol," in Costantino Marmo, ed., *Vestigia, Imagines, Verba* (1997), pp. 223–53; "The Intelligibility of Faith and the Nature of Theology: Peter Auriole's Theological Programme," *Studia Theologica* 53 (1999), pp. 26–39; idem, "The Debate between Peter Auriol and Thomas Wylton on Theology and Virtue," *Vivarium* 38.1 (2000), pp. 35–98; "Peter Auriol's Way with Words. The Genesis of Peter Auriol's Commentaries on Peter Lombard's First and Fourth Books of the *Sentences*," in Evans, ed., *Commentaries on Peter Lombard's Sentences*, forthcoming; Robert Pasnau, *Theories of Cognition in the Later Middle Ages* (Cambridge 1997), pp. 69–85; Dominik Perler, "Peter Aureol vs. Hervaeus Natalis on Intentionality. A Text Edition with Introductory Remarks," AHDLMA 61 (1994), pp. 227–62; idem, "What Am I Thinking About? John Duns Scotus and Peter Aureol on Intentional Objects," *Vivarium* 32.1 (1994), pp. 72–89; Bert Roest, *Reading the Book of History. Intellectual Contexts and Educational Functions of Franciscan Historiography 1226 – ca. 1350* (Groningen 1996), pp. 183–92; Chris Schabel, "Place, Space, and the Physics of Grace in Auriol's *Sentences* Commentary," *Vivarium* 38.1 (2000), pp. 117–61; Reijo Työrinoja, "Auriol's Critique of Henry of Ghent's *Lumen medium*," in Aersten and Speer, eds., *Was ist Philosophie*, pp. 622–8.

²   A group of scholars attached to the Universities of Iowa and Copenhagen was created in 1991 to critically edit Auriol's *Sentences* commentary and *Quodlibet*. See the description of the project in Lauge Olaf Nielsen, "The Critical Edition of Peter Aureoli's Scholastic Works," in Alvaro Cacciotii and Barbara Faes de Mottoni, eds., *Editori di Quaracchi 100 anni dopo. Bilancio e prospettive* (Rome 1997), pp. 217–25, and Tachau, "The Preparation of a Critical Edition," with manuscript list for the *Sentences* commentary on pp. 214–16.

³   Based primarily on the works cited in the Introduction, n. 3.

work, published two centuries later in 1511.[4] In 1312, while lecturing on the Bible and/or the *Sentences* at the Franciscan *studium generale* of Bologna, he wrote the incomplete treatise *De principiis naturae*, now being critically edited by Martin Bauer in Stuttgart. Auriol then went on to teach theology at the order's *studium generale* in Toulouse, in 1313 or 1314, for at least two years. There he wrote his extremely influential *Tractatus de conceptione Beatae Mariae Virginis*, composed in 1314, and his *Repercussorium editum contra adversarium innocentiae matris Dei*. Three Early Modern editions of this work exist, and a modern edition was published in 1904.[5]

Also probably at Toulouse Auriol completed the writing of his monumental *ordinatio* on the first book of the *Sentences*, the so-called *Scriptum in primum librum Sententiarum*. A beautiful presentation copy of this huge work for Pope John XXII, Vatican Borghese 329, was completed in Auriol's hometown of Cahors on 19 May 1317, according to the colophon, and it would have taken several months to copy the work in the elegant Gothic textura script. The *Scriptum*, therefore, pre-dates Auriol's period as Franciscan Bachelor of the *Sentences* at the University of Paris, a task to which he was assigned at the 1316 Franciscan General Chapter at Naples. No doubt he had already established a reputation as an important scholar because of his early works and of the *Scriptum*, which Cardinal Costantino Sarnano published in Rome in 1596, on the basis of a mediocre manuscript. In the 1950's Eligius Buytaert published a substantial portion, i.e. the Prologue and the first eight distinctions, using the very accurate, but still imperfect, Borghese manuscript. Aside from very small sections, nothing else was edited until the undertaking of the critical edition a decade ago.[6]

Auriol lectured on the *Sentences* at Paris in the academic years 1316–18, on books I and IV in the first year, and on II and III in the second. During this time students took down reports of his lectures, i.e. *reportationes*, and Auriol began reworking these texts afterwards. For the most part, the reworked *reportationes*

---

[4] In *Firmamenta trium ordinum beatissimi Patris nostri Francisci*, part IV (Paris 1511), ff. 116r–129r.

[5] In *Fr. Gulielmi Guarrae, Fr. Ioannis Duns Scoti, Fr. Petri Aureoli Quaestiones Disputatae de Immaculata Conceptione Beatae Mariae Virginis* (Quaracchi 1904), of which 85 percent is Auriol, the Ware and Scotus texts being mere introductory material. Only five of the many extant manuscripts were used in the edition, which has no apparatus criticus, and so there is a need for a new, critical edition. See Duba, "The Immaculate Conception," pp. 10–11 and 34.

[6] The 1596 edition is *Commentariorum in Primum Librum Sententiarum* in two parts, and the newer one is Buytaert, ed., *Peter Aureoli Scriptum Super Primum Sententiarum*, 2 vols. Otherwise, there is only the Boehner edition of d. 38, a. 3, transcribed from one of the poorer manuscripts (*The Tractatus*, pp. 118–24); Jan Pinborg's edition of most of d. 23, a. 2, from Borghese 329 ("Radulphus Brito on Universals," CIMAGL 35 [1980], appendix III, pp. 133–7). Since 1991 the following have appeared: much of dd. 40 (aa. 1 and 4), 41 (aa. 1 and 3), and 45–47 in James Halverson, "Peter Aureol and the Re-emergence of Predestinarian Pluralism in Latin Theology, 1317–1344" (PhD Dissertation, University of Iowa 1993), pp. 295–436, based on four mss.; excerpts of d. 23, which Pinborg did not publish, in Perler, "Peter Aureol vs. Hervaeus Natalis," pp. 242–62, based on Borghese 329; a critical edition of dd. 38–39, with manuscript study, in Schabel, "Peter Aureol on Divine Foreknowledge," pp. 87–212; and Friedman's editions of d. 9, part 1, and d. 27, with manuscript study, in "*In principio erat Verbum*," pp. 365–496.

for books II-IV were the basis for Peter Capullius's edition of these books, published in Rome in 1605, except that the printed book III, unfortunately, is a confusing mix of material following the textual tradition of the extant manuscript in Sarnano; some of this mix may even date from Auriol's pre-Paris days. The more popular tradition is, therefore, unedited. Moreover, the manuscript used for book II was worse than most or all of the extant witnesses.[7] Of course Auriol also lectured on book I, where he covered the problem of divine foreknowledge and future contingents in distinction 38–40. But because of the existence of the earlier *Scriptum*, which survives in some fourteen complete or almost complete witnesses, the Parisian lectures were never published. What survives is rather confusing, and will be discussed below.

In November of 1318, with John XXII's help, Auriol became master of theology, and he remained in Paris during the academic years 1318–20 as Franciscan *magister regens*, or professor of theology, during which time he completed his famous Bible commentary, the *Compendium sensus litteralis totius Sacrae Scripturae*, which was published in 1896.[8] He also held one Quodlibetal debate in 1320 as regent master, the questions of which were published in 1605 along with the commentaries on books II-IV of the *Sentences*.[9] Auriol now embarked on an ecclesio-political path, becoming first the provincial minister of Aquitaine for the Franciscans, and then archbishop of Aix-en-Provence in 1321, nominated in February and consecrated by John XXII in June. By the later fourteenth century it was commonly thought that Auriol had become cardinal, and authors frequently refer to him as *Cardinalis Petrus Aureoli*, rather than *magister* or *doctor*. This does not seem to have actually happened, however, and his new career was cut short when he died in January 1322.[10]

---

[7]   Aside from the 1605 Rome edition, entitled *Commentariorum in Secundum, Tertium, Quartum Libros Sententiarum (Tomus Secundus)*, there is a critical edition of book II, d. 2, part 3, q. 1, with manuscript study for this and the *Scriptum in primum*, in Schabel, "Place, Space, and the Physics of Grace," and Buytaert's critical edition of the unprinted (and more popular) version of book III, d. 3, qq. 1–2 ("Aureoli's Unpublished *Reportatio* III, Dist. 3, q. 1–2," FcS 15 [1955], pp. 159–74). For the confusing situation of book III, see Valens Heynck, "Die Kommentare des Petrus Aureoli zum dritten Sentenzenbuch," FzS 51 (1969), pp. 1–77, and Duba, "The Immaculate Conception." On book IV, see Nielsen, "Peter Auriol's Way with Words." Ms. Padova, Universitaria 1580 (ff. 167r–230r) was reported to contain Auriol's questions on the *Metaphysics*, but in fact the material is excerpted from his commentaries on books II and III of the *Sentences*, two of the questions being also in ms. Padova, Biblioteca Antoniana 173 (ff. 45vb–47rb and 57ra–b).

[8]   Petrus Aureoli, *Compendium Sensus Litteralis Totius Divinae Scripturae a Cl. Theologo Fr. Petri Aureoli Ord. Min.*, ed. P. Seeboeck (Florence 1896). Frederick Stegmüller also published Auriol's *Compendiosa Expositio Evangelii Johannis* in an article in FzS 33 (1951), pp. 207–19. Nancy Spatz is editing what appears to be Auriol's *Recommendatio et divisio sacrae Scripturae* from ms. Paris BN lat. 14566.

[9]   On the *Quodlibet*, see Nielsen, "Peter Auriol's Way with Words."

[10]   Peter de Rivo calls Auriol "Cardinal," and Peter of Candia refers to him as "*Dominus*." Some modern authors have been confused by this, as Christian Trottman, *La vision béatifique des disputes scolastiques à sa définition par Benoît XII* (Rome 1995), p. 873a. Auriol certainly might have become cardinal had he lived, if we are to judge by the example of Elias of Nabinaux, who followed a similar career path a decade later: Franciscan from southwest France, provincial minister of Aquitaine (1324), bachelor of the *Sentences* at Paris (1328 to 1329 or 1330), master of theology with John XXII's help in 1331, archbishop (of Nicosia in Cyprus) in

Auriol does not return to the problem of divine foreknowledge and future contingents in his quodlibetal questions, and so our sources for his theory are the versions of his commentary on book I of the *Sentences*. The *Scriptum* for book I presents no serious problem, but the *reportationes* do. For the first 32 distinctions three manuscripts carry one tradition (the short commentary on book I, or "SC1") that parallels in some ways the reworked Parisian *reportationes* of the other books, and one manuscript, Vat. lat. 6768, contains nine selected questions from these distinctions and is probably a less polished version (the Vatican questions, or "VQ") of what appears in the other manuscripts. For distinction 33, however, there is much confusion, and we have three different texts. Lauge Nielsen has already analyzed the various versions of the first thirty-three distinctions carefully, and in any case they do not concern us directly.[11]

The later distinctions, from distinction 34 to the end of book I, encompass the material of present concern and pose different problems. Two of the manuscripts carrying SC1 diverge from the third, Vat. Borghese 123. Between these two manuscripts, from Berlin (Staatsbibliothek, Theol. Fol. 536) and Padua (Antoniana, 292 scaff. xiii), there are some differences, but they carry essentially the same material, mostly verbatim. Where they differ, either Berlin's text has been more extensively reworked, or it is a different and somewhat more detailed *reportatio* of the same lectures. In general, this section in Berlin-Padua is less polished than the first thirty-two distinctions, i.e. SC1. Moreover, the last ten questions from book I found in Vat. lat. 6768 correspond to the full text of selected questions from the tradition that the Berlin manuscript carries in the later distinctions.[12] As a result, we can tentatively conclude that for these later distinctions this tradition is a less reworked *reportatio* than SC1, somewhat in the tradition of VQ for the selected questions from the first thirty-two distinctions. Borghese 123, on the other hand, carries a different text for the last fifteen distinctions. The manuscript is very corrupt, suggesting a hurried composition, and many passages match the *Scriptum* verbatim, which implies some authorial reworking.

There is evidence that all three versions had an impact on later theologians, and so a comparison of the three (*Scriptum*; SQ1 + later distinctions in Borghese 123; and VQ + later distinctions in Berlin-Padua-Vat. lat. 6768, or "BPV") is important to help clarify their nature and perhaps their relative chronology. The *Scriptum* takes up over 1100 large pages of the 1596 edition, and it would take up about 5000 pages of a book like the present one. By contrast, SQ1 + Borghese 123 consist of roughly 1250 pages, still substantial, but

1332, again with John's assistance, and cardinal in 1342. On Elias, see my "Archbishop Elias and the *Synodicum Nicosiense*," *Annuarium Historiae Conciliorum* 32 (2000).

[11] For the first thirty-three distinctions of the *reportationes* on book I, see Nielsen, "Peter Auriol's Way with Words," which nicely presents the earlier attempts to sort out book I by F. Pelster (who discovered SC1), Anneliese Maier (who found VQ), and Stephen F. Brown (who has edited part of SC1). At present, Nielsen, Russell Friedman, and I are editing the *reportationes* on book I.

[12] Not a contracted text, as Brown, "Petrus Aureoli," p. 202, suggests.

not monumental. Extrapolating from what we have of BPV, the 'complete' text would probably take up about 1000 pages. Distinctions 38 and 39 of the *Scriptum* require 126 pages in my edition, a sizeable amount, but given that there are forty-eight distinctions plus a Prologue, this amount is less than proportional. This may be because these distinctions occur near the end of the book: Auriol may not have had time to pay the same attention here as he had earlier, and he also saves space by referring to earlier material. Still, in Borghese 123 these two distinctions are almost half of the size of the *Scriptum's* treatment, i.e. twice the usual ratio, while BPV, which spills over into distinction 40, is only one fourth as large, as we would expect. These differences become more striking when we consider that a full fourteen pages of the *Scriptum* are devoted to the description of Lombard's text (the *divisio textus*) and the principal opening arguments and their refutation, and BPV assigns five pages to the opening arguments, although it has no *divisio textus*. By contrast, Borghese 123 gives only three pages over to this material, having only eight lines total of *divisiones textus* for the two distinctions. This means that it goes straight to the point. When we look at the most famous and controversial part of Auriol's treatment, concerning future contingent propositions, we find that the Borghese 123 version roughly *equals* the *Scriptum's* discussion in size. Significantly, BPV is about two thirds the size of the others on this particular issue, which constitutes nearly half of its entire treatment of foreknowledge.

The inclusion of large *divisiones textus* in the *Scriptum*, of smaller ones in Borghese 123, and of none at all in BPV does highlight the stylistic differences among the three redactions. These variations become more apparent when we look at Auriol's method of citation.[13] The *Scriptum*, apparently a literary composition from the start, has proportionally many more explicit citations of Aristotle and patristic authors in these distinctions than do the other versions. Moreover, and this is highly unusual for the 1310s, Auriol routinely cites recent and contemporary authors by name in the *Scriptum*, and where there might be confusion he provides detailed information about the specific locus he is referring to, such as "Henry [of Ghent], *Quodlibet* VIII, second question." It is no surprise that later figures would use the *Scriptum* as a mine for the opinions of others. Francis of Meyronnes, in his own *Sentences* commentary from 1320–21, remarked, "If you want to see the opinions of others presented distinctly, look everywhere in Auriol,"[14] and this may be evidence that Meyronnes was using the *Scriptum*, an issue to which I shall turn shortly. In contrast, the Borghese 123 version uses honorific titles only (*Doctor Communis* for Aquinas, *Doctor Solemnis* for Henry, and *Doctor Subtilis* for Scotus), and only these three recent thinkers are mentioned, as opposed to seven in the *Scriptum*. There is one explicit citation of a work, but it is merely to Henry's "*Quodlibet* VIII.*" BPV has *no* such explicit citations, all references use the vague *quidam*

---

[13] I discuss this in my "*Haec Ille*: Citation, Quotation, and Plagiarism in 14th-Century Scholasticism," in Taifacos, ed., *The Origins of European Scholarship*, forthcoming.

[14] Brown, "Walter Burley, Peter Aureoli and Gregory of Rimini," p. 381.

dixit or *aliqui dicunt*, i.e. "some say...," and occasionally Auriol refers to his adversary simply as "*tu.*"

There are other differences in presentation and terminology between the three versions. For example, Borghese 123 differs from the other versions in that the other redactions refer repeatedly to the passage of time as including a *linea successionis*, which God does not perceive directly, although we do. Borghese 123 always employs the phrase *differentia temporis* to contrast our time with God's eternity. In the sections of the *Scriptum* containing his treatment of foreknowledge and future contingents, Auriol mentions *linea successionis* at least seventeen times, and in only one instance does he say *differentia temporis*, in that case discussing *our* knowledge, not God's. BPV follow suit: Berlin has *linea successionis* sixteen times, and the shorter Padua says it on eight occasions, but neither manuscript has *differentia temporis* at all. Borghese 123, in contrast, has no fewer than twenty-five mentions of the term *differentia temporis* and no instances of *linea successionis* at all.[15]

Moreover, BPV and Borghese 123 are somehow to be associated with Paris. As will be explained in Part III, I have found ample evidence that some theologians writing in the first few years after Auriol at Paris were using the terminology and presentation of the Borghese 123 version and a few indications that BPV was used. Because (a) the *Scriptum* comes before the Paris lectures, (b) BPV reflects the *Scriptum* terminology, and (c) Landulph Caracciolo OFM, who lectured on the *Sentences* at Paris most likely just after Auriol in 1318–19, uses the Borghese version, therefore I think the Borghese 123 version is the last of the three. Because (a) Francis of Marchia, who read the *Sentences* at Paris in 1319–20, appears to make use of the BPV redaction, (b) BPV appears to be connected to VQ, i.e. the earlier distinctions in Vat. lat. 6768, and (c) VQ is probably a Paris *reportatio*, therefore I am inclined to think that BPV is also connected with Auriol's Paris years. Moreover, the Borghese version bears signs of being at least partially a written work, because of the *divisiones textus* (like SQ1) and the passages taken from the *Scriptum*, whereas BPV has the appearance of a relatively unpolished *reportatio*.

Finally, in distinction 41 of all versions Auriol describes a position that is attributed to Thomas Anglicus, i.e. Thomas Wylton, in the manuscripts of the *Scriptum* (although not in the Rome edition). Like the passage quoted above in chapter two, this comes from Wylton's question on predestination and foreknowledge in Tortosa 88 and Ripoll 95. Although we cannot be sure, this question is probably from Wylton's December 1315 *Quodlibet* or just afterwards. Here are the parallel passages in Wylton and in all three versions of Auriol's commentary on book I of the *Sentences*:

---

[15] See my "Peter Aureol on Divine Foreknowledge," pp. 79–81.

Scriptum, d. 41, a. 1 (Vat. Borghese 329, f. 437rb):
Opinio Thome Anglici: Et ideo dixerunt alii quod usus liberi arbitrii potest intelligi quod sit bonus dupliciter: primo quidem bonitate moris qui est in potestate nostra supposita influentia generali Dei, qua bonitate operationes virtutum moralium de quibus tractat Philosophus bone sunt; et in illam potest homo ex puris naturalibus. Secundo vero bonitate supernaturali et gratuita per quam aliquis dicitur Deo gratus, dilectus, et acceptus. Loquendo ergo de bonitate prima, bonus usus predestinationis esse causa potest, non quidem de condigno, sed de congruo et dispositive. Loquendo vero de bonitate secundo modo, sic bonus usus est predestinationus effectus.

Wylton, a. 2 (Ripoll 95, f. 40ra; Tortosa 88, f. 116vb–117ra:
Dico distinguendo de usu bono liberi arbitrii quod usus bonus liberii arbitrii potest intelligi dupliciter: uno modo quod sit bonus bonitate moris, que bonitas est in potestate nostra ex naturalibus, supposita influentia generali Dei, qua bonitate operationes virtutum moralium, de quibus determinat Philosophus, bone sunt. Alia est bonitas supernaturalis, que dicitur bonitas gratuita, per quam aliquis dicitur gratus et acceptus Deo. Primo modo intelligo quod precognitio usus boni liberi arbitrii est causa predestinationis ex congruo, non ex condigno. Bonus usus secundo modo dictus est effectus predestinationis.

BPV (d. 41, q. 1)
Tertia opinio est quod bonus usus liberi arbitrii — non ut bonus bonitate gratuita, sed bonitate morali, que bonitas simpliciter est in potestate nostra que de congruo meretur salutem, licet non de condigno — hic usus talis liberi arbitrii previsus a Deo est causa praedestinationis in habente istum, et hoc ab eterno.

Borghese 123 (d. 41, q. 1, a. 2)
Alius doctor modernus, quod bonitas liberi arbitrii potest intelligi esse duplex: una quidem moralis que est in potestate nostra, <alia> vero supernaturalis gratifica que est ex gratia. Bonitas igitur usus liberi arbitrii moralis previsa ab eterno causa est predestinationis, non quidem de condigno, sed de congruo et dispositive.

Given these new considerations, I tentatively suggest that the following is the case: early and unrecorded reactions to Auriol's lectures at Toulouse and perhaps Bologna and to his *Scriptum* suggested that Auriol's stance on future contingent propositions was controversial and deserved emphasis, which he gave in his Parisian lectures on book I, given starting in the autumn of 1316. These lectures are more or less recorded in VQ-BPV. At some time thereafter Auriol began to rework the *reportationes* of his lectures, intending to place particular stress on his controversial theory of divine foreknowledge and, in particular, on future contingent propositions. But the last distinctions, with their new terminology and copious borrowing from the *Scriptum*, were not completed satisfactorily but rather left in a rough state. This version was available to Landulph Caracciolo, but exactly when he used it depends in part on when Caracciolo's surviving commentary was put in final form, which could be anywhere after the fall of 1318. Since this last section of Auriol's *reportatio* was never polished like the earlier distinctions, Berlin and Padua represent a tradition that attempted to fill the gap with the relatively unpolished *reporta-*

tio (or *reportationes*) preserved, in selected questions, in Vat. lat. 6768. The full text of book I contained in the Berlin and Padua manuscripts circulated more than that of Borghese 123, as is suggested by Vat. lat. 6768, a question list in Toulouse, Bibliothèque municipale 243, and an abbreviation in Vat. lat. 946, all of which in the later distinctions correspond to BVP. The more popular *Scriptum* eventually eclipsed the *reportationes*, perhaps as early as 1320–21 in some cases, if Francis of Meyronnes used it.[16]

All three versions are, therefore, pertinent to our story, especially given the particular attention paid in them to divine foreknowledge and future contingents. Certain terminological similarities between Marchia's portrayal of Auriol's opinion and the BVP text lead me to conclude that Marchia used that version. Further, its overwhelming stress on future contingent propositions may also explain why that is virtually the only element of Auriol's theory that Marchia and, by extension, his followers the Augustinians Michael of Massa and Gregory of Rimini deal with. Caracciolo, who was not without followers of his own, employed the Borghese 123 version, which placed a more even emphasis on the various aspects of the problem. Finally, the *Scriptum* soon became the favored redaction and has remained so until today. In analyzing Auriol's doctrine, I will focus on the *Scriptum*, since it is both longer and clearer than the other redactions. Whenever I find an important difference in the other versions, however, I will bring attention to them, both because they probably represent in some rough way his more mature thought, and because they played a role in the early years at Paris. In later chapters, I will draw attention to which version(s) Auriol's successors appear to be reading.

The second difficulty in approaching Auriol's doctrine is finding his starting point. A writer faced with the task of giving a detailed presentation and explanation of a theologian's views on such a subject as divine foreknowledge and future contingency must make awkward decisions. Philosophically it might be preferable to sift out Auriol's views and present them as coherently as possible. Historically it is important to tell the reader the order in which Auriol himself presents his specific arguments, the opponents whom Auriol opposed and how he tried to refute them, and the examples that Auriol used to clarify his refutations and explanations. One can fit Auriol's discussion into the proper historical context in both the philosophical and historical presentation, though one more easily performs such contextualizing in a historical approach.

---

[16]   Another, less likely, scenario is that Berlin-Padua is a pre-Paris *reportatio* to which Marchia had access, and the Borghese 123 is closer to the Paris lectures. There is a reference to "indeterminate truth" in the Berlin-Padua version which makes little sense considering Auriol's position, and this might indicate it represents his immature thoughts on the matter. This would mean, however, either that all questions in Vat. lat. 6768 are from earlier lectures, or that it carries questions from two different lecture series, one for before distinction 33 and one for after. Both of these possibilities seem to me more unlikely than my scenario. A closer comparison of the relationship between SQ1 and VQ, on the one hand, and between Borghese 123 and BPV for the later distinctions, on the other, could help clarify matters.

Auriol was a synthetic thinker, and did indeed constantly return to synthetic views to clarify his position. Thus distinctions 38 and 39 form a unit, but a unit interwoven with discussions of immutability in distinction eight, God's will in distinction 47, divine knowledge in distinction 35, and so on. Article one of distinction 38 is not the starting place for his discussion. In choosing a point to begin, one unavoidably chooses to emphasize that point as the impetus for what follows, and this might not be what Auriol intended. Is human free will and contingency the proper place to start? The nature of God? God's foreknowledge in particular? The truth status of future contingent propositions? The definitions of modal terms?

I will try to present Auriol's position following the basic conceptual order I presented in the introduction to chapter two: (1) Since God is immutable, and immutability is the same as necessity, He cannot know the future as future in any way, otherwise everything would happen of necessity; (2) God knows the future not as future but as present, or rather indistant to Him in His eternity; (3) future contingent propositions are not true or false, and God's knowledge of the future does not make them true or false; (4) there must be a distinction between God's active, extrinsic will, and His passive, intrinsic will.

Immutability Equals Necessity

Does Auriol think God is foreknowing of future contingents? Many medieval and some modern scholars have said that he does not, but Auriol begins distinction 38 by saying that although Aristotle, Averroes, Seneca, and others deny divine foreknowledge because of its apparent incompatibility with the contingency of things, it is orthodox to concede that God determinately foreknows contingent things, because it is a "common conception of the mind" and is necessary for divine perfection [38.1:144–50].[17] Nevertheless, Auriol uses distinction 39, building on statements in Boethius and Anselm, to show that foreknowledge, strictly speaking, is incompatible with contingency, and that their distinction between the different types of necessity is not applicable to the matter at hand. Here Auriol clarifies how modal terms like possible,

---

[17]   In the my discussion of Auriol I will refer in square brackets to my edition of the *Scriptum* (in "Peter Aureol on Divine Foreknowledge") by distinction, article, and line numbers, so that [38.1:144–50] refers to *Scriptum* I, d. 38, a. 1 (ed. Schabel, ll. 144–50). Medieval thinkers commonly used three Latin words for 'knowledge': *scientia, notitia,* and *cognitio.* Sometimes the author wishes to draw a distinction between different types of knowledge, but more frequently, in the context of future contingents, authors use the three terms interchangeably. In this book I will translate all three terms as 'knowledge', unless it is clear that the author means something else, such as 'cognition'. It would be awkward for the reader to use verbs such as 'cognize' on a regular basis. Unfortunately, common spoken English is not as rich as Latin in this specific regard, and even when the medieval author means to make a distinction, our 'knowledge', vague as it is, has enough nuances to cover that author's meaning. Luckily, 'foreknowledge' is almost always rendered *'prescientia'* in Latin. See for example Tachau, *Vision and Certitude,* for discussions of the different meanings of the terms, in a context (epistemology) where such distinctions in English are more frequently necessary.

immutable, contingent, and necessary apply to God and creation. As we have seen, in distinction 39 of the *Sentences* Peter Lombard had asked whether God's knowledge could increase or decrease, and in the fourteenth century this forum provided space for questions concerning not only the definitions of those terms, but also discussions of God's power and the proper contents of knowledge.

Auriol says he is first going to inquire about the immutability and necessity of divine foreknowledge [39:156–7]. Auriol held to a particularly emphatic concept of divine simplicity and necessity that pervaded his entire œuvre, and affected his solution to every theological problem. In essence, his was the God of the philosophers, rather than the anthropomorphic God of Scripture, especially the Old Testament.[18] Thus in issues surrounding the Trinity or predestination, for example, Auriol's doctrine of simplicity led him to his extensive development of the 'connotative' distinction to explain the 'differences' between the three persons or the divine attributes.[19] Simplicity coupled with Auriol's stress on *absolute* divine necessity — the meaning of which I will explain — in turn led him to the belief that God's foreknowledge is absolutely necessary, a tenet that would have profound repercussions for Auriol's entire teaching on foreknowledge and future contingents.

Following Augustine, Auriol argues that God's foreknowledge is the same as God's essence. Since God's essence is absolutely necessary, so is His foreknowledge, because being and knowing are the same in God. Here Auriol is in direct opposition to Scotus, who grounded contingency in God. For Scotus, although God is necessary, His will wills contingently, and thus God knows contingently. Scotus agreed that God's knowledge is immutable, but asserted that this immutability and contingency were compatible. In the instant of eternity, God has the capacity to will, and hence know, the opposite of what he does in fact will. The basis for the solutions of Scotus and of most other theologians depends on the inequality of immutability and necessity, and it is precisely this inequality that Auriol denies.

Scotus's claim was not new: in the *Sentences* Peter Lombard had asked the question whether God could know more or less than he knows. We have seen that the answer was affirmative if one took the question in the divided sense, but negative in the composite sense. Let us say that what God knows is X and

---

[18]   This is perhaps the main point of Alessandro Conti's "Divine Ideas and Exemplar Causation in Auriol," pp. 115–16, although in accusing Auriol of "evident heresy" for supposedly claiming that creation is necessary, Conti fails to notice Auriol's patent desire to stress contingency and freedom.

[19]   The connotative distinction can be explained as follows: something absolutely simple, like the divine essence, can have no parts, no internal distinctions, but our intellect can conceive of distinctions within that simple thing on the basis of the way it relates to or connotes other things that are in some way different or distinct from it. For example, one could say that the divine intellect and will are distinct because the former knows (connotes) both good and evil but the latter wills (connotes) only good, so there is a connotative distinction between them. On simplicity and connotation in Auriol's Trinitarian theology, see Russell Friedman, "*In Principio Erat Verbum*," pp. 293–340; in his doctrine of predestination, see James Halverson, *Peter Aureol on Predestination*, passim.

only X. 'God can know more than He knows' is true in the divided sense, because it means merely that it is not logically incoherent for God to be able to know X + 2, where X is simply an amount unconnected to any supposition that God knows that amount. In the composite sense, however, the proposition entails that God can know both X — and only X — and X + 2 at the same time, which implies a contradiction, since God is supposed to in fact know X and only X already, and X is not the same as X + 2. In effect, Lombard employed the distinction between the composite and divided senses to prove the inequality of immutability and necessity when applied to God's willing.

By Scotus's time, this distinction was sometimes applied to questions involving the difference between God's power considered absolutely, and His power as it is actually ordained for the world, although, obviously, this difference was already implicit in Lombard's own discussion. Since when God's power is considered absolutely (Dei potentia absoluta, or DPA), it was logically possible, though it is not now possible in reality, for God to will and know differently from how He in fact wills and knows, therefore 'God can know more than He knows' is true in the divided sense. Considering and assuming God's power as it is ordained in the world (Dei potentia ordinata, or DPO), it would be a contradiction for God to will or know differently, because God would will something and not will something at the same time. Hence in the composite sense the proposition is false. Conversely, 'God cannot know more than He knows' is true in the composite sense, but false in the divided sense.[20]

Scotus took the distinction further by saying that since God wills eternally in one instant of eternity, He retains the capacity to will and know other than He does, although He cannot will and not will the same thing in that instant of eternity. Scotus thus grounds contingency in this very capacity itself. The will wills contingently and the intellect knows contingently. Along with this, Scotus clarified the definition of 'possible' that had been developing for some time. For Scotus, as we have seen, 'possible' is what does not entail a logical contradiction.[21] And what was consistent with God's absolute power was coextensive with what was logically possible, since God, according to DPA, could do anything that did not entail a contradiction.

Scotus further demonstrated his position by saying that not every contingent thing is mutable, so not every immutable thing is necessary. Although Socrates's running, while he runs, is immutable (by the conditional necessity of the present), says Scotus, Socrates runs contingently nevertheless. So it is with divine foreknowledge. It is contingent in the 'now' of eternity, but it is immutable in that entire instant of eternity [Auriol's summary in 39.1:195–204].

---

[20]   A good, although not universally accepted account of the DPA/DPO distinction is William J. Courtenay, Capacity and Volition: A History of the Distinction of Absolute and Ordained Power (Bergamo 1990). See also Francis Oakley's review in Speculum 68.3 (1993), pp. 739–42 and the works of Eugenio Randi in this regard, particularly Il sovrano e l'orologiaio: Due immagini di Dio nel dibattito sulla 'potentia absoluta' fra XIII e XIV secolo (Florence 1987), which includes an edition of pertinent questions from Hugh of Novocastro.

[21]   For Scotus's modal ideas in this context see Simo Knuuttila, "Modal Logic," in CHLMP (pp. 342–57), pp. 353–5, and idem, Modalities in Medieval Philosophy, pp. 139–49.

Auriol flatly rejects Scotus's position [39.1:280–87]. Divine foreknowledge is absolutely necessary, because it is the same as God's essence, which is absolutely necessary, as Scotus would agree. Auriol asserts explicitly that "necessity and immutability are the same, so that in positing that foreknowledge is immutable, one necessarily posits that it is necessary,"[22] something he had showed in distinction eight:

> Those things are one-and-the-same that have in common a definitive nature (*ratio*), since a definition points out what the thing's being is. But the definition of necessary is that it is impossible for it to be otherwise; [the definition] of immutable is that it is impossible for it to change; but changing is being otherwise now than before. Therefore immutable and necessary are the same.[23]

In the case of Socrates' running, this is immutability *ex suppositione*. Auriol claims this is the same as necessity *ex suppositione*, and many theologians agreed. With God, Auriol maintains that Scotus has made a distinction between absolute necessity and immutability *ex suppositione*, but that this is not the proper distinction. Besides, with God there is *absolute* immutability.

> [T]he same holds for immutable just as for necessary. Socrates's running is not something absolutely immutable (*simpliciter*), just as it not necessary, but it is necessary and immutable with this qualification: the simultaneity of contradictories is impossible, and their non-simultaneity is something necessary, and also immutable. So those who spoke in this way have been deceived, because they posited that incommutable *ex suppositione* is not necessary *ex suppositione*, and they signalled a difference between absolutely necessary and incommutable *ex suppositione*, not noticing that incommutable without qualification is the same as necessary without qualification, and that incommutable *ex suppositione* is the same as necessary *ex suppositione*.[24]

Auriol continues this line of argument later against Bonaventure, where he asserts that in the case of God there is no difference between absolute necessity

---

[22] [39.1:280–82]: "Tertia quoque propositio est quod necessitas et immutabilitas idem sunt, ita quod ponendo prescientiam immutabilem necesse est eam ponere necessariam."

[23] Petrus Aureoli, *Scriptum* I, d. 8, q. 2, a. 1 (ed. Buytaert, vol. 2, p. 935): "Illa namque sunt unum et idem, quae communicant in definitiva ratione. Nam definitio indicat quid est esse rei. Sed definitio necessarii est quod impossible est aliter se habere; immutabilis autem quod impossibile est mutari; mutari autem est aliter nunc se habere quam prius. Ergo immutabile et necessarium est idem."

[24] [39.1:303–12]: "...idem enim est de immutabili sicut de necessario. Non enim Sortem currere est quoddam immutabile simpliciter, sicut nec necessarium, est tamen necessarium et immutabile cum ista determinatione: Simultas enim contradictoriorum est impossibilis, et non simultas est quoddam necessarium, sicut et immutabile. Unde decepti sunt sic dicentes, quia putaverunt incommutabile ex suppositione non esse necessarium ex suppositione, et assignaverunt diversitatem inter necessarium absolute et incommutabile ex suppositione, non attendentes quod incommutabile simpliciter idem sit quod necessarium simpliciter, et incommutabile ex suppositione idem quod necessarium ex suppositione."

and necessity *ex suppositione*. Against Richard of Middleton, who is cited as calling the distinction that between 'caused necessity' and 'concomitant necessity', which is conditional necessity [39.3:756–72], Auriol replies that since God exists always and is immutable, there is no point in making such a distinction in His case [39.3:782–87]. He repeats against Durand of St. Pourçain that God's knowledge has been immutable from eternity:

> Something necessary *ex suppositione*, even if it is contingent simply speaking (*simpliciter*), is nevertheless necessary and completely inevitable, while the given supposition stands; but the foreknowledge of causes and of all things that come together with respect to the future effect itself stands from eternity (*ab eterno*) and immutably, and He knows immutably that all things will come together in that way; therefore it is no use deliberating about what cannot change.[25]

And thus, finally, against Lombard and most theologians, one cannot find a time or occasion when the divided sense obtains. The composite sense and the supposition of God's essence (and hence will and knowledge) are always the case.[26] Of course, because this could imply that God's willing to create is necessary, Auriol will have to draw a distinction between the different aspects of divine will, as we shall see.

By equating immutability with necessity, Auriol thus changes considerably Scotus's notion of modality. For Auriol, God is absolutely necessary, and it is absolutely impossible for God to be otherwise. Whereas Scotus defined 'impossible' as that which implies a logical contradiction, Auriol extends the definition of 'impossible' to include what God does not know or will, because God is absolutely necessary. Of course, this may simply be a particular case of Scotus's definition, because for Auriol, God's knowing more or less, or being different, does imply a contradiction. In a sense Auriol is putting 'metaphysical' impossibility on par with Scotus's logical impossibility. I think, for Auriol, God's being absolutely necessary means that He is the way He is in eternity, and that both in our time and in eternity not only was He not, is He not, or will He not be different *de facto*, but also He never was, is, or will be *able* to be different.

Along with this claim comes Auriol's stress on the complete lack of possibility in God. Because God is absolutely necessary, and cannot be other than He is, anything that is possible must in fact be the case. There is no potency in

---

[25] [39.3:840–44]: "Necessarium enim ex suppositione, etsi sit contingens simpliciter, est tamen immutabile et omnino inevitabile, stante predicta suppositione; sed ab eterno stat et immutabiliter prescientia causarum et omnium que concurrunt ad ipsum effectum futurum, et novit immutabiliter quod omnia sic concurrent; igitur consiliari non oportet de eo quod mutari non potest."

[26] [39.3:871–5]: "Sed nec iste modus evadit, quia semper stat suppositio et sensus compositus. Immutabile enim est hodie quin sit prescius Deus, et per consequens immutabile erit quin eveniat. Et qui vult conari ad oppositum deberet conari ad immutandam divinam prescientiam et eius intuitum de quo consiliari vanum est et superfluum."

God, but pure act. So anything that is possible in God, is in God, and hence is really necessary in God, not possible.[27] Thus it is difficult to see how Scotus's 'logical possibility' applies to God.

This entails a rejection, then, of the distinction between DPA and DPO. God's power considered absolutely is the same as His power as ordained. Any real possibility to will otherwise, as the distinction supposes, involves imperfection in God, according to Auriol. Therefore any attempt to ground contingency in the world somewhere in God, using the distinction between the composite and divided senses or between DPA and DPO, is useless. Contingency comes from elsewhere. In grounding contingency in the divine will, Scotus emphasized the contingency of the world, of everything God willed. Auriol did not think this contingency existed from the divine will, or if it did, it was not real contingency.

In twentieth-century historiography, Scotus and the thinkers of the fourteenth century were considered to have introduced a radical contingency into the world, based on the need to stress God's absolute freedom. It has been mentioned that in the 1270s, most importantly at Paris in 1277, a series of condemnations were issued that proscribed philosophical and theological opinions that seemed to say that things other than God were necessary and that God was constrained in some way. It was thought that these condemnations led later thinkers to stress the radical contingency of the world considered with respect to God's power taken absolutely. It is more likely, however, given the research of recent decades, that these condemnations were more complex, and that they represent tendencies in thinkers such as Henry of Ghent that were already there, perhaps even as far back as Peter Lombard, as we have observed.[28] It is easy to see that radical contingency, for the most part, was *not* propounded. Scotus's contingent world does not seem very contingent to non-philosophical eyes, for, supposing the eternal determination of

---

[27] See [39.4:1072–89]: "Sed hic modus dicendi, quamvis videatur esse Magistri *Sententiarum*, et communiter sic dicatur, nihilominus stare non potest in multis. Primo quidem in hoc quod dicit divinum velle semper esse quasi in egrediendo a voluntate. Probabitur enim infra quod Deitas est quoddam velle subsistens purum absque omni potentia volitiva, sicut et intelligere purum. Ubicumque enim est ratio potentie volitive, ibi est ratio imperfectionem importans, quia omnis possibilitas dicit imperfectionem maxime; susceptiva voluntas autem dicitur velle suscipiendo volitionem formaliter et non eliciendo; sed constat quod in Deo non est aliqua ratio imperfectionem importans; ergo non est in Eo potentia volitiva, sed velle inelicitum, actus purus, et subsistens.

Secundo vero in eo quod ait quod Deus potest non velle quod vult, non quod simul velit et non velit, nec etiam quod postmodum non velit. Secundum hoc enim sequeretur quod aliquod velle esset in Deo quod potuisset non esse, et aliquod velle non esset in Eo quod tamen esse potuisset; sed hoc est impossibile, quia quicquid umquam possibile est esse in Deo, totum est actu, et quod non est actu, est impossibile simpliciter in Eo esse, alioquin, cum quicquid sit in Deo sit Deus, esset aliquis Deus possibilis qui non est, et aliquis Deus possibilis non esse Deus; igitur poni non potest quod isti dicunt."

[28] On the condemnations of 1277 and their impact see for example various places in Pierre Duhem, *Le système de monde*, 10 vols. (Paris 1913–59); Hissette, *Enquête sur les 219 articles condamnés à Paris le 7 mars 1277*; Grant, "The Condemnation of 1277"; and the more recent study by J.M.M.H. Thijssen, *Censure and Heresy at the University of Paris, 1200–1400* (Philadelphia 1998).

God's will, some would say that Scotus's world has been predetermined. This is the opinion of John Hiltalingen of Basel, for example, from the 1360s. Peter Auriol does not seem to be constrained by the condemnations issued by the Bishop of Paris, Etienne Tempier, when he criticizes Scotus's view of divine contingency, eliminates the distinction between DPO and DPA, and emphasizes the necessity of God and the impossibility for Him to be different.

The contingency that does lie in the world is very little. It does not lie in natural events. Auriol agrees with Scotus that natural causes bring about their effects necessarily. If they are impeded, it is either by another natural cause, or by free will. For Auriol, a natural cause cannot not cause, and natural causes, such as celestial events that affect things on earth, are "necessary with respect to the concourse of causes" [39.3:855–8]. This is not very different from the position held by scientists today, or at least before Heisenberg. The only real contingency in the world arises from the use of humans' free will.

That there is contingency is something that cannot be proven by something more known than contingency itself. Following Scotus, Auriol says contingency is a *per se notum*, something obvious and known directly. We simply know that the things we do we do freely by the use of our free will. This fact is as obvious to someone as the fact that she is awake, or exists, or lives. Auriol gives the typical response to the skeptics who say that everything they do they do necessarily, and that events occur of necessity: one can tell them that they are sleeping even when they speak, because it is not more known to them that they are awake then that they do things freely. He cites Avicenna that these people should be thrown into fire or cold water, and then we shall see if they still think everything happens of necessity [39.2:489–510].

As a result of the existence of contingency in the world, we take trouble with our affairs. If everything happened of necessity, why would we bother trying to do or not to do something, asks Auriol. All attempts to take steps to run our own lives would be futile. The immutability of divine foreknowledge will bring about without fail the immutable and necessary coming about of all futures, Auriol maintains, if the traditional concept of divine foreknowledge is true [39.2:511–6].

Given all of this, Auriol presents and refutes seven explanations of how the immutability of divine foreknowledge could coexist with the contingency of things. Auriol presents this consequence: 'If God foreknows this to be future, therefore it will exist'. As on many occasions, he claims that this is a necessary consequence. The antecedent, it is commonly agreed, is at least immutable (for Scotus, see above, chapter one), and for Auriol this is the same as necessary.[29] Auriol now attempts to show that no solution other than his own can avoid the conclusion that the consequent is also necessary.

---

[29]   See [39.3:691–96]: "Circa tertium vero considerandum quod immutabilitas divine prescientie videtur imponere necessitatem rebus futuris pro eo quod necessario sequitur: 'Si Deus prescit hoc esse futurum, igitur illud erit'. Constat enim quod hec consequentia necessaria est; antecedens autem videtur necessarium ex quo supponitur quod Dei scientia immutabilis sit, et ita consequens erit necessarium et eveniet de necessitate."

Aquinas and his followers hold the antecedent and consequent to be necessary, but Aquinas adds that when the antecedent pertains to an act of the soul, the consequent must be taken as it is in the soul. An example is this: 'If a soul understands, what it understands is immaterial'. In this example the object of understanding is immaterial only as it is in the intellect, and not in itself. With 'If God knows something, it will exist', the consequent must be taken as it is in God's knowledge, which, for Aquinas, is as it is present in eternity. As such the consequent is necessary, as is the antecedent. This does not mean the object of knowledge is necessary in itself, but only as it is present to God [39.3:697–707].

Auriol responds by pointing out that Aquinas also says that 'God knew that this was future' is a necessary antecedent, and that 'this will be future' is the corresponding consequent. If Aquinas holds that the object of knowledge is in the divine understanding in its presentiality, and not as future, then Aquinas must deny that God knew this was future, since this implies knowledge of something as future. The consequent, 'this will be future', cannot be in the divine intellect except as future. Besides, when we say 'I know that a stone is immaterial', we mean that the stone is immaterial in itself. A passage in Auriol's Paris Borghese 123 *reportatio* makes this clearer:

> One thing is to be said about knowledge as it applies to a thing as something incomplex, and another concerning knowledge applied to a proposition or a complex thing. Thus 'I know a thing; therefore the thing exists' does not follow, but 'I know that a thing is in external reality; therefore it exists in external reality' does indeed follow. And in his example, 'I know that a thing is immaterial; therefore the thing is immaterial' does in fact follow, but 'I know an immaterial; therefore that thing is immaterial' does not follow. And the reason is that when knowledge applies to a proposition or to something complex, it applies to the being that expresses the truth according to which the proposition (*complexio*) conforms to the thing in external reality; indeed it is not true unless it conforms to the thing in external reality. And consequently knowledge applied to that proposition, if it is true, argues that the thing exists thus in accordance with its being in external reality.[30]

Auriol here draws a contrast between propositional and non-propositional knowledge, a topic that does not appear to become a fundamental issue of contention in the context of foreknowledge until Walter Chatton. I shall deal

---

[30] Aureoli, *Reportatio Parisiensis* I, d. 39, q. 3 (ed. Nielsen-Schabel, Borghese 123, f. 172ra): "Aliud est enim dicendum de notitia cadente super rem ut super incomplexam, aliud est de notitia cadente super propositionem vel super rem complexam. Unde non sequitur 'scio rem; igitur res est', sed bene sequitur 'scio rem esse extra; igitur res est extra'. Et in exemplo suo sequitur bene 'scio rem esse materialem; igitur res est materialis', sed non sequitur 'scio immateriale; igitur illud est immateriale'. Et ratio <est> quia quando notitia cadit super propositionem sive super complexum, cadit super esse quod exprimit veritatem secundum quam complexio conformis est rei extra, imo non est vera nisi sit conformis rei extra, et per consequens notitia cadens super propositionem illam, si est vera arguit rem esse ita secundum esse extra."

with it in greater depth in chapter ten, but briefly, for Auriol, 'God knows that X is future' concerns propositional knowledge, signifying that X is future. Auriol claims that no one would agree that 'I *know* that a triangle does not have three angles' is true, although a triangle's not having three angles might be the non-propositional 'knowledge' contained in a mind with a false understanding of 'triangle'. If the understanding were true, it would be necessary for the triangle actually not to have three angles in itself. Thus if God *knows* that X is future, then X must really be future. So Aquinas's solution will not avoid the necessary coming about of the future, and all attempts to deliberate about future things would be useless [39.3:708–47].

Bonaventure and Richard of Middleton, as noted above, had tried to show that things happen necessarily only by necessity *'ex suppositione'*, roughly the same as conditional necessity, the necessity of the consequence, subsequent necessity, and concomitant necessity. Auriol responds to both, again, that the supposition that God knows something is immutable and inevitable, so things happen of necessity, and there is no reason to bother about things. Auriol cites, via Richard, Aquinas's example of a person viewing a road from above who sees everything, while someone walking along the road cannot see what is happening far in front or behind. For Aquinas, this vision did not impose necessity on the actions in the road, but Auriol claims that God's vision is always there, and if He sees things as future long before they happen, then they must happen as they do, and in that case Auriol still does not see reason to deliberate concerning anything [39.3:779–87].

Auriol considers Scotus's position, too, as completely failing to avoid the problem. If the divine will wills contingently, which Auriol does not hold, and if things are not necessary, it is nevertheless true under Scotus's model that the divine will determines things. If the coming of futures is determined, though not necessary absolutely speaking, Auriol says that there would still be no reason to bother. God's will is immutable, and "it is as stupid to take troubles about something immutable as about something necessary, because these are one-and-the-same" [39.3:796–802].

The position of Henry of Harclay, as reported in his *Sentences* commentary, is one found in the works of Augustine and Anselm, as Harclay and Auriol realize. According to this opinion, the reason God does not impose necessity on things is because He knows that events, such as one's sinning, will occur through the use of free will. Thus He does not simply know that one will sin, but that he will sin contingently by his own deliberation and decision. In this way one must still deliberate and be concerned, because "the entire process" comes under divine foreknowledge [39.3:803–11].[31] Auriol, however, does not

---

[31] This is a position many Christians hold today, and some determinists agree with it. One could say that although things are foreordained, or even predetermined, and in some way happen necessarily, nevertheless we do not perceive this, and our very efforts are part of this predetermination. To some, it makes no difference whether they are predetermined or not, though to theists, with a notion of just rewards and punishments that are eternal, this position presents more trouble.

think this solves the problem. If the whole process is necessary, it is the same for him as if one event taken alone were necessary. It is not free will for Auriol if God foresees that one person will deliberate and another will not, because that deliberation or non-deliberation is unavoidable.[32]

As we have seen in chapter two, Durand of St. Pourçain's position is a slight variation on Harclay's, in that God knows all things that will impede, not impede, determine, and not determine our use of free will. Durand falls back on the argument about the benignity of the necessity *ex suppositione* that comes along with this knowledge [39.3:820–38]. For Auriol, however, if God foreknows our use of 'free' will or what will determine it, then the will is not really free, and there is no reason to bother about events. Moreover, Durand begs the question, Auriol claims, by not explaining *how* God can foreknow impediments governed by human free will [39.3:839–54].

Finally Auriol attacks the common opinion, that of Peter Lombard, which states that 'If God knows some future thing, that will come about' can be taken in the divided or composite sense. We have seen that Auriol denies this distinction for God, and thinks it does nothing to explain why we should take trouble. Under Lombard's position, any effort to deliberate would be "vain and superfluous" [39:871–5].

Auriol's predecessors agreed that God's willing was immutable, but in their attempt to avoid determinism they refused to accept that it was also necessary. The array of terms and distinctions they developed was in order to defend the inequality of immutability and necessity, and thereby preserve the common view of divine foreknowledge and the existence of contingency in the world. For Auriol, however, all of these attempts fail: immutability is identical with necessity, and if God's willing is immutable, it is also necessary. As we shall see, this means Auriol will also have to abandon the common conception of foreknowledge.

Auriol's arguments about necessity did not convince most of his successors, who either repeated the distinction between necessities, or, like Francis of Marchia and his followers Michael of Massa and William of Rubio, developed new explanations to sidestep Auriol's reasoning (see chapter nine). Nevertheless, Auriol thinks he has destroyed his opposition, and now claims that only his position will work:

> The question of foreknowledge, concerning which Boethius, in *The Consolation of Philosophy*, book V, said that it is an ancient and long standing quarrel, "which was passionately pursued by Cicero when he treated divination and has been for a long time a subject of my own in-

---

[32] See [39.3:812–9]: "Sed nec iste modus dicendi sufficere videtur, quia secundum hoc totus processus et decursus eventus futuri cadit sub Dei prescientia. Quare non est minor difficultas respectu totius decursus quam respectu unius effectus precise sumpti. Unde dicetur quod Deus previdit quod iste sollicitabitur, ille non; et ita immutabile est quin iste sollicitetur et ille non. Hoc autem facto, tollitur persuasio. Non oportet enim persuadere isti quod sollicitetur, quia faciet sine hoc; nec illi, quia previsum est quod non sollicitabitur. Unde patet quod remanet difficultas."

vestigation," cannot be solved except by saying that foreknowledge does not make a proposition about a future contingent determinately true.[33]

Aristotle, Auriol asserts, in the beginning of this ancient quarrel, proved that all things would happen of necessity, and there would be no point in deliberating or bothering about things, if propositions about the future were determinately true or false. He reached this demonstrated conclusion [38:829–32], Auriol stresses, based only on a consideration of philosophical truth, without any appeal to divine foreknowledge [39:901–5]. Since immutability equals necessity, Auriol sees no way to avoid the necessary coming of events other than to show that God does not know future contingents as future. By separating God's knowledge from the futurition of things, Auriol thinks he can preserve divine perfection, immutability, and omniscience, as well as contingency and free will. And since God is omniscient, future things simply cannot be known as future, for as future things they are indeterminate.

Auriol lists all of the things that God knows, and how he knows them:

(1) The 'whatness' (quiddities) of things. These are known the same way whether they exist or not.

(2) The actual existence of things. While things actually exist they can be known immutably.

(3) The existences of things that will come about naturally, such as rain and wind. These things are all found within the universal causality of the whole of nature, which cannot escape God's knowledge.

(4) The existences of things that will come about freely and indeterminately. They are known as they are in actuality indistantly, by God, who is the abstracted exemplar.

(5) Necessary complexes of things. Even we know these, e.g. 'a triangle has three angles'.

(6) Contingent complexes of things. These are known immutably when they are put in actuality.

(7) The shifting of time. Like us, He does not *know* futures while they are future, but unlike us, He does know them *indistantly by abstraction*.[34]

---

[33] [39.3:925–30]: "Secunda vero propositio est quod questio de prescientia, de qua dicit Boetius V *De consolatione* quod est vetus et antiqua querela, 'que a Tullio cum divinationem distribuit vehementer est agitata, michique ipsi res diu multumque quesita, nec ab ullo actenus satis diligenter ac firmiter expedita,' hec utique questio non aliter solvi potest nisi dicendo quod prescientia non dat propositioni de futuro contingenti quod sit determinate vera."

[34] See [39.4:1196–1234]: "Preterea, scientia Dei attingens Deitatem dicitur attigisse rerum quidditates; rerum existentias actuales; rerum existentias futuras naturaliter, ut pluvias, ventos, et talia; rerum existentias futuras libere et ad utrumlibet, ut mores hominum, merita, et peccata; rerum complexiones necessarias, ut quod triangulus habet tres; rerum complexiones contingentes, ut quod Sortes sedet; inflexiones temporum, ut quod Cesar fuit, et quod Antichristus nondum est — sciet autem, quando erit, quod est, et dum fuerit mortuus, sciet quod fuit. Sed manifestum est quod nullum istorum cognitorum inducit mutabilitatem in divina scientia. Constat enim quod non facit hoc cognitio quidditatum; ille enim, sive sint sive non sint, uniformiter cognoscuntur.

What Auriol means by "indistantly by abstraction," that is, what sort of divine knowledge can know the future but not as future, he had already made clear in distinction 38.

Nec etiam existentie actuales, quia res, dum existit, immutabiliter est et invariabiliter cognosci potest. Nec etiam existentie futurorum que naturaliter fiunt, ut in pluribus vel raro, quia talia reducuntur in causalitatem universalem totius nature et supra celestium corporum, et sic subterfugere non possunt cognitionem divinam.

Nec etiam futura libere, quia licet reduci non possint in causas determinatas, quia liberum arbitrium est ad utrumlibet, tamen ut posite sunt iam in actu, quedam cognoscibilia sunt, et possunt habere similitudinem presentantem, coexistentem, ut dum cadunt sub sensu, vel abstractam et indistantem, quia precedentem vel subsequentem habere non possunt quin fallax et deceptoria sit. Deitas autem est exemplar abstractum, et ideo potest representare res positas in actu, non quidem ut preteritas vel futuras vel simultaneas, sed solum pro illo tunc in quo posite sunt. Et ita mores hominum, et merita ac demerita, immutabiliter sunt Deo cognita, quia et ipsa immutabilia sunt prout ponuntur in actu.

Nec etiam facit varietatem in divina scientia cognitio complexionum et compositionum que necessarie sunt, ut quod triangulus habet tres, quia ille semper uniformiter cognoscuntur etiam a nobis. Nec etiam complexionum contingentium, quia ille immutabiliter possunt cognosci, dum ponuntur in actu. Nec etiam inflexiones temporum, licet enim non sit eadem enunciatio: 'Antichristus est natus', 'Nascetur', et 'Natus fuit', quia una est vera, reliqua existente falsa, tamen eadem res est cognita sub diverso modo cognoscendi, nunc quidem expectative, ut cum dicitur 'nascetur', nunc vero memorative, ut cum dicitur 'natus est', nunc vero intuitive vel simultanee, ut cum imaginamur quod nascitur — in intellectu ergo sic apprehendente rem, varietas enunciationum inducit varietatem scientiarum sicut in nobis; sed ubi res cognoscitur abstrahendo a futuritione, preteritione, et simultate, non oportet quod inflexio rei secundum tempora inducat varietatem in tali scientia, et sic Deus immutabiliter mutabilitates istas cognoscit; enunciationes enim istas non format, sed a nobis formabiles, vel formatas, cognoscit cognita Deitate. Ergo nullum est scibile quod in divina scientia mutabilitatem inducat."

Chapter 4

Indistant Knowledge of the Future

What kind of divine knowledge can know the future, but not as future, and thus preserve free will? When Auriol begins his distinction 38 in the usual way, by citing many authorities and giving the basic positions on the subject, he is very careful and precise in his wording. He does not say that Lombard here began to treat God's *fore*knowledge, but only the divine understanding as it is expressed by the name 'foreknowledge' [38:3–5]. It is this sort of precision of usage that calls upon us to analyze his positive stance closely. The main question is whether God is foreknowing of future contingents [38:62], but Auriol's first two articles ask specifically how He knows future contingents, and whether His knowledge of future things is properly intuitive or rather expective — and thus *fore*knowledge.[1] Of course Auriol does not think it can be expective foreknowledge, for that would entail the necessary coming about of all futures.

As we have seen, the primary element of Henry of Ghent's solution and the sole foundation of John Duns Scotus's theory rely on God's knowledge of the determinations of His will. Auriol correctly recognizes the relationship between Henry and Scotus on question of future contingents. As Auriol sees it, Henry held that the divine will was the cause of future contingents, and by knowing this unimpedible cause, the divine intellect could know the future effects with certainty.[2] Scotus maintained that this seemed to introduce a certain discursiveness into God, and to add to his own, perhaps less complicated, version of eternity, Scotus (or Scotists) says that this is the order of events in God's eternity: (1) The divine intellect presents the divine will with both parts of a contradiction (e.g., 'Bubba will get tenure'; 'Bubba will not get tenure'); (2) the will accepts one part (i.e., 'Bubba will get tenure') and from this acceptance that part becomes knowable as determinate and certain; and (3) through the divine essence the intellect knows that part with certitude. This addition of Scotus's, according to Auriol, prevents the will from seeming to be the direct basis of knowing and makes it merely "something leading the way [as] required on the part of the knowable thing, giving itself certitude and

---

[1] [38:133–7] "Primo namque, supposito tamquam vero determinato per fidem quod Deus sit prescius futurorum, inquiretur modus secundum quem potest cognoscere futura. Secundo vero inquiretur an notitia futurorum in Deo sit proprie intuitiva vel potius expectativa et quedam prescientia."

[2] Auriol cites Henry of Ghent correctly [38.1:173–8]: "Opinio Henrici VIII *Quolibeta*, questione secunda, et Scoti. Dixerunt vero alii quod Deus potest cognoscere futurum contingens certitudinaliter propter hoc quod voluntate Sua causa est contingentium futurorum; qui autem novit causam impossibilem impediri, certitudinaliter novit effectum; novit autem Deus determinationem voluntatis Sue et omnia per consequens ad que determinat se, propter quod infallibiliter novit futura."

the basis of knowability."³ For Scotus and Henry, God knows future contingents not as they are present, but as they are future, through their cause, the divine will, which is unimpedible on account of divine omnipotence. This sort of knowledge, for Auriol, is not intuitive of something present, but "rather a knowledge of something future as distant and to be brought about later."⁴

Auriol probably borrows his refutation of the position of Scotus and Henry from Thomas Wylton: the simple and obvious response is that the divine will is not the cause of all, if any, future contingents, because it is not the cause of acts of free will, especially sins. God is not an evil doer, so knowing the determination of the divine will does not provide certain knowledge of what the divine will has no hand in, such as evils. Neither does the divine will determine a created will to sin.⁵

A defense of the Scotus/Henry position, from Scotus's distinction 47, is the popular notion that God permits the created will to sin, even if He does not determine it. In this way God's knowledge that Judas will sin in instant A stems from His willing Himself to allow it. For Auriol, however, even if God permits a sin, this does not mean the sin will happen. The free created will is still indeterminate with respect to sinning and not sinning, since it is still possible for it to sin and not to sin. So knowing what the divine will permits will not give certitude to the divine intellect with respect to future contingents. Auriol gives other possible defenses of the position, but in every case either (1) the created will is left free and indeterminate with respect to bringing something about or not bringing it about, or (2) the divine will would be the author, at least partially, of sin and evil, or (3) only future contingents not having to do with free will are known. The first case does not provide certain knowl-

---

    ³ [38.1:179–87]: "Opinio Scoti in speciali. Dixerunt quoque alii addentes ad predicta quod intellectus divinus non novit tantum futura ex determinatione Sue voluntatis ne discursivus ponatur, sed novit ea in se, tamen previa voluntate et acceptatione ipsius, ut iste sit ordo: Quod intellectus presentat utramque partem contradictionis voluntati, voluntas vero alteram acceptat, et ex hoc illa pars facta est scibilis tamquam quid determinatum et certum, et tunc per essentiam suam intellectus divinus cognoscit certitudinaliter partem illam. Et secundum hoc voluntas non erit sibi ratio cognoscendi, sed aliquid previum, requisitum ex parte cognoscibilis et dans sibi certitudinem et rationem scibilitatis."
    ⁴ [38.2:614–15]: "et ita notitia Dei non erit intuitiva, sed potius futuri ut distantis et posterius fiendi."
    ⁵ [38.1:200–211]: "Deus enim non cognoscit futura per cognitionem illius quod non est futurorum causa, cum omnis cognitio vel sit rei in se vel rei per suas causas; sed manifestum est quod determinatio voluntatis divine non est causa contingentium futurorum — saltem omnium — quia non est causa actuum qui eliciuntur a libero arbitrio, et maxime peccatorum, quia Deus non est actor malorum; ergo non potest dici quod cognoscat omnia futura contingentia cognoscendo determinationem aut nutum Sue voluntatis.

    Preterea, illud non cognoscit Deus per determinationem Sue voluntatis respectu cuius non est determinatio Sue voluntatis; sed manifestum est quod voluntas divina non determinat creatam voluntatem ad peccandum; ergo dici non potest quod cognoscendo determinationem Sue voluntatis cognoscat Deus Iudam in tali nunc fuisse peccaturum."

edge, the second is untenable, and the third is irrelevant, since we are concerned with *all* future contingents.[6]

Auriol also criticizes Henry and Scotus's notion of the relationship between God and time. Although Auriol disagrees with Aquinas's eternal presence mechanism for divine foreknowledge, Auriol nevertheless is more sympathetic to Aquinas's and Boethius's image of God's eternity where nothing is future or past to God (or even really simultaneous with Him, according to Auriol, as we shall see). For Auriol, Henry and Scotus connect God's knowledge too closely with the actual passage of time, and do not follow what "the saints say everywhere, that nothing becomes past and nothing is future to God, but all is present." Of course, as we will see, the 'present' that Auriol is thinking of differs in significant ways from that of previous theories [38.2:707–31].

---

[6] [38.1:212–60]: "Sed forte dicetur quod licet Deus non determinet voluntatem ad peccandum, nichilominus permittit, et secundum hoc habet voluntatem permissionis, secundum quam novit quod Iudas in tali instanti peccabit quia Ipse permittet.

Sed si ita dicatur, non valet. Illud enim, quo posito, adhuc remanet effectus indeterminatus ad utramque partem contradictionis — quia possibile fieri vel non fieri — non ducit per certitudinem et determinate in alteram partem contradictionis; sed voluntate permissionis posita, adhuc remanet voluntas creata indeterminata, et peccatum possibile est fieri vel non fieri, non enim permissio determinat ad peccandum, sed exigitur ultra hoc determinatio voluntatis create que penitus remanet indeterminata quantumcumque permittatur; ergo Deus non novit determinate peccatum futurum in tali nunc ex hoc quod novit permissionem Sue voluntatis Et confirmatur, quia causa que non ponit effectum determinate non ducit certitudinaliter in cognitionem illius.

Ulterius forte dicetur quod in peccato semper est aliquid positivum, videlicet actus substractus deformitati; licet ergo divina voluntas non determinet ad deformitatem peccati, determinat tamen ad actum substractum, cum sit aliquid positivum.

Quod si ita dicatur, non valet. Impossibile est enim quod aliquid determinet ad actum quin determinet ad deformitatem inseparabilem ab illo actu; sed deformitas est inseparabilis ab illo actu numerali in quo est, et omnino ab actu odii divini deformitas separari non potest; ergo si determinet Deus voluntatem creatam ad actum, determinabit et ad deformitatem ac peccatum.

Et confirmatur, quia nec voluntas creata intendit deformitatem per se, sed delectationem et id quod est positivum in actu — nullus enim ad malum aspiciens operatur, secundum Dionysium, immo displicet quod est actui annexa deformitas, et si posset, vellet peccator perfrui delectatione et habere quicquid est positivum in actu exclusa deformitate; et tamen hoc non obstante, dicitur actor peccati propter hoc quod est causa actus quem deformitas necessario comitatur; quare si Deus determinaret voluntatem creatam ad talem actum, necessario esset actor peccati. Et iterum non deberet peccatori imputari si determinaretur ad huiusmodi actum positivum a voluntate divina, que est efficax et que semper impletur.

Ulterius forte dicetur quod Deus novit quibus proposuit gratiam Se daturum et quibus non daturum; cognoscendo ergo huiusmodi propositum, cognoscet quis peccabit, quia cui non dabit gratiam; qui vero habebit gratiam non peccabit.

Quod si ita dicatur, non valet, quia contingit habentem gratiam peccare et non habentem gratiam aliquando non peccare.

Ulterius forte dicetur quod licet per determinationem voluntatis Deus non possit mala cognoscere, potest tamen alia futura.

Sed nec etiam istud valet, tum quia remanet nobis difficultas quomodo novit actus liberi arbitrii in quibus contingunt peccata; tum quia difficultas est generalis circa omnia futura, et si aliquod novit in se absque determinatione voluntatis, videtur quod omnia possit etiam sic cognoscere; tum quia licet aliquorum futurorum Deus sit actor per Suam voluntatem, non tamen est omnium, unde non ideo quia Deus prenovit, futura sunt, secundum Magistrum in presenti distinctione.

Sic igitur demonstrative concluditur cuilibet fideli quod Deus non novit futura omnia per cognitionem nutuum Sue voluntatis et determinationis ipsius."

For Auriol, Scotus's theory is the most objectionable and the most easily refuted, but Auriol has to deal more carefully with Thomas Aquinas's solution
based on eternal presence and with divine Ideas, because his own position has
much in common with both of them. Auriol gathers together Aquinas's opinion
on this matter from his *Summa theologiae*, *Sentences* commentary, and *Summa
contra gentiles*. Aquinas, says Auriol, thinks that God cannot know future
things through their causes, since some causes are contingent and not determinate. No certitude can come from the knowledge of indeterminate causes, such
as causes arising from free will. Instead, God must know future things as they
have determinate being, as they are actually placed in the world. Because, as
Boethius maintains, knowledge is according to the mode of the knower, and
God is outside of time, therefore His intellect intuits every contingent as present in eternity, although with regard to each other the contingents are successive. The same necessity of the consequence that holds when we say, "I see
that Socrates is running; therefore he is necessarily running" also holds when
God intuits future contingents in this way, and from this necessity comes absolute certainty.

Auriol uses the verb 'intuit' because for Aquinas God knows the futures
when their being, as it is actually exhibited and placed in the world, is *present*
to eternity. Here Auriol is simply distinguishing between the knowledge of the
past, present, and future, rather than making any important epistemological
declarations about the nature of divine knowledge. Later Auriol distinguishes
between the different types of knowledge, following Augustine in the *Confes-
sions*, for whom there is memorative knowledge of what has passed, expectative knowledge of what has yet to come, and attentative knowledge of what
the mind 'attends' presently. The knowledge humans have of something
changes as that something goes from being past to present to future
[38.2:626–33].

Auriol refutes Aquinas's position first by saying that future things are not
actually present in eternity. Mindful of Scotus's criticisms of Aquinas on this
point, Auriol nevertheless tends to present different criticisms, probably because Scotus's critique could be applied to Auriol's indistance solution, which
resembles Aquinas's in many respects. By separating himself from Aquinas,
Auriol thinks he can escape Scotus. Thus Auriol begins by asserting that, even
if the existences of futures were present to eternity, God would not have certain knowledge of them because of that. Citing Augustine, he holds that the
doctrine of divine simplicity, to which Auriol always wishes to adhere closely,
dictates that God does not intuit anything outside himself. That is, God's intuition in eternity does not end directly (*terminatur*) at something outside
Himself, which would be the case if the existences of future contingents were
present in eternity. The existence of things cannot add anything from outside to
the divine intellect.[7]

---

[7]   [38.1:354–71]: "Quarta autem propositio est quod non ideo Deus futura cognoscit quia
eorum existentia exhibita in rerum natura presens est eternitati, sic quod divinus intuitus feratur

For Auriol, another difficulty with Aquinas's position is that it does not fully explain how the divine intellect could ascertain the actuality of the future contingent present in eternity. Auriol claims that Aquinas must hold that the intellect, essence, or at least something else, is the medium by which such knowledge is obtained, but he does not. Here Auriol takes up a possible correction of Aquinas's views by Durand of St. Pourçain, whom Auriol treats merely as a follower and apologist of Aquinas rather than as an independent thinker. According to Auriol, Durand believes that those who put forth this mode of divine knowing did not mean that things are really present to eternity in their actual existences, but that their causes are the basis of God's determinate knowledge of those future effects. As we have seen, Durand holds that, by knowing the causes, whether they are necessary or impedible, and, if they are impedible, by what they can and will be impeded, God can know what effects will and will not come about.[8] Auriol again refutes this with his frequent appeal to free will. Perhaps God knows what can and cannot impede the causes of future contingents, but He cannot know what will or will not, be-

---

super eas in sua existentia actuali. Hoc enim verum non est, ut supra visum fuit, quod scilicet res future actualiter sint presentes eternitati. Et, dato quod sic esset, adhuc divinus intuitus non ferretur in eas ut sic, nec haberet earum certam cognitionem quia sic essent presentes. Constat enim quod divinus intuitus nullo modo terminatur ad aliquid extra se, sed tantum ad essentiam suam, ut Augustinus dicit *LXXXIII questionum*, questione XLVI — ait enim quod, 'Deus nichil extra se positum intuetur'; sed existentia futurorum est aliquid realiter positum extra Deum; ergo quantumcumque presentialiter existeret ab eterno, non ex hoc Deus habebit certam notitiam de futuro contingenti.

Preterea, non magis tribuit divino intellectui existentia futuri contingentis ut presens eternitati quam cum est presens etiam cum hoc in certo tempore; sed futurum contingens iam positum in actu in certo tempore, ex hoc quod est sic presens et positum, non dat divino intellectui ut certitudinaliter ipsum cognoscat, immo habet hoc intellectus a se, alias vilesceret divinus intellectus et mensuraretur a rebus, cum traheret certitudinem ab ipsis; ergo nec futurum presens eternitati tribuit divino intellectui quod certitudinaliter cognoscatur ab eo."

[8]   John D. North claims that Durand, along with Auriol and Robert Holcot, "held that God was ignorant of future contingents until the moment they happened" ("Astronomy and Mathematics," in J. I. Catto and R. Evans, eds., *The History of the University of Oxford. Volume II: Late Medieval Oxford* [Oxford 1992], p. 111). While this perhaps could be said of Holcot (though based only on some passages in his œuvre; see chapter 4), it certainly needs qualification when said of Auriol, and is simply not true of Durand, unless one means simply that Durand held that God does not know future contingents as present (which North says on the next page), but only through their causes. Even so, Durand still held that God has determinate knowledge of future contingents, before they occurr, via their causes.

What North goes on to say is equally puzzling: "Others, such as Thomas Buckingham and Adam Woodham, adopted the weaker position that God's knowledge must be as contingent as the contingents themselves. Note the differing opinions of the two Mertonians, Bradwardine and Buckingham, and the broad agreement between the Franciscans Auriol and Woodham." The fact is that many theologians in the fourteenth century, Franciscans, Dominicans, Augustinians, etc., held that the basis for contingency was in God. Auriol, on the other hand, did not call God's knowledge contingent, and Wodeham even had much more in common with Bradwardine in this respect (see below, chapter 10). Unfortunately, on a complex and confusing matter such as this, we are still far from being able to communicate clearly to those engaged in important synthetic work, such as North.

cause some of these causes and their impediments are based on the free and indeterminate use of the will.[9]

Besides the fact that no creature is present in the divine view as an end, terminating that view directly, Auriol gives an interesting argument based on the infinite. God would intuit as presently existing either an actual infinite or a finite multitude of the "thoughts of people" and "wails of the damned." It cannot be infinite, because an actual infinite is impossible. Nor can it be finite, "because that [finite] multitude of thoughts and wails would be cut short and consumed in a finite time, beyond which the wails and thoughts would still continue," since, for example, the damned have eternal suffering, infinite in duration.[10] Auriol of course gives other refutations of Aquinas's position, but their substance is better discussed while treating Auriol's own position. Still, in the end Auriol's position shares many similarities with Aquinas's, and Auriol could not or would not refute the stance entirely, but just enough to

---

[9] [38.1:372–401]: "Preterea, quantumcumque res future sint presentes eternitati, adhuc restat querere ex parte divini intellectus, quid est sibi ratio attingendi actualitatem futuri positi in sua presentialitate? Et oportet dicere quod essentia — ut idea — vel voluntas, vel aliquid aliud; sed iste modus dicendi non ponit; igitur ad propositum nichil scire nos facit.

Ex quo etiam patet quod vana est interpretatio aliquorum qui dicunt non intellexisse positores istius modi quod res in sua existentia actuali presentes essent eternitati realiter, sed tantum secundum esse cognitum, ita quod intellectus divinus intuetur presentialiter existentiam actualem contingentis futuri. Cum enim non intueatur immediate, oporteret eos dedisse per quid Deus intuetur, an scilicet cognoscendo determinationem Sue voluntatis aut ideas. Quod enim dixerunt: Quod per essentiam ut est causa cognoscuntur determinate futura, quia sicut ex causa necessaria sequitur effectus infallibiliter, sic ex causa impedibili — si non impediatur — sequitur infallibiliter suus proprius effectus. 'Quare cognita causa impedibili, et omnibus que eam impedire possunt et insuper iis que eam impedient vel non impedient, certitudinaliter potest cognosci quis effectus eveniet vel quis non eveniet'; nunc autem Deus cognoscit causas omnium contingentium futurorum et omnia que determinare eas possunt et que determinabunt, et insuper cognoscit que impedire possunt et que impedient vel non impedient; ergo cognoscit certitudinaliter futura contingentia, cognoscendo enim suam essentiam cognoscit causas futurorum contingentium et si impedientur vel non impedientur.

Quod utique sic dixerunt, non valet quia, dato quod per essentiam cognoscat causas contingentium et que impedire possunt vel non impedire, non tamen potest scire quid impediet actu vel non impediet, quia in actibus liberi arbitrii potest contingere utraque pars contradictionis ex sola determinatione voluntatis; huius autem determinationis Deus causa non est effective et determinative immediate, sed tantum mediante voluntate; voluntas autem penitus indeterminata est et potest ad utramque partem, et sic ea cognita a Deo nescitur ad quam partem contradictionis determinabitur, nisi aliquid aliud ponatur ex parte Dei ratione cuius illam determinationem cognoscat."

[10] [38.2:666–79]: "Secunda vero propositio est quod Deus non cognoscit futura ut presentia aut coexistentia Sue eternitati ita quod Eius intuitus ad futurorum existentias terminetur. Visum est enim supra quod nulla creatura est in divino prospectu terminative; sed existentie futurorum contingentium sunt et creature; ergo Suus intuitus non fertur in eas, nec terminatur ad earum presentialitatem.

Preterea, cogitationes hominum succedent sibi in infinitum et similiter eiulatus dampnatorum; si igitur Deus istorum existentias intuetur quasi presentes, aut ipse ut existentes in divino intuitu sunt secundum multitudinem finitam aut in multitudine infinita; sed non potest dari secundum, quia infinitas et presentialitas vel actualitas mutuo sibi repugnant, ut infra dicetur et iam apparuit supra; nec potest dari primum, quia illa multitudo cogitationum aut eiulatuum finita resecaretur et consumeretur in tempore finito, ultra quod adhuc eiulatus et cogitationes adhuc sibi succederent; igitur poni non potest quod divinus intuitus feratur in res futuras tamquam in presentialiter existentes."

show that his own differed. It is Auriol's different understanding of the implications of Aquinas's position that is most important as we shall see in our treatment of propositions. Auriol probably thinks that Aquinas did not realize the riches of his own solution, and Auriol transferred that wealth to his indistance theory.

Concerning how God knows the future Peter Auriol also discusses and refutes the solution based on divine Ideas, a theory that can be ascribed to Thomas Aquinas and Bonaventure, among others, although Auriol's immediate source is Henry of Ghent. The position holds that God knows the future through Ideas He has within Him which represent both simple terms and complexes of terms "with all the circumstances of time and place," a phrase Aquinas employed. To use Henry and Auriol's example, 'Antichrist', 'a future instant', 'sitting', and 'temple' are simple terms, whereas 'the Antichrist sits in the temple at time X' is a complex of terms. The situation of the Antichrist sitting in the temple at time X is 'complexly signifiable' (*complexe significabile*), to use anachronistically a phrase popular later. "So God, having in him the Ideas of the Antichrist and of a future instant and of sitting and of the temple, knows determinately through them that the Antichrist will sit in the temple at such and such a time, as if he himself were God."[11]

Auriol has to proceed with caution in his rebuttal, because he must find a way around Scotus's objections without destroying his own solution, which shares elements with the Ideas position. In fact Auriol's successors *will* use Scotus's arguments against him. Thus Auriol takes almost seventy lines of text to deal with this position, and in the end, perhaps not accidentally, he does not give the appearance that he is certain about his refutation. Following Scotus, he asserts that Ideas represent terms and complexes of terms without regard to whether what they represent will come about. Auriol gives an example from his theory of vision: "A species of a rose represents 'rose' whether [the rose] exists or not."[12] Similarly, a complex of terms can be either true or false, so it cannot provide certainty [38.1:309–14]. Auriol goes on, however, to attempt to demonstrate that Scotus's arguments against Ideas are not conclu-

---

[11] [38.1:188–93]: "Dixerunt autem alii quod Deus novit futura per ideas quas habet penes Se que quidem non solum representant simplices terminos, immo complexiones terminorum cum omnibus circumstantiis temporis et loci. Unde Deus, habens penes Se ideas Antichristi et instantis futuri et sessionis et templi, novit per eas determinate quod Antichristus in tali nunc sedebit in templo, quasi ipse sit Deus." Cf. Henricus de Gandavo, *Quodlibet* VIII, q. 2 (ed. Venice, f. 4ra): "... ipso sedente in regio throno, Deus videbit ipsum secundum corpus et animam, eius sessionem in throno, ipsum thronum, instans illud, et circumstantes ipsum."

[12] [38.1:288–99]: "Tertia quoque propositio est quod per representationem idearum quas Deus habet de omnibus simplicibus terminis, non potest certitudinaliter cognoscere futura. Illud enim quod abstrahit ab esse et non esse in representando non ducit determinate in rem ut est existens; sed idee simplicium terminorum representant indeterminate sive sint sive non sint, sicut et species rose representat rosam sive sit sive non sit; ergo dici non potest quod per ideas cognoscantur futura.

Et si dicatur quod immo per ideas non solum representantes terminos sed complexionem terminorum in tali nunc vel tali, non valet, quia adhuc talis representatio possibilis est, sive sic eveniat sive non eveniat, et per consequens nescietur determinate per ideas representantes futurum in tali nunc utrum sic erit vel non erit."

sive. The gist of the discussion is that Auriol is unclear about whether God could somehow have a mechanism by which He could know with certainty, through perfect Ideas, which things will come about and which things will not.[13] Later, based on this uncertainty, a confused Pierre d'Ailly would claim that Auriol actually accepted the Ideas stance. He did not, however:

> Thus there is no way to attack and destroy Ideas of this sort except the one touched upon above, namely that if there were an Idea in God that represented a future *complexio* in this or that 'now', it would follow that God, in representing, would be material, for He would be within the line of succession.[14]

God abstracts from the local and temporal modes when representing, otherwise He would be material, having been dragged into time and place. If He represented, through Ideas, with 'before' or 'after', or 'now' or 'then', He would "be within the line of succession with respect to which there would be something prior and something posterior." God is supposed to abstract from 'now' and 'then', what the Borghese version calls the "*differentiae* of time" in the language of Henry of Ghent, and what the *Scriptum* refers to as the temporal "line of succession." One must not think that God is in the line of succession. But if through Ideas God did represent a future situation in a particular

---

[13] [38.1:315–45]: "Est autem sciendum quod processus aliquorum in ista conclusione non valet. Arguunt enim quod per ideas non possit Deus cognoscere futura quia rationes sive idee terminorum non causant sufficientem notitiam, nisi illam que est nata ex terminis haberi; notitia autem contingentium non est nata haberi ex terminis, cum complexio terminorum non oriatur ex ipsis in materia contingenti, immo termini sunt indifferentes ad utramque partem contradictionis; et ita per ideas non possunt futura certitudinaliter cognosci.

Dicerent tamen alii quod complexio terminorum futura est aliquid aliud a terminis, propter quod habet ideam in Deo ultra ideas simplicium terminorum, et sic per ideam huiusmodi illa futura complexio certitudinaliter cognoscetur.

Iterum arguunt quod idee quicquid representant naturaliter representant, cum sint in divino intellectu ante omnem actum voluntatis; aut ergo due idee — utpote hominis et albi — representant complexionem hominis et albi, aut divisionem, aut utrumque; si compositionem, igitur necessaria est propositio: 'Homo erit albus', quia naturaliter et non libere est representata, et per consequens non est futurum contingens; si vero divisionem, impossibilis est propositio: 'Homo erit albus', quia ex terminis naturaliter presentatis oritur oppositum illius propositionis, et ita non est futurum contingens; si vero utrumque, sequitur quod Deus neutram partem novit determinate.

Dicerent tamen illi quod idee terminorum representant utrumque sub quadam indifferentia, sed idea complexionis representat alterum tantum; nec tamen propter hoc est futurum necessarium, immo remanet contingens, sicut manet contingentia, dato quod actus divine intellectionis attingens ea immutabilis sit.

Arguunt iterum sic: Deus eque perfectas ideas habet respectu possibilium fieri que non fient, sicut respectu fiendorum; sed non habet respectu non fiendorum ideas que representent ipsas aliquando futuras, quia tunc Deus falleretur; igitur nec habet respectu fiendorum ideas representantes quod sint futura.

Dicerent tamen isti quod quia fienda futura sunt, idcirco in Deo est idea representans complexionem pro illo tunc pro quo fient."

[14] [38.1:346–7]: "Sic ergo non est via ad impugnandum et tollendum huiusmodi ideas nisi que supra tacta est, videlicet quod si in Deo esset idea representans complexionem futuram in tali nunc vel tali, sequeretur quod Deus in representando esset materialis; esset enim infra lineam successionis."

instant, and these Ideas were within Him, Auriol thinks He would be material and "within the line of succession"[15] Throughout his 'attacks' on the opinions of his recent predecessors, Auriol utilized his own extreme emphasis on divine simplicity, which we discussed in the previous chapter. He begins his determination in the fifth of five negative propositions, the first four being the refutations. Here we begin to see more clearly Auriol's allegiance to Augustinian and Platonic notions of God, together with Aristotelian definitions of perfection. For Auriol, God is the exemplar and eminent similitude (like an Idea?) of all, and He is 'indistant' to the actualities of the existences of future contingents. His position is hard to grasp, and his presentation is long and complicated. This perhaps explains why most later figures virtually ignore much of this section of his discussion of divine foreknowledge and future contingency, and perhaps even ignore his conclusion in article one: God *is* foreknowing of future contingents.

Auriol states that those who have previously asked the question have got the question wrong. Instead of seeking some sort of medium of knowing by which God infallibly knows future contingents, the question should be why God, with the divine intellect knowing the divine essence, knows all future contingents with equal strength (*equipollenter*) and denominatively. Any medium would have to be either between potency and act in God, or between the act and the object of knowledge. It cannot be between potency and act, because in God there is no potency of intellect, but only pure act. It cannot be between the act and the object, because God has only His essence in his view, and no creature. So God knows futures by knowing His essence. Auriol says that God, or the Deity, to use his word here, "is the eminent similitude and exemplar of all, and is in all so eminently that all things that are known are known with equal strength and more than if they were known in themselves."[16] Now we must ask what this means exactly, and how God can tell between what will come about and what can come about but will not.

---

[15] [38.1:300–308]: "Preterea, sicut Deus abstrahit a modo situali in representando — non enim representat ut hic vel ibi, alioquin esset materialis, ut supra dictum est — sic abstrahit a linea temporali et successionis, unde non representat ut ante vel post aut nunc vel tunc, alioquin esset infra lineam successionis respectu cuius esset aliquid prius et aliquid posterius; sed si Deus haberet ideam representantem talem rem futuram in tali nunc, sequeretur quod representaret secundum lineam temporalem, nec abstraheret a nunc vel tunc in representando; ergo poni non potest quod representet huiusmodi complexionem terminorum in tali nunc futuram." Cf. Henricus de Gandavo, *Quodlibet* VIII, q. 2 (ed. Venice, f. 6va): "... nunc eternitatis prout abstrahit ab omni differentia temporis..."

[16] [38.1:407–28]: "Quinta vero propositio est quod nulla ratio tamquam medium cognoscendi ponenda est quare Deus futura contingentia infallibiliter novit. Istud enim medium aut poneretur inter potentiam et actum aut inter actum et obiectum tamquam obiectum primarium per quod actus transiret in futura contingentia ut in obiecta secunda, sicut videntur imaginari ponentes quod vel idee vel determinatio voluntatis sit ratio cognoscendi futura; sed constat quod horum neutrum poni potest; primum siquidem non, quia in Deo non est intellectus potentia nec intelligere elicitum, etiam secundum rationem, sed purus actus subsistens, ut alias dictum fuit; nec etiam secundum, quoniam supra dictum est quod in divino prospectu est sola sua essentia et non aliqua creatura, etiam ut obiectum secundum; ergo non est querenda talis ratio tamquam medium cognoscendi.

Auriol now gives three positive propositions:

(1) God is the exemplar of the actuality of a future contingent such that God is its eminent similitude [38.1:429–30].

(2) The actuality of a future contingent is able to have an infallibly present similitude, if such a similitude is either coexistent and simultaneous with it, or if the similitude and actuality are not distant from each other in accordance with the line of succession [38.1:468–71].

(3) Only God is able to be the similitude representing without error the actuality of a future contingent [38.1:537–9].

As his solution to article two, Auriol adds one further proposition: knowledge of future things is not called foreknowledge because the knowledge precedes what is known, but rather because one known thing precedes another [38.2:732–4].

While defending the propositions, Auriol does not really attempt to demonstrate that the *only* solution to the main question of how God knows is that He is the eminent similitude, but Auriol does try to show that his solution is logically coherent. Taking for granted, based on the previous refutation of the evident alternatives, that God is an exemplar and similitude, Auriol shows the coherence of proposition (1) in several arguments. The first argument attempts to explain why God can be the eternal and immutable similitude of the actuality of something which is future, and it repeats why God must know it through His essence:

1a. God is not the similitude of anything in time without also being its similitude immutably and from eternity, otherwise there would be change in God.

1b. While the actuality of a future contingent is put into reality in time, necessarily God is its similitude and exemplar, because God knows a contingent being when it is in actuality.

1c. God does not know except through his (1) essence, (2) will, or (3) some other similitude. It is not through his (2) will, because, as we have seen, the determination of God's will does not provide certain knowledge of the actuality of contingent sins, for example. Besides, even if God knew the actuality of every future contingent through the will's determination, God would know it not directly, but via mental dis-

---

Sed quia supra dictum est quod Deitas est similitudo omnium eminens et exemplar, et est in tantum omnia eminenter quod ea cognita cuncta sunt cognita equipollenter et amplius quam si cognoscerentur in seipsis, idcirco dubium est quomodo sit similitudo futurorum que fient quoad eorum existentias in aliquo nunc determinato ponendas, et tamen non sit similitudo multorum possibilium que non fient quantum ad existentias eorum. Videtur enim quod uniformiter sit similitudo omnium possibilium fieri — sive fiant sive non fiant — alioquin aliqua viderentur habere prerogativam aliquam apud divinam essentiam, per quod sequeretur quod impossibile esset ista non fieri et impossibile illa fieri. Unde in hoc consistit punctus questionis et difficultas istius inquisitionis."

course, as the effect is known through its cause when an astronomer knows an eclipse before it occurs. This knowledge seems imperfect. It cannot be through (3) another similitude, for God does not intuit anything outside Himself.

1d. Thus God knows the actuality through (1) His essence, and God is the exemplar and eminent similitude of that actuality, immutably and from eternity.[17]

Thus, if one holds that God, as a similitude, knows that something exists while it exists (and most do hold that God knows singular things when they exist), and if one holds that God is immutable, then one has to agree that God, throughout eternity, must know that thing and be the similitude of that thing as it exists.

The next two arguments rely on the notion of exemplars. If something is the exemplar of some trait, then all manifestations of that trait must be contained in that exemplar, because, one might say, the exemplar is the most perfect example of that trait. The second argument concerns the trait 'necessity':

2a. God is the similitude of every necessary entity, since God is the exemplar of necessity.
2b. The actuality of a future contingent is a certain necessary entity, while it is in reality, because "everything which is, when it is, necessarily is."
2c. God is the eternal exemplar of the actuality of a future contingent.[18]

The third and final argument attempts to demonstrate in a stronger sense that Auriol's position must be true, although it is perhaps weak in that it relies

---

[17] [38.1:431–49]: "Prima quidem quod actualitas futuri contingentis exemplatur a Deitate ita quod Deitas est eminens similitudo illius. Hoc autem potest multipliciter declarari. Constat enim quod nullius est Deitas similitudo ex tempore quin sit ab eterno et immutabiliter illius similitudo, alias esset apud Deum vicissitudo et variatio; sed manifestum est quod dum actualitas futuri contingentis ponitur et exhibetur in tempore, Deitas de necessitate est similitudo et exemplar illius, certum est enim quod Deus cognoscit contingens esse quando actu est; non cognoscit autem nisi vel per essentiam Suam, vel per voluntatem, vel per similitudinem aliam. Per voluntatem autem non, quia determinatio voluntatis non extendit se ad actualitatem omnis contingentis — unde peccatum Iude actualiter positum, non potuit Deus cognoscere intuendo determinationem Sue voluntatis, et iterum sequeretur quod Deus non cognosceret actualitatem directe, sed quasi arguitive ex Sua voluntate, sicut effectus arguitive cognoscitur ex causa — unde cognosceret sicut astrologus eclipsim cognoscit antequam sit, notitia quasi absenti, que videtur imperfectionem importare; nec potest dici quod per similitudinem aliam ab essentia cognoscat actualitatem futuri exhibiti iam in actu; et ideo relinquitur quod per essentiam illam cognoscat. Et ita Deitas est exemplar et eminens similitudo illius actualitatis; ergo ab eterno et immutabiliter erat similitudo."
[18] [38.1:450–55]: "Preterea, Deitas est similitudo omnis necessarie entitatis, cum omnis necessitas exempletur ab Ea — est enim una de conditionibus entitatis necessitas perfectionem importans; sed manifestum est quod actualitas futuri contingentis, dum est exhibita, est quedam necessaria entitas, quia 'esse quod est quando est necesse est esse', secundum Philosophum primo *Peryarmenias*; ergo Deitas est exemplar eternale actualitatis futuri contingentis."

on an Aristotelian topic (accepted premise) concerning exemplar *causation*, which is defended elsewhere:[19]

> 3a. Every lesser entity and every truth is caused by the first entity and truth by exemplar causation. (Auriol here warns that this sort of causation should not be confused with efficient causation. The example given is that of fire and heat. Fire is not the efficient cause of all heat, because heat is made by the sun and other stars, and even by motion; but fire is the exemplar of all heat on account of 'an excess' of heat.)
>
> 3b. While it is in reality, the actuality of a future contingent is a certain determinate entity, and for that time it has determinate truth in it.
>
> 3c. God is the eternal exemplar and immobile similitude of that actuality which the future contingent has while in reality.[20]

Hence Auriol adopts a solution resembling the divine Ideas and eternal presence positions, but with special differences.

Having explained how God knows future contingents, Auriol must show how his solution answers two further questions: (1) How does God know *when* a future contingent actually exists in reality (without introducing mutability into God)? (2) How does God's knowledge not precede the future event in any way? Auriol answers by appealing to his crucial notion of indistance. He gives proof that it is logically coherent for there to be an 'infallibly present similitude' of the actuality of a future contingent, such that the similitude and actuality are not *distant* along a line of succession in time. This is the most important positive element in his account of how God, in His eternity, knows future contingents with certitude. Auriol is aware that the greatest difficulty with this positive element is that it is negative, because it relies on 'in distance'.

The similitude must be coexistent, or simultaneous, with the actuality of the existence of the future contingent, or rather it must be indistant, or not distant, from it. Because a simultaneous similitude represents the existence only while its actuality is presently exhibited in the world, and not before or after, it gives infallible certainty to God, the knower:

> And it is apparent by the example of sensory knowledge that an existing simultaneous similitude represents the actuality of a future contin-

[19] That is d. 35; on exemplar causation in Auriol, see Conti, "Divine Ideas and Exemplar Causality in Auriol," although Conti's general conclusion should be treated with caution.

[20] [38.1:456–67]: "Preterea, omnis entitas diminuta et omnis veritas causatur a prima entitate et veritate causalitate exemplaritatis, ut Philosophus dicit secundo *Metaphisice* — illa enim propositio: 'Primum in entitate et veritate est causa omnium aliorum que sunt istius dispositionis', que scilicet sunt vere entia, intelligi debet non de causalitate efficientie sed exemplaritatis, secundum mentem Philosophi, quod patet in exemplo quod ponit: Non enim ignis est causa efficiens omnium calidorum, cum calor generetur a sole et aliis stellis et quandoque a motu, est tamen ignis exemplar omnium calidorum propter excessum caloris; sed manifestum est quod actualitas futuri contingentis, dum est exhibita, est quedam determinata entitas, et pro tunc est determinata veritas in ipso contingenti; ergo Deus est eternale exemplar et similitudo immobilis illius actualitatis quam habet futurum contingens dum exhibetur in actu."

gent with certitude: Socrates, when he sits, is through vision judged with certitude to be sitting, for it impresses a similitude coexisting with the sitting itself, and not preceding or following or remaining in that vision after the sitting; otherwise, if it preceded or remained, it would represent the sitting falsely and fallibly. Therefore a similitude that stays only while the actuality of the contingent is shown as present, and did not exist before and does not remain afterwards, is a similitude that truly and infallibly leads to the knowledge of the actual existence of the future contingent.[21]

Auriol wants to avoid simultaneity, however, which he thinks is close to the eternal present position of Aquinas that he refuted earlier. Auriol asserts that the opposite of temporal distance is not only simultaneity, or 'durative coexistence', which is the contrary of temporal distance, but also the negation of distance, or indistance, which as a privation is the contradictory of temporal distance. As in the case of exemplars and similitudes, Auriol is not the first to employ the term 'indistant'. For example, Richard of Middleton uses it in the context of a discussion of the tenses of verbs, and Alexander of Alessandria, while not using 'indistant', does state, "Past and Future are distant from each other, but with respect to a third, namely eternity, they are non distant."[22] Auriol is, however, responsible for the extensive development of the term. Auriol gives several arguments to show how a similitude that abstracts from before and after — so that it is indistant but is not simultaneous — infallibly gives such certitude. One argument is that Auriol thinks the only reason a similitude can be false is if there is a distance, or temporal duration, between it and the actuality of the future contingent. In this case, the similitude will necessarily be erroneous, because it will represent the existence for a time in which the actuality does not exist. Thus the similitude must be indistant, so it

---

[21] [38.1:471–85]: "Secunda vero propositio est quod actualitas futuri contingentis potest habere similitudinem certitudinaliter presentantem, si vel talis similitudo sit coexistens simultanee cum illa actualitate vel, dato etiam quod non sit existens simultanee, dum tamen existat indistanter secundum lineam successionis, ita quod similitudo illa non representet actualitatem ut distantem in posterius, sed vel per modum simul coexistentis vel saltem non distantis; et quod similitudo existens et simultanea actualitatem futuri contingentis certitudinaliter representet apparet in notitia sensitiva: Sortes enim quando sedet, certitudinaliter iudicatur per visum sedere, imprimit enim similitudinem coexistentem ipsi sessioni, nec precedentem in visu nec subsequentem seu remanentem post sessionem — alioquin si precederet vel remaneret, falso et fallibiliter representaret sessionem; similitudo ergo que manet precise dum actualitas contingentis presentialiter exhibetur, nec fuit ante nec manet post, illa est que veraciter et infallibiliter ducit in notitiam existentie actualis futuri contingentis."

[22] Alexander de Alessandia, *In primum Sententiarum*, d. 35, q. 4 (ms. Firenze, Bibl. Laurenziana, cod. Fesul. 133, f. 125v): "Ita quod preteritum et futurum inter se sunt distantia, sed tamen respectu tertii, id est eternitatis, *distantia non sunt*" (cited in Rossini, "*Quod coexsistit exsistit*," p. 1055). Russell Friedman also finds Alexander employing the term in book I, d. 28 (personal communication). Middleton uses the term in *IV Sent.*, d. 8, a. 3: "Idem autem significatum per modum distantis non restringit quod significatum per modum *indistantis* restringit..." (cited in Irène Rosier and Alain de Libera's handout for their respective papers "Les difficultés logico-grammaticales de la formule 'Hoc est corpus meum'" and "Les enjeux logico-sémantiques de la formule de consécration eucharistique." Auriol himself uses 'indistance' when treating God's ubiquity in d. 37, a. 3 (ed. Rome 1596, p. 871a).

represents only *while* the actuality exists. An indistant similitude cannot be mistaken in representing.[23]

The indistant similitude, in fact, abstracts from simultaneity, as well as from prior and posterior and the entire line of succession in time, in representing the existence of the future contingent as present, while it exists.[24] Auriol goes on to list exhaustively and sometimes repetitively the attributes of this indistant similitude, "connected in existing with the actuality of the future contingent": it abstracts from prior, but is opposed to prior, so that the similitude represents the actuality but not before it exists; it abstracts from posterior, but is opposed to posterior, so that it represents the actuality but not after it exists; it is able to function like a simultaneous similitude, so that it represents the actual and simultaneous and present existence, but rather than being simultaneous positively, it is indistant negatively, such that it retains its opposition to prior and posterior, yet also keeps the form of a similitude; it abstracts from simultaneity so that it does not represent it as coexisting. Auriol's conclusion is that the indistant similitude will represent a future thing's existence for that time X when its actuality exists, because it is indistant from time X negatively, but not "at the same time" positively. For Auriol, such a similitude cannot be the basis for mistaken judgements.[25]

---

[23] [38.1:490–503]: "Remota enim causa, removetur effectus; sed tota causa et ratio quare aliqua similitudo representans futuri contingentis existentiam actualem fallax esse potest consurgit ex hoc: Quia existentia futuri distat ab existentia similitudinis illius quadam distantia durativa, et econverso similitudo distat ab existentia; si enim detur oppositum, quod impossibile sit distare, utpote quia in essendo mutuo sunt connexa, tunc similitudo non precedet existentiam, et per consequens non fallet, quia non representabit nisi dum erit, et tunc similiter existentia representata erit; si autem distat, necessario fallax est, quia pro illo tunc non erit actualitas pro quo illa similitudo existentiam presentabit; nunc autem oppositum distantie est non solum simultas sive coexistentia durativa, que opponitur contrarie, immo et negatio distantie vel indistantia que opponitur privative et contradictorie; ergo similitudo indistans ab actuali existentia futuri contingentis, dato quod non sit coexistens et simultanea, sed tantummodo non distans, habere non poterit unde fallat in presentando."

[24] [38.1:509–17]: "unde si non existit similitudo illa per modum prioris et distantis ab existentia, manifestum est quod non presentabit illam antequam sit; iterum nec presentabit eam postquam non est, quia nec similitudo illa distat in post, cum sit positum quod omnino non distet; nec presentabit existentiam illam ut simul cum similitudine ipsa, quia supponitur quod abstrahat a simultate, et a priori et posteriori, et a tota linea successiva, et quod sic se habeat ad existentiam quod non distet ab ea, non tamen sit simul cum ea; presentabit ergo existentiam non ante nec post nec simul, sed indistanter dum erit; ergo talis similitudo vera erit et certa et impossibilis ad fallendum."

[25] [38.1:518–36]: "Preterea, similitudo simultanea et connexa in existendo cum actualitate contingentis futuri aliquid habet unde similitudo, et aliquid unde opposita priori et posteriori, et aliquid unde similitudo simultanea; nam unde similitudo habet quod representet existentiam actualem futuri contingentis; unde vero opponitur priori, ita quod non precedit existentiam, habet quod representet illam, sed non antequam sit; unde vero opponitur posteriori, quia non sequitur, habet quod representet existentiam contingentis futuri, sed non postquam non est; unde autem simultanea est, habet quod representet existentiam actualem ut simultaneam secum atque presentem. Sed manifestum quod similitudo, si ponatur indistans negative, nec tamen simultanea positive, retinet oppositionem ad prius et posterius et similiter rationem similitudinis. Et abstrahit a simultate, ergo, inquantum similitudo representabit existentiam actualem futuri contingentis; inquantum vero abstrahit a priori, non representabit eam antequam sit; inquantum vero a posteriori, non representabit postquam non est; inquantum vero a simultate, non representabit eam ut

Auriol does not mean here that God's knowledge is 'abstractive' as in Scotus's notion of 'abstractive cognition', which is often taken to be the 'normal' medieval definition. While it is true that God's knowledge is 'abstracted' from prior, posterior, and simultaneous, this knowledge is closer to Scotus's intuitive cognition, in which the object is immediately present. It is more complex than that, however, for the object is neither immediately present nor absent, as it may be in abstractive cognition, but rather simply indistant. Auriol's concept of intuitive and abstractive cognition differs from Scotus's in any case. For Auriol, knowledge that acts without intermediaries, as God's indistant knowledge of future contingents, is intuitive, because God's knowledge of His essence is direct.[26] God knows the actuality of a future contingent via his intuitive knowledge of His essence, not 'terminatively', because the divine essence alone ends or terminates God's intuition, but rather 'denominatively'. Auriol uses the term 'denominatively' to distinguish between the object of God's intuition, the divine essence, and what is known via that object:

> Finally the fourth proposition is that the knowledge God has of future things can be called 'intuitive' with respect to the object intuited and terminating [God's] gaze. As it relates to the object known denominatively, however, i.e. the existences of future things, although it cannot strictly be called 'expectation' of the future or simultaneous intuition, it is still called 'foreknowledge', because one thing that is known follows upon another such thing that is known, not of course upon the knowledge [of it], since that is completely indistant [from it].[27]

For Auriol, only Deity can be the similitude that represents the actuality of a future contingent without error. Most of his argument here is repeated in brief from what he had said earlier: God abstracts in being from every time and duration, and nothing is past or future to, or simultaneous or positively coexisting with Him; He is indistant from every time, and yet, against Aquinas, not at the same time or presently coexisting; the actuality of a future contingent

---

coexistentem; et per consequens, cum sit indistans ab actualitate futuri contingentis, presentabit eam pro illo tunc pro quo est, quia supponitur quod ab illo tunc sit indistans negative, licet non simul positive. Talis igitur similitudo non poterit esse fallax, sed cum omni certitudine infallibiliter representans."

[26] Scotus's distinction between intuitive and abstractive cognition, primarily in human epistemology, is examined in Tachau, *Vision and Certitude*, especially pp. 68–75. Tachau inspects Auriol's definitions in chapter 4, "Peter Aureol," pp. 85–112. In this context Boehner interprets Auriol as I do: "Aureol, of course, does not deny the prescience of God as to future contingent facts. He refers it to the intuitive knowledge of God, which abstracts from all temporal connotation" (*The Tractatus*, p. 82).

[27] [38.2:734–9]: "Quarta demum propositio est quod licet notitia futurorum quam Deus habet possit dici intuitiva in ordine ad obiectum intuitum et terminans aspectum, in ordine vero ad obiectum denominative cognitum, que sunt existentie futurorum, licet non possit dici proprie futuri expectatio nec simultanea intuitio, dicitur tamen prescientia quia scitum subsequitur — non quidem scientiam, cum omnino sit indistans, sed quia sequitur aliud in proprio genere." On the difference between denominative and terminative, see also Conti, "Divine Ideas and Exemplar Causation in Auriol."

can have a similitude that cannot be mistaken, if it is not distant according to prior and posterior, but either indistant or coexisting simultaneously; therefore Deity, existing wholly indistantly from the actuality of the future contingent, could infallibly represent and be its exemplar with certainty.

The proposition that Auriol defends in article two is that foreknowledge is so-called because one known thing precedes another, and not because the knowledge precedes the known. Thus God's knowledge of the existence of futures is not expectative knowledge (nor, of course, is it simultaneous intuition). Auriol here takes the opportunity to raise and refute some possible objections to his position. One objection, at which Francis of Meyronnes would hint later (see below, chapter seven), is that although indistance is a relative negation, it exists before the *relata*, since the actualities of future contingents do not yet exist. Thus God cannot be the similitude indistant from those non-existent actualities. As Auriol remarks, this is just as much of a problem for positive simultaneity.[28] Auriol's clever response is that although there cannot be a positive simultaneity in the case of actualities which do not, and even will not, exist, indistance *can* exist as a relative negation. He gives the example of a chimera and a tragelaf (goat-stag), which do not exist and so cannot exist at the same time, yet are not distant, since there is no distance between things that do not exist at all.[29] Regardless of this retort's effectiveness, Nicolas Bonet would agree with this argument around 1330 (see chapter seven).

The second objection is that if one negates contraries with a positive middle, one necessarily posits that positive middle to be the case. So if one negates distance from prior and posterior, one must posit their positive middle, which is simultaneity. If X is neither before nor after Y, it must be temporally together with Y. Thus if one holds that God by negation is indistant from the actualities of futures, thus denying that He is before or after, one necessarily agrees with Aquinas that God is in between, i.e. He is coexistent and simultaneous with them.[30] Auriol responds that the negation of the extremes posits

---

[28] [38.2:742–8]: "Hiis tamen que dicta sunt videntur aliqua obviare. Indistantia namque, cum sit negatio relativa, videtur preexigere existentiam terminorum; sed actualitates futurorum contingentium non existunt; ergo non videtur quod Deitas sit similitudo indistans ab actualitatibus contingentium futurorum. Unde videtur eadem difficultas de indistantia et de simultate positiva, quare sicut Deitas non potest per modum simultatis attingere actualitates futurorum, sic videtur quod non possit eas attingere per modum indistantis."

[29] [38.2:767–73]: "considerandum quod actualitates que non sunt, possunt fundare aut etiam terminare negationem relativam importatam per indistantiam, et tamen non relationem positivam importatam per simultatem; chimera enim non distat a tragelafo, non tamen potest esse simul; sic igitur Deus non distat nec est propinquus aut simul cum existentiis futurorum; et idcirco si eas representat, representabit ut non distantes nec simul existentes."

[30] [38.2:749–57]: "Preterea, inter contraria immediata aut inter contraria habentium medium positivum, non reperitur medium per abnegationem omnium tam medii quam extremorum, immo abnegatio extremorum de necessitate ponit illud medium positivum, sicut nec album nec nigrum ponit aliquem colorem medium; sed distare per prius ab aliquo et distare tamquam posterius sunt opposita, esse vero simul est medium inter illa; ergo cum negatur distantia prioris et posterioris respectu alicuius, ponitur de necessitate simultas respectu illius. Et ita dicendo quod Deus est indistans ab actualitatibus futurorum, necessario ponitur quod sit coexistens et simultanee attingens, et redit opinio prima."

the positive middle only when the subject is naturally able to accept that middle; when the whole genus is negated, however, then negating the extremes does not posit a positive middle. In the subject of an angel, for example, and the genus color, the negation of the extreme contraries black and white does not posit a middle color, for *all* color is being negated. So in the case of God, indistant means He abstracts from the extremes, i.e. prior and posterior, and from the middle, simultaneity, and it is not necessary to posit positive coexistence [38.2:774–80].

The third objection questions God's ability to be the exemplar of a possible that will come about and a possible that will not, and still distinguish between the two [38.2:758–61]. This was also an objection to the 'Ideas' solution, and Meyronnes would repeat it. Auriol responds that although God uniformly represents things insofar as they are possible, he represents existences differently depending on whether they will exist today, for example, or never. Thus X, which will exist, has a similitude of its *actuality* in God from eternity, but Y, which will not exist but is only possible, does not have such a similitude of its actuality.[31] To a final objection Auriol reiterates that although possible futures, both those that will and will not come about, are equally possible and nothing, nevertheless the actuality of the one that will come about, while it exists, gives it the ability to have an immutable, indistant similitude in God, providing infallible certitude of its existence.[32]

A twentieth-century student of the period may find herself bewildered by the sheer amount of abstract terminology. These concepts were familiar to and understood by his contemporaries, however. The terminology of similitudes and exemplars was present in the works of such thirteenth-century theologians as Richard of Middleton, Bonaventure, Thomas Aquinas, and Henry of Ghent, and in many ways Auriol's use of 'similitude' and 'exemplar' resembles a combination of the solution based on Ideas in the divine mind and the one based on God's atemporal eternity. There are, of course differences, but it is

---

[31]　[38.2:781–6]: "Non procedit etiam tertia. Licet enim uniformiter representet Deus creaturas inquantum possibiles sunt, non tamen similiter representat existentias, quia rem que hodie existit representat ut existentem, et tamen rem que numquam existet non representat ut in aliquo nunc existentem; res igitur que hodie existit habet in Deo similitudinem sue actualitatis etiam ab eterno; ea vero que numquam fient non habent talem similitudinem ab eterno." Friedman, "Conceiving and Modifying Reality," pp. 312–14, treats a parallel discussion in d. 8 on the difference between existence and essence: a cognition of a really existing object has some kind of existential indicator attached to it so we know that it is not merely timeless, changeless essence.

[32]　[38.2:787–96]: "Non procedit etiam quarta, quia difformitas ista oritur ex parte existentiarum. Licet enim res equaliter sint possibiles et equaliter nichil in actu, actualitas tamen rei dum existit dat sibi quod possit habere similitudinem immutabilem, tamen indistantem, quia ut sic existentia immutabilis est, que tamen ut futura mutabilis erat; propter quod res ut future eque representantur, sed tamen ut indistanter existentes non eque representantur. Et tota ratio consistit in hoc quod res posite in actu habent ex suis actualitatibus quod possint habere similitudinem infallibilem, et hoc vel coexistentem vel eternam, eternitate non ponente precessionem aut distantiam vel simultatem, sed non distantiam solam. In hoc ergo secundus articulus terminetur." Conti, "Divine Ideas and Exemplar Causality in Auriol," pp. 111–15, also discusses this and quotes further passages from d. 35 that show how Auriol's theory works.

telling that Auriol himself had difficulty refuting the Ideas argument.[33] For a long time after Auriol, the use of this type of terminology diminished in the context of divine foreknowledge, and later discussions are easier for modern students to understand, with some exceptions, such as John of Ripa's. Just as one gets the impression that Auriol was one of the last great system builders of the Middle Ages, one also feels ('feels' is the correct term) that Auriol was one of the last theologians to be a constructive speculative thinker, whose project was at times a metaphysical exploration, a philosophical essay rather than technical argument. Still, around 1380 Peter of Candia would say that the solution based on 'eminent similitudes' was rather popular in his time, but he criticized it for failing to explain things, and merely responding to arguments, as if to fill in the holes (see chapter twelve). Of course, it was necessary for Auriol to show how a system of divine knowledge could preserve free will and divine perfection, even if it was not proven demonstratively.

What *is* important to keep in mind is Auriol's element of indistance, which some of his contemporaries would find objectionable. Auriol perhaps emphasized indistance to avoid the arguments aimed at Aquinas, but indistance also helped explain how God's knowledge does not precede the future. An obvious problem with the notion of indistance is that, since it is negative, it could easily be replaced with something like "not entailing a contradiction between the eternal, immutable, and certain foreknowledge of God and the contingency of the future," a cumbersome but equally vague phrase, which begs the question. Still, although Auriol occasionally says humans cannot really understand how God knows, one cannot conclude that Auriol's use of the *via negativa* is simply an a priori emphasis on divine transcendence. Rather it is the result of a long and complex process of syllogistical elimination.

Auriol's position on how God knows future contingents is intriguing, but difficult to analyze. One modern commentator has called it "logically coherent but theologically preposterous, if not impossible."[34] Was Auriol himself pleased with it? Did he repeat definitions exhaustively because he thought his contribution was important, noteworthy, and demonstrated, or because it was weak and needed the benefit of familiarity for the readers? At any rate, although a few of Auriol's successors, such as Meyronnes, Bonet, and Landulph Caracciolo, attacked the concept of indistance, some of Auriol's successors paid little attention to articles one and two of his distinction 38, for what they found in article three gave them fuel enough.

---

[33] See for example Hoenen's chapter 5, "Divine Ideas," in *Marsilius of Inghen*, pp. 121–56, for a discussion of the topic generally throughout the period.

[34] Jos Decorte, "*Sed Modum Exprimere Nescio*," p. 152. But Decorte has not given Auriol a complete reading, ignoring d. 38, aa. 1–2 completely. Thus he states of Auriol's position: "Hence divine knowledge of an event... cannot grasp in advance something that definite actuality had not yet given to that preceding moment at which God knows" (p. 151); and (p. 152) "God cannot anticipate the determinateness of the future contingent event on the basis of His divine way of knowing," and "Aureoli clings to foreknowedge in the literal sense regardless of the queer logical consequences this may entail." All of these statements are to a degree accurate, but they also oversimplify Auriol's theory of how God knows the future.

Chapter 5

Neutral Propositions

The Philosophical Problem

Peter Auriol was a highly original thinker, and he showed his innovative skills in articles one and two of distinction 38, where he largely invented a new solution to the problem of how God knows future contingents. It is in article three, however, that Auriol makes his biggest mark on the future history of the problem. In the introduction and principal arguments for distinction 38, when Auriol discusses the basic authorities on the question of whether God is foreknowing of future contingents, one finds that in less than fifty lines of text Auriol cites Aristotle eleven times, from the *Posterior Analytics*, *Metaphysics*, *Nicomachean Ethics*, and *Peri Hermeneias*. Auriol knows Aristotle well, and interprets him as saying that there is no determinate truth in singular propositions about future contingents. Given that his third article concerns this very question, it becomes apparent that Auriol's treatment of the problem of divine foreknowledge and future contingency will be quite different from those of his predecessors. Articles one and two serve as an important preface to the third article, and they explain how God, by being a similitude indistant from the existence of future contingents, can know the actuality of those future contingents, while He remains immutable in His eternity, despite the passing of time with respect to creatures. Article three is nothing less than a classic of western medieval thought, and it is this article that vilifies Auriol for most of his successors, and perhaps stimulates them to concentrate more of their efforts on the problem, which, after Auriol, takes on a new dimension.

In Article three Auriol asks whether a singular proposition about a future contingent is determinately true or false in one side of a contradiction.[1] For example, with respect to England's defeating or not defeating France at future time X, is the singular statement "England will defeat France at future time X" true or false, in a way that has been determined? Auriol first discusses the problem of future contingent propositions and determinism, from the point of view of Aristotle, without reference to God; next he discusses whether God's foreknowledge adds anything drastic to the problem; then he gives a brief general rule about what one should say to resolve the problem.

As for the main question, Auriol begins with the common Christian opinion, which he ascribes to Scotus: yes, there is determinate truth in propositions about future contingents, not in their own nature, but with respect to God's knowledge. In propositions about the present and past, whether the proposi-

---

[1]   [38.3:798–800]: "An propositio singularis de futuro contingenti sit determinate vera vel falsa in altera parte contradictionis."

tions correspond to what actually inheres and has been established in reality determines whether they are true or false. No such inherence yet exists for the future. Nevertheless God knows them to be future, that they will be.[2] Supporters of this view go to great lengths to explain why this fact does not lead to determinism, which, for a Christian, is not comfortably compatible with free will and divine justice.

Auriol starts his own determination with the thinker who, in the minds of fourteenth-century scholars, introduced the problem of future contingents: Aristotle. Auriol interpreted Aristotle as saying in *Peri Hermeneias*, chapter nine, that propositions about the future are not determinately true or false, for if they were it would lead to determinism, and all effort, planning, and consultation would be destroyed.[3] We are now faced with over 200 lines of text without reference to God or the faith. As was often the case in theological lectures of the later Middle Ages, the mendicants (mostly Franciscans, we can assume), monks, canons, and seculars in the audience that day heard no theology, but in this instance only talk of logic and propositions, with five brief, direct references to Aristotle, and none, even indirect, to anyone else. Auriol here defends the proposition that "No singular proposition about a future contingent, whether affirmative or negative, is determinately true, but rather completely indeterminate; whence one can form no [such proposition] that one can concede to be true or false, contrary to the common opinion."[4] His defense of this proposition is more exhaustive than even Aristotle's, and one can see that the problem had grown more significant in the intervening 1600 plus years. Auriol was aware that some scholars had been discussing future-contingent propositions as being 'indeterminately' true, and he certainly knew that for Scotus and his followers, such propositions were neutral in the first instant of nature in God's eternity, before the determination of the divine will.

2   [38.3:801–16]: "Opinio Scoti. Circa tertium vero considerandum quod aliqui dixerunt quod de futuris contingentibus est determinata veritas, non quidem in sui natura, sed in ordine ad divinam notitiam. Ubi considerandum quod non eodem modo veritas determinata est in futuris sicut in presentibus et preteritis, quia in istis est tanta determinatio quod non est in potestate cause posse in oppositum illius effectus, in illis vero, pro instanti quo ponuntur futura, potest poni oppositum illorum, quia non necessario ponitur in effectu ab aliqua causa aliqua pars contradictionis contingentis futuri. Sed non propter hoc sequitur, si veritas contingentis futuri sit <in>determinata* quantum ad esse, quin determinata illius sit; immo est determinata pro eo quod non est de se posita in esse, sed ponenda; nec Deus habet aliquid pro obiecto futuro, quin illud habeat pro obiecto cognito. Sic igitur secundum istos concedi potest quod Deus scit Antichristum futurum et quod hec propositio est determinate vera: 'Antichristus erit'. Nec propter hoc tollitur consilium, immo tolleretur si altera pars non esset futura; si enim neutra vel utraque esset futura, non oporteret consiliari; sed quia altera, non tamen de necessitate futura est, ideo consiliari oportet." * The fifteenth-century Bologna ms. is the only one with the correct reading here.
3   [38.3:817–22]: "Opinio Philosophi, primo *Peryarmenias*. Fuit vero mens Aristotelis opposita, sicut patet primo *Peryarmenias*. Et arguit ad hoc quia si singularis de futuro contingenti erit vera determinate iam, nunc determinatum est quid fiet, et ita impossibile est non fieri; et per consequens tollitur omnis sollicitudo, quia sive sollicitemur, sive consiliemur, sive negotiemur, vel non, id quod determinatum est fiet."
4   [38.3:824–8]: "Et primo quod nulla propositio singularis de futuro contingenti est determinate vera, nec affirmativa nec negativa, sed penitus indeterminata. Unde nulla potest formari de qua possit concedi quod sit vera vel falsa, contra opinionem communem."

Moreover, Thomas Wylton's opinion, although not expressed with great clarity, approaches Auriol's own and probably influenced it. Nevertheless, it is with Auriol that we have the first definitive Christian defense of neutral propositions in a theological context, and it is beautifully constructed.[5] Auriol's point of departure reminds us that even without reference to an omniscient being who knows the future, there is still a problem. For Auriol, no proposition about the future, such as 'Socrates will exist', is true or false, but all are neither true nor false. If one grants, says Auriol, that any and every such proposition is determinately true, or determinately false, then every contingent thing (for that matter, everything) will inevitably come about. Inevitability takes away any need to deliberate about our actions. According to Auriol and just about everyone else in the Middle Ages and before, one cannot deny that we do in fact deliberate; denying this would be denying something obvious and instead supporting an idea opposed to the principles of ethics and to human experience [38.3:829–39].

Auriol defends two propositions of his own about what would happen if future contingent propositions were true or false. The first is that, "if such a proposition is true, then it will immutably and inevitably be true" [38.3:842–4]. Here Auriol introduces a set of rules that describe the possible and real changes in the truth status of future contingent propositions, assuming they are determinately true.[6] If such a proposition, for example, "The Antichrist will exist,"[7] is true, it is immutably and inevitably true, for no instant can be found when it could change into falsity. Switching from the Antichrist to Socrates, Auriol runs through the possible times when proposition X: 'Socrates will exist in time Z', could go from truth to falsity, assuming it is true at time A, which is before Z:

(1) Instant A: if X changed in A, X would be both true and false in the same instant, which is impossible.
(2) The instant preceding A: (1) if X is true in A as assumed, then X was true in every instant before A; e.g., "If it is true today that Socrates will exist tomorrow, then it was true yesterday that Socrates would exist tomorrow, and if it could change into falsity, it would change in an in-

[5]   Boethius defends Aristotle's position in his commentaries on *Peri Hermeneias*, and in the second commentary Boethius discusses some of the theological implications of the view. In both commentaries, however, Boethius denies 'determinate truth' while sometimes appearing to accept 'variable' truth. See Boethius, *Boethii Commentarii in librum Aristotleles Peri Hermeneias*, ed. C. Meisner (Leipzig 1877–80), especially vol. 1, p. 126. I have benefitted from a preliminary translation by Norman Kretzmann.

[6]   Auriol's rules precede and may be the instigation for a set of rules that will become popular as the fourteenth-century progresses, one which is connected to the incipit/desinit and instant of change problems. Hoenen (*Marsilius of Inghen*, pp. 192–3) finds the origins of these rules in Ockham, and does not mention Auriol. He does discuss briefly the future path of these rules, which may very well have gone through Ockham. Whether Ockham got them from Auriol is difficult to say (see below, chapter 10).

[7]   This example is as close as Auriol gets here to theology per se, but it is *only* by way of example. Many would have served the same purpose, but Auriol's example would have been the briefest and most understandable for his audience.

stant in which it had been true, and consequently it would be true and not true at the same time." (2) "It would follow that it would lose beforehand the truth it had" in A, which is absurd.

(3) An instant between A and Z: "if in any such instant, say tomorrow, 'Socrates will exist' is false, then it is impossible for it to have been true yesterday, for if the opposite is granted, namely that yesterday it was true and today it is false, this will be because of some mutation made in the thing; but no change is made, because the thing does not yet exist, nor does it come under any power in actuality, and consequently, since nothing is changed concerning the thing, nothing will be changed concerning the proposition."

(4) Instant Z: it cannot change from true to false in Z, because (1) the truth of the proposition goes into the past in Z, and thus becomes immutable,[8] or because (2) either (a) "the thing signified [by the proposition] is put into being in reality, and then it will not change but indeed be confirmed in its truth, or (b) the opposite of what it signifies is put [into being], and in that case it will not change, because it never was true, but always false."[9]

Auriol then explains succinctly what would happen to the truth of such a proposition in the passage of time. To make it clear, I shall use an example with a specific date, although Auriol certainly does not do this: if 'Japan will bomb Pearl Harbor on 7 December, 1941' is true on 1 September 1939, then it was true on 11 November 1918, and was always true beforehand even on 25

---

[8]   Here Auriol cites Aristotle in the *Nicomachean Ethics*, where he says that Agathon was right in saying even God cannot undo what has been done.

[9]   [38.3:845–73]: "Primum ergo assumptum patet ex multis, scilicet quod si hec propositio vera est: 'Antichristus erit', immutabiliter et inevitabiliter est vera. Si enim mutari potest ne sit vera, aut mutabitur in illo instanti quo est vera, aut in instanti precedenti, aut in instanti subsequenti usque ad instans quo res fiet, aut in instanti quo res fiet. Sed manifestum est quod non potest mutari in illo instanti quo est vera, quia pro eodem instanti esset vera et non vera, quod impossibile est. Nec in instanti precedenti, tum quia si in instanti dato est vera, et in omni precedenti fuit vera, quia si hodie verum est quod Sortes erit cras, et heri verum fuit quod Sortes esset cras, et ita si tunc poterat mutari in falsitatem, mutaretur in illo eodem tunc quo esset vera, et per consequens simul esset vera et non vera; tum quia si in instanti precedenti suam veritatem mutaretur, sequeretur quod ante amitteret veritatem quam haberet, quod nichil est dictu. Nec potest dici quod mutari possit in aliquo instanti subsequenti in tempore signabili inter instans propositionis et instans quo res fiet, quia si in aliquo instanti, utpote cras, falsa sit hec propositio: 'Sortes erit', impossibile est quod fuerit heri vera; detur enim oppositum, scilicet quod heri fuit vera et hodie falsa, hoc erit propter aliquam mutationem factam in re; nulla autem mutatio facta est, quia nondum res est nec subest alicui potentie in actu, et per consequens, cum nichil mutetur circa rem, nichil mutabitur circa propositionem. Nec potest dici quod in illo instanti in quo res fiet vel non fiet mutabitur illa veritas, tum quia veritas illa transit in preteritum, nam usque ad istud instans verum fuit quod Sortes erit, quod autem transit in preteritum immutabile est, secundum Philosophum VI *Ethicorum*, Agathonis sententiam approbantis, qui dixit quod hoc solo privatur Deus: Ingenita facere que facta sunt; tum quia si mutetur in instanti factionis rei, aut hoc erit quia significatum eius ponetur in esse, et tunc non mutabitur sed potius confirmabitur in sua veritate, aut oppositum sui significati ponetur, et tunc non mutabitur, quia numquam fuit vera, sed semper falsa. Ergo, cum non inveniatur instans in quo possit mutari propositio de futuro a veritate in falsitatem, necessario immutabiliter erit vera, si aliquo modo ponatur vera."

December 800. It will also be true up until Japan actually does bomb. At a certain time on 7 December 1941, the truth of the future-tensed proposition will be transferred to this present-tensed proposition: 'Japan is bombing now, 7 December 1941'. When the bombing is over, the truth will be transferred to this past-tensed proposition: 'Japan bombed on 7 December 1941'. That past-tensed proposition will then be true on 8 December 1941, on 6 August 1945, and afterward forever until the end of time. Here also he anticipates the aforementioned rules:

> ... if 'Socrates will exist' is true today, it was also true yesterday, and it was true a thousand days ago, and whenever it is formed, even *ab eterno*, it was true up until the instant in which Socrates will be put into being. And then the truth will be changed from futurition into presentiality, and it will be true that Socrates exists. And afterwards [it will be changed] into preterition, and it will be true from then on to eternity that Socrates existed. Therefore if for any instant truth is put in a proposition about the future, that truth is posited to remain eternally, because even for the entire time of futurition that one can imagine preceding backwards to infinity, that truth will remain in the proposition about the future, then in the proposition about the present, and from then on afterward to infinity in that proposition about the past.[10]

Thus, Auriol concludes, there exists no instant at which a change from truth into falsity could occur, and the proposition will of necessity be immutably true, although the truth of the future-tensed proposition will be transferred at the time of the event to a corresponding present-tensed one, and after the event finally to a proposition in the past tense. That is, if 'Socrates will drink hemlock' is true in 420 BC, then it will always be true until 399 BC, when its truth will be applied to 'Socrates is drinking hemlock', after which time the truth will go to the proposition 'Socrates drank hemlock', and that will remain true forever. At each stage one proposition becomes false and another becomes true. For Auriol, it is simply impossible for a future-tensed proposition to *become* true, without it always beforehand having been true.

The second proposition Auriol defends is that "it inevitably and necessarily follows that if a proposition about the future is true, its significate will be

---

[10]   [38.3:873–89]: "Preterea, illud quo posito pro aliquo nunc in esse, de necessitate ponitur pro semper in esse, immutabiliter ponitur esse. Et hoc patet, quia predicatum clauditur in subiecto. Quod enim determinat sibi sempiternitatem in essendo, in nullo tempore mutari potest, unde immutabilitatem sibi determinat; sed manifestum est quod si propositio singularis de futuro pro aliquo instanti ponitur vera, de necessitate pro omni instanti ponitur vera, donec veritas illa transeat in presens et a presenti in preteritum, quia si ista vera est hodie: 'Sortes erit', et heri fuit vera, et in millesimum diem ante fuit vera, et quandocumque formaretur, etiam ab eterno fuit vera usque ad illud instans quo Sortes ponetur, et tunc mutabitur veritas a futuritione in presentialitatem, et erit verum quod Sortes est, et postmodum in preteritionem, et erit verum deinceps in eternum quod Sortes fuit; igitur si veritas ponatur in propositione de futuro pro aliquo instanti, veritas illa ponitur eternaliter permanere, quia et pro toto tempore futuritionis quod potest ymaginari infinitum in ante permanebit veritas illa in propositione de futuro, deinde in propositione de presenti, et deinceps in illa de preterito in infinitum a parte post."

put into reality."[11] This Auriol proves easily first by appeal to a simple logical rule about necessary consequences, found in book I of the *Prior Analytics*. A consequence, e.g. (X -> Y), is necessary if the opposite of the consequent entails the opposite of the antecedent, (~Y -> ~X). The consequence 'Socrates will exist; therefore Socrates will be put into reality', contains a proposition about the future, and 'Socrates will not be put into reality' (~Y) entails 'Socrates will not exist' (~X) [38.3:899–907]. Therefore if either antecedent is true, the future follows necessarily.

Second, Auriol seems to reach back to a definitional/tautological explanation found in Anselm (see above, chapter one). If two propositions signify the same thing using different terms, one necessarily entails the other. In Auriol's example, Marcus and Tullius, Cicero's first names, signify the same thing, so anything said about one is also necessarily said about the other. In 'Socrates will exist; then Socrates will be put into being', 'will exist' and 'will be put into being' signify the same thing.[12]

Now a necessary consequence does not mean a necessary antecedent or consequent, as in 'Socrates is running; therefore Socrates is moving', since it is not necessary for Socrates to be running, but rather contingent. His running, however, once assumed, necessarily entails his moving, by the necessity of the consequence. Recall that this is the 'benign' sense of necessity, which is called by many other names, such as accidental necessity and conditional necessity. But in his first proposition Auriol has already established that if a proposition about the future is true at all, it is immutably and inevitably true, and thus the antecedent, 'Socrates will exist', is necessary, since, as we have seen in chapter three, Auriol equates immutable with necessary. And in a necessary consequence, a necessary antecedent entails a necessary consequent, so 'Socrates will be put into being' follows necessarily, and everything occurs of necessity. Auriol, of course, considers this absurd and obviously false. Therefore, no proposition about a future contingent is true or false, but only 'true or false' disjunctively.[13]

---
[11] [38.3:843–4]: "Prima quidem quod si talis propositio vera est, illa immutabiliter et inevitabiliter erit vera; secunda vero quod ex illa inevitabiliter et necessario sequitur quod tale futurum ponetur in esse."

[12] [38.3:908–13]: "Preterea, quando per duas propositiones significatur idem sub aliis terminis, ex una infertur alia de necessitate; sequitur enim, si Marchus disputat, quod Tullius disputet, quia Marchus et Tullius sinonima sunt et significant idem; sed futurum et venturum idem significant; ergo de necessitate sequitur, si Sortem esse est futurum, quod hoc eveniet, et si hec vera est: 'Sortes erit', de necessitate istud est verum: Quod sic eveniet."

[13] [38.3:914–30]: "Ex hiis ergo demonstrative sequitur quod omnia futura immutabiliter evenient, si propositio de futuro determinate sit vera. In omni enim consequentia necessaria et immutabili, si antecedens est contingens, consequens potest remanere contingens, sicut patet cum dicitur: 'Sortes currit, ergo movetur', consequentia enim est necessaria, sed antecedens et consequens sunt contingentia; si vero antecedens est necessarium, consequens erit necessarium; si vero antecedens sit immutabile et inevitabile, consequens erit inevitabile et immutabile; sed propositione ista: 'Sortes erit', vel Antichristus, existente vera, sequitur de necessitate: 'Ergo ita eveniet', ut patet ex secundo assumpto.

Ex primo autem apparet quod antecedens est immutabile et inevitabile, scilicet veritas istius propositionis: 'Antichristus erit', si aliquo modo sit vera; ergo consequens erit inevitabile. Unde

Auriol's purely philosophical argument is rather convincing, yet he now gives some purely philosophical objections to his stance. The first two say that by insisting that singular propositions about the future are neither true nor false determinately, he is breaking two fundamental rules of logic: The First Principle and the Law of Contradictories. The First Principle (obviously fundamental to logic, as its name indicates: *'primum principium'*) states that "concerning anything whatever either the affirmation or negation is true." The objection deduces from it what we call the Principle of Bivalence, *except* that Auriol himself carefully replaces 'false' with 'not true': "Supposing any singular proposition, it is either true or not true." Thus every proposition is either true or it is not true. But if it is not true, the objection concludes, then it is false: it can have only one of two truth values; hence Bivalence. The argument recalls an objection to Auriol's position in article one, when it was said that in the case of a negation of two contrary extremes that have a positive middle, one necessarily posits the middle in a subject that is naturally apt to receive that middle. Here the argument says that in the case of two immediate contraries, which obviously have no middle, if one negates one of the contraries one necessarily posits the opposite contrary in a subject to which it can apply naturally. In the case of a line, which is naturally apt to receive curvature and rectitude, if it is not straight, it is curved. In article one Auriol refuted the objection by asserting that he was negating the entire genus, which was time and the line of succession, and not just the contrary extremes, prior and posterior, because the subject, God, was not naturally apt to receive either the extremes or the positive middle, which was simultaneity. Here, however, the objection goes that propositions are the very things that are naturally apt to receive truth and falsity, so that negating one is necessarily positing the other. If the proposition about the future is not true, then it is wholly false.[14]

Auriol responds by simply saying that the rule does not hold for a proposition about a future contingent, which is not naturally apt to receive truth or falsity, except disjunctively, as e.g. 'Socrates will exist or will not exist'. That is to say, a *singular* proposition about a future contingent has no truth-value, otherwise a contingent thing would be determined, and determination is repugnant to contingency.[15] This is a rejection of Bivalence. A disjunctive propo-

---

immutabiliter ita eveniet et idem potest concludi de omni futuro; igitur omnia futura immutabilia sunt et evitari non possunt. Hoc autem dicere dementissimum est, ergo et illud unde sequitur, scilicet quod aliqua propositio de futuro sit vera. Unde ista non est vera: 'Antichristus erit', nec etiam ista: 'Antichristus non erit', sed bene disiunctiva: 'Antichristus erit vel non erit'."

[14] [38.3:931–9]: "primum principium: 'De quolibet esse vel non esse', falsum esse non potest; assumpta ergo propositione singulari, aut est vera aut non vera; si vera, habetur propositum; si non vera, ergo est falsa, quia verum et falsum sunt contraria immediata; ex negatione autem unius contrarii immediati sequitur positio alterius in subiecto apto nato; sequitur enim: 'Linea non est recta; ergo est curva'; sed constat quod omnis propositio est subiectum aptum natum recipere veritatem vel falsitatem; ergo sequitur, si singularis propositio de futuro non est vera, quod omnino sit falsa."

[15] [38.3:984–99]: "Sic igitur, cum natura contingentis omnino indeterminata sit pro quolibet instanti precedente suam existentiam actualem, necessario utraque pars contradictionis absque ulla determinatione sibi debetur pro tunc. Et ideo nulla propositio est vera, nisi que claudit utramque partem contradictionis sub indifferentia et disiunctim. Que vero determinate alteram

sition about a future contingent, on the other hand, does have a truth-value, and so the Law of the Excluded Middle holds.[16]

The second principle, the Law of Contradictories, states that if one of a pair of contradictories, as 'Socrates will exist', is false, the other, 'Socrates will not exist', is true, and that necessarily one is true and the other false.[17] Auriol refutes this objection by saying that Aristotle made an exception for the rule in the case of future contingent propositions in *Peri Hermeneias* [38.3:1000–1003]. Gregory of Rimini (see chapter eleven) would agree that Aristotle did make an exception, but like Francis of Meyronnes, Rimini would use Aristotle against Aristotle and defend the laws.

Auriol explains in greater detail that the rules do not apply, since singular propositions receive their truth or falsity depending on whether what they signify inheres in reality (that is, the actuality of their significates gives them truth or falsity), and since contingent things are indeterminate with respect to inhering in reality, and their causes, far from determining them beforehand, are altogether indifferent. Auriol is worth quoting on this point:

> The actuality that gives determination to the contingent can be referred to every instant preceding and distant *in ante* from the actuality, or to every instant succeeding and distant *per posterius* from that actuality. Thus the actuality gives determination to the contingent in any instant whatever following the actuality, although [the actuality] does not exist in those instants. From that point it is always determinately true that such an actuality existed. But [the actuality] does not confer determination for any preceding instant. Thus it is never determinately true that it will exist, for the determination that the actuality gives the contingent is extended to subsequent instants, but not to preceding instants. And the reason for this is because the actuality, with respect to future instants that follow, puts the contingent beyond its causes, and so it does not remain within anything's causality, nor can any active power be applied to it. Conversely, however, in all instants that pre-

---

partem exprimit non est vera nec etiam falsa, quia si falsa esset, pars opposita esset determinata; et hinc est quod hec propositio vera est: 'Sortes erit vel non erit', et ista falsa: 'Sortes nec erit nec non erit'; et ista vera: 'Aliquod istorum indeterminate eveniet', quod scilicet Sortes erit vel non erit, et illa falsa, scilicet quod: 'Neutrum determinate eveniet'. Hec tamen: 'Sortes erit', neque vera neque falsa; similiter nec illa: 'Sortes non erit'. Statim enim dum hoc concederetur, poneretur determinatio in ipso contingente, que ponibilis non est; immo repugnat sue nature.

Non procedunt ergo instantie. Prima siquidem non, quia propositio de futuro contingenti sumpta precise sub altera parte contradictionis non potest esse subiectum veritatis vel falsitatis, alioquin res contingens esset determinata."

[16] See Normore, "Petrus Aureoli and His Contemporaries," pp. 90–91. The Principle of Bivalence and the Law of the Excluded Middle are similar, but not exactly the same, and neither are they exactly the same as their medieval counterparts, the First Principle and the Law of Contradictories. See discussion above on Aristotle, chapter 1, and Craig *The Problem of Divine Foreknowledge*, p. 10.

[17] [38.3:940–43]: "Preterea, lex contradictoriarum est quod si una sit vera, reliqua sit falsa, et quod de necessitate una sit vera, reliqua sit falsa; ergo necessario vel ista est vera: 'Antichristus erit', et reliqua falsa, scilicet: 'Antichristus non erit', vel econverso, cum contradictorie opponantur."

cede it, the actuality leaves the contingent within the causality and power of its originators (*principia*). These, however, are indeterminate and can go either way, and consequently the determination, having its origin from the actuality, cannot be extended to the instants, which precede [the actuality].[18]

Auriol gives another quick explanation by saying that when B arises or results from A, then B follows and cannot precede A. Therefore, since the determination of a contingent arises or results from its actuality, that determination cannot be applied to instants prior to the actuality from which it arose [38.3:981–4].

Thus Auriol has revived, adopted, and further articulated what he took to be Aristotle's non-bivalent logic for singular propositions about future contingents, for since the nature of contingents is indeterminate, propositions about them are not determinately true or false. Although it is true to say 'Socrates either will be or will not be', and false to say 'Socrates neither will be nor will not be', it is neither true nor false to say 'Socrates will be' or 'Socrates will not be'. Rather, any such proposition is wholly indeterminate.

Mention should be made here of some peculiarities in the other two versions of Auriol's treatment. The *Scriptum* only mentions 'disjunctive' once in this section of text, and there are only two instances in the Borghese 123 version. In BPV, by contrast, Auriol makes an effort to emphasize that Excluded Middle holds disjunctively, mentioning the word 'disjunctive' no less than eight times. This opens the door for Francis of Marchia, reading the BPV version, to criticize Auriol and use his acceptance of Excluded Middle to defend Bivalence. Thus Auriol's phrasing in BPV may have led indirectly to Rimini's thorough critique a quarter of a century later.[19]

---

[18] [38.3:960–80]: "Sed hiis non obstantibus dicendum est sicut prius, ubi considerandum quod veritas propositionis sumitur ex entitate rei, quia veritas signi sumitur ex conditione signati; unde ab eo quod res est vel non est dicitur oratio vera vel falsa, ut patet in *Predicamentis*. Constat autem quod contingens ad utrumlibet nullam determinationem habet ad alterum ex ordine ad suas causas, cause namque illud respiciunt sub omnimoda indifferentia; tunc ergo primo determinatur contingens ad utrumlibet quando actualiter ponitur et existit. Actualitas autem, que dat contingenti determinationem, potest referri ad omne instans precedens et distans in ante, vel ad omne instans succedens et distans per posterius ab illa actualitate. Dat ergo actualitas determinationem contingenti in quolibet instanti sequente actualitatem, quamvis non sit in illis instantibus; unde semper est determinate verum quod talis actualitas fuit. Non dat autem sibi determinationem pro aliquo instanti precedente; unde numquam est determinate verum quod erit. Trahitur enim determinatio quam dat actualitas contingenti ad instantia subsequentia, non autem ad instantia precedentia, cuius ratio est quia actualitas respectu futurorum sequentium ponit contingens extra suas causas; unde non remanet infra causalitatem alicuius, nec cadere potest super ipsum activa potentia. Econverso autem, in omnibus instantibus que precedunt, relinquit actualitas contingens infra causalitatem et potentiam suorum principiorum; illa autem sunt ad utrumlibet et indeterminata, et per consequens determinatio, ortum habens ab actualitate, trahi non potest ad instantia que precedunt."

[19] I'll quote some of the interesting passages for those with a special interest in logic. BPV *Reportatio* I, d. 39, q. 1 (ed. Nielsen-Schabel, forthcoming): "Circa distinctionem 39 quero primo utrum propositio singularis de futuro contingenti sit determinate vera vel falsa secundum alteram partem contradictionis. Videtur quod sic: ubi est vera contradictio, ibi est lex contradictoriorum... Confirmatur, quia primum principium tenet in omni materia... Contra; Aristoteles, 1

The Theological Problem

If Peter Auriol was concerned about the deterministic implications of the non-theistic and philosophical problem of future contingents, he was positively obsessed by the severity of the problem when divine foreknowledge was added into the equation. Auriol had gone to great lengths to show that God did not have expectative or intuitive knowledge (i.e. of something present in a positive sense) of future contingents, as he considered Scotus and Aquinas, respectively, to have held. He holds that God is wholly indistant. Now Auriol defends the proposition that "the knowledge that God has of the actualities of future contingents does not make it so that a proposition that is only affirmative or only negative, formed about the future, is true or false, but rather [that knowledge] leaves the proposition neither true nor false."[20]

Auriol explains that God has knowledge of the actuality of a future contingent in two ways. As far as a thing is considered as future in itself and with respect to the present now, it is indeterminate for now, and the divine knowledge (*notitia*) does not know if that thing will come about or not when the divine knowledge compares the thing's actuality to the present now. But when the divine knowledge considers it by abstracting from the thing's futurition, then God's knowledge determinately knows that actuality. That actuality, however, as determinately known by the divine knowledge, is not future.[21] We

---

Peryarmenias... Primo pono punctum questionis. Dico enim quod in questione 'utrum propositio singularis de futuro contingenti sit determinate et precise vera vel falsa in altera parte contradictionis', dico 'precise' et 'determinate', non utrum cognoscit indeterminate, sed precise determinatum ad partem veritatis vel falsitatis. Dico etiam 'in altera parte contradictionis determinate' ut excludatur disiunctiva, quia disiunctiva semper est vera, quia certum est quod navale bellum vel erit vel non erit. Opposita enim huius semper est falsa. Solum ergo accipio cathegorice ut istam: 'Antichristus erit', 'Antichristus non erit' — utrum in istis sit veritas determinata?"

Of course the answer is negative, but I shall quote the conclusion: "Respondeo quod 'possibile' potest sumi dupliciter: vel pro possibili ad utrumlibet, id est ad alteram partem contradictionis... Si primo modo, sequitur... quia illa sub disiunctione utriusque partis contradictionis est vera, quia vel erit vel non erit. Ita hec est vera, 'Possibile est cras', quia dicit utrumlibet sub disiunctione. Hoc non sonat contingens ad utrumlibet vel possibile. Sensus ergo est propositionis illius, 'Possibile est esse cras navale bellum', hoc est, 'Erit vel non erit'. Sic ad questionem. Ad argumentum de lege contradictoriorum, potest dici quod verum est quod ibi sunt contradictoria 'erit', 'non erit', tamen non deffinit ibi lex contradictoriorum quod una sit determinata vera et altera falsa, et illas excipit Philosophus ab illa lege. Vel dicitur, et forte melius, quod lex contradictoriorum est quod si una est vera, reliqua est falsa, sed non quod illa sit determinate vera et reliqua determinate falsa, maxime in istis quas Philosophus excipit primo *Peryarmenias*. Et quando dicitur de primo principio, dico quod primum principium non dicit quod de quolibet sit altera pars determinate vera contradictoriorum, sed semper sub disiunctione ad utrumlibet de quolibet verum est dicere quod sit vel non sit."

[20] [38.3:1023–5]: "notitia divina quam de actualitatibus futurorum contingentium habet non dat ut propositio affirmativa precise vel negativa precise formata de futuro sit vera vel falsa, immo relinquit utramque neque veram neque falsam."

[21] [38.3:1249–58]: "res, etsi futura sit in se et per comparationem ad nunc presens, non tamen ut sic est determinata, immo est ad utrumlibet pro isto nunc; propter quod divina notitia comparans actualitatem ad istud nunc non novit determinate si erit vel non erit, quia ut sic ad utrumlibet est; sed prout apprehendit eam modo abstracto a futuritione, novit determinate actualitatem predictam, et ita verum est quod actualitas ut cognita non est futura. Unde Deus habet cognitionem de huiusmodi actualitate dupliciter: Primo quidem ut abstracta est a futuritione in Sui

might call this 'Auriol's catch': of course God can have determinate knowledge of the actuality of a future contingent, if it is not considered as future, and God's knowledge does not therefore give determinate truth to the future-tensed proposition about that actuality; if one considers it as future, however, as it is with respect to us and in the proposition about the future, then God does not have determinate knowledge at all, and still cannot give determinate truth to such a proposition.

So Auriol defends this by saying such a determination must come either from the mode of knowing or from what is known, both of which possibilities have been ruled out in previous discussions [38.3:1036–8]. "The knowledge that gives something determination for some instant, must coexist with that instant."[22] Of course God's knowledge, being wholly indistant from the actuality of the future contingent, is not coexistent with any instant (even the present one, for it abstracts from simultaneity, as it does from all *differentiae* of time, in the language of Borghese 123). It abstracts from prior, so that it is not expectative, distant knowledge, extending into the future and giving determination in instants preceding the actuality. So it cannot make a future tensed proposition true or false. What is known, of course, is the actuality of the future contingent, but as we have seen, for Auriol this actuality cannot confer determination on instants preceding that actuality. Thus propositions about future contingents are not made true or false because of what is known.[23]

Auriol now faces a barrage of objections, which would seem to be overwhelming. He lists ten, the first few having to do with prophecy: there are many cases in Scripture where God, through prophets, forms propositions about future contingents. Surely these must be determinately true because of the infallibility of divine omniscience. Auriol gives examples from Isaiah, "Behold a virgin shall conceive and bear a son," and the Gospels, "the cock shall not crow this day, till thou thrice deniest that thou knowest me" and "You know that after two days shall be the pasch: and the son of man shall be delivered up..."[24]

If such prophecies (future contingent propositions) were not true, it would be impossible to distinguish between true and false prophets, since they would all be giving prophecies equally indeterminate toward truth and falsity. Auriol gives examples from Scripture that distinguish between true and false

---

notitia, et illa est determinata; secundo vero ut futura est, non quidem Sibi sed isti nunc presenti, et illa indeterminata est et ad utrumlibet, quia et natura rei sic habet."
    [22]   [38.3:1027–8]: "notitia que dat determinationem alicui pro aliquo instanti, debet coexistere illi instanti."
    [23]   [38.3:1031–5]: "declaratum est supra quod notitia Dei non est expectativa futuri, nec tendit in ipsum tanquam in distans — unde non precedit actualitatem futuri; ergo non dabit determinationem illi actualitati pro aliquo instanti precedenti, et per consequens nec propositio formanda habebit a divina notitia quod sit vera vel falsa."
    [24]   [38.3:1052–8]: "Hiis tamen videntur aliqua obviare. Certum est enim quod prophetie non potest subesse falsum; propositiones ergo prophetice sunt determinate vere; sed propositiones huiusmodi sunt de futuro contingenti, ut illa Ysaie: 'Ecce Virgo concipiet et pariet filium', et illa Christi: 'Non cantabit gallus, donec ter abneges nosse me', et illa: 'Scitis, quia post biduum Pascha fiet, et filius hominis tradetur', et sic de omnibus prophetiis; ergo videtur quod ex infallibilitate divine prescientie propositiones de futuro contingenti habeant quod sint vere."

prophets, commending the former and reprehending the latter: "Ezechiel 13 speaks of 'foolish prophets' who 'see nothing' and 'foretell lies', and in Deuteronomy 18, Moses defines the false prophet saying 'Thou shalt have this sign: Whatsoever that same prophet foretelleth in the name of the Lord, and it cometh not to pass: that thing the Lord hath not spoken.'" Thus such propositions which come from God's foreknowledge must be determinately true or false, "otherwise Isaiah's having said 'Behold a virgin shall not conceive and bear a son' would have been worth the same as saying 'Behold a virgin shall conceive and bear a son'."[25] Moreover, every proposition must be determinately true if it must be believed according to the faith, because objects of faith are infallibly true; 'the resurrection of the body will come' and 'the last judgment will happen' are examples of such propositions [38.3:1070–73].

There are several other objections. For example, since knowledge is of true things, every known thing is true; God knows some propositions about the future, otherwise he would not have predicted them and revealed them; therefore they must be true propositions [38.3:1074–7]. Some objections assert that God's knowledge, even though it is not expectative and distant from the actuality, still gives determination to such propositions. Indeed, the fact that God's knowledge is indistant should provide *more* determination, not less.[26]

Perhaps the most important objection is one based on God's knowledge of the passage of time with respect to us:

> Moreover, the knowledge God has of the future, even if it is not simultaneous or coexistent with that 'now', is nevertheless indistant from that 'now'; but in so far as it is indistant from that 'now', it views the future contingent under the form of future and distant. Thus God knows that that actuality is future, even if not to Him, at least to that thing that exists in the present instant. For God not only knows the actuality

---

[25] [38.3:1059–69]: "Preterea, si propositiones tales non essent vere, nullus predicens futura esset mendax, et per consequens non esset differentia inter prophetas veridicos et sanctos, et prophetas mendaces, quia neuter dicit verum vel falsum; sed scriptura sacra reprehendit prophetas falsos et commendat veros, Ezechielis XIII, dicens de 'prophetis insipientibus' qui 'nichil vident' et 'divinant mendacium', et Deuteronomii XVIII, Moyses diffiniens quid sit falsus propheta, dicit quod: 'Hoc habebis signum quod in nomine Domini propheta ille predixerit et non evenerit, hoc Dominus non est locutus'; ergo dici non potest quin propositiones de futuro ex divina prescientia. habeant quod sint vere alique et earum opposite false, alioquin tantum valuisset Ysaie dixisse: 'Ecce virgo non concipiet,' sicut dicere: 'Ecce virgo concipiet'."

[26] [38.3:1078–92]: "Preterea, illa notitia dat determinationem propositioni illi cum cuius opposita illa notitia stare non potest; sed cum illa notitia quam Deus habebat de trina negatione Petri non poterat stare veritas istius propositionis: 'Petrus non negabit ter Christum'; igitur predicta notitia dabat determinatam veritatem propositioni opposite.

Preterea, illa notitia dat propositioni de futuro quod sit determinate vera in qua notitia est veritas determinata; sed veritas futuri contingentis determinata est in divina notitia quomodocumque hoc sit, sive per modum futuritionis sive per modum non futuritionis; ergo veritas sic determinata dat propositioni de futuro quod sit vera.

Preterea, si id quod minus videtur inesse inest, et id quod magis; sed scientia expectativa, que tendit in rem ut futuram, si esset certa, daret quod propositio de futuro esset determinate vera; ergo multo fortius notitia Dei, que tendit in actualitatem futuri ut in presentem, vel saltem ut in non distantem, dabit quod propositio sit vera, cum presentialitas sit potior quam futuritio."

of the Antichrist, but He knows that it is future at least to us, otherwise He would not know when a thing becomes past or is future or exists presently. Thus He knows the future Antichrist in relation to this 'now', and consequently this proposition is true: 'The Antichrist is future'.[27]

Auriol responds that the only way that knowledge can make a proposition true is if the proposition's significate is objectively within that knowledge. The significate of the proposition 'the Antichrist will exist', for example, is not within the divine knowledge. Although 'Antichrist' may be within His knowledge, the copula joined with it is not, because the verb 'will exist' (erit) is future and is necessarily viewed distantly as future by the one with the knowledge. As we have seen, of course, God's knowledge is not extended to anything "as distant in post or in the future."[28]

> God does not apprehend this proposition through His way of understanding, but only in so far as He apprehends all propositions that we form. Thus the proposition, 'The Antichrist will exist', does not receive its being true or false from the divine knowledge, since it does not fall in the divine knowledge immediately as if God formed it, but rather mediately, namely because we form it (for every knowledge immediately forming it is expectative). Rather it is left indeterminate, because it is neither true nor false.[29]

Humans view as future such things as the Antichrist's being. Since God has *knowledge* of the Antichrist's being, which is future to humans, people therefore assume that God also knows the corresponding future-tensed proposition, 'the Antichrist will exist'. For Auriol this is incorrect: God's knowledge is *indistant* from the Antichrist's being and therefore has determinate truth, but as we view it, i.e. as future, there is no truth or falsity. Humans, then, are always deceived concerning the way God determinately knows what we consider future. In order for us to understand how God apprehends futures, our

---

[27] [38.3:1093–1100]: "Preterea, illa notitia quam Deus habet de futuro, etsi non sit simultanea et coexistens isti nunc, est tamen indistans ab isto nunc; sed prout est indistans ab isto nunc, aspicit futurum contingens sub ratione futuri et distantis; unde scit Deus quod actualitas illa est futura, etsi non Sibi, tamen isti rei que existit in presenti instanti; non enim solum novit actualitatem Antichristi, immo novit quod est futura saltem nobis, alioquin nesciret quando res preteriit vel futura est aut presentialiter existit; igitur scit Antichristum futurum per comparationem ad istud nunc, et per consequens propositio ista vera est: 'Antichristus est futurus'."

[28] [38.3:1112–18]: "Nulla enim notitia dat alicui propositioni quod sit vera nisi quatinus significatum illius est in ipsa notitia obiective; sed significatum istius propositionis: 'Antichristus erit', non cadit in divina notitia. Qui enim dicit in mente sua quod Antichristus erit, necessario respicit ipsum ut futurum. Hoc enim habet copula de futuro importata per li 'erit' quod esse copuletur cum subiecto ut futurum. Declaratum est autem sepe quod divina notitia non tendit in rem ut in post distantem vel in futurum."

[29] [38.3:1119–26]: "Unde nec Deus istam propositionem apprehendit ex Suo modo intelligendi, sed quatinus apprehendit omnes propositiones quas nos formamus; et ideo hec propositio: 'Antichristus erit', cum non cadat immediate in divina notitia, quasi Deus eam formet, sed mediate, scilicet quia nos formamus — omnis enim notitia ipsam immediate formans est expectativa — utique cum sit ita, non recipiat a divina notitia quod sit vera vel falsa, sed relinquitur indeterminata, quia nec vera nec falsa."

intellect would have to abstract from futurition, presentiality, and preterition, as God's does. Even then, apprehending God's knowing the futures and understanding that His knowledge is not extended to it as if into the future, but rather indistantly, "our intellect itself co-understands the futures as if distant and future."

> And all the difficulties arise from this fact, and a non-cause is interpreted as a cause; for it is thought that the divine knowledge introduces what expectation (which of necessity accompanies our way of understanding) introduces. And the reason is that God has knowledge of the contingent future which is somehow *ineffable and incomprehensible* to us, except via a discursive process only, namely through abstraction from every knowledge either expectative, memorative, or intuitive. Although when we say this we always use expectative [knowledge], and on account of this it seems to us that our expectative [knowledge] is true, because his [knowledge], abstractive from all expectation, is determinately true.[30]

For Auriol, then, we cannot really understand how God's knowledge of what is future to us does 'cause' to be true a future-tensed proposition about that future. We can only view His knowledge of the future as expecting the future, as our knowledge would if we actually did know the future: and in that case, such knowledge would indeed entail the truth of the future-tensed proposition about that future. But God's knowledge is *not* of this sort, and we do not *know* the future.

Thus the objections to Auriol's position fail. It is at this point that Auriol's statements, perhaps taken out of context, become controversial later. He says that prophetic propositions about the future are neither true nor false, not

---

[30] [38.3:1027–52]: "Est tamen hic attendendum quod intellectus noster semper decipitur in apprehendendo quomodo veritas futuri contingentis est determinata in divina notitia. Si enim comparetur actualitas contingentis ad notitiam precedentem, nullo modo potest esse determinata, nec veritatem aut falsitatem dare illi notitie, sicut nec propositioni. Si vero comparetur ad notitiam subsequentem aut etiam coexistentem, quarum una est memorativa et alia intuitiva, utique dat determinationem veritatis. Si vero comparetur ad notitiam simpliciter abstractam que nec precedat nec subsequatur nec coexistat, talis notitia potest habere determinationem pro eo quod non distat secundum precedentiam et prioritatem; unde perinde est ac si sequeretur vel coexisteret. Et secundum hoc patet quod nulla notitia quam nos habeamus de futuro, cum precedat actualitatem futuri, est vera vel falsa, sicut nec propositio de futuro, adhuc nec aliqua notitia, secundum quam apprehendamus Deum cognoscere futura, est plene vera; oporteret enim quod apprehendens Deum cognoscere illa abstraheret illa futura a futuritione, presentialitate, et preteritione, sicut et notitia Dei abstrahit. Intellectus autem noster, dum apprehendit Deum cognoscere actualitatem futuram, quantumcumque dicat quod notitia Dei non tendit in illa tamquam in futura, immo sicut in non distantia, nichilominus ipse intellectus noster cointelligit illa tamquam distantia et futura. Et ex hoc oriuntur omnes difficultates et conicitur non causam ut causam; putatur enim quod divina notitia inferat quod infert expectatio illa que de necessitate concomitatur nostrum modum intelligendi; et hinc est quod Deus habet notitiam futuri contingentis quodammodo a nobis incomprehensibili et ineffabili, nisi tantum arguitive, per abstractionem scilicet ab omni notitia vel expectativa vel memorativa vel intuitiva; quamvis cum hoc dicimus, utamur semper expectativa, et ob hoc videtur nobis quod nostra expectativa sit vera, quia Sua abstractiva ab omni expectatione est determinate vera."

even more true than their contradictory opposites. In light of the many prophecies in the Bible, this position would seem awkward or even dangerous to defend. First Auriol remarks that it is often the case in scripture that, for example, some propositions are phrased about the past when they are really about what is future to us. An example is Isaiah 9.6: "For a child is born to us, and a son is given to us," which could also be translated "For a child was born to us, and a son was given to us." Auriol says that "Behold a virgin shall conceive," though it is in the future tense about something future to the listeners, is no more true than the previous proposition in the past tense, which is about the same thing, the coming of Christ, a future thing for Isaiah [38.3:1153–9].

This is not to say that Auriol interprets Isaiah and others to have been *deliberate* with regard to the tenses they chose in making prophecies. Rather it is an introduction to Auriol's reasoned explanation. Auriol states that utterances, in the form of propositions, are signs of the impressions (*passiones*) that are in one's soul, according to Aristotle. In the case of God and divine knowledge, however, it is impossible for prophets, who are human, to utter a proposition not in some tense, a tense which is certainly lacking in the divine knowledge, which abstracts from past, present, and future. A proposition about the future cannot express the truth about a future contingent that is in the divine knowledge. Such propositions, then, are neither true nor false.[31]

Yet prophetic propositions do not signify only by the nature of the proposition itself, which does not contain truth or falsity; they also "give understanding from the intention of the prophet." They inform the listener or reader that in the divine knowledge there is "a certain ineffable truth and a certain determination of the matter about which the proposition is formed," although this determination does not make the proposition about the future contingent true or false. In fact, adds Auriol, this determination in the divine knowledge is not even what gives truth to propositions about the past, because God still abstracts from the past. Rather the past actuality confers truth and falsity on past-tensed propositions.[32]

So it is still possible to distinguish between true and false prophets, because the former "mean to express a certain determination in the divine knowledge with respect to the matter about which they speak." Even when

---

[31] [38.3:1160–66]: "Sciendum est ergo quod, cum voces sint note earum passionum que sunt in anima, ut dicitur primo *Peryarmenias*, significant enim propositiones res ut conceptas, impossibile est quod aliqua propositio exprimat veritatem futuri contingentis prout est in divina notitia; omnis enim propositio vel est de presenti vel de preterito vel de futuro, illa vero abstrahit a quolibet istorum et ideo non plus dicebat verum propheta dicendo: 'Ecce Virgo concipiet', quam si diceret 'concipit' vel 'concepit.'"

[32] [38.3:1166–74]: "Propositiones ergo prophetice aliud significant ex institutione et ex natura propositionum, aliud vero dant intelligere ex intentione prophete; secundum enim naturam propriam et significationem quam exhibent, nec sunt vere nec sunt false; secundum autem intentionem prophete, vere sunt, quia dant intelligere quod in divina notitia est quedam veritas ineffabilis et quedam determinatio illius materie de qua formantur, que quidem determinatio non plus dat propositioni future quod sit vera quam illi de preterito, cum abstrahat simpliciter ab omni tali; et hoc est quod nititur gestiendo ut cumque exprimere propheta." This idea was later developed more fully by Peter de Rivo.

they do this, what they prophesy may not come to pass, so that if prophetic propositions about the future were true or false, Jonah would have been a liar and a false prophet when he said: "Yet forty days and Ninivah shall be destroyed." True and false prophets are thus distinguished by what moves them: God or the "vanity of their hearts." It makes no difference, as Auriol's examples show, whether what is prophesied comes to pass. If Christ had said Peter would not deny him three times, Auriol says, he would not have said something false, because Peter was still able to not deny him.[33]

This last argument is one way to help explain why articles of faith that concern the future are to be believed, even though their corresponding propositions may not be true or false now. They express that the believer means that there is some determination in the divine knowledge that is "ineffable and inexpressible through any proposition." On the other hand, Auriol says, it could also be said that the resurrection of the body and the last judgment, for example, are not future contingents at all, because God determines them completely. Auriol plays it safe, however, and suggests that his first explanation is better.[34]

And so fail other objections. The argument about knowledge was that since God knows, for example, that the Antichrist will come, and knowledge concerns only what is true, 'the Antichrist will come' is true. Auriol responds that God does not know "that the Antichrist will come, or any proposition about the future." Future-tensed propositions express an expectative knowledge of the future qua future, from which, among others, God abstracts. With respect to the nature of the propositions, they cannot express anything about the divine knowledge, which is indistant. So although if it were accompanied by certainty, and if God had it, expectative knowledge would give determinate truth

---

[33] [38.3:1175–88]: "Non valet etiam secunda, quia propheta verax et mendax non differunt penes veritatem propositionum, alioquin mendax fuisset Ysaias dicendo: 'Parvulus natus est nobis', quia non erat tunc natus, et Ionas cum dixit: 'Adhuc XL dies et Ninive subvertetur', hoc enim non evenit, quia 'misertus est Dominus super malitia, quam locutus est ut faceret et non fecit', ut dicitur Ione tertio. Est ergo differentia prophete veri a mendace ex hoc quod intendunt exprimere, scilicet determinationem quamdam in divina notitia respectu illius materie de qua loquntur. Unus enim movetur a Deo, alius vero a vanitate cordis sui, sicut Ezechielis dicit. Propter quod unus est sompniator et alius verax. Quod ergo dicitur, si evenerit, quod est propheta Domini, si vero non, quod est propheta falsus, dicendum quod sive evenerit sive non, propheta non dixit falsum, quia propositio de futuro nec est vera nec est falsa. Unde Christus non dixisset falsum, dato quod Petrus non abnegasset ter ipsum, immo potuit non negare."

[34] [38.3:1192–1200]: "Non valet etiam tertia, quia propositiones alique future cadunt quidem sub fide quantum ad id quod exprimunt ex intentione credentis, videlicet quod determinatio quedam est de illa materia in divina notitia ineffabilis et inexpressibilis per quamcumque propositionem et sic sunt vere, non autem ut rem respiciant in proprio genere. Vel dicendum quod carnis resurrectio et generale iudicium non sunt futura contingentia ad utrumlibet, quia Deus determinavit omnino quod sic fiat; et sic forte fuit de multis propositionibus propheticis ad quas determinaverat Se Deus. Melius tamen dicitur primo modo, si tamen debeat salvari contingentia ad utrumlibet, et eventus necessitas evitari." Many later scholars, such as Ockham, Rimini, and Marsilius of Inghen, were to use the words 'ineffabilis' and 'inexpressibilis' in connection with divine foreknowledge (cf. also above, n. 30), but with different conclusions. Again, Peter de Rivo was to articulate further the idea that the intention of the believer is expressed in such propositions, and thus they contain a type of 'truth'.

to propositions about the future, God's indistant knowledge does not, because it cannot be expressed in terms of such propositions. Indeed, indistant knowledge cannot even give determinate truth to propositions about the present and past, because it abstracts from past, present, and future, and is not expressed in propositions in any such tense.[35]

Perhaps the strongest objection to Auriol's theory was that, even though things that are future to us are not future to God, God could nevertheless give determinate truth to propositions about the future in comparison to us. We could imagine some sort of chain. Perhaps God could make this known to a human: "Antichrist, sitting in the temple, 7 December 2441," and then that human could form a proposition that would be determinately true: "The Antichrist will sit in the temple on 7 December 2441."

This presents a serious difficulty. Auriol of course accepts the validity of prophetic prediction and foretelling, as his Apocalypse commentary attests,[36] and he thinks that God does make it so prophets have some sort of understanding of the determination of a future contingent in God's knowledge. Nevertheless, Auriol denies that the transfer from determinate indistant knowledge to prophetic expectative knowledge includes the application of the determination of God's indistant knowledge to the future viewed expectatively.[37] Moreover, Auriol does not even tell us how this transfer of knowledge to prophets works, so we cannot really imagine this sort of relay. In fact later, in distinction 39, Auriol asks "is abstracted knowledge of this sort communicable to the mind of a prophet, or does only God have [such knowledge] and He assures the prophet that He has it through some impressions or indications?" He replies that it is not "of the present speculation"![38] Many of Auriol's successors would attack his opinion on prophecy, and Auriol's only true defender, Peter de Rivo, would find these objections difficult and even dangerous to refute.

Auriol's third proposition in article three is discussed only briefly as a conclusion: "What we must hold as a general rule on this matter, because the divine knowledge does not give more to a contingent in the future than its own actuality gives to preceding times which regard [the contingent] as future":[39]

---

[35] [38.3:1201–9]: "Non valet etiam quarta, non est enim concedendum quod Deus sciat Antichristum futurum, vel aliquam propositionem de futuro, quasi expectet eum et apprehendat ut distantem a Se; immo non aliter novit quam ipsum cognoscat dum actu est; et ita illa notitia non cadit super Antichristum futurum. Iste igitur propositiones concedende non sunt quantum ad id quod de sui natura significant, sed quatinus intenditur per ipsas exprimere quod non minus novit Deus futura quam presentia et quod eodem modo cognoscit sicut cognoscet dum erunt in actu. Certum est autem quod ex notitia indistante ab actu non licet inferre de huiusmodi actu quod erit."

[36] On this, see Roest, *Reading the Book of History*, pp. 183–92.

[37] See above, n. 21 [38.3:1249–58].

[38] [39.4:1310–12]: "Utrum autem huiusmodi notitia abstracta sit communicabilis menti prophete, vel solummodo Deus habeat eam et certificet prophetam Se habere illam per impressiones aliquas et indicia, non est presentis spectulationis."

[39] [38.3:1266–9]: "Quid pro regula generali sit tenendum in hac materia, quia non plus divina notitia dat contingenti in futurum quam ipsamet actualitas posita dedit precedentibus seculis eam respicientibus in futurum."

It is clear from this rule that no proposition about the future is true on account of the divine knowledge, because the actuality of today's lecture does not make the proposition 'the lecture will take place' true in preceding times either. And, from the same rule, it is clear that neither the proposition 'God knows that the lecture will take place' nor 'God knows a future actuality' is true. And whoever holds this rule in all cases, so that he takes recourse in the actuality by comparing it to the times *in eternum*, can most easily avoid the objections that stems from the eternal divine knowledge of that actuality.[40]

Strictly speaking then, any statement indicating that God knows something future, such as 'God knows that the Antichrist will be', is *false*, since 'the Antichrist will be' is neither true nor false, and knowledge is only of the true. Auriol will repeat this often in distinction 39. Taken out of context, the statement seems blasphemous, and later figures would find Auriol's remarks abhorrent.

---

[40] [38.3:1276–82]: "Ex ista ergo regula patet quod nulla propositio de futuro est vera propter divinam notitiam, quia nec actualitas lectionis hodierne dedit precedentibus seculis quod hec esset vera: 'Lectio erit'. Et ex eadem patet quod nec ista est vera: 'Deus scit quod lectio erit', nec ista: 'Deus scit actualitatem futuram'. Et in omnibus qui tenet hanc regulam ut recurrat ad actualitatem, comparando eam ad secula in eternum, facillime potest omnem instantiam vitare que procedit ex divina notitia eterna de illa actualitate. Et per hunc modum salvatur contingentia ad utrumlibet futuri, et tollitur eventus immutabilis, ut magis apparebit in questione sequenti. In hoc ergo tertius articulus finitur."

Chapter 6

Intrinsic and Extrinsic Willing

Let us review the main elements of Auriol's position: (1) Immutability and necessity are the same, and so immutable God cannot know what is future to us as future to Him, for in that case all would happen of necessity. (2) Therefore God does not, strictly speaking, have foreknowledge: He does not view things as future, but as indistant. Although the actuality of the existence of a future contingent does not exist in itself, it has an eminent similitude in God. (3) Thus in God, and in no other way, the actuality of the existence of a future contingent is determinate, but this does not make future contingent propositions true, nor are propositions that imply that God knows futures true.

A difficulty remains with God's will. Because God is absolutely necessary, there is no potency, no possibility, in Him. All in God is pure, subsisting act.[1] God's will, therefore, must remain indeterminate toward contingent things. If God's will were determined, that determination would be as necessary as God, and those 'contingent' objects of his will would come about necessarily, both because of the fact that God willed them, and, absolutely, because God in that case would not have been able to will the opposite, without introducing an imperfection into God. Of course Auriol cannot leave it at that, at the God of the philosophers. If he did, God would seem to be too distant from the world for orthodox Christians, and all contingent events would occur outside of God's will, with God neither willing nor nilling. The Christian God of the Bible does in fact will some things in a determinate manner, Auriol agrees. In distinctions 40 and 41 Auriol will discuss predestination, a convenient way to make the transition to his treatment of the divine will. As God, in a way, wills some people to be saved, and perhaps others to be damned, predestination involves a particular case of foreknowledge.

Auriol holds that the conditional necessity of our present actions, which he calls the necessity of immutability (*ex suppositione*), does not affect the free-

---

[1]   [39.4:1075–89]: "Probabitur enim infra quod Deitas est quoddam velle subsistens purum absque omni potentia volitiva, sicut et intelligere purum. Ubicumque enim est ratio potentie volitive, ibi est ratio imperfectionem importans, quia omnis possibilitas dicit imperfectionem maxime; susceptiva voluntas autem dicitur velle suscipiendo volitionem formaliter et non eliciendo; sed constat quod in Deo non est aliqua ratio imperfectionem importans; ergo non est in Eo potentia volitiva, sed velle inelicitum, actus purus, et subsistens.

Secundo vero in eo quod ait quod Deus potest non velle quod vult, non quod simul velit et non velit, nec etiam quod postmodum non velit. Secundum hoc enim sequeretur quod aliquod velle esset in Deo quod potuisset non esse, et aliquod velle non esset in Eo quod tamen esse potuisset; sed hoc est impossibile, quia quicquid umquam possibile est esse in Deo, totum est actu, et quod non est actu, est impossibile simpliciter in Eo esse, alioquin, cum quicquid sit in Deo sit Deus, esset aliquis Deus possibilis qui non est, et aliquis Deus possibilis non esse Deus; igitur poni non potest quod isti dicunt."

dom of our actions. Those actions are free if we are complacent in them, or accept them positively, for what comes about complacently comes about freely [39.1:314-6]. But if *God* actively wills or knows beforehand our 'free' actions as future, then this benign necessity of immutability becomes absolute necessity, destroying both free will and the need to deliberate. Since God is somehow involved in our eternal salvation or damnation, however, Auriol must explain how it is that God can do this without affecting His neutral will towards our free acts.

Auriol therefore distinguishes between what is an intrinsic act and an extrinsic act of the divine will. An intrinsic act of the will is carried to both sides of a contradiction equally and indeterminately. Auriol uses the example of the creation of the world. If God willed the creation of the world by an intrinsic act of his good pleasure, then either (1) He created the world of necessity, and He was not able to will the non-creation of the world, or (2) it was possible for Him to will the non-creation of the world; and in that case He did in fact will the world's non-creation, because anything possible in God, is in God; otherwise there could be a different God, and God would not be absolutely necessary, etc. Number one cannot be the case, because this entails determinism. Number two cannot be the case, because this involves a contradiction, for God would will the entity and non-entity of the world at the same time.[2]

Hence it remains that He did not will the creation of the world by an intrinsic act of His good pleasure, but rather His will was carried to both sides of the contradiction equally. "According to this it is necessary to say that God no more wills that some contingent thing come about than that it not come about. But whatever comes about pleases him." So God's intrinsic will is indeterminate with respect to both sides, and cannot, as a cause, produce a determinate effect. A possible objection based on Scotus's simultaneous capacity for opposites does not change matters, for Auriol denies that capacity.[3]

---

² [39.2:563-75]: "Tertia quoque propositio est quod res contingentes non profluunt in esse nec trahunt contingentiam effective ab aliquo actu intrinseco existente in divina voluntate. Actus enim intrinsecus divine voluntati fertur simul in utramque partem contradictionis, et non magis in unam partem quam in aliam; complacet enim Deus necessitate nature eque in creatione mundi sicut in non creatione, et eque vult actu intrinseco, et econverso. Quod patet, quia quicquid est possibile in Deo est de necessitate in Eo, nam in necesse esse, quicquid est possibile est necessarium; constat autem quod Deus potest complacere et velle non entitatem mundi, saltem potuit ab eterno, alioquin de necessitate mundum fecisset, et dum mundus non erat, Suum beneplacitum non fuisset impletum; igitur si potuit ab eterno velle non entitatem mundi actu intrinseco beneplaciti, et hodie de necessitate vult eam, alias posset aliquid esse in Deo quod actu non esset, et posset aliquid esse Deus quod actu non esset Deus."
³ [39.2:575-82]: "Et secundum hoc necesse est dicere quod Deus non magis vult de aliqua re contingenti quod fiat quam quod non fiat, sed placet Sibi quodcumque fiat, nec desiderat plus unum quam aliud. Sed manifestum est quod a tali causa non potest determinatus effectus sequi, quia qua ratione unum contradictoriorum sequeretur, eadem ratione sequeretur et aliud, vel utrumque simul, quod impossible est; ergo nullus effectus contingens producitur ex determinatione divine voluntatis sic quod illa determinatio sit aliquis actus intrinsecus existens formaliter in Deo."

On the other hand, there is an extrinsic determination, which is called 'operation'.[4] Thus "in God one must understand a two-fold necessity and one contingency with respect to the production of creatures."

> Indeed the first is the necessity that in the same act in which He wills His essence, He wills creatures, not only with respect to their essences, but also their existences, not that He desires their existences, but He is complacent in them. But the second necessity is that in the same act He wills both sides of a contradiction with indifference and indeterminately, as that the world should exist or should not exist. Thirdly, however, contingency arises, because since God's will is indeterminate to both sides of a contradiction, God's operation, through which He comes into contact with creatures, is wholly contingent, because there is nothing in God through which He is determined toward doing or not doing. But it is in His power either to do or not to do, except that He may not intrinsically determine Himself, because no such intrinsic determination is possible without it being necessary, because it is the same as God. And therefore the contingency that a creature has in existing does not arise from the contingency of the intrinsic will, but of a certain extrinsic thing, namely operation, which is called the will of sign.[5]

One of the significant differences between the *Scriptum* and the Borghese 123 *reportatio* in this context is that in the later *reportatio* version Auriol gives an instants of nature account of divine willing vis-à-vis future contingents, in the manner of Scotus. As this account was attacked by some of Auriol's immediate successors, such as Landulph Caracciolo, and was even remembered over a century and a half later by Francesco della Rovere, the future Pope Sixtus IV, it is worth quoting here:

> There is therefore this order in its determination: first the divine will wills its own essence and is pleased with it, and in the same act, as it were in the second sign, all creatures please it both with respect to their essences and with respect to their existences, but not determinately to one side, but rather to both sides of a contradiction with indifference

---

    [4]   [39.2:657–9]: "Oritur autem hec contingentia quia res non sunt a se, nec sunt ex aliqua determinatione intrinseca existente in Deo, sed ex determinatione quadam extrinseca que appellatur 'operatio'."
    [5]   [39.2:665–80]: "Est igitur considerandum quod in Deo debet intelligi duplex necessitas et una contingentia respectu productionis creaturarum: Prima quidem necessitas quod eodem actu quo vult Suam essentiam, vult creaturas, non solum quoad essentias, sed quoad existentias earumdem, non quod desideret earum existentias, sed complacet in eis. Secunda vero quod eodem actu vult utramque partem contradictionis sub indifferentia et indeterminate, ut quod mundus sit vel non sit. Oritur autem tunc tertio contingentia, quia cum indeterminata sit voluntas Dei ad utramque partem contradictionis, operatio Dei per quam attingit creaturas omnino contingens est, quia non est aliquid in Deo per quod determinetur ad operandum vel non operandum. Sed est in Sua potestate utrumque et operatur vel non operatur, absque hoc: Quod intrinsece determinet Se, quia nulla talis intrinseca determinatio est possibilis quin esset necessaria, quia id ipsum quod Deus. Et ita contingentia quam habet creatura in existendo oritur non ex contingentia intrinsece voluntatis, sed cuiusdam extrinseci, scilicet operationis, que appellatur 'voluntas signi', ut magis inferius apparebit."

and even indetermination, e.g. that the world should exist or should not exist. With this complacency remaining determined to both sides and undeterminable, however, there follows thirdly the first contingent determination actively in an operation in external reality, through which determination the will comes into contact with creatures. And this determination is contingent because of the fact that God's will, from which it proceeds, is determined to both sides of a contradiction. Nor is [the will] in itself passively determined to this or that, but the first determination is completely in the operation that comes forth, through which [the will] actively comes into contact with creatures. And in the fourth sign the contingent determination of a passive determination arises, by which a creature is said to be produced and preserved [in being].[6]

Auriol further develops the distinction between God's intrinsic will, by which God is pleased with everything that comes about or does not come about, and His extrinsic will, by which He efficaciously wills particular things to come about. Auriol's position on the intrinsic will saves divine perfection and simplicity, while avoiding determinism. Although God's intrinsic will does not actively will, say, the creation of the world, it is pleased by the creation. For this reason God's intrinsic will can be said to be free and not constrained, on Auriol's definition of freedom. As we have seen, for Auriol what is willed complacently is willed freely [39.3:314-16]. God's extrinsic will, on the other hand, wills particular things and is efficacious. Though his extrinsic will could will otherwise, and is free, this does not suggest potentiality in God, because this will is extrinsic to God.[7]

Of course Auriol does not originate these distinctions for the will. It was customary to distinguish between the will proper, i.e. the will of good pleasure, and the will taken metaphorically, that is, the will of sign. The will of sing, moreover, could be understood as prohibition, precept, counsel, and permission, besides operation. In the present context we have even seen that Thomas Wylton employed the distinction between God's "efficacious" will of good

---

    6   Petrus Aureoli, *Reportatio Parisiensis* I, d. 39, q. 1, a. 3 (ed. Nielsen-Schabel, Borghese 123, f. 170vb): "Est igitur ordo iste in huius determinatione: primo enim voluntas divina vult essentiam suam et complacet in ea; et eodem actu, quasi in secundo signo, placet omnis creatura tam quo ad suas essentias quam quo ad existentias, non quidem determinate ad alteram partem, sed quo ad utramque partem contradictionis sub indifferentia tam etiam indeterminatione, ut quod mundus sit vel non sit. Ista autem complacentia remanente sic determinata ad utrumlibet indeterminabili, sequitur tertio prima determinatio contingens in operatione active extra, per quam attingit creaturas; quae quidem determinatio contingens est ex hoc quod voluntas Dei, e qua profluit, determinata est ad utramque partem contradictionis. Nec tamen in se passive determinatur ad hoc vel illud, sed omnino determinatio prima est in operatione egrediente per quam active attingit creaturam. Et in quarto signo fit determinatio contingens determinationis passivae, qua dicitur creatura produci et conservari."

    7   James Halverson discusses the distinction between God's intrinsic and extrinsic will in chapter 2 of *Peter Aureol on Predestination*, esp. pp. 61-70, while chapter 3 concerns in part how this distinction fits with predestination. See Halverson's dissertation, "Peter Aureol and the Re-Emergence of Predestinarian Pluralism," Appendix E, pp. 405-32, for an edition of Auriol's distinction 47, which contains his discussion. See also the important discussion of the distinction in Vignaux, *Justification*, pp. 71-80.

pleasure, which cannot be impeded, and His permissive will, which allows humans indeterminate freedom. Perhaps influenced by Wylton, Auriol's distinction is nevertheless different and applied in a different way.[8]

The distinction between the intrinsic and extrinsic will of God is explained at length in, among other places, Auriol's distinctions 40 and 41, where he treats predestination, the paradigm of divine efficacy, as James Halverson calls it.[9] Auriol defines predestination as the "operation, foreknown from eternity, whereby God confers grace and glory upon the saved." This definition, as Halverson points out, does not concern God's intrinsic will, which is distinct from operation, as we have seen.[10] This is not to say that predestination does not involve God's intrinsic will, however. Auriol's doctrine of predestination is what Halverson labels General Election. With help from a passage in I Timothy 2.4, "God wills that all men be saved,"[11] Auriol holds that this willing all men to be saved is the role of God's intrinsic will, although he adds that God does not will to be saved those who have an impediment or "obstacle to grace," blocking their reception of grace. In this way Auriol claims God's intrinsic will sets up necessary rules that refer to types of people, rather than individuals, and by this intrinsic, general will, God is pleased by both the predestination of the elect and the reprobation of the damned. The actual predestination and reprobation of individuals are "temporal actions extrinsic to Deity itself." The presence in some of an obstacle to grace — not sin per se — is a sort of positive cause of their reprobation, whereas its absence is a privative or negative cause in those who are predestined.[12]

Auriol's account of predestination, which is much more complex than has been presented here, is consistent with his account of the will's role in foreknowledge. In foreknowledge generally, God's intrinsic will is directed toward both sides of a contradiction equally, and it is pleased by whatever is actualized. On the other hand, the creation of the world, for example, involved also an operation of the extrinsic will. In the important particular case involving foreknowledge, predestination, God by His intrinsic will wills toward both sides of the contradiction equally, and is equally pleased by what is actualized; i.e. He is pleased by the salvation of those with grace and the damnation of those without it, on account of an obstacle to grace. The criteria for salva-

---

[8]   On the traditional distinctions for the will, cf. for example Thomas Aquinas, *Summa theologiae* I, q. 19, aa. 11–12. On Wylton, see above, chapter 2.

[9]   Halverson, *Peter Aureol on Predestination*, p. 76.

[10]   Halverson, *Peter Aureol on Predestination*, p. 188. The quotation is translated from his edition in "Peter Aureol and the Re-Emergence of Predestinarian Pluralism," p. 305.

[11]   Halverson, *Peter Aureol on Predestination*, p. 83; cf. Vignaux, *Justification*, p. 49.

[12]   Halverson, *Peter Aureol on Predestination*, p. 90. On Auriol's soteriology, and the interesting element of the obstacle to grace (*obex gratiae*) in the reprobate, see also Vignaux, *Justification*, especially pp. 80–95, and Friedman, "The *Sentences* Commentary, 1250–1320," which has a good discussion of the historical context of the development of Auriol's theory. Like his discussion of future contingents, Auriol's soteriological treatment, and the idea of the *obex gratiae*, came under fire immediately after Auriol's lectures, in the works of, for example, Landulph Caracciolo, Francis of Marchia, and Walter Chatton. On this, see my chapters "Parisian Commentaries from Peter Auriol to Gregory of Rimini" and "Oxford Franciscans after Ockham: Walter Chatton and Adam Wodeham," in Evans, ed., *Commentaries on Peter Lombard's Sentences*, forthcoming.

tion are intrinsic to God and absolutely necessary, but the determination of specifically who does and who does not fulfill the criteria is extrinsic to God.

Auriol goes on in distinctions 45 through 47 to treat the will in general, and although he discusses the difference between God's intrinsic will of complacency and His extrinsic will of operation at much greater length there, especially in distinction 47, the basic foundation is the same:

> Furthermore, that disposition is necessary which is impossible and was impossible *ab eterno* not to be; but if the intrinsic divine willing has a disposition toward the creation of the world such that God may have willed for that instant that the world would come about, then it was impossible for that disposition not to be, even *ab eterno*, because given the opposite, that it was possible for it not to be, it follows that the opposite disposition was able to inhere, namely that God was able *ab eterno* not to will to create the world for that instant at which He created it. If, however, He was able not to will, it follows that that notwilling was able to be God, because God *is* His willing and His notwilling and whatever is in Him. It is established, however, that whatever was able to be God, of necessity is God and today is God; wherefore if by any intrinsic willing God was able *ab eterno* not to will ever to create the world, then today it is necessary for Him to have that not-willing. Therefore, since He does not have that [not-willing], because He already created [the world], it follows that He would not be able to have such a not-willing, and thus He had the will of creating necessarily, such that it was impossible for things to be any other way. But this is totally discordant and erroneous; therefore it cannot be said that the divine willing has a contingent disposition, or any disposition, according to which it would be true to say that God willed or did not will to create the world.[13]

Extreme divine simplicity, in Auriol's case, leads him to deny any active intrinsic willing, though it is still the case that God does freely will creatures by His intrinsic will of complacency, though indifferently:

---

[13]   Petrus Aureoli, *I Sent.*, d. 47, a. 1 (ed. Halverson, pp. 408–09, ll. 224–48): "Preterea, illa habitudo est necessaria quam impossibile est non esse et fuit impossibile ab aeterno, sed si divinum velle intrinsecum habet habitudinem ad creationem mundi, ita quod Deus voluerit pro illo instanti quod mundus fieret, habitudinem illam impossibile fuit non esse etiam ab aeterno, quia detur oppositum quod fuit possibilis non esse, sequitur quod habitudo opposita potuit inesse, videlicet quod Deus potuit ab aeterno nolle mundum creare pro illo instanti quo creavit. Si autem potuit nolle, sequitur quod illud nolle potuit esse Deus, quia Deus est suum velle et suum nolle et quicquid est in seipso. Constat autem quod quicquid potuit esse Deus, de necessitate est Deus et hodie est Deus, quare si aliquo velle intrinseco potuit Deus ab aeterno nolle mundum umquam creare et hodie oportet quod habeat illud nolle. Cum ergo non habeat, cum iam creaverit, sequitur quod habere non potuerit tale nolle et ita habuit voluntatem creandi de necessitate, sic quod impossibile fuit aliter se habere. Sed hoc est totaliter absonum et erroneum. Ergo dici non potest quod velle divinum habeat habitudinem contingentem immo nec aliquam habitudinem secundum quam sit verum dicere quod voluerit Deus aut noluerit mundum creare."

It is clear how God is said to will creatures and their production, for He is said to will them by the will of a certain complacency, inasmuch as He is complacent in their being, and consequently in every creatable or created entity. This complacency, however, is immutable and absolutely necessary, and God is not determined by it to produce or not produce, because He is equally complacent whether they come about or not. He does not have, however, any willing by which He intrinsically strives for or chooses, or desires... Nevertheless God is said to will freely and voluntarily to produce what He produces; indeed freely because He produces complacently, for He is complacent in the entity of the creature and in the entity that its production entails, whether it exists or not.[14]

Thus God's intrinsic will does not lean to one side of a contradiction more than to another, for God's will of complacency is inefficacious, does not move, and "has the nature of spiritual rest."[15] It is because God's intrinsic will was unable to choose one side of a contradiction that Auriol proposes the extrinsic will of operation, by which God actually does things, like create the world.

This 'solution', however, creates as many questions as it answers, but one must admit that, in his treatment of predestination in particular, Auriol makes an ingenious attempt to preserve free will and divine omnipotence and immutability, and therefore to avoid fatalism and Pelagianism both. Auriol's ideas on this subject provoked much discussion in the rest of the fourteenth century. In the context of future contingents, Landulph Caracciolo and his anonymous Franciscan follower would attack his distinction of the will (see chapter seven). Thus Auriol's rather 'ad hoc' solution drew immediate fire for the new problems it created. That it was a fundamental element of Auriol's position is still attested early in the next century, when Peter of Nugent presented Auriol's position on divine foreknowledge and future contingents *solely* by quoting most of Auriol's distinction 47, article one. A few years later John Capreolus would also oppose this notion in his defense of Aquinas's solution to the problem (see below, chapter twelve).

---

[14]   Aureoli, *I Sent.*, d. 47, a. 1 (ed. Halverson, p. 413, ll. 494–512): "Ex praemissis itaque patet qualiter Deus dicitur velle creaturas et productionem earum, dicitur enim eas velle voluntate cuiusdam complacentiae, inquantum sibi complacet in sua entitate, et per consequens in omni entitate creabili et creata. Haec autem complacentia est immutabilis et necessaria absolute, nec ex illa determinatur Deus ad producendum vel non producendum quia aequaliter complacet sive fuerint sive non. Non habet autem aliquod velle quo appetat intrinsece aut optet vel concupiscat... Nihilominus tamen Deus dicitur libere et voluntarie producere quae producit. Libere quidem quia complacenter producit, complacet enim in entitate creaturae et in entitate quam importat productio, sive sit sive non sit."
[15]   Aureoli, *I Sent.*, d. 47, a. 2 (ed. Halverson, p. 417, ll. 770–72; p. 418, ll. 794–7): "Quid dicendum secundum veritatem, et primo quod velle complacentiae non habet in Deo activitatis seu efficaciae rationem... complacentia non movet immediate, nisi pro tanto excitat desiderium, et huius ratio est quia complacentia habet rationem spiritualis quietis et non alicuius motionis."

Conclusion

We shall have to wait until the critical, annotated edition of Peter Auriol's *Scriptum* is finished really to analyze his thoughts on, for example, God's knowledge via similitudes and the different types of divine willing. These topics deserve lengthy treatment in themselves. And until we edit more texts from Auriol's successors, we shall not be able to evaluate fully his impact on these related issues. We can say a few things about that, however. Auriol's solution was closer to Aquinas's than to Scotus's and could not have helped Auriol gain acceptance in his own Franciscan order; the fact that Auriol made important modifications to Aquinas's theory would not have helped his cause with the Dominicans. In addition, each of the main elements of Auriol's position was, to a certain degree, new to Auriol. He faced a struggle if he were to gain approval for his innovative ideas, which, in a system such as Auriol's, were so interwoven that attacking one point would mean attacking the whole. It may even be the case that Auriol 'overarticulated' his position, so by conscientiously drawing all of the conclusions to his arguments that he could, he opened himself up to further attacks.

Auriol tried more than most Christian theologians in the Middle Ages to emphasize the 'God of the philosophers'. Divine simplicity and necessity was his point of departure all along in the context of divine foreknowledge and future contingents. The perfect, unchanging, undesiring God of the philosophers, who "fancies nothing," as has been said, was quite close to Auriol's God, indistant from all, not in time and without a relation to time, not willing or nilling in an intrinsic way, not 'learning' when events had actually come to pass and thus not changing in His knowledge. To save human free will, Auriol denied Bivalence in singular categorical propositions about future contingents, and the God of the philosophers allowed Auriol to maintain this denial on metaphysical grounds. Auriol's employment of God's will of operation was the one concession to the revealed God of Scripture.[16]

This was too much for his successors at Paris to swallow. They could not give up their Christian notion of an anthropomorphic God, attested perhaps by Scripture, desired certainly by the common man. Auriol's destruction or at least modification of basic logical axioms made Auriol's solution even more difficult to accept. The only evidence of anyone looking favorably upon his position in the fourteenth century is a couple of anonymous abbreviations of Auriol's *Sentences* commentary, and perhaps one theologian reading *secundum*

---

[16]   Perhaps in his attempt to distinguish between the will of complacency and the will of operation, Auriol is an exception to Jos Decorte's generalization that "Misled by a Greek (Platonic) prejudice medieval theologians failed to conceive a concrete and relative divine nature, to which alone the activity of knowing what is happening in time can be ascribed. Hence the problem of explaining divine foreknowledge of contingent events must become, sooner or later, insoluble." Certainly Auriol is an exception to Decorte's statement that "The Franciscan solution paid more heed to the concrete elements (Franciscans having always been more attracted to what is concrete and individual than to what is philosophically abstract) and tried out the other way. Starting from a conception that attributed more objectivity and ontological reality to time they framed a more concrete notion of eternity" (Decorte, "*Sed Modum Exprimere Nescio*," p. 166).

Aureoli.[17] In those cases, however, the material on divine foreknowledge and future contingents was probably just abbreviated or copied along with the rest, and tells us nothing about the positive reception of Auriol's opinion. Certainly no one whose name we know adopted his position, at least until the late-fifteenth century. Instead, all aspects of his stance came under immediate attack in Paris.

---

[17]   As was said, Vat. lat. 946 contains an abbreviation of SQ1-BPV. Clermont-Ferrand, Bibliothèque municipale 109 abbreviates the *Scriptum* questions. The anonymous commentary on book one in Pelplin 53/102 is probably from a Franciscan reading *secundum* Auriol, to such an extent that most of the material is merely a verbatim and slightly rearranged abbreviation of the *Scriptum*. Wladislaw Senko, "Quelques contributions à l'histoire de la littérature philosophique de XIVᵉ siècle d'après le ms 53/102 de la Bibliothèque du Grand Seminaire de Pelplin," MPP 11 (1963), pp. 69–85, esp. pp. 70–80, had described the commentary contained on folios 14ra–129vb as that of a Parisian lecturing in the mid-1320's, but Senko's question list and transcription of part of q. 19, "Utrum in omni alio citra Deum differat esse et essentia," match Auriol's question titles and d. 8, pars 1, respectively, verbatim. In the first couple of questions, however, Auriol is actually cited explicitly and the copying is reduced, and so it may be someone reading *secundum alium*. See my "Parisian Commentaries between Peter Auriol and Gregory of Rimini."

PART THREE

The Reaction to Auriol's Theory at Paris

Chapter 7

Franciscans against the God of the Philosophers

Peter Auriol left his successors with a third basic theory of divine foreknowledge and future contingents, adding his to Aquinas's and Scotus's. In the half decade or so after Auriol's lectures on the *Sentences*, his junior colleagues at the University of Paris collectively attacked all of the main elements of his position on future contingents and divine foreknowledge: his view that fatalism resulted from the traditional opinions on foreknowledge; the notion of indistance; the neutral truth value of future contingent propositions; and the distinction between God's intrinsic and extrinsic will. For the next quarter of a century, until Gregory of Rimini in the 1340's, Auriol's treatment of the problem set the agenda for theologians at Paris, who usually attacked him in favor of some sort of Scotist stance, which they modified to various degrees depending on their evaluation of the strength of Auriol's arguments. Moreover, treatments of divine foreknowledge generally become longer after Auriol and there is a greater emphasis on how God foreknows contingents, more focus on propositions, and a greater use of technical vocabulary.[1] This period was thus a lively and interesting chapter in the history of the problem of divine foreknowledge and future contingents.

It is a common assumption, however, that the University of Oxford outshone the University of Paris in the 1320s and 1330s.[2] The story goes that after Peter Auriol a vibrant period in the history of the leading center of theological learning on the European continent came to an end. That earlier period saw Paris at the zenith of its influence, represented by figures like Thomas Aquinas, Bonaventure, Giles of Rome, Henry of Ghent, and John Duns Scotus. Now names like Peter of Aquila, Bernard Lombardi, and William of Brienne, little known to most intellectual historians, indicate a stagnant period in the

---

[1] These changes are charted in my "The Quarrel with Aureol," pp. 130–33.

[2] On this assumption, the historical literature, and its relationship to the historiography on Peter Auriol, see Tachau, *Vision and Certitude*, pp. 315–17. The reaction to Auriol's thought at Paris in the period 1318–45, with respect to his epistemological ideas, is the subject of Tachau's chapter 11, "Paris 1318–1345: The Interpreters of Scotus and Auriol," pp. 315–52. William J. Courtenay's *Parisian Scholars in the Early Fourteenth Century. A Social Portrait* (Cambridge 1999) is a recent attempt to shed some light on this era, although it deals with seculars and therefore considers virtually none of the major theologians of the day. Schwamm, *Das göttliche Vorherwissen*, and Dettloff, *Die Entwicklung der Akzeptations- und Verdienstlehre*, both deal with these decades, although neither does so both at length and for its own sake. Halverson, *Peter Aureol on Predestination*, does not take the opportunity to examine Paris between Auriol and Rimini, and devotes less than ten pages to it.

university's history when scholars simply repeated the old ideas of their predecessors, not even taking up the intellectual challenge brought by Auriol.

At the same time, however, the University of Oxford was experiencing a vitality that, we are told, carried it to a role of intellectual leadership. William of Ockham, Adam Wodeham, Thomas Bradwardine, Robert Holcot, and many others were the scholastic avant-guard of the time. The philosophers and theologians at Oxford developed new concepts in logic and mathematics, for example, and then used these ideas to stimulate new treatments of old theological problems, sometimes inventing new problems. It was at Oxford in this era that the solutions of Scotus and Auriol were scrutinized with the most ingenuity and skill.

Around 1340, however, Paris began to reassume its role as the queen of universities, as the new English developments slowly made their way across the channel. Now, figures such as Gregory of Rimini came to prominence at Paris, and Oxford's period of leadership ended. Although Paris remained for decades the focus of theological inquiry, its position of undisputed leadership faded somewhat with the founding of new universities, especially in the wake of the Great Schism.

This scenario may not be entirely true. It is partly based on the interests of modern scholars. There is a tendency for scholars to appreciate the ideas of those whom they know, then to investigate those theories further, thus compounding what may at first have been a subjective selection. It may also be the case that not all theological discussions after 1340 were enriched solely by the developments at Oxford; perhaps a Parisian tradition continued in some contexts with little influence from outside. At the same time the use of the printing press, as Damasus Trapp has noted, has affected the availability of sources for the modern scholar:

> The art of Gutenburg had two opposite effects: it made printed medieval authors accessible but condemned those who by 1600 had not been printed to inaccessibility. The printers who strove after an ideal of perfect readability gradually dropped scholastic stenography from their columns, and by unintentional chain-reaction destroyed the art of writing and reading scholastic shorthand. By 1600 only a few theologians were able to plow through shorthand texts in manuscripts which became more and more museum pieces, kept in jealously locked and practically inaccessible libraries.[3]

And the printing press had another effect. Those authors who were most famous in the late fifteenth and sixteenth centuries were printed. This choice was often conservative, and fell upon those who had been the early intellectual leaders of religious orders, such as Aquinas, Bonaventure, and Giles of Rome. In times of great change and, especially, the proliferation of universities,

---

[3]   Damasus Trapp, "Augustinian Theology," p. 178.

later fourteenth-century and fifteenth-century authors were largely ignored, in favor of those whom everyone knew well, who had universal reputations.

Several scholars active in these decades at Paris did have their theological works printed in the late-fifteenth and sixteenth centuries, but it was precisely those who had the most conservative views, probably because of those views. For the Franciscans it was the Scotists, in this case the "Prince of the Scotists," Francis of Meyronnes, and Peter of Aquila, known as "Little Scotus." For the Augustinians it was Gerard of Siena and Thomas of Strasbourg, hardly revolutionary thinkers. The Carmelites had Baconthorpe, whose lack of innovation we shall see. Auriol himself had to wait until 1595, probably because after John Capreolus in the early fifteenth century Auriol is no longer a primary focus of attacks, with the exception of the Louvain quarrel. The theologians mentioned, who had their *Sentences* commentaries printed, all dealt with Auriol at one point or another, but usually not with any flare. This is yet another reason why Auriol's impact has not drawn much scholarly attention. The scholars of the period whose commentaries on book I remained only in manuscript form, however, have the most interesting things to say: Francis of Marchia, Landulph Caracciolo, Michael of Massa, and Gerard Odonis. One can include Nicholas Bonet here, since one has to dig for his stance in various printed philosophical works; his *Sentences* commentary has not been found.

There is no easy way to organize the discussion of the period. It would be useful to group scholars based on common ideas, but they refuted different parts of Auriol's position, often in different ways, and such an arrangement would perhaps mean dividing up the treatment of one scholar into several separate sections. Another way would be to take a strict chronological approach, which has the benefit of keeping the treatments of individual theologians intact, while preserving the historical perspective. This has the disadvantage of jumping from one argument to another, from one topic to another and back again. Furthermore, it is not always easy to tell exactly when someone first had or last wrote an idea. *Sentences* commentaries were often years in revision.

Therefore I have decided on the following arrangement: in this chapter I shall treat Franciscans, most of whom can be described as 'Scotists' to one degree or another on this issue, who concentrated on attacking Auriol's theory of the will and indistance and defended a more anthropomorphic image of God. In the next chapter I deal with scholastics outside the Franciscan order, and continental Franciscans outside Paris, who were usually conservative in their reactions to Auriol. Finally, I will look at the Franciscan Francis of Marchia and what I call the 'Marchist School'. Marchia put forth an interesting alternative solution to the problem, and he was followed by a group of Franciscans and one Augustinian, Michael of Massa. Thomas of Strasbourg and Peter of Aquila will be treated later as conservative predecessors of Rimini from the 1330s. There are shortcomings in this arrangement, but I hope the positive outweighs the negative.

Landulph Caracciolo

Several Franciscans focussed their arguments against Auriol's emphasis on extreme divine simplicity. Auriol's God of the philosophers was in no way connected to time, and hence He was indistant from rather than present to the actualities of future contingents. Moreover, God's will, intrinsically, desired nothing. Taking their lead from Landulph Caracciolo, several theologians attacked the weak points of these elements of Auriol's solution, and reaffirmed the more anthropomorphic, or at least worldly, side of the Christian God.

Landulph Caracciolo, the *Doctor Recollectus*, was born in Naples and, after his academic career, became first bishop of Castellammare in 1327 and then archbishop of Amalfi in 1331, serving in the latter capacity until his death in 1351.[4] Caracciolo most likely lectured on the *Sentences* at Paris immediately after Auriol, in the academic year 1318–19. Others have suggested that he taught slightly later, perhaps in 1321–22, but Valens Heynck has shown that he lectured at least on book IV between the summers of 1318 and 1321. Since his confrères Francis of Marchia and Francis of Meyronnes read the *Sentences* in 1319–20 and 1320–21 respectively, this leaves 1318–19. He was a master of theology by February 1325, at which time he was Franciscan provincial minister of Terra Laboris in southern Italy.[5]

Caracciolo was a major theologian, and among his surviving works are numerous sermons and a popular commentary on the *Sentences*. At least two dozen extant manuscripts contain at least one of the four books of Caracciolo's commentary.[6] Book II was printed in Venice before 1500, and it shows Caracciolo to have been a pivotal figure on the subject of change and instants of time and nature. Book I has been the subject of investigations concerning grace, epistemology, and predestination. In each of these cases Caracciolo,

---

[4]   See Ehrle, *Der Sentenzenkommentar Peters von Candia*, p. 260, and Dettloff, *Die Entwicklung der Akzeptations- und Verdienstlehre*, p. 192.

[5]   See Valens Heynck, "Der Skotist Hugo de Novo Castro, OFM," FzS 43 (1961), pp. 244–70, esp. pp. 250–52, basing himself on Caracciolo's citations of a consistory of 1318 (probably July) against John de Polliaco, and Caracciolo's lack of reference to the July 1321 consistory that condemned John. Knuuttila and Lehtinen, "Change and Contradiction," pp. 196–7, also support the earlier date, which Anneliese Maier, *Metaphysische Hintergründe der spätscholastische Naturphilosophie* (Rome 1955), p. 127, had suggested as a possibility. The fact that Caracciolo incorporated sections of Hugh de Novocastro's pre-Auriol commentary into his own supports the earlier 1318–19 date (cf. Heynck, p. 263). As Heynck notes (pp. 248, 252–3), no matter how one looks at it, the 1295 statute of the Franciscan order's general chapter that every three years a friar from the French province should be bachelor of the *Sentences* at Paris appears to have been ignored or bypassed, as allowed by the 1316 general chapter's statute. Thus the 1295 statute is not especially helpful in dating Franciscan *Sentences* commentaries.

[6]   See Fridericus Stegmüller, *Repertorium commentariorum in Sententias Petri Lombardi* I (Würzburg 1947), pp. 253–4, and Doucet, *Commentaires sur les Sentences*, p. 58. Landulph's question on the immaculate conception from book III was published by D. Scaramuzzi, "L'immaculato concepimento di Maria. Questione inedita di Landolfo Caracciolo, O.F.M. (†1351)," *Studi Francescani* 28 (1931), pp. 33–69.

usually defending Scotus, responds to Auriol's position as presented in the latter's Parisian *reportatio* for book I represented by Borghese 123.[7] Caracciolo's treatment of divine foreknowledge in distinctions 38–40 is rather long, taking up thirty-two pages in the edition. Although this is still perhaps half of the length of his successor Francis of Marchia's, Caracciolo devotes almost all of his discussion to two objectives: affirming a basically Scotist position, and refuting Peter Auriol's arguments in a comprehensive way. In distinction 38 he makes the claim — which becomes something of a cliché after Auriol — that contingency in the world is a *per se notum*. Caracciolo also ascribes to the notion that God has a simultaneous capacity for opposites, and that He knows future contingents via the determinations of the divine will. Nevertheless, nowhere does he put forth the entire Scotist position comprehensively, e.g. he does not present the 'four instants of nature' element clearly, so Caracciolo is perhaps less a Scotist than Meyronnes would be.[8]

Presenting and attacking Auriol's stance takes up over half of his text, but even when he deals with the ideas of others, such as Thomas Aquinas, he does so via the writings of Scotus and Auriol on the subject, giving what can begin to be called 'stock arguments'. Thus in distinction 39 Caracciolo quickly refutes the divine Ideas solution, the argument based on the 'presentiality' of

---

[7]   On Caracciolo and change, see Knuuttila, *Modalities in Medieval Philosophy*, pp. 160–62. On grace, see W. Dettloff, *Die Entwicklung der Akzeptations- und Verdienstlehre*, pp. 192–6 (pp. 193–4 for Caracciolo's use of Auriol's Borghese 123 *reportatio*). On epistemology, see Tachau, *Vision and Certitude*, pp. 320–22 (on Auriol's *reportatio*, p. 322, n. 19). On predestination, see my "Parisian Commentaries from Peter Auriol to Gregory of Rimini." Schwamm, *Das göttliche Vorherwissen*, pp. 276–89, treats Caracciolo on future contingents with respect to his Scotism, although he does recognize that Caracciolo's main opponent here is Auriol. A critical edition of Caracciolo's dd. 38–40, which determines that ms. ÖNB 1496 is the best, is contained in my "Landulphus Caracciolo," pp. 307–338.

[8]   Caracciolo's defense of contingency as a *per se notum* is in Landulphus Caracciolo, *I Sent.*, d. 38, a. 1 (ed. Schabel, "Landulphus Caracciolo," p. 308). Caracciolo's Scotist position can be pieced together from various places, e.g. *I Sent.*, d. 38, a. 2 (ed. Schabel, pp. 312–13): "Prima propositio: Omnis complexio de contingenti est neutra intellectui divino ante actum divine voluntatis. Ista probatur: Ante actum voluntatis divine omnia que sunt in Deo sunt necessaria. Si igitur complexio de contingenti ante actum voluntatis non esset neutra, sed determinata, esset necessaria, quod est impossibile. Antecedens patet, quia quidquid representatur in divina essentia, intellectus in ea intelligit necessario. Consequentia patet, quia determinatio ante actum voluntatis esset vel in essentia representante vel in intellectu intelligente, que omnia sunt necessaria et non contingentia... Quarta propositio, quod actus divine voluntatis circa opposita contingentia non est liber ex hoc quod habeat in sua potestate utrumque oppositum successive, puta 'hodie pluere et cras non', ymo quod simul pro eodem signo habet utrumque oppositum in sua potestate...'" Caracciolo, *I Sent.*, d. 39, a. 2 (ed. Schabel, p. 332): "Tertia, quod intellectus divinus infallibiliter cognoscit futurum contingens determinate cognoscendo determinationem divine voluntatis. Formo igitur rationem: Illud cognoscit infallibiliter intellectus divinus quod divina voluntas infallibiliter determinat. Sed divina voluntas determinat infallibiliter futurum contingens. Igitur ipsum infallibiliter cognoscet intellectus divinus. Maior patet, quia ad intelligendum determinatum effectum, non requiritur nisi intelligere determinatam causam. Causa determinata futuri contingentis est divina voluntas, ut patuit." He also uses the composite/divided sense distinction to defend his stance.

things with respect to God's eternity, and the stance distinguishing between something's being necessary to God but contingent in its proximate causes.[9]

Caracciolo's attack on Auriol comes in many places, but two stand out, one against Auriol's intrinsic/extrinsic will division, and one against indistance. In distinction 38 Caracciolo presents Auriol's position on the divine will in the first of three "conclusions":

> The first opinion to be presented is one that states that contingency exists in things only from the contingent determination of something extrinsic to God. And this is exterior 'operation'... And this opinion imagines four instants: in the first the divine will is complacent in His essence; in the second sign it is complacent in itself with respect to all creatures, both with regard to their essences and to their existences — not with regard to one side of a contradiction, but rather to each side with indifference, "as whether the world should exist or not"; in the third sign there is a contingent determination in things through an active operation *extra*, with the will remaining altogether indeterminate *ad intra*; in the fourth sign there follows a passive determination *extra* when things are passively put into being.[10]

Clearly Caracciolo is responding to the *reportatio* version of Auriol's *Sentences* commentary contained in Borghese 123, and not the *Scriptum*, as the quotation stems from the passage cited above from Borghese 123 (see above, chapter six). Other passages in Caracciolo's questions on foreknowledge contain verbatim quotations from Auriol's Borghese *reportatio*, and one can also discern this in the phrasing of the questions, general content, and specific terminology of Caracciolo's text. Finally, concerning the divine will, only the Borghese 123 version asks a specific related question in this context.[11]

As has been noted, Auriol's distinction between God's intrinsic, passive will of complacency, and his extrinsic, active will of operation would seem to have been an obvious target for opponents, and Caracciolo gives some obvi-

---

[9]   See Caracciolo, *I Sent.*, d. 39, a. 2 (ed. Schabel, pp. 323–5).

[10]   Caracciolo, *I Sent.*, d. 38, a. 2 (ed. Schabel, pp. 310–11): "Prima ponenda est opinio una que dicit quod contingentia in rebus precise est ex determinatione contingenti alicuius extrinseci a Deo, et hoc est exterior operatio. 'Exemplum: Si ignis haberet in sua potestate' comburere et non 'comburere ex sola contingenti determinatione combustionis' active, ex qua sequeretur contingens determinatio combustionis in passo, diceretur contingenter comburere. Ita Deus, per nihil intrinsecum, nec per actum, nec per obiectum vel voluntatis vel intellectus — nec ex ordine cuiuscumque intrinseci ad obiectum oritur contingentia in rebus —, ymo stante voluntate intrinsece in suo actu indeterminata, sola extrinseca operatione determinat ipsum contingens.

Et ymaginatur opinio ista quatuor instantia: In primo voluntas divina complacet sibi in essentia sua. In secundo signo complacet sibi in omnibus creaturis tam quo ad essentias quam quo ad existentias — non quo ad alteram partem contradictionis, ymo quo ad utramque partem sub indifferentia, 'ut quod mundus sit et non sit'. In tertio signo est contingens determinatio in rebus per operationem activam extra, manente voluntate omnimode indeterminata ad intra. In quarto signo sequitur determinatio passiva in rebus extra cum res ponuntur passive in esse."

[11]   That is, d. 39, q. 1 (ed. Nielsen-Schabel, Borghese 123, f. 170ra): "Utrum contingentia rerum oriatur ex causa extrinsica earum vel intrinsica ipsarum nature."

ous objections: it is pointless and contradictory for God's intrinsic will of complacency to be at once pleased both with something's being and its non-being, for this indifference is the same as "being pleased with nothing, and therefore being both pleased and not pleased." Moreover, how could God actively will anything at all intrinsically? Before the world was created, either God had a determinate act of the will or not. An affirmative answer would seem to posit an intrinsic act before operation. If the response is negative, then Caracciolo wonders if God ever had an act of willing the world's being. If so, this would make God mutable, since He did not have that act beforehand. If not, God never willed or nilled the world's being, which is ridiculous, since the world does exist. Another possibility is that the world, produced by the extrinsic, active will of operation, is produced involuntarily and negatively with respect to God's intrinsic will, which is also absurd. Again, says Caracciolo, one might also ask why the world was created in one instant and not another, if God remained intrinsically indifferent throughout. Finally, Caracciolo wonders about this extrinsic will of operation, does it will necessarily or contingently? Obviously not necessarily, but if it wills contingently, "it is necessary to understand beforehand (*preintelligere*) the operation extrinsically determining the act of the will toward a determinate operation and toward a determinate operable."[12] This mechanism Auriol does not explain.

---

[12]   Caracciolo, *I Sent.*, d. 38, a. 2 (ed Schabel, pp. 311–12): "Secunda conclusio est ostendere istam opinionem multa impossibilia et repugnantia implicare. Probo primo sic: Actum amoris et complacentie cadere super utroque contradictorio de eodem et pro eodem instanti est contradictio. Sed tale quid ponit ista opinio. Igitur ponit contradictionem. Maior est manifesta, quia velle utrumque contradictorium de eodem simul est nihil velle, cum una pars interimat aliam. Unde complacere mihi quod tu sis et non sis simul est nihil complacere, et per consequense complacere et non complacere. Minor patet per eos, quia Deus complacet sibi in creaturis sub omnimoda indifferentia ad alteram partem contradictionis.
    Secundo sic: Ad entitatem mundi totius presentatam in divina essentia antequam esset productus mundus, aut Deus habuit determinatum actum volitionis aut non. Si sic, habeo propositum, quia iam ponis intrinsece determinatum Deum ante operationem. Si non, quero utrum Deus umquam habeat vel habere debeat actum volendi ita mundi entitatem quod nolit eius non entitatem? Si sic, efficietur de non determinato determinatus intrinsece, quod est absurdum. Si non, igitur Deus numquam volet mundi entitatem, et numquam volet eius non entitatem, quod est absurdius.
    Tertio, et istud pondero, cum Deus per operationem activam extrinsece determinat contingens ad unam partem, aut est intrinsece determinate volens aut nolens, aut nec volens nec nolens. Si nolens aut volens determinate intrinsece, habetur propositum. Si non, sequitur alterum duorum: Vel quod Deus produxit res involuntarius negative, puta nec volens nec nolens, vel sequitur quod produxit volens eas esse et non esse simul, nec magis esse quam non esse, que sunt absurda.
    Quarto, Deus ab eterno intrinsece in actu voluntatis fuit magis determinatus quod voluerit mundum esse pro instanti quo fuit quam pro alio instanti pro quo non fuit—da oppositum, mundus non fuisset in instanti quo fuit. Igitur determinatio verissima intrinsece in actu voluntatis divine fuit ante illam extrinsicam operationem.
    Quinto, et istud pondero, operatio activa extrinseca per quam fit determinatio contingentis egreditur a voluntate. Quero si voluntas vult istam operationem extrinsecam determinantem vel non? Si non, igitur operatur non volens. Si sic, igitur est intrinsece determinata per actum volitionis ex quo vult operari determinate ad determinatam partem contradictionis.
    Ultimo, operatio activa extrinseca egreditur a suo principio, scilicet voluntate, aut necessario aut contingenter. Non potest dici quod necessario, quia Deus nihil ad extra necessario operatur."

It is difficult to guess how Auriol would have responded. He might have seen some difficulties in Caracciolo's conception of God's eternity, a conception that seems to view eternity as durative. Unlike many others, Auriol equates necessity with immutability and, in a sense, has a special abhorrence of any sort of duration in God's eternity. This of course makes his position on the divine will more difficult; he might not have been able to explain convincingly how God could have remained intrinsically indifferent to the creation of the world, and yet created the world via His active, extrinsic will of operation, with the until-then-non-existing world playing, obviously, no causal part.

Reading Auriol's text, Caracciolo anticipates these objections based on divine necessity and the impossibility of duration in eternity. Caracciolo must make his own distinctions: it is true that there is no potency in God's intrinsic will, but there is potency and intrinsic determination with respect to external objects:

> Because it is certain that God can annihilate the world and that He could will this intrinsically, and He was able beforehand to produce and to will to produce the world, and yet there is not any potency in Him from the fact that He did not do it [beforehand]. Thus when you say, 'whatever is possible in God is actually posited', it is false for the efficient potency, because He can create another world.[13]

Auriol and Caracciolo have reached an impasse, and Caracciolo knows it. Auriol maintains intrinsic necessity and cannot explain extrinsic operation well; Caracciolo maintains extrinsic operation and cannot explain the lack of intrinsic potency well. Caracciolo asserts that God immutably wills contingently in an instant; Auriol declares that contingency requires succession and mutability. Thus Caracciolo retorts,

> I respond that the act of the divine will never changes intrinsically, because it is the same act in number. You say yes [it would]. I deny it. When you give your proof, I say that if your proof is good, all theologi-

---

Si contingenter, oportet necessario preintelligere operationem extrinsece actum voluntatis determinantem ad operationem determinatam et ad determinatum operabile. Voluntas enim nulla exit in aliquam operationem contingenter nisi per actum volitionis preintellectum quo contingenter et libere vult operari. Tolle actum volendi mediantem inter operationem et voluntatem operantem, numquam voluntas operabitur."

[13] Caracciolo, *I Sent.*, d. 38, a. 3 (ed. Schabel, p. 315): "Quicquid est possibile in Deo est positum in actu. Sed per te in Deo est potentia simul ad utrumque oppositum. Igitur simul erunt posita in actu, quod est impossibile... Respondeo. Maior est falsa. Certum est enim quod in determinatione actus voluntatis intrinsece, ut est purum velle, non est in Deo potentia, quia actus suus est idem cum substantia, nec penes talem determinationem accipitur libertas voluntatis sicut in nobis in quibus est alius actus volendi, alius nolendi. Sed quod in ordine ad obiectum extrinsecum non sit potentia et determinatio intrinseca in Deo est falsum, quia certum est quod Deus potest mundum adnihilare et posset hoc intrinsece velle, et potuit mundum ante producere et velle producere, et tamen non est in eo potentia ex hoc quod non fecit. Cum igitur dicis, 'Quicquid est possibile in Deo, est positum in actu', falsum est potentia effectiva, quia potest mundum alium creare, et tali potentia effectiva potest determinare contingens ad utrumque oppositum..."

cal discussion ceases. For the divine volition from eternity was indifferently able to will that Christ be incarnated or that He not be incarnated, so if He willed Him determinately to be incarnated, therefore He changed. [It is] thus with producing and not producing the world, so if He determined Himself to will to produce it, He changed.[14]

Having proven that there is an impasse, Caracciolo is free to declare that God can contingently determine Himself in one act in the durationless instant of eternity, without any mutation and with the simultaneous capacity to will the opposite. The fact that an impasse has been reached is made manifest in Caracciolo's response to Auriol's objection that "if God, by His will, is the cause of contingents, then God will be the cause of evil acts and sins, which are chosen contingently, not necessarily." Caracciolo answers: "This difficulty follows from every position, because every position posits that God is the primary cause of all entities, but evil acts are entities, at least with respect to the substance of the acts." Because Christians have no way around this problem, Caracciolo is content to give the "common" response, knowing that the fundamental problem remains.[15] The God of the philosophers will not suffice, even for knowledge alone, because the anthropomorphic God created the world and became incarnate.

In distinction 39 Caracciolo continues his attack on Auriol. Caracciolo begins with three conclusions, the first of which gives the three main points of Auriol's positive stance: (1) God has (Auriol would say 'is') a similitude of the contingent; (2) the similitude represents the actuality of the contingent as it

---

[14]   Caracciolo, *I Sent.*, d. 38, a. 3 (ed. Schabel, pp. 315–16): "Videris implicare contradictoria. Primo dicis quod instans eternitatis est sine successione. Sed determinatio contingentis includit necessario successionem... Respondeo quod instans eternitatis cum sui omnimoda simplicitate et permanentia compatitur secum utramque partem contradictionis, sicut et modo totum temporis fluxum. Unde non est ymaginandum quod cum esse est post non esse quod in eternitate sit aliqua divisio, vel successio — ymo idem indivisibile in eternitate aspicit utrumque...
In actu divine voluntatis non potest poni mutatio intrinsece. Sed si ponatur ista positio, hoc sequitur... Respondeo quod actus divine voluntatis intrinsece numquam mutatur, quia idem actus est numero. Dicis quod sic. Nego. Cum probas, dico quod si probatio est bona, cessat omnis propositio theologica. Divina enim volitio indifferenter ab eterno potuit velle quod Christus incarnaretur vel non incarnaretur. Igitur si voluit eum determinate incarnari, igitur est mutatus. Ita mundum producere et non producere. Igitur si determinavit se velle producere, est mutatus."
[15]   Caracciolo, *I Sent.*, d. 38, a. 3 (ed. Schabel, pp. 316–17): "Ideo dico: Quamvis sit ibi determinatio, non est tamen aliqua mutatio, quia non in actu, cum eodem actu numero velit et voluit. Non in potentia voluntatis, quia actum unum habet eundem cum substantia. Non in essentia, patet. Nec est ymaginandum quod Deus primo sit indeterminatus et postea fiat determinatus, ymo ab eterno fuit determinatus. Sed ista determinatio non tollit potentiam quin posset in oppositum, quia contingens erat a potentia libere determinante...
Sed contra predicta remanet maxima difficultas, quia si Deus voluntate sua est causa contingentium, Deus erit causa actuum malorum et peccatorum, que non necessario, ymo contingenter eliciuntur. Respondeo: Ista difficultas sequitur omnem positionem, quia omnis positio ponit Deum esse causam primariam omnium entium. Actus autem mali sunt aliqua entia, saltem quo ad substantiam actus. Ideo dico, ut communiter dicitur, quod Deus causat positivum in actu peccati co-agendo voluntati peccantis. Istud positivum non est malum. Sed non coagit sibi quo ad privationem consequentem, que est malitia."

is exhibited in reality, not following it, by abstracting from pastness, present-
ness, and futurition, and not representing it as present but as indistant by
negative indistance; (3) the divine essence displays this similitude by which it
represents indistantly and therefore infallibly.

Caracciolo's immediate response rejects the theory that the divine essence
can represent contingents for many of the same reasons that the Ideas solution
fails: the divine essence represents all things necessarily, in a simple apprehension, before any act of the will or intellect. In order to distinguish between
contingents that will happen and those that will not, propositional knowledge
is required, and propositions are formed by the intellect. But the intellect cannot even provide knowledge of which side of a contradiction is true until the
divine will makes its determination, since "a future contingent is neither
knowable nor representable before the act of the divine will."[16]

Auriol had anticipated this refutation, which presupposes in part the acceptance of a Scotistic position and a denial of indistance. For Auriol, a future
contingent is determined when the *human* free will puts it into being, and God
does not know it 'beforehand' but indistantly. Caracciolo therefore goes on to
battle indistance. This time Auriol's stance is given in a series of seven conclusions, which although taken in sequence from Auriol's own distinction 38, appear here to be unconnected, and Caracciolo brings to bear a wide variety of
similarly unconnected responses, based on reason and authority.[17]

Auriol's first 'conclusion' states that there is a controversy between theologians and philosophers on the matter of foreknowledge and future contingency. Caracciolo relates that Augustine holds that one should follow the
theological opinion as the truer one, accepting both foreknowledge and future
contingency.[18] Taken out of context, the fifth conclusion, which Caracciolo
calls the main conclusion, appears heretical to one who does not know Auriol:
"God does not know (*intelligit*) the future insofar as it is future, and so this is
not true: 'God knows the Antichrist is future',"[19] and Caracciolo first re-

---

[16]   Auriol's position is given on pp. 319–20, and refuted on pp. 320–21. See Caracciolo, *I
Sent.*, d. 39, a. 1 (ed. Schabel, p. 320–21): "Ostendo quod impossibile est futurum contingens rep-
resentari in divina essentia... Omne illud cuius divina essentia est representativa potest apprehendi simplici apprehensione. Sed hoc impossibile est de futuro contingenti... quia divina essentia est representativa termini, non complexionis. Complexionem autem causat actus intellectus. Illud autem quod divina essentia obiective representat, precedit omnem actum intellectus divini.
Minor patet, quia impossibile est representare futurum nec apprehendi nisi simul apprehendatur
ipsum esse possibile esse et non esse. Hoc autem est complexio... aliqua futura contingentia sunt
possibilia que numquam erunt, aliqua erunt. Quero unde proveniat ista differentia? Non a repre-
sentativo. Igitur ab aliquo altero, scilicet a voluntate determinante." And giving his own opinion
(p. 322): "Futurum contingens nec est cognoscibile nec representabile ante actum divine voluntatis."
[17]   See Caracciolo, *I Sent.*, d. 39, a. 2 (ed. Schabel, pp. 325–7).
[18]   Caracciolo, *I Sent.*, d. 39, a. 2 (ed. Schabel, pp. 327–8): "Contra quamlibet conclusionem opinionis istius arguo sic: Contra primam est plana auctoritas Augustini..."
[19]   Caracciolo, *I Sent.*, d. 39, a. 2 (ed. Schabel, p. 326–7): "Quinta conclusio: Quod Deus
non intelligit futurum in quantum futurum, ita quod ista non est vera: 'Deus intelligit Antichristum futurum'..."

sponds again through Augustine, citing his statements against Cicero. Caracciolo is aware, however, that Auriol's position is more complex than the conclusion appears to allow, because Auriol maintains indistant knowledge. Nevertheless, Caracciolo denies this and gives more authorities.[20]

Two conclusions concern indistance, which Caracciolo rejects with reasoned arguments. In distinction 38 he had declared that God cannot abstract from futurition indistantly, because some distance is necessary for and implied by the object's being possible and contingent, and not necessary. By 'possible' Caracciolo understands that the contingent is distant from its real actuality.[21] Now he reiterates that there is a distance between the object of foreknowledge and its *actuality*, but that this does not affect foreknowledge. On the other hand, cognition touches every known thing immediately through the act of knowing, according to Caracciolo, and therefore there is no distance between knowledge and its *object*.[22]

Caracciolo refutes other conclusions with scriptural citations. These conclusions state that humans cannot properly express divine knowledge, and they give Auriol's solutions to the problem posed by revelation. Caracciolo's arguments based on Scripture are nothing new, but it is noteworthy that he knows Auriol's text well enough to cite the latter's three possible explanations of revelation: (1) Such revealed things are necessary and not contingent; (2) God does know the future actuality indistantly, so He can reveal it somehow; (3) it

---

[20] Caracciolo, *I Sent.*, d. 39, a. 2 (ed. Schabel, p. 329): "Contra quintam conclusionem, que est principalior, ostendo primo quod est contra Augustinum... Si dicas quod hoc est verum per indistantiam, non in quantum futurum, contra, quia Augustinus dicit ibidem quod Deus scit quid voluntates nostre facture sint, quid valiture. Unde si homo peccat, hoc est quia Deus peccaturum esse prescivit, et si omnino non peccat, hoc etiam ille prescivit. Secundo, est contra opinionem Magistri... Sed forte dices quod hoc est per indistantiam quia cognoscit actualitatem, sed non in ordine ad instans temporis. Contra, quia subdit quod licet ex aliquo tempore Deus non cognoverit, tamen cognovit futura omnia temporalia atque in eis etiam quid et quantum et quando et quos et de quibus rebus exauditurus et non exauditurus esset, sine initio quando prescivit. Igitur in obiecto intellexit quando... Tertio, ostendo quod repugnat diffinitioni prescientie posite ab Hugone, *De Sacramentis*... Quarto, quod est contra Ieronimum, *Super Ieremiam*...*"
[21] Caracciolo, *I Sent.*, d. 38, a .1 (ed. Schabel, p. 310): "Quinta conclusio, quod intelligere futurum contingens per indistantiam ad futuritionem est contradictio. Probatio: Quia eo ipso aliquod est contingens et futurum quo potest poni et non poni in esse — da oppositum, non erit contingens futurum. Sed abstrahere hoc a futuritione est contradictio, quia ipso facto quod intelligo illud esse ponibile, intelligo ipsum distare a sua reali actualitate, et per consequens sub futuritione."
[22] Caracciolo, *I Sent.*, d. 39, a. 2 (ed. Schabel, pp. 328): "Contra secundam conclusionem ostendo quod procedit in equivoca. Notitiam enim esse expectativam vel rememorativam est dupliciter: Vel quod includat distantiam actus ad obiectum, vel quod obiectum includat distantiam ad suum esse, puta entitas Antichristi in esse cognito distat ab illo tunc quando ponetur in esse reali. Prima distantia non includitur in cognitione futuri contingentis, ymo nullius cognoscibilis, quia omne cognitum attingitur immediate per actum. Secunda distantia includitur in cognitione futuri, sed istud non repugnat intellectioni divine quia Deus intelligit animam Antichristi in esse cognito distare a nunc in quo ponetur in esse reali, alias Deus nesciret pro quanto debet producere Antichristum realiter."

is the intention of the believer that is important, not that propositions about future contingents revealed by God are true. Caracciolo discards all of these.[23]

Landulph Caracciolo goes on to refute Auriol's position yet again in distinction 40.[24] In sum, he knew Auriol's position well, and did not leave much of Auriol's solution untouched, although his most potent arguments were directed at Auriol's notion of the intrinsic will of complacency and the extrinsic will of operation. The fundamental difference between Auriol and Caracciolo lies in their conceptions of God. Auriol strives to preserve God's simple necessity and His atemporality, but Caracciolo thinks that this fails to account for the facts of existence and of revelation. The best alternative, then, is Scotus's theory, and whatever weaknesses remain are common to all solutions.

Caracciolo's treatment of the problem of divine foreknowledge and future contingents presages in some ways what we shall find in Meyronnes and even Marchia. As we shall see, Marchia will develop an important and popular distinction between a human free will's determining itself *de inesse* toward one side of a contradiction without removing its indetermination *de possibili*, and its contingency. On one occasion Caracciolo clearly leans in this direction, and one wonders whether he influenced Marchia.[25] Moreover, it is interesting to note that in Caracciolo's arguments against Auriol there is a strong hint of the controversial tendency at Oxford and later at Paris to appear to dissolve the difference between past and future by focussing on the immutability of God's power in His eternity with respect to creation:

---

[23] Caracciolo, *I Sent.*, d. 39, a. 2 (ed. Schabel, pp. 331–2): "Contra septimam conclusionem, ostendo quod natura termini responsionum salvat quod Deus Pater potuerit predicere futura. Primo quia non cognoscens futurum in quantum futurum non potest ipsum revelare. Secundo, et istud pondero, Deus revelando futurum aut habet de eo determinatam notitiam aut non. Si non, non poterit revelare. Si sic, contradicunt sibi. Dicunt enim, ut patebit in distinctione sequenti, quod nulla propositio de futuro est determinata in divina notitia.

Prima etiam solutio quam ponit ista conclusio est falsa, videlicet quod illa que revelavit Deus determinavit ab eterno, quia tunc Petrus necessario negasset Deum, et Christus fuisset necessario incarnatus etiam secundum eos, quia ex hoc ipsi deducunt quod ex hoc cessaret omne consilium et omnis libertas, si contingens esset determinatum in divina notitia. Secunda responsio non est ad propositum, quia concesso quod Deus cognoscit actualitatem futuri per indistantiam perfectissime, queritur utrum cognoscat distantiam futuri quam revelat, puta 'Christus incarnabitur post mille annos'? Si sic, habetur propositum. Si non, non poterit revelare. Et tamen Christus per distantiam revelavit cum dixit de Petro 'Priusquam gallus cantet', etc. Tertia responsio etiam non valet. Propositiones enim alique de futuris revelatis in scriptura non solum ponuntur ut fide credamus Deum intelligere per indistantiam et modo ineffabili, ymo ut sciatur hora determinata qua fient revelata, et quod tantum tempus preteribit vel erit futurum, ut fiant, quod horam et distantiam Deus revelans non ignorat, sicut Danieli revelatum est tempus ebdomodarum."

[24] See Caracciolo, *I Sent.*, d. 40, a. 1 (ed. Schabel, pp. 334–6).

[25] Caracciolo, *I Sent.*, d. 38, a. 1 (ed. Schabel, p. 310): "Sexta conclusio, quod determinatio futuri ad partem unam sue contingentie per causam libere et contingenter determinantem non tollit ab ipso futuro contingentiam et indeterminationem que competit sibi ex se formaliter. Exemplum: Cum determino quod cras legam per voluntatem meam libere determinantem, quamvis ista, 'me legere', sit determinate partis contradictionis, tamen, quia ista determinatio est in potestate voluntatis determinantis, non tollitur contingentia a futura lectione — ymo remanet indeterminatio sibi formaliter debita, quia possum non legere et possum velle non legere."

Just as in the beginning of the instant of eternity God freely determined a contingent toward one side in a way that He was able to determine toward the opposite, so also He can now. For example, just as in the beginning of eternity He determined Peter to be saved and was able to determine him to be damned, so also He is able to now.[26]

This is because the measure of eternity is absolutely simple and not successive, and whatever 'was' in God's power in the 'beginning', still is, because it is the same 'now' of eternity. Although this idea can be seen less explicitly in the works of, for example, Scotus himself, and perhaps even Lombard, Caracciolo more expressly foreshadows what is to be the heart of the discussion in Adam Wodeham, Thomas Bradwardine, and others a decade or so later, both at Oxford and at Paris.

An Anonymous Caracciolist

There is no doubt that Caracciolo influenced the anonymous author of a commentary in manuscript Vienna, ÖNB 1439 (ff. 1–50), where we also see his slight modifications of Scotus's system. Based on citations, we can guess that this author was a Franciscan who read the *Sentences* at Paris around 1325. His main adversary was Peter Auriol, whom he cites even more frequently than Scotus, "the Doctor."[27] In our author's short question on future contingents, Auriol is again his primary opponent. In this case, he often follows the criticism of Caracciolo, whom he cites very frequently against Auriol in general. Like Caracciolo, this Franciscan responds to Auriol's Borghese *reportatio*.

The second question for distinctions 38 and 39, "Whether God's knowledge with respect to contingents is infallible," is only about 200 lines in length, but in giving various ways in which God can know future contingents, the author presents Auriol's position first, at the end of which he relates in brief Caracciolo's 'four signs of nature' characterization of Auriol's position.[28] Following Caracciolo, our author attacks Auriol's notion of God's extrinsic will of operation. He has two basic criticisms. First, whatever God wills by His will of op-

---

[26]   Caracciolo, *I Sent.*, d. 38, a. 2 (ed. Schabel, p. 314): "Quinta propositio, quod sicut in principio instantis eternitatis Deus libere determinavit contingens ad unam partem ita quod potuit determinare ad oppositum, ita et modo potest. Exemplum: Sicut in principio eternitatis determinavit Petrum salvari, et potuit determinare ipsum dampnari, ita potest modo. Probatio: Agens in mensura simplicima et non successiva eodem modo se habet ad suam determinationem. Eternitas est talis mensura, quia ibi nulla successio. Ideo sicut concipimus modo nostro quod Deus in principio eternitatis libere determinavit ad alteram partem, ita quod potuit determinare ad oppositum, ita et modo potest, cum sit eodem modo in principio eternitatis."

[27]   On the Franciscan identity of the author, his dates, and a complete list of marginal citations and questions, see Russell L. Friedman and Chris Schabel "The Vitality of Franciscan Theology at Paris in the 1320's: MS Wien, Palatinus 1439," AHDLMA 63 (1996), pp. 357–72. For the text of his question on future contingents, see my "Landulphus Caracciolo," pp. 339–43.

[28]   Anon. OFM, *I Sent.*, dd. 38–39, q. 2, a. 1 (ed. Schabel, "Landulphus Caracciolo," p. 339).

eration, like the creation of the world, He wills determinately, otherwise He would produce something determinately without willing it determinately, which is ridiculous. Thus whether this willing is intrinsic or extrinsic, the author seems to say, it is determinate willing.[29] The second criticism attacks Auriol's own idea of divine simplicity and necessity in identifying God's actions with God: either this operation *is* the Creator or a creature:

> That operation is not the Creator; therefore a creature. Therefore it is put into being via a simple willing, and this proves my point, because by the same reasoning another [operation as a creature] will be put into being through that willing or through another operation, and one will ask about that [operation] *ad infinitum*.[30]

According to this author, then, God's activities *ad extra* have to be grounded in God, *ad intra*, at some point.

The author then asks in article two how God's foreknowledge is infallible. Following Scotus, Auriol, and probably Caracciolo, he treats the positions based on Ideas and the presence of things to eternity, rejecting them both. Then he presents Auriol's position based on abstraction and indistance. Following Caracciolo he rejects this stance and defends with Augustine, other *antiqui*, and Scripture, the strict interpretation of God as *fore*knowing, suggesting even that Auriol's view is heretical. It is true, he says, that God's knowledge abstracts from every difference of measuring time, but it is also true that God knows things objectively and His knowledge exists along with every temporal difference. God gets infallible certainty because His intellect knows the determinations of His will, and our author gives a Scotist explanation, based on no less than five instants of nature.[31] Likewise, contingency is in the world from

---

[29] Anon. OFM, *I Sent.*, dd. 38–39, q. 2, a. 1 (ed. Schabel, pp. 339–40): "Contra Petrum Landulphus: Contra: Quicumque vult utrumque contradictoriorum in eodem instanti de eodem, nihil vult. Sed hoc ponit ista opinio. Ergo voluntas divina nihil vult de re. Sed ulterius ponit quod per operationem ponit rem in esse determinato. Ergo implicat contradictionem. Secundo, voluntas divina ab eterno voluit mundum esse in tali instanti. Quero utrum voluit vel non voluit, propter primum principium. Si sic, habetur propositum. Si non, ergo non fuit productus. Tertio, voluntas per te elicit operationem. Vel ergo vult illa determinate vel non. Si sic, habetur propositum. Si non, ergo producit determinate quod non vult determinate, quod est ridiculosum."

[30] Anon. OFM, *I Sent*, dd. 38–39, q. 2, a. 1 (ed. Schabel, p. 340): "Motivum alterius doctoris non valet. Quando enim dicit quod Deus operetur ad operationem elicitivam, hoc falsum est. Sed per suum velle simplex eternum ponit rem in tali esse. Probo: Illa operatio non est creator; [vel] ergo creatura. Ergo ponitur in esse per simplex velle, et habetur propositum, quia pari ratione alia ponetur in esse per illud velle vel per aliam operationem, et queretur de illa ad infinitum."

[31] Anon. OFM, *I Sent.*, dd. 38–39, q. 2, a. 2 (ed. Schabel, pp. 342–3): "Contra: Augustinus… Item, Magister in littera… Item, Ieronimus *Super Ieremiam*… Item, Hugo…. Item, negare revelationem de futuris contingentibus est hereticum, quia contra sacram scripturam, nam revelavit incarnationem, negationem Petri, activam proditionem etiam Iude. Sed hoc totum negat illa opinio. Ergo etc. Deus nihil revelat quod ignorat. Ad motivum suum dicendum quod cognitio Dei abstrahit ab omni differentia temporis mensurative, sed cognoscat obiective et stat cum omni differentia temporis, sicut essentia Dei."

God's free and contingent will, although our author carefully states that in the case of created wills, they *concause* their effects.[32]

Francis of Meyronnes

Francis of Meyronnes (or de Mayronis, ca. 1288– ca. 1330), nicknamed among other things the 'Prince of the Scotists', was yet another Franciscan who attacked directly Auriol's 'positive' solution to the problem and his refutations of Scotus. An extremely prolific author, Meyronnes was well known in the later Middle Ages for a variety of theological and philosophical writings. Many of these works were edited in the Early Modern period, but very little has received modern philological treatment, with the notable exception of his dispute as Franciscan bachelor of the *Sentences* with his Benedictine *socius* of the 1320–21 academic year, Pierre Roger, later Pope Clement VI. He became master of theology at Paris in 1323, having like Auriol the help of Pope John XXII. In 1324, as Franciscan provincial minister of his native Provence, he was with John in Avignon, but he died in Piacenza a few years later.[33]

Doctor: Doctor ergo dicit quod Deus determinate cognoscit omnia preterita, presentia, et futura. Probatio: Ille intellectus qui cognoscit determinate rationem determinantem, determinate <cognoscit> quodcumque contingens futurum. Sed intellectus divinus cognoscit illam rationem, scilicet voluntatem divinam. Ergo etc. Ymaginatur Doctor quod intellectus in primo signo cognoscit omnia ad intra in divinis, et obtulit voluntati et complacuit voluntati complacentia simplici; in secundo obtulit obiecta secundaria, et complacuerunt; in tertio, obtulit ista fienda; in quarto, voluntas determinavit; in quinto intellexit et cognovit determinate instans in quo <erunt>."

[32]   Anon. OFM, *I Sent.*, dd. 38–39, q. 2, a. 1 (ed. Schabel, p. 340): "Ponuntur quatuor conclusiones secundum principia doctoris. Prima, quod prima et principalis causa determinationis contingentie contingentis est voluntas divina libera. Probatur: Quidquid potest Deus mediante causa secunda effective, potest per se et voluntatem. Voluntas ergo divina vel causat necessario vel contingenter sive libere. Si necessario, causabit quantum potest. Ergo cum sit prima, causabit totum et tolletur ordo essentialis. Ergo est causa prima causans contingenter. Secundo, in causis essentialiter ordinatis, si prima est necessaria, et omnis; et tunc nulla erit in rebus contingentia.

Secunda conclusio, quod voluntas creata est causa concausans sive partialis. Probo: In rebus creatis video effectum necessarium et contingentem. Ergo reducuntur in aliquam causam priorem; non in primam, quia illa solum contingenter causat. Ergo in aliam que potest utroque modo causare.

Tertia conclusio, quod omnis alia causa in creaturis preter voluntatem causat necessario. Probo: Omnis causa causans naturaliter causat necessario. Omnia alia causa in creaturis preter voluntatem liberam causat naturaliter. Ergo etc.

Quarta conclusio est quod quamquam causat naturaliter et necessario, tamen causat effectum contingentem. Probo: Quandocumque ad effectum concurrunt due cause, una partialis a qua omnis alia causa dependet, effectus sortitur denominationem ab illa. Sed prima est semper libera et contingens. Ergo qualitercumque causa esset, effectus est semper contingens et etiam naturalis."

[33]   See Jeanne Barbet, ed., *François de Meyronnes — Pierre Roger: Disputatio (1320–1321)* (Paris 1961). Girard Etzkorn has recently edited another text from Meyronnes: "Franciscus de Mayronis: A Newly Discovered Treatise on Intuitive and Abstractive Cognition," FcS 54 (1994–7), pp. 15–50. For a list of Meyronnes's philosophical works and the secon-

Not surprisingly, Meyronnes has left us one of the most popular *Sentences* commentaries of the period. The main version, the so-called *Conflatus*, was printed several times early on and survives in over one hundred manuscripts containing at least one of the four books, book I being by far the most popular. Other redactions survive in a couple of dozen manuscripts. His success, however, may be due to his conservativism and clarity of presentation. As his sobriquet indicates, he tended to defend Scotus, having probably studied under the Subtle Doctor in Paris in 1304–07. In the fifteenth century a particular Meyronnist branch and school of Scotism was attributed to him. This gives the impression, however, that he was not completely dependent on the Subtle Doctor for answers, and instead developed Scotus's theories, a hypothesis that appears to have been born out by some recent studies.[34]

Pierre Roger's *Sentences* commentary, however, has not been identified, but William Courtenay has studied his disputation with Meyronnes in light of the distinction between God's absolute and ordained powers. Because Roger saw it as impossible and implicitly contradictory for a *beatus* to experience the beatific vision without experiencing the persons of the Trinity or one of the persons without the others, Courtenay infers that Roger rejected the Scotist position that God can do otherwise than He actually does.[35] As Courtenay states, this rejection of DPO/DPA reminds one of Peter Auriol's rejection, and one might speculate that Roger's position on future contingents was influenced by Auriol's treatment, which included a rejection of the position that God, at least via His intrinsic will, could know or will other than He does. This rejection of the contingency of God's intrinsic will, as we have seen, was accompanied by a denial of foreknowledge per se.

The Franciscan Meyronnes upheld the Scotist distinction between DPO and DPA, and Scotus's four instants of nature, or 'signs', in the process of divine willing and foreknowing.[36] It is not surprising then to find Meyronnes attacking Auriol's position in the context of future contingents, both on indistance and on the neutrality of propositions.[37] I shall concentrate on the expanded treat-

---

dary literature, see Olga Weijers, ed., *Le travail intellectuel à la faculté des arts de Paris: textes et maîtres (ca. 1200–1500)*, II, C–F (Turnhout 1996), pp. 94–8.

[34] For a discussion of Meyronnes's commentaries and question lists from the unprinted versions, see H. Rossmann, "Die Sentenzenkommentare des Franz von Meyronnes OFM," FzS 53 (1971), 129–227. For a recent analysis of his thought, see e.g. Tachau, *Vision and Certitude*, 327–32, on epistemology.

[35] Courtenay, *Capacity and Volition*, p. 128.

[36] Courtenay, *Capacity and Volition*, p. 127. On future contingents and Meyronnes's relation to Scotus, see Schwamm, *Das göttliche Vorherwissen*, pp. 151–67. See Marco Rossini, "*Scientia Dei conditionata*: Francesco di Meyronnes e i futuri contingenti," *Medioevo* 19 (1993), pp. 287–322, for a fresh and lengthy look at Meyronnes's views and the general context. Rossini does not relate Meyronnes to his immediate Franciscan predecessors Auriol, Caracciolo, and Marchia, however.

[37] Boehner calls him a faithful disciple of Scotus in this regard (Boehner, *The Tractatus*, p. 84). Tachau (*Vision and Certitude*, pp. 327–32) sees him taking a Scotist stance epistemologically, against Auriol, though Meyronnes develops Scotus's position, as he does with foreknowledge. Halverson ("Peter Aureol and the Re-emergence," pp. 211–13) holds that Meyronnes simply

ment in the *Conflatus*, which, although not overly long in absolute terms, goes straight to the heart of the disagreement between Scotus and Auriol: question one, "Whether God has certain knowledge (*certam notitiam*) concerning future contingents;" two, "Whether the act of the divine will precedes the act of the intellect in future contingents;" three, "Whether the mutability of contingents can stand with the infallibility of divine knowledge;" and four, "Whether future contingents have determinate truth."[38]

In question one, article four, Meyronnes quickly refutes the solutions based on the divine essence, Ideas, and eternal presence, then attacks Auriol's notion of indistance, without naming Auriol explicitly. Meyronnes understands Auriol's position, but remarks that such a negative solution to the problem of God's knowledge of things outside Himself does not avoid the difficulties. Like Caracciolo, Meyronnes believes that there cannot be such indistance between God and things, for in that case God would know them necessarily, and He would not be able to distinguish between futures and non-futures, and possibles and non-possibles. God does so distinguish, and only through a positive distance. Although this was the same objection Scotus directed at the Ideas solution, Meyronnes would be noted for it explicitly 150 years later by Francesco della Rovere and John Foxal during the Louvain dispute.[39] Auriol did try to explain how God distinguished between what was future and what was not by saying, basically, that they differed, just as an ass and a man differ, whether they exist now or not. Still, the objection about his negative solution attacks a true weak point in Auriol's defense. Meyronnes opts for the Scotist position that God knows future contingents through the determination of the divine will, which is contingent. He is careful to point out, immediately after refuting Auriol, that his own solution is an affirmative one.[40]

---

reiterated Scotus's argument in his related treatment of predestination.

[38] Franciscus de Mayronis (Meyronnes), *In primum Sententiarum foecundissimum scriptum sive conflatus nominatum*, dd. 38–39, q. 1 (ed. Venice 1520,fol. 112rbH): "Utrum Deus habeat certam notitiam de futuris contingentibus," q. 2 (fol. 113vbQ): "Utrum in futuris contingentibus actus voluntatis divine precedat actum intellectus," q. 3 (fol. 114rbG): "Utrum cum infallibilitate divine scientie poterit stare mutabilitas contingentium," and q. 4 (fol. 114vaM): "Utrum futura contingentia habeant veritatem determinatam." I have inspected what is apparently a *Reportatio* in ms. Admont, Bibliothek der Benediktinerabtei 91, which does not appear to contain anything absent in the *Conflatus*. In Admont the one question for d. 38 (ff. 67rb–68vb) corresponds to the *Conflatus*, dd. 38–39, except that a. 4 combines material in the *Conflatus*, q. 1, a. 4, and q. 2. At 68vb Admont gives d. 39, which goes back to the *Conflatus*, d. 36, q. 5 (!), and then for d. 40 Admont has the *Conflatus's* d. 40–41, q. 3 (69vb–70va).

[39] Cf. Georgius Benignus Salviati, *De Arcanis Dei* III, cc. 10 and 19 (ed. Etzkorn, p. 153, ll. 587–8, p. 174, ll. 482–8).

[40] Meyronnes, *I Sent.*, dd. 38–39, q. 1, a. 4 (ed. Venice, fol. 113vaK–L): "Quarta conclusio, quod non cognoscit ea per indistantiam sicut dicunt aliqui quod Deus per indistantiam ea cognoscit. Quod probant, licet enim ea que non sunt presentia Deo esse non possint positive, tamen nullatenus distant a Deo, cum ipse sit indistans omni dimensioni temporis, sicut et loci. Sed istud non potest stare. Ratio enim negativa non videtur esse sufficiens representativum alicuius positivi, sed bene e converso. Et preterea, talem indistantiam respectu omnium habet, et ideo necessario talia cognosceret, et per consequens talia necessario essent. Preterea, talem indistantiam habet respectu omnium futurorum et non futurorum, possibilium et non possibilium, quia nullum

Unlike Caracciolo, Meyronnes explicitly accepts Scotus's theory of instants of nature, or signs, in the account of God's knowledge of future contingents, and thus can be called more a true Scotist in this context, justifying his fifteenth-century reputation. Meyronnes's version here looks a bit like Scotus's first way, however, because Meyronnes de-emphasizes the role of the divine essence, which Scotus added in his second way to avoid the 'discursiveness' of the first way, attributed to Henry of Ghent.[41] Perhaps Meyronnes plays down the role of the divine essence because of Auriol's criticisms of Scotus on this point.[42]

Meyronnes brings up one of Auriol's objections to his position: the will is the same as the essence and knowledge, which are immutable and hence necessary, so how can it be the basis of contingency? Meyronnes makes a rather odd distinction:

> I maintain that one must understand an active determination in the divine will and a passive one in the determined creature. But what is this active determination in God's will? I claim that it is nothing but the active production by which the will itself produces the objects in willed being (*esse volito*). There is therefore in the will a respect of reason consequent on the will, just as there is in the intellect a respect of reason consequent on the intellect... Thus when the intellect intuitively knows

ab eo positive distat. Et tamen dicimus quod aliter novit futura quam non futura; ergo etc. Confirmatur, quia omnis ratio negativa reducitur ad affirmativam, nec etiam aliqua negativa potest esse simpliciter prima.
    Dico ergo conclusionem affirmativam, scilicet quod Deus cognoscit omnia futura contingentia et etiam presentia per voluntatem suam, sive per determinationem proprie voluntatis, quia per propriam causam cognoscitur effectus; sed voluntas divina est propria causa contigentis; ergo etc." Rossini, "*Scientia Dei conditionata*," pp. 313–14, discusses Meyronnes on Auriol's indistance solution, but he does not identify it with Auriol.
    [41] Meyronnes, *I Sent.*, dd. 38–39, q. 3 (ed. Venice, fol. 114rbG–H): "Sed ad intelligendum istam veritatem oportet imaginari in complexionibus de quibus est scientia quatuor signa. Primum est in quo divina essentia representat intellectui divino terminos simplices complexionum tam necessariarum quam possibilium vel contingentium. Secundum signum est in quo divinus intellectus format complexiones talium terminorum determinate possibiles et necessarias, quia ille sunt ex terminis note, quia vero contingentes non habent evidentiam ex ipsis terminis ipsas concepit ut neutras. Tertium signum est in quo divina voluntas tales complexiones ut neutras sibi per intellectum presentatas determinat ad alteram partem, dicens 'hoc erit,' 'hoc non erit.' Quartum signum est in quo divinus intellectus aspiciens ad divinam voluntatem determinatam videt illam propositionem quam sibi ut neutram presentavit, et ex tali determinatione quam videt cognoscit propositiones contingentes, scilicet 'hoc erit,' 'hoc non erit.'" Recall that Scotus held that in sign four the intellect knew the determination of the will through the essence, as the basis of knowing.
    [42] Thus in q. 1, a. 4 (ed. Venice, fol. 113rbH–vaI), Meyronnes says: "Deus non cognoscit futura contingentia per suam essentiam, sicut aliqui dixerunt moti, ex hoc quod ipsa est primum obiectum intellectus divini. Probo sic: Nam divina essentia cuiuscumque est principium vel representativum necessario et uniformiter representat, et divinus intellectus necessario intelligit quantum est ex se quicquid intelligit; et ideo si divina essentia futurum contingens representaret, ipsum uniformiter et necessario representaret, et divinus intellectus necessario intelligeret. Et sic sequeretur vel quod esset necessarium, sicut esset necessario notum, vel quod divinus intellectus deciperetur, quorum utrumque est impossibile. Evenirent enim omnia de necessitate."

this respect, it knows the term, because a respect cannot be known except through a true term.[43]

Meyronnes's phrasing and terminology are very much like the passage in Auriol's Borghese *Reportatio* (quoted in chapter six) that Caracciolo presented and attacked. The difference is that Auriol calls this active determination of the divine will an external operation, while the will *ad intra* remains indifferent, but Meyronnes aims at something that is internal, not the will itself, but something by which the will determinately produces and determines future contingents "in willed being." Meyronnes reveals his debt to Caracciolo here, as when he repeats these words in question four in a passage that Fernando of Cordova would copy during the Louvain quarrel 150 years later (see Epilogue), concluding:

> Just as something productive requires a producible, a determined productive thing required a determined producible. In the same way, just as something determinative requires a determinable, what determines requires something determined. But the divine will determines, so something else is determined. But this can only be a future contingent.[44]

By thus modifying the Scotistic position, in response to Auriol's objections based on divine simplicity, Meyronnes thinks he can retain the basis of contingency and foreknowledge in the divine will. Since he holds that God knows future contingents via the will's determinations such that they have determinate truth in God, Meyronnes believes that, by resorting to the distinction between necessity *secundum quid* and *simpliciter*, and by employing the composite and

---

[43] Meyronnes, *I Sent.*, dd. 38–39, q. 1, a. 4 (ed. Venice, fol. 113vaL): "...quia divina voluntas ita videtur ex se invariabilis sicut essentia et intellectus; ergo videtur quod quicquid representat uniformiter et necessario representabit, sicut essentia," to which Meyronnes responds (fol. 113va-bM–N): "Dico quod oportet intelligere unam determinationem activam in voluntate divina, et unam passivam in creatura determinata. Sed quid est illa determinatio activa in voluntate Dei? Dico quod non [13vb] est nisi productio activa qua voluntas ipsa obiecta producit in esse volito. Est ergo respectus rationis consequens voluntatem in voluntate, sicut respectus rationis est in intellectu consequens intellectum. Sed quomodo ens rationis potest esse principium cognoscendi rem? Dico quod non est inconveniens quod respectus rationis non confictus a ratione, sed derelictus, sit ratio cognoscendi rem. Tunc ergo intellectus intuitive cognoscendo respectum istum cognoscit et terminum, quia respectus cognosci non potest nisi per verum terminum."

[44] Meyronnes, *I Sent.*, dd. 38–39, a. 2 (ed. Venice, fol. 114vbP–Q): "Omni productioni active correspondet necessario aliqua passiva; sed divina voluntas active producit ista futura contingentia in esse volito, quod non est aliud nisi active ea determinare; ergo necessario aliquid est productum. Non aliquid quod sit in Deo formaliter; ergo necessario aliquid est in creatura vel in futuro contingenti. Sed ipsummet producitur in esse volito; ergo determinatur passive. Ergo etc.

Confirmatur, quia sicut productivum requirit producibile, ita determinatum productivum determinatum producibile. Et eodem modo sicut determinativum requirit determinabile, ita determinans determinatum. Voluntas autem divina est determinans; ergo aliquid <aliud> est determinatum. Illud autem non potest esse nisi futurum contingens."

divided senses, we can retain contingency in the world.[45] In fact, given that God's *contingent* willing is the basis of what exists and the foundation of foreknowledge, Meyronnes even accepts that God's knowledge is therefore "conditional."[46]

When Auriol denied this contingency in God's will and the validity of the distinction between the composite and divided senses in propositions pertaining to God's intrinsic willing, he considered it necessary to deny both foreknowledge per se and the determinate truth of future contingent propositions. Meyronnes has already explained how the determination of the divine will does not entail the necessity of the future, and in question four he accompanies this with a defense of Bivalence, probably following his Franciscan brother Francis of Marchia, who lectured the previous year (see chapter nine). Although in his Scotist account such propositions are neutral in the second sign, Meyronnes defends determinate truth in future contingent propositions against Auriol's assault. Meyronnes emphasizes that scriptural revelations require determinate truth,[47] but he also asserts on purely logical grounds that the Law of Contradictories holds universally, such that of any pair of contradictory propositions, one is true and the other is false. Meyronnes supplies Auriol's objection that the law does not hold for propositions about the future, although Meyronnes does not mention Auriol or Aristotle explicitly. In a short passage given almost in dialogue form, Meyronnes simply refuses to agree with Auriol, and says the law is obvious, known in itself. Then Meyronnes sidesteps the issue by saying that the Law of Contradictories is irrelevant anyway, because they are not talking about a pair of contradictory propositions, but a singular proposition only. By the First Principle, the Principle of Bivalence, any singular proposition is either true or false, he claims. Auriol had denied even this, so Meyronnes finally states that Auriol's arguments could just as well be applied to present-tensed propositions: in the moment in which God produces grace, "Grace exists" is determinately true, but it can be false in the divided sense since God can do other than He does dividedly. Likewise, "The Antichrist will exist" is determinately true, and yet it can be false in the divided sense, and contingency is thereby saved along with determinate truth. Here Meyronnes approaches some contemporary Oxford opinions (see chapter ten), although, again, his source may be Caracciolo.[48]

---

[45]   In q. 4, a. 1 (ed. Venice, fol. 114vb, N), Meyronnes defends the determinate truth of future contingents in God, beginning "Dico quod futura contingentia habent veritatem determinatam in Deo." In q. 4, aa. 3–4 (fol. 115raC–rbF), Meyronnes explains how contingency is in the divine will and in the world by using distinction between the composite and divided senses, a distinction he employs quite often.

[46]   See Meyronnes, *I Sent.*, dd. 38–39, q. 3 (ed. Venice, fol. 114vaK–L). On this, the distinction between necessity *secundum quid* and *simpliciter*, and the use of composite and divided senses in Meyronnes, see Rossini, "*Scientia Dei conditionata.*"

[47]   See Meyronnes, *I Sent.*, dd. 38–39, q. 4, a. 1 (ed. Venice, fol. 114vbN) and a. 2 (fol. 114vbQ).

[48]   Meyronnes, *I Sent.*, dd. 38–39, q. 4, a. 2 (ed. Venice, fol.114vbQ–115raB), letting (M) be Meyronnes's position, and (A) Auriol's: "Quarto, quia cuiuslibet contradictionis altera pars

Meyronnes concludes his entire treatment of the problem with another passage that Fernando of Cordova would quote verbatim, including an assertion that parallels Aristotle's and Auriol's but with the opposite intent: "Concerning anything about which it was once true to say 'it will exist' it was always true to say it would exist, because for the same reason it was true to say this an hour beforehand, it was also true a thousand years beforehand, and a thousand thousand years beforehand, and so on to infinity."[49] What Auriol found intolerable, Meyronnes embraces.

In sum, then, perhaps because of the extensive refutations of his predecessors Caracciolo and Marchia, Meyronnes's counterattack on Auriol amounts to a flat-out rejection of some of the main points of Auriol's stance, from a Scotistic perspective, borrowing from both Caracciolo and Marchia. Nevertheless, Meyronnes's impact on this issue was immediate and enduring.[50]

Two Meyronnists: Himbert of Garda and Pastor of Serrescuderio

Landulph Caracciolo was not the only Franciscan successor of Auriol who developed a following on the issue of foreknowledge and future contingents. As we shall see, Francis of Marchia was the most successful in attracting adherents, but Francis of Meyronnes's exposition of Scotus drew its own imitators. Judging from his explicit citations and the examples he gives, the Francis-

---

est vera. Sed nunc est ista vera vel falsa: 'Antichristus erit.' Si vera, habetur propositum. Si falsa, tunc eius contradictoria erit vera: 'Antichristus non erit,' et hoc est propositum. Et eo modo possunt fieri Deo subcontrarie in contingenti materia false, eo quod ambe negarentur, sicut predicte.

(A) Dicunt tamen aliqui quod non est contradictio in propositionibus de futuro. (M) Sed contra, quia in eis est affirmatio et negatio. (A) Ideo concedunt. Sed tamen dicunt quod nec sunt vere nec false determinate. (M) Contra, quia altera pars contradictionis vel est vera vel falsa. (A) Sed isti dicunt quod lex contradictoriorum ibi non tenet. (M) Contra, quia propositio per se nota in aliqua materia negari non debet. Ideo dico quod necessario est tenendum tamquam conclusum per principium primum complexum quod altera sit determinative vera, quia 'de quolibet est affirmatio vel negatio vera'. (A) Dicunt tamen aliqui quod alterutra est vera, sed non altera. (M) Sed hoc nihil est, quia licet aliquod commune possit esse indifferens ad utrumque contradictoriorum, non tamen aliquod singulare. Sed hic est questio de ista singulari propositione. Preterea, negato determinate altero contradictoriorum, ponitur reliquum, aliter non essent opposita immediata. (A) Sed tamen instantur contra hoc, quia si est ista vera determinate, 'Antichristus erit', ponatur oppositum inesse, quia hoc est possibile Deo. Ergo quando ista propositio prolata fuit, fuit vera et falsa, et sic simul vera et falsa. Et similiter de ista, 'Mundus semper movebitur'. (M) Dico quod iste instantie ita bene concluderent de presenti sicut de futuro, quia in eodem instanti quo Deus producit gratiam, ista propositio est vera, 'Gratia est'; et in eodem instanti posset eam non producere, et tunc esset falsa illa que prius erat vera. Dico quod ista que nunc est vera de presenti, potest in eodem instanti esse falsa in sensu divisionis, non tamen in sensu compositionis. Deus enim in sensu compositionis in illo instanti in quo produxit gratiam non potest non producere, sed bene in sensu divisionis."

[49] Meyronnes, *I Sent.*, dd. 38–39, a. 4 (ed. Venice, fol. 115rbE): "De omni de quo fuit verum dicere quandoque 'erit' semper fuit verum dicere quoniam erit, quia eadem ratione qua fuit verum a mille annis et a mille millibus, et sic in infinitum sicut de una hora."

[50] In Vat. lat. 4269 (ff. 1–72) there is an abbreviation of a text which, based on a quick reading, may come from Paris in this period. It deals with the ideas of Meyronnes, but appears not to have material related to Auriol on future contingents.

can Himbert of Garda probably lectured on the *Sentences* in the early or mid-1320s somewhere on the continent, perhaps in Italy, but probably not in Paris, although he had been a student of theology at Paris before 1320.[51] Himbert is almost certainly to be identified with the author of the commentary in manuscript 1584 of the Jagiellonska library in Krakow, which is probably another redaction of the same lectures.[52]

---

[51] Vat. lat. 1091 contains books I–III, for which one volume would suffice for a critical edition. Books I and III are called *reportationes* in the explicits (ff. 73v, 182r). Labelled a Franciscan twice (75r, 182r), he is called Garda twice (75r and 182r), Gardia once (136v, book II's explicit), and *magister* Himbertus twice (183v). Himbert refers to the time he "*was* in Paris," with Master Guy Terrena, the Carmelite, who left before 1320 (7r; cf. Dumont, "New Questions," p. 341, n. 2). Although he follows Meyronnes (whether the *Conflatus* or another redaction, I cannot tell), he changes some examples. In the context of predestination, where Meyronnes mentions the "paterfamilias" with two sons, only one of whom will inherit (*I Sent.*, dd. 40–41, q. 3 [ed. Venice 1505–07, fol. 126rb]), Himbert adds "sicut fit in Anglia ubi fit ex consuetudine" (69v), and when citing an Oxford scholar, he says, "Et hic dicit unus Oxon. quod sic" (19v). Thus he was on the continent. Where Meyronnes gives a general example of inferiors appealing to superiors in secular and ecclesiastical affairs (ed. Venice 1505–07, fol. 125vb), Himbert adds, "sicut quando secularum appellatur ad imperatorem, regularum ad papam" (68v), which may indicate that he was at an Italian (or, less likely, German) *studium*.

[52] That is, on ff. 39ra–106va. Tachau, *Vision and Certitude*, p. 318, n. 11, quotes a passage from this ms. (ff. 42vb–43ra), and it is found essentially verbatim in Vat. lat. 1091 (16v), although the order of the second and third arguments is reversed. The text of Krakow 1584 and Vat. lat. 1091 closely match in the context of future contingents as well. The question lists (Krakow, ff. 106vb–108ra; Vatican, ff. 74r–75r) are also virtually identical, with two exceptions: (1) Krakow's d. 48, which ends book I, is placed between dd. 29–30 and dd. 31–32 in the Vatican ms., thus causing the explicits to differ, although the end of d. 47 is the same in both mss.; (2) their prologues, and hence incipits, also differ: Vat. lat. 1091 has five questions, and only the brief q. 2 (10r–11r) and q. 5 (16r–) are contained in Krakow, matching its q. 3 (40rb–41ra) and q. 5 (42rb–). Stegmüller, *Repertorium* I, pp. 169–170, gives incipits, explicits, and questions from the Vatican manuscript, but notes that Vat. lat. 1091's large question one (1r–10r) is contained separately in two fragments (Assisi 659 and Paris BN 1010), whereas the whole of book I is extant in Chambéry, Bibliothèque de la ville 23. The Chambéry ms., Stegmüller notes, has a different incipit from Vat. lat. 1091, and in fact it matches the Krakow ms.

Here is the probable explanation: Himbert lectured on the *Sentences* after Meyronnes (1321) but probably before the summer of 1323 and perhaps, in the case of book one, in the fall of 1321. This redaction is witnessed by Chambéry and Krakow, in which, as Tachau notes, Aquinas is referred to as simply "Thomas," and in her quotation Auriol is "magister" and presumably still alive. Himbert soon began reworking the first two questions of the prologue into one large question, which has its own explicit, stating that the work is subject to the "correctione doctorum nostrorum" and for the honor of Christ "cui est honor et gloria per infinita secula eterna seculorum, amen." This appears to have been a separate treatise then, contained by itself in the Assisi and Paris mss., and in the Vatican ms. it replaced the first two questions of the Krakow-Chambéry version. Since Auriol is still "magister" (6v), perhaps it also predates his death. Himbert then changed two of the next three questions, and rewrote the rest of the commentary with minor alterations. Vat. lat. 1091 is the sole witness for this redaction, in which Aquinas is now sometimes "Sanctus Thomas" (e.g. 20r, 32v, 34v, 69r), but often the simple "Thomas" is left as it was (e.g. 10r, 35v, 69r). It is notable that Krakow's question list skips its first four questions and only begins with the final question of the prologue where it joins Vat. lat. 1091. The table's explicit reads "Explicit tabula super primum *Sententiarum* de reportationibus" (108rb), i.e. *re-*

Oddly, Himbert combines distinctions 37 and 38 and asks "whether there is contingency in things." Like Meyronnes, he answers this question in the conventional Scotist way in the small article one, but he then turns to predestination. Here Himbert paraphrases Meyronnes's distinctions 40–41, specifically question three, although he is a little clearer than Meyronnes about the severity of the problem: "Why did God create my soul after He knew that I would die in mortal sin and be damned in the end?" Meyronnes admits that it all boils down to the inscrutable will of God, but Himbert is more blunt, repeatedly stating that it is "Because He willed it," "Because He likes it," and "He willed it because it pleased Him." In other words, "Just because." Although Himbert still holds to a vague notion that sin is involved in reprobation, he nearly approaches the double-predestinarian stance we shall find in Rimini.[53] After Auriol, predestinarian views multiply.

Although Himbert does cite Auriol on occasion in other contexts, he does not in his brief discussion of foreknowledge and predestination. Pastor of Serrescuderio does, however. Like Meyronnes, Pastor was from southern France, and he probably studied in Avignon at the Franciscan *studium*, perhaps under Meyronnes himself, in the 1320s. Finding himself on the papal side of the dispute between John XXII and Michael of Cesena, Pastor became Franciscan provincial minister for Provence, probably in early 1329, but he resigned his position before lecturing on the *Sentences* in Paris in 1332–33. After his lectures Pastor was once again provincial minister of Provence from 1334–37, having become master of theology in 1333. In this period he reworked his commentary on all four books of the *Sentences*, which survives solely in his autograph. He afterwards rose to the rank of bishop, archbishop, and finally cardinal at the end of 1350, and he died in 1356.[54]

Pastor proves conclusively that administrative success is not closely connected to scholarly brilliance, and he seems to have been an unoriginal theologian. The reason he cites Auriol is because he chose to paraphrase Meyronnes's *Conflatus*, distinction 38–39, more fully than had Himbert, and so along with the attacks on the solutions based on the representation in the divine essence, divine Ideas, and eternal presence, Pastor follows Meyronnes's refutation of Auriol's indistance theory, before giving his Scotist opinion based on the determinations of the divine will. The only notable difference I can find between Pastor's abbreviated paraphrase and Meyronnes's original, besides an

---

portationes plural. The remark that Himbert "was in Paris" is contained in the *new* prologue, so it does not rule out the possibility that he lectured on the *Sentences* at Paris in 1321–22.

[53] Himbertus de Garda, *I Sent.*, dd. 37–38, a. 2 (Vat. lat. 1091, f. 68v): "Cur Deus creavit animam meam postquam sciebat me mori in peccato mortali et finaliter dampnatum? ... de hoc nulla causa est nisi voluntas divina... nisi quia vult... 'fecit quia voluit'... sic placet... quia placuit sic voluit." A. 4: "Forte diceris, 'Quare Iudas non resurrexit a peccato sicut Petrus?' Dico quod non habuit voluntatem bonam. Itam enim potuisset sicut Petrus quantum ad liberum arbitrium. Unde dico quod licet predestinationis non sit causa, tamen reprobationis bene potest esse."

[54] See William J. Courtenay, "Pastor de Serrescuderio (d. 1356) and MS Saint-Omer 239," AHDLMA 63 (1996), pp. 325–56, for a discussion of Pastor's career, a description of the ms., and a question list.

interesting example about the rotation of the Earth, is that Pastor likes to add a fifth instant of nature to Meyronnes's four signs account. This seems to correspond, in a sense, to Auriol's will of operation: in the fifth instant of nature, the "will wills," or, "the executive power, with foresight, carries out Peter's salvation in accordance with the determination of the divine will."[55]

Gerard Odonis

Gerard Odonis (ca. 1285–1349) was, like Meyronnes, from present-day southern France. He is best known for his long and controversial term as minister general of the Franciscans in a turbulent time (1329–42) and his support of John XXII in the dispute surrounding the beatific vision. Gerard's investigation into the alleged heretical ideas of some Franciscan confrères and his opposition to his predecessor, Michael of Cesena, won him many enemies who did not hesitate to accuse him in turn of heresy. Nevertheless Clement VI, Pierre Roger, made Odonis Latin patriarch of Antioch in 1342, drawing his income as acting bishop of Catania, where died of the plague.[56]

As a scholar, Odonis is better known for his philosophical works, which are now being critically edited.[57] Indeed it is primarily his commentary on the

---

[55]   For dd. 38–39, Pastor asks two questions, and the questions and articles match Meyronnes, dd. 38–39, qq. 1–2 (ed. Venice 1520, ff. 112raH–114raF), except that Pastor's q. 2 is Meyronnes's q. 1, a. 4 (according to Pastor's *pes quaestionis*, q. 2 is actually considered q. 1, a. 4), and Pastor's q. 2, a. 2, is actually Meyronnes q. 2. Cf. Pastor de Serrescuderio, *I Sent.*, dd. 38–39, q. 1 (ms. Saint-Omer, Bibliothèque municipale 239, f. 42v): "Utrum intellectus divinus habeat certam notitiam de futuris contingentibus... hic quatuor videnda: primo an sit dare contingentiam in rebus...; secundo, unde provenit; tertio de quesito; quarto, supposito quod sic, per quem modum Deus cognoscit futura contingentia. Quantum ad primum..." A. 2: "Secundo principaliter videndum unde venit contingentia" (including the statement, on f. 43r: "Tertio, quidquid convenit uni globe, et toti terre; sed uni globe convenit moveri circulariter; ergo sicut secundum naturam producta est, etiam tota terra potest moveri circulariter et actu movetur"); a. 3 (43r): "Tertio videndum est si intellectus divinus cognoscat ista futura contingentia." Q. 2 (43v): "Consequenter queritur per quem modum Deus cognoscit contingentia futura, secunda utrum actus intellectus preveniat actum voluntatis, tertia quomodo stet infallibilitas scientie Dei cum contingentia rerum. Quantum ad primum..." (a. 1 argues against indistance on 43v); a. 2 (44r): "Secundo principaliter videndum an actus intellectus preveniat actum voluntatis..." giving the fifth instant of nature: "Quinto potentia executiva exequatur providendo salutem Petri iuxta determinationem divine voluntatis"; a. 3: "Tertio principaliter de infallibilitate divine scientie quomodo stet cum contingentia rerum..." giving again the fifth instant of nature (44v): "Quinto, voluntas vult."

[56]   On Odonis as minister general, see e.g. Clément Schmitt, *Un Pape réformateur et un défenseur de unité de l'Eglise. Benoît XII et l'Ordre des Frères Mineurs (1334–1342)* (Florence 1959). On Odonis and the beatific vision controversy, see for example Trottmann, *La vision béatifique*, pp. 718–22 and passim. Anneliese Maier edited a key text of Odonis's in "Die Pariser Disputation des Geraldus Odonis über die Visio beatifica Dei," *Archivio italiano per la storia della pietà* 4 (1965), pp. 213–51.

[57]   The first volume is Odonis's *Logica*, ed. Lambert M. de Rijk (*Giraldus Odonis O.F.M., Opera Philosophica* I) (Leiden 1997); volume two, including de Rijk's edition of Odonis's *Tractatus de esse et essentia*, a question that is also in book I of the *Sentences* commentary, is forthcoming. See in addition de Rijk's "Works by Gerald Ot (Gerardus Odonis) on Logic, Metaphysics

Ethics, printed in 1500, that earned him the title *Doctor Moralis*. Still, his *Sentences* commentary had a part in earning Odonis his name, and is beginning to receive some attention.[58] A dozen or so manuscripts, mostly containing one book each, preserve Odonis's commentary on all four books of the *Sentences*. Although there is some question about when he taught theology, there should not be, because according to the incipits and explicits of various manuscripts, Odonis was a bachelor of theology lecturing on the *Sentences* in the Franciscan *studium* in Paris in the academic years 1326–27 and 1327–28, on books I and probably IV in the first year, and on books II and probably III during the second year. He probably became master of theology just afterwards.[59]

Odonis not only maintained a radical position on the beatific vision, but he tends toward atomism in physics and semi-Pelagianism in soteriology. The reader who appreciates extreme theories will not be disappointed in the present context. In distinction 38 and 39 of book I of his *Sentences* commentary, Odonis asks three brief questions on the subject of divine foreknowledge that, taken together, constitute a not insubstantial treatment of the problem. Since Odonis's lectures took place about five years after the debate among Auriol's successors, Caracciolo, Marchia, and Meyronnes, had subsided, in a sense Odonis was left free to explore the problem without any pressing need to refute anyone in particular. Thus the first question of distinction 38 is essentially a quick introduction to and rejection of solutions based on eternal presence, divine Ideas, and the distinction between primary and proximate causes.

Significantly, unlike the five Scotists treated above, Odonis rejects each of Scotus's two ways of saying that the basis of divine foreknowledge is the de-

---

and Natural Philosophy Rediscovered in Madrid, Bibl. Nac. 4229," AHDLMA 60 (1993), pp. 173–93, and his "Gerardus Odonis O.F.M. on the Principle of Non-Contradiction and the Proper Nature of Demonstration," FcS 54 (1994–97), pp. 51–67.

[58] See Gedeon Gál, "Geraldus Odonis on the Unity of the Concept of Being," FcS 52 (1992), pp. 23–51 (with an edition of Gerard's book I, d. 3); Lambert M. de Rijk, "Guiral Ot (Giraldus Odonis) O.F.M. (1273–1349): His View of Statemental Being in His Commentary on the *Sentences*," in Marmo, ed., *Vestigia, Images, Verba*, pp. 355–69 (in his other works, de Rijk gives 1285 as Odonis's birthdate); See also Joke Spruyt, "Gerard Odonis on the Universal," AHDLMA 63 (1996), pp. 171–208, based on questions parallel to Odonis's *I Sent.*, d. 19, qq. 1–2. There are four manuscripts for book I, on which I base my edition of d. 38 and d. 39, q. 1, in *"Non aliter novit facienda quam facta."* Unfortunately, the least accessible witness, Valencia, Biblioteca del Cabildo 139, appears to be the best. Gedeon Gál provided me with a provisional question list for Odonis's commentary.

[59] For dating, see my *"Non aliter novit facienda quam facta,"* and my "Parisian Commentaries between Peter Auriol and Gregory of Rimini," which deals with Odonis on predestination. Some of the works mentioned in the previous notes, without citing a primary source, state that Odonis was made regent master in 1326, which contradicts the mss. Anneliese Maier, for her part, merely states that he was surely master at Paris before becoming his order's general in 1329 (*Zwei Grundprobleme der scholastischen Naturphilosophie* [Rome 1968], p. 348, n. 52). In one instance de Rijk, *Logica*, p. 1 and nn. 2–3, is tempted by remarks in A. Teetaert, "Ot Guiral," DTC XI (1932) (cols 1658–63), cols. 1658 and 1660, to date Odonis's lectures to the 1310's, but elsewhere he gives the correct dates.

terminations of the divine will.[60] Like Auriol, Odonis argues on the basis of sin: the will is in fact determined *away* from sins and evil deeds, not toward them, and so it can provide the intellect with no certitude about such acts. In fact, it would tend to give the *opposite* impression by its prohibitions and counsel against sinning. Far from providing knowledge, the will offers erroneous aid to the intellect in these cases.[61]

Gerard's own position is based on John of Damascus's notion of divine immensity:

> Every intellect that is the same in reality as an ocean of infinite substance, and that includes through identity every perfection without qualification, has essentially and really every perfection that is possible for it from that ocean of infinite substance; but the divine intellect is the same as an ocean of infinite substance; therefore it is in its nature to have knowledge of future contingents.[62]

This is rather vague, but in the next question Odonis expands on this in explaining how God's knowledge of what is contingent and future can nevertheless be infallible. The key lies in Augustine's statement in *City of God*: "Non aliter novit facienda quam facta."[63] Here Odonis shows the positive influence of Peter Auriol in saying that God *abstracts* from the *differentiae* of time, but he adds an odd twist to Auriol's theory, with a different interpretation of Augustine's maxim: if God does not know differently what is to be done from what has been done, then God knows what is to be done *as having been done*. Odonis's reasoning is simple. Human beings in time have 'knowledge' of past, present, and future things, but it is only with the past that we can have certitude. Now this certitude with respect to the past, for example the creation of the world, is a perfection without qualification. Since by the Damascene's dic-

---

[60] I thus modify my previous remarks about Gerard's attitude toward Scotus's position in "The Quarrel with Aureol," p. 242.

[61] Gerardus Odonis, *Lectura super primum librum Sententiarum*, d. 38, q. 1, a. 3 (ed. Schabel, "*Non aliter novit facienda quam facta*," par. 28-9): "Quinta conclusio probatur dupliciter. Primo sic: nullius voluntatis determinatio certificat de proposito que magis est determinata ad oppositum quam ad propositum; sed voluntas divina in multis, puta in peccatis et in malis operibus, magis est determinata ad oppositum quam ad propositum, quia prohibet mala fieri, precipit, et consulit non fieri; ergo voluntas divina prohibens propositum fieri, precipiens, et consulens propositum non fieri, magis certificabit de opposito quam de proposito, scilicet de peccatis vel de malis operibus.

Secundo arguitur sic: omnis voluntas certificans aliquid futurum est efficax ad ponendum illud futurum; sed voluntas divina non est efficax ad ponendum peccatum; ergo voluntas divina non certificabit de peccato futuro. Minor apparet, quia tunc necessitaret et cogeret homines ad peccandum." The earlier positions are presented in a. 2 (par. 11-17) and rejected in a. 3 (par. 18-30).

[62] Odonis, *I Sent.*, d. 38, q. 1, a. 3 (ed. Schabel, par. 31): "Sexta conclusio probatur sic: omnis intellectus qui est idem realiter pelago substantie infinite includente per ydempnitatem omnem perfectionem simpliciter, habet essentialiter et realiter ab illo pelago infinite substantie omnem perfectionem sibi possibilem; sed intellectus divinus est idem pelago substantie infinite, et est natus habere notitiam de futuris contingentibus."

[63] Cf. Odonis, *I Sent.*, d. 38, q. 2 (ed Schabel, par. 34), a. 2 (par. 44), and a. 3 (par. 50).

tum any such perfection under any *differentia* of time is also a perfection without qualification in God's eternity, and God therefore possesses it, then God has certitude of future contingents "as the future falls under preterition." Thus Odonis agrees with Auriol that God abstracts from time, and does not know futures as future, because as such they are not knowable; but Odonis abandons much of what Auriol had tried to maintain:

> ... certain knowledge concerning any thing whatsoever, inasmuch as it is knowable, is a perfection *simpliciter*, and such knowledge of the thing, inasmuch as it is knowable, exists in God; but the knowledge of past things under the *differentia* of preterition, for example the creation of the world, pertains to the knowledge of certitude; therefore such knowledge is a perfection *simpliciter*. Then thus: everything that is a perfection *simpliciter* within any *differentia* of time is a perfection *simpliciter* in the state of eternity; but knowing that the world has been created with respect to now is a perfection *simpliciter* right now, because it is knowledge of a thing that is knowable with certitude; therefore it is a perfection *simpliciter* in the state of eternity. But God has every knowledge that is a perfection *simpliciter*; therefore God has certitude concerning future things, not as they come under futurition, but in the way that at some time they will have gone into preterition.[64]

It seems that Gerard Odonis agrees with Auriol that futures cannot be known as future to the knower. For Auriol, however, the most important reason for holding to this point was to avoid the necessity of the future. Gerard, on the

---

[64] Odonis, *I Sent.*, d. 38, q. 2, a. 2 (ed. Schabel, par. 42–4): "Tertia consideratio est quod nullum futurum contingens nec temporale aliquod est certitudinaliter noscibile secundum quod cadit sub differentia futuritionis, sed tantum ut cadit sub differentia presentialitatis vel preteritionis, quia ad certitudinem scientie requiritur rem scibilem impossibile aliter se habere. Quarta consideratio est quod status eternitatis abstrahit ab omni differentia temporis. Istud patet, quia eternitas est interminabilis vite tota simul et perfecta possessio. Si tota simul, ergo abstrahit ab omni differentia temporis, quia non extenditur preteritione vel futuritione.

Ex prima consideratione sequitur quod omnis perfectio simplex est in Deo. Ex secunda consideratione sequitur quod notitia certa de quacumque re secundum quod est noscibilis est perfectio simpliciter in Deo. Ex tertia consideratione, quod notitia certa de quacumque re secundum quod est noscibilis est perfectio simpliciter, et quod talis notitia de re secundum quod est noscibilis est in Deo; sed notitia preteritorum sub differentia preteritionis, puta mundi creatio, cadit sub notitia certitudinis; ergo talis notitia est perfectio simpliciter. Tunc sic: omne quod est perfectio simpliciter sub quacumque differentia temporis est perfectio simpliciter in statu eternitatis; sed nosse mundum creatum pro nunc nunc est perfectio simpliciter, quia notitia de re certitudinaliter noscibili; ergo perfectio simpliciter est in statu eternitatis. Sed Deus habet omnem notitiam que est perfectio simpliciter. Ergo Deus habet certitudinem de futuris, non ut cadunt sub futuritione, sed eo modo ut aliquando ceciderint sub preteritione, et ut modo sumus sub memoratione, non sub expectatione. Unde nos habemus notitiam sub triplici differentia temporis, scilicet futuri, presentis, et preteriti. Modo Deus non habet notitiam de futuris contingentibus ut cadunt sub futuritione et Ipse sub expectatione sicut nos, sed secundum quod cadunt sub differentia preteritionis vel presentie. Et hoc est quod dicit Augustinus ubi supra: 'Non aliter novit facienda quam facta'. Sed facta novit non sub expectatione, quia Deus abstrahit ab omni expectatione, sicut et ab omni differentia temporis."

other hand, appears to use God's immensity in eternity to explain that He can know futures in their *pastness*, though they are not yet past in time. This position defeats Auriol's purpose, but accepts some of his reasoning, especially in that for both Odonis and Auriol God abstracts from all *differentiae* of time.

Odonis is, of course, aware of the already existing difficulty that his position has made even worse, and he addresses the issue in the first question of distinction 39: God's foreknowledge of the future, e.g. of the future coming of the Antichrist, is *as certain* and determinate as ours is of the past creation of the world — which God *knew* determinately as past *ab eterno*.[65] Earlier he had even gone so far as to say that "God foreknew all things necessarily" is *always true*, because after things occur He knows them necessarily and His knowledge never changes.[66] Odonis's solution, however, would have been wholly unsatisfactory to Auriol: everything may be necessary with respect to God's knowledge, but in themselves they happen contingently and remain contingent until after they have occurred.[67] Here Odonis agrees with Boethius that they are necessary with respect to God's knowledge but contingent in their own natures.[68] For those combating Auriol, Gerard merely further complicated matters. Using Auriol's argument for the atemporal God of the philosophers, Odonis actually intensifies God's knowledge of particulars, hinting at a notion of a relationship between God and time that Nicolas Bonet would develop more fully.

Nicolas Bonet and Poncius Carbonell

The Franciscan Nicolas Bonet, the "Peaceful Doctor," was probably born in central France around 1280. His *Sentences* commentary has not been identified,

---

     [65]   See Odonis, *I Sent.*, d. 39, q. 1, a. 1 (ed. Schabel, par. 64): "Tertia difficultas est de necessario, ex qua arguitur sic: Dictum est quod Deus ab eterno habuit talem notitiam de creatione mundi qualem habeo ego nunc, scilicet determinatissimam sicut de preterito. Tunc sic: illud de quo habetur talis notitia et ita determinata sicut ego habeo de creatione mundi et de incarnatione Christi est necessarium et impossibile aliter se habere — sicut enim impossibile est mundum non esse creatum et Christum non esse incarnatum, sic impossibile est aliter esse illud quod sic est notum, ut sunt ista duo; sed Deus habet talem notitiam de ista: 'Antichristus est venturus', et ita determinata sicut ego nunc de ista: 'Mundus est creatus', 'Christus est incarnatus et passus'; ergo sicut nunc impossibile est mundum non esse creatum, Christum non esse incarnatum et passum, sic impossibile est Antichristum non esse venturum. Et eodem modo de quibuscumque futuris contingentibus. Quare omnia futura contingentia erit impossibile aliter se habere et necessaria."

     [66]   See Odonis, *I Sent.*, d. 38, q. 2, a. 3 (ed. Schabel, par. 39 and 50): "Quarta difficultas est hec: omne quod necessario Deus prescivit, necessario eveniet; sed omnia necessario prescivit; ergo omnia necessario evenient," and (par. 50): "Ad quartam difficultatem, 'omne quod necessario Deus prescivit necessario eveniet' etc., multi dicunt quod ista est vera sed minor est falsa. Mihi tamen videtur quod minor semper sit vera, dicente Augustino ubi supra quod 'non aliter novit facienda quam facta'; sed postquam legi necessario novit me legisse; ergo necessario prescivit me lecturum esse."

     [67]   See Odonis, *I Sent.*, d. 39, q. 1, a. 2 (ed. Schabel, par. 74).

     [68]   See Odonis, *I Sent.*, d. 38, q. 2, a. 2 (ed. Schabel, par. 44).

although we can guess that he taught theology in Paris in the late 1320s. It is certain that Benedict XII sent him on a mission to Kublai Khan in 1338. He returned before the rest of the mission and Clement VI appointed him bishop of Malta in 1342, but he died in 1343. As a scholar, Bonet was known for a variety of writings, and several of his Aristotelian commentaries were printed in Venice in 1505. Interestingly, he is well known for following Gerard Odonis's atomistic theory. More importantly for present purposes, there is evidence that Peter Auriol influenced Bonet's physical theories, which were not forgotten in the Early Modern period.[69]

On the subject of foreknowledge, Bonet is noteworthy for his lasting impact and for his attitude toward Auriol's ideas. Despite Vassili Zoubov's claim that "Bonet's writings were almost forgotten around the beginning of the sixteenth century," in Giorgio Benigno Salviati's late fifteenth-century dialogue on God's freedom and immutability, Francesco della Rovere, the Franciscan cardinal and future Pope Sixtus IV, cites a variety of Bonet's works rather frequently, alongside Scotus and Francis of Meyronnes, as does Cardinal Bessarion, for whom the dialogue was written. Francesco names Francis of Meyronnes and Bonet as two who argue against Auriol's notion of indistance.[70] Bessarion says, however, that Bonet admitted neutral propositions,[71] and the anonymous author of the *Sentences* commentary in the beginning of Vat. lat. 986 (ff. 1–31) suggests that Bonet had much in common with Auriol:

> From these follows a fourth opinion, which nevertheless I do not assert, that is against the Master and practically against all who speak in the common way concerning this matter: that the consequence 'God knew that the Antichrist would exist; therefore the Antichrist will exist' is not necessary is clear from the fact that for us, although by reason of pastness the antecedent, 'He knew that the Antichrist would exist', is necessary, nevertheless the consequent, 'The Antichrist will exist', is

---

[69] For Bonet's career, see Steven Donovan, "Bonet, Nicholas," *The Catholic Encyclopedia* II (New York 1911), p. 665, and George Sarton, *Introduction to the History of Science, Volume III: Science and Learning in the Fourteenth Century* (Baltimore 1947), p. 532. Like Odonis, Bonet was involved in the early 1330s in the dispute with John XXII over the beatific vision. On Bonet's scientific thought, see e.g. Duhem, *Le système du monde*, vol. 6, pp. 474–509, and vol. 7 throughout. On Bonet's atomism see Vassili P. Zoubov, "Walter Catton, Gérard d'Odon et Nicolas Bonet," *Physis. Revista di storia della scienza* 1 (1959), pp. 261–78. For his connection with Auriol on physical questions, see my "Place, Space, and the Physics of Grace in Auriol's *Sentences* Commentary," pp. 140-41.

[70] Salviati, *De arcanis Dei* III, c. 19 (ed. Etzkorn cit., p. 174, ll. 482-7): "Franciscus: 'Per indistantiam futura Deus evidenter agnoscit... Verum, quia Franciscus noster, pariter et Bonetus, hanc refellunt opinionem...'" For Zoubov's remark, see his "Walter Catton, Gerard d'Odon et Nicolas Bonet," p. 264, n. 27. The fact that some of Bonet's works were published in 1505 is evidence enough that Zoubov's statement is false. Moreover, John Foxal, another participant in Salviati's dialogue, labelled one group of fifteenth-century Scotists "Bonetists."

[71] Salviati, *De arcanis Dei* I, c. 4 (ed. Etzkorn cit., p. 74, ll. 238–42): "Bessarion: ... 'E theologis vero Scotum, quem sublimem et esse et appellari constat, Aureolumque invenio neutras propositiones posse dari opinatos. Idemque fere Bonetum, qui etsi non fundamentaliter, formaliter tamen neutras dari posse et dicit et probare nititur.'"

contingent; otherwise it would follow, if such a consequence were necessary, that a conclusion about what is contingent would follow from two
propositions about what is necessary. And although this is against the
Master, it is nevertheless the opinion of Poncius, Peter Auriol, and N.
Bonet.[72]

Bonet is lumped together with Auriol and Poncius (probably Poncius Carbonell; see below) in denying that the consequence as necessary, contrary to
those who commonly assert its necessity. Although the author confuses
Auriol's doctrine, he is exactly right about Bonet. We have not located Bonet's
Sentences commentary, but we have his *Natural Theology*, which was printed in
Venice with his commentaries on Aristotle.[73] In book III of that work Bonet
discusses the Prime Mover's knowledge. Chapter three concerns future contingents, and after setting down several propositions stating that the Prime
Mover has certain and infallible knowledge of simple terms, necessary complexes of terms, past contingents, and present contingents, Bonet states that
the difficulty lies in determining whether God's knowledge of future contingents is infallible.[74] Bonet declares that it is not infallible *simpliciter*, but only
"under a condition." Drawing a close connection between infallible and necessary, Bonet asserts that, because infallible knowledge *simpliciter* is necessary in
such a way that it cannot be wrong, what God knows would not be contingent, but necessary.[75] He goes on to agree with Auriol that the distinction be-

---

[72]   Anonymus OFM, *I Sent.*, d. 33 et sequentes (Vat. lat. 986, fol. 28rb): "Ex istis sequitur
quarta, que est contra Magistrum et quasi contra omnes communiter loquentes de ista materia —
quam tamen non assero — quod hec consequentia non est necessaria: 'Deus scivit Antichristum
fore; igitur Antichristus erit' patet; ex quo in nobis, licet ratione preteritionis hoc antecedens
'scivit Antichristum fore' sit necessarium, tamen hoc consequens 'Antichristus erit' est contingens, aliter sequeretur, si consequentia talis esset necessaria, quod ex duabus propositionibus de
necessario sequitur conclusio de contingenti. Et licet hoc sit contra Magistrum, est tamen opinio
Poncii et Petri Aureoli et N. Bonet."
[73]   Nicolaus Bonetus, *Habes Nicholai viri perspicacissimi quattuor volumina: Metaphy-
siciam videlicet, Naturalem phylosophiam, Predicamenta nec non Theologiam Naturalem* (henceforth *Theologia naturalis*) (ed. Venice 1505). 1330 is the date John Murdoch suggests for the *Theologia naturalis*, with a question mark, in *"Mathesis in philosophiam scholasticam introducta*: The
Rise and Development of the Application of Mathematics in Fourteenth Century Philosophy and
Theology," in *Arts libéraux et philosophie au moyen âge* (Montreal-Paris 1969) (pp. 215–54), p.
216, n. 2.
[74]   Bonetus, *Theologia naturalis* III, c. 3 (ed. Venice, ff. 108va–b): "Tota difficultas est de
notitia futurorum contingentium, an sit infallibilis. Propter hoc enim introductum est hoc capitu-
lum."
[75]   Bonetus, *Theologia naturalis* III, c. 3 (ed. Venice, fol. 108vb): "Propositio ergo quinta
sit talis: Primus motor non habet notitiam omnino et simpliciter infallibilem (propter hoc enim dicitur habitus conclusionis demonstrate simpliciter infallibilis et necessarius necessitate opposita
falsitati, quia non potest esse falsus, ex hoc quod est ex necessaria complexione et impossibili
aliter se habere) nec habitus erit simpliciter infallibilis. Amplius autem manifestum est quod si
notitia primi motoris de futuro contingenti est infallibiliter vera, sic quod non possit esse falsa,
necessario infert futurum in esse (quoniam si non inferret futurum in esse, sequitur quod <noti-
tia> esset falsa et non vera), et sic illud quod ponebam contingens erit necessarium."

tween the necessity of the consequent and of the consequence is useless here, for he holds that the antecedent is also necessary:

> If the consequence is necessary and the antecedent is necessary, it follows that the consequent is necessary; but it is like this here, since you say that the knowledge is infallibly true, and consequently necessarily true, and it is already posited and in a formal consequence, because it impels its object into being; therefore it follows that the consequent will be necessary.[76]

This is a *reductio ad absurdum*, and so the necessity of the consequence must be denied.

In real agreement with Auriol, however, as Bessarion relates in the dialogue, Bonet claims near the end of the chapter: "Still, one can infer from what has been said that no true proposition about the future is compatible with contingency, and similarly no false proposition about the future is compatible with contingency."[77] One might expect, then, that Bonet would agree with Auriol that because of God's indistance to the actualities of future contingents in His eternity, God knows them determinately, but not in a way that precedes their coming about, or makes future-tensed propositions about them true or false. Bonet explicitly rejects this, however, and at length. Instead, he accepts a difference between certitude with respect to necessary futures and contingent futures, such that God's knowledge of the latter is not infallible *simpliciter*, but only *sub conditione*:

> Namely supposing that He determines Himself to one side [of a contradiction], and because that to which He has all at once and *quasi* always determined Himself does not change the determination, but rather He always keeps [the determination] and He could *change* it and determine Himself to the opposite side. It is like when we speak of a wise and true man: when he promises to do something, he is not considered true and certain and unchangeable *simpliciter*, but [because] the opposite is never or hardly ever found, namely that he would fail in his promise, although *simpliciter* and absolutely he could fail if he wished. In this way one says under a *condition* that the Prime Mover has infallible knowledge of future contingents. It is clear to anyone who understands this that for every intellect the certitude of necessary things that come about necessarily and for which it is impossible not to come about is one

---

[76] Bonetus, *Theologia naturalis* III, c. 3 (ed. Venice, fol. 108vb): "Etsi dicas quod non erit necessarium necessitate consequentis, sed necessitate consequentie, istud non valet, quoniam si consequentia est necessaria et antecedens est necessarium, sequitur quod consequens est necessarium; sic autem est hic, quoniam tu dicis quod notitia est infallibiliter vera, et per consequens necessario vera, et est iam posita et consequentia formali, quia infert suum obiectum in esse; ergo sequitur quod consequens erit necessarium."

[77] Bonetus, *Theologia naturalis* III, c. 3 (ed. Venice, fol. 108vb): "Adhuc autem fertur ex dictis quod nulla propositio vera de futuro stat cum contingentia, et similiter nulla propositio falsa de futuro stat cum contingentia."

thing, and the certitude of contingents that come about possibly and for which it is possible not to come about is another, since the certitude of necessary things is true and necessary in such a way that it is *simpliciter* impossible for it to be false, but the certitude pertaining to contingent things is certain such that it can be false and dubious.[78]

Clearly, Peter Auriol's reevaluation of the problem leads Bonet to such a conclusion. While it was common to hold that God could know other than He did, or more or less than He did, it was very unusual for someone actually to use the transitive verb 'to change' in this context. Bonet actually admits that God's certitude with respect to future contingents can be false, and that He can 'change" (*mutare*) His eternal determination. So the antecedent 'God knew that the Antichrist would exist', which is necessary because of its pastness, does not necessarily entail the consequent 'The Antichrist will exist', not even by necessity *ex suppositione*. This did not escape the attention of the anonymous author of Vat. lat. 986, who says that Bonet admitted variation in divine knowledge.[79]

To a certain extent, Bonet is in agreement with Auriol that God does not know the future qua future with absolute certitude, but his analogy of the wise man must have seemed repulsive to some. Bonet realizes that most others hold both that things come about necessarily in the way that future-tensed propositions expressing God's knowledge state, and that those future things are contingent, concluding: "This last point is quite discordant with what was said above in this chapter; therefore I assert no conclusion here. Because of the great difficulty I would rather listen than say anything." And thus he presents

---

[78] Bonetus, *Theologia naturalis* III, c. 3 (ed. Venice, fol. 108vb): "Propositio sexta sit talis: Primus motor habet scientiam certam de futuris contingentibus et infallibilem non simpliciter, sed sub conditione, scilicet supposito quod ad partem [aliam] <alteram> determinet se, et quia istud ad quod determinavit se semel quasi semper determinationem non mutat, sed in ea semper stat et eam posset mutare, et ad partem oppositam se determinare, sicut dicitur de sapiente et vero homine, cum aliquid promittit se facturum, reputatur pro vero et certo et immutabili non simpliciter, sed vix aut numquam est inventum oppositum, scilicet quod deficeret in promisso, licet simpliciter deficere posset et absolute si vellet, sic dicitur sub conditione primum motorem habere scientiam infallibilem ex futuris contingentibus. Palam autem cuilibet intelligenti quod apud quemcumque intellectum alia est certitudo necessariorum que necessario eveniunt et que impossibile est non evenire, et alia est certitudo contingentium que possibiliter eveniunt et que possibile est non evenire; quoniam certitudo necessariorum sic est vera et necessaria quod impossibile simpliciter est quod sit falsa; certitudo autem contingentium sic est certa quod potest esse falsa et dubia."

[79] Anon., *I Sent.*, d.33 et sequentes (Vat. lat. 986, fol. 28va): "Sed contra, si sit verum quod Deus potest noviter aliqua scire, etc., et ab eterno predestinatum scire esse prescitum, in quo est mutatio non video ego, sive Deus et non mutor nec in creatura, quia creatura nondum est; igitur. Respondetur secundo: secundum enim Bonet, qui ponit res ab eterno subesse Dei nuto: In esse cognito tunc esset variatio que sic est tunc sub tali esse ita quod actus notitie divine prius ferebatur in tali re sub tali esse ad salutem et nunc noviter ex parte sui uniformiter se habens fertur super eandem rem nichil esse ad dampnationem."

"with doubts" Auriol's propositions that deny truth to future contingent propositions.[80]

While Bonet recognizes Auriol's criticisms of the common positions, he prefers adopting no solution to choosing Auriol's, which he attacked in the previous chapter. In book III, chapter two, Bonet discusses God's knowledge *ad extra*, concluding that God's understanding ends (*terminatur*) in His essence as the primary object, and then ends at things outside Himself as secondary objects; and God first knows necessary complexes and simple terms, then contingent complexes.[81] As we have seen, future contingent complexes would present a problem in the next chapter of the *Natural Theology*, but already in chapter two Bonet treats God's knowledge of future contingents while discussing whether God knows futures, pasts, and presents qua future, past, and present. Here again Bonet says the problem is difficult, because the 'new philosophers' speak in many ways about it. Although this may be true, Bonet gives only Auriol's position, and at length, first in three propositions which in sum say that God is the eminent similitude and exemplar of all, and represents the actuality of future contingents indistantly, while they exist, and not before, after, or simultaneously, because God abstracts from all parts of time.[82] Bonet even refutes in brief what he considers the most important previous objection to indistance, that it is a relative negation requiring two relata, one of which is an as yet non-existent future contingent. To this objection, which we have seen in Auriol's own *Scriptum*, Bonet thinks Auriol's refutation sufficient, that a pure negation does not require such relata in actuality. Just as a chimera is not distant from a tragelaf, because in not existing at all they certainly do not exist simultaneously, so also God can be negatively indistant from the actuality of the future contingent.[83]

---

[80] Bonetus, *Theologia naturalis* III, c. 3 (ed. Venice, fol. 108vb): "Ideo illas sub dubio trado, quia nonnulli existimant quod illa simul stant: Primum quod altera pars contingenter eveniet et quod possibile esset evenire; secundum quod illius partis contingentie que eveniet potest haberi notitia que representat intellectui quod talis pars futura eveniet; tertium quod talis notitia de parte futuri contingentis que eveniet est vera: Ita erit sicut per propositionem enunciatur; ergo a primo ad ultimum propositio vera et necessaria de futuro contingenti potest stare cum contingentia. Et illud ultimum est multum dissonum dictis superius in hoc capitulo; ergo hic nullam conclusionem assero. Plus vellem audire propter magnam difficultatem quam aliquid dicere."

[81] Bonetus, *Theologia naturalis* III, c. 2 (ed. Venice, fol. 108va): "Concludamus ergo propositionem affirmativam: Quod primus motor intelligit non tantum se formaliter, sed intelligit alia que sunt extra se formaliter; primo tamen terminatur intellectio sua ad essentiam propriam, deinde ad alia que sunt extra se. Et hoc est quod aliqui volunt dicere, quod essentia primi motoris est obiectum primarium, et creature obiectum secundarium, et primo intelligit complexiones necessarias et simplices terminos quam complexiones contingentes."

[82] Bonetus, *Theologia naturalis* III, c. 2 (ed. Venice, fol. 107rb): "Dubitatio vero quarta est de notitia futurorum contingentium, an primus motor intelligat futurum sub ratione futuri, et preteritum sub ratione preteriti, et presens sub ratione presentis; valde difficilis est ad solvendum, de hoc enim varie loquuntur novi philosophi." Bonet's description of Auriol's stance follows immediately, and takes up much of fol. 107va.

[83] Bonetus, *Theologia naturalis* III, c. 2 (ed. Venice, fol. 107va): "Etsi dicis: 'Quod nihil est, a nullo potest esse indistans, quia indistantia, cum sit [necessario] <negatio> relativa, requirit extrema; contingens autem futurum est penitus nihil; ergo essentia primi motoris non potest

Bonet agrees with Auriol to the extent that he accepts that God is the eminent similitude of all simple terms and necessary complexes, and as such He
represents them with certitude. Bonet does not see the difference between
similitudes, exemplars, and Ideas, however, and as a Franciscan he is aware,
probably via Scotus if not Auriol himself, of the criticism that Ideas necessarily represent whatever they represent. Thus Ideas are only suited to representing things that are necessary. If for some reason such Ideas could represent
contingently, and only when the actuality exists in reality, then either the Ideas
would still represent such an actuality before and after, and thus incorrectly,
or they would not, and God would be mutable, representing at one time and
not at another. Bonet concludes that God does not represent the actuality of
future contingents in this way distantly or indistantly.[84]

Bonet in fact has a common sense, almost human view of God's knowledge
of contingent things in time, which is consistent with the 'wise man' analogy
discussed above. He flatly rejects the notion that similitudes do not represent
before or after an event, drawing yet another analogy, this time with an astronomer who has a similitude of an eclipse a year before it occurs, and retains it afterwards. Certainly prophets and prognosticators have such similitudes before events, and retain them in their intellect. The only variation is in
what is connoted, namely the different parts of time. Such similitudes represent the future qua future, and are not, obviously, infallible, when what they
represent is contingent.[85]

Therefore, somewhat like Gerard Odonis, Bonet asserts that although God
abstracts from time, He is also aware of the differences in time. To explain

---

esse indistans a futuro contingenti', responditur quod licet simultas sit relatio positiva et requirit extrema, indistantia tamen, cum sit pura negatio seu privatio, non requirit extrema in actu,
sicut chymera non distat a tragelapho, cum non sit simul cum eo."
    [84] Bonetus, *Theologia naturalis* III, c. 2 (ed. Venice, fol. 107vb): "Primus motor simpliciter
est exemplar et ydea simplicium terminorum et complexionum necessariarum, nullo autem modo
contingentium, quoniam si representaret contingentia, cum necessario et invariabiliter representet quicquid representat, contingentia necessario evenirent... Palam autem quod si representat actualitatem contingenter, quando actu est, sequitur quod antequam esset et postquam non esset eius
actualitatem representabit, alias esset mutatio et variatio in Eo, quia de representante fieret non
representans, et sic non erit simpliciter immutabilis... Palam autem ex dictis quod ratio eius assu-
mit falsum cum dicit quod essentia representat indistanter, quoniam non representat futurum contingens nec distanter nec indistanter. Aliud enim dictum non est verum cum dicit quod primus motor non intelligit aliter quam essentia representat. Hoc non est verum de cognitione contingentium,
licet sit verum de terminis simplicibus et complexionibus necessariis."
    [85] Bonetus, *Theologia naturalis* III, c. 2 (ed. Venice, ff. 107va–b): "Alius intellectus potest
esse talis: Quod si similitudo futuri ad hoc quod vere representet nec debet precedere nec sequi futurum, sed simul esse cum actualitate futuri vel indistans ab Eo, et ille sensus non est verus. Palam
autem quod in intellectu astrologi est similitudo eclypsis future vere ipsam pro nunc representans
per mensem vel per annum <precedentem> ipsam, et transacta eclypsi, adhuc remanet similitudo
ipsam representans fuisse preteritam... Nec est ibi variatio subiecta alicuius, licet forte sit variatio in connotato, scilicet in partibus temporis... Certum est tamen quod similitudo aliquid ponit in
intellectu representans futurum sub ratione futuri, quam similitudinem certitudinaliter representantem habere dicuntur pronostici et prophete veridici, similiter similitudinem representantem
preteritum sub ratione preteriti."

this, Bonet draws an analogy with God's understanding of place. Although God is not *in* any place, that is subjectively, nevertheless he is related to place 'terminatively', because He is a terminus of distance or presence for diverse places, and can understand 'here', 'there', 'in that direction', and 'in this direction.' It is the same way with time:

> Although the Prime Mover abstracts from the entire successive line of time, because He is neither measured by time, nor decays in time, nor is contained in time, nevertheless via the intellect He will be able to point out present, past, and future, and under the nature (*ratio*) of present, past, and future.[86]

Nicolas Bonet exemplifies the difficulty a twentieth-century historian or philosopher or theologian has in evaluating the minds of past figures. How bright was Bonet? Those who think that there is no solution to the problem will admire Bonet's intelligence and intellectual honesty in understanding Auriol's deep critique of previous views, while giving no positive solution himself. They will also admire his rejection of indistant similitudes, based on the argument against Ideas that Scotus made popular. Bonet accepts an explanation of God's relation with time that might have disturbed Auriol and others, but Bonet does so to avoid depriving God of what certitude He could have of the future. That certitude is analogous to a wise man's certitude of his own promise, or an astronomer's surety about a future celestial event. It may be that God, the perfect intellect, will never be wrong about the future, but this does not mean even God has the same certitude about the future as He does about the past. Seeing the future qua future, He cannot have absolute certitude, for that would eliminate contingency for Bonet. Allowing God to see the future indistantly or presently only, disregards God's awareness of time, which is analogous to His awareness of space. If He had such indistant knowledge, certainly God would be able to put two and two together, and know with absolute certitude the future qua future as well as indistantly. Certainly Francesco della Rovere and Bessarion would have respect for Bonet's thought in 1471, for they cite him frequently. Whatever they thought of his opinion on God and time, they considered his attack on indistance effective.

Some people today, however, will find Bonet's treatment cowardly, or too simplistic, or even stupid, and will prefer any number of previous solutions to Bonet's seeming non-solution. This is the difficulty for the intellectual historian, who is neither obliged to evaluate nor merely to present the ideas of past thinkers. The quality of a mind in any period, even one's own, is hard to

---

[86]   Bonetus, *Theologia naturalis* III, c. 2 (ed. Venice, ff. 107vb–108ra): "Palam autem ex his quod licet primus motor se non habeat ad locum subiective, tamen se habet terminative, quia est terminus distantie vel presentie sub diversis, ubi potest demonstando dicere 'hic', 'ibi', 'istuc', 'illuc'. Manifestum est autem quod modo simili et conformiter est dicendum de tempore, quod licet primus motor abstrahat a tota linea successiva temporis, quia non mensuratur tempore, nec tabescit in tempore, nec sub tempore continetur, poterit tamen per intellectum demonstrare presens, preteritum, et futurum, et hoc sub ratione presentis, preteriti, et futuri."

measure, and this is all the more true for the Middle Ages, so distant from us in so many ways. Along with this problem comes the problem of deciding the relative merits of originality and conservativeness. Peter Auriol's treatment of the problem was as original as anyone's, although many may reject it. Bonet's 'solution' has some sources in, for example, Caracciolo and Odonis, yet it is rather original. Still, it seems more negative than positive.

Brief mention can also be made here of another theologian who may have been active at Paris at this time. The anonymous author of the first commentary in Vat. lat. 986 gives the opinion of a certain Poncius. This is probably Poncius Carbonell, a Franciscan born in Barcelona perhaps around 1260, although there are perhaps a half-dozen candidates with the name Poncius active in Paris in this time. Earlier his death was given as ca. 1320, but he wrote an important Apocalyse commentary in 1335, and was Franciscan provincial minister for Aragon from 1336 until his death in 1350.[87] Poncius's opinion is apparently that God can know something *de novo*, and stop knowing what He knew before.[88] Perhaps our author misinterprets Poncius, however, for the author goes on to say:

> And he continues to argue in this way: while uniformity exists in the cause, uniformity obtains in the effect; but *ab eterno* uniformity obtains in the cause, which is God's foreknowledge; therefore if *ab eterno* He contingently willed that the Antichrist would come about, and He was able to will that he would come about, then He is also now able to will contingently that he not come about, because the indifference remains now just as it did then. Another proposition of his: it is clear that predestination can be changed so that it is possible that he who was predestined is not saved, and he who was foreknown (*prescitus*) etc., because otherwise there would be the necessity of futures.[89]

These statements may have been taken out of context, for we will see them frequently in the 1340s, and interpret them benignly (see below, chapter eleven). Nothing like this appears to be in his Apocalyse commentary, at least,

---

[87] Gregory Cleary, "Pontius Carbonell," *The Catholic Encyclopedia* XII (New York 1911), p. 234, gives his dates as ca. 1250–ca. 1320, but Roest, *Reading the Book of History*, p. 177, dates his Apocalypse commentary to 1335, and gives further information in his and Maarten van der Heijden's important website "Franciscan Authors, 13th–18th Century."

[88] Anon., *I Sent.*, d. 33 et sequentes (Vat. lat. 986, fol. 28rb): "Ponit etiam Poncius quod Deus potest noviter aliqua scire que numquam ante scivit, ex quo sequitur quod predicta consequentia non est necessaria, quia potest desiderare scire illud quod ante scivit, et eius oppositum scire et velle."

[89] Anon., *I Sent.*, d. 33 et sequentes (Vat. lat. 986, ff. 28rb–29va): "Et adhuc arguit sic: uniformitate stante in causa, stat uniformitas in effectu; sed ab eterno stat uniformitas in causa que est prescientia Dei; igitur si contingenter ab eterno voluit Antichristum fore, et [fol. 28va] poterat velle illum non fore, igitur et modo potest contingenter velle illum non fore, quia nunc manet indifferentia sicud tunc. Alia propositio eius: quod predestinatio potest immutari sic quod possibile est quod ille qui fuit predestinatus non sit salvatus, et qui fuit prescitus etc., patet, quia aliter esset necessitas futurorum."

although the subject matter is definitely related.[90] It is unlikely that Poncius said in those exact words "predestination can be changed," for if he did, his position would be radical. Nevertheless it is important that the author, saying "*sed contra*," opposes Poncius for jeopardizing God's immutability, and, as we have seen, Bonet also held perhaps heterodox views about the infallibility and immutability of divine foreknowledge, as our author realizes. Thus our author appears to think Poncius denied the necessity of the consequence and consequent in 'God knew the Antichrist would be; therefore the Antichrist will be', on account of the mutability of God's knowledge, which would otherwise be, in some way, a cause.

Franciscans at Paris in the 1320s were reluctant to accept Auriol's radical departure from traditional stances toward the problem of foreknowledge and future contingency. Auriol placed too little emphasis on the God of Scripture, active in history and the world. Caracciolo, Meyronnes, and their followers rejected Auriol entirely and defended a more or less traditional Scotist position that maintained the compatibility of God's immutability and contingency. Odonis, Bonet, and Poncius were both much more receptive to the new view and more innovative, but their innovations departed even further from Auriol's God. Odonis strengthened divine knowledge of the future by asserting that God knows it as past, and Bonet and Poncius took the opposite approach. Perhaps they reasoned that if immutability and necessity are the same, it is best to deny absolute immutabilty. What unites them all is the fact that Auriol's theory played an important role in their treatments.

---

[90] Roest, *Reading the Book of History*, pp. 177–83 deals with the commentary at some length, and in a private communication he stated that he has not seen this position in that work. It may, of course, come from a lost work. Interestingly, Roest treats Poncius right before Auriol.

Chapter 8

The Reaction outside the Franciscan Convent at Paris

A majority of the extant comprehensive theological works written in the decade or so after Peter Auriol's Paris lectures were authored by Franciscans. All
Franciscans who are known to have taught at the University of Paris ꞏuring
this time show the impact, positive or negative, of Auriol's theory of divine
foreknowledge. In England, as we shall see, the same can be said for the most
important Franciscans who lectured on the *Sentences* in the 1320s: Walter
Chatton and Adam Wodeham. The overall impression, and not just on this issue, is that during this decade Auriol's teaching was a focal point in theology
on both sides of La Manche — to take the Parisian perspective. This image
might be slightly skewed, however, for when we examine the few extant *Sentences* commentaries of Parisian theologians from outside the Order of Friars
Minor, or of Franciscans who taught elsewhere on the continent, it is difficult
to find this obsession with Auriol's position. For that, one has to wait until
the 1330s, when the Order of the Hermits of Saint Augustine takes over the
refutation of Auriol's theory.

Peter Thomae and Peter of Navarre

As we have seen, Franciscans' knowledge or ignorance of Scotus and Auriol,
especially in controversial contexts, is a good indicator of when, and perhaps
where, they lectured. Dating the commentaries of the two Iberian Franciscans
Peter Thomae and Peter of Navarre is especially complicated, but it is important to investigate this question because it concerns the reception of Auriol's
thought in and out of Paris. Both Peter Thomae and Peter of Navarre deal
with Scotus's position on future contingents, and neither of them displays
awareness of Auriol's stance, but traditionally they read the *Sentences* at Paris
after Auriol. This tradition should therefore arouse immediate suspicion. Peter
of Navarre (or de Atarrabía, ca. 1275–1346), born near Pamplona, may have
studied at Paris under Scotus at the beginning of the fourteenth century. He
was probably teaching in the Franciscans' Barcelona *studium generale*, perhaps
already a master of theology, when he became provincial minister of Aragon in
1317. He was replaced in 1320, and probably spent the next three years
teaching again in Barcelona, where he had contacts with Aufredo Gonteri Brito
(see chapter nine) and Peter Thomae, and most likely worked on the writing of
his commentary on the *Sentences*, called a *Scriptum*. He once again served as

provincial minister of Aragon from 1323 to 1327, and is mentioned as "professor of theology" in 1325. Only his commentary on book I survives, in five manuscripts, and in fact it is the only 'Parisian' *Sentences* commentary from the period between Scotus and Peter of Aquila to have been critically edited.[1] Book I of Peter Thomae's commentary is also the sole survivor, in this case in only one manuscript, Vat. lat. 1106, although he authored several other works still extant, including a critically-edited *Quodlibet*.[2] Like Peter of Navarre, Peter Thomae (ca. 1280–1340) was from northern Spain. He studied theology in Paris, probably not under Scotus, and was teaching at the Barcelona *studium generale* by 1316. In the late 1320s he was in Avignon working for John XXII, but he was accused of sorcery in 1336 and died in prison.[3]

In their *Sentences* commentaries, in which they treat the problem of foreknowledge and future contingents, both Peters cite or directly quote Auriol's *Scriptum*, calling him a doctor, a title Auriol only received in late 1318.[4] However, Navarre cites Aquinas simply as Thomas, and not Saint Thomas, and so he supposedly finished the work before 1323, when Thomas was canonized. Thomae's *Quodlibet* has extensive citations of Auriol's *Scriptum*, includes internal references to his own *Sentences* commentary, which therefore predates the *Quodlibet*, and refers to Aquinas as Thomas. But Navarre appears to know Aufredo Gonteri Brito's *Sentences* commentary, and so he seems to have written after Gonteri's 1322 Barcelona lectures. In turn, Thomae alludes to Navarre's *Sentences* commentary in his own.[5] If we try to save all of the phe-

---

[1]   *Doctoris Fundati Petri de Atarrabia sive de Navarra, OFM, In Primum Sententiarum Scriptum*, 2 vols., ed. Pius S. Azcona, OFM (Madrid 1974). See Azcona's introduction, vol. 1, pp. 14*–28* for Navarre's life and the dating of his *Scriptum*.

[2]   For a description of Thomae's writings, see Eligius Buytaert, "The Scholastic Writings of Petrus Thomae," in J. Auer and H. Volk, eds., *Theologie in Geschichte und Gegenwart* (Munich 1957), pp. 927–40. Significant editions of his writings include *Petrus Thomae O.F.M. Quodlibet*, eds. M.R. Hooper and E.M. Buytaert (St. Bonaventure, NY 1957); for the treatise *De ente*, Stephen D. Dumont, "The Univocity of the Concept of Being in the Fourteenth Century: II. The *De ente* of Peter Thomae," *Mediaeval Studies*, 50 (1988), pp. 186–256; and from the *Sentences* commentary, Alfonso Maierù, "Logica e teologia trinitaria nel commento alle *Sentenze* attribuito a Petrus Thomae," in J. Jolivet, Z. Kaluza, and A. de Libera, eds., *Lectionum Varitates. Hommage à Paul Vignaux (1904–1987)* (Paris 1991), pp. 177–198 (d. 2, q. 8, a. 4, dubia 9–10), and Gedeon Gál, "Petrus Thomae's Proof for the Existence of God," FcS 56 (1998), pp. 115–51 (d. 2, q. 2, plus question list).

[3]   Despite the fact that they use the same sources, and Gal cites Dumont, Gal ("Petrus Thomae's," p. 115) and Dumont ("The Univocity... II," p. 187, n. 3) disagree on important items, Gal maintaining that Peter Thomae is from Catalonia and that "Between 1317 and 1332 he was teaching philosophy and theology" in Barcelona, whereas Dumont has him hail from the Franciscan province of St. James of Compostela (in the west), teaching in Barcelona in 1316 (with solid evidence), and working in Avignon "a decade later." Dumont's contention that Thomae's commentary and *Quodlibet* are from his earlier Paris years is incorrect, however, as we shall see.

[4]   For Thomae's quotation "illius doctoris novi qui invehitur contra Scotum," see Maierù, "Logica e teologia trinitaria," p. 189 (par. 2). For Navarre's explicit citation, cf. Azcona ed., vol. 1, p. 63, l. 77: "quidam doctor in *Scripto* suo."

[5]   For Thomae's citation of Navarre's *Sentences* commentary his own, Navarre's ignorance of Aquinas's canonization, and Navarre's relationship with Gonteri, see Azcona's introduction, vol. 1, pp. 20*, 26*–27*, and 74*–75*. For Thomae's citation of his own commentary in his *Quodlibet* and his referring to Aquinas as "Thomas," see Buytaert's introduction, pp. xi–xii.

nomena, we get Gonteri lecturing in 1322, then Navarre and then Thomae all before 1323, each citing the previous lector. This is implausible.

Thomas's canonization is therefore not a very useful *terminus ante quem* for Franciscan authors, and I submit that knowledge of Auriol's theories is a better criterion for dating and locating their works.[6] Ignoring Aquinas, we can have Gonteri lecturing in Barcelona in 1322, Navarre finishing his commentary in 1323, and Thomae some time later. The fact that they cite the *Scriptum* rather than the *reportationes*, which were more popular among Auriol's immediate successors at Paris, is in keeping with this scenario, but their use of the *Scriptum* could also indicate that they were never writing in Paris, but rather in Barcelona, where the *reportationes* may not have circulated.

Or we could even ignore Gonteri's 1322 date. As we have seen in the case of Auriol, *Sentences* commentaries as we have them today were sometimes purely written works unconnected with any actual lectures, sometimes rough *reportationes* from lectures, and sometimes-reworked *'ordinationes'*. Gonteri's commentary is unmistakably a written work, since he incorporates extremely large sections of previous authors' writings verbatim, as we shall see. Moreover, Peter of Navarre's commentary is also called a *Scriptum*. Therefore it is very plausible that they had access to earlier versions, 'works in progress', of each other's commentaries. Thomae's *reportatio*, in fact, may have been the first work of these three to be 'finished'.

I think that these *Sentences* commentaries were *begun* at a fairly early date, in Barcelona. All three authors knew Auriol's *Scriptum*, but there is no reason to suppose that they were able to make extensive use of the entire work. This is why on the subject of future contingents, where we would expect a reaction to Auriol, Navarre and Thomae appear to be ignorant of Auriol's opinion, and Gonteri merely inserts a brief refutation into his copying of previous commentaries. Instead, Navarre refutes the solutions based on eternal presence and divine Ideas, which he explicitly links to Aquinas and Richard of Middleton. Here he betrays John of Bassol's influence as well as Scotus's. In the end, Navarre describes both of Scotus's ways, defending the second way, for which he describes no less than six signs, or instants of nature. Navarre, therefore, can be termed a true 'Scotist' on this issue.[7]

Peter Thomae is only slightly less a Scotist: he refutes eternal presence and Ideas, maintains that the existence of contingency is a *per se notum*, defends God's real capacity for opposites in the instant of eternity, and posits a two instants of nature solution based on the determinations of the divine will. He passes over "the Doctor's" second way, however, and accepts the first way.

---

[6]   Victorin Doucet, "Der unbekannte Skotist des Vaticanus Lat. 1113, Fr. Anfredus Gonteri O.F.M. (1325)," FzS 25 (1938) (pp. 201–240), p. 207, speaking of Gonteri, also argues against Schmaus that the Aquinas-title criterion is no strong proof for dating. Buytaert is of the same opinion in his introduction to Thomae's *Quodlibet*, p. xii. Stephen D. Dumont works on the basis of their ignorance of Auriol in other contexts, as in his "The Scotist of Vat. lat. 869," *Archivum franciscanum historicum* 81 (1988) (pp. 254–83), pp. 272–3.

[7]   Cf. Petrus de Atarrabia, *Scriptum* I, d. 38, qq. 1–2 (vol. 2, ed. Azcona, pp. 867–86, positing the Scotist stance on pp. 884–5, ll. 60–87).

He thus avoids making explicit his tacit criticism that the divine essence is only the intellect's basis of knowing what is necessary, including future contingents independently of whether they will actually exist or not. Nevertheless, Thomae's clear explanation of Scotus's opinion and critiques of others is a real contribution to the *Scotist* program.[8] Given the two Peters' Scotist stances, intentionally ignoring Auriol would seem ridiculous.

John Baconthorpe the Carmelite

Of the four mendicant orders, the Carmelites leave the fewest traces in the history of the problem of foreknowledge and future contingents, although they surpass the Dominicans in the period at Paris between 1316 and 1345. Unlike the Augustinians, Dominicans, and Franciscans, the Carmelites do not develop a distinctive doctrine in this context. Two Carmelite masters of theology at Paris dealt with the issue in the 1310s: Guy Terrina in *Quodlibeta* of 1313 and 1318, and Gerard of Bologna in his *Summa theologica* written between 1313 and his death in 1317. The scribe of Auriol's Borghese 123 manuscript also penned the sole surviving witness of Guy's *Quodlibeta*, Borghese 39, and although Guy's 1313 question only indirectly concerns future contingents, the very wording of his second effort, "Whether God knows one side of a future contingent determinately," appears directed at Auriol. Aside from the question itself, however, Guy exhibits no awareness of Auriol's position. His perfunctory 'refutation' amounts to a simple declaration of God's greatness and perfection, although he does presage Gerard Odonis's use of Augustine. Guy concentrates instead on following Durand against Aquinas in asserting the knowability of futures via their causes, and on rejecting the Scotist account by claiming that the judgement of the divine intellect must precede the will's determination.

Guy places himself more squarely in the Dominican camp, against the Franciscan voluntarists, than did his confrère Gerard of Bologna, who prefers to steer a middle course between the two traditions; that is, Gerard appears to try to reconcile the views of the giants, Thomas Aquinas and John Duns Scotus. Gerard's *Summa* was not forgotten: at the end of our period, in 1345, Gerard's confrère Paul of Perugia would cite Gerard's *Summa* in his discussion. The most prominent Carmelite of this era, however, was the Englishman John Baconthorpe, whose treatment fails to inspire admiration for his order's

---

[8]   See Petrus Thomae, *Reportatio* I, d. 39 (Vat. lat. 1106, ff. 294v–300v). I will publish this distinction in the near future: "Utrum Deus habeat de omnibus rebus quantum ad omnes conditiones existentie notitiam determinatam, certam et infallibilem, immutabilem et necessariam, cum qua determinatione et certitudine stare possit aliqua contingentia ex parte rerum in existentia actuali" (fol. 294v). Thomae refutes Ideas and presence to eternity on ff. 295v–296v, and defends Scotus on ff. 297r–299v); the real capacity for opposites is discussed on fol. 299r, and instants of nature on fol. 299v, where he adds: "Intellectus enim divinus in primo instanti futura contingentia intelligit, sed coniunctionem futurorum cum esse actualis existentie intelligit in secundo instanti, scilicet quo illud determinatur fore per voluntatem divinam. Et sic essentia divina est intellectui ratio intelligendi quecumque necessaria, et hoc ante omnem actum voluntatis."

intellectual prowess: as we have seen, he mostly copies Thomas Wylton's presentation verbatim.[9] The one Parisian Carmelite *Sentences* commentary to survive from this era is that of Baconthorpe, the 'Prince of the Averroists'. Baconthorpe was probably from Norfolk, where he received his early education at a Carmelite convent. From there he went to Oxford and then to Paris, reading the *Sentences* there in 1319–20, or perhaps the following year, making him a *socius* of Francis of Marchia or of Meyronnes and Pierre Roger. He was promoted to master between 1322 and 1324. Returning to England, he was put in charge of the English Carmelites in 1329–33, becoming involved in such matters as the conflict between William of Ockham and Pope John XXII. He died in 1346. He was perhaps the most important Carmelite theologian of the Middle Ages. He wrote many works on theology and philosophy, and gained a reputation for his political ideas. The modern Carmelite historian Xiberta devotes more space to Baconthorpe than to any other fourteenth-century Carmelite.[10]

We have two redactions of his *Sentences* commentary on the first three books, and two separate commentaries on book IV, the second dating from as late as 1340. There is only one witness for what might be a *reportatio* on the first three books, but an *ordinatio* redaction of the first three books, for which there are no manuscripts, was published in Paris in 1484, the later commentary on book IV the following year. In later printings his quodlibetal questions were included. The *Ordinatio in primum* was completed around 1325, according to an *explicit*, which explains why he is able to cite books II–IV as well as his first two quodlibetal debates, held in Paris against, among others, Pierre Roger, in 1322–23.[11] There are indications that the *Ordinatio* was completed in England, because where Wylton says "Seine" and "King of France," Baconthorpe inserts "river" and "King of England." Moreover, all of Baconthorpe's manuscripts are now in London, and the English scribe of Tortosa 88 instructs the reader to "look in John" at one point.[12]

In his printed *Ordinatio in primum*, and in his quodlibetal questions, Baconthorpe "battled Auriol sharply." In fact, Auriol was his main adversary,

[9]   For Guy's *Quodlibeta*, see Glorieux, *La littérature quodlibétique* I, pp. 169-74. The 1313 question is *Quodlibet* I, q. 2, and the one from 1318 is *Quodlibet* VI, q. 3 (ms. Borghese 39, ff. 220vb–222va). Gerard of Bologna's question in the *Summa*, "Utrum Deus cognoscat futura contingentia," is in mss. Borghese 27 (ff. 91rb–93va) and Oxford, Merton College 149. On Paul of Perugia, see chapter 11; on Wylton and Baconthorpe, see above, chapter 2. I plan to publish an article with editions of the pertinent questions of the three Carmelites.
[10]   See Bartholomaeus Maria Xiberta, *De scriptoribus scholasticis saeculi XIV ex ordine Carmelitarum* (Louvain 1931), pp. 167–240, which I follow. On the applicability of Baconthorpe's nickname, see James P. Etzwiler, "John Baconthorpe, 'Prince of the Averroists'?" FcS 36 (1976), 148–76.
[11]   On the *Sentences* commentary, see Xiberta, *De scriptoribus*, pp. 177–83. Ernst Borchert, *Die Quaestiones speculativae et canonicae des Johannes Baconthorp über den sakramentalen Charakter* (Munich 1974), provides a question list for the first commentary on book IV, the *quaestiones speculativae*, an edition of qq. 1, 4, 5, and 13 based on the sole ms., British Library, Royal 9 C VII, and an edition of dd. 4–6, 8, 17, and 24–25 of the second commentary, the *quaestiones canonicae*, based on Baconthorpe's autograph, British Library, Royal 11 B XII.
[12]   See chapter 2, nn. 24 and 34.

Baconthorpe citing him over seventy times, only four or five times not to attack Auriol. A similar thing could be said for the *Reportatio in primum*, where in the text itself Baconthorpe has detailed citations of Auriol's *Scriptum*.[13] Baconthorpe thus joined his Franciscan contemporaries whose works are extant in making Peter Auriol his main opponent. However, the situation is more complicated in the context of future contingents and predestination.

Baconthorpe's treatment of divine foreknowledge and future contingency in book I is a rather long discussion. It is unusual in that he devotes distinctions 38 and 39 to the question of how God knows things outside Himself, d. 38: "Whether divine Ideas are distinguished on the basis of the nature of the object (*rei*)," and d. 39: "What must be held concerning divine Ideas, attributes, and emanations *ad intra* in the way of the Commentator."[14] In these distinctions Baconthorpe lives up to his reputation as the 'Prince of the Averroists', supporting the Commentator's position. Other than Aristotle, Themistius, Averroes, and Richard of Middleton once, Baconthorpe cites only Auriol, devoting about six columns to attacking Auriol's stance on God's knowledge.

Although Baconthorpe held to the sort of theory of divine Ideas that Auriol had attacked in his own distinction 38, for our purposes the heart of the disagreement between them is a differing conception of the will. Both agree that God does not know creatures terminatively, with His knowledge ending directly at the creatures, but based on Auriol's distinction 35 Baconthorpe knows Auriol holds that God knows creatures only denominatively, through apprehending Himself, the eminent similitude of all.[15] For Baconthorpe, this is

---

[13]   For the *Scriptum*, cf. Xiberta, *De scriptoribus*, pp. 202–203. For the *Reportatio in primum* I count the following marginal citations: Scotus (39), Henry of Ghent (26), Auriol (25), Aquinas (19), Guy Terrina (10), Gerard of Bologna (7), Robert Walsingham, OCarm (6), Wylton (6), Hervaeus Natalis (6), Giles of Rome (5), Godfrey of Fontaines (5), Durand (3), and fourteen others with fewer references. For a *Scriptum* reference, cf. e.g. d. 27 (ms. British Library, Royal 11 C VI, fol. 114vb): "Concordat Aureolus, d. 27, q. 1, a. 1, prop. prima, et d. 3, q. de ymagine, a. 1, prop. prima," referring to a text in ed. Friedman, "*In principio erat Verbum*," pp. 377-81. For books II and III I count only two such references to Auriol, while Scotus (23), Aquinas (15), Henry (15), Godfrey (9) Durand (8), Hervaeus (4), Wylton (3), and Giles (3) have more. This might suggest that Baconthorpe knew only the *Scriptum in primum*, but in the one place I have inspected carefully I have found a lengthy section taken verbatim from Auriol's *Reportatio* II, d. 2, without attribution; see Schabel, "Place, Space, and the Physics of Grace in Auriol's *Sentences* Commentary," p. 139

[14]   Johannes Baconthorpe, *I Sent.*, d. 38, q. 1 (ed. Cremona, p. 376bC): "Utrum ideae divinae distinguantur ex natura rei," and d. 39, q. 1 (p. 379aF): "Quid sentiendum sit de divinis ideis, attributis, et emanationibus ad intra in via Commentatoris." Hoenen, *Marsilius of Inghen*, mentions Baconthorpe's opinions on divine knowledge in many places.

[15]   Baconthorpe, *I Sent.*, d. 39, q. 1, a. 1 (ed. Cremona, p. 382–first p. 382; after 383 the edition returns to 380-83 again bC–D): "In ista via videtur Aureolus concordare mecum, d. 35, q. 2, a. 2, sed tamen in re totaliter discordat. Negat enim Deum cognoscere creaturas terminative, sicut et ego, sed vult per hoc quod Deus non intelligat eas aliquo actu apprehensivo quoquo modo attingente eas, sed solum dicuntur intelligi a Deo denominative; puta quod Deus apprehendendo se, qui est tota entitas eminenter, ab illa apprehensione denominantur entia participata fore intellecta," and (first p. 383aB): "essentia est similitudo eminens omnium." Baconthorpe's interest in the question of the object of God's knowledge spills over into several quodlibetal questions, i.e. *Quodlibet* I, qq. 9–12, and *Quodlibet* II, qq. 1–3 and 5–7. Cf. Glorieux, *La littérature quodlibétique* II, pp. 149–51.

not enough, because he holds that God must 'touch' creatures in an apprehensive act. He gives an argument from salvation, saying that if God wills someone to be saved, He must judge him to be saved, and judgement involves active apprehension, and practical willing. Baconthorpe thus does not accept, or rather understand, Auriol's specific distinction between the intrinsic and extrinsic will of God, a distinction crucial to Auriol's account. Baconthorpe therefore explicitly does not accept what he calls 'contrary volitions', which God has according to Auriol's theory of General Election. Auriol held that God wills, by His will of complacency, that those who qualify be saved, and that those who do not qualify be damned. For Baconthorpe, who requires a more active will and hence knowledge, these are contrary volitions.[16] Baconthorpe goes on to say that denying God such apprehensions is theologically dangerous.[17] The sort of divine will Baconthorpe and most others have in mind is not one that would agree with Auriol's conception of God's absolute necessity. So Baconthorpe is free in distinction 40 to return to the Lombardian method of compounding and dividing, and the distinction between God's absolute and ordained powers, which Auriol had rejected in arguing for one of his main points: God cannot have foreknowledge per se, because everything would happen of necessity.

In distinction 40, Baconthorpe asks "Whether divine foreknowledge destroys our freedom." As we have seen (see above, chapter two), in the 'Reportatio' Baconthorpe was content to copy Thomas Wylton and accept his determination, but in the Ordinatio he changed his mind. Here his procedure with Wylton is similar to Peter of Palude's with respect to Durand: he first presents nearly the whole of Wylton's treatment, deleting on occasion some material present in his Reportatio, before turning to oppose Wylton in a somewhat brief determination.

Not surprisingly, Baconthorpe does not mention Auriol explicitly in distinction 40. Baconthorpe thought Wylton's position included a couple of contradictions, namely that in the consequence, 'God knows that X will exist; therefore X will exist', Wylton accepted the necessity of the antecedent and yet considered the consequent contingent because of God's permissive will and our free will. And Baconthorpe had already shown an aversion to a similar distinction in God's will that Auriol posited. Wylton also denied that the consequent is determinate, then later allowed for a lesser degree of determination. Perhaps Baconthorpe deemed Auriol's theory of future contingent proposi-

---

[16] Baconthorpe, I Sent., d. 39, q. 1 (ed. Cremona, p. 383 bA–C — i.e. the first p. 383, following which the edition goes to 380–83 again): "Deus vult me salvandum: sed si solum cognitus sum ab eo denominative, non apprehensive, hoc non erit, quia voluntas ferretur in non apprehensum. Confirmatur, quia quod apprehenditur ut Deus non est volitum salvari, immo quod apprehenditur ut non Deus est volitum salvari. Sed Deus non est natus simul habere tales contradictorias apprehensiones et tales contradictorias volitiones... Quod aliquid sit volitum salvari oportet iudicari ut salvandum; iudicium enim est in apprehensione; sed Deus non iudicatur salvandus, sed aliud; igitur. Confirmatur, quia velle salvari pertinet ad praxim, quia est circa factibile; sed ad praxim concurrit apprehensio cum velle."
[17] Baconthorpe, I Sent., d. 39, q. 1 (ed. Cremona, second p. 380aB): "Periculosum est negare a Deo, quod est perfectionis in anima..."

tions to be a version of Wylton's stance. Baconthorpe himself grounds contingency in God's will, although unlike Scotus he asserts that the divine will is contingent only as it extends itself to contingents in creation.[18]

Not only does Baconthorpe's procedure lack innovation, but his solution is neither new nor insightful: God knows the future, but He knows that contingent events will occur contingently, not just that Adam will sin, but that Adam will sin by a bad use of his free will. So the consequence should be, 'God knows that X will come about contingently; therefore X will come about contingently'. That is, "the consequent requires some added conditions, both in the antecedent and in the consequent."[19] One could still claim that these events are still inevitable, but Baconthorpe counters that they are only "conditionally or concomitatively inevitable, although in themselves they are avoidable, as are all things which come under God's general influence and permissive will."[20] He borrows Wylton's terms, but Baconthorpe's solution is the familiar one from Boethius based on the distinction between absolute and conditional necessity.

It is not clear why Baconthorpe quoted the arguments of Wylton so extensively. Perhaps it was because of Wylton's modifications of Scotus. Baconthorpe chose to refute Auriol's conception of God's knowledge of things outside Himself in distinction 38. In distinction 40, he concentrated on refuting Wylton's claims about the necessity that resulted from foreknowledge strictly taken, and Baconthorpe had a different interpretation of the truth-value of future contingent propositions. In this distinction, Baconthorpe is forced to re-evaluate Scotus's stance in light of Wylton's and Auriol's attacks. Baconthorpe fell back on the position that God foreknows the use of free will when He foreknows contingent events in the future, but not before Baconthorpe drew further distinctions on the term 'inevitability'.

---

[18]   Baconthorpe, *I Sent.*, d. 40, q. 1, a. 2 (ed. Cremona, pp. 390bE–391aA): "Miror de Gilton. Prima quia vult quod hec est necessaria: 'Deus scit hoc fore,' ut patuit supra, ubi arguit contra principalem conclusionem, et tamen concedit quod consequens est contingens, quia solum dependens a sola voluntate permissiva Dei et nostra libera... Secundo miror quod neget quod sit determinate vera, licet non sit necessaria, quia infra in positione sua concedit esse determinate veram... Sine preiudicio ergo dico quod antecedens est contingens, sed non accipiendo contingentiam quamcumque ex parte divine voluntatis et intellectus (ut videtur Scotus imaginari) sed accipiendo contingentiam intellectus divini ut extendit se ad contingens in creatura."
[19]   Baconthorpe, *I Sent.*, d. 40, a. 3 (ed. Cremona, p. 391aB–C): "Tertius articulus: quomodo valeat ista consequentia, 'Deus scit hoc fore; ergo erit'. Ubi dico quod consequentia requirit aliquas conditiones additas et in antecedente et in consequente. Et premitto quod Augustinus in libello *De triplici habitaculo* concedit Deum ab eterno scivisse Adam peccaturum, negat tamen quod propter hoc Adam necessario peccaverit. Et ratio sua est hec: quia Deus scivit Adam peccaturum sic quod non peccaret nisi secundum modum secundum quem Deus scivit eum peccaturum; sed Deus non scivit Adam peccaturum nisi quia prescivit ipsum male usurum suo libero arbitrio; ergo..."
[20]   Baconthorpe, *I Sent.*, d. 40, a. 4 (ed. Cremona, p. 391bC): "Dico enim quod triplex est inevitabile... quoddam inevitabile concomitative seu conditionaliter, sed in se vitabile, ut sunt omnia que subsunt generali influxui Dei et voluntati permissive eius."

Walter Burley

Another Englishman, the secular theologian Walter Burley (ca. 1275–1344/5), was a prominent scholar at Paris, staying there from 1310 to 1327, and it is interesting to note that he was a student of Thomas Wylton. Burley's *Sentences* commentary, like most of Wylton's, has not been identified. We do have more than one commentary on *Peri Hermeneias* from Burley, however, and in the final one he speaks of God. His so-called 'Middle Commentary' is relatively brief, approximately 260 lines, and in it he does not treat God, but he does discuss Aristotle's position as Wylton and Auriol saw it.[21] Burley's final commentary, from his later Oxford years, is several times longer, and in it he treats God's knowledge, discusses and refutes at length what Auriol held to be Aristotle's position, and implies, according to Boehner, that Aristotle did not hold that position.[22]

It is tempting to put forth the following scenario: Burley wrote his Middle Commentary unaware of Auriol's position. Later, perhaps, either through his master, Thomas Wylton, or directly, Burley became cognizant of Auriol's radical position. In his final commentary of 1337, Burley went into much greater detail, discussing the implications of divine foreknowledge, and rejecting Auriol's position on neutral propositions, even going so far as to *omit* a discussion of Aristotle's final opinion on the matter.[23]

Bernard Lombardi the Dominican

Perhaps unjustly, the period in Paris between Auriol and Rimini has been labeled one of 'school traditions', where most theologians simply reiterated, defended, and sometimes elaborated on the positions of the great masters of their orders, Aquinas for the Dominicans, Scotus for the Franciscans, and Giles of Rome for the Augustinians. For the Carmelites, Baconthorpe had no such towering figure to stifle innovative tendencies; he simply lacked originality on this issue. The Franciscans had the distinct advantage of having no offi-

---

[21] Thus Burley concludes his Middle Commentary: "Igitur sic erit in propositionibus de futuro quod nec erunt determinate verae nec determinate falsae, et sic non oportet in illis de futuro quod affirmatio et negatio sit vera vel falsa" (Brown ed., "Walter Burley's Middle Commentary," p. 96). For a recent bibliography and list of Burley's works, see Gerhard Krieger, "Studies on Walter Burley 1989–1997," *Vivarium* 37.1 (1999), pp. 94–100, who continues Rega Wood's bibliography from *Bulletin de philosophie médiévale* with the help of Olga Weijer's bibliography.

[22] Boehner, *The Tractatus*, pp. 82–3. Boehner quotes some of the relevant passages in Burley's Latin text. I have not seen the actual text, and have relied on Norman Kretzmann's English translation, preliminary draft, from the Oklahoma Translation Clearing House. For discussion of the role of divine foreknowledge, see pp. 11–17 of Kretzmann, or fol. 68rb–69rb of the 1497 Venice edition of Burley's text.

[23] For example pp. 11–12 of Kretzmann's translation (fol. 68rb): "And according to that view 'God knows that A will be' would have to be denied (let A be a future contingent); for nothing is known unless it is true... and that A will be is not true. And so God does not know that A will be, nor does he know that A will not be." For the dates of Burley's *Peri Hermeneias* commentaries, see Brown, "Walter Burley's Middle Commentary," pp. 42–3.

THE REACTION OUTSIDE THE FRANCISCAN CONVENT   181

cial teaching doctor, however, and this allowed for diverging views. The Dominicans and Augustinians, on the other hand, were obliged to defend Aquinas and Giles respectively. Since Giles's position resembled Aquinas's, de
facto both orders were officially required to defend Thomist theories of divine
foreknowledge.

A few Dominicans active during or just after Auriol's Parisian *Sentences* lectures have left quodlibetal questions, namely John of Naples, Henry of Lübeck,
and Raymond Bequini, the latter of whom also wrote a *Correctorium* of
Auriol's errors. Only John of Naples's brief *Quodlibet* X, question six, concerns
future contingents, however.[24] The one securely identifiable surviving Parisian
Dominican *Sentences* commentary from the period between Auriol and Rimini
is that of Bernard Lombardi, who lectured in 1327–28. Bernard was probably
from Provence, despite his name. He had been the Preaching Friars' prior provincial of Provence since 1323 when the 1327 general chapter at Perpignan assigned him to read the *Sentences* at Paris. He became a master in 1331–32, but
his date of death is unknown. His main surviving works are a *Quodlibet* and a
Sentences commentary on all four books.[25] Like Peter of Palude, Bernard's
practice in his *Sentences* commentary was to incorporate large passages of Durand of St. Pourçain's commentary, in this case Durand's third redaction, and
in fact Bernard gives us the *terminus ante quem* of 1327 for this version.[26] Bernard usually goes on to refute Durand, however, and in the only part of his
Sentences commentary printed so far, a question on being and essence, Bernard
also copies lengthy passages from Peter Auriol before turning to oppose him.[27]

---

[24]   Hervaeus Natalis's brief *Quodlibet* V, q. 6, "Utrum angeli cognoscant futura contingentia" (ed. Venice 1513, ff. 119vb-120rb) may date to this period, but it is not very pertinent, nor
is John of Naples's question, which I inspected in ms. Tortosa, Archivo de la Catedral 244 (ff.
152rb-vb). Henry of Lübeck probably read the *Sentences* outside of Paris just after Auriol, but
the commentary does not survive, since the manuscripts that Stegmüller (*Repertorium* I, p. 156)
claimed contained this work apparently do not, although they do contain his *Quodlibeta*. Cf. Waclaw Bucichowski, "Le principe d'individuation dans la question de Henri de Lubeck 'Utrum
materia sit principium individuationis'," MPP 21 (1975), p. 92. For a question list, see Glorieux,
La littérature quodlibetique II, pp. 134–7, and for Bequini's *Quodlibet* from ca. 1320, see p. 238. On
Bequini, see recently William Duba, "The Afterlife in Medieval Frankish Cyprus," *Epetirida of
the Cyprus Research Centre* 26 (2000) (pp. 167–94), pp. 179–84, and for the questions in his *Correctorium*, F. Pelster, "Zur ersten Polemik gegen Aureoli," FcS 15 (1955), pp. 30–47.
[25]   For Bernard's life and question lists of his works, see Stanislaw A. Porebski, "La
question de Bernard Lombardi concernant la différence réelle entre l'essence et l'existence," MPP
17 (1973), pp. 157–85. There are four mss. for his *Sentences* commentary, of which only Leipzig,
Univ. 542, contains all four books.
[26]   See Fumagalli, *Durando di S. Porziano*, p. xi-xii.
[27]   This is *I Sent.*, q. 21, in Porebski's edition, from Leipzig, in "La question de Bernard
Lombardi," pp. 169–85. Porebski's edition is problematic, because although he is basically
aware of the positions presented, he gives no indication that over half of Bernard's text is taken
verbatim from Durand and Auriol. Compare ll. 2–35, 59–76, 116–29, 135–59, and 196–287 with
Durandus, *I Sent.*, d. 8, q. 2 (ed. Venice, ff. 35ra–vb), paragraphs 1–2, 5–7, and 9–16. Ll. 350–501
is Auriol's determination verbatim from *Scriptum* I, d. 8, q. 1, aa. 2–3 (vol. 2, ed. Buytaert), pp.
898, 901–2, 907–12, and 914, although it is merely attributed to an "auteur anonyme... dont les
conceptions se rapprochent de celles de Pierre Aureoli et Durand" (Porebski, p. 167). One oddity
with Bernard's text is that although he copies down most of Durand's opening arguments, he
fails to refute them, even though Durand had! The reason for this is probably because Durand's
third version entirely lacks a determination. It ends with Durand's presentation of Hervaeus Na-

Thus Bernard Lombardi at least partially employs the technique of reading *secundum alium*, or "according to another." In the 1310s and 1320s at Paris it was common for one scholar to follow another. Thus many Franciscans followed Scotus, the anonymous Franciscan of Vienna ÖNB 1439 followed Caracciolo, Himbert of Garda and Pastor followed Meyronnes, and we shall see that Michael of Massa and others followed Francis of Marchia. In some cases the later theologian was presenting his own work, often with significant modifications on his 'model'. There are some instances of paraphrasing, and even of major verbatim copying, apparently especially among the Dominicans, but also with the Augustinian Dionysius de Burgo Sancti Sepulchri and the Carmelite Baconthorpe. The 'best' example, however, was the Franciscan Aufredo Gonteri Brito, as we shall see.

In the context of divine foreknowledge and future contingents, question 47 of book I, Bernard Lombardi basically summarizes Durand's pertinent questions, usually verbatim, copying some sentences and paragraphs and omitting others. Occasionally Bernard actually says he is giving Durand's position, but only when Bernard is about to make one of his brief 'original' contributions to theology, and in those cases he gives a defense of Aquinas's position against Durand.[28] Thus unlike in the question on being and essence, Bernard shows no knowledge of Auriol on future contingents.

How much this tells us about the Dominican order at Paris and the extent of Auriol's influence is hard to say. It is only a sample of one, and we have seen two Franciscans from this period who did not show evidence of Auriol's influence on this issue. Perhaps it is true that Dominicans were simply satisfied with what Aquinas had to say on many topics, and even with Durand's contribution, except where the two clashed, in which case they defended Aquinas. If this scenario is true, then there was not merely one conversation going on at Paris, just as a different one was going on in Oxford. It is probably the case, however, either that the Dominican order was stagnant, or that Bernard is simply a poor representative of Dominican scholarship at Paris.

---

talis's position, "Alii autem sunt qui dicunt quod," which Bernard reproduces in full. I am not prepared to say that the rest of Bernard's text is original with him. It appears that Wladislaw Senko later reedited this question in *Opera philosophorum medii aevi* 2 (1978), pp. 103–20, but I have not seen this edition.

[28]   He does the same in his treatment of predestination. In Bałcoyiannopoulou, Friedman, and my edition of Palude's book I, distinction 38, q. 3, on future contingents, in "Peter of Palude," the text de facto also covers Durand's versions two and three of the corresponding d. 38, q. 3. Whatever Bernard Lombardi adds to Durand is given in an appendix on the basis of Erfurt, Wissenschaftliche Bibliothek C.A. 2° 368 (fol. 118vb–122rb). The same is done for Dionysius de Burgo Sancti Sepulchri, on whom, see below, and we hope to include John of Naples's quodlibetal question on future contingents and James of Lausanne's material from the second version of his *Sentences* commentary of ca. 1315.

Augustinians

Bernard was not the only theologian, however, to copy Durand. The Augustinian Dionysius de Burgo Sancti Sepulchri (†1342), a *socius* of Auriol, had also done so when he was lecturing on the *Sentences* at Paris in 1316–17. In the period between Auriol and 1345, besides the Franciscans only the Augustinians had collectively a major impact on Parisian theology, with a half dozen surviving commentaries on book I attributed to named Augustinians. There are in addition an anonymous commentary, Henry of Friemar the Younger's popular book IV, and the *Quodlibeta* of Prosper de Reggio Emilia, William of Cremona, and James of Pamiers, none of which contain material on divine foreknowledge.[29]

However, Dionysius, who became master of theology in about 1323, is not among the most significant Augustinian theologians, although he is interesting for his ties with Petrarch and for his humanistic tendencies, being the author of a commentary on Valerius Maximus, for example. Dionysius's commentary on books I–II of the *Sentences* survives in only one manuscript, but a question list has been published along with an analysis of the marginalia of Erfurt Amplon. 2° 131, and so it is worth looking at the state of his order at the beginning of our period. Not surprisingly we find that Dionysius supports Giles of Rome, "Our Doctor," often in relation to Aquinas, with whom Giles sometimes agreed and sometimes did not. Henry of Ghent figures prominently as an opponent, as does Durand.

But marginalia and even explicit citations in the text can only tell part of the story. For example, in his distinction 38, question three, "Whether God knows future contingents," Dionysius in fact copies columns of Durand's distinction 38, question three, verbatim, without any textual or marginal attribution at all. Dionysius only strays from verbatim copying when he wants to shorten his discussion, at which point he paraphrases. It is humorous to note that he even reproduces Durand's opening arguments without their corresponding refutation at the end! Of course, Dionysius merely likes Durand's presentation, because when it comes to Durand's determination, he inserts a brief defense of Aquinas's eternal presence solution instead. Despite the fact that it does not fit with what he had just copied from Durand, Dionysius

---

[29] On Dionysius, see Damasus Trapp, "Augustinian Theology," pp. 156–60, and, for the question and citation list, idem, "The *Quaestiones* of Dionysius de Burgo O.S.A.," *Augustinianum* 3 (1963), pp. 63–78. For a recent bibliography, see Weijers, ed., *Le travail intellectuel... C-F*, pp. 47–8. The Parisian lectures of Friemar, whose book IV survives in over a dozen complete witnesses, may have taken place in 1318–19; for Henry and Dionysius, see Adolar Zumkeller, "Die Augustinerschule des Mittelalters: Vertreter und philosophisch-theologische Lehre," *Analecta Augustiniana* 27 (1964) (pp. 167–262), pp. 207–8. The anonymous commentary on book I in Wien, Dominikanerkloster 160/130 (ff. 1–24vb, on which see Tachau, *Vision and Certitude*, p. 318–20) stops before d. 38. On the *Quodlibet* of James of Pamiers, from about 1332, see Glorieux, *La littérature quodlibétique* II, pp. 142–3, and for dating, William Courtenay, "The *Quaestiones in Sententias* of Michael de Massa, OESA. A Redating," *Augustiniana* 45 (1995) (pp. 191–207), pp. 195–6. For William of Cremona's *Quodlibet*, from before 1326, and Prosper de Reggio Emilia's, from 1317–18, see Glorieux, *La littérature quodlibétique* II, pp. 116 and 233–4, respectively.

adds that God also knows future contingents because his will and intellect are their causes. In this he is following another branch of Aquinas interpreters.[30]

In sum, Dionysius shows that the Augustinians in this time are closely connected to the Dominicans and Aquinas, that Durand had considerable influence outside his order, and that Dionysius's own *Sentences* commentary is conservative. But there are doubts about the precise nature of that conservativism, because one cannot say much about a text based solely on marginalia without knowing the text itself and the texts of many previous thinkers as well. Unfortunately for the historian, scholastics tended to cite chronologically-distant figures both when they agreed and disagreed with them, but when it came to citing more recent thinkers with whom they agreed, they often kept the credit for themselves. Thus not only does Dionysius not mention Durand at all in the question of future contingents, where Dionysius does mention Durand, as in a marginal note in distinction 38, question one, he simply says "against Durand," and he cites Giles favorably in question two.[31]

Gerard of Siena's Parisian *Sentences* commentary was considerably more popular and, although it is not saying much, more original. Gerard (†1336) was an important Augustinian author, who has left us with a few quodlibetal questions, a treatise on the principal of individuation, and works on moral theology and canon law. The latest person he cites in his *Sentences* commentary is Landulph Caracciolo, and his lectures have been dated as early as 1322–3, although some put them in about 1325. At any rate he was a bachelor of theology in the spring of 1327, and a master in about 1329.[32] Book I was printed in Padua in 1598, and survives in more than twenty manuscripts, while book II is extant in perhaps a half dozen, making this work one of the most widely circulated of the era.[33]

According to Damasus Trapp's general analysis of the text and marginalia from Gerard's and Michael of Massa's commentary, Gerard's main opponent generally was Auriol, through whom he also attacked Scotus. Gerard often supported Giles of Rome, calling him '*doctor noster*'. Michael of Massa in turn

---

[30] The *entire* 'original' contribution of Dionysius can be quoted here! Dionysius, *I Sent.*, d. 38, q. 3, a. 2 (ms. Erfurt C.A. 2° 131, fol. 90vb), continuing from Durand's "Deus novit ab eterno illam propriam et actualem existentiam quam se habent processu, sic quod Deus cognoscit futura" (cf. Durandus, ed. Venice, p. 104va, para. 11), he adds "Quod patet tripliciter…" the first way being in agreement with Durand, then "… Secundo sic: illa Deus cognoscit quorum est causa; sed est causa futurorum contingentium; ergo etc. Maior supponitur, cum sit causa per intellectum et voluntatem. Minor probatur, quia nihil habens aliquam entitatem Dei subterfugit causalitatem; ergo etc. Tertio sic: eternum non concernit tempus; ergo omnia, sive futura sive presentia sive preterita, sunt presentia eternitati; sed Deus est eternus et eternitate mensuratur; ergo etc."

[31] Dionysius cites Durand in *I Sent.*, d. 38, q. 1 (Erfurt 131, fol. 90ra).

[32] According to Courtenay, 'The *Quaestiones in Sententias* of Michael de Massa," p. 195. Trapp, "Augustinian Theology," pp. 161 and 172–3, puts his lectures in about 1325–26, and Zumkeller, "Die Augustinerschule des Mittelalters," pp. 208–9, concurs with Trapp. There is some disagreement about the authorship of Gerard's *Quodlibet*, from about 1330, but Glorieux, *La littérature quodlibétique* II, pp. 97–8, lists no question on divine foreknowledge.

[33] Cf. Stegmüller, *Repertorium* I, pp. 115–16, and Doucet, *Commentaires sur les Sentences*, p. 33. Doucet claims that mss. Coimbre, Univ. 727, and Roma, Biblioteca Angelica 338, both contain books I through *III*.

criticized Gerard for his critique of Auriol, and for his failure to represent his opponents fairly. In contrast, Michael supported Auriol, explicitly against Gerard. Trapp further claimed that Massa's support of Auriol and attack on Gerard, and hence Giles, may partly explain the impression that most later Augustinians ignored Massa, and that his order did not make him a master, though he left a large body of writings.[34] As we shall see here and in the following chapter, Trapp's analysis is not fully justified in the context of divine foreknowledge.

Gerard's discussion of the problem of future contingents and divine foreknowledge is found in his distinction 38, and in distinction 39 he deals with providence. The discussion is rather brief, and in it Gerard does not treat future contingent propositions. He does focus on Auriol's discussion, however. In fact, all of Gerard's treatment, with the exception of the criticisms of Auriol, could have been gleaned from Auriol's own commentary. Gerard asks "whether future contingents are immutably represented in the divine essence," and he divides this question into two articles, "whether future contingents are infallibly represented in the divine essence," and "whether future contingents are present to the divine intellect and infallibly known by it."[35]

In article one Gerard first gives the opinion involving divine Ideas, attributed here to Aquinas and Giles of Rome, then Scotus's refutation of this position, which Gerard partially opposes and partially supports. Next Gerard gives Scotus's own opinion and the order of the instants of nature in which Scotus presents his solution. Gerard ends the article in a way consistent with Trapp's analysis, by giving Auriol's refutation of Scotus. Gerard says along with Auriol that Scotus's solution introduces possibility into the divine essence in several ways, and Gerard seems to agree here with Auriol's description of the simplicity and necessity of the divine essence.[36]

If one were to stop here one would think Trapp that had it wrong, and that Gerard was really an Auriolist, because Gerard agrees with Auriol when concluding:

---

[34]   Trapp, "Augustinian Theology," pp. 161–4 and 170–73.

[35]   Gerardus de Senis, *Super primum librum Sententiarum*, d. 38 (ed. Padua 1598, p. 573b; Chicago, University Library 22, fol. 143ra): "Utrum futura contingentia in divina essentia immutabiliter repraesententur," and a.1: "Utrum in divina essentia infallibiliter repraesententur futura contingentia," and (p. 575a; Chicago 22, fol. 143rb) a.2: "Utrum futura contingentia sint divino intellectui praesentia et infallibiliter ab eo cognita." The Padua edition incorrectly has 'praesententur' in the question in article one; I have read 'repraesententur,' following Chicago.

[36]   Senis, *I Sent.*, d. 38, a. 1 (ed. Padua, pp. 574a–575a), e.g. p. 574b (Chicago 22, fol. 143rb): "Primum est quia aliqua limitatio et possibilitas esset in representatione divinae essentiae, quod omnino est inconveniens." Trapp has indicated that the Padua edition, which I have looked at, is "of very doubtful value" ("Augustinian Theology," p. 161). The edition is quite coherent, but Trapp's assessment is borne out by the fact that Scotus's opinion is ascribed to Auriol in the margin, and Auriol's opinion is labelled "contra Auriolum" in the margin. The correct attribution is given in Chicago, in which distinction 38 is found at fol. 143ra–143vb. Chicago correctly has "contra Scotum" instead of "contra Auriolum," but does not ascribe the refutation of Scotus to Auriol, as it could. The incorrect ascription in the edition is either the 16th-century editor's, or an error of the manuscript(s) from which he was working. In general, however, the Padua edition is not unreliable for distinction 38.

It seems therefore that one must answer in another way, namely that future contingents are represented immutably in the divine essence because of its highest actuality, to which it is repugnant to expect anything in the future. And therefore whatever it represents, it represents invariably and immutably. Thus it must either be said that future contingents are in no way represented in the divine essence, which is clearly false, since it itself is the exemplar form of all beings; or it must be said that they are represented in it naturally and immutably. And this is, briefly, what I understand concerning this article.[37]

It is in the second article, however, that Gerard opposes Auriol. Contrary to what Michael of Massa may charge generally, Gerard gives an accurate description of Auriol's stance on how God knows future contingents, and the position is attributed to Auriol explicitly in the Chicago manuscript ("Opinio Aurioli," fol. 143rb). He cites Auriol's phrase that the divine essence is the "eminent similitude and exemplar of the actuality of every future thing whatever," but Gerard stretches Auriol's words in saying that by 'ending' in the divine essence, the divine intellect is 'ended' (*terminatus*) in the actuality of a future thing, because the divine essence is at least as capable of providing knowledge as the actuality itself. Auriol was careful not to say that the divine intellect 'ended' at these actualities. Using language from Auriol's *Scriptum*, Gerard also sees that in Auriol's account the divine essence "abstracts from the entire successive line," that is from preterition and futurition, and that nothing is therefore coexistent with the divine essence, but rather the divine essence is indistant from the actuality of the future thing.[38]

As elsewhere, however, Gerard cites Auriol, ultimately, as his principal opponent, giving several points in which he claims Auriol's account fails.[39] Gerard holds that in fact the divine intuition does not simply end at the es-

---

[37] Senis, *I Sent.*, d. 38, a. 1 (ed. Padua, p. 575a; Chicago 22, fol. 143rb): "Videtur ergo aliter esse dicendum, scilicet quod futura contingentia representantur immutabiliter in divina essentia propter suam summam actualitatem, cui repugnat expectare aliquid in futurum. Et ideo quicquid representat, invariabiliter et immutabiliter representat. Quapropter vel erit dicendum quod futura contingentia nullo modo represententur in divina essentia, quod patet esse falsum, cum ipsa sit forma exemplaris omnium entium; vel erit dicendum quod represententur in ea naturaliter et immutabiliter. Et hoc est breviter quod intelligo de isto articulo."

[38] Senis, *I Sent*, d. 38, a. 2 (ed. Padua, p. 575b ; Chicago 22, fol. 143va–vb): "Quapropter tota causa quare* cognoscuntur est quia divina essentia potest esse et est eminens similitudo et exemplar actualitatis cuiuscumque futuri, et ideo intellectus terminatus ad essentiam dicitur terminatus ad actualitatem cuiuscumque futuri, ex eo quod terminatur ad aliquod aequipollens et plusquam aequipollens. Quod autem divina essentia sit similitudo et exemplar actualitatis cuiuscumque futuri probant per hoc, quia divina essentia (secundum eos) abstrahit a tota** linea successiva, et per consequens abstrahit a praeteritione, ita ut nihil sit ei praeteritum; abstrahit etiam a futuritione,*** ita ut nihil sit simultaneae coexistentiae. Et ita abstractio est tota causa (secundum eos) quare divina essentia non potest distare ab aliqua differentia temporis, nec etiam aliqua differentia temporis sibi simultaneae coexistere. Quapropter videtur relinqui quod sine omni falsitate possit representare actualitatem cuiuscumque futuri tanquam indistans ab ea." For * Chicago adds "infallibiliter" (fol. 143rb). At **, Chicago has "totali" instead of 'tota' (fol. 143va). The *** represents an omission *per homeoteleuton*, of "ita ut nihil sit ei futurum; abstrahit insuper a simultate coexistentie et presenti," which is in fact found in Chicago (fol. 143va).

[39] Chicago 22 introduces this section with "contra Auriolum" (fol. 143va).

sence, but also ends at something besides the essence as a secondary object.[40] Here Gerard opposes both Auriol and one of Auriol's main critics on this point, John Baconthorpe. In addition, Gerard follows Francis of Meyronnes in attacking Auriol's position as a negative solution in its emphasis on abstraction from time.[41]

Gerard's last points of criticism foreshadow his own solution. Auriol's account is deficient in that it denies that anything can coexist with God simultaneously. Gerard's position is that of Aquinas and Giles: all things are in fact present to God. One reason is that God causes some things, and there must be coexistence of some kind between the cause and the effect. Another argument asserts that because the divine essence is present to the divine intellect, and is the exemplar of future contingents, these future contingents must also be present to the intellect. Gerard is also opposed to Auriol in that he holds that future things can be revealed, and can be known as future, as revelations to angels demonstrate.[42]

To the objection that these futures would really be present, Gerard gives the old Dominican response that they would only be present "by a presentiality giving them knowability *as if* they were really existing," not a presentiality giving them real and actual existence.[43] Hence there is no reason for Gerard to argue at length with Auriol's position about the truth content of future contingent propositions, because he sees no difficulty with that, and only admits in the end that God's foreknowledge of future contingents confers conditional

---

[40]   Senis, *I Sent*, d. 38, a. 2 (ed. Padua, p. 575b; Chicago 22, fol. 143va): "... supponit quod divinus intuitus non terminetur ad aliquid ultra divinam essentiam, tanquam ad secundarium obiectum, cuius contrarium fuit ostensum superius contra eos..."

[41]   Senis, *I Sent*, d. 38, a. 2 (p. 575b; Chicago 22, fol. 143va): "... representatio futuri est aliquod positivum; abstractio vero divinae essentiae a linea successionis est aliquid negativum; affirmatio autem non debet reduci in negationem."

[42]   Senis, *I Sent.*, d. 38, a. 2 (ed. Padua, p. 576a; Chicago 22, fol. 143va): "Tertio, ponit quod nihil potest simultanee coexistere ipsi Deo. Ad quod dictum sequuntur duo inconvenientia; primum est quia Deus non erit causa in actu respectu creaturae, quod est falsum... quia de ratione effectus est quod coexistat simultanee suae causae," and "Quarto deficit quia ponit quod per illam representationem qua futura contingentia representantur in divina essentia non redduntur intellectui divino praescientia, quod etiam est falsum propter duo. Primo, quia alio modo obijcitur essentia divina intellectui suo, ut essentia est, et alio modo ut exemplar futurorum contingentium est, et per consequens aliquid redditur sibi praesens per hoc... per hoc vero quod obijcitur secundo modo efficiuntur ei praesentia, ultra hoc etiam futura contingentia. Secundo, quia... potest reddere futura contingentia praesentia intellectui creato, sicut patet in revelationes Angelorum," and "Et ideo adhuc est alia opinio quae ponit quod... totus descursus temporis ei praesentialiter coexistit." In margin, next to this last line, Chicago has "Opinio Thome et Egidii." After giving objections to this position, Gerard says (p. 576b; Chicago 22, fol. 143va): "Illis tamen non obstantibus dico quod si bene intelligatur illa opinio videtur omnino rationalis."

[43]   Senis, *I Sent*, d. 38, a. 2 (ed. Padua, p. 576b; Chicago 22, fol. 143va–vb): "Et ideo ad evidentiam huius est notandum quod futura contingentia esse praesentia vel coexistentia intellectui divino potest intelligi dupliciter. Uno modo quod sint ei praesentia praesentialitate dante eis realem et actualem existentiam in natura, et isto modo non intelligo opininionem. Nec unquam intellectus huius opinionis potest esse talis, nam si futura contingentia essent praesentia divino intellectui isto modo, iam non essent amplius futura, sed simpliciter praesentia. Alio vero modo potest intelligi quod sint praesentia praesentialitate dante eis tantam cognoscibilitatem, ac si essent realiter existentia, ita ut eorum perfecta cognoscibilitas nullo modo expectet eorundem existentiam, et isto modo intelligo quod opinio sit simpliciter vera."

necessity on the futures, not absolute necessity.[44] Gerard's response seems to be an early defense, against Auriol, of Boethius, Aquinas, and Giles's position that things are eternally present to God. One might also note that the many positive remarks Gerard makes about Auriol's stance underscore the probability that Gerard recognized Auriol's solution to have much in common with that of Aquinas and Giles.

Dionysius and Gerard indicate that the Augustinians maintained a close connection to the conservative Parisian Dominicans in the 1310s and 1320s. The history of Parisian theological *development* in the 1320s is almost solely the history of Franciscan theology. The primary figure in this development is another Franciscan, Francis of Marchia, but as we shall see, Augustinian theology at Paris would be revitalized in the 1330s by Michael of Massa, who gave a closer and, with regard to Marchia, more sympathetic reading of the Franciscans. By the mid-1330s the Augustinian order was on its way to assuming the role of intellectual leadership it was to hold at Paris in the 1340s and perhaps beyond. It does not appear that the Dominicans had a similar revitalization at the University of Paris in the fourteenth century.

---

[44] Senis, *I Sent.*, d. 38, a. 2 (ed. Padua, p. 577a; Chicago 22, fol. 143vb): "Infallibilis cognitio Dei non dat futuris contingentibus necessitatem absolutam, sed necessitatem conditionatam; necessitas autem conditionata bene potest stare cum contingentia..."

Chapter 9

The Marchist School

Francis of Marchia

Life and Works

I will draw three basic conclusions about Francis of Marchia's treatment of the problem of divine foreknowledge and future contingents: (1) his main opponent was Peter Auriol, (2) he developed an interesting new theory, and (3) his theory was among the most influential in the later Middle Ages. That these are *my* original conclusions might come as a surprise, but until recently very little attention has been given to Marchia's thought. Indeed, I count only two studies published before 1986 that devote more than ten pages to Marchia. Significantly, Hermann Schwamm's *Das göttliche Vorherwissen* is one of these, but as in the case of Peter Auriol, Schwamm accidentally serves to cloud Marchia's doctrine and his historical importance.[1]

Francis of Marchia, also known as Francis de Pignano, Francis de Esculo, Franciscus Rubeus, and the *Doctor Succinctus*, may be the most important Parisian theologian from the period between Auriol and Rimini.[2] Born around 1290 in the province of Ascoli Piceno in the area south of Ancona, Marchia lectured on the *Sentences* at Paris in 1319–20, according to the explicit of a manuscript carrying his *Reportatio* on book I. Another manuscript, however, provides this explicit for book IV: "Explicit the *Reportatio* on the fourth book done (*facta*) under (*sub*) Master Francis of Marchia the Anconite, of the Order of [Friars] Minor, by W[illiam] of [Rubio] in the year of the Lord 1323, also."[3] The odd choice of words allows for various interpretations, but we can probably maintain that the two versions of books I–II and the one version of books III–IV were composed in Paris between 1319 and 1323. His questions on the *Metaphysics* also belong to this period. Marchia may have become master of theology by 1323, but he certainly was by 1324 when he was lector at the Franciscan *studium* in Avignon, where he remained until 1328. Since James of Pamiers reports that "master Francis of Marchia" determined a question in

---

[1] Schwamm, *Das göttliche Vorherwissen*, pp. 240–55. The other study is Anneliese Maier, *Zwei Grundprobleme*, pp. 161–200. There is also the unpublished dissertation of R. Ferguson, "Francis of Marchia: the Historical Context of His Understanding of the Nature of Theology" (University of Wisconsin 1973). For a bibliography of most of the few works on Marchia before 1986, see Weijers, ed. *Le travail intellectuel... C–F*, pp. 91–2 (and 92–4 for his own writings).

[2] Biographical information can be found in the introductions to the works listed below, n. 8, and in A. Teetaert, "Pignano (François de)," DTC XII (Paris 1933), cols. 2104–9.

[3] The first from ms. Napoli, BN VII. C. 27, fol. 126va, the second from ms. Vat. Chigi. B. VII 113, fol. 233ra.

Avignon,[4] perhaps his lone *Quodlibet* comes from his Avignon years. His literal *Physics* commentary probably stems from his Paris or Avignon period.

In 1328, Marchia ran into trouble with Pope John XXII for supporting the excommunicated ex-minister general of the Franciscans, Michael of Cesena. Apparently Marchia first went to Paris, because in February of 1329 the pope wrote to Elias of Nabinaux, the Franciscan bachelor of the *Sentences* at Paris at the time, instructing him to arrest Marchia. He remained at large, however, penning a polemical treatise, the *Improbatio*, against the papal bull *"Quia vir reprobus"* the following year, and at some time writing a *Responsio* against the new minister general, Gerard Odonis. In 1331 he followed the Emperor Louis of Bavaria to Munich with his more famous fellow refugees, William of Ockham and Marsilius of Padua. Finally Marchia was captured in 1340, and after confessing and retracting his errors before the Inquisition in 1341, he was reconciled with the Church, and he died some time after 1344.[5]

The fact that Marchia's *Quodlibet* survives, for the most part, in only one manuscript has been attributed to his difficulties with the Church between 1328 and 1341, and, as we shall see, this might also be a reason why his followers on the issue of divine foreknowledge do not cite him. Nevertheless, it has been claimed that Marchia had an explicit, immediate, and lasting impact, negative and positive, on both sides of the channel. Among his alleged followers or opponents we can count the Franciscans Walter Chatton and John Rodington in England, the Augustinians Alphonsus Vargas of Toledo and Gregory of Rimini in Paris, and Henry Totting of Oyta and John Brammart later on. The large number of surviving manuscripts of his *Sentences* commentary, some two dozen, further attests his significance. In addition, Marchia has long been well known as a natural philosopher. In particular, historians have attributed an interesting theory of the cause of motion, especially of projectiles, to Marchia, which foreshadows the fascinating discussions of motion to be found in the works of his famous Parisian successors John Buridan, Nicole Oresme, and Albert of Saxony.[6]

---

[4]   See Courtenay, "The *Quaestiones in Sententias* of Michael de Massa," p. 195, n. 13, quoting James's remark that "Contra istas raciones <Michaelis de Massa> arguit magister Franciscus de Ma<rchia> in quadam questione, quam determinavit in curia..." But could not the "Franciscus de Ma" refer to "Maronis" who was also at the curia in 1324? Unfortunately, an inspection of James's *Quodlibet* in Padova, Biblioteca universitaria 2006 (ff. 144r–166v) revealed references to "magistro Francisco de Marchia" (f. 152rb), "magister Franciscus de Maronis" (f. 157rb), and "Magister Franciscus de Ma" (ff. 161ra and 162rb)! This difficulty with the two Francisci occurs frequently.

[5]   For the possibility of the alternative date of 1336 for the inquisitorial procedure, see Eva Luise Wittneben and Roberto Lambertini, "Un teologo francescano alle strette. Osservazioni sul testimone manoscritto del processo a Francesco d'Ascoli," *Picenum Seraphicum* 18 n.s. (1999) (pp. 97–122), pp. 102–5.

[6]   His scientific reputation is largely due to many short passages in the major works of Pierre Duhem and Anneliese Maier. See e.g. Duhem, *Medieval Cosmology. Theories of Infinity, Place, Time, Void, and the Plurality of Worlds*, trans. Roger Ariew (Chicago 1985), esp. pp. 200–202 and 321–3; and Maier, *Die Vorläufer Galileis im 14. Jahrhundert* (Rome 1949), pp. 133–6 and 241–7; eadem, *Metaphysische Hintergründe*, pp. 200–209 and 250–56, which discusses the earliest Parisian reaction to Ockham's physics; eadem, *An der Grenze von Scholastik und Naturwissenschaft* (Rome 1952), pp. 82–7; eadem, *Zwischen Philosophie und Mechanik* (Rome

And yet until 1986 almost nothing substantial on Francis of Marchia was published. This is in part because his works were not printed in the Early Modern era, and in modern times he has often been labeled a dogmatic Scotist, something which may have limited his appeal for scholarship.[7] In truth, however, he shows remarkable, systematic creativity and independence of thought on a number of issues, and was prepared to refute the Subtle Doctor. His originality and importance are beginning to be recognized, and if we can talk about a renaissance in Auriol studies in the past decade or so, then we can speak of the naissance of Marchia studies in those same years — and the present study attempts to link these two trends: Marchia's *Improbatio*, *Physics* commentary, and *Quodlibet* have been critically edited, the critical edition of his *Metaphysics* commentary is underway, and parts of book II of the *Sentences* commentary have been published.[8]

Work has also begun on book I of the *Sentences* commentary, which contains his only treatment of divine foreknowledge and future contingents. But here the task is daunting, because as in the case of Auriol, there are multiple redactions: a "*Reportatio*" from Marchia's lectures of 1319–20, and what is called a "*Scriptum*" in at least one manuscript, probably put into final form a couple of years later. Moreover, some manuscripts mix the two versions. The *Scrip*-

---

1958), pp. 350–54; and especially Maier's chapter "Franciscus de Marchia" of her "Die Impetustheorie," in eadem, *Zwei Grundprobleme*, pp. 161–200, on pp. 166–80 of which is a transcription of much of the question presenting the impetus theory, the first question of book IV. Part of the question was translated into English in Marshall Clagett, *The Science of Mechanics in the Middle Ages* (Madison 1959) pp. 526–30, and partially reedited twice by Schneider and Mariani, as in note 8 below.

 [7]   For example, Teetaert, "Pignano (François de)," col. 2108, writes: "François de Pignano s'est montré toujours un disciple fidèle et un défenseur convaincu des théories et des doctrines du vénérable Jean Duns Scot."

 [8]   The first volume devoted to Marchia is Notker Schneider, *Die Kosmologie des Franciscus de Marchia: Texte, Quellen, und Untersuchungen zur Naturphilosophie des 14. Jahrhunderts* (Leiden 1991), which includes (pp. 37–78) a partial manuscript study for book II of the *Sentences*, a critical edition of questions 29–32 of that work, question nine of Marchia's *Metaphysics* III commentary, and part of the question Maier published. Cf. also the review article by Jean-Michel Counet, "La cosmologie de François de Marchia. À propos d'un livre récent," *Bulletin de philosophie médiévale* 34 (1992), pp. 215–20. Schneider announced the edition of the entire *Metaphysics* commentary (p. 29, n. 92), and he had already published three articles concerning Marchia, including "Franciscus de Marchia über die Wirklichkeit der Materie (Metaph. VII q. 5)," FzS 71 (1989), pp. 138–58 (for the other two, from 1986 and 1991, see Weijers, *Le travail intellectuel... C-F*, p. 92). Since then the Franciscan Nazareno Mariani has produced critical editions of the *Improbatio*, the *Quodlibet*, and the *Physics* commentary: *Francisci de Esculo, OFM Improbatio contra libellum Domini Johannis qui incipit 'Quia vir reprobus'* (Grottaferrata 1993); *Francisci de Marchia sive de Esculo, OFM Quodlibet cum quaestionibus selectis ex commentario in librum Sententiarum* (Grottaferrata 1997); *Francisci de Marchia sive de Esculo OFM, Sententia et compilatio super libros Physicorum Aristotelis* (Grottaferrata 1998). The *Physics* edition contains a transcription (pp. 66–77) of parts of the question Maier published, and a reprint (pp. 85–95) of the proceedings of Marchia's examination of 1341. The *Quodlibet* edition contains transcriptions of many questions from Marchia's commentary on book I of the *Sentences* (see next note) and qq. 3 (pp. 346–50) and 25 (pp. 317–23) from book II. For book IV, see Bakker, *La raison et le miracle*, pp. 86–93 and 399–408. Another scholar who works on Marchia (see Weijers, *Le travail intellectuel... C-F*, p. 92), Roberto Lambertini, now edits *Picenum Seraphicum*, which promises to be a forum for studies on Marchia and other Franciscan theologians from the Ancona area. Cf. Wittneben and idem, "Un teologo francescano," and the next note.

tum was left unfinished: it stops at distinction 40, and in many places the reader is directed to the *Reportatio* to fill in the blanks. This was done for one part of the *Scriptum* tradition, but the other main branch of the stemma simply omits the text. No less than thirteen complete witnesses survive for the *Scriptum*, making it one of the most popular theological works of the period. The *Reportatio* is extant in three manuscripts, but there is a divergence after distinction 20. Therefore we have three versions of distinctions 35–39 concerning future contingents: the *Scriptum*, and two *reportationes*.[9] Since the *Scriptum* is by far the most popular and the differences between the three versions are minor, I will concentrate on the *Scriptum* in what follows.

Marchia on Divine Foreknowledge and Future Contingents

Significantly, Marchia devotes all of distinctions 35, 36, and 38 to the issue of foreknowledge and future contingents. When Hermann Schwamm treated Francis of Marchia's views, he did so only vis-à-vis Scotus. Schwamm usually attempted to be thorough, but in Marchia's case he discussed only distinction 36, article four, and distinction 38, article three, which together constitute just one fifth of Marchia's material on the problem — and by no means the most important fifth. Moreover, Schwamm's selection of texts hampered his analysis in other ways: he chose two articles where the *Scriptum* tradition is unfinished, and for whose text he relied on the two worst manuscripts of the thirteen *Scriptum* witnesses! Not surprisingly he opted to follow the less important *Reportatio*.[10] In the end, Schwamm failed to notice Marchia's opposition to Auriol, his innovation, and, except for William of Rubio, his later impact.

In general Francis of Marchia opposed Peter Auriol, and this is also the case in the context of divine foreknowledge. Like Caracciolo, Marchia does

---

[9]   One *reportatio* is contained in ms. Napoli, BN VII. C. 27, and Vaticano Ross. lat. 525, and the other in Paris, BN 3071. For the manuscripts and question lists for the versions of book I, see Friedman, "*In Principio Erat Verbum*," appendix 11, pp. 573–91. Friedman and I, who are editing all redactions of book I, intend to publish shortly a description of the versions of all four books and of the manuscripts of book I in "Francis of Marchia's Commentaries on the Sentences." In his dissertation, Friedman provides (pp. 555–72) a preliminary edition of the *Scriptum*, d. 27, based on three mss, and he includes long excerpts from d. 11 in "Francis of Marchia and John Duns Scotus on the Psychological Model of the Trinity," *Picenum Seraphicum* 18 n.s. (1999), pp. 11–56. In the same volume, pp. 57–95, and in volume 19 (2000), pp. 3–55, see my "Il Determinismo di Francesco di Marchia," for a critical edition of the *Scriptum* dd. 35, 36, and 38, based on all known mss., together with a probable stemma and study of the redactions. In his *Quodlibet* edition mentioned in the previous note, Mariani makes a substantial contribution to our understanding of Marchia as a theologian by offering a transcription of 18 questions from the *Scriptum* of book I, using Vat. Chigi. B. VII 113 (pp. 295–560), which he supplements with Vat. lat. 1096 where Chigi has lacunae. The questions include nos. 1, 2, 14–16, 18, 20, 22a, 23, 24, 27, 28, 42–46, and 50 from Friedman's qq. list noted above; cf. my review, "Notes on a Recent Edition of Parts of Marchia's *In primum librum Sententiarum*," *Picenum Seraphicum* 19 n.s. (2000), forthcoming.

[10]   See Schwamm, *Das göttliche Vorherwissen*, pp. 240–55. For the *Scriptum* he used Naples VII. C. 23 and parts of Vat. lat. 1096, the two worst manuscripts (cf. my "Il determinismo" I, pp. 66–8). He therefore considered the Naples ms. of a *Reportatio* more pure, sharp, and logical, containing additional arguments (pp. 240–41).

not reply to Auriol's *Scriptum*, but rather to a *reportatio* version. There is evidence that in other contexts Marchia used the version contained in Borghese 123,[11] but here it is probable that he is reading the BPV redaction (see above, chapter three), i.e. the least developed version. My evidence is based primarily on a comparison of terminology between Marchia's *Scriptum*, distinctions 35–40, and Auriol's texts, but also on the fact that Marchia does not deal with indistance or the distinction in the will, and instead concentrates his energies on defending Bivalence, the refutation of which absorbs a much greater share of Auriol's BPV *Reportatio* than of the other versions. In addition, Marchia exploits Auriol's admission that future contingent propositions are true *disjunctively*, something Auriol only emphasized in BPV.[12]

Throughout Marchia lives up to his reputation as an innovative natural philosopher, always emphasizing the determinism of the chain of natural causation, and the psychology of human willing. In distinction 36 Marchia examines natural causation, and answers affirmatively in articles one and two that God can know future contingent effects through contingent causes. In distinction 35 Marchia explains how this is possible with respect to future contingents stemming from the free decisions of the human will. In articles three and four of distinction 36, Marchia shows that he has trouble with the Scotist account of divine foreknowledge, and presents his own view of *how* God knows the future. Finally, in distinction 38, Marchia reviews his position.

The first thing Marchia does, however, is attack Auriol, in distinction 35, "Whether before it is put into being a future contingent is determinate in reality to one side of a contradiction."[13] The question itself suggests Auriol's influence, and the entire 500 lines are devoted to refuting Auriol's arguments and explaining how something determined in advance can still be free from necessity. Marchia thinks Auriol's criticisms of previous views concerning necessity can be circumvented, and hence there is no reason to agree with Auriol in denying truth and falsity to future contingent propositions. After giving preliminary arguments, Marchia states:

> One doctor maintains, and he takes it from the Philosopher, I *Peri Hermeneias*, that a future contingent can be considered in two ways: either as it has being in actuality in itself, and as such it is not considered as future, but as present, and in this way it is determinate to one side of a contradiction. Or it can be considered as it has being virtually in its contingent cause, and in this way it is considered as future, not as present, and thus is indeterminate to both sides of a contradiction in a dis-

---

[11] See Werner Dettloff, *Die Entwicklung der Akzeptations-und Verdienstlehre*, p. 191, discussing Book I, distinction 17, and questions of grace.

[12] See also my "Parisian Commentaries from Peter Auriol to Gregory of Rimini," on Marchia's theory of predestination and its reception, in which context I think Marchia also employs BPV and maybe Borghese 123 as well.

[13] Franciscus de Marchia, *Scriptum* I, d. 35 (ed. Schabel, "Il Determinismo," p. 69, ll. 1–4): "Circa distinctionem 35ᵃᵐ, in qua Magister agit de prescientia Dei respectu futurorum, quero primo ex parte obiecti contingentis utrum futurum contingens, antequam ponatur in esse, sit determinatum in re ad alteram partem contradictionis?"

junction. And so although the principle "concerning anything whatever the affirmation or negation [is] true" is valid in any context, it is true differently for propositions about the past and present than for contingent propositions about the future... [in which] neither side of a contradiction is true determinately, but only in the disjunction 'this or that'... because if one side were determinately true, then that side would come about necessarily and not contingently, and so all would happen of necessity...[14]

Marchia gives six arguments in support of Auriol's position, showing that contingent effects are indifferent to being and not being and their causes indeterminate toward acting and not acting before the effect comes about. If the effects were determinate, that determination would precede the coming of the effect, and would thus be something past, over which that cause would have no power. The final argument is that this conditional is necessary: "'If this side of a contradiction is determined with respect to the future, this side of the contradiction will come about'... necessarily and not contingently."[15]

Marchia has two objectives: to show Auriol's position to be incoherent and to show his own position to be coherent. The arguments against Auriol's stance occasionally show a lack of awareness of Auriol's notion of God's knowledge being indistant from its objects, although they probably influenced his successor Francis of Meyronnes, as we have seen. Marchia first attacks Auriol's claim that under a disjunction, the "principle of contradiction," as Marchia calls it here (he says "Law of Contradictories" in the *reportationes*), holds for future contingents. Marchia asserts that if either of the members of the disjunction individually is falsely said of the subject, then the disjunction is false also. He gives an example: "This proposition is absolutely false: 'Man is wood', and similarly this is absolutely false: 'Man is stone', so this proposition is false disjunctively: 'Man is stone or wood'." The argument is forceful, but Marchia holds implicitly that 'not-true' equals 'false', whereas Auriol

[14]   Marchia, *Scriptum* I, d. 35 (ed, Schabel, pp. 70–71, ll. 19–37): "Responsio: hic dicit unus doctor, et accipit a Philosopho, primo *Peryarmenias*, quod futurum contingens potest considerari dupliciter: vel ut habet esse actu in seipso, et sic non consideratur ut futurum, sed ut presens, et sic est determinatum ad alteram partem contradictionis. Vel potest considerari ut habet esse virtualiter in sua causa contingente, et sic consideratur ut futurum, non ut presens, et sic est indeterminatum ad utramque partem contradictionis sub disiunctione. Et ita licet illud principium, 'de quolibet affirmatio vel negatio vera', teneat in omni materia, tamen aliter verificatur in propositionibus de preterito et de presenti quam in propositionibus contingentibus de futuro; quia in propositionibus de preterito et presenti altera pars contradictionis est determinate vera et absolute in re, licet aliquando lateat nos; sed in propositionibus contingentibus de futuro, neutra pars contradictionis est vera determinate, sed solum sub disiunctione 'hec vel illa', puta, 'Navale bellum erit cras vel non erit cras'; quia si altera pars esset determinate vera, tunc illa pars eveniret necessario et non contingenter, et ita omnia evenirent de necessitate." Vat. Chigi. B. VII 113 has "opinio Aurioli" in the margin.
[15]   Marchia, *Scriptum* I, d. 35 (ed. Schabel, pp. 72–3, ll. 72–7): "Item, omnis conditionalis vera necessaria est; sed ista conditionalis est vera: 'Si hec pars contradictionis est determinata de futuro, hec pars contradictionis eveniet', quia sicut determinatum est, eveniet; ergo hec conditionalis est necessaria; ergo, si hec pars est determinata, necessario eveniet et non contingenter, et ita perit tota contingentia."

would simply deny that the 'principle of contradiction' obtained at all in the case of future contingents and instead claim that such propositions were neither true nor false. Marchia goes on to give other arguments against the neutrality of propositions in a similar vein.[16]

Marchia also maintains that something that is not determinately true is not determinately knowable, and if it were known beforehand under a disjunction only, God's knowledge would not be any greater than ours.[17] In this he makes no mention of Auriol's argument that God's knowledge does not precede the coming about of a future event. For Auriol, an event or its cause need not be determinate *beforehand* for God to know it, for God is eternally indistant to both cause and effect. Auriol would even agree with Marchia that for a future to be known qua future, it would have to be determined beforehand, either in its cause or in some other way. In this case, however, Auriol holds that such a future could not be contingent *ad utrumlibet*, and free will would be destroyed.

Marchia disagrees, and holds that even in contingent human willing there is some prior determination. Before we look at Marchia's account of human willing in distinction 35, let us examine distinction 36; there he makes clear at the outset that he is not going to follow Aquinas line's theory that God knows future contingents in themselves as they are present to eternity.[18] Therefore Marchia needs to explain contingency somewhat exhaustively: he wishes to

---

[16]   Marchia, *Scriptum* I, d. 35 (ed. Schabel, pp. 73–4, ll. 78–94): "Contra istam opinionem arguo primo ex parte contradictionis: de quocumque alterum membrum disiunctionis est absolute falsum de subiecto, sub disiunctione est falsum de illo subiecto. Patet exemplo et ratione. Exemplo: quia hec est falsa absolute: 'Homo est lapis', similiter hec est falsa absolute: 'Homo est lignum'; ideo hec est falsa sub disiunctione: 'Homo est lapis vel lignum'. Ratione: quia illud quod absolute removetur a re, sub nulla disiunctione inest sibi, quia cum disiunctio sit quedam species compositionis, et modus compositionis presupponit extrema, ideo si utrumque extremum absolute est nihil, sub disiunctione etiam est nihil; sed si neutra pars contradictionis effectus contingentis est determinata, tunc quelibet pars absolute accepta sine disiunctione est falsa, quia si non, tunc quelibet absolute esset vera; ergo utraque sub disiunctione erit falsa, et ita *principium contradictionis* falsificabitur in eis tam absolute quam sub disiunctione." In both *Reportationes*, Marchia says "*lex contradictoriorum*" (mss. Paris 3071, f. 70ra; Napoli 27, f. 112ra — Ross. 525, f. 108rb). This is a minor difference, but the fact that Massa does not refer to the *lex contradictoriorum* suggests he used Marchia's *Scriptum*.

[17]   Marchia, *Scriptum* I, d. 35 (ed. Schabel, pp. 75–6, ll. 130–44): "Item, illud quod non est determinate verum non est determinate scibile, quia nihil est determinate scibile nisi quod est determinate verum; sed futurum contingens est determinate scibile a Deo quantum ad alteram partem contradictionis; ergo illa pars contradictionis est determinate vera. Probatio minoris: quia si Deus ab eterno non cognovisset determinate alteram partem contingentis, sed solum disiunctive, tunc Deus non cognovisset aliter futurum contingens quam ego, quia ego cognosco quamlibet partem contradictionis cuiuscumque esse veram sub disiunctione, et cum tali cognitione stat in me omnimoda ignorantia futurorum contingentium. Et ita Deus non habuisset aliam notitiam futurorum contingentium quam ego, quod est absurdum, quia tunc non potuisset aliter predicere certitudinaliter futura contingentia quam ego, nec revelare prophetis certitudinaliter antequam eveniret."

[18]   Marchia, *Scriptum* I, d. 36 (ed. Schabel, Parte II, ll. 12–19): "Contra: Deus habet certam scientiam futurorum contingentium, cum non habeat notitiam opinativiam vel suspicativam nec creditivam, quia quelibet istarum est imperfectionis, imperfectio autem non est in Deo; sed Deus non habet notitiam certam de futuris contingentibus per se ipsa antequam sint, quia antequam sint non sunt ratio cognoscendi se ipsa; ergo cognoscit effectus futuros contingentes per suas causas contingentes."

show how God can know future contingents via their contingent causes, but he must take care to avoid the confusion of Durand and others.[19] There are two types of contingency in the world. The first, in Marchia's words, is contingency *per accidens, secundum quid, privativa,* and *extrinsica.* This is the contingency of natural causation. A natural effect, say for example an avalanche, takes place as the result of many accidental causes. Some of these causes may be impeded by other natural, accidental causes, and so with respect to a small, limited number of causes a natural effect may be considered 'contingent'. This does not mean that the natural effect is really and truly contingent without qualification, however; i.e. it does not have contingency *per se, simpliciter, positiva,* and *intrinseca,* to use Marchia's terms again. This is because, if we take *all* of the natural effect's causes into account, the effect will necessarily follow, or not follow, as the case may be. Natural causation works necessarily, and so with all of an effect's causes taken together, what happens in nature is necessary.[20] Hence Aquinas and Wylton had confused the issue.

Durand, on the other hand, is absolutely correct in assuming God can know such effects by knowing all the causes that can and will affect the natural outcome of the chain of causation. In fact, assuming that by his "general influence" God allows this chain of causation to continue to exist and function, these 'contingent' effects can even be known by a *created* intellect. This is because the number of natural causes, which of course cause necessarily, is not infinite. Thus a finite, created intellect can know the natural future with certainty. Francis of Marchia in essence is laying down one of the bases of modern science, at least before Heisenberg: predictability is theoretically obtain-

---

[19] Anneliese Maier recognized Marchia's importance in this debate. In the chapter "Notwendigkeit, Kontingenz und Zufall" of *Die Vorläufer Galileis,* pp. 241–4, she quotes an extensive section of Marchia's *Scriptum* I, d. 36, a. 2 (erroneously called "38. Distinktion"), suggesting that Siger of Brabant may have influenced his treatment, but that "Der erste, der mit vollem Bewusstsein und voller Klarheit diesen neuen Standpunkt eingenommen hat, scheint uns Franciscus de Marchia gewesen zu sein."

[20] See Marchia, *Scriptum* I, d. 36, a. 1 (ed. Schabel, ll. 26–70): "... dico quod duplex est contingentia: quedam est contingentia per accidens, quedam per se. Contingentia per accidens est qua effectus est contingens in ordine ad causas per accidens concurrentes cum causis per se, et non est contingens ex causis per se. Et hec est contingentia effectuum naturalium generabilium et corruptibilium, qui propter concursum varium causarum accidentalium cum causis per se possunt impediri et non impediri. Ideo eveniunt contingenter non ex causis per se quantum est ex se — quia cause per se necessario agunt quantum est ex se, quia presente activo et passivo, necessario sequitur actio, secundum Philosophum, 9 *Metaphysice* — sed eveniunt contingenter propter causas per accidens, que tamen cause per accidens, licet sint cause per accidens respectu unius effectus, sunt tamen cause per se alterius effectus. Et ideo talis contingentia est contingentia secundum quid, non simpliciter, quia effectus solum est contingens in ordine ad unam causam partialem comparatus. Non autem est contingens comparatus ad totum ordinem causarum simul concurrentium, quia positis omnibus causis, effectus naturalis necessario sequitur. Nec potest impediri per aliquam causam naturalem, quia tunc illa causa faceret ad positionem illius effectus, et ita sine illa causa non haberentur omnes cause... Est contingentia privativa et non positiva quia non est contingens in ordine ad causas in ultima dispositione in qua possunt agere effectum, sed est in ordine ad causas in dispositione in qua non possunt pro tunc ponere effectum... Ideo est contingentia privativa et non positiva quia provenit ex privatione debite dispositionis causarum requisite ad agendum, et non provenit ex dispositione debite perfectionis. Est contingentia extrinsica et non intrinseca quia provenit ex impedimento extrinsico alterius cause concurrentis et non ex dominio cause impedibilis. Ideo talis contingentia venit ab extrinsico...."

able in natural systems because natural causes are finite and act necessarily. This is Marchia's physical or natural determinism, and he lives up to his reputation as an able natural philosopher. The only hitch, says Marchia, is that we humans have a short life and an intellect that is bound with the body.[21]

Correct or not, however, Durand has missed the important point, because he was not discussing contingency *per se*. Contingency *per se, simpliciter, positiva*, and *intrinseca* is the contingency by which something is still able to occur or not occur even when all the required accidental, natural causes have been posited. This is contingency without qualification, with respect to all accidental causes and not just a limited number.[22]

There are only two sources of such contingency: the human will and God. Marchia maintains that all natural events would come about necessarily if there were not a truly *per se* contingent basis. This contingent basis cannot be the human will, obviously, because most natural effects are independent of the human will. Therefore God, the first cause, is the source of this contingency, as Scotus maintains. For Marchia it is important to defend the freedom of divine causation, which, as he hints, can cease its "general influence" that

[21]   See Marchia, *Scriptum* I, d. 36, a. 2 (ed. Schabel, ll. 262–77): "Ideo dico aliter quod, sicut dictum est, effectus contingens est duplex: quidam naturalis, quidam voluntarius. Et secundum hoc pono duas conclusiones. Prima conclusio est quod effectus contingens naturalis, stante generali influentia prime cause, potest determinate cognosci ab intellectu creato, licet non ab humano, per suas causas contingentes. Quod declaro sic: Omnis effectus dependens ex causis finitis necessario ipsum inferentibus potest cognosci determinate per suas causas ab aliquo intellectu finito — patet, quia ex quo cause sunt finite, omnes possunt comprehendi ab intellectu finito, et <si> necessario causant effectum, potest concludi determinate effectus ex talibus causis; sed quilibet effectus contingens naturalis dependet ex causis finitis modis finitis concurrentibus et necessario causantibus, stante generali influentia; igitur quilibet effectus contingens naturalis, stante generali influentia, potest determinate cognosci ab aliquo intellectu finito per suas causas contingentes.

... Et cause in ultima dispositione existentes necessario causant, si possunt, vel necessario impediunt, si possunt. Ergo quilibet effectus contingens naturalis dependet ex causis finitis modis finitis concurrentibus necessario ad ipsum, cuius signum est quod frequenter intellectus humanus precognoscit aliquos effectus contingentes futuros per causas contingentes. Quod autem non possit plene attingere, hoc est propter imperfectionem intellectus coniuncti et brevitatem vite."
[22]   Cf. Marchia, *Scriptum* I, d. 36, a. 1 (ed. Schabel, ll. 71–100): "Contingentia vero per se est qua effectus est contingens in ordine ad causas essentiales, non in ordine ad causas accidentales, quia remotis omnibus causis accidentalibus, vel eis positis, potest effectus poni ab eis et non poni, sicut Augustinus ponit exemplum, 12 *De civitate Dei*, capitulo 6, de duobus hominibus eandem corporis pulchritudinem videntibus, mente et corpore pariter affectatis, quod unus eorum moveatur illicite ad fruendum, alius vero in recta voluntate perseveret. Et ista est contingentia actuum liberi arbitrii, qui actus, positis omnibus causis in ultima dispositione, potest poni et non poni ab eis... Et talis contingentia est contingentia per se et non per accidens quia quod effectus non ponatur in esse non venit ex concursu alicuius cause accidentalis impedientis, sed venit ex contingentia talis cause. Ideo est contingentia simpliciter, non secundum quid, quia ista contingentia non est in ordine ad unam causam impedibilem per aliam, sed est in ordine ad totum ordinem causarum requisitarum, quia positis omnibus causis requisitis, potest effectus poni et non poni, ut patet in exemplo Augustini preallegato. Ideo est contingentia positiva et non privativa quia ista contingentia non provenit ex privatione debite dispositionis causarum in qua nate sunt agere, sed provenit ex plenitudine perfectionis causarum que in ultima dispositione existentes possunt agere et non agere — patet in priori exemplo Augustini. Ideo est contingentia intrinseca et non extrinseca quia talis contingentia non venit ex impedimento alicuius cause extrinsice, sed venit ex predominio talis cause super effectum, et hec est contingentia perfecta."

keeps the natural world in being. As Marchia has already pointed out in distinction 35, the important source of contingency in the context of the problem of divine foreknowledge of future contingents is human free will. Does this even exist? Marchia says that it does, because otherwise human actions could not be blamed or praised, and virtue and vice would not exist. Humans would be mere brutes if they did not have free will.[23]

Now certainly God knows the future of the natural world: He is the first cause, the natural world depends on His general influence, and all natural secondary causes act necessarily. Even a created intellect can know these 'future contingents'. Until Peter Auriol, however, no one — not Aquinas, not Scotus — had made it absolutely clear that the real issue is how God can know *per se* future contingents that have their origin not in the divine will but in the human will. Auriol denies that God could know *these* future contingents beforehand via their contingent causes.

Marchia's response is an addition to his distinction 35, where he had shown that the human will does determine itself *de inesse* beforehand in making decisions to act. Therefore the effect is determined in the cause, the human will, before it exists in reality. By knowing the human will's prior determination, God can know the future effect. There still remains the major difficulty of how God can know these effects *ab eterno* by knowing the human will as a contingent cause even before the creation of that will, but Marchia has hit on a real problem in Auriol's theory: How do humans freely act at all?[24]

For Auriol, any predetermination before a future decision tends to destroy freedom and contingency. Things would therefore occur of necessity, and in that case, as Aristotle says in chapter nine of *Peri Hermeneias*, there would be no need to deliberate or take trouble about the future. Marchia, however, turns the argument around against Auriol: If there were no predetermination in the human will at all, then the will would act, if it acted, randomly and by chance. This is obviously not the case. Instead, we plan our actions, focussing, as Scotus says, on the end and then putting the means to that end into effect:

> Every contingent effect is 'dispositionally' determined in the cause before it is formally determined in itself; otherwise every agent would act randomly and by chance. And so everyone who posits that a contingent effect is not determined in the cause before it is determined in itself has to posit that all contingents in human actions are random and by chance. And so all deliberation and human effort is lost, because there is neither deliberation nor prudence with respect to random things.[25]

---

    [23] See Marchia, *Scriptum* I, d. 36, a. 1 (ed. Schabel, ll. 101–142).
    [24] See Marchia, *Scriptum* I, d. 36, a. 2 (ed. Schabel, ll. 180–260), and below.
    [25] Marchia, *Scriptum* I, d. 36, a. 2 (ed. Schabel, ll. 225–32): "Ergo effectus quicumque contingens prius est determinatus in causa habitualiter quam in se ipso formaliter, aliter agens omne ageret a casu et a fortuna. Et ita omnis qui ponit quod effectus contingens non est prius determinatus in causa quam in se habet ponere quod omnia contingentia in actibus humanis sint a casu et fortuna. Et ita perit omne consilium et omnis sollicitudo humana, quia de casualibus non est consilium nec prudentia."

Just as there is no point in deliberating or taking trouble about what happens necessarily, as Aristotle and Auriol emphasize, there is also no reason to deliberate or take trouble about what occurs completely at random. In fact, deliberating and taking trouble would not even occur in a random world.

Here then is the counterpart to Marchia's physical determinism: his psychological determinism.[26] He does not wish to destroy free will and contingency by any means, but he does realize that some determinism is even required for free human action. Now although a created, finite intellect cannot know these contingent predeterminations of the human free will and their effects, the divine intellect can and does. As we shall see, Marchia devotes the final two articles of distinction 36 to explaining how it does and does not.

Marchia articulates this psychological determinism more fully back in distinction 35, arguing against Auriol's position. There also he asserts that in fact a contingent effect, before it comes about, is determinate in its contingent cause, for it could not be the case that the cause is determinate to both sides simultaneously. For things to happen at all, says Marchia, there must be some determination in their causes prior to their occurrence. Marchia explains:

> And I ask about that determination in the cause, was it in the cause before the placing of the effect [into reality] or not? If yes, then I have my point. If not, I ask, how is the effect determined in its cause before it is put into being, necessarily or contingently? If necessarily, then it comes about necessarily, according to this opinion. If contingently and a contingent is not determined to one side in its cause, then that determination is not determined except through some prior contingent determination. And I would ask of this just as before, will it go on infinitely, or is it necessary to stop at some contingent determination in the cause before the effect?[27]

Marchia may have a point here, but in the case of God's foreknowledge, if 'foreknowledge' is taken strictly for knowledge preceding the future event, we

---

[26] I am not claiming this is entirely original, just insofar as it is applied to the problem of foreknowledge and future contingents. For a philosophical discussion of a kind of psychological determinism already in Aquinas, see Scott MacDonald, "Ultimate Ends in Practical Reasoning: Aquinas's Aristotelian Moral Psychology and Anscombe's Fallacy," *The Philosophical Review* 100.1 (1991), pp. 31–66.

[27] Marchia, *Scriptum* I, d. 35 (ed. Schabel, p. 75, ll. 111–29): "Item, a causa indeterminata equaliter ad utramque partem contradictionis non provenit determinate altera pars contradictionis — patet, quia effectus non habet esse determinatum in se nisi prius sit determinatus in causa; sed a causa contingente provenit determinate una pars contradictionis et non alia, cum utramque partem simul evenire sit impossibile; ergo illa pars contradictionis prius natura fuit determinata in causa quam in effectu; igitur effectus contingens prius est determinatus in causa quam in seipso. Et quero de illa determinatione in causa, aut prefuit in causa ante positionem effectus aut non? Si sic, habetur propositum. Si non, quero quomodo effectus sit determinatus in causa antequam ponatur in esse, aut necessario aut contingenter? Si necessario, ergo necessario evenit, secundum istam opinionem. Si contingenter, et contingens non est determinatum in sua causa ad alteram partem, ergo illa determinatio non est determinata nisi per aliam determinationem priorem contingentem. Et queram de illa sicut de priori, vel ibitur in infinitum, vel oportet stare ad aliquam determinationem contingentem in causa priorem effectu?"

are not talking about a determination in the cause an hour beforehand, a month beforehand, or even one hundred years beforehand. Since Marchia does not appeal to an argument based on eternity here, one could say that under his scheme, God has determinate knowledge of what I will do on Bastille Day 2039, before I am born. How can this determinate knowledge arise from a contingent determination in the contingent cause, me? Moreover, if there is a determination in me on say, 7 July 2039, does that determination preclude my ability to do otherwise than I have determined during the following week, and if so, am I still acting freely and contingently? Marchia does not answer the question about God's knowledge *ab eterno*, but his answer to this last question constitutes the major portion of the rest of his question.

Francis of Marchia's elegant solution is aimed directly at Auriol. It is perhaps not entirely new, as it reminds one of, for example, Anselm's stance, and one can find hints in Scotus. Nevertheless, Marchia expresses it more clearly and in greater depth than anyone before. Essentially, Marchia draws a distinction between indetermination and determination with respect to being able to act and not to act, and indetermination and determination with respect to being and not being the case in reality. Auriol demands that contingent causes and effects be indeterminate before the future event. Marchia holds that there must be some determination beforehand for God to know the future and for the future to come about via contingent causes. Marchia thus compromises. It is true that before an event, say eating breakfast, I determine myself toward eating breakfast. This determination makes my eating breakfast knowable beforehand, and indeed makes it so I eat breakfast. Nevertheless, I still remain indeterminate with respect to being able to eat breakfast and being able not to eat breakfast. Until the event, there remains in me an indetermination with respect to being able to do something or not to do something, although there is a determination in me toward actually doing it (or actually not doing it): "This indetermination is different from the first indetermination just as being able to do is different from doing, and potency is different from act."[28]

The indetermination 'about the possible' (*de possibili*), with respect to being able to act and being able not to act, is prior to the indetermination 'about inhering' (*de inesse*), with respect to what will be the case in reality, and it is this prior indetermination remaining in us until the event that makes us free,

    [28] Marchia, *Scriptum* I, d. 35 (ed. Schabel, pp. 78–9, ll. 181–91): "Ideo dico aliter ad questionem quod duplex est indeterminatio cause contingentis et effectus similiter: quedam est indeterminatio cause contingentis de possibili, qua scilicet causa est indeterminata ad posse agere et posse non agere, et hec indeterminatio pro tanto dicitur 'de possibili' quia respicit posse agere et posse non agere. Alia est indeterminatio cause de inesse, qua scilicet causa est indeterminata ad agere et non agere, que pro tanto dicitur 'de inesse' quia respicit agere de inesse et non agere. Et hec indeterminatio est alia a priori indeterminatione, sicut posse agere est aliud ab agere, et potentia est aliud ab actu." Schwamm (*Das göttliche Vorherwissen*, pp. 248–52) also treats this distinction about indetermination and determination, based on d. 38, a. 3. Cf. Scotus, *Ordinatio* I, d. 38, pars 2 and d. 39, qq. 1–5 (ed. Balic, p. 432, ll. 5–10): "Talis autem non est determinatio ex parte futuri, quia licet alicui intellectui sit una pars vera determinate (et etiam una pars sit vera in se, determinate, licet eam nullus intellectus apprehenderet), non tamen ita quin in *potestate causae* est pro illo instanti ponere oppositum. Et ista *indeterminatio* sufficit ad consiliandum et negotiandum."

and allows us to act contingently and not necessarily. The posterior indetermination toward what will inhere in reality, however, is an obstacle to foreknowledge and, for us, to acting. Thus this posterior indetermination *de inesse* is not required for freedom and contingent acting, and it must be replaced by a determination in the contingent cause toward acting, for the future to be known and for us to act. The determination *de possibili*, toward being able to act or being able not to act, is absent from free causes, until the event comes to pass, at which time our freedom, and power, is removed, since there is no power with respect to the past. This prior indetermination *de possibili*, before the event, is no obstacle either to foreknowledge or to acting, and preserves contingency.[29]

Marchia's solution resembles Anselm's in that, in effect, it accepts for the sake of foreknowledge that something will indeed happen, and that its opposite possibility will not happen. At the same time, however, our *ability* to act in the opposite way is not impaired, although we will not in fact do so. All of Marchia's positive arguments and refutations of Auriol's attacks are based on this distinction between indetermination *de inesse*, with respect to what inheres in reality, and indetermination *de possibili*, with respect to what an agent is able to do or able not to do. Of course Auriol would have said that Marchia has merely sidestepped the problem, and Peter de Rivo, Auriol's defender in the Louvain quarrel, will have the opportunity to refute Marchia.

Although, as we shall see, Marchia is not a Scotist in this context, he continually makes use of the Scotist notion of a simultaneous capacity for opposites to make this distinction, which Marchia in turn uses effectively to establish better than just about everyone the cogency of the argument based on the

---

[29] Marchia, *Scriptum* I, d.35 (ed. Schabel, pp. 79–80, ll. 204–24): "...agere et non agere sunt alia a posse agere et posse non agere et posteriora ipsis, sicut actus sunt alii a potentiis et posteriores eis; ergo secunda indeterminatio est alia a prima indeterminatione et posterior ipsa. Prius autem potest absolvi a posteriori absque contradictione quando prius non est idem cum posteriori; ergo prima indeterminatio, cum sit prior secunda, potest absolvi ab ea. Et sic causa contingens potest esse indeterminata prima indeterminatione, et determinata determinatione opposita secunde indeterminationi. Igitur quod causa sit indeterminata ad posse agere et posse non agere de possibili, et sit determinata de inesse ad alteram partem ad agere vel non agere, nulla est contradictio. Et in hoc stat contingentia cuiuscumque cause contingentis, scilicet in prima indeterminatione et non in secunda. Quia causa contingens potest agere et potest non agere, ideo agit contingenter et sic est indeterminata solum de possibili — non autem de inesse, quia nulla causa de mundo est indeterminata de inesse, quia omnis causa de mundo de inesse est sub altero extremo contradictionis, quia vel agit, et tunc est determinata ad agendum, vel non agit, et tunc est determinata ad non agendum... (pp. 81–2, ll. 240–55) Quod autem ista secunda indeterminatio de inesse nihil faciat ad contingentiam rerum probo: illud quod sublatum per possibile vel impossibile stat totalis ratio contingentie, illud nihil facit ad contingentiam; sed posito hoc solo, quod aliqua causa possit agere et possit non agere, remoto quocumque posteriori per possibile vel impossibile, hoc solo stante quod possit agere et non agere, talis causa agit contingenter — patet, quia causa non potest magis contingenter agere quam quod sit in potestate sua agere et non agere; sed indeterminatio de inesse ad agendum et non agendum est posterior natura indeterminatione de possibili ad posse agere et posse non agere, sicut extrema sunt posteriora natura extremis, ut probatum est; ergo remota secunda indeterminatione per possibile vel impossibile, et stante prima indeterminatione, habetur totalis et perfecta ratio contingentie; ergo secunda indeterminatio nihil facit ad contingentiam; igitur frustra ponitur."

composite and divided senses.[30] Marchia deals with one of the Auriolist objections to this at some length. The objection states that on Marchia's account, the effect is determinate in the cause before the action of the cause, and thus that determination is 'presupposed' in the subsequent action of the cause. Since it is 'presupposed', that determination is not in the cause's power, and thus is not contingent.[31] Marchia responds in various ways. First he repeats that the effect is only determinate *de inesse*, and in the future and not in the present, since it does not exist yet. It is not determinate at all *de possibili*, either in the future or present. This determination *de inesse*, or about inhering, involves only the necessity of the consequence.[32]

Marchia then gives another explanation for this determination:

> ... it can be said in another way, that 'action' can be taken in three ways: either it can be taken actually, namely when an agent is actually acting; or it can be taken potentially, when an agent can act although he is not acting; or it can be taken in a middle way, not purely actually nor purely potentially, but in a middle way as 'dispositionally' or 'aptitudinally', namely when an agent is not acting but is determined toward acting, although in actuality he is not acting — and he not only can act, but is also determined to be acting later.
>
>   Similarly there is a threefold 'determination' of the agent: One actual, by which an agent actually determinately puts one part of a contradiction in the effect; another is a potential determination by which an agent posits or can determine any part of a contradiction dividedly;

[30] Marchia, *Scriptum* I, d. 35 (ed. Schabel, pp. 83–4, ll. 278–97): "Item tertio, illa que coniunctim simul non repugnant, nec divisim seorsum repugnant, ut si currere et sedere coniunctim non repugnant, multo magis nec divisim repugnant; sed determinatio effectus ad unam partem et contingentia illius partis coniunctim simul in eodem instanti non repugnant; ergo nec divisim determinatio illius partis precedentis tempore eius positionem repugnat sibi. Probatio minoris: quando effectus contingens ponitur a causa, in illo instanti in quo ponitur, in illo instanti ponitur contingenter a causa (probatio: quia si in illo instanti non poneretur contingenter, in nullo instanti poneretur contingenter, quia in illo instanti in quo non ponitur, nec contingenter ponitur nec necessario; sed in nullo instanti alio ponitur nisi in illo in quo ponitur; ergo si in illo non ponitur contingenter, in nullo ponitur contingenter); sed in illo instanti in quo ponitur, ponitur determinate secundum unam partem contradictionis et non sub disiunctione, quia una pars ponitur determinate et non alia; ergo in illo instanti ponitur contingenter et ponitur determinate; ergo determinatio unius partis et contingentia eiusdem non repugnant simul coniunctim; ergo multo magis nec divisim."

[31] Marchia, *Scriptum* I, d. 35 (ed. Schabel, pp. 71–2, ll. 50–57): "Item, illud quod presupponitur actioni cause non subest eius potestate; sed si effectus contingens esset determinatus in causa ante actionem et alteram partem contradictionis, tunc determinatio illius partis presupponeretur actioni cause sequenti; ergo illa determinatio non esset in potestate cause. Et effectus provenit a causa secundum quod est determinatus in causa; ergo talis effectus non esset in potestate cause, et ita non eveniret contingenter sed necessario."

[32] Marchia, *Scriptum* I, d. 35 (ed. Schabel, p. 85, ll. 310–18): "Dico quod effectus contingens futurus est determinatus in causa contingenti antequam ponatur de inesse, non de presenti, quia nondum est, sed est determinatus de inesse ad alteram partem de futuro, quia erit, si sit determinatus ad istam partem, vel non erit, si sit determinatus ad aliam partem. De possibili autem non est determinatus nec de presenti nec de futuro, quia non est determinatus ad posse produci nec ad posse non produci, sed est indeterminatus de possibili de futuro ad utrumque... (p. 86, ll. 332–4) Per hoc ad aliud, quod omnis conditionalis vera est necessaria, concedatur pro nunc necessaria necessitate consequentie, quia de hoc alias"

the other is, as it were, a 'dispositional' or 'aptitudinal' determination, by which an agent is determined with respect to the future to putting one part of a contradiction [into effect]. Each determination presupposes the action corresponding to it, because an actual determination follows the action in actuality; the dispositional determination follows the action dispositionally, although it precedes the actual action; the potential determination follows the potential action, although it precedes that actual and dispositional action.[33]

Thus when an agent is determined *de inesse* to doing something in the future, that determination is like a disposition, and neither actual, because the event has not yet occurred, nor potential, because the possibility to do otherwise is not removed. Such a determination is not 'actually' in the agent's power, Marchia grants, but it is in his power 'dispositionally', for although the agent cannot act before he acts, he can be disposed to act so that he will in fact act.[34]

Marchia makes a similar distinction when answering the question of whether that determination can change or not. This is a complex issue: it is one thing to say that things can be other than they are, and it is quite another to say that they can *change*, i.e. be one way and *then* another. In his *Reportationes* Marchia placed the objection among Auriol's opening arguments, and gave an unsatisfactory response: it can change but it will not.[35] Marchia rearranges things in the *Scriptum*, placing greater emphasis on the difficulty, and providing a more subtle answer. Corresponding to the threefold action and threefold determination, there is a threefold change or mutation: actual, potential, and dispositional. Since there is no actual determination, there can be

---

[33] Marchia, *Scriptum* I, d. 35 (ed Schabel, pp. 89–90, ll. 392–411): "Propter quod potest dici aliter, quod actio potest sumi tripliciter: vel potest sumi actualiter, quando scilicet agens actu agit; vel potest sumi potentialiter, quando agens potest agere licet non agat; vel potest sumi medio modo, non pure actualiter nec pure potentialiter, sed medio modo quasi habitualiter vel aptitudinaliter, scilicet quando agens non agit sed est determinatum ad agendum, licet actu non agat; et non solum potest agere, sed est etiam determinatum ad fore agendum.

Consimiliter est triplex determinatio agentis: una actualis, qua agens ponit actu determinate in effectu unam partem contradictionis; alia est determinatio potentialis, qua agens potest determinare divisim quamlibet partem contradictionis; alia est determinatio quasi habitualis, vel quasi aptitudinalis, qua agens est determinatum de futuro ad ponendum unam partem contradictionis. Quelibet autem determinatio presupponit actionem sibi correspondentem, quia determinatio actualis sequitur actionem in actu; determinatio habitualis sequitur actionem habitualiter, licet precedat actionem actualem; determinatio potentialis sequitur actionem potentialem, licet precedat actionem actualem et habitualem."

[34] Marchia, *Scriptum* I, d. 35 (ed. Schabel, pp. 90–91, ll. 420–8): "Determinatio autem de inesse effectus futuri contingentis non est determinatio mere actualis, nec est determinatio mere potentialis, sed est determinatio mere quasi habitualis, vel aptitudinalis, que licet precedat actionem actualem, sequitur tamen actionem habitualem et etiam potentialem. Ideo, licet illa determinatio non sit in potestate agentis actualiter, est tamen in potestate eius habitualiter, quia eo modo debet queri qualiter sit in potestate quomodo est ipsa determinatio."

[35] Marchia gives six arguments for Auriol in the *Scriptum*, repeated from the Naples-Ross. lat. *Reportatio* (the Paris *Reportatio* omits the fifth one), which adds two more, the first of which concerns change. The response is (ms. Napoli 27, f. 113vb): "Ad 7, quando arguitur, 'Aut huiusmodi determinatio potest immutari aut non', dico quod potest immutari. Potest enim contingere quod hoc quod determinatum est non eveniat, tamen de facto sive de inesse numquam immutabitur. Secus enim est aliquid posse immutari et secus est ipsum immutari."

no actual mutation, but the determination can change dispositionally through a dispositional action, a mutation which "puts nothing intrinsically in secondary causes before the effect is put in reality, but which only puts something extrinsically, according to reason":

> For example: when a king determines something in his power, by the very fact that it is determined in the king's will, it is determined extrinsically in all his subjects who are willing to obey him, because from the very fact that some are disposed to obey every edict of the king, immediately following the determination in the king's will, that matter is determined concerning the future in all his inferiors. But this determination in his subjects puts nothing *de novo* intrinsically in them, but only speaks of an ordering with respect to the first thing proposed and to the future effect. This is how it is with the ordering of the universe: because all secondary causes follow the ordering of the first cause, therefore by the fact that something is determined in the first cause actually, it is determined dispositionally in all causes from the ordering to the first cause. Nevertheless the secondary causes act contingently, just as the subjects of the king also contingently carry out the king's decree.[36]

The analogy with the king, of course, should not be taken too strictly. Auriol would not have found Marchia's solution acceptable, for reasons mentioned above, namely because God would know such a disposition *ab eterno*, and if such dispositions were not absolutely certain, one could not have *knowledge* of the effects of the disposition. Marchia did put it very eloquently, however.

Marchia's main innovation is in explaining how future contingents can be known via their causes, but he still has to provide a mechanism for divine foreknowledge. Not surprisingly, it is not via eternal presence or divine Ideas, but what is striking, for an alleged Scotist, is that Marchia rejects Henry of

---

[36] Marchia, *Scriptum* I, d. 35 (ed. Schabel, pp. 91–2, ll. 432–61): "Per hoc ad aliud, 'aut illa determinatio potest immutari aut non', dico quod sicut est triplex actio et triplex determinatio, ita est triplex mutatio, scilicet mutatio actualis, mutatio potentialis, et mutatio quasi habitualis. Dico quod illa determinatio de futuro non potest immutari actualiter, quia non est determinatio actualis. Sed potest immutari habitualiter per ipsam actionem, non actualem, quia actio actualis sequitur, sed potest immutari per actionem habitualem habitualiter, quia illa precedit; quia sicut aliquid potest immutari actualiter et immutari per actionem actualem, ita potest immutari habitualiter per actionem habitualem, quia sicut se habet actio actualis ad mutationem actualem, ita actio habitualis ad mutationem habitualem. Tamen ista mutatio nihil ponit intrinsece in causis secundariis antequam effectus ponatur, sed solum ponit aliquid extrinsece, secundum rationem.

Exemplum: rege determinante aliquid apud se, eo ipso quod illud est determinatum in voluntate regis, est determinatum extrinsece in omnibus sibi subiectis volentibus sibi obedire, quia eo ipso quod aliqui sunt in proposito obediendi omni edicto a rege, statim facta determinatione in voluntate regis, est determinatum de futuro illud in omnibus inferioribus eius. Ista autem determinatio in suis subiectis nihil ponit de novo intrinsece in eis, sed solum dicit ordinem ad primum propositum et ad effectum futurum. Sic est de ordine universi: quia omnes cause secunde sequuntur ordinem cause prime, ideo eo ipso quod aliquid est determinatum in causa prima actualiter, est determinatum habitualiter in omnibus causis ex ordine ad causam primam. Et tamen cause secunde agunt contingenter, sicut etiam subditi regis execuntur contingenter decretum regis."

Ghent and Scotus's position. For Marchia, the main impediment to the theory that God knows future contingents via the determinations of the divine will is not because it appears to destroy human free will, since Marchia accepts and even requires some prior determination in the human will anyway. The real flaw with Henry and Scotus is that the divine will appears to be nobler than the divine intellect. And not only is it an issue of a possible hierarchy of divine attributes, it also connects with the persons of the Trinity:[37]

> In God the intellect is the principle of producing the Word, and the will is the principle of producing the Holy Spirit, according to this position. Therefore the Holy Spirit's principle is nobler than the Word's principle, which is absurd. Therefore the intellect is as apt as the will to determine one side of a contradiction.[38]

Moreover, since the intellect has only one act by which it understands all, Marchia cannot understand how it first knows necessary things and only later knows contingent things after the will's determination.[39]

Against Scotus's 'second way', that the intellect knows the future contingents that the will has determined as they are reflected in the essence, Marchia sees further problems: it seems that the essence obtains something and is therefore dependent on the will in some way, which is absurd. In any case the will still appears nobler than the intellect.[40] Interestingly, Marchia does make

---

[37] Interestingly, Marchia also makes this point and connects it with the problem of foreknowledge in his discussion of the production of the Holy Spirit and the Son in d. 11. See Friedman, "Francis of Marchia and John Duns Scotus," pp. 25–7 for commentary, and pp. 51–3, pars. 29–35 for Marchia's text.

[38] Article four contains the arguments against eternal presence, Ideas, and Henry and Scotus's stance, see Marchia, *Scriptum* I, d. 36, a. 4 (ed. Schabel, ll. 742–62): "Contra: Potentia determinans alteram partem contradictionis est nobilior potentia que non est nata determinare alteram partem — patet, quia ideo voluntas ponitur in nobis nobilior quam intellectus eo quod voluntas nata est determinare alteram partem contingentie ad utrumque, intellectus autem non — alia ratio non est; sed voluntas divina determinat alteram partem contingentis, intellectus autem non est natus determinare alteram partem, secundum istam opinionem; ergo voluntas in Deo est nobilior intellectu respectu obiecti secundarii. Et si est nobilior respectu obiecti secundarii, erit etiam nobilior respectu obiecti primi, quia potentie que non respiciunt obiecta secundaria nisi virtute obiecti primi, si non habent aliquam preeminentiam inter se respectu obiecti primi, non habent preeminentiam respectu obiecti secundarii, cum preeminentia potentiarum respectu obiecti secundarii non veniat nisi ex preeminentia respectu obiecti primi. Et intellectus in Deo est principium producendi Verbum et voluntas principium producendi Spiritum Sanctum, secundum istam opinionem. Ergo principium Spiritus Sancti est nobilius principio Verbi, quod est inconveniens. Ergo intellectus ita natus est determinare alteram partem contingentis sicut voluntas."

[39] See Marchia, *Scriptum* I, d. 36, a. 4 (ed. Schabel, ll. 763–75): "Item, intellectus qui unico actu formaliter intelligit quodlibet intelligibile, eodem medio intelligendi intelligit quodlibet intelligibile (patet, tum quia actus intelligendi non est illimitatior medio intelligendi, sed magis e converso; tum quia unitas actus dependet ab unitate rationis intelligendi); sed intellectus divinus eodem actu formaliter intelligit quicquid intelligit, et non diversis actibus formaliter, quia si sic, tunc actus intelligendi esset formaliter limitatus in Deo; ergo Deus eodem medio intelligendi intelligit formaliter necessaria et contingentia. Sed necessaria non intelligit per determinationem voluntatis, nec presupponendo determinationem voluntatis; ergo nec contingentia intelligit per determinationem voluntatis nec presupponendo ea."

[40] See Marchia, *Scriptum* I, d. 36, a. 4 (ed. Schabel, ll. 776–805): "Item, aut intellectus divinus intelligit contingentia intelligendo determinationem voluntatis obiective in voluntate, aut

an attempt to straighten out the relationship between the intellect and will, but he aborts it. Here the *Scriptum* remains unfinished, and the passage from the *Reportatio* that fills in the lacuna in some manuscripts offers no solution.[41] So what is Marchia's solution? The intellect knows future contingents via the essence. Here Marchia borrows from Auriol and others and opposes many Franciscan Scotists. In wording very close to Auriol's own, Marchia declares that the "limitless" divine essence is "eminently all being," containing things "in a more perfect way than they have being in their own nature." And so the intellect, knowing the essence, knows all things "not just in universal and in general" but also "in particular," in a more perfect way than by knowing them in themselves. Thus "God's one action is formally equivalent and su- perequivalent to an infinite number of possible intellections occurring succes-

---

intelligendo determinationem illam obiective resultantem in essentia, sicut aliqui ponunt. Non primo modo, tum quia per aliud medium intelligeret contingentia quam necessaria, et ita alio actu formaliter, quod est inconveniens. Tum quia intellectus divinus acciperet notitiam contingentium a voluntate et perficeretur ab ea, et sic voluntas divina determinaret intellectum suum et intellectus divinus determinaretur passive a voluntate, quod est inconveniens in Deo. Nec secundo modo, quia illud quod representat aliquid representat per aliquid sibi intrinsecum quod est formaliter in ipso, non per aliquid extrinsicum quod non est formaliter in ipso; determinatio autem volunta- tis nihil ponit formaliter intrinsice in essentia; ergo essentia per illam determinationem non plus representat contingentia post determinationem quam ante.

Item, intellectus non intelligit perfecte aliquid nisi intelligendo primam causam eius; sed prima causa determinationis contingentium est voluntas et non essentia, secundum istam opinionem; ergo intellectus divinus non intelligit perfecte contingentia per essentiam nisi resolvendo ultimate ad voluntatem sicut ad primam causam.

Confirmatur, quia quicquid est causa cause, est causa causati; sed determinatio contingentium a voluntate est causa determinationis resultantis obiective in essentia, et resultatio eorum in essentia determinate est causa cognitionis determinate apud intellectum; ergo a primo ad ultimum, determinatio contingentium a voluntate est causa notitie contingentium, et ita intellectus intelligit contingentia per voluntatem, quod est inconveniens."

[41] See Marchia, *Scriptum* I, d. 36, a. 4 (ed. Schabel, ll. 831–61): "Sicut voluntas in nobis comparata ad alias potentias est prima potentia libera, sed comparata ad essentiam est secundo libera virtute essentie que est primo libera virtualiter, sicut agens principale est primo liberum virtualiter et instrumentum est secundo liberum participative — est autem voluntas in nobis instrumentum anime, secundum Anselmum in libro *De concordia predestinationis*, capitulo 3 — ita correspondenter dico in Deo, si ista distinguantur, quod voluntas divina respectu intellectus est primo libera et primum principium contingentie, sed respectu essentie in qua includitur perfec- tionaliter est secundo libera et secundum principium contingentie, quia ipsa essentia, si ponatur distincta a voluntate, est primo virtualiter et eminenter libera, voluntas autem est secundario et quasi formaliter libera. Ideo essentia est prima ratio determinandi contingentiam et non voluntas. Et sic intellectus divinus, intelligens perfecte essentiam, intelligit contingentia per determina- tionem contingentium in essentia virtualiter et eminenter, non per determinationem contingentium a voluntate.

Sed semper iste modus habet annexam illam difficultatem: Quod voluntas est nobilior intel- lectu ex quo voluntas determinat alteram partem contingentis primo vel secundo, intellectus au- tem non determinat primo nec secundo. (The *Scriptum* proper ends here.) Et ideo dico quod intel- lectus divinus non sic potest intelligere contingentia. Iste tamen ordo determinationis facte per voluntatem et intellectionis contingentium determinate sequentis determinationem voluntatis est in nobis. Non enim est simile de intellectu creato et divino, quoniam intellectus noster perficitur ab obiecto et est ignobilior voluntate, et ideo potest presupponere, sicut et presupponit, determina- tionem voluntatis precedentem antequam intelligat determinate aliquam partem complexionis contingentis. Non sic autem est in Deo"! What follows are two sentences refuting the *argumen- tum in oppositum*.

sively in us."[42] There still remains a problem: how can the essence, which is absolutely necessary, be the basis of understanding what is contingent? Marchia basically resorts to the distinction between the essence in itself, formally necessary, and the essence as it is "virtually" every other being. He also appeals to the notion that foreknowledge considered in itself is necessary, but not as it relates to its future contingent object.[43] Since for Marchia immutability is not the same as necessity, this solution has more attraction for Marchia than it did for Auriol.[44]

Some aspects of Marchia's treatment, especially divine knowledge, deserve more consideration than they have been given here. This holds true for Marchia's thought in general. He gains our attention in this context for his independence from Scotus, his refutation of Auriol, his own innovations, and, not least, for his impact on the succeeding generation of Parisian theologians.

Aufredo Gonteri Brito

Francis of Meyronnes seems to have adopted elements of Marchia's defense of Bivalence the year after Marchia's *Sentences* lectures. I have already men-

---

[42]   See for example Marchia, *Scriptum* I, d. 36, a. 3 (ed. Schabel, ll. 410–85): "Intellectus comprehendens perfecte et adequate aliquod obiectum, comprehendit omne intelligibile per ipsum; sed intellectus divinus comprehendit perfecte et adequate suam essentiam quantum est intelligibilis, sed per essentiam suam est intelligibile quodlibet ens sub propria ratione; ergo intelligendo essentiam suam, intelligit quodlibet ens sub propria ratione... Sed non est ratio cognoscendi tantum in universali et generali, quia cognoscere aliquid tantum in universali est cognoscere ipsum imperfecte et confuse; ergo est ratio cognoscendi omnia in particulari...

... Si ergo obiectum intellectus divini est totum ens eminenter, sequitur quod obiectum eius includat quodlibet ens multo perfectius quam habeat esse in propria natura. Quod autem includit aliud perfectiori modo quam habeat esse in propria natura est ratio cognoscendi ipsum perfectiori modo quam sit cognoscibilis per se ipsum, quia non ob aliud notitia per causam est nobilior quam notitia per effectum nisi quia causa nobiliori modo continet effectum quam effectus contineat causam. Ergo Deus nobiliori modo cognoscit quodlibet ens per essentiam suam quam sit natum cognosci quodlibet per se ipsum...

... Confirmatur, quia actio equivalens in perfectione diversis actionibus potest nobiliori modo in omnia illa in que possunt actiones plures; sed actio Dei unica formaliter equivalet et superequivalet infinitis intellectionibus possibilibus nostris successive se habentibus, sicut essentia divina superequivalet infinitis animabus possibilibus ad invicem succedentibus..."

[43]   See for example Marchia, *Scriptum* I, d. 36, a. 3 (ed. Schabel, ll. 575–81): "Ad tertium dico quod necessarium formaliter et virtualiter non est immediata ratio intelligendi contingens, tamen formaliter necessarium et virtualiter contingens est immediata ratio intelligendi contingens. Deus autem, licet sit formaliter necesse esse, est tamen virtualiter quodlibet aliud ens etiam possibile, quia licet necessarium non possit esse causa univoca contingentis, potest tamen esse causa equivoca eius." See also Marchia, *Scriptum* I, d. 38, a. 1 (ed. Schabel, Part II, ll. 55–62): "Dico quod prescientia futurorum potest considerari dupliciter: vel quantum ad actum prescientie in se, et sic est necessaria simpliciter... vel potest considerari ut transit super obiectum contingens futurum, et sic... est in se contingens et non necessarium."

[44]   For example Marchia, *Scriptum* I, d. 38, a. 1 (ed. Schabel, ll. 138–47): "Ab opposito in oppositum non est transitus sine mutatione alterius extremi; sed esse contingenter prescitum et esse non contingenter prescitum sunt contradictoria circa idem; ergo obiectum non transit de esse contingenter prescito ad esse non contingenter prescitum sine aliqua mutatione. Sed Deus ab eterno contingenter prescivit. Ergo, si nunc non prescit contingenter, est ibi aliqua mutatio, vel e converso est ibi aliqua mutatio circa obiectum, et tunc minor assumpta est falsa. Vel si non est ibi mutatio, sequitur quod contingenter presciat nunc sicut ab eterno."

tioned another of Marchia's followers on this issue when speaking of Peter of Navarre and Peter Thomae: the Franciscan Aufredo Gonteri Brito, who lectured at Barcelona in 1322 and then at Paris in 1325. His commentary on the first three books survives in two witnesses for books I–II and one manuscript for book III. As has long been known, more drastically than had Palude, Dionysius, and Baconthorpe, Gonteri read *secundum alium*, in this case Henry of Harclay, on book I and probably II, since Gonteri literally absorbed almost the whole of Harclay's commentary into his own. Gonteri makes significant additions to Harclay, however, including many new questions. In his own material he often attacks Auriol in the latter's *reportatio*, and apparently Marchia.[45]

In the context of future contingents and predestination, the situation is both different and more complex.[46] Based on the contents of these questions, especially the last one of distinction 38, Hermann Schwamm, discussing what he took to be the anonymous author of Vat. lat. 1113, thought that Auriol was the author's main adversary in his defense of Scotus.[47] While one could not say that Auriol was Gonteri's *primary* opponent, it is true that where Gonteri's commentary adds to Harclay's in the two large questions on future contingents taken out of Harclay, Auriol's position is attacked. The same is the case when Gonteri treats predestination.[48]

Therefore Aufredo Gonteri Brito in his slavish copying of Harclay is perhaps even of greater importance than, say, a Gerard of Siena with respect to Auriol's impact on the Paris discussion: Gonteri takes time out to attack Auriol. What Gonteri says, however, should not detain us. We might expect that such a plagiarizer would have little new to say, and in fact in the material I have edited this is exactly the case. Even Gonteri's additions to Harclay, both where they attack Auriol and where they do not, are merely paraphrases of Francis of Marchia, whom Gonteri *follows* here. The same conclusion holds for predestination. In one short quotation Gonteri borrows the whole of Mar-

---

[45] Studies of Gonteri's commentary that conclude that he was refuting, directly or indirectly, Auriol's *reportatio*, include Tachau, *Vision and Certitude*, pp. 317–18 and 322–7, and Dettloff, *Die Entwicklung der Akzeptations- und Verdienstlehre*, pp. 180–85. Dettloff follows Doucet, "Der unbekannte Skotist des Vaticanus lat. 1113," p. 202, in naming Marchia (along with Auriol) as a major opponent. Doucet's article includes an edition of Gonteri's book I, d. 34, q. 3. An edition of Gonteri's book III, d. 3, is in J. Alfaro, "La Immaculada Concepción en los escritos de un discípolo de Duns Escoto, Aufredo Gontier," *Gregorianum* 36 (1955), pp. 590–617.

[46] In my "Aufredo Gonteri Brito *secundum* Henry of Harclay" I discuss Gonteri and Marchia and present a composite critical edition of Harclay's *I Sent.*, dd. 38–39 and Gonteri's additions, using Gonteri's mss. as well. Without noting the Auriol connection, Michael Schmaus, "Uno sconosciuto discepolo di Scoto. Intorno alla prescienza di Dio," *Rivista di Filosofia Neoscolastica* 24 (1932), pp. 327–55, had edited Gonteri's book I, d. 41, q. 1, on predestination, from Vat. lat. 1113, and also transcribed parts of the questions I later re-edited. Schwamm, *Das göttliche Vorherwissen*, pp. 187–206, analyzed Gonteri's stance in these and his additional questions in Vat. lat. 1113, although he and Schmaus were unaware of Gonteri's and Harclay's identities.

[47] Schwamm, *Das göttliche Vorherwissen*, pp. 186–7.

[48] Cf. Halverson, "Peter Aureol and the Re-Emergence of Predestinarian Pluralism," pp. 213–16, who, unaware of Harclay's text, realizes the limited nature of Gonteri's attack on Auriol.

chia's *de inesse/de possibili* distinction as a conclusion to his main 'addition' to Harclay:

> Furthermore, an agent's deliberation about things that are to be done contingently would be in vain unless the contingent cause were determined *before* it contingently caused. Therefore, although in an absolute sense a contingent cause is indifferent to being able to act and not being able to act, and to acting and not acting, nevertheless it is freely and contingently determined *before* it acts. And I say that by itself it determines itself toward acting, and while it determines [itself] it is able not to determine itself, in the divided sense.[49]

Gonteri will not go so far as to accept as compelling Marchia's direct critique of Scotus, however. In Gonteri's second addition, when Marchia objects that Scotus's theory makes the will nobler than the intellect, Gonteri sees "nothing absurd" in this. Gonteri also provides a weak defense of the "Subtle Doctor" against Marchia's charge that on Scotus's account the divine intellect knows necessary things in one act and future contingents in another, after the determinations of the divine will. So Gonteri retreats to a Scotistic position, tacitly accepting the 'second way' where the essence plays a major role.[50]

What about the three brief, additional questions Gonteri asks on future contingents, distinction 39, questions one, three, and four? They too should arouse suspicion, and I have been able to establish that they are mere paraphrases of Hugh of Novocastro's distinction 38, questions five and six, and distinction 39, question two, respectively.[51] Since there are two versions of book II of Hugh's commentary, and of part of book III and perhaps book IV, it is possible that there was a second version of book I as well, which Gonteri

---

[49] Aufredus Gonteri Brito, *I Sent.*, d. 38 (q. 7) (ed. Schabel, "Aufredo Gonteri Brito *secundum* Henry of Harclay," pp. 167–8): "Preterea, frustra esset consilium in agente a proposito de agendis contingenter, nisi prius esset causa contingens determinata quam causet contingenter. Licet ergo absolute causa contingens sit indifferens ad posse agere et non posse agere, et ad agere et non agere, prius tamen determinatur libere et contingenter quam agat. Et dico quod ex se determinat se ad agendum, et dum determinat potest se non determinare in sensu diviso." It turns out that, not surprisingly, Anneliese Maier already noticed Gonteri's "kleiner Exkurs" which "ist aus Franciscus de Marchia entlehnt" (*Ausgehendes Mittelalter* I [Rome 1964], p. 482, note to p. 290), and which she had described in *Die Vorläufer Galileis*, pp. 244–5.

[50] Gonteri, *I Sent.*, d. 38 (q. 7) (ed. Schabel, pp. 172): "Dico quod nullum est inconveniens voluntatem divinam secundum rationem esse nobiliorem intellectu, sicut in nobis realiter actus voluntatis est nobilior actu intellectus, cum sint diversarum specierum. Et species in perfectione necessario sunt inequales, quia qualem ordinem habent aliqua in priorate et perfectione ubi distinguuntur realiter, talem habent ubi distinguuntur secundum rationem." And against the second objection (p. 173): "Dico quod causa representativa activa veritatis determinate futurorum contingentium in intellectu divino est determinatio divine voluntatis, quia non sunt nata sciri esse determinate vera nisi quia sunt volita. Sed ratio formalis qua representantur ut obiecta secundaria est actus divini intellectus invariabilis et unus formaliter ex unitate obiecti sui primi, quod est essentia divina."

[51] Both Hugh's and Gonteri's questions will be published in Friedman and my "Hugh of Novocastro's Questions." Interestingly, Stephen D. Dumont, "The Scotist of Vat. lat. 869," has shown that the author of several Scotist treatises in that manuscript is probably either Hugh or Gonteri. Given the relationship between the two in the questions on foreknowledge, it may be impossible to tell that the author is *not* Hugh.

copies verbatim. At any rate, these small questions tell us nothing about the reaction to Auriol, only about Gonteri's lack of originality.[52]

William of Brienne

Lecturing at Paris in 1330–31, the Franciscan William of Brienne has left us a brief *reportatio* on all four books that survives in only one manuscript, in which he also reveals Marchia's impact and appears to react to one of Auriol's *reportationes*, directly or only via Marchia. In his very short question for dd. 38–41 of book I, Brienne adopts Marchia's *de inesse/de possibili* scheme in relation to future contingents. Given that Brienne does not appear to copy, even in its brief form his commentary shows more 'originality' than Gonteri's.[53]

A close look at theological texts from 1315 and 1330 has revealed some interesting, innovative, and influential treatments of the problem of divine foreknowledge, as in the case of Thomas Wylton, Peter Auriol, Landulph Caracciolo, and Francis of Marchia, for example, but it has also shown that besides the normal conservative element, there was a considerable amount of verbatim copying, albeit sometimes merely to refute the copied material in the end. Peter of Palude, Dionysius de Burgo Sancti Sepulchri, John Baconthorpe, Bernard Lombardi, and, especially, Aufredo Gonteri Brito engaged in reading wholly or partly *secundum alium*, a practice that represents the negative aspect of Parisian theology in the period.

William of Rubio

The Franciscan William of Rubio was probably born in Aragon around 1290. While a student at Paris he was Francis of Marchia's secretary of sorts, taking down *reportationes* of Marchia's commentaries at least on books II and IV, the latter in 1323. His own lectures on the *Sentences* took place at some time after this, not only because it is unlikely that a Parisian bachelor of the *Sentences* would still be making *reportationes* for others, but also because he is the first continental theologian to make extensive use of the commentary of the English Franciscan Walter Chatton, whose first *Sentences* lectures were in 1321–23. In May 1333, while Rubio was Franciscan provincial minister of Aragon, a commission set up by the minister general, Gerard Odonis, examined for errors Rubio's commentary on all four books of the *Sentences*. Although Rubio could

---

    [52]   On the redaction problem for Hugh's *Sentences* commentary, see Heynck, "Der Skotist Hugo de Novo Castro, OFM," pp. 258–60.
    [53]   See Guillelmus de Brienna, *Reportatio in libros Sententiarum* I, dd. 38–41 (ms. Praha, Universitní knihovna [Statní knihovna], VIII. F. 14, fol. 65r): "Ad illa est notandum quod duplex est determinacio et indeterminacio opposita: quedam de inesse, quedam de possibili, et similiter de indeterminacione. Modo determinacio de inesse stat cum indeterminacione de possibili. Modo nulla determinacio de inesse excludit contingentiam de possibili." Tachau, *Vision and Certitude*, pp. 333–4, treats Brienne in brief on intuitive and abstractive cognition, and concludes that he probably did not use Auriol's *Scriptum*.

therefore have lectured any time between 1323 and 1332, something closer to the latter date is more likely: the commission, which approved the work, described it as *novum*, and Rubio replies to Auriol's *Scriptum* rather than a *reportatio* when he attacks him.[54]

Rubio's commentary on all four books survives, but not in any known manuscripts: it was printed in Paris in 1518. Not surprisingly Rubio's solution to the problem of divine foreknowledge and future contingents reflects that of his master, Francis of Marchia. In his distinction 38 he follows Marchia's presentation and refutation of Auriol's position in a series of arguments, sometimes verbatim, other times paraphrasing, and occasionally expanding. In fact, there are no indications that Rubio is reading Auriol's *Scriptum* here, but merely Marchia's text. For that matter, he is not reading Marchia's *Scriptum* either, but rather, as we might expect, the *Reportatio* for which he himself is probably responsible.[55]

Rubio also adopts Marchia's distinction between the determination *de inesse* and determination *de possibili*, holding with his master that the former determination does not endanger the contingency of the future, but is needed for foreknowledge. The latter determination does not exist for future contingents until after they come about, but the corresponding indetermination *de possibili* is required for contingency.[56] This distinction for Rubio, as for Marchia, is his main bastion against the attacks of Peter Auriol. Moreover, Rubio basically accepts Marchia's theory of *how* God knows future contingents through the essence.[57]

---

[54] For the commission, cf. fol. i of the Paris 1518 edition. For dating, see Zénon Kaluza, "*Serbi un sasso il nome*: une inscription de San Gimignano et la rencontre entre Bernard d'Arezzo et Nicolas d'Autrecourt," in Burkhard Mojsisch and Olaf Pluta, eds., *Historia Philosophiae Medii Aevii*, vol I (Amsterdam 1991) (pp. 437–66), pp. 445–8. Dettloff, *Die Entwicklung der Akzeptations- und Verdienstlehre*, pp. 196–200, touches on Rubio's doctrine of grace and declares his reliance on the *Scriptum* (p. 197). For future contingents, see Schwamm, *Das göttliche Vorherwissen*, pp. 255–75. Rubio also apparently wrote *Quodlibeta*, edited by Rubert Candau, *Archivo Ibero-Americano* 15 (1928), pp. 5–32; 16 (1929), pp. 145–81; and 17 (1930), pp. 5–42; and by L.M. Farré, "La conceptió inmaculada de la Verge segons Fr. G. Rubió," *Analecta Sacra Tarraconensia* 7 (1931), pp. 95–138. Candau also authored *La filosofia del siglo XIV a través de G. Rubió* (Madrid 1952). I have not seen these works, however.

[55] For example, while the *Scriptum* initially presents Auriol's position in six arguments, Rubio follows the *Reportatio* in Napoli 27 and Ross. lat. 525 in giving those six plus two more. See above, n. 35. Auriol's opinion is given and then refuted in Guillelmus de Rubione, *Disputata in quatuor libros Magistri Sententiarum*, I, d. 38, q. 1, a. 1 (vol. 1, ed. Paris 1518, ff. 219ra–b, and ff. 221rb–222ra).

[56] Rubione, *I Sent.*, d. 38, q. 1 (ed. Paris, fol. 220ra): "Secundum premittendum est, quod determinatio est duplex; est enim una de possibili, qua aliquid est determinatum ad posse tantum vel ad non posse agere vel ad posse agere ita hoc, quod non aliud; et est alia determinatio de inesse, qua videlicet aliquid est determinatum de facto ad agere vel ad non agere, existens tamen indeterminatum indeterminatione de possibili ad agere et non agere; licet enim sit aliquis determinatus ad agere, non tamen propter hoc est necessitatus, sed potest agere vel non agere, et ista indeterminatione de possibili, cum qua est determinatio de inesse, stat ratio contingentie." Also cited in Schwamm, *Das göttliche Vorherwissen*, p. 260.

[57] Thus Rubione, *I Sent.*, d. 38, q. 2 (ed. Paris, ff. 222rb–224ra) has much in common with Marchia, *I Sent.*, d. 36, a. 3 (ed. Schabel). In Rubio's d. 39, qq. 1–2 (ed. Paris, ff. 224rb–225vb), where he treats modal questions, there are the normal appeals to different types of necessity.

The main difference between Rubio and Marchia lies in Rubio's emphasis on how God, the first cause, fits into Marchia's schema. Instead of a defense of Bivalence and an explanation of how contingent causes are predetermined, Rubio's general presentation revolves around divine determinism from eternity (*ab eterno*). One of the potential objections to Marchia's theory was that it only explained how some prior determination is in a contingent cause, while the problem with divine foreknowledge involves determination *ab eterno*. Instead of avoiding this problem, Rubio accepts it:

> The first omnipotent cause established and eternally ordained that these things come about and not others, and consequently it was determined toward this. From this my point follows, namely that each one of all possibles was determined *ab eterno* to one side of a contradiction, some toward coming about or existing, and others toward not coming about, as with all other possible non-futures.[58]

When Rubio has explained this at length, he posits four conclusions, incorporating Marchia's determination division and inserting his own general analysis of causation. The first conclusion sums up the previous passages: "The first cause was determined *ab eterno* by determination *de inesse*, but not by determination *de possibili*; rather in that way it was indeterminate."[59]

The second conclusion tackles the issue of secondary causation. Of course secondary causes are determined *de inesse* in the way Marchia said, but Rubio asserts that they are also determined *de possibili* in a certain way (*aliqualiter*), because not everything is possible for each cause. This determination *de possibili* is not absolute and without qualification, but rather in a certain respect (*secundum quid*). Rubio's point is best understood through his illustrations. In the case of natural causes, fire, for example, is determined even *de possibili* toward producing fire, but it is still more determined *de possibili* to not producing water, "because it is so determined toward not producing water that in no way can it produce it." With respect to fire, however, it still requires God's coaction to burn — as the scriptural example of the three boys who did not burn demonstrates —, so it is less determined *de possibili*.[60] More impor-

---

[58]   Rubione, *I Sent.*, d. 38, q. 1, a. 1 (ed. Paris, f. 219va): "Ista fieri et non alia causa prima omnipotens statuit et eternaliter ordinavit, et per consequens ad hoc determinata fuit. Ex quo sequitur propositum, videlicet quod quodlibet possibilium fuit ab eterno ad alteram contradictionis partem determinatum, aliqua videlicet ad fiendum seu essendum et alia non fiendum, ut omnia alia possibilia non futura."

[59]   Rubione, *I Sent.*, d. 38, q. 1, a. 1 (ed. Paris, f. 220ra): "Prima est quod prima causa fuit determinata ab eterno determinatione de inesse, non autem determinatione de possibili, sed hoc modo fuit indeterminata..."

[60]   Rubione, *I Sent.*, d. 38, q. 1, a. 1 (ed. Paris, f. 220rb): "Secunda conclusio est quod omnis causa secunda est determinata determinatione de inesse et etiam determinatione de possibili uno modo et non alio ad effectum sibi possibilem producendum... Hoc apparet in exemplo de igne qui, habito passo, non potest non producere ignem, nec, passo habito vel non habito, potest producere aquam. Et ideo determinatione de possibili arguitur esse determinatus et ad producendum ignem et ad non producendum aquam. Magis tamen ad non producendum aquam quam ad producendum ignem, quia ad non producendum aquam et sic determinatus quod nullo modo potest eam producere, ad ignem autem producendum non sic est determinatus, cum possit non producere vel passo

tantly, this is also the case for created wills, for which Rubio briefly remarks, "Similarly, I maintain this for a created will that is acting toward this act of willing or nilling in such a way that it does not act toward something else that is produced by another created will."[61]

Rubio's third conclusion brings God into the picture, because the first cause determines the secondary causes.[62] Rubio gives the obvious objection: what about the freedom of the will?

> When one calls a cause 'free' or 'freely acting' only that which by itself is able to act and not to act, every other agent set aside, then no cause acts nor is able to act freely except the first cause, since no cause can [produce] any effect without it. Nevertheless the created will, and no other secondary cause, is called free from the fact that, when the first cause assists, it can choose or suspend an act, will it or nill it.[63]

Rubio further describes God's connection with created willing in the fourth conclusion, where is it objected that, since the first cause determines the secondary cause, how can the secondary cause determine itself in any way toward an exterior effect? Rubio's solution is to claim that God does not participate in the actual act of bringing about the effect, but He only coacts through the secondary cause, the created will, so that the creature actually brings about the effect.[64]

Perhaps Rubio noticed that Marchia's treatment left a few matters unresolved, especially with regard to the role of the first cause in the determination *de inesse* and *de possibili* schema. He therefore extended the distinction to God, and even completed his exposition by applying it to the problem of Bivalence, perhaps as a concession to Auriol. In all propositions, even those

---

deficiente vel etiam existente, prima causa sibi non coagente... ut apparet de igne trium puerorum."

[61] Rubione, *I Sent.*, d. 38, q. 1, a. 1 (ed. Paris, f. 220va): "Consimiliter dico de ista voluntate creata ita agente ad istum volendi vel nolendi actum quod non ad alium ab alia voluntate creata productum."

[62] See Rubione, *I Sent.*, d. 38, q. 1, a. 1 (ed. Paris, f. 220va): "Tertia conclusio est quod causa secunda, modo predicto in conclusione alia determinata, est determinata non ab alio quam a prima."

[63] Rubione, *I Sent.*, d. 38, q. 1, a. 1 (ed. Paris, f. 220vb): "sed contra istam conclusionem arguatur, quia sequi videtur quod nulla sit libertas in aliqua causa, cum non possit ex se sed ex alio ad effectum esse determinata. Dico quod vocando causam liberam seu agentem libere solum illam que ex se potest agere vel non agere, omni agente alio circumscripto, nulla causa secunda est agebs nec agere potens libere nisi prima, cum nulla causa secunda possit in effectum aliquem sine ipsa. Ex hoc tamen voluntas creata dicitur libera et non aliqua alia causa secunda quia potest assistente sibi prima actum elicere vel suspendere, velle vel nolle."

[64] See Rubione, *I Sent.*, d. 38, q. 1, a. 1 (ed. Paris, f. 221rb): "et si contra hoc obiiciatur quia superius fuit dictum quod nulla causa secunda determinatur a se ipsa, nec ab alia causa secunda, sed a prima, cum omnis causa secunda sit ex se ad omnes effectus eiusdem rationis consimiliter indeterminata, Dico quod hoc est verum, et intelligendum de omni causa naturaliter secunda et etiam de causa libere et contingenter agente, videlicet de voluntate creata respectu actus interioris, non autem respectu operis exterioris... Non tamen sic Deus ipse statuit ipsum coagere immediate ad exteriorem effectum, videlicet ad artificiatum ipsum. Non enim statuit coagere ad istum effectum ipsi nisi volenti ipsum."

about future contingents, there is determinate truth and falsity *de inesse*. *De possibili*, however, there is determinate truth only in necessary propositions, because with respect to future contingents, "in such propositions that announce the future, *each* side [of a contradiction] is true, namely that it can come about and that it is able not to come about."[65] Rubio's attempt to pursue the matter, however, may have served merely to draw attention to the main flaw in Marchia's argument, rather than remove it.

Michael of Massa

Although he may have opposed Francis of Marchia on other issues, the Augustinian Hermit Michael of Massa (†1337) was Marchia's truest follower on the subject of divine foreknowledge. Like his confrère Gerard of Siena, Massa was from the Siena area. He is mentioned as being his province's definitor at the Augustinian order's general chapter in Venice in 1322, and he probably died in Paris. Massa's Parisian *Sentences* commentary on books I–II survives in only a handful of manuscripts. Massa's commentary was once dated to about 1325, but recently it has been shown that he is much more likely to have lectured in the 1330's, and indeed the written version was not yet completed at Massa's death. The new dating explains why his fellow Augustinian, Thomas of Strasbourg, never cites Massa in his *Sentences* commentary, since Strasbourg's work may actually precede Massa's. In any case, Massa's role in the history of Augustinian thought needs to be re-evaluated.[66]

---

[65] Rubione, *I Sent.*, d. 38, q. 1, a. 1 (ed. Paris, f. 221rb): "Ex predictis omnibus sequitur quod tam in necessariis quam in contingentibus est altera pars contradictionis determinate vera non tantum de presenti et de preterito, sed etiam de futuro, et hoc de inesse, videlicet quod erit vel non erit, non tamen de possibili... Nec sic autem est in materia contingenti, quoniam in tali, licet altera pars sit determinate vera et alia falsa in propositionibus de inesse sive annunciantibus futurum sive presens sive preteritum, non tamen in propositionibus de possibili, sed in talibus annunciantibus futurum utraque pars est vera, videlicet quod potest fieri et quod potest non fieri."

[66] Book II has only one witness: Vat. lat. 1087, but book I is extant in three manuscripts, of which ms. Napoli BN VII. C. 1 goes only to distinction eight. Of the 'complete' manuscripts, the better of the two, i.e. Bologna, Collegio di Spagna 40, is physically missing about 60 percent of its folios. Finally, two abbreviations of book I were made in the fifteenth century, witnessed by two manuscripts each. On the commentary and the manuscripts, see Damasus Trapp, "Augustinian Theology," pp. 163-75, and idem, "Notes on some Manuscripts of the Augustinian Michael de Massa (†1337)," *Augustinianum* 5 (1965), pp. 58-133, which has a question and citation list; Courtenay, 'The *Quaestiones in Sententias* of Michael de Massa," on the authenticity of book II and dating questions; and my "Questions on Future Contingents," *Augustiniana*, 48 (1998), pp. 165-229, which includes a critical edition of Massa's *Scriptum*, dd. 35, 36, and 38, and a discussion of the abbreviations. Massa apparently also wrote a life of Christ; see Walter Baier, "Michael von Massa OESA (†1337) — Autor einer *Vita Christi*. Kritik der Diskussion über ihre Zuordnung zur *Vita Christi* des Kartäusers Ludolf von Sachsen (†1378)," in Adolar Zumkeller and Achim Krümmel, eds., *Traditio Augustiniana. Studien über Augustinus und seine Rezeption* (Würzburg 1994), pp. 495-524, which I have not seen.

Trapp, "Augustinian Theology," dated Massa's lectures to 1325-26, just after Gerard of Siena, whom Massa cites. This is because (a) in his *Quodlibet* James of Pamiers cites Massa and refers to Durand as bishop of Le Puy, which was not the case after 1326, and (b) in book I Massa calls Alexander of St. Elpidio the prior general of the Augustinians, which was not true

Book I of Massa's commentary, labeled a *Scriptum*, unfortunately stops in mid-sentence in the beginning of the second question for distinction 38. Ordinarily, without a complete distinction 38 and 39, we would not know a thinker's views on future contingents. We do, however, know what questions Massa asks in distinction 38: "Whether God knows future contingents?" "Whether God's knowledge or foreknowledge imposes necessity on future contingents — and this question has a special difficulty on account of future contingents depending on free choice —?" "Whether God knows future contingents via Ideas of the known things themselves?" and "Whether God knows propositions both of necessary truths and contingent truths through Ideas of complex truths?"[67] In the course of the first question, Massa refers matters to the next question on three occasions, but whether he meant the next *distinction* or simply the next *question* in distinction 38 is difficult to say, as the second question breaks off in the first sentence, and the third and fourth questions are left untouched. The title of the last question implies that Massa actually defended the Ideas solution, but we shall probably never know.

Some clue is gained from Massa's distinction 37, where Massa deals at length with God's knowledge of things outside Himself (*ad extra*). His exposition here is consistent with Trapp's opinion that Massa explains Auriol in attacking Gerard of Siena. After brief preliminary arguments, Massa goes straight to Auriol's position, and this remains the focus throughout. Gerard thought that Auriol's opinion was that God knows creatures *terminatively* in

---

after February 1326. Trapp then explained that Strasbourg's refusal to cite Massa in his Paris lectures of 1336, Massa's own failure to become master of theology, and the dearth of citations of Massa by later Augustinians, are the result of Massa's opposition to Gerard and therefore to Giles of Rome. Courtenay, however, asked why in book II Massa mentions Ockhamists (*Occamistae*) and their physical theories, and there are no other references to such a group at Paris until 1339. So Courtenay refuted Trapp's evidence: the reference to Durand is in the margin in a *later* hand; Pamiers was still a Parisian *bachelor* of theology in 1329, and so the *Quodlibet* should probably be dated to ca. 1332, when he was a master (the first citation of the *Quodlibet* is only in 1344–5, our real *terminus ante quem*); the prior general of the Augustinians may be William of Cremona (1326–42), which would explain Massa's marginal reference to "O.G.," i.e. "O<pinio> G<uillelmi>." Based on references to Aquinas as "frater Thomas" in one manuscript of book I but "sanctus Thomas" in another, Courtenay concluded that Massa probably (a) wrote a pre-Paris version, before 1323, (b) lectured on the *Sentences* around 1332, so that his never becoming master is not unusual, and (c) began to rework his commentary before his death in 1337. I then suggested that abandoning the Aquinas criterion for non-Dominicans (which forced Courtenay to push Gerard's lectures as far back as 1322–23), we are free to date all redactions of Massa's commentary to the 1330s. Zénon Kaluza put Strasbourg's commentary at an earlier date, 1334–35, and so Strasbourg's reticence concerning Massa is the normal scholastic reluctance to cite close contemporaries by name. Alternatively, if Strasbourg does not deal with Massa's opinion at all (which has not been proven), we could maintain that either Massa's lectures post-date Strasbourg's, or they did not circulate yet in written form.

[67] Michaelis de Massa, *I Sent.*, d. 38 (ed. Schabel, "Questions on Future Contingents," p. 224, ll. 3–11): "Et ideo tractande essent hic quatuor questiones, quarum prima est utrum Deus cognoscat futura contingentia. Secunda questio est utrum scientia seu prescientia Dei imponat necessitatem futuris contingentis, et habet specialem difficultatem ista questio propter futura contingentia dependentia ex libero arbitrio. Tertia questio est de modo cognoscendi futura contingentia, utrum videlicet per ydeas ipsarum rerum cognitarum cognoscat Deus futura contingentia. Quarta questio est utrum complexiones tam veritatum necessariarum quam veritatum contingentium cognoscat Deus per ydeas veritatum complexarum."

the essence, and Gerard held against Auriol that it in fact goes beyond the essence. Massa corrects Gerard, showing that Auriol held that God knows creatures *denominatively*, and Massa agrees with Auriol that it does *not* go beyond the essence. But in an important way Massa also sides with Gerard. Along with Auriol and, significantly, Francis of Marchia, Massa maintains that the essence is eminently the similitude of a creature,[68] but contrary to Auriol, Massa thinks that in knowing the essence, the intellect is able to 'end' (*terminare*) at the creatures, so that the intellect knows the creatures terminatively and not only denominatively. So Massa corrects Gerard's understanding of Auriol's opinion, and then goes on to adopt the position that Gerard had wrongly assigned to Auriol and criticized.[69]

What about future contingents? Fortunately, Michael of Massa refers the refers back to distinction 35, and in fact he moved much of his discussion on this issue to distinctions 35 and 36, as had Francis of Marchia. The questions of distinction 38 hint at a relationship between the works of the earlier Franciscan and the Augustinian. All doubts are dispelled when one looks at distinctions 35 and 36, in both of which Massa follows Marchia's corresponding distinctions. In many respects Massa expands on and clarifies Marchia's presentation. I shall note two: his treatment of Auriol, and his discussion of the origin of contingency. Massa has not simply followed Marchia's outline of Auriol's position; he has taken a fresh look at it, explicitly citing the latter's *Scriptum*, rather than the *Reportatio* that Marchia used. What Marchia describes in sixty lines, Massa lays out in 260.[70] He gives Marchia's basic description of Auriol's stance as it regards the denial of the univocal application of the First Principle to propositions about the past and future, and he repeats Marchia's argument that if the principle is only true 'disjunctively' of the future, God would be as knowledgeable, and as ignorant, as we are about the future. Like Marchia, he also argues in support of the First Principle and against the neutrality of propositions. But then, anticipating Gregory of Rimini, Massa is the first thinker to focus on Auriol's two propositions: "If a categorical proposition by which it is said absolutely and without a disjunc-

---

    [68] Massa gives Auriol's position thus, Massa, *I Sent.*, d. 37 (ms. Bologna, Universitaria 2214, f. 232ra): "Et ideo tandem iste doctor, volens ostendere secundum quem modum slavari possit quod Deus intelligat alia extra se, dicit quod hoc est verum, non quidem sistenter et terminative, sed solum equipollenter et denominative," adding later that in understanding the essence the intellect "intelligit id quod est eminenter et plus quam equipollenter similitudo creature."

    [69] See Massa, *I Sent.*, d. 37 (ms. Bologna, Biblioteca Universitaria 2214, f. 232va): "Ergo per te sequitur quod cognitio Dei simpliciter loquendo non terminetur ad creaturas, sed solum secundum quid et aliquo modo. Sed hoc est inconveniens et est incidere in errorem..." and "Sed per te creature non sunt cognite ab intellectu divino nisi denominative et ab extrinseco et in suo superequivalenter; ergo non sunt vere et simpliciter cognite ab intellectu divino. Sed hoc est falsum et periculosum in fide." Massa's opinion is e.g. ibidem: "Ergo mutlo magis divina essentia est ratio cognoscendi perfecte a priori quodlibet aliud ens ab ipsa, et hoc cognitione distincta se tenente a parte obiecti, non solum denominative, sed terminative." His conclusion to the first question is on fol. 233rb: "Et dico quod Deus habeat notitiam rerum fissibilium (?) se attingentem eas terminative in seipsis, ut distinguuntur a divina essentia in ratione obiecti cogniti..."

    [70] Massa, *I Sent.*, d.35 (ed. Schabel, p. 176, l. 39): "...unus doctor in *Scripto* suo..." See ibid. (pp. 176–86, ll. 38–300), for Massa's general presentation of Auriol's position.

tion, 'Socrates will exist', is true determinately, then it is necessarily and inevitably true," and "If the truth of any proposition about a future contingent is inevitably true, then its significate is inevitably and necessarily put into being." He also explains Auriol's reasoning that no instant can be found when true propositions about the future can possibly be false before the future event's coming about.[71]

Massa argues against neutral propositions by saying, contrary to Auriol, that propositions naturally contain the 'habit of truth or falsity', just as natural bodies necessarily have either the 'habit' of motion or rest. All natural bodies are either resting or in motion, and there is no middle ground. Likewise, all propositions are either true or false, but not neither. Auriol flatly denied this, saying that propositions about future contingents were in fact not 'naturally apt' to receive truth and falsity.[72] Also interesting, and beyond Marchia's treatment, are Massa's objections involving prophecy and his hypothetical example of how God might reveal a determinately true proposition about a future contingent which expressed His determinate knowledge about that future contingent: "By the cracking of the sky."[73]

The other issue where Massa surpasses Marchia's exposition, the existence of contingency in the world, may be further evidence for a late date for Massa's commentary, because in the early 1330s many critics charged that Pope John XXII was a fatalist, and thus the problem came to the fore.[74] Of course it had already become a commonplace at Paris by the 1320s to include a section refuting fatalism, but at the same time showing that the existence of contingency was a *per se notum*, that is, not something provable but rather plainly obvious. These discussions usually ended with Avicenna's exhortation that those who deny contingency and hold instead that all things happen of necessity should be beaten until they admit, by their pleading, that the one who tortures has the free will to desist. Massa's discussion follows along

---

[71] Massa, *I Sent.*, d. 35 (ed. Schabel, p. 179, ll. 117–19): "Si propositio cathegorica que absolute et sine disiunctione dicitur, 'Sortes erit', sit determinate vera, ergo est necessario et inevitabiliter vera"; (p. 181, ll. 161–3): "Si veritas alicuius propositionis de futuro contingenti sit inevitabiliter vera, ergo significatum eius ponetur inevitabiliter et necessario in esse"; and (p. 181, ll. 158–60): "Cum ergo non possit eveniri aliquod instans in quo possit mutari propositio habens determinatam veritatem de futuro contingenti, sequitur quod inevitabiliter sit vera."

[72] Massa, *I Sent.*, d. 35 (ed. Schabel, pp. 189–90, ll. 376–88): "Preterea, accipio istam propositionem: 'Antichristus erit', et quero, aut est determinate vera aut determinate falsa, aut neutra, possibilis tamen subesse tam habitudini veritatis quam etiam habitudini determinationis ad veritatem... Si vero detur tertium, contra: non minus determinat sibi propositio complexa habitudinem veritatis et habitudinem falsitatis, habentes se sicut passiones propositionis, quam corpus naturale determinet sibi motum et quietem, que sunt passiones corporis naturalis; sed corpus naturale, saltem naturaliter, non potest se habere ut neutrum, ita ut non insit sibi actualiter vel motus vel quies; ergo nulla potest esse propositio complexa habens se ut neutra ita ut non insit sibi actualiter vel veritas vel falsitas."

[73] Massa, *I Sent.*, d.35 (ed. Schabel, p. 188, ll. 340–44): "Preterea, suppono quod Deus habeat de futuro contingenti pro illo instanti pro quo ponatur in esse notitiam determinatam ad unam partem contradictionis, et quod pro tunc formare potest Deus, vel per aeris fractionem vel per aliquem alium modum, propositionem cathegoricam determinatam ad unam partem contradictionis." Massa's prophecy objections are on p. 187, ll. 325–39, and p. 189, ll. 358–75.

[74] On this issue, see Courtenay, *Capacity and Volition*, pp. 147–61.

these lines, but he is unusual in the lengths to which he goes. Massa appears to be talking about a real *adversarius* who defends fatalism, and real opponents who attempt anew to refute necessity with logical arguments.[75]

Recall that Marchia maintains that all natural events would come about necessarily if there were not a truly *per se* contingent basis, which must be God. Massa points out that an adversary would claim that Marchia is merely assuming that natural events do not occur of absolute necessity.[76] But it is not at all clear that this is so, and indeed for practical purposes it makes little difference for the natural world and natural philosophy, so Massa instead falls back on the idea in Scotus, Auriol, and others that such contingency is a *per se notum* that cannot be proven.[77]

Again, when Marchia asserts that, unless the human will were also a source of contingency, an absurdity would follow, namely that humans would be mere brutes and not responsible for their actions, Massa responds that an adversary, "on account of the corruption of the [sensitive] appetite and other extrinsic difficulties," would respond that Marchia is begging the question, and that this is not absurd.[78] Instead, this also is a mere unproven assumption, to be taken as a *per se notum* and unprovable. Moreover, Massa makes a move similar to Rubio's assertion that secondary causes are determined *de possibili* in a certain respect, but not absolutely, whereas only God is completely indeterminate *de possibili*. Massa's version is to turn Marchia's twofold division of contingency into a more precise three-fold contingency. Since God can remove or impede contingents having their source in human free will by supernaturally impeding the human will itself, then while human free will

[75] See Massa, *I Sent.*, d. 36, q. 1 (ed. Schabel, pp. 212–14, ll. 81–154).

[76] See Massa, *I Sent.*, d. 36, q. 1 (ed. Schabel, pp. 212–13, ll. 92–104): "Sed ista ratio non concluderet evidenter adversariis, ymo diceret adversarius quod ratio petit quod est in principio, scilicet quod contingentia dividatur per predicta duo membra. Nam non videretur sibi quod in rerum natura sit possibile esse aliqua contingentia positiva nec aliqua contingentia simpliciter, quia omnis contingentia est propter defectum alicuius cause non habentis plenarium vigorem ad tollendum omnia impedientia, et ideo omnis contingentia pertinet ad defectum. Et ex hoc ipso sequitur quod non sit dare contingentiam simpliciter, quia non est dare defectum vel malum simpliciter, sed solum secundum quid. Supponit ergo ratio quod contingentia in communi dividatur per contingentiam simpliciter, que est contingentia positiva, et per contingentiam secundum quid, que est privativa, et quamvis hoc verum sit, tamen ratio supponit quod principaliter vertitur in dubium."

[77] See Massa, *I Sent.*, d. 36, q. 1 (ed. Schabel, pp. 215–16, ll. 157–86).

[78] See Massa, *I Sent.*, d. 36, q. 1 (ed. Schabel, p. 214, ll. 143–54): "Sine dubio ista ratio est bona; tamen propter corruptionem appetitus et propter quasdam extrinsecas difficultates non haberet adversarius pro inconvenienti illud quod concluditur pro inconvenienti. Quicquid tamen sit de conclusione que intenditur, quia infallibiliter est vera, tamen illud quod assumitur pro medio, scilicet quod actus humani sint laudabiles et vituperabiles eo modo quo loquimur hic de laude et vituperio, prout videlicet debentur agentibus habentibus in potestate sua agere et non agere, etiam positis in esse omnibus per se causis requisitis ad agendum, est eque dubium sicut sit conclusio principaliter intenta, scilicet quod homo agat contingenter actus suos contingentia simpliciter accepta, que est libertas arbitrii ad agere et non agere, positis in esse omnibus per se causis requisitis ad agendum."

can be termed contingent *simpliciter*, it is not, however, *prima* contingency. Only God's will is *prima* contingency, unimpedible.[79] The most important element, however, of Massa's position, is his solution to Auriol's arguments, and in this he follows Marchia most closely. "Determination to one part of a contradiction," he says, "is common to the necessary and the contingent":

> And therefore it seems to me that we must speak in another way concerning this question. Wherefore one must consider that a twofold indetermination is found in things: One, indeed, is an indetermination about what can be put into being, namely that by which the thing is indeterminate toward being able to be put into being and being able not to be put into being; but the other one is the indetermination toward being de facto or toward having been put into being de facto, namely that by which a thing is indeterminate toward being de facto in being and not being de facto in being.[80]

---

[79] See Massa, *I Sent.*, d. 36, q. 2 (ed. Schabel, pp. 217–19, ll. 228–62): "In universo contingentia dicitur tripliciter: Uno modo contingentia secundum quid, qualis videlicet cóntingentia est effectuum naturalium, que non est contingentia in ordine ad omnes suas per se causas requisitas, sed solum in ordine ad hanc causam particularem vel illam impedibilem per concursum alterius cause. Alio modo dicitur contingentia simpliciter, tamen non prima, et ista est contingentia actuum humanorum qui sunt contingentes in ordine ad omnes suas per se causas requisitas pro quanto, positis omnibus per se concurrentibus ad agendum, adhuc potest homo ex libertate arbitrii agere et non agere, et ideo simpliciter loquendo agit contingenter et non necessario. Et talis est contingentia quorumcumque actuum elicitorum ex libertate arbitrii creati et existentium in potestate voluntatis create, sive sit voluntas hominis sive angeli, sive sit voluntas viatoris sive comprehensoris. Dicitur autem talis contingentia esse contingentia simpliciter, non tamen prima, quia licet impediri non possit ab aliquo agente naturali, potest tamen impediri divinitus et ab agente supernaturali. Nam supposito quod voluntas divina subtraheret suam influentiam generalem voluntati create ad eliciendum aliquem actum volendi, sive posito quod Deus non coexisteret voluntati create in ratione agentis naturalis respectu cuiuslibet actionis, saltem quantum ad id bonitatis quod reperitur in actione, tunc voluntas creata actionem suam, et specialiter actionem bonam, absque omni malitia non posset per facultatem naturalem sui arbitrii causare. Et hoc non solum loquendo de actu elicito exteriori, sed etiam de actu voluntatis elicito interiori, quia sicut dicit Apostolus ad Romanos, capitulo <9>, 'Non est volentis velle nec currentis currere, sed Dei miserentis'.
Sed tertio modo dicitur contingentia simpliciter et penitus independens et prima, et ista est contingentia rerum productarum a Deo in ordine ad voluntatem divinam cuius efficatia et propositum efficax impediri non potest. Verum est tamen quod voluntas divina non respicit contingenter substantiam sui actus, quia actus qui est velle divinum est ipsamet Dei voluntas et Dei substantia, et ideo est summe necesse esse. Ac per consequens voluntas divina non respicit contingenter actum sicut facit voluntas creata, sed mediante actu qui est ipsum velle respicit contingenter obiecta volibilia extra se. Patet ergo quod generaliter loquendo contingentia tripliciter reperitur in rebus."
[80] Massa, *I Sent.*, d.35 (ed. Schabel, p. 193, ll. 470–71): "...determinatio ad unam partem contradictionis est communis necessario et contingenti..." (p. 194, ll. 494–9): "Et ideo videtur mihi aliter esse dicendum circa istam questionem. Ubi est advertendum quod in rebus reperitur duplex indeterminatio: una quidam est <in>determinatio de ponibili in esse, qua videlicet res est determinata ad posse poni in esse et posse non poni in esse; alia vero est <in>determinatio de facto esse vel de posito in esse, qua videlicet res est indeterminata ad esse de facto in esse et non esse de facto in esse."

When indetermination with respect to actually inhering (*de inesse*) goes over contingently to determination, as it must for things to take place at all by contingent causes, this does not affect that contingency, as is clear from the use of the term 'contingent'.[81] As long as the indetermination with respect to being able to be put or not be put into being (*de possibili*) remains, contingency and foreknowledge also remain. Massa makes himself clearer in a series of six conclusions, which repeat Marchia's solution, with slightly different terminology, for example admitting 'conditioned necessity' where Marchia said 'the necessity of the consequence'. Massa uses the composite and divided senses in the same way and sees the same prior and posterior relationship between the two determinations and indeterminations, *de inesse* and *de possibili*.[82]

The Franciscan Francis of Marchia's new solution, prompted by Peter Auriol's treatment of the problem, thus had a positive impact a few years later on Michael of Massa, of the Augustinian order. Because Marchia had an impact on Gregory of Rimini, there is the probability that Massa was the path Marchia's ideas on the subject took to reach Massa's junior Augustinian brother. Moreover, like Rimini, Massa responded explicitly to Auriol's *Scriptum* on book I, and evidence also suggests that Massa's own innovations in his attack on Auriol influenced Rimini, specifically Massa's defense of Bivalence where he focuses on the same lines of Auriol's text that Rimini does later. If this is the case, then Massa may be a key figure in the Augustinian movement away from Dominican-oriented theology and toward the Franciscans. Through Massa, probably, Marchia's position passed to Gregory of Rimini, and Marchia's own substantial direct influence was supplemented by Rimini's popularity in the Late Middle Ages. It is the Augustinians, notably Rimini and Alphonsus Vargas, who would deal with Auriol most decisively two decades later, when the Franciscans virtually ignored him. Looking back on the 1320s at Paris, then, especially among the Franciscans, one can draw some conclusions. First, it was a lively debate, and Peter Auriol had provided that stimulus. Second, no one was prepared to accept Auriol's radical departure from traditional stances toward the problem of foreknowledge and future contingency. Auriol placed too little emphasis, perhaps, on the God of Scripture, active in history and the world. Third, Gregory of Rimini would have much 'local' material to draw upon when he went on to refute Auriol yet again in the Paris tradition, this time using the new ideas from Oxford.

---

[81]   Massa, *I Sent.*, d.35 (ed. Schabel, p. 192, ll. 433–57).
[82]   Massa, *I Sent.*, d.35 (ed. Schabel, pp. 197–201, ll. 568–655).

PART FOUR

The Reaction in England and in the Late Middle Ages

Chapter 10

London and Oxford 1317–1344

This book primarily concerns the debate of the Faculty of Theology at the University of Paris over the problem of divine foreknowledge and future contingents from Peter Auriol's lectures on the *Sentences* there, starting in the fall of 1316, to Gregory of Rimini's and Alphonsus Vargas of Toledo's lectures in 1343–45. A parallel debate went on in England during these same years, from William of Ockham's Oxford lectures on the *Sentences* beginning in 1317 to the 1344 publication of Thomas Bradwardine's *De causa Dei* which, among other things, allegedly attacked Auriol's views on future contingents. Historians have rightly seen these years as the Golden Age of Oxford thought, and correspondingly modern critical editions and doctrinal studies are available for the opinions of many of the participants on the question of foreknowledge and contingency. There are two reasons why the present excursion to England is required here: first, to determine what impact, if any, Auriol and other Parisian scholars from these decades had on the English discussion; second, to highlight the basic English developments, because they in turn would affect the Paris debate starting with Rimini. Thus this an essay with limited goals.[1]

The flow of ideas from Paris to Oxford was steady until about 1320, as English scholars studying at Paris brought back the innovations of the continental university's great masters. If that trend had continued, one would expect Oxford scholars in the 1320s and 1330s to be debating the merits of Auriol's indistance theory, Marchia's *de inesse/de possibili* distinction, neutral future-contingent propositions, the equation of necessity and immutability, and God's intrinsic and extrinsic willing. But it did not continue, mostly because of the growing tension between England and France which culminated in what we call the Hundred Years' War. The last important English scholars left Paris in the 1320s, and they were not replaced. As a result one finds only a couple of Auriol's fellow Franciscans, active at London in the early 1320s, discussing a small segment of Auriol's theory. Conversely, the new English developments on this issue do not appear in Paris until Gregory of Rimini. Clearly in this context the notion of the relative isolation of the two universities from each other in the late 1320s and 1330s is verified.[2]

---

[1] A broad overview of the English problem has yet to be written, but one can combine Jean-François Genest, *Prédétermination et liberté créée à Oxford au XIVᵉ siècle. Buckingham contre Bradwardine* (Paris 1992) and Hester G. Gelber, *It Could Have Been Otherwise: Modal Theory and Theology among the Dominicans at Oxford, 1310–1340* (Princeton, forthcoming).
[2] I discuss this problem in my "Paris and Oxford between Aurioli and Rimini," building on the works of William J. Courtenay, e.g. *Schools and Scholars in Fourteenth-Century England* (Princeton 1987). See also idem, "Foreign Study in a Time of War: English Scholars at Paris 1325–1345," *History of Universities* 14 (1995–6), pp. 31–41. Unfortunately, one result is that

Unlike the case of Paris in these decades, I have not inspected all of the Oxford texts, but based on what I have examined, the following appears to be a likely scenario of the Oxford debate as it relates to Auriol: William of Ockham first treated future contingents in his Oxford *Sentences* lectures before 1320, but his extant writings on the subject were probably all produced at the Franciscans' London *studium* in 1321–24, while his confrères Walter Chatton and Adam Wodeham were also in residence. Thus Chatton's and Ockham's pertinent works are contemporary, and, indeed, there is a complex and intricate relationship between them.[3] In his *Scriptum* or *Ordinatio* on book I of the *Sentences* and in his *Tractatus* on predestination and foreknowledge, Ockham formulated what would become the common opinion on the matter at Oxford and in the Late Middle Ages generally, without direct knowledge of Auriol's discussion. Chatton reacted negatively to this *opinio communis* in his *Reportatio*, and he proposed a radical alternative that owes much to Auriol's doctrine. Ironically Chatton, the one important English theologian from this period who has received almost no attention on this issue, is the one who owed the greatest debt to Auriol. Perhaps as a result of Chatton's critique, Ockham modified his theory in his *Quodlibeta*, and for the next decade Oxford theologians took up positions that fit into this Chatton-Ockham spectrum. In the early 1330s, however, perhaps in connection with the conflict with Pope John XXII over the beatific vision, Adam Wodeham considered Auriol's position again, and Thomas Bradwardine adopted a rather deterministic stance that sparked off a new controversy. Along the way there developed some particularly Oxonian sub-issues, the seeds of which are contained already in the treatments of Ockham and Chatton: propositional analysis, the contingency of the past, knowledge of propositions vs. knowledge of states of affairs (*complexe significabilia*), and prophecy and revelation. So, if our story in Paris begins with Auriol and ends with his refutation in Rimini, in Oxford it starts with Chatton and ends with his rejection by Bradwardine.

William of Ockham

In the period after Peter Auriol's lectures on the *Sentences* at Paris, Oxford claimed some of the most famous figures in the history of medieval thought.

---

scholars sometimes completely ignore Paris, as does Eugenio Randi, "Onnipotenza divina e futuri contingenti nel XIV secolo," DSTFM 1.2 (1990), pp. 605–30, which is really only about Oxford, except for John of Mirecourt in the 1340s.

    [3] It is not my purpose to explore this relationship in detail, but see for example Stephen F. Brown, "Walter Chatton's *Lectura* and William of Ockham's *Quaestiones in Libros Physicorum Aristotelis*," in William A. Frank and Girard J. Etzkorn, eds., *Essays Honoring Allan B. Wolter* (St. Bonaventure, NY 1985), pp. 81–115, and Tachau, *Vision and Certitude*, esp. pp. 149–53, 180–81, and 207–8. It should be stressed that it is only probable and not certain that Ockham, Chatton, and Wodeham were in London in 1321–24 rather than at the Franciscan convent just outside the walls of Oxford; cf. William J. Courtenay, "Ockham, Chatton, and the London *Studium*: Observations on Recent Changes in Ockham's Biography," in Wilhelm Vossenkuhl and Rolf Schönberger, eds., *Die Gegenwart Ockhams* (Weinheim 1990), pp. 327–37.

None of these looms larger in the historiographical tradition than the Franciscan William of Ockham (ca. 1285–1347), who lectured on the *Sentences* at Oxford 1317–19, almost the same time Auriol did so in Paris, although his writings on the subject all date from 1321–24, as was mentioned. In 1324 he was called to Avignon for an investigation into some of his ideas before incepting as master of theology, hence his nickname the 'Venerable Inceptor'. Ockham had to flee Avignon in 1328 in connection with the Franciscans' conflict with Pope John XXII, and as a refugee in the Emperor Louis of Bavaria's court he wrote mostly political treatises in his later life.[4]

Ockham did know some of the views of Peter Auriol, but in the context of future contingents it does not appear that he was directly familiar with Auriol's ideas. Tachau has shown that Ockham's admission that he had not been able to examine Auriol's *Scriptum* carefully is probably true.[5] In his earliest work on the subject, the *Ordinatio* on book I, Ockham shares Auriol's assessment of Aristotle's position, and he even goes so far as to say that Aristotle would have denied foreknowledge to God.[6] Ockham deals almost exclusively with Scotus's position: he denies that there is a real capacity for opposites without succession, i.e. in an instant, and he denies the existence of instants of nature. Instead, he holds that the present is necessary.[7] Ockham also

---

[4]   The literature on Ockham's thought, and his position on foreknowledge, is extensive. In 1945 Boehner (*Tractatus*) published a critical edition of Ockham's *Tractatus de praedestinatione et de praescientia Dei et de futuris contingentibus*, along with an edition of distinctions 38 and 39 of his *Sentences* commentary, his commentary on chapter nine of *Peri Hermeneias*, and the part of his *Summa Logicae* dealing with the problem. In 1969 Marilyn McCord Adams and Norman Kretzmann published an English translation, William of Ockham, *Predestination, God's Foreknowledge, and Future Contingents* (New York 1969), further facilitating study. Although all of these texts put together still represent a smaller, and certainly more disjointed, treatment of the problem than Auriol's distinctions 38 and 39, much more scholarly attention has been devoted to Ockham's thought on the matter than to Auriol's. For many historians of the problem, in fact, Ockham is the end of the medieval story. Although Boehner's texts have been reedited, he included a lengthy study in his edition, *The Tractatus*, pp. 41–75, as did Adams and Kretzmann in their translation, pp. 1–33. Streveler (pp. 54–64) is useful, and the standard work on Ockham, Adams's two volume *William Ockham* (Notre Dame 1987), contains various discussions of Ockham's thought on this subject and related ones. Craig's philosophical treatment, *The Problem of Divine Foreknowledge*, pp. 146–68, is valuable also for its dialogue with the secondary literature. See also Dominik Perler, "Notwendigkeit und Kontingenz. Das Problem der 'futura contingentia' bei Wilhelm von Ockham," in Olaf Pluta, ed., *Die Philosophie im 14. und 15. Jahrhundert* (Amsterdam 1988), pp. 39–65; his much expanded discussion in idem, *Prädestination, Zeit und Kontingenz: philosophisch-historische Untersuchungen zu Wilhelm von Ockhams 'Tractatus de praedestinatione et de praescientia Dei respectu futurorum contingentium'* (Amsterdam 1988); and Decorte, "Sed modum exprimere nescio."
[5]   See Tachau, *Vision and Certitude*, for example p. 136. Halverson, *Peter Aureol on Predestination*, pp. 111–22, discusses Ockham's theory of predestination and finds that he shows Auriol's influence (via Chatton?), although "buried by indigenous [to Oxford] issues" (p. 122).
[6]   Guillelmus de Ockham *Ordinatio in primum librum Sententiarum*, d. 38 (eds. Girard Etzkorn and Francis Kelley, *Guillelmi de Ockham Opera Theologica IV* [St. Bonaventure NY, 1979], p. 572, ll. 5–11): "Circa distinctionem trigesimam octavam quaero utrum Deus habeat scientiam determinatam et necessariam omnium futurorum contingentium. Quod non: Quia illud quod non est in se determinate verum, nulli est determinate verum; sed futurum contingens non est in se determinate verum," and later (p. 584, ll. 3–5): "Et dico quod Philosophus diceret quod Deus non scit evidenter et certitudinaliter aliqua futura contingentia."
[7]   Ockham, *Ordinatio* I, d. 38 (ed. Etzkorn-Kelley, p. 581, ll. 9–17): "Ex isto patet quod

contends, as does Auriol, that Scotus's position may work well for things governed by natural causation, but it cannot explain how God knows the effects of our free will by resorting to the determination of the divine will, unless the divine will determines our will. In that case, our will would not be free.[8] Perhaps as a result of Ockham's criticism, Scotus's theory does not play the role in Oxford that it does in Paris after Auriol. This critique of Scotus is as far as the similarity with Auriol's views goes, however, for Ockham's stance for the most part still resembles that of Peter Lombard, although it is argued more vigorously, as Calvin Normore has pointed out.[9] Ockham agrees with Scotus that God does will contingently in an instant, and he is of the same mind as Lombard that a statement of the type 'God willing X is able not to will X' is true in the divided sense.[10] Auriol would ask him how God could will otherwise, since He only exists in one eternal instant that is not subdivided by 'real' instants of nature.

Ockham holds that God knows future contingents. Although he admits that he cannot explain exactly how, he does assert that the "divine essence is one intuitive cognition" of everything, so that God even knows "which side of a contradiction will be true and which will be false."[11] Ockham's position on the truth-value of future contingent propositions is not well developed in the *Ordinatio*, and Ockham here does not go on to treat the necessity *ex suppositione* that most agree would result from God's foreknowledge. Presumably Ockham would resort to the composite and divided senses of 'It can be otherwise than as God has foreknown'. Thus, in the *Ordinatio*, Ockham avoids some important issues that Auriol takes on.

---

non est convenienter dictum quod voluntas divina, ut prior naturaliter, ita ponit suum effectum in esse in A quod potest eum non ponere in esse in eodem instanti. Quia non sunt talia instantia naturae sicut iste imaginatur, nec est in primo instanti naturae talis indifferentia ad ponendum et non ponendum. Sed si in aliquo instanti ponit effectum suum in esse, impossibile est quod per quamcumque potentiam sit illud instans et quod in illo non sit, sicut est impossibile quod per quamcumque potentiam contradictoria sint simul vera."

[8]   Ockham, *Ordinatio* I, d. 38 (ed. Etzkorn-Kelley, p. 582, ll. 9–18): "Praeterea, quantumcumque posset salvari certitudo scientiae per determinationem voluntatis respectu omnium effectuum productorum a voluntate, et etiam respectu omnium effectuum causarum naturalium quibus voluntas divina coagit, non tamen videtur quod certitudo actuum futurorum ipsius voluntatis creatae possit per praedictam determinationem salvari. Quia si respectu omnium est voluntas divina determinata, quaero: aut illam determinationem necessario sequitur determinatio vel productio voluntatis creatae vel non. Si sic, igitur ita naturaliter agit voluntas creata sicut quaecumque causa naturalis."

[9]   See Normore, "Future Contingents," p. 370.

[10]   Ockham, *Ordinatio* I, d. 38 (ed. Etzkorn-Kelley, p. 586, ll. 13–18): "'... Deum volentem A fore possibile est velle non fore', est distinguenda secundum compositionem et divisionem. In sensu compositionis denotatur quod haec sit possibilis 'Deus volens A fore non vult A fore', et hoc est impossibile quia includit contradictionem. In sensu divisionis denotatur quod Deus volens A fore, potest non velle A fore, et hoc est verum."

[11]   Ockham, *Ordinatio* I, d. 38 (ed. Etzkorn-Kelley, pp. 584, l. 20–585, l. 10): "Ista tamen ratione non obstante, tenendum est quod Deus evidenter cognoscit omnia futura contingentia. Sed modum exprimere nescio. Potest tamen dici quod ipse Deus, vel divina essentia, est una cognitio intuitiva, tam sui ipsius quam omnium aliorum factibilium et infactibilium, tam perfecta et tam clara quod ipsa etiam est notitia evidens omnium praeteritorum, futurorum et praesentium... etiam scitur quae pars contradictionis erit vera et quae erit falsa."

Soon after his *Ordinatio*, Ockham wrote an entire *Tractatus* consisting of questions on the related matters of predestination, foreknowledge, and future contingents. The discussion in the *Tractatus* is twice the size of that in the *Ordinatio*, but in the *Tractatus* Ockham mainly expands upon what he set down in the *Ordinatio*. Nevertheless, certain points are made in the *Tractatus* that were not present, or at least were much less evident, in the *Ordinatio*. First, in order to preserve the necessity of the past,[12] Ockham holds in several places that statements like 'God knew Scott was predestined' are really contingent, since they are really about the future, and only vocally about the past.[13] One can find this idea in several earlier scholars, such as Bonaventure, and refuted by others, such as Wylton, but the view has become associated with Ockham in the historiography. A second point that Ockham develops in the *Tractatus* is on prophecy. Ockham claims that prophecies are merely disguised conditionals, whose condition is not always expressed. Thus, Ockham would have to say that Peter would deny Christ only if some condition obtained, and that Peter was able not to deny Christ even after Christ's 'prophecy'.[14] This opinion resembles one Boethius set down in his second commentary on *Peri Hermeneias*.[15] That there are difficulties with the concept of prophecy is obvious, and I have found only one person who follows Ockham on this, Angelus de Dobelin, and he wrote many decades later.[16]

---

[12]   Not the absolute necessity of the past, for Ockham agreed that everything but God was ultimately contingent.

[13]   Guillelmus de Ockham, *Tractatus de praedestinatione et de praescientia Dei et de futuris contingentibus*, q. 1 (ed. Philotheus Boehner and Stephen F. Brown, *Guillelmi de Ockham Opera Philosophica* II [St. Bonaventure, NY 1978], p. 509, ll. 59–67): "... illa propositio quae est sic de praesenti quod tamen aequivalet uni de futuro, et cuius veritas dependet ex veritate unius de futuro, non habet aliquam de praeterito necessariam; immo ista contingens est illa de praeteritio sicut sua de praesenti. Et tales sunt omnes propositiones in ista materia, sicut patet ex quarta suppositione, quia omnes aequivalenter sunt de futuro, quamvis vocaliter sint de praesenti vel de praeterito. Et ideo ita contingens est illa 'Petrus fuit praedestinatus' sicut ista 'Petrus est praedestinatus.'"

[14]   Ockham, *Tractatus*, q. 1 (ed. Boehner-Brown, p. 513, ll. 170–82): "Dico quod nullum revelatum contingens futurum evenit necessario sed contingenter. Et concedo quod fuit aliquando vera 'hoc est revelatum', et sua de praeterito fuit postea semper necessaria. Et concedo quod non fuit revelatum tamquam falsum, sed tamquam verum contingens et non tamquam verum necessarium, et per consequens tale potuit et potest esse falsum. Et tamen Prophetae non dixerunt falsum, quia omnes prophetiae de quibuscumque futuris contingentibus fuerunt condicionales, quamvis non semper exprimebatur condicio. Sed aliquando fuit expressa, sicut patet de David et throno suo; aliquando subintellecta, sicut patet de Ninive destructione a Iona prophetata: 'Adhuc post quadraginta dies et Ninive subvertetur', nisi scilicet poeniterent; et quia poenituerunt, ideo non fuit destructa."

[15]   See Boethius, *Boethii Commentarii in librum Aristotelis Peri Hermeneias* (vol. 2, ed. Meiser, Leipzig 1880, p. 225).

[16]   See Angelus de Dobelin, *In libros Sententiarum* I, d. 38, a. 1 (Jena, Univ. El. Fol. 47, fol. 54ra): "Sexta conclusio: nullus debet aliquod futurum asserere nec revelatum futurum credere, nisi solo conditione tacita vel expressa, sicud quod iudicium mortuorum erit nisi Deus aliter disponat. Probatur, quia utramque partem contradictionis divisim Deus potest facere et unam partem revelatam facere. Ergo ex ista conclusione et precedenti, sequitur quod questio est vera. Et ex hoc sequitur quod verba et propositio que annunciant futura absolute dicta, non debent absolute intelligi nec credidi, quia nihil est sic revelatum esse futurum absolute de quo Deus aliter non possit disponere."

This position on prophecy is not the same as Auriol's, but it might suggest that Ockham was indirectly aware of Auriol's criticisms of earlier positions. This is also the case when Ockham gives a very brief refutation of the statement "whatever can be in God, of necessity is God," which could have stemmed from Auriol, who held to an extreme view of divine necessity and simplicity. The brevity of Ockham's refutation, wholly inadequate, suggests no close acquaintance with Auriol's distinctions 38 and 39. Here Ockham simply does not address Auriol's position fully, and he does not *explain* how God could know differently, stating only that God knows contingently. Of course for Ockham, knowing differently is not as important in God as it is for Auriol. This is not the place for a long discussion of ontology, but it cannot be denied that Ockham tends toward nominalism. Although they do not discuss universals in their treatments of foreknowledge, Auriol and Ockham implicitly hold to differing views of the ontological status of mental entities. For Auriol, a God who knows X is not the same as a God who does not know X — the two Gods are intrinsically different. Ockham makes it clear that 'knowing X' is merely a concept, a name, which is in God only through predication. It is not necessary for it to be in God, it is not part of God, and it can be predicated of God "contingently and *ex tempore.*"[17]

Ockham also discusses the possible equation of immutability and necessity, and refutes it by denying that everything immutable is necessary, although accepting the converse.[18] Ockham then rejects necessity *ex suppositione* with respect to God's foreknowledge, claiming that syllogisms appearing to have as a necessary consequent statements like 'X will come about', are mixed syllogisms; that is, their premises and conclusions are not all in the same mode.[19] This treatment also fails to demonstrate an adequate examination of Auriol's opinion, although Gregory of Rimini would use it.

Thus Ockham composed his *Ordinatio* and *Tractatus* with only abstract cognition of Auriol's position. Nevertheless, in Ockham's treatment of the

---

[17] Ockham, *Tractatus*, q. 2 (ed. Boehner-Brown, p. 531, ll. 300–307): "Tertio sic: quidquid potest esse in Deo de necessitate est Deus, quia est immutabilis; sed scire A potest esse in Deo; igitur necessario est in Deo, igitur necessario scit A. Dico quod illud quod est in Deo vel potest esse in eo formaliter necessario est Deus; sed scire A non est sic in Deo sed tantum per praedicationem, quia est quidam conceptus vel nomen, quod <aliquando> praedicatur de Deo. Et aliquando non; et non oportet quod sit Deus, quia hoc nomen 'Dominus' praedictur de Deo contingenter et ex tempore et tamen non est Deus."

[18] Ockham, *Tractatus*, q. 2 (ed. Boehner-Brown, p. 530, ll. 284–8): "Et quando probatur consequentia, quod ibi non est necessitas nisi immutabilitatis, concedo, quia alii modi necessitatis, scilicet coactionis etc., non ponuntur in Deo propter imperfectionem. Et ideo bene sequitur 'ibi est necessarium, igitur est immutabilie', et non e converso, quia omne necessarium est immutabile, et non econverso..."

[19] Ockham, *Tractatus*, q. 2 (ed. Boehner-Brown, p. 532, ll. 329–38): "Quinto sic: omne scitum a Deo fore necessario erit; A est scitum a Deo fore; igitur A necessario erit. Maior est de necessario, quia praedicatum necessario inest subiecto; et minor est de inesse simpliciter, quia est vera pro aeternitate; igitur sequitur conclusio de necessario. Dico quod maior est falsa, quia exprimit sensum divisionis, et multa scita a Deo fore contingenter erunt et non necessaria, et ideo sequitur conclusio falsa. Si autem maior accipiatur in sensu compositionis, ita quod haec sit necessaria 'omne scitum a Deo <fore> erit', tunc mixtio non valet, quia minor est de inesse ut nunc, et ideo non sequitur conclusio."

truth-value of future contingent propositions, on which Auriol held such an extreme position, the Venerable Inceptor develops the common opinion. In his distinction 38 of his *Ordinatio*, Ockham makes a statement that Chatton would attack: "To the first principal argument it can be said that one of two (*altera*) sides of a contradiction is determinately true, such that it is not false. It is nevertheless contingently true, and therefore it is true such that it can be false, and can never have been true."[20] Hester Gelber has written a monograph stressing the ultimate contingency of the world as seen by theologians at Oxford in the first half of the fourteenth century, and one could add that most theologians at Paris, as we have seen, saw it the same way. In this case, any statement that a proposition determinately true about the contingent future is contingently true can be taken as obvious. As Gelber notes, Ockham repeats this reasoning in several places, but in no case is there any hint that Ockham is suggesting some sort of new truth-value. He merely makes the remark, directed perhaps at Auriol even, that in an ultimately contingent world, all statements about the future are contingently true if true. Thus they can be false. Gelber also notes that Ockham does not seem to mean that such propositions are indeterminately true or false.[21] For him, and for most scholars who held that God had determinate knowledge of future contingents, the determinate truth of future contingents was always contingent absolutely, although, to some, necessary *ex suppositione*. These are two elements of the *opinio communis*.

The other important element is that the past is necessary. Some later thinkers, such as Thomas Bradwardine and Alphonsus Vargas of Toledo, will say that both the past and future are necessary *ex suppositione* of God's eternal will, but contingent with respect to God's freedom. At first glance, this move appears to dissolve the differences between the past and future, and to make way for real past contrary-to-fact reasoning, in the sense that God can *change* the past. This would be an incorrect understanding, however, for no medieval theologian, not even Peter Damian, believed that once an event has happened, it can come about later that it did not happen, assuming that event.[22]

---

[20]   Ockham, *Ordinatio* I, d. 38 (ed. Etzkorn-Kelley, p. 587, ll. 21–4): "Ad primum principale potest dici quod altera pars contradictionis est determinate vera, ita quod non est falsa. Est tamen contingenter vera, et ideo ita est quod potest esse falsa, et potest numquam fuisse vera."

[21]   Gelber, *It Could*, ch. V.

[22]   The questions of the contingency of the past and of the possibility to change the past (two different questions) are often conflated, because of the ambiguity of the language used to express possibility in terms of both time and eternity. Damian never makes it clear that he thinks that once I have existed, God can make it so I never existed; in fact Damian denies this, and says *for us* we must say God *could* have made me not exist. On Damian I am in agreement with Toivo Holopainen, *Dialectic and Theology in the Eleventh Century* (Leiden 1996), pp. 6–43, and John Marenbon, "Philosophy and its Background in the Early Medieval West," in idem, ed., *Medieval Philosophy*, pp. 112–13, against, among many others, Irven Michael Resnik, *Divine Power and Possibility in St. Peter Damian's De divina omnipotentia* (Leiden 1992), pp. 77–111, and Richard Gaskin, "Peter Damian on Divine Power and the Contingency of the Past," *British Journal of the History of Philosophy* 5.2 (1997), pp. 229–47. Gaskin (p. 245) may be correct that if we take eternity to be completely atemporal, then "talk of God's eternal abilities will sustain no translation into explicitly temporal terminology." Nevertheless, statements to the effect that the past can never have existed were often made, but with some equivocation: in the sense that (a) if the contradictory of the past had in fact existed, nothing impossible would follow, *and* (b) God *in his*

Ockham makes statements about partial past contrary-to-fact reasoning when he says that past-tensed propositions that are only vocally about the past, but really about the future, have no necessary truth, and are still contingent just as their present and future-tensed counterparts.[23] But statements really about the past have necessary truth.[24] Because Ockham holds that God has determinate knowledge of future contingents, his distinction is between true statements about the past, which are determinate and necessary, and true statements about the future, which are determinate and contingent. Then what does he mean when he says that past-tensed statements that are really about the future are able never to have been true? And what kind of necessity is Ockham attributing to true statements about the past? Ockham has not worked out his thought clearly, but perhaps the *opinio communis* is like this: (1) Following Scotus, everything but God is contingent, and God's will is free; (2) since all things other than God are contingent, their being other than they are is not impossible in the divided sense; (3) God knows these things determinately, so that in the composite sense it is impossible that things occur other than as God knows them — they are 'necessary' *ex suppositione*; but (4) after things occur, some sort of new 'necessity' is attached to them. When speaking of past-tensed propositions really about the future, Ockham holds that they maintain whatever degree of contingency is eventually removed when the event (the proposition's significate) takes place. Whether this position is intelligible is not the issue here, but it is certain that Ockham did not make himself clear in this case. Given Ockham's stance on the contingency of the world, however, any time he says something is contingent, we are warranted to assume that he is talking in an absolute sense, from God's eternal perspective.

This position was destined to become the common opinion, especially at Oxford, and as Normore and Genest have pointed out, it is mainly Ockham's formulation. In Genest's words, this opinion consists of three points: (1) There is determinate truth in future contingents, (2) that truth is, in an absolute sense, no less contingent for being determinate, and (3) the truth of present and past things is not only determinate but necessary.[25]

---

eternity cannot be said to have the power to will that contradictory at one point and not at another, given God's immutability. We shall see more of this discussion later, but speaking philosophically, one might say here that if God can change the past, it would jeopardize the truth of the statement 'Cogito ergo sum'. If I exist today, and tomorrow God can make it so I never existed, then I cannot be sure I exist today. This seems ridiculous to me. Although he does not use this argument, William Lane Craig has a very interesting discussion of the issue, including the possibility of time travel, in his *Divine Foreknowledge and Human Freedom*, especially chapter 6.

[23] Ockham, *Tractatus*, q. 1 (ed. Boehner-Brown, p. 509, ll. 59–63): "... illa propositio quae est sic de praesenti quod tamen aequivalet uni de futuro, et cuius veritas dependet ex veritate unius de futuro, non habet aliquam de praeterito necessariam; immo ita contingens est illa de praeterito sicut sua de praesenti."

[24] Ockham, *Tractatus*, q. 1 (ed. Boehner-Brown, p. 509, ll. 50–52): "Item, secundo sic: omnis propositio de praesenti semel vera habet aliquam de praeterito necessariam, sicut haec 'Sortes sedet', si est vera, haec semper postea erit necessaria 'Sortes sedit'."

[25] Genest, *Prédétermination et liberté créée*, p. 34. Genest discusses the common opinion and Ockham's and Richard Campsall's role on pp. 34–8. Normore, "Future Contingents," p. 370, also identifies Ockham as the main originator of the stance.

Walter Chatton

Ockham's fellow Franciscan Walter Chatton (1285-1344) probably lectured at the London convent from 1321-24 while Ockham was there working on his *Ordinatio, Tractatus,* and *Quodlibeta,* and Chatton was certainly aware of both Ockham's and Auriol's views generally.[26] Chatton devotes all of distinctions 38-41 of his extant *Reportatio* (from either 1321-23 or, more probably, 1323-24) to future contingents, and much interesting material comes, surprisingly, in distinctions 40 and 41, nominally given over to the standard issue of predestination. The entire discussion is set against the background of Auriol's, Ockham's, and, to a lesser degree, Scotus's *ordinationes.* Chatton's presentation is fascinating and probably quite influential, but for two reasons it is difficult to be certain about Chatton's own opinion: first, the text really appears to be more or less a true *reportatio,* without many signs of authorial reworking; second, Chatton repeatedly disassociates himself from what he states on such a "dangerous matter," and he only wishes to proceed by reciting and investigating, asserting nothing for himself. In fifty pages of text (ca. 1500 lines) there are no less than eight such disclaimers, and it is worth quoting the timid pun he makes with regard to the question "Is the proposition 'this man will be saved' true?"

> I do not want to speak for myself. Above I recited some ways to put an answer, of which one way maintains that a proposition about a future contingent is determinately true, and another, namely Peter Auriol's, posited that it is not. In this section, because I wish to explain *each side of a contradiction* on this matter, I shall recite this last way, namely how it could be sustained that it is not determinately true. But no opinion should be attributed to me, but rather to those to whom belong the opinions which I recite.[27]

The resulting snarl of opinions can only be untangled with the help of a critical edition, which Girard Etzkorn is providing. Examining the text, one finds that Chatton is perhaps right to be fearful, given what appears to be his position as presented in the first person singular. Chatton reveals himself to be rather semi-Pelagian on predestination, who does not believe in foreknowledge.[28] In-

---

[26]   On Chatton and the secondary literature to 1988, see Tachau, *Vision and Certitude,* chapter 7, "The Early Reaction to Auriol and Ockham: The Views of Walter Chatton," pp. 180-208, which has long discussion of Chatton's reaction to the epistemological views of Ockham and Auriol. For dating, see my "Oxford Franciscans after Ockham: Walter Chatton and Adam Wodeham," and the works cited there.

[27]   Gualterus de Chatton, *Reportatio* I, dd. 40-41, q. 1, a. 1 (*Reportatio in primum librum Sententiarum vol. III: distinctiones 10-48,* ed. Girard Etzkorn [Toronto, forthcoming], par. 7-8): "Primo, an sit vera 'iste salvabitur'... nihil volo dicere de meo. Recitavi supra aliquos modos ponendi, quorum unus salvat quod propositio de futuro contingenti sit determinate vera; alius posuit quod non, scilicet Petri Aureoli. In parte ista recitabo ultimam viam, quia volo declarare utramque partem contradictionis in hac materia, quomodo scilicet possit sustineri quod non sit vera determinate. Nulla tamen opinio mihi imponatur sed illis quorum sunt quas recito."

[28]   Girard Etzkorn has kindly allowed me to use his forthcoming critical edition, which

deed Chatton, while hiding behind Auriol, actually exceeds him in denying foreknowledge.

In distinction 38 Chatton gets to what he considers the heart of the matter, the consequence 'God knew the Antichrist would exist; therefore the Antichrist will exist'. The ensuing 'propositional analysis' exemplifies one of the Oxford trends in the years that follow Chatton's lectures. In this question Chatton gives Auriol's theory, claiming that Aristotle supports it. He states that this opinion holds that there is no determinate truth in future contingents, and it denies that God knows that something will come about. Chatton adds that this position does not take God's knowledge to be one that expects a thing as future, so His knowledge does not make the thing come about in any way, or make a future-tensed proposition true, because otherwise things would come about necessarily, for at no time could a true proposition about the future be false. Significantly, however, Chatton misrepresents Auriol, stating that God's knowledge is "apt to be obtained *after* the thing [known] exists," which Auriol would reject. Moreover, although he knows Auriol's opinion on prophecy, i.e. that prophets signify one thing and intend to signify another, Chatton remarks that in prophesying "we intend to signify that the thing comes *before* the knowledge," which is not at all what Auriol means.[29]

Chatton stretches Auriol's meaning, perhaps because he wishes to adopt the theory that he is describing. In fact there are indications that Chatton knew more of Auriol's treatment, certainly his position on predestination, but Chatton ends up concentrating all his energy on Auriol's distinction 38, article three, on future-contingent propositions. Chatton states explicitly that Auriol's opinion would be a good way to solve the problem, if it were true. Ostensibly Chatton considers Auriol's interpretation of Aristotle to be irrational, because when we say that a proposition about the future is true, we mean that something will come about, and when it comes about, it will come

replaces the very preliminary edition of d. 38 in my "Quarrel with Auriol," pp. 744–50. The fact that dd. 40–41 are also given over to future contingents had escaped me, and so my discussion in "Quarrel with Aureol," pp. 184–7, should be ignored. Although future contingents are the focus of dd. 40–41, Chatton still finds space to react to Auriol on predestination. Cf. my "Oxford Franciscans after Ockham: Walter Chatton and Adam Wodeham."

[29]   Chatton, *Reportatio* I, d. 38, a. 1 (ed. Etzkorn, par. 12–13): "Alius modus dicendi directe innititur Aristoteli, et tenent quod nulla propositio de futuro est determinate vera in contingentibus, tum per Aristotelem, tum quia si haec sit vera 'Sortes sedebit', non est dare quando incepit esse vera, igitur ab aeterno fuit vera, igitur est necessaria; quia si non, sed posset esse falsa, aut igitur antequam sedebit, et hoc non, quia ante est vera etiam ab aeterno; nec simul nec post, planum est. Sustinent igitur istam consequentiam 'Sortes sedebit', igitur necessario sedebit', sed negant antecedens. Similiter, cum dicitur 'Deus scit A fore', falsum est, quia 'A fore' non est verum. Imaginantur quod scientia et notitia Dei est talis qua nata est haberi postquam res est, non quasi exspectans futuritionem rei, et ideo nec tribuit rei quod eveniat, nec propositioni quod sit vera, nec aufert contingentiam a rebus. Et quomodo tunc est de prophecia? Dicunt quod aliud significamus et aliud intendimus significare. Significamus quasi scientia praeveniret, sed intendimus significare quod res praeveniat notitiam. Et addunt, et bene, quod nullus est modus congruus exprimendi prescientiam Dei."

about as the true proposition about the future said it would.[30] But on closer inspection one finds that Chatton actually agrees with Auriol:

> What does Aristotle mean when he says that a proposition is not determinately true? Either that *nothing* in the world exists that makes it so this proposition about the future is determinately true, and this is *correct*; or that some proposition signifies that something will be, so that *when* that thing is put into being it would be true *at that time* that it is *then* in reality just as the proposition signified it would be, and in this way one cannot deny that a proposition about the future is determinately true. Because *when* Socrates is actually sitting, it cannot be denied that it is *at that time* in reality just as this proposition signified *earlier*: 'Socrates will sit'.[31]

Chatton asserts this on numerous occasions, and the natural interpretation of Chatton's statement is that he does not think future-contingent propositions are determinately true or false *now*. According to this rather benign definition of determinate truth, which Chatton himself abandons anyway, even Auriol might have agreed that such propositions are 'determinately true'. But if when one says 'determinately true' one means it according to Auriol's definition, i.e.:

> that there is or was some thing, or something said or written, or some cognition, which when posited makes it so this proposition is true *now*, and it is now just as the proposition signifies, this is *not* true, but only a condition of a proposition about the present or past, and *no* proposition about the future, speaking thus, is determinately true.[32]

[30] Chatton, *Reportatio* I, d. 38, a. 1 (ed. Etzkorn, par. 14–15): "Si ista conclusio esset licita, bene esset clarus modus quantum ad primum, quod propositio de futuro nulla est vera, nec scita a Deo esse vera. Sed contra istam: quod non sit vera conclusio, probo: primo per primam rationem contra praecedentem opinionem. Suppono quod propositionem esse veram est ita esse in re sicut propositio significat esse, si est de praesenti; vel ita fore sicut significat fore, si est de futuro. Quid igitur intelligis per istam propositionem esse veram 'Sortes sedebit'? Aut quod sic sit modo in re sicut propositio significat, et hoc est illud quod exigit veritas propositionis de praesenti, non autem de futuro, et ita non est ad propositum. Vel quod aliqua res erit, qua posita in sua mensura, sic est sicut propositio de futuro significavit, et sic loquendo nec Aristoteles nec aliquis <alius> potest rationabiliter negare eam esse veram."

[31] Chatton, *Reportatio* I, d. 38, a. 1 (ed. Etzkorn, par. 8): "Quid igitur vocat Aristoteles propositionem non esse determinate veram? Vel quod nihil sit in rerum natura, quo posito haec propositio de futuro est determinate vera, et hoc <est> verum; vel quod aliqua propositio significat aliquid fore, quo posito in esse, verum esset tunc dicere quod sic est modo in re sicut propositio fore, et sic non potest negare propositionem de futuro esse veram determinate, quia quando Sortes actu sedet, non potest negari quin tunc ita sit in re sicut significavit ista prius 'Sortes sedebit'."

[32] Chatton, *Reportatio* I, d. 38, a.1 (ed. Etzkorn, par. 24): "Aut quod aliqua res sit vel fuerit, vel dictum vel scriptum vel cognitio, quo posito, haec propositio sit modo vera, et ita sit modo sicut propositio significat, et hoc non est verum, sed ista solum est condicio propositionis de praesenti et de praeterito; et nulla propositio de futuro est, sic loquendo, determinate vera."

This remark Chatton makes against an opinion that was popular "in Villa," i.e. in Oxford, when he was attending lectures there.[33] According to this common position, one could deny the equivalence of 'This is true, "Socrates will sit"' and 'This will be true, "Socrates is sitting"'. Chatton refuses the first and accepts the second, but only when pointing to the proposition about the present contained in it.[34] He completely denies that its future-tensed version is true now:

> And when you say that this proposition was true in the past, 'Socrates will sit', by what truth? Certainly never by such truth as with 'Socrates is sitting'; indeed the truth of the former was dependent on the future, and so before it is put into being, both God and creature can do the opposite. I will not grant you any other truth.[35]

This is very much Auriol's position. But will Chatton continue to follow this line of thinking when the opponent adds divine foreknowledge into the equation, and asks about the proposition 'God knows that X will exist'? Chatton splits it into a copulative, 'God knows X and X will exist', made up of a necessary and a contingent. It would appear that Chatton is following a traditional Franciscan method here and abandoning Auriol; but this is deceptive, because when Chatton accepts that 'X will exist' is true he does not mean it in Auriol's sense of true, and Chatton only admits that 'God knows X' is true — even necessary — "when knowledge is taken as *cognition*." This is because, in this case, God's knowledge is not the sort that will change if 'X will exist' changes from truth into falsity.[36] What is Chatton claiming? It appears that he agrees with Auriol completely that nothing precedes the coming about of the future — not even God's knowledge — which predetermines the future, and yet he allows for God's cognition of the future.

As we shall see, the key lies in the distinction between 'cognition' and 'knowledge'. Somehow if God has *cognition* of the future, the future is still indeterminate *ad utrumlibet*. This becomes clearer when Chatton deals with the

[33]   Chatton, *Reportatio* I, d. 38, a. 1 (ed. Etzkorn, par. 22): "Tertia opinio, quae currebat in Villa, tempore quo audivimus in Villa..."
[34]   Chatton, *Reportatio* I, d. 38, a. 1 (ed. Etzkorn, par. 25): "Et qui vellet sic dicere, posset dicere iuxta tertiam opinionem quod istae sunt distinctae propositiones 'Haec est vera "Sortes sedebit"', et 'Haec erit vera "Sortes sedet"'. Et de prima dicerem quod non, quia tunc, ex quo iam vera est, non esset necessarium consiliari nec negotiari circa hoc quod foret. Secundam concedo, ubi demonstratur propositio de praesenti."
[35]   Chatton, *Reportatio* I, d. 38, a. 2 (ed. Etzkorn, par. 49): "Et cum dicis, haec fuit vera de praeterito 'Sortes sedebit', quali veritate? Nunquam certe tali quali haec 'Sortes sedet'; immo veritas illius dependebat a futuro, et ideo antequam ponatur, et Deus et creatura potest facere oppositum. Aliam veritatem non dabo tibi."
[36]   Chatton, *Reportatio* I, d. 38, a. 1 (ed. Etzkorn, par. 28): "Sed cum quaeris utrum Deus sciat futura contingentia, quid intelligis per istam 'Deus scit A fore'? Aut quod scientia Dei est aliquid, quo posito A erit, ita quod si mutaretur ista 'A erit', a veritate in falsitatem mutaretur scientia Dei, et hoc nego. Aut quod tota ista 'Deus scit A fore' aequivalet isti copulativae 'Deus scit hoc, et hoc erit', istud concedo, ita quod scientia accipiatur pro cognitione. Tunc enim dicere quod Deus scit A fore aequivalet huic copulativae 'Deus cognoscit A et A erit', cuius prima pars est necessaria, et secunda contingens."

more difficult proposition, 'God fore*knew* that X will exist in A'. The common method of dissolving this, including Ockham's, was to claim that the statement is only verbally about the past and in reality depends on the contingent future. Chatton rejects this, because if 'X will exist' is truly contingent, then it is still possible for X not to come about, and for us to make it so God did not know it *ab eterno*. Other theologians, e.g. John of Mirecourt, would indeed assert this — suggesting some power over the past, but in reality merely claiming that the past is absolutely contingent but necessary *ex suppositione*. Chatton, however, really means to note the power over the past, and his statement should be taken as a *reductio ad absurdum*. Instead, Chatton asserts that the statement should be expand thus: 'God *cognized* X', which is necessary, 'and X will exist', which is contingent, and he means contingent in Auriol's sense.[37] For he declares, against the *opinio communis*:

> Where the truth of a proposition depends on the future and its being true is a thing that is to be posited in being in that future, I do *not* see how that proposition *cannot* be false at all times before the thing of this sort is posited in being in that future. Nor can these men avoid this, namely that as long as the proposition is contingently true it can be false, because they maintain that God knew from eternity that X will come about, and they claim that this was eternally and *contingently* true.[38]

For Chatton, using the example 'Socrates will sit in time A', the truth of the proposition is always in Socrates's power before A: he can make it true or false.[39] Other theologians may have said this, but they also declared that *de facto* Socrates will sit, that he will sit by necessity *ex suppositione*, and that, in the composite sense, he cannot not sit. Therefore such theologians — and Chatton explicitly has Ockham in mind — believed that they could maintain

---

[37] Chatton, *Reportatio* I, d. 38, a. 2 (ed. Etzkorn, par. 41): "Dices: accepi istam de preterito 'Deus scivit A fore in A' — Resolvo istam in copulativam, ubi prius, 'Deus cognovit hoc', et haec pars est necessaria, et 'hoc erit', et istud secundum est contingens; nec est de praeterito ista pars contingens, sed de futuro. Isto modo non possunt illi respondere de alia via, quae ponit quod scit quod deliberabis etc.; sed illi habent dicere quod sicut est in potestate tua ne hoc sit in A, ita est in potestate tua ne Deus ab aeterno sciverit A, et tunc cum arguitur quod omne verum de praeterito est necessarium, habent dicere quod verum <est>, ubi illud praeteritum non dependet a futuro, cuius oppositum est in proposito."

[38] Chatton, *Reportatio* I, d. 38, a. 3 (ed. Etzkorn, par. 60): «Responsio: Non video quin, ubi veritas propositionis dependet a futuro et ipsam esse veram est rem esse ponendam in tali futuro, quin semper antequam in illo futuro res huiusmodi ponatur, possit propositio illa esse falsa. Nec ipsi etiam possunt hoc vitare, quin scilicet pro eadem mensura pro qua propositio contingenter est vera, posset esse falsa; quia dicunt quod Deus aeternaliter scivit A fore, et quod aeternaliter fuit haec vera et contingenter vera."

[39] Chatton, *Reportatio* I, d. 38, a. 2 (ed. Etzkorn, par. 43): "Dico quod pro toto tempore ante A, voluntas Sortis aequaliter se habet ad utrumque, et ideo ista 'Sortes sedebit in A' non est vera pro sedere vel non sedere ante A, sed pro sedere in A, non quod ante A aliquid ponatur propter quod positum ipsa sit vera..." (Par. 45–6): "Sed non est sic de contingenti veritate de futuro... cum hoc stat quod Sortes potest non stare in A, quia semper ante A est in potestate Sortis facere propositionem non esse veram. Ad aliud, dico quod contingenter est vera, quia suo modo est vera pro re ponenda, ante cuius positionem semper potest impediri."

contingency, divine foreknowledge, and determinate truth in future-contingent propositions.

Like Ockham and Auriol, Chatton does not admit that Socrates's power to do otherwise exists at A, only before, so he rejects Scotus's simultaneous capacity for opposites.[40] But like Auriol and explicitly against Ockham, Chatton refuses to acknowledge the effectiveness of appeals to the composite and divided senses of propositions, or of declaring that *de facto* such propositions are true, although their truth depends on the future, in order to preserve determinate truth. If the proposition 'this man will be saved' is true now, Ockham "will be syllogizing in vain." And if the truth depends on something that does not yet exist, Chatton does not see how it is true.[41]

Discussing God's role, then, Chatton offers two ways of looking at contingency, hiding behind Auriol: one can support Scotus's theory that God's will, in predetermining everything in particular, is the only source of contingency: He would be the total cause, and so the created will would not be free and a source of contingency, and 'future-contingent' propositions would have determinate truth. If however God did not predetermine human wills, our created wills would be completely undetermined, and such propositions would not be determinately true or false because their truth would depend on the future itself. Or one could, like Auriol, mix the two methods, and claim that God predetermined conditionally or generally, by making conditions (e.g. if the first man sins, the Son of God will be born of a virgin) or general rules (e.g. those well disposed will be saved). In this case there would still be no determinate truth in future-contingent propositions.[42]

> But I am not speaking about a proposition about the future where there is determination in a created cause, as in the sun's rising tomorrow, or in an uncreated cause either, as when God determined that it would exist, because in those cases there already exists a thing whereby such a proposition will be true. But taking this sort of proposition, 'Socrates will sit', where there is plain indifference without the determination of any cause toward one side of a contradiction, in that case neither is this proposition true, 'Socrates will sit at A', nor is this one true, 'Socra-

[40] Chatton, *Reportatio* I, d. 38, a. 3 (ed. Etzkorn, par. 63): "Non est igitur potentia ad ponendum opposita in A, sed semper ante A est potentia ad ponendum <in> A vel non ponendum indifferenter."

[41] Chatton, *Reportatio* I, dd. 40–41, a. 1 (ed. Etzkorn, par. 4–7): "Primus igitur articulus erit videre an iste sit contingenter praedestinatus… et dicit unus quod sic… Et distinguunt propositiones de modo in hac materia secundum compositionem et divisionem etc. Vide in Ockham. Et iste est communis modus respondnedi hic, ponere quid de facto est vera, et vitare argumenta per compositionem et divisionem. Sed talis modus non est clarus, quia remanet tota difficultas circa quam vertitur quaestion, quomodo scilicet istae duae conclusiones simul stant, quod iste fuit praedestinatus quantumcumque contingenter, et tamen quod possit damnari. Et stant argumenta facta in contrarium, quia si haec modo sit vera 'Iste salvabitur' vel 'Iste est praedestinatus', frustrabitur syllogizando. Dices, de facto est vera, eius tamen veritas dependet a futuro. — Dico quod haec videntur opposita, quod modo de facto sit ista vera 'Iste salvabitur', et tamen quod eius vertias dependeat a re quae iam non est; nulla enim est res extra animam, qua posita haec sit vera."

[42] Chatton, *Reportatio* I, dd. 40–41, q. 1, a. 1 (ed. Etzkorn, par. 10–13).

tes is sitting at A', because the copula 'is' denotes that it is now true for that time. And therefore I say that no such proposition, however you specify it, is true which signifies a future thing, where there is plain indifference to both sides.[43]

Like Auriol, Chatton realizes that it is not enough to simply deny determinate truth in future-contingent propositions: he must also deny foreknowledge. Auriol's solution was to deny the prefix 'fore' and assert his indistance theory. We have seen that Chatton misrepresented Auriol on this point, and I think it is because he rejected indistance but nevertheless wished to shield himself from attacks by claiming to be merely reciting Auriol's opinion. At any rate, Chatton's answer is to first remove the 'knowledge' part of foreknowledge, and claim it is mere cognition: "But is God's cognition assent or knowledge, and not only apprehension? It could be said that God's cognition is not an assent except when the thing is put into being. And when the thing is future, it can be said that [God's] cognition is *not* knowledge."[44]

In article one of distinction 39 Chatton treats the solutions based on the determinations of the divine will, divine Ideas, and eternal presence, but it is risky to take his rejection or acceptance out of context. For example, someone objects to Scotus that God's infinite cognition knows the future even without the will's determination, and Chatton responds that God's infinite cognition represents things indifferently.[45] In fact Chatton is stating his own position about how God cognizes future contingents: indifferently. In article two Chatton gives his own definition of 'to know' (*scire*): to cognize (*cognoscere*) the thing signified by a true complexum (proposition), or to assent to something that is signified by a true complexum. Interestingly, an affirmative proposition and its negative contradictory signify one and the same thing for Chatton. This means that every state of affairs is signified, and is always signified, by a true complexum. Indeed, it is impossible for it not to be so signified.[46]

---

[43]   Chatton, *Reportatio* I, dd. 40–41, q. 1, a. 2 (ed. Etzkorn, par. 60): "Non loquor autem de propositione de futuro ubi est determinatio causae creatae, puta quod sol orietur cras, vel increatae etiam, puta quando Deus determinavit quod erit, quia in illis casibus iam est res quare propositio talis erit vera. Sed accipiendo talem 'Sortes sedebit', ubi est plena indifferentia absque determinatione alicuius causae ad unam partem contradictionis, ibi nec ista est vera 'Sortes sedebit pro A', nec haec est vera 'pro A Sortes sedet', quia copula 'est' denotat quod modo sit vera pro isto tempore. Et ideo dico quod nulla talis propositio, quomodocumque specificies, quae significat rem futuram, ubi est plena indifferentia ad utramque partem, est vera."

[44]   Chatton, *Reportatio* I, d. 38, a. 2 (ed. Etzkorn, par. 42): "Utrum autem cognitio Dei sit assensus vel scientia, et non solum apprehensio, possit dici quod cognitio Dei non est assensus nisi re posita; et quando res est futura, potest dici quod cognitio non est scientia."

[45]   Chatton, *Reportatio* I, d. 39, a. 1 (ed. Etzkorn, par. 8 and 11): "Cognitio Dei ex se est infinita, igitur ex se est omnis cognitio, etiam circumscripta quacumque determinatione cuiuscumque voluntatis" and "Cognitio infinita Dei indifferenter repraesentaret lapidem, sive erit sive non erit."

[46]   Chatton, *Reportatio* I, d. 39, a. 2 (ed. Etzkorn, par. 25): "Scire apud me est cognoscere rem significatam per complexum verum..." (Par. 26): "Item, scire stricte est assentire alicui quod per complexum verum significatur; sed impossibile est unquam aliquid esse verum quin modo per complexum verum significetur... nam illud idem quod significatur per propositionem affirmativam, significatur per negativam contradicentem." (Par. 29): "Rem scitam esse veram non est nisi

For example, let us take the complexum "Socrates is sitting." According to Chatton, this signifies the exact same thing that the complexum "Socrates is not sitting" signifies. In later terms, this thing, or state of affairs, signified by a complexum is a 'complexly signifiable' (*complexe significabile*), which will play an important role in discussions of foreknowledge at Oxford. Obviously, the idea is already here in Chatton, but he does not differentiate between negative and positive states of affairs. This is for good reason. Let us call the thing signified by both affirmative and negative complexes TS. God cognizes TS from eternity, and moreover God assents to TS for any given time A. "And yet no such proposition, 'Socrates is sitting for A' is true, since this entails more," namely that Socrates will sit in A.[47] The object of God's cognition, TS, is neither true nor false but indifferent, since truth and falsity are only in complexa. Before Socrates sits, this complexum is true, 'Socrates is not sitting', and God has *knowledge* of that. When Socrates actually sits, the complexum 'Socrates is sitting' is true, and God's cognition becomes *knowledge* of that.[48]

But unlike people, God does not have to assent to propositions, but He can assent directly to the thing signified by them. Until the thing comes to be, God's assent is neither true nor false, but only becomes an affirmative assent if the thing comes about, or negative if it does not. Moreover, people have it in their power to make God's assent negative or affirmative:

> Let us take this proposition, 'Socrates is sitting'. God eternally assents to this complex. And this assent is true and necessary for the one assent- ing to it, for this reason the first contradictories, namely 'Socrates is sit- ting', 'Socrates is not sitting', signify the same thing, and that thing is necessarily true by the truth of the thing, and the assent is necessarily true by the affirmative or negative truth, because it is in conformity with the affirmative or negative complex signifying the same thing in external reality. It is the same with God's unique assent that corre- sponds to these contradictories that signify the same thing in the soul 'this proposition is true «Socrates is sitting»', 'this proposition is not true'. And so I concede that it is impossible for God not to assent to that thing in the soul by an affirmative or negative assent... and further I concede that it is in my power for God's assent to be affirmative or nega-

---

significari per complexum verum, et impossibile est aliquid significari per complexum verum quin modo significatur per contradictoria, et impossibile est quin alterum sit verum."

    [47] Chatton, *Reportatio* I, dd. 40–41, q. 1, a. 2 (ed. Etzkorn, par. 61): "Quomodo igitur est certitudo? Dico quod in hoc quod Deus assentit ab aeterno pro A rei significatae per hoc com- plexum 'Sortes sedet', et similiter propheta firmiter assentit pro A rei significatae per istam 'Sortes sedet'; et tamen nulla talis propositio est vera 'Sortes sedet pro A', quia plus importat, sicut dictum est."

    [48] Chatton, *Reportatio* I, dd. 40–41, q. 1, a. 1 (ed. Etzkorn, par. 31): "Sed si vis loqui de hac copulativa 'Deus cognoscit hoc et hoc est verum', primum est necessarium indifferenter, sit complexum possibile sive impossibile; sed secunda pars nec est vera nec falsa... Cognitio igitur praefuit, sed illa cognitio non erat scientia donec res ponatur, et hoc loquendo in illo casu, ubi est indifferentia aequalis ad utramque partem contradictionis."

tive, because without any change in Him it is now equivalent to the affirmative assent, now the negative, when the thing is different.[49]

This implies an entirely different theory of prophecy as well, perhaps more extreme than Auriol's. When God assents to something, is not His assent either
true and hence knowledge or false and thus erroneous? No, Chatton answers,
because it is neither, until the thing is put into being.[50] "A prophet very firmly
assents that you will do X, and yet you know by experience, and it is seen to
be the case, that the act is in your complete indifferent control." So even if
God assents to something, it does not make the thing necessary, because we
experience otherwise. Chatton does not know how this could be, but he knows
it is true from experience.[51] In fact, Chatton maintains, a person can make it so
a prophecy is false. One can also make the prophet's assent false, because it
is caused and expressed by a proposition. God's assent is always true, however, since His assent is to the thing and the thing is signified by *both* sides of
a contradiction. This allows Chatton to speak of our actions as merely "conditionally ordained."[52]

Chatton's position, it appears to me, is as amazing and radical as his
rather Pelagian stance on predestination, namely that human merit and demerit are positive causes of predestination and reprobation. Chatton adopts
Auriol's notion of the completely undetermined created will, and the intrinsically indifferent God of the philosophers, but without seriously attempting to
accommodate the anthropomorphic God of Scripture. Revelation does occur,
but it is of an odd sort. God's eternal neutral cognition 'becomes' *de facto*

[49] Chatton, *Reportatio* I, dd. 40–41, q. 2, a. 2 (ed. Etzkorn, par. 26): "Accipiamus igitur istam 'Sortes sedet'. Huic complexo assentit Deus aeternaliter, et hoc assensu vero et necessario
assentienti huic, quia sicut prima contradictoria, videlicet 'Sortes sedet', 'Sortes non sedet', significant eandem rem, et illa res necessario est vera veritate rei, et assensus necessario verus veritate affirmativa vel negativa, quia conformi complexo affirmativo vel negativo significantibus
rem eandem extra. Ita est de assensu unico Dei correspondente istis contradictoriis significantibus rem eandem in anima 'haec est vera "Sortes sedet"', haec non est vera'. Et ideo concedo quod
impossibile est quin Deus assentiat illi rei in anima assensu affirmativo vel negativo... Et concedo ultra quod in potestate mea est quod assensus Dei sit affirmativus vel negativus, quia modo
sine omni mutatione sui aequivalet assensui affirmativo, modo negativo, quando res aliter se habet."
[50] Chatton, *Reportatio* I, dd. 40–41, q. 1, a. 2 (ed. Etzkorn, par. 79): "Contra: Ex quo firmiter assentit, aut igitur ille assensus est scientia, et tunc veridicus; aut error, et tunc est falsus.
— Dico quod nec est scientia nec error, nec verus nec falsus, sed est quo firmiter assentitur, et
quando in A res ponitur, tunc est assensus verus."
[51] Chatton, *Reportatio* I, dd. 40–41, q. 1, a. 2 (ed. Etzkorn, par. 72–3): "Firmissime
propheta assentit quod tu facies hoc, et tamen per experientiam scis, et videtur, quod actus est in
plena indifferenti potestate tua. Istam igitur consequentiam nego 'Deus firmiter assentit, et
propheta firmiter assentit, quod ita erit, igitur non potest esse falsum', quia experior quod potest
esse falsum. Quomodo autem et quae sit causa, ego nescio, sed regulabor per experientiam meam."
[52] Chatton, *Reportatio* I, dd. 40–41, q. 2, a. 2 (ed. Etzkorn, par. 32–3): "De actibus nostris,
dico quod habet providentiam condicionaliter ordinatam... Concedo quod in potestate mea est
quod prophetia sit falsa, si absolute assentiat quod ego faciam hoc. Possum enim facere oppositum, quod si faciam, assensus suus falsus erat. Et ratio est quia assensus suus est talis qualis
natus est causari mediante complexo. Sed non est sic de Deo, sed per eundem assensum assentit,
sive una pars contradictionis sit vera sive opposita pars."

knowledge when anything actually happens, without any real change happening in God, and humans are free from any necessity, even *ex suppositione*, to choose. Further analysis of related questions in Chatton's œuvre is required, however, and Chatton did make sure that the reader would not impute anything of what he said to him. Nevertheless, the position he puts forward is not really anyone else's, despite his occasional attempts to attribute it to Auriol. Moreover, in his *Quodlibet* from about 1330, Chatton seems to retain the same opinion. Question 28 is, quite characteristically for that time, on the revelation of future contingents: "Does the certitude of revelation about future contingents stand along with their contingency?" Chatton lists fifteen different answers, and in question 29, which is only one page long, he provides his own analysis of the test case: "Christ asserted that Peter would deny Him; therefore Peter was going to deny Christ":

> Either that denial proceeded from the fact that God knew that Peter would deny him, or it proceeded from the fact that God knew that Peter's soul was in such a state that from it, in such a situation, such a denial follows, according to the 'common law'. In the first way, the antecedent is contingent and the consequence is necessary. But in the second way the antecedent is necessary and the consequence is contingent. Nor therefore does it follow that Christ asserted something false, because i t does not follow.[53]

As we shall see, two decades after Chatton's London lectures on the *Sentences*, Thomas Bradwardine remarked in his *De causa Dei*, published in 1344, that he had heard Aristotle's opinion that future contingent propositions are neither true or false defended at the Papal Curia in Avignon and at Oxford. Very possibly Walter Chatton was the man whom Bradwardine heard defend it a t Oxford, and perhaps Chatton was also one of the new Pelagians against whom Bradwardine composed his great work. Unlike in Paris, where Auriol met an almost universally negative reception among known theologians, and hence remained a focus of attention, in England Walter Chatton appears to have adopted Auriol's radical stance on propositions and his ideas about necessity and contingency, actually going well beyond Auriol in his image of divine cognition. If Oxford had such a radical in Chatton, why should scholars have looked directly at Auriol? Most did not, but Auriol's indirect influence via Chatton may have stimulated the Oxford discussion of a multi-valent logic that developed in the later 1320s and 1330s.[54]

---

[53] Gualterus de Chatton, *Quodlibet*, q. 29 (ed. Girard Etzkorn and Chris Schabel, forthcoming; ms. Paris, BN lat. 15805, f. 60rb): "Christus asseruit Petrum se negaturum, ergo Petrus fuit Christum negaturus... aut illa negatio Petri processit ex hoc quod Deus scivit Petrus se negaturum, aut processit ex hoc quod Deus scivit animam Petri esse tali condicionis quod ex ea in tali casu sequitur talis negatio de communi lege. Primo modo, antecedens est contingens et consequentia necessaria. Sed secundo modo, antecedens est necessarium et consequentia est contingens. Nec ideo sequitur Christum asseruisse falsum, quia non sequitur."

[54] The following analysis of Richard Campsall, Arnold of Strelley, Robert Holcot, and William Crathorn, is mostly based on Gelber, *It Could*, ch. V, although I am familiar with the ed-

A Multi-Valent Logic in Oxford

Richard Campsall, whose *Sentences* commentary has not survived, on one occasion actually used the terms 'indeterminately true' and 'indeterminately false' before 1306, in his commentary on the *Prior Analytics*. In this he may have been influenced by the commentary on *Peri Hermeneias* in the *Opus secundum*, traditionally attributed to Scotus, or by other, vaguely phrased, *Peri Hermeneias* commentaries, perhaps even Thomas Aquinas's.[55] As we have seen, Antonius Andreas, Thomas Wylton, and even Peter Auriol had at least mentioned the term 'indeterminately true' at Paris, and undoubtedly others had employed it as well. Later, however, in Campsall's *Notabilia pro materia de contingencia de prescientia Dei*, perhaps written in the late 1310s, he uses language that might have influenced Ockham's, stating: "Some proposition is contingently true and, nevertheless, is *not* able to change from truth into falsity, although it can be false."[56] So by Auriol's time Campsall was committed to Bivalence, and also to the contingent truth of determinately true statements about the future, although he did not make a great effort, as Auriol had, to make his position clear.

Ockham himself, however, in *Quodlibet IV*, question four, appears to depart from this opinion. As Calvin Normore has noted, Ockham here gives an account of prophecy different from that of the *Tractatus*, stating that an utterance by God concerning the future is not a revelation unless what is seemingly revealed by the utterance comes about. The mere fact that God utters something in the form of a proposition does not make the proposition true or false, even if God made the utterance in the past. This suggests Walter Chatton's influence, and comes closer to Auriol's denial of the determinate truth of future contingent propositions. Ockham says there:

> You might object that the proposition 'God is causing this', referring to some future-tense proposition, was once true and does not depend upon the future. Therefore, 'God caused this' will always be necessary from now on. In reply I claim that if by 'this' one means the future-tense proposition or the quality that *is* the proposition, then the proposition 'God caused this' is necessary after the moment at which it is caused, since its present-tense counterpart does not depend upon the future. On the other hand, if by 'this' one means the revealed thing or an evident

---

ited works of all four figures. Gelber has generously allowed me to see a very preliminary version of this book.

[55] See above, chapter 1, and Gelber, *It Could*, ch. V, citing Normore's "Petrus Aureoli and His Contemporaries." Boehner has a discussion of the view put forth in the *Opus Secundum* (*The Tractatus*, pp. 77–82). The Campsall citation is from *Quaestiones datae a Ricardo de Camsale super librum priorum analeticum*, q. 3, in Edward Synan ed. *The Works of Richard Campsall* vol. 1 (Toronto 1982), p. 70: "Similiter, hec esset vera: 'omne quod erit est determinata futurum' et tamen ex ista et alia indeterminate vera sequitur unum indeterminate falsum..."

[56] Richardus de Campsall, *Notabilia pro materia de contingentia et prescientia Dei* I, in Synan, *The Works* vol. 2, p. 38: "Aliqua proposicio est contingenter vera et tamen non potest mutari a veritate in falsitatem, quamvis possit esse falsa."

cognition thereof, then the past-tense proposition is contingent because its present-tense counterpart does depend upon the future. For the proposition 'God is causing this revealed thing (or this evident cognition)' implies that the revealed thing will come to be, since what is false can be caused but cannot be revealed. But 'God is causing this proposition or quality' does not imply that the proposition referred to will be true or that it will be false.[57]

Moreover, in some manuscripts and in the 1491 Strasbourg edition, instead of "since what is false can be caused but cannot be revealed," we find, "since what is false can neither be evidently known nor revealed." Fortunately, the variants are recorded in Joseph Wey's critical edition, and we find that the more extreme position suggested by the variants did not go unnoticed: Ockham's fellow Franciscan Adam Wodeham, who was associated with Ockham at the time, later used it to argue (against Wodeham's own position) that future contingents are not determinately true. In fact, Wodeham places this position before Aristotle's:

> The second article is to present certain doubts against the said [opinion]. The first doubt is because it seems that since some futures are contingent with respect to both sides (*ad utrumlibet*), they are not determinately true, and consequently they cannot be evidently known or foreknown to be true. And Ockham holds this and proves this to be the opinion of the Philosopher, although in this [matter] the truth of the faith contradicts the Philosopher... Again, in book I, *Peri Hermeneias*... with respect to these things that are and that have been done it is necessary that the affirmation or negation be true or false, but in singular [propositions] about the future it is not...[58]

---

[57] William of Ockham, *Quodlibetal Questions Volume I, Quodlibets 1–4*, trans. Alfred J. Freddoso and Francis E. Kelley (New Haven 1991), pp. 261–2. In Normore's words, "...for while 'God says that P; therefore P' is a valid inference 'God utters P; therefore God reveals that P' is not. If Peter had not denied Christ three times, Christ's utterance 'Peter, you will deny me three times' would not have been a revelation that Peter would deny him three times" ("Future Contingents," p 373). The citation from Ockham is as follows in the new critical edition (Normore cites the Strasbourg edition of 1491): "Dico quod haec propositio 'Deus causavit hoc', si per li hoc demonstratur illa propositio de futuro vel illa qualitas quae est propositio, est necessaria post instans causationis, quia sua de praesenti non dependet a futuro. Sed si demonstratur per li hoc revelatum vel notitia evidens, tunc est illa de praeterito contingens, quia illa de praesenti dependet ex futuro. Nam ista propositio 'Deus causat hoc revelatum sive notitiam evidentem' importat quod hoc revelatum erit, quia falsum potest causari, non revelari. Sed ista 'Deus causat hanc propositionem vel qualitatem' non importat quod illa propositio erit vera neque falsa," in Ockham, *Quodl. IV*, q. 4, in idem, *Quodlibeta septem* (ed. Joseph Wey, *Opera Theologica* IX [St. Bonaventure, NY 1980], p. 317, ll. 64–74).

[58] Adam Wodeham, *In libros Sententiarum. Opus oxoniense*, III, d. 14, q. 2, a. 2 (Paris, Bibliothèque Mazarine 915, fol. 174ra): "Secundus articulus est movere aliqua dubia contra dictam. Primum dubium est quia videtur quod eo ipso quod aliqua sunt futura contingentia ad utrumlibet, non sunt determinate vera, nec per consequens possunt evidenter sciri vel presciri esse vera. Et hoc tenet Okam et probat hoc esse opinionem Philosophi, quamvis in hoc Philosopho veritas fidei contradicat... Item in primo *Perihermenias*... in hiis, inquit textus, que sunt et que facta sunt, necesse est affirmationem vel negationem veram esse vel falsam. In singularibus vero futuris non..." Normore, "Future Contingents," p. 373, uses and cites (n. 37) the Strasbourg edition.

It is probable, as Wodeham recognized, that in both cases Ockham was refer-ring to our knowledge only, and not God's; one cannot establish a clear con-nection between Ockham's remarks and Auriol's notions.

Hester Gelber, however, has found two Dominicans who defend, even if not at length, a different sort of multivalent logic: Arnold of Strelley and Rob-ert Holcot. Like Chatton and Wodeham, Strelley was associated with Ock-ham in the 1320s. Gelber considers him to be the author of the *Centiloquium theologicum*, written about the time of his *Sentences* commentary, between 1323 and 1330. Gelber has also shown that a separate question of Strelley's on predestination and foreknowledge is "almost an abbreviation of Ockham's *Tractatus.*"[59] In his *Sentences* commentary, Strelley followed Ockham in stating that the Philosopher would have denied foreknowledge to God[60] but, whether he was influenced by Campsall's brief statement in his earlier *Prior Analytics* commentary, by Antonius Andreas, Thomas Wylton, Auriol, or Chatton, Strelley reasoned contrary to Ockham that God has indeterminate knowledge of future contingent events.

In the *Centiloquium*, the main points of Strelley's position are as follows:[61] (1) There is no determinate truth in future contingents, or past and present-tensed propositions depending on future contingents; (2) God knows future contingents; (3) true future contingent propositions and true propositions in the past/present tenses but depending on future contingents are *indetermi-nately* true; (4) God knows future contingents as *indeterminately* true, and after their actualization as determinately true; and (5) God's knowledge is immuta-ble. Strelley's opinion looks very much like Chatton's, especially Chatton's idea that God's indifferent cognition 'becomes' knowledge, without any change, when something comes to be.

Strelley's position also seems similar to Ockham's in that they both deny the equation of immutability and necessity, and that they say a true proposi-

---

[59] Hester G. Gelber, "Ockham's Early Influence: A Question about Predestination and Foreknowledge by Arnold of Strelley, O.P.," AHDLMA 55 (1988) (pp. 255–89), p. 255. For Strel-ley as author of *Centiloquium* see ibid. pp. 256–66. It should be noted that Gelber's attribution of the *Centiloquium* to Strelley is not universally accepted. For Strelley's dates see Gelber, *It Could*, ch. I, and for his ideas on future contingents, ch. V. I will deal with Holcot later in this chapter.

[60] Arnoldus de Strelley, *I Sent.*, q. 7: "Ad septimum, dico quod futura contingentia sunt vera secundum rei veritatem, non tamen secundum Aristotelem, qui non posuit aliquam esse causam futurorum contingentium nisi solam voluntatem humanam... Estimavit autem Aristoteles quod nec Deus intellexit futura talia nec eorum causa fuit propter mutabilitatem in eis..." Erfurt, Wissenschaftliche Bibliothek, C.A. F, 180, fol. 29vb, cited in Gelber, *It Could*, ch. V.

[61] See Gelber, *It Could*, ch. V: Strelley, *Centiloquium theologicum*, concl. 12, in ed. Philotheus Boehner, "The *Centiloquium* Attributed to Ockham, Part III," FcS 1.3 (1941), p. 68: "Et totum istud dico secundum opinionem illorum qui ponunt quod in futuris contingentibus non est aliqua veritas determinata, nec in aliqua propositione de praesenti vel de praeteri[t]o cuius veri-tas dependet a veritate propositionis de futuro contingenti." *Cent.* concl. 85, in ed. Boehner, "The *Centiloquium...* Part VI," FcS 2 (1942), p. 293: "Ista consequentia est plana et antecedens declara-tur: quia A est falsum contingens et indeterminate falsum; ergo ..." *Cent.* 12, in ed. Boehner, "The *Centiloquium...* Part III," p. 68: "Et si dicatur: ergo Deus potest mutari ab una voluntate ad aliam voluntatem, negatur consequentia. Quia quamvis ista propositio 'Sortes damnabitur in A in-stanti' sit vera et poterit esse falsa, non tamen poterit mutari de veritate in falsitatem..."

tion about a future contingent is able never to have been true.[62] Yet while Ockham held that true propositions about the future were determinately true, yet
contingently true, Strelley, in at least one place in his *Sentences* commentary,
seems to equate 'contingently true' and 'indeterminately true'.[63] We assume,
then, that Strelley would equate 'determinately true' with 'necessarily true'
when considering propositions about the past. If future-tensed propositions
were determinately true, as Ockham said, although absolutely contingent, then
for Strelley the future would be the same as the past, and its opposite impossible (*ex suppositione*). If this is the case, one can see why Strelley had to avoid
determinate knowledge of future contingents. Strelley and Auriol have similar
worries, but their solutions to the problem are very different, perhaps because
of Chatton. Auriol would have considered 'indeterminately true' a meaning-
less phrase, but Strelley would not have held Auriol's solution in high regard
either. Auriol would also have rejected Strelley's contention — which appears
to be another version of Chatton's theory — that God's knowledge changed
from indeterminate to determinate with the actualization of the future event,
and that God's knowledge was not thereby mutated.

Variety rather than consensus characterizes the debate in the fruitful years
between about 1328 and 1335, when Oxford is at its theological peak. We
have more sources from this period than from the period before, or for the
same period at Paris, and it has been investigated more fully. During this time,
William Crathorn, Richard Fitzralph, Robert Holcot, Adam Wodeham, Thomas Bradwardine, and others lectured on the *Sentences*. Looking at the Franciscan John of Rodington, who read the *Sentences* 1328–29, one can observe
some trends that were already present in Walter Chatton and even William of
Ockham.[64] First, although Rodington is a Franciscan, there is a decrease in the
discussion of God's will and essence in connection with the problem, along
with less frequent use of the Scotistic ideas of instants of nature and the capacity for opposites in an instant. This indicates that Scotus's position had
been abandoned. Another trend is a tendency to differentiate explicitly between different types of divine knowledge, described by different words (e.g.
scientia, cognitio, notitia) and different nuances for the same word. Accompanying this is a new answer to the question of whether God can know more
than He knows. The answer is a flat no in some cases, taking knowledge (*scientia*) for knowledge of *complexa* signifying states of affairs. In that case, if
God knows 'the Antichrist will be', He could not know less or more, for if He
knew differently, it would only be 'the Antichrist will not be', and the number

---

[62] Strelley, *Cent.*, concl. 12, in ed. Boehner, "The *Centiloquium*...Part III," pp. 68–9: "Et
radix istius est quia propositio vera nunc et quae prius fuit vera, potest numquam fuisse vera,"
as cited in Gelber, *It Could*, ch. V. "Sed illud quod est contingens, licet una pars sit semper vera et
erit semper vera, tamen intrinsice potest non esse vera..." Erfurt 180, fol. 30ra, as cited in Gelber,
It Could, ch. V.
[63] Strelley, *I Sent.*, q. 1: "Dici igitur potest quod talis peccat in primo instanti emissionis
voti, ista tamen: 'iste peccat', in primo instanti est indeterminate vera et contingenter vera quia
dependet a veritate unius de futuro..." Erfurt 180, fol. 2vb, as cited in Gelber, *It Could*, ch. V.
[64] On Rodington, see Tachau, *Vision and Certitude*, p. 209 and pp. 216–36.

of *complexa* in God's knowledge would be the same in any possible world.[65] A final trend that can be mentioned in passing is an emphasis on issues concerning revelation, and what can or cannot be revealed. Perhaps this is an effect of Chatton's and Ockham's provocative remarks that seemed to endanger the certainty of prophecy.

On the other hand, although he adopts the *opinio communis*, Rodington fits in the pre-Auriol Franciscan tradition at Paris. To the question in distinction 38, "whether God has knowledge of future contingents," after immediately giving Aristotle's denial of determinate truth,[66] Rodington presents his own solution in three articles and a series of eleven doubts, which cover many questions connected with the problem, including whether God's knowledge is determinate, infallible, immutable, etc. Rodington's position is a combination of many we have seen, and in some ways it is more similar to those defended at Paris, for he makes continual use of the composite and divided senses of propositions to show that in the divided sense things can be other than as God knows them.[67] Unlike Strelley, Rodington holds that God has determinate knowledge of future contingents,[68] and he saves contingency only by saying that God can know other than He does know, but not in an instant, and not successively, because God's knowledge is immutable. Rodington even says at one point that the 'necessity of immutability' or 'necessity of inevitability' holds for God's knowledge, phrases we have heard at Paris and in Scotus.[69] So what seems to be reasoning based on a really possible counterfactual past at one point is not.[70] Nevertheless, Rodington does distinguish between

---

[65] An example of this in Rodington: "...impossibile est quod sciat plura quam scit, quia tot sunt contradictoria affirmativa quot sunt negativa. Si non sciat istam: 'Antichristus est futurus', scit istam: 'Antichristus non est futurus'... Johannes de Rodington, *In primum librum Sententiarum*, d.38, a.3 (ms. Brussel, Koninklijke Bibliotheek 11578 [1552], fol. 85va).

[66] Rodington, *I Sent.*, d. 38, a. 1 (Brussel 11578, fol. 83vb): "Circa distinctione 38 quero utrum Deus habeat scientiam de futuris contingentibus. Videtur quod non, quia secundum Philosophum, primo *Periermenias*, in futuris contingentibus non est veritas determinata; igitur nec scientia."

[67] For example Rodington, *I Sent.*, d. 38, a. 3 (Brussel 11578, fol. 85rb): "Ad primum argumentum respondeo quod non plus sequitur ista conclusio: 'Deus decipitur', quam ista: 'Deus non decipitur;' sed sequitur quod scitum a Deo potest esse falsum, et hoc est verum in sensu divisionis; et sicut res scita potest non esse, ita Deus potest eam non scire, et si non erit non sciet," and (fol. 84rb): "Ad illud: 'hoc est scitum a Deo et potest esse falsum; igitur scitum a Deo potest esse falsum', dico quod conclusio est distinguenda; et in sensu composito est falsum, quia iste est sensus 'hec est possibilis: scitum a Deo est falsum'. Alius sensus est iste quod ista stant simul: 'istud est scitum a Deo' et tamen 'potest esse falsum'." There are several other examples where the terms 'divided sense' and 'composite sense' are used.

[68] Rodington, *I Sent.*, d. 38, a. 1 (Brussel 11578, fol. 83va): "Dico igitur quod Deus habet determinatam notitiam de futuro contingenti sicut de presenti..."

[69] Rodington, *I Sent.*, d. 38, a. 2 (Brussel 11578, fol. 84ra): "Preterea, alia propositio sequitur quod quia utrumque contradictoriorum potest esse verum, et tamen nec simul nec successive, sicut 'iste est predestinatus' et 'iste non est predestinatus', utramque potest esse vera, et tamen nec simul nec successive. Et est ibi secundum Iohannem <Scotum> necessitas immutabilitatis, quia impossibile est quod unum succedat alteri; sed non nisi necessitas inevitabilitatis."

[70] Rodington, *I Sent.*, d. 38, a. 2 (Brussel 11578, fol. 84ra–rb): "Preterea, sequitur quod Deus ab eterno scivit aliquid et tamen possum facere quod non sciat illud, quia Deus scit ab eterno me sessurum cras, et sedere cras est in libera voluntate mea; igitur possum non sedere cras, et ista propositio est vera in sensu divisionis."

propositions really about the past and ones only verbally about the past, as Ockham does,[71] and he retains a basically Lombardian solution to the overall problem.

The increasing tendency at Oxford to discuss future contingents in terms of revelation reaches a high point with the Irishman Richard Fitzralph (ca. 1295–1360), who phrases entire questions along those lines. Fitzralph was a secular theologian with a long career.[72] He read the *Sentences* at Oxford from 1328–29, and wrote a *quaestio biblica* in that time dealing with future contingents. In the 1340s he took up the issue at length again in his treatise on the 'errors' of the Eastern Churches, the *Summa de quaestionibus Armenorum*. In his *Sentences* commentary, Fitzralph asked two questions on the subject: Question 15, "whether God is foreknowing of futures," and question 16, "whether God can reveal future contingents to a rational creature." His *quaestio biblica* asks "whether a rational creature can foreknow any future contingent in the divine Word," and is thus similar to question 16.[73] One might expect to find Fitzralph's position on Bivalence and other matters directly pertinent to our project in question 15, but the short question pertains mostly to how God's essence represents future contingents. There is no discussion of either Scotus's or Auriol's stance on the matter.[74] Question 16 is massive, and the *quaestio biblica* is also lengthy. Still, even in 3000 lines of text, it is difficult to find evidence of Auriol's or even Aristotle's position. What is certain, however, is that the problem at Oxford had definitely shifted to discussions of revelation. Of all those at whom Genest and I have looked, Fitzralph is the first to devote entire questions to revelation. This fact and the sheer size of his questions may point to Fitzralph as the catalyst behind this trend in the 1330s, when Robert Holcot and Adam Wodeham, for example, give much space to the problem.

---

[71] Rodington, *I Sent.*, d. 38, a. 2 (Brussel 11578, fol. 84ra): "Preterea, alia propositio erit ubi est proprie de futuro vocaliter cum verbo (?) credendi vel reverendi illa propositio non est de preterito nisi vocaliter. Verbi gratia 'anima Christi scivit Antichristum esse futurum' non est de preterito nec de futuro, sed compositum isti copulative: 'talis scientia fuit in anima Christi et Antichristus est futurus'."

[72] Fitzralph (Archbishop of Armagh 1347–60) has been the subject of much study recently. A good biography is Katherine Walsh's *A Fourteenth-Century Scholar and Primate: Richard FitzRalph in Oxford, Avignon, and Armagh* (Oxford 1981), and for his thought see Tachau, *Vision and Certitude*, pp. 236–42.

[73] Books 15–17 of Fitzralph's *Summa* deal with foreknowledge. This takes up 42 folios (over 7000 lines) of ms. Padua, Biblioteca universitaria 1439! Genest has edited the *quaestio biblica* in Jean-François Genest, "Contingence et révélation des futurs, la *Quaestio biblica* de Richard FitzRalph," in J. Jolivet, Z. Kaluza, and A. de Libera, eds, *Lectionum varietates, Hommage à Paul Vignaux (1904–1987)* (Paris 1991), pp. 199–246: "Utrum creatura racionalis possit prescire in Verbo divino aliquod futurum contingens." I have looked at the *Sentences* commentary, question 16, in several manuscripts, including Vat. Ottob. lat. 869; Vat. Ottob. lat. 179; Oxford, Oriel College 15; and Firenze, BN centrale A111 508: "Utrum Deus possit revelare creature rationali futura contingentia." For question 15 I have looked at only Vat. Ottob. 869 and Firenze, BN centrale A111 508. The Florence ms. (fol. 49rb) has "Utrum Deus necessario sit prescius futurorum," but Vat. Ottob. 869 (fol. 77r) has: "Utrum Deus sit prescius futurorum."

[74] A sample of Fitzralph's discussion in question 15: "Dico quod ex hoc quod divina essentia habet in se talem representantem respectu futuri cuiuslibet, ipse cognoscit omne futurum esse futurum quia ipsa est in se sufficiens in qua et propter quam sufficienter ostenditur res..." Richardus Fitzralph, *In libros Sententiarum*, I, q. 15 (Ottob. lat. 869, fol. 78v).

With these developments, Auriol and Scotus fade from the picture, though the ideas of Ockham on prophecy and on propositions only vocally about the past retain their place in the new discussions.[75] William Crathorn, a Dominican who read on book I of the *Sentences* in 1330–31, just after Rodington and Fitzralph, did not follow Fitzralph's lead in devoting a question to revelation, or in devoting much space to the problem of future contingents.[76] Nor did he follow his fellow Dominican Arnold of Strelley in assigning indeterminate truth to true propositions about the future. Crathorn agrees that everything except God is ultimately contingent, such that everything was able to be otherwise.[77] He follows Strelley, however, in contrasting 'contingently true' with 'determinately true', and he seems to attach some sort of necessity *ex suppositione* to determinately true propositions.[78] He does not accept a multivalent logic, however, nor does he accept counterfactual pasts with respect to God's knowledge. When God knows X will be, then afterwards God knew X would be and God cannot not have known X would be, even if X has not come about yet.[79] In fact, given God's eternity:

> Therefore, I say that, if A is future in B, God from eternity knew that A is future in B, nor can He now not have known that A is future in B, nor in any instant before B can God not know or not have known that A is future in B.[80]

---

[75] See Genest, "Contingence et révélation," for a discussion of thinkers who devote questions to the revelation of future contingents, and of the issues involved.

[76] On Crathorn see Tachau, *Vision and Certitude*, pp. 255–74, and Gelber, *It Could*, ch. I, and on future contingents, ch. V.

[77] Guillelmus Crathorn, *Quästionen zum ersten Sentenzenbuch*, q. 19 (ed. Fritz Hoffmann, [Münster 1988], p. 484, ll. 16–19): "...omne quod est, excepto deo, est contingenter. Patet, quia omne id est contingenter, quod potuit non fuisse et poterit non esse. Sed omne quod est aliud a deo, aliquando potuit non fuisse et poterit non esse. Igitur omne quod est aliud a deo, est contingenter." Also cited in Gelber, *It Could*, ch. V.

[78] Crathorn, *I Sent.*, q. 19 (ed. Hoffmann, p. 496, ll. 15–20): "Ad primum istorum dicendum quod haec propositio formata: 'A est in b', non est futurm (sic) contingens ad utrumlibet, licet formetur de futuro contingenti ad utrumlibet, nec est vera contingenter ad utrumlibet, sed est determinate vera, et impossibile est quod sit falsa respectu illius significati stante significatione terminorum citra instans vel tempus, in quo a est; et tamen ex hoc non sequitur quod a necessario est." Cited also in Gelber, *It Could*, ch. V.

[79] Crathorn, *I Sent.*, q. 19 (ed. Hoffmann, p. 490, ll. 1–11): "Decima octava conclusio est: si a est futurum in b, deus scivit ab aeterno quod a erit in b, et tamen a posse non fore in b non arguit deum posse nescivisse a futurum in b. Et probatur ista sicut praecedens, quia a posse non fore in b est consequens ad istam: Deus scivit ab aeterno a fore in b. Secundo probatur sic, quia verum non infert impossibile. Sed haec est vera: 'A potest non fore in b', haec autem impossibilis: Deus potest nescivisse a fore in b, igitur etc. Quod autem sit impossible hanc esse veram: Deus potest nescivisse vel non scivisse a futurum in b in aliquo instanti citra b, si deus scivit a futurum in b, probo primo, quia haec est de praeterito: Deus scivit quod a erit in b; igitur postquam a est futurum in b, deus non potest non scivisse a futurum in b." Passage also cited in Gelber, *It Could*, ch. V.

[80] Crathorn, *I Sent.*, q. 19 (ed. Hoffmann, p. 490, ll. 22–4): "Ideo dico, si a est futurum in b, deus ab aeterno scivit quod a est futurum in b, nec potest modo non scivisse quod a est futurum in b, nec in aliquo instanti citra b potest deus non scire vel non scivisse quod a est futurum in b..." I translate 'modo' as 'now', instead of as 'in mode [i.e. possibly]' as Gelber has it (*It Could*, ch. V).

Although Crathorn emphasizes the world's contingency in an absolute sense, he leaves little room for it in reality. Crathorn then agrees with the *opinio communis* that what has happened is now necessary, but unlike most he extends that necessity to propositions that Ockham and others considered to be only vocally about the past, but really depending on the contingent future.

How then does Crathorn avoid the Parisian conclusion that the future is necessary *ex suppositione* of God's foreknowledge? He does not. Crathorn does everything but use the Parisian terminology: he admits that 'God knew that A will be in B; therefore A will be in B' is a necessary consequence, if it is true. In Paris, the truth of the antecedent is the supposition. Of course the antecedent, though true, is not necessary, so the consequent is not necessary for that reason, and no such proposition is necessary absolutely.[81]

In contrast to Crathorn, Robert Holcot (ca. 1290–1349) eventually followed his fellow Oxford Dominican Arnold of Strelley in attributing indeterminate truth and falsity to true and false propositions about the future, but not in his *Sentences* commentary.[82] Interestingly, Holcot moves the main treatment in his *Sentences* commentary to book II, where he asks the very long question "whether God from eternity knew He would produce the world." Basically following the *opinio communis*, Holcot accepts Ockham's distinction between true propositions about the past and present and those only vocally about the past or present which are equivalent to propositions about the future.[83] True

---

[81] Crathorn, *I Sent.*, q. 19 (ed. Hoffmann, p. 491, ll. 17–18; 26–9): "... ista: 'Deus scivit quod a erit in b', bene infert istam: 'A erit in b' ita quod consequentia ista est bona et necessaria, si fiat... Concedo... si a est futurum in b, quod haec: 'Deus scivit ab aeterno quod a erit in b', erit vera in quolibet instanti, si formetur in quolibet instanti citra b, et impossibile est hanc esse falsam in aliquo instanti citra b: 'Deus scivit ad aeterno quod a erit in b'." Gelber (*It Could*, ch. V) has a different interpretation of Crathorn's goals here. I do not think our two discussions have to be mutually exclusive, however. I am merely assessing Crathorn's treatment of the problem in the terms of the Parisian debate centering on Auriol, of which Crathorn himself may not have been aware.

[82] For Robert Holcot's life and ideas on future contingents, see Gelber, *It Could*, ch. I, and ch. V; Katherine's Tachau's introduction to Paul Streveler and eadem, eds., *Seeing the Future Clearly: Questions of Future Contingents by Robert Holcot* (Toronto 1995), pp. 1–55; and Tachau's "Logic's God and the Natural Order in Late Medieval Oxford: the Teaching of Robert Holcot," *Annals of Science* 53 (1996), pp. 235–67, which also concerns Fitzralph. Joseph M. Incandela, "Robert Holcot, O.P., on Prophecy, the Contingency of Revelation, and the Freedom of God," *Medieval Philosophy and Theology* 4 (1994), pp. 165–88, takes an interesting approach. For Holcot's related soteriological views, see Halverson, *Peter Aureol on Predestination*, pp. 122–9.

[83] Robertus Holcot, *In quatuor libros Sententiarum quaestiones* II, q. 2 (ed. Streveler-Tachau, p. 112): "Queritur secundo utrum Deus ab eterno sciverit se producturum mundum." Aristotle's position is given on p. 122, ll. 233–5: "Confirmatur iste modus arguendi per processum Aristotelis, 1 *Perihermenias*, in fine, ubi ostendit quod in propositionibus contradictoriis de futuro in materia contingenti, neutra pars est determinate vera."

Holcot's basic position (also cited by Gelber) is on p. 127, ll. 324–41: "Et haec est differentia inter propositiones de futuro in materia contingenti et eis aequivalentes, sive sint de praesenti sive de praeterito, et propositiones de praesenti et de praeterito quae non aequivalent talibus nec tales virtualiter includunt; quia si aliqua sit propositio vera de praesenti vel de praeterito, necessario postea erit semper verum dicere quod illa fuit vera... Sed in propositionibus de praesenti et de praeterito quae aequivalent propositionibus de futuro vel exponi habent per aliquam de futuro, secus est. Nam ista propositio: 'A fuit scitum a Deo'... potest numquam fuisse vera."

propositions about the past and present are necessarily true, but a proposition about the future is true in a way that it is able never to have been true.[84]

Holcot read on book II of the *Sentences* in the 1332–23 academic year. In the next year he held quodlibetal debates with William Crathorn, and we find that Holcot has changed his mind and opted for a position more like Chatton's or Strelley's. Four questions deal with future contingents, and the question where we would expect to see a discussion of Auriol's views is *Quodlibet* III, question two, "whether this consequence is necessary: 'God knows that A will exist; therefore A will exist'." But the question is only about thirty lines long, and Holcot merely states that the antecedent is contingent, and can never have been true, basically the same position he defended the previous year. But he adds, somewhat like Chatton, that a proposition such as 'God knows that A will exist' is contingent because it can be made into a copulative such as 'God gives assent to this proposition: "A will exist," and it will be that A will exist'. The first part may be necessary in some sense, as it is in the present, but the second part is definitely contingent, as it is about the future.[85]

Most of the other quodlibetal questions deal with revelation, and as such they fit into the Oxford tradition, but in *Quodlibet* III, question one, Holcot says that there is no determinate truth or falsity in propositions about the future, and that they are true or false *indeterminately*.[86] This is Strelley's position. In addition, Katherine Tachau, in a provocative paper, points out that by the time of the quodlibetals Holcot, as had Chatton, denied foreknowledge to God, if one took foreknowledge (*prescire*) in the strictest sense of a demonstrated conclusion, which could not be otherwise (*non possit aliter se habere*). This may again reflect Chatton's influence, via Strelley. Holcot does not work out the implications of this stance for *how* God knows the future, a fact that testifies to Oxford's ignorance of Auriol's important treatment. Auriol always

---

[84] Holcot, *II Sent.*, q.2 (ed. Streveler-Tachau, p. 145–6, ll. 745–63): "Septimus articulus est, an in propositionibus de futuro in materia contingenti sit veritas determinata in uno contradictoriorum et falsitas in reliquo. Et videtur esse sententia Philosophi quod non, sicut allegatum fuit... Sed sententia theologorum est huic contraria... Dico hic, sicut communiter dicetur, quod propositio de futuro est vera, sic tamen quod potest numquam fuisse vera. Et ideo aliter est vera quam illa quae est simpliciter vera de praeterito vel de praesenti, sic quod nullo modo ad suam veritatem requirat aliquam de futuro esse veram. Nam si aliqua talis est vera, necessarium est postea quod illa fuit vera."

[85] Holcot, *Quodlibet III*, q. 2 (ed. Streveler-Tachau, p. 73–4, ll. 2–4, 19–27): "Utrum ista consequentia sit necessaria: 'Deus scit A fore; ergo A fore'. 'Ad rationem in oppositum, quando accipitur quod antecedens huius consequentiae est necessarium, ista videlicet: 'Deus scit A fore', dicendum quod haec est contingens: 'Deus scit A fore', quia sic scit A fore quod potuit numquam scivisse A fore... Modo, ista propositio: 'Deus scit A fore' aequivalet isti copulativae: 'Deus assentit huic complexo: "A erit", et ita erit quod A erit', cuius secunda pars est contingens per positum."

[86] Holcot, *Quodlibet III*, q. 1 (ed. Streveler-Tachau, p. 60, ll. 29–33): "Secundo, distinguo de isto termino 'futura contingenti', quia uno modo futura contingentia dicuntur propositiones de futuro quarum non est veritas determinata vel falsitas, quia, licet sint vera vel falsae, illae tamen quae sunt verae possunt numquam fuisse falsae..." and (p. 63, ll. 93–6) "Quarta conclusio est quod non omnis videns clare Deum videt omnia futura contingentia, accipiendo 'futura contingentia' primo modo, videlicet, pro propositionibus de futuro quae sunt verae vel falsae indeterminate..." Also cited by Gelber, *It Could*, ch. V.

took 'foreknowledge' in the strict sense, and that is why he made such efforts to put forth a new theory of divine knowledge of the future. For Auriol, if the object of foreknowledge could turn out differently, then it was not fore*knowledge* at all, and this could not be said of God. Instead of attacking 'knowledge', Auriol aimed his arrows at the 'fore'. Perhaps Holcot leans to his own compromise in his *Sentences* commentary, but it is not until the quodlibetal disputations that it is spelled out.[87] Why was there a change in Holcot's position during the year?

Before answering that question it might be useful to look at Adam Wodeham (ca. 1298–1358), who was lecturing on books II–IV of the *Sentences* in the same year in which Holcot held the quodlibetal debates, 1333–34.[88] Oddly, Wodeham moved his treatment to book III, distinction 14, questions two, three, and four. One gets the feeling reading Wodeham's *Sentences* commentary that although he participates in the Oxford discussion, he is also aware of the discussion on the continent. While Wodeham cites Ockham frequently, and deals with revelation in great depth, he is also conversant with different types of necessity in the context of future contingents, makes use of the composite and divided senses of propositions, and sees the difficulty of the problem as expressed by Peter Auriol, whose *Scriptum* Wodeham knew well.[89]

We are not concerned here with Wodeham's solution to the problem, which in many ways is the *opinio communis*, except that he often states things in terms more used in Paris than in Oxford. We are interested for the present in Wodeham's role in the history of the problem as it relates to Peter Auriol. In one way he functions as a conduit bringing Ockham's ideas on the subject to Gregory of Rimini, who as we shall see devoted much of his discussion to a refutation of Auriol's views. When Wodeham mentions such items as Ockham's opinion that we cannot in this state know how God knows future contingents, Rimini, who knew Wodeham's work, picks up on those points.

More important is Wodeham's presentation of the problem. The second article to distinction 14, question two, concerns doubts with respect to the normal opinion on the matter. The first doubt is whether there is any truth in future contingent propositions (in this case, so that they can be revealed). After mentioning that Ockham seemed to deny such truth and said that such revela-

[87] Katherine Tachau, "Logic's God," pp. 253–4. Tachau also explains (p. 254) that "it is apparent that Holcot's treatment of the perplexing issues bound together under the rubric 'future contingents' translates into the very activity of 'propositional analysis,' with its attendant semantic and epistemological commitments, that scholars now accept as characteristic of Oxford thought from ca. 1315 onwards." Quite so, yet, as Tachau knows, those same scholars have to realize that Auriol's work preceded the Oxford discussion, and was perhaps one of the best developed expression of such 'propositional analysis' until Gregory of Rimini.

[88] On Wodeham's life and works, see William J. Courtenay, *Adam Wodeham: An Introduction to His Life and Writings* (Leiden 1978), and Tachau, *Vision and Certitude*, especially pp. 275–312. For dating, see my "Oxford Franciscans after Ockham: Walter Chatton and Adam Wodeham." For his ideas on future contingents, see Hoenen, *Marsilius of Inghen*, various places in chapter 7.

[89] Tachau, *Vision and Certitude*, p. 290, discusses Wodeham's knowledge of Auriol's ideas and works.

tions were not possible (as we have seen), Wodeham presents at some length Aristotle's arguments, mentioning Peter Auriol by name in connection with Aristotle's position.[90] The second doubt concerns the seeming incompatibility of God's unchanging and determinate foreknowledge and the freedom of the human will. These doubts take up considerable space.[91] In question three he discusses the difference between necessity and immutability,[92] and as we have seen discusses the types of necessity and uses the composite and divided sense.[93] His presentation of the problem, and his explicit reference to Auriol, may have helped trigger Rimini's interest in Auriol's position.

John XXII and Thomas Bradwardine

Why do Robert Holcot and Adam Wodeham signal a change of emphasis in the Oxford discussion in 1333–34, as I contend? It could simply have come from the reaction to Auriol and Ockham of Walter Chatton, whom Wodeham knew well from London in the early 1320s and whose Oxford *Quodlibet* was fresh in scholars' minds.[94] There is a possibility, however, that the stimulus for both Holcot's change and Wodeham's interest in the Parisian terms of the debate came from outside academia. It is difficult to discuss the impact of society on intellectual currents, especially in a context such as the history of the treatment of divine foreknowledge and future contingents, where little in the way of historical overview has been written. Analyses of individual thinkers' ideas, based on the present state of research on future contingents, provides no occasion to see trends. Only in looking at many figures over a period of time can one see developments, and then look for outside influences. One such outside influence, although not really 'societal', was the controversy surrounding Pope John XXII.

As Courtenay has explained,[95] John effectively attacked the distinction between God's absolute and ordained power when he claimed, for example, that baptism was absolutely necessary for salvation, in sermons in 1330 and 1333.

---

[90] Adam Wodeham, *In Libros Sententiarum. Opus Oxoniense* (hereafter as *Ordinatio*) III, d. 14, q. 2, a. 2 (Paris, Bibl. Mazarine, 915, fol. 174ra): "Probatio primi prima est secundum eum <Ockham> hac distinctione 38 primi sui, et Petrum Auriolum, quia illud quod non est verum non potest sciri pro illo tunc pro quo non est verum; sed futurum contingens dependens simpliciter a potentia libera non est in se verum..."

[91] After giving these doubts Wodeham adds (Paris 915, fol. 175ra): "Ad istud dubium difficillimum, respondet Okam et bene in hac distinctione 38 primi sui, 'indubitanter est intelligendum quod Deus certitudinaliter et evidenter scit omnia futura contingentia; sed hec declarare,' inquit, 'et modum quo scit omnia futura contingentia exprimere est impossibile omni intellectui pro statu isto.'" Wodeham's own description of God's knowledge has to do with God's immensity.

[92] Wodeham, *Ordinatio* III, d. 14, q. 3, a. 1 (Paris 915, fol. 177vb).

[93] Wodeham, *Ordinatio* III, d. 14, q. 3, a. 1 (Paris 915, fol. 178ra–b) discusses the opinions of Boethius, Augustine, Anselm, etc., and their notions of necessity.

[94] Tachau, *Vision and Certitude*, p. 276, suggests that Chatton stimulated Wodeham to look into Auriol's ideas.

[95] Courtenay, *Capacity and Volition*, pp. 147–54.

In his opponents' view, John denied contingency in the world in agreeing with what was basically Auriol's view of the necessity and immutability of God's will and intellect. As we have seen, Michael of Massa may have had John in mind when discussing contingency. Auriol also denied the DPA/DPO distinction, but John and Auriol had vastly differing views of God's will. In order to save contingency and maintain God's necessity, Auriol made a distinction between God's intrinsic and extrinsic will. God's intrinsic will was absolutely necessary, and could not be other than it was, but because it was indifferent to what happened in the world, there was still contingency in the world. God's extrinsic will, on the other hand, enabled God to actively do things in the world, while preserving God's intrinsic necessity.

Auriol was in fact something of a client to Pope John. What is more, as we have seen, Auriol presented a copy of his *Scriptum* to John in Avignon. It is possible that John saw Auriol's distinction between the intrinsic and extrinsic will of God as too problematic to accept, or it is possible that he was not aware of that distinction, which is given near the end of the *Scriptum*. John stressed the absolute necessity of the habit of grace, as Auriol did but for God's intrinsic will. Without Auriol's distinction between the absolutely necessary intrinsic will and the contingent active will of operation, and without the larger context of a *Sentences* commentary, John made himself open to the objection that his position meant that all things happen of necessity, including future contingents, which could not very well be called 'contingent' at all. After wondering "Whether John's position had developed independently or through his association with Peter Auriol," Courtenay rightly cautions in a footnote that "In assessing any compatibility between the view of Peter Auriol and John XXII, one needs to keep in mind that John's view of the infallibility of divine foreknowledge and the consequent necessity of future events is in striking contrast to Auriol's position on the issue."[96]

Still, there are grounds for thinking that Auriol had an important impact on the thought of John XXII, and therefore there are grounds for thinking that Auriol had a further important, if indirect, impact on Oxford thought in the

---

[96]   Courtenay, *Capacity and Volition*, p. 149, and p. 162, n. 8. Courtenay's assessment of Auriol's position is slightly problematic. Citing Vignaux, Schwamm, Oberman, and Genest, Courtenay states (p. 154) that at Oxford between 1331–37, "in contrast to the debate on the habit of grace, majority opinion on future contingents favored Auriol's approach over that of Scotus..." Both men had few adherents at Oxford on the subject of future contingents, but it is true that Auriol's attacks on Scotus may have been influential in both Oxford and Paris, as Genest mentions, "Le *De futuris contingentibus* de Thomas Bradwardine," *Recherches Augustiniennes* 14 (1974) (pp. 249–336), p. 255. Courtenay goes on to say that "[F]or Auriol, foreknowledge precedes any action of the divine will (*post praevisa merita*), which remains undetermined as to which part of a contradiction ('X' will or will not be saved) is true until events make one or the other true. God knows future events as future, not as present, and one cannot on the basis of divine foreknowledge conclude anything about the truth of future contingent propositions. Although in agreement with Auriol on the integrity of human freedom and the idea that God's foreknowledge precedes predestination, Ockham and others were reluctant to say that future contingents had no determined truth." These statements need some qualification. Auriol held that God knows future contingents indistantly, not as future, and that God's knowledge does not 'precede' anything, temporally speaking.

early 1330s via that route. Courtenay's impression of the issue of future contingents at Oxford in the period is as follows: (1) The problem of future contingents had an important place in Oxford theology between 1328 and 1334,[97] as is evidenced by the work of Fitzralph, Holcot, Wodeham, and Bradwardine; (2) "Ockham's modifications on Auriol's position influenced the expositions of Richard Fitzralph, Robert Holcot, Adam Wodeham, and others until the middle of the 1330's";[98] (3) news of John XXII's position probably reached England by 1333; (4) "although perhaps not a factor in discussions among Fitzralph, Crathorn, Holcot, and Wodeham... [John XXII's position] was probably known to Bradwardine and Buckingham";[99] (5) after 1333 almost every Oxford theologian took issue with Bradwardine's views.[100]

Perhaps this assessment has some truth to it, although Ockham's knowledge of Auriol appears slight and Chatton's reaction Auriol and Ockham himself also played a role in the development of the Oxford debate. Moreover, since Bradwardine first put forth his rather deterministic doctrine in 1332–33, if he was influenced by John XXII's position, then Holcot's and Wodeham's works of 1333–34 could very well have been negative reactions to John, not only directly, but also via Bradwardine. We now need to turn Bradwardine.[101]

Thomas Bradwardine (ca. 1295–1349), the Profound Doctor, probably lectured on the *Sentences* in 1332–33. Genest and Tachau have shown that his question on future contingents was part of his commentary.[102] At one point in this long question (about 2000 lines), Bradwardine gives nine opinions on the matter of future contingents, one of which may be that of Peter Auriol: "The fifth is the opinion that something is a future contingent *ad utrumlibet*, but that that thing is not foreknown by God, because if it is, God's knowledge can be mistaken and God can be deceived, which is false." This is part of Peter Auriol's position, and also Holcot's. It is not exactly the same one expressed later in *De causa Dei*. Bradwardine ascribes the opinion to Averroes, and says that he (Averroes or the *modernus* to whom Bradwardine is referring) also says God does not know singulars.[103] This is not Auriol at all, although limited ac-

---

[97] Courtenay, *Capacity and Volition*, p.165, n. 30. Courtenay adds that "unfortunately, most of these texts remain unedited."
[98] Courtenay, *Capacity and Volition*, p. 154.
[99] Courtenay, *Capacity and Volition*, p. 155.
[100] Courtenay, *Capacity and Volition*, p. 157.
[101] On Bradwardine generally, see Gordon Leff, *Bradwardine and the Pelagians*; Heiko Oberman, *Archbishop Thomas Bradwardine: A Fourteenth-Century Augustinian, A Study of His Theology in Its Historical Context* (Utrecht 1958); and recently Edith Wilks Dolnikowski, *Thomas Bradwardine. A View of Time and a Vision of Eternity in Fourteenth-Century Thought* (Leiden 1995). For Bradwardine's views on the related topic of predestination, see Halverson, *Peter Aureol on Predestination*, pp. 129–33.
[102] Jean-François Genest and Katherine H. Tachau, "La lecture de Thomas Bradwardine sur les *Sentences*," AHDLMA 57 (1990), pp. 301–6.
[103] Thomas Bradwardinus, *De futuris contingentibus* (ed. Genest, "Le *De futuris contingentibus*," p. 291, 16a–c): "Quinta est opinio quod aliquid est futurum contingens ad utrumlibet, sed illud non prescitur a Deo, quia si sic, sciencia Dei potest falli et Deus potest decipi, quod est falsum. Confirmatur per Commentatorem in *De sompno et vigilia*, quod sompnia vera non sunt in nobis nisi de illis que accidunt in majore parte, et ideo non de futuris contingentibus ad utrumlibet. Similiter dicit quod Deus non cognoscit singularia, quia sunt infinita, et constat quod non

quaintance with his ideas might have produced such confusion. In any case, as Genest points out,[104] in fact it is the *third* opinion in *De futuris contingentibus* that corresponds to the later one attacked in *De causa Dei*, which has been attributed to Auriol.

Bradwardine's own position is one that eliminates the difference between the past and future.[105] He holds that God wills freely, so that there is no absolute necessity in the world. Since God wills, however, everything must happen as He wills it, and His will is naturally prior to His foreknowledge. The past and future are equally contingent, and equally necessary: the past cannot be changed, but neither can the future, and yet they are both contingent. The *opinio communis* of Ockham and of others at Oxford was that the world was ultimately contingent, but that the past received a necessity, almost an absolute necessity, which the future did not. Some had admitted that the future received necessity in some sense from God's foreknowledge, or will, but they did not equate whatever 'weak' necessity might attach to the future with the 'strong' necessity attached to the past. Bradwardine, on the other hand, emphasizes the fact that since God's power in His atemporal eternity cannot be said to change, it does not change with respect to what becomes our past.

In his *Sentences* commentary, Thomas Buckingham opposed the apparent determinism of Thomas Bradwardine.[106] In 1344 Bradwardine responded again with his huge *De causa Dei*, in which he again declared his views on the necessity and contingency of the past and future. Bradwardine attacked on the one hand those like John XXII who said that all things happened of necessity, and on the other those who took the common position, ascribing too much necessity to the past and too much contingency to the future, thus taking away some of God's immutability, Bradwardine thought.

I have noted that Bradwardine declares in his *De causa Dei* that he heard what looks like Peter Auriol's position defended in Oxford and at the Papal Curia in Avignon by a "famous Toulousan philosopher." Let us quote the passage at length:

> The sixth opinion supposes that something is 'future *ad utrumlibet* or not future' in the composite sense, not however in the divided sense,[107] to which they make a great effort to add 'no simple proposition about the future in contingent matter is, equally, true or false', with the Philosopher, I *Peri Hermeneias*, in the end, attesting. Thus neither is anything future or not future *ad utrumlibet* dividedly. I heard this opinion, however, defended completely in the open by a famous Toulousan philoso-

---

loquitur de singularibus presentibus, quia illa sunt finita et non infinita, sed de futuris loquitur; igitur."

[104] Genest, "Le *De futuris contingentibus*," p. 262.

[105] For Bradwardine's position on future contingents, see Genest, "Le *De futuris contingentibus*," and *Prédétermination et liberté créée*. For more brief discussions, see Normore, "Future Contingents," pp. 374–7, and de la Torre, *Thomas Buckingham*, 91–101.

[106] I have seen Buckingham's *Sentences* commentary in Vaticano, Palat. lat. 329.

[107] I take this to mean that the disjunctive (composite sense) "either X will exist or X will not exist" is true, but neither "X will exist" nor "X will not exist" is true (divided sense).

pher in the Roman Curia in a certain solemn disputation concerning future contingents. And similarly I also used to hear (*audiebam*) the opinion in Oxford. But this opinion is easily refuted. For according to this opinion nothing is future *ad utrumlibet* contingently, but everything that comes about comes about by completely absolute necessity, which [chapter] 12 of this [book] damns. Again, someone who holds this opinion is trapped, for it holds that nothing is contingently future or not future in the divided sense; therefore nothing is contingently future; therefore the Antichrist is not contingently future, which goes against the opinion. It also follows that this is true: 'The Antichrist is not future', and its opposite is false, which makes clear the irrational nature of the position.[108]

Bradwardine goes on to say that according to this opinion, God would not know that the Antichrist will come, or that he will not come, but only that he will either come or not come, "as any illiterate person knows."[109]

As I mentioned in the introduction to this book, Michalski appears to be the first modern scholar to claim that this passage is directed at Auriol. I noted there that Michalski was unfortunately unaware of the other aspects of Auriol's doctrine, because he approached Auriol via Rimini and his *sequaces* Pierre d'Ailly and Henry of Langenstein, who concentrated on Auriol's view on propositions and his apparent denial of foreknowledge. Michalski reasoned as follows: (1) Rimini, d'Ailly, and Langenstein attacked Auriol's stance on the neutrality of future contingent propositions; (2) Bradwardine also attacked a position that denied determinate truth to such propositions; (3) Rimini knew Bradwardine; therefore (4) Bradwardine was attacking Auriol. Oberman, agreeing, made this reasoning more explicit:[110]

Michalsky has argued very plausibly, especially by his reference to the *Sententiae* commentary of Henry of Hessen [or Langenstein], that when Gregory of Rimini and afterwards Peter of Ailly take the side of

---

[108] Thomas Bradwardinus, *De causa Dei, contra Pelagium, et de virtute causarum, ad suos Mertonenses, libri tres* III, chapter 17 (ed. London 1618, p. 692): "Opinio sexta fingit quod aliquid est futurum ad utrumlibet vel non futurum in sensu composito, non autem in sensu diviso, quam sic astruere moliuntur: 'Nulla propositio simplex de futuro in materia contingente aequaliter est vera vel falsa', Philosopho I *Perihermenias* ult. attestante; quare nec aliquid est futurum ad utrumlibet vel non futurum divisim. Hanc autem opinionem audivi in Curia Romana a quodam famoso Philosopho Tolosano in quadam disputatione solenni de contingentia futurorum, secundam eam totaliter publice respondente, quam et Oxoniae similiter audiebam. Sed haec faciliter convincetur: Nam secundum eam nihil est futurum ad utrumlibet contingenter, sed omnia que evenient evenient de necessitate penitus absoluta, quod 12 huius damnat. Item sic opinans propriae opinionis laqueo irretitur; dicit enim nihil esse contingenter futurum vel non futurum in sensu diviso; ergo nihil est contingenter futurum; ergo Antichristus non est contingenter futurus, quod opinioni repugnat; sequitur quoque hanc esse veram: 'Antichristus non est futurus', et eius oppositam esse falsam, quod rationem positionis irrationabilem manifestat."
[109] Thomas Bradwardine, *De causa Dei* III, c.17 (ed. London, p. 692): "Item, tunc nec Deus, nec Angelus aut Propheta sciret Antichristum, nec quicquam possibilium contingenter esse futurum divisim vel non futurum, sed tantum esse futurum vel non futurum contiunctim, sicut et scit quilibet idiota."
[110] Oberman, *Archbishop Thomas Bradwardine*, p. 32.

Bradwardine in the controversy on the necessary happening of the "futura contingentia", they direct their attack against Auriolus. They remind us in such a direct way of Bradwardine's arguments (in III. 17.692f.), that it is safe to presume that Auriolus should be classed as one of Bradwardine's most important antagonists.

As we shall see, however, Rimini had *direct* and extensive knowledge of Auriol's works in Paris, so there is no reason to infer that Bradwardine had, since he was certainly not Rimini's source for Auriol's doctrine. Moreover, it is rather doubtful that Bradwardine meant Auriol when referring to the famous Toulousan philosopher. Oberman himself thinks it improbable, relating Weisheipl's opinion that "it would be very extraordinary and nearly unthinkable for Bradwardine to call the archbishop, a doctor of theology, 'philosophus'."[111] On the other hand, Gordon Leff, writing in the same year, says that it was "almost certainly" Auriol.[112] Since, however, Auriol was master of theology in the summer of 1318, and died in 1322, Bradwardine's opponent was almost certainly *not* Auriol.

This mystery philosopher could have been another scholar, most likely a master of arts, teaching later on. The case of Peter de Rivo shows that in the fifteenth century one could find a master of arts defending Aristotle's position with or without reference to theological concerns. It is even possible that John XXII was aware of the same Toulousan's teaching at Avignon. As for Oxford, we have seen that at least Walter Chatton, Arnold of Strelley, and Robert Holcot denied determinate truth in future contingent propositions at some point, so Bradwardine could have been referring to one of them.

Perhaps the 1618 edition is quite corrupt at this point. I have translated it so that it could refer to Auriol as much as possible, but nevertheless it is certain that Auriol would not have said that everything happens of absolute necessity. Perhaps it is significant that manuscript Klosterneuberg 317 does not include the word "famous."[113] Genest has shown that Bradwardine was in Avignon at the end of 1335, and considers this to be the time he heard the Toulousan philosopher speak.[114] Since Avignon is close to Toulouse, there may have been many Toulousan logicians in Avignon. In addition, the *absurdum* to which Bradwardine reduces the opinion actually looks like John XXII's position that all things happen of necessity.

Thomas Buckingham reacted again to Bradwardine's thesis, returning fire with roughly 4500 lines devoted to the problem in his treatise *On the Contingency of Futures and the Freedom of Choice*.[115] Both men, and Ockham, died just

---

[111] Oberman, *Archbishop Thomas Bradwardine*, pp. 20–21.
[112] Leff, *Bradwardine and the Pelagians*, p. 2.
[113] Bradwardinus, *De causa Dei* III, ch. 17 (ms. Klosterneuberg, Augustinerehorherrenstift 317, fol. 207v): "Hanc opinionem audivi in curia Romana a quodam philosopho Tholosano et etiam Oxoniense."
[114] Genest, "Le De futuris contingentibus," p. 252.
[115] De la Torre has recently edited and published with a study Buckingham's *De contingentia futurorum et arbitrii libertate* (de la Torre, *Thomas Buckingham*), but the fact that a mere five years later Genest also published an edition of the same text attests to the extreme complexity

before or during the plague. Thus ended a lively debate at Oxford that spanned over a decade and involved such thinkers as Holcot, Fitzralph, Wodeham, Bradwardine, and Buckingham, but one can hardly conclude without quoting the famous passage in Chaucer's later "The Nun's Priest's Tale":

> But that which God's foreknowledge can foresee
> Must needs occur, as certain men of learning
> Have said. Ask any scholar of discerning;
> He'll say the Schools are filled with altercation
> On this vexed matter of predestination
> Long bandied by a hundred thousand men
> How can I sift it to the bottom then?
> The Holy Doctor St Augustine shines
> In this, and there is Bishop Bradwardine's
> Authority, Boethius' too, decreeing
> Whether the fact of God's divine foreseeing
> Constrains me to perform a certain act
> — and by 'constraint' I mean the simple fact
> Of mere compulsion by necessity —
> Or whether a free choice is granted me
> To do a given act or not to do it
> Though, ere it was accomplished, God foreknew it,
> *Or if his wityng streyneth never a deel*
> *But by necessitee condicioneel.*[116]

I have only given the barest outlines of this Oxford "altercation" as it involved Peter Auriol.[117] It is certainly not true that Bradwardine and Buckingham

---

of this type of material (see Genest, *Prédétermination et liberté créée*, p. 182, for an explanation of the need for a new edition). On Buckingham's life and stance of future contingents, see de la Torre, pp. 3–25 and 103–40; and Genest, pp. 87–182.

William J. Courtenay, "John of Mirecourt and Gregory of Rimini on Whether God Can Undo the Past," RTAM 39 (1972), pp. 224–56, and 40 (1973), pp. 147–74, in Part II, p. 151, implies that Buckingham agrees with Auriol that "propositions about the future are neither true nor false; propositions about the past are not necessarily true or false," but the conclusion about propositions about the future is not contained in the quotation from Buckingham on which Courtenay bases his remark (n. 106): "Voluntas divina respectu futurorum contingentium quamdiu sunt futura, est libera libertate contradictionis; sed cum fuerint praesentia in praeteritumve labuntur desinit esse libera huiusmodi libertate et incipit esse necessaria necessitate opposita respectu eorum, sine mutatione in Deo posita vel ponenda." Auriol would have agreed with Courtenay's inference that such propositions are neither true nor false, but it is not clear that Buckingham would have, and nothing is said of truth, falsity, or propositions in the quotation.

[116] Geoffrey Chaucer, *Canterbury Tales*, trans. Nevil Coghill (Harmondsworth 1951), pp. 243–4. I have kept the two lines in the original to preserve the reference to conditional necessity. Genest, *Prédétermination et liberté créée*, p. 25, gives the Middle English. For a good discussion of how "The Nun's Priest's Tale" connects to the related instants of nature or incipit/desinit issue, see Peter W. Travis, "Chaucer's *Chronographiae*, the Confounded Reader, and Fourteenth-Century Measurements of Time, " in Carol Poster and Richard Utz, eds., *Constructions of Time in the Late Middle Ages* (= *Disputatio* 2) (Evanston, Illinois 1997), pp. 1–34, esp. pp. 15–26.

[117] A full-length history of this debate at Oxford is needed, but the amount of work necessary is tremendous. First more texts need to be edited to facilitate study. Given this, it will be a long time before we will be able to take a close look at anonymous texts, but I will take this op-

moved their debate to Paris, as was once thought, but in the 1340s this Oxford debate did reach a high point at the University of Paris with the *Sentences* commentary of Gregory of Rimini, heir to both Paris and Oxford traditions.[118]

---

portunity to mention a few. The same manuscript that contains Buckingham's *Sentences* commentary, Vatican, Palat. lat. 329, also has an anonymous commentary on fol. 1r-37r, which asks (fol. 25v) "Utrum immutabilis determinatio divine scientie tollat libertatis indifferentiam et futurorum contingentiam," which mentions Aristotle's position in "*Peryarmenias*" (fol. 27r). The author knows Aquinas well, citing him as "Doctor Sanctus" on fol. 6r, so the commentary is from after 1323. He also cites Giles of Rome and Peter of Tarantasia. The commentary may be from a Parisian Dominican, anywhere after 1323. The anonymous commentary in Vat. lat. 829 (fol. 149–201) does not go to distinctions 38 and 39. It argues against Ockham occasionally, and appears to be in an English hand — though not the same hand throughout. Finally, Vat. lat. 1112 contains a very brief commentary (fol. 3–21) whose anonymous author asks (fol. 17vb) "Circa distinctionem 38 queritur utrum Dei scientia sit respectu futurorum contingentium determinata et necessaria evidentia," and (18ra) "Circa distinctionem 39 queritur utrum Deus per suam scientiam possit habere plurimum quam habeat scientie ille (?) evidentiam." This author cites Aristotle's opinion, uses the composite and divided senses, and makes the distinction between propositions about the past and those really depending on the future. This last item may suggest the author was writing at Oxford, perhaps between 1325 and 1350.
    [118] Zénon Kaluza has shown that the opinion that Bradwardine and Buckingham debated in Paris is erroneously based on a misreading of a question by Etienne de Chaumont in Paris, BN lat. 16409 (Zénon Kaluza, "La prétendue discussion parisienne de Thomas Bradwardine avec Thomas de Buckingham: Témoignage de Thomas de Cracovie," RTAM 43 [1976], pp. 219–36).

Chapter 11

Paris 1343–1345

The 1330s were a great decade for Oxford, but Parisians appear to have had other things to worry about than the normal theological lectures. Except for Michael of Massa's work, what we have from the decade, even in printed form, does not betray much of the earlier interest in Auriol or of the influence of Oxford developments. With Gregory of Rimini in 1343-44, however, Auriol returns to prominence and Oxford ideas and themes join the Parisian debate, and a number of theologians contributed enriched this discussion in the academic year 1344-45. Rimini's treatment was to be standard reading in late-medieval universities, unhappily for Auriol and his memory. Nevertheless, the influx from Oxford helped remove Auriol from the center of Parisian theology.

The Background: Thomas of Strasbourg and Peter of Aquila in the 1330s

Zénon Kaluza has recently redated the lectures on the *Sentences* of the Franciscan Peter of Aquila and of the Augustinian Hermit Thomas of Strasbourg (de Argentina), assigning the latter's lectures to 1334–35 at the latest.[1] Strasbourg's *Sentences* commentary, surviving in some fifty manuscripts, was one of the most popular of the fourteenth century, due in part to his term as general of the Augustinian order from 1345 to his death in 1357. Trapp reports that Strasbourg cites no one who read the *Sentences* after 1326,[2] and because distinctions 38 and 39 together only amount to about three columns in the Venice edition of 1564, and only involve the question "whether God's knowledge causes things," one expects that Strasbourg has little to say, and nothing new, on the issue. Like his later Augustinian brother Hugolino of Orvieto, however, Strasbourg moves most of his discussion to distinction 40, where article three, the longest, "whether someone predestined can be damned," contains Strasbourg's main treatment of the problem.[3]

---

[1] See Zénon Kaluza, *"Serbi un sasso il nome,"* especially pp. 460–62, for a discussion of Strasbourg's dates. For Strasbourg's soteriology, see Halverson, *Peter Aureol on Predestination,* pp. 134–44.

[2] Trapp, "Augustinian Theology," pp. 175–82. On the number of Strasbourg's manuscripts, see my "Parisian Commentaries between Peter Auriol and Gregory of Rimini."

[3] Thomas de Argentina (Strasbourg), *Commentaria in IIII libros Sententiarum* I, dd. 38–39, (ed. Venice 1564, fol. 109ra): "An scientia Dei causet res," or "Utrum scientia Dei sit causa rerum ad extra productarum." I, d. 40 (fol. 110ra): "An possibile sit praedestinatum tandem non salvari," or "Utrum possibile sit praedestinatum ad salutem finaliter non salvari." I, d. 40, a. 3 (fol. 110rb): "Quantum ad tertium articulum, utrum praedestinatus possit damnari?"

Strasbourg's solution is in many ways a combination of older ones. He gives the common statement that someone who is predestined can be damned, but that in reality he will never be damned. He discusses the various types of necessity, those named by Boethius, Anselm, and 'moderns', and admits that a 'consequent necessity', or necessity of the consequence, obtains with respect to the coming about of futures foreknown by God. He is also partial to Boethius's formulation of God's eternity and of the relationship of past, present, and future things to God, a position that recalls that of Aquinas and Giles of Rome.[4]

Unlike his recent predecessors, however, Strasbourg does not appeal to God's contingent willing to explain how there is contingency in the world, but is satisfied simply to say that things must, by the necessity of the consequence, come about *in the way* that God foreknows them, and that is contingently, in the case of things dependent on human free will. Strasbourg's phrase "Necessarily it is contingently future" is similar to Anselm's words, which Alphonsus Vargas will later repeat, saying that it is necessary for the future to come about without any necessity.[5]

There are several interesting aspects of Strasbourg's discussion. One is his use of metaphor, which may reflect the classicizing (proto-humanist?) tendencies of the Augustinians at the time. For example, after listing a dozen or so arguments against the compatibility of foreknowledge and contingency, some supporting the necessity of God's foreknowledge, others denying foreknowledge in order to save contingency, Strasbourg concludes:

> And one can conclude in the same way about any future that you posit to be contingent, and thus it is clear that according to these two extreme opinions one who desires to avoid Charybdis crashes into Scylla. Therefore, in this vast and spacious sea, in which there are reptiles, that is doubts, without number, we must avoid the danger of each of these and affirm God's foreknowledge with respect to all futures in such a way that we do not deny the contingency *ad utrumlibet* of any futures.[6]

---

[4] Strasbourg, *I Sent.*, d. 40, a. 3 (ed. Venice, fol. 110rb): "Secunda conclusio est quod quamvis praedestinatus modo predicto possit damnari, tamen de facto nunquam damnabitur..." and (fol. 111va): "Ad octavum dicendum quod Anselmus, *Metalogicon*, dat intellectum illius dicti, dicens quod verum est necessitate consequente, non autem necessitate antecedente, et appellat necessitatem antecedentem illam quae ex natura rei provenit, quam Boethius, 5 *De consolatione*, vocat necessitatem absolutam. Necessitatem vero consequentem appellat illam quae ex vi sermonis innascitur, quam Boethius vocat necessitatem conditionatam seu conditionalem; et hanc doctores moderni vocant necessitatem consequentiae et non consequentis." Strasbourg's preference for the eternal presence solution is on fol. 111va, top half of column.

[5] Strasbourg, *I Sent*, d. 40, a. 3 (ed. Venice, fol. 111rb): "Et quia Deus ab aeterno cognovit futura contingentia ex causis mutabilibus dependere, quae possunt in causando multipliciter impediri, ideo cognovit talia contingenter esse ventura, quo antecedente sic modificato in esse posito, non sequitur quod consequens absolute necessario sit venturum, sed quod necessario contingenter sit futurum." Also on 111vb: "Ad tertium dicendum quod, ut patet ex dictis superius, non plus hic concluditur nisi quod tale futurum non potest non contingenter evenire, ex quo Deus ab aeterno praescivit ipsum contingenter esse futurum; propter quod per divinam praescientiam non tollitur contingentia a rebus, sicut intendunt dicere Stoici, sed magis confirmatur."

[6] Strasbourg, *I Sent.*, d. 40, a. 3 (ed. Venice, fol. 110vb): "Et eodem modo potest concludi

Was Strasbourg aware of, and in agreement with, any developments in the debate at Oxford? He does liken the divine essence to a perfectly clear mirror for the divine intellect, which wholly comprehends the essence and thus most lucidly represents all things, including their actual existences, be they past, present, or future.[7] Although Auriol himself makes this analogy, the Parisian doctor John Hiltalingen of Basel later attributes the perfect mirror analogy to Richard Fitzralph, in the latter's *Summa de quaestionibus Armenorum*, written after Strasbourg's lectures. There is a slight possibility Strasbourg knew of Fitzralph's earlier works, but probably he developed this idea on his own, building on the imagery of such Parisian figures as Auriol.

More striking is Strasbourg's use of 'indeterminate truth' to describe the truth status of propositions about future contingents. In language reminiscent of Arnold of Strelley, and to a lesser extent Robert Holcot, he says:

> To the fourth it must be said that a proposition's being true can be understood in two ways, one way by determinate truth, another way by indeterminate truth. Then I say to the consequence that in the way in which this proposition was true: 'Peter, predestined, will be saved', it is necessary for Peter to be saved; but before Peter was beatified, that proposition was true by indeterminate truth, because there is no determinate truth in singular future contingent propositions, as the Philosopher says in I *Peri Hermeneias*...[8]

Strasbourg goes on to use the term 'indeterminate truth' to stress the non-necessity of the significate of a proposition about the future.[9] Nevertheless, with respect to God, who sees things as present "according to their own actuality," these things have determinate truth.[10] Of course there were potential

---

de quolibet futuro quod tu ponis esse contingens; et sic patet quod secundum has duas extremas opiniones incidit in Scyllam cupiens vitare Carybdim. Nos igitur in hoc mari magno et spacioso, in quo sunt reptilia, id est dubia, quorum non est numerus, utrumque illorum periculum vitantes, sic affirmare debemus respectu omnium futurorum Dei praescientiam, ut ex hoc aliquorum futurorum non negemus ad utrumlibet contingentiam."

[7]   Strasbourg, *I Sent.*, d. 40, a. 3 (ed. Venice, fol. 111va): "Et hoc sufficit ad habendum infallibilem notitiam seu scientiam futurorum ei qui adaequate comprehendit huiusmodi exemplar, scilicet ipsam divinam essentiam, quae tanquam clarissimum speculum intellectui divino qui ipsam comprehendit omnimode et adaequate omnia lucidissime representat." And also 111ra: "Etiam haec omnia in speculo clarissimo santae trinitatis aequaliter representantur, non solum quantum ad suas quidditates et essentias, verumetiam quantum ad suas proprias et individuas seu* actuales existentias..."

[8]   Strasbourg, *I Sent.*, d. 40, a. 3 (ed. Venice, fol. 111rb–va): "Ad quartum dicendum quod propositionem esse vera<m> potest intelligi dupliciter: uno modo veritate determinata; alio modo veritate indeterminata. Tunc ad consequentiam dico quod eo modo quo vera fuit illa propositio: 'Petrus praedestinatus salvabitur', illo modo necesse est Petrum salvari; sed illa propositio antequam Petrus esset beatus erat vera veritate indeterminata, quia de singularibus et futuris contingentibus non est determinata veritas, ut dicit Philosophus, I *Perihermenias*..."

[9]   Strasbourg, *I Sent.*, d. 40, a. 3 (ed. Venice, fol. 111va): "Illa autem non repugnat antecedenti, quia indeterminat veritas propositionis de futuro poterit bene stare, dato quod suum significatum non sit necesse esse."

[10]   Strasbourg, *I Sent.*, d. 40, a. 3 (ed. Venice, fol. 111vb): "Ad quartum dicendum quod quamvis de singularis et futuris contingentibus non sit determinata veritas apud intellectum nos-

Parisian sources for his remarks,[11] and Arnold of Strelley did not hold this last point of Strasbourg's to be true. Strasbourg's stance looks like a combination of those of Strelley or Antonius Andreas, Auriol or Fitzralph, Aquinas, and others. The fact that he does not appeal to God's freedom and contingent will to explain contingency in the world may reflect Auriol's criticism of the distinction between necessity and immutability. He does affirm that whatever God was able to do from eternity, He can do at any time, and that His power does not decrease over time,[12] but he also admits that de facto there is no power over the past. Strasbourg's position on how God knows the actuality of futures is similar to Auriol's, but his willingness to suggest that things necessarily (ex suppositione) must happen contingently allows him to keep foreknowledge, and forego the argument from 'indistance'. He essentially agrees with Anselm's notion of free will, which Auriol would not accept.

Kaluza has also shown that the Franciscan Peter of Aquila (†1361) lectured on the Sentences at Paris after his term as Franciscan provincial minister of Tuscany ended in the summer of 1337, a few years later than was previously thought.[13] His popular commentary went through several early printed editions, the Speyer edition being as early as 1480. More than anything else, this was probably for his conservative orthodoxy, which gave him the nickname 'little Scotus' (Scotellus). It is not surprising, then, to find that Aquila's treatment is brief; he asks in distinction 38 older questions, "whether God's knowledge is the cause of things" and "whether God has knowledge of future contingents";[14] and he basically defends Scotus's position.[15] Aquila brings up

---

trum, qui ex suo modo cognoscendi non habet de talibus futuris evidentiam certam, donec sint praesentia secundum suam propriam actualitatem; tamen talium futurorum potest esse determinata veritas apud intellectum Dei, qui aeque evidenter et clare videt omnia futura, sicut videt ea, cum actualiter sunt praesentia."

[11] Perhaps Strasbourg looked at Peri Hermeneias commentaries. In Buridan's Questiones longe super librum Perihermeneias, ed. Rita van der Lecq, probably written in the last half of the 1320s (see p. xiii), he says that propositions about future contingents are not determinately true, but are true such that it is still possible that they are or were never true (p. 49, ll. 6–9): "Quarta conclusio est quod non omnis propositio de futuro affirmativa kategorica de inesse est determinate vera vel falsa, quia que est vera, adhuc possibile est quod numquam est vel fuit vera sed falsa, sed que est falsa, possibile est quod non est nec fuit falsa sed vera." Buridan uses 'determinate' in Strelley's sense, but he does not use the term 'indeterminately true' at any point. As we shall see in the Epilogue, the arts faculties in medieval universities may often have had ideas different from those of the theologians, though it is not always certain that they would have retained those ideas in theological contexts.

[12] Strasbourg, I Sent., d. 40, q. 1, a. 1 (ed. Venice, fol. 110ra): "Probo antecedens, quia quicquid Deus potuit ab aeterno, hoc potest omni tempore, nam ex successu temporis non diminuitur divina potentia."

[13] Kaluza, "Serbi un sasso il nome," p. 446 and n. 18. I have not seen the critical edition, Commentarium in libros Sententiarum, ed. C. Paolini (books I–III, Recco 1907; book IV, Levanto 1909).

[14] Petrus de Aquila, In libros Sententiarum I, d. 38, q. 1 (ed. Speyer 1480, fol. 43rb): "Utrum scientia Dei sit causa rerum;" and q. 2 (fol. 43vb): "Utrum Deus habeat scientiam futurorum contingentium."

[15] Halverson ("Peter Aureol and the Re-Emergence of Predestinarian Pluralism," p. 216) finds that Aquila "describes both the majority Dominican account [of predestination] and the Scotist 'instants of nature' account... as doctrinally acceptable. He does not cite Auriol's... account at all..."

and refutes several opinions popular before Scotus, including Aquinas's. He also holds, along with most Parisian theologians, that God has determinate foreknowledge.

There are indications, however, that he is not completely isolated from the main issues as they stood in 1337. For one thing, he states that Aristotle's position would deny foreknowledge.[16] Second, he draws a distinction between knowing (*cognoscit*) future contingents and expecting (*expectat*) their existences.[17] This appears to refer to issues with which Auriol was concerned. Third, he is aware of the criticism that Scotus's position seems to destroy free will, though he attempts to defend it.[18]

In distinction 39 he asks "Whether some things in the universe come about contingently," and "Whether God has necessary knowledge of future contingents."[19] One could interpret these questions as extremely conservative returns to pre-Auriol days, or as new attacks on John XXII, the controversy surrounding whom must have been fresh in the minds of scholars. As we recall, the Pope's opponents claimed that his position held everything to come about necessarily, and that God necessarily was as He was. In the first question Aquila not only gives the basic arguments for contingency in the world, he is also careful to add that the opinion to the contrary is "false and against the saints and the philosophers."[20] Aquila then makes the popular Parisian distinction between necessity *ex suppositione* and absolute necessity, specifically using the word 'absolute'.[21] Nevertheless, Aquila does not argue at length on the subject.

The fact that Aquila makes reference to Auriol in his book II, distinction 37, lends support to the notion that scholars had to be selective about where they were going to be original, since theologians had so little time to lecture over so much material. Although Aquila does not seem worried in distinctions 38 and 39 of book I about Auriol's critique, in book II he shows his awareness of Auriol's refutation of a Scotist position on the relationship of God's will to sinning. A possible escape for those following Scotus's brand of divine voluntarism was to say that God's will determined only the positive substrate of

---

[16]   Aquila, *I Sent.*, d. 38, q. 2 (ed. Speyer, 43vb): "Et quod non, quia de eo non habetur scientia de quo non habetur determinata veritas; sed de futuris contingentibus non est determinata veritas per Philosophum, primi *Perihermeniarum*..."
[17]   Aquila, *I Sent.*, d. 38, q. 2 (ed. Speyer, 43vb): "Preterea, aut Deus cognoscit futura contingentia aut expectat existentiam eorum." He of course opts for the first choice.
[18]   Aquila, *I Sent.*, d. 38, q. 2 (ed. Speyer, fol. 44rb): "Sed hic sunt duo dubia, quia ex dictis videtur quod Deus determinaret voluntatem meam ad actum meritorium qui actus est contingens, et sic tollitur libertas voluntatis."
[19]   Aquila, *I Sent.*, d. 39, q. 1 (ed. Speyer, fol. 44rb): "Utrum in universo eveniant contingenter aliqua," and q.2 (fol. 45ra): "Utrum Deus habeat scientiam necessariam de futuris contingentibus."
[20]   Aquila, *I Sent.*, d. 39, q. 1 (ed. Speyer, fol. 44va): "Ista opinio est falsa et contra sanctos et philosophos..."
[21]   Aquila, *I Sent.*, d. 39, q. 2 (ed. Speyer, fol. 45ra): "Ideo est alia opinio et distinguit de necessario, quia ut patet circa finem secundi *Phisicorum*, necessarium est duplex, scilicet absolutum et ex suppositione. Et sic dicuntur ad questionem due conclusiones: prima quod Deus non habet scientiam necessariam de contingentibus necessitate absoluta vel simpliciter. Secunda quod Deus habet scientiam necessariam de contingentibus necessitate ex suppositione vel conditionata."

the act of sinning, and not the deformity of the act. Aquila agrees with Auriol that the act of sinning and its deformity are inseparable, so Aquila has to take a different path to defend Scotus.[22]

Gregory of Rimini

Aquila's treatment of Auriol was buried for centuries, while Rimini's discussion may have helped bury Auriol's. The Augustinian Gregory of Rimini (ca. 1300–1358) was perhaps the most important theologian in the period between Auriol and Ockham's time and the Reformation, and Martin Luther apparently considered Rimini to be the only medieval thinker completely devoid of 'Pelagian' tendancies.[23] Rimini studied arts at Paris from 1323 to 1329, and then taught at various Augustinian *studia* in central and northern Italy, including Bologna, Padua, and Perugia. Almost certainly while in Italy, Rimini came into contact with theological works of Oxford scholars from the 1320s and 1330's. Rimini returned to Paris in 1342 to prepare to lecture on the *Sentences*, which he did in 1343–44. Becoming master of theology in 1345, Rimini revised his lectures, removing certain passages that until recently were considered later *additiones*. Rimini continued to play an important role at Paris, and later followed Thomas of Strasbourg as the Augustinians' prior general after the former's death in 1357, but he himself died in 1358.[24]

Rimini's commentary on books I–II of the *Sentences* is, practically speaking, his only major work, which makes it clear that Rimini's later reputation and impact as a theologian rests on his *Sentences* commentary. As we shall see, in the Late Middle Ages Rimini's work was the frequent object of plagiarism, and his ideas spread via that route. Thus the twenty complete manuscripts of book I and eleven of book II can only begin to indicate his importance, although the half dozen or so early modern editions are more in keeping with his historical stature.

Rimini was the first Parisian theologian to make extensive use of a number of Oxford works from the 1320s and 1330s, and this has tended to obscure his debt to the Parisian context. If we look at the direct and indirect citations

---

[22]   Petrus de Aquila, *II Sent.*, d. 37, q. 1 (ed. Paris 1585, p. 554): "Praeterea arguit contra hoc Auriolus fortiter sic: Si Deus ageret quantum ad substratum actus, ergo necessario ageret quantum ad deformitatem actus. Probatio consequentie: quando aliqua sic se habent, quod impossibile est illa ab invicem separari, quod agit in unum, agit in reliquum. Sed sic se habet deformitas ad substratum actus. Ergo. Minor patet in odio Dei, ubi ad actum necessario sequitur deformitas. Ideo forte opinio quarta in 2. art. dist. 34 est verior, etc.," cited in Schwamm, *Das göttliche Vorherwissen*, p. 295.
[23]   Steven Ozment, *The Age of Reform, 1250–1550: An Intellectual and Religious History of Late Medieval and Reformation Europe* (New Haven 1980), p. 232.
[24]   The secondary literature on Rimini is too extensive to note here; see for example *Gregor von Rimin: Werk und Wirkung bis zur Reformation*, ed. Heiko Oberman (Berlin 1981); Heiko Oberman, *The Harvest of Medieval Theology: Gabriel Biel and Late Medieval Nominalism* (Cambridge, Mass. 1963; reprint Durham, NC 1983); and Gordon Leff, *Gregory of Rimini. Tradition and Innovation in Fourteenth Century Thought* (Manchester 1961).

that the editors of the critical edition found, we get an idea of Rimini's knowledge of Oxford, but not of Paris after Auriol. For scholars after Scotus, Rimini has by far the most references to Auriol and Ockham, approximately 200 each. Next, Rimini cites theological works of Wodeham (66 times) and Fitzralph (34) most frequently, and the number decreases sharply after this. The number of Oxford citations may exaggerate Rimini's preoccupation with the English *studium generale*. Rimini may have wanted to show off the novel ideas, or perhaps they required more explanation to the Parisians. Accordingly, Rimini's reliance on Parisian theologians after Auriol was probably much heavier than a citation count shows, both because historians know less about these theologians and would not easily recognize such influences, and because Rimini may, in common scholastic practice, have been reluctant to give credit to his immediate Parisian predecessors. What is certain is that Rimini marks the merging of the Oxford and Parisian traditions, and therefore opens a new era in Parisian theology.[25]

In the context of foreknowledge and future contingents, Rimini also represents the closing of the 'Auriolcentric' era and the beginning of the English-influenced period. Moreover, the critical edition of Rimini's text has been available for some time, and it is soon to appear in English translation. Finally, Rimini's treatment of the problem has received considerable attention already. For these reasons, I will focus on how Rimini deals with Auriol, and, more briefly, how the new Oxford ideas shape Rimini's discussion.[26]

Even given his apparent concentration on Oxford, Rimini's principal adversary on the subject of foreknowledge and future contingents was Peter Auriol. Rimini's response to Auriol, therefore, is significant. It is especially significant considering the scale and focus of Rimini's project. Rimini devotes what amounts to about ninety pages of the critical edition to distinctions 38 and 39. He is also one of the most systematic of medieval thinkers, as we shall see. What may be surprising, in light of recent historiography, is that very little of what Rimini says in his discussion against Auriol demonstrates the impact of Oxford thought. There are exceptions, but for the most part Rimini cites Auriol and to a lesser extent his predecessors Scotus, Giles of Rome, and Aquinas. We have already seen that theologians at Oxford had developed a tradition different from that of the Parisians with respect to future contin-

---

[25]   See for example William J. Courtenay, "The Role of English Thought in the Transformation of University Education in the Late Middle Ages," in J.M. Kittelson and P.J. Transue eds., *Rebirth, Reform and Resilience, Universities in Transition 1300-1700* (Columbus, Ohio 1984) (pp. 103–62), pp. 121–33.

[26]   The critical edition is *Gregorii Ariminensis OESA Lectura in I et II libros Sententiarum*, ed. D. Trapp, V. Marcolino, W. Eckermann, M. Santos-Noya, M. Schulze, W. Simon, W. Urban, and V. Vendland, 6 vols. (Spätmittelalter und Reformation Texte und Untersuchungen, vols. 6–11) (Berlin-New York 1979–84). For the material on future contingents in English, see *Modality, Order, and Transcendence*, trans. Friedman and Schabel. For Rimini's ideas on divine foreknowledge and future contingents, see especially Hoenen, *Marsilius of Inghen*, pp. 196–214, who exploits the vast amount of material published since Leff's analysis in *Gregory of Rimini*, pp. 105–18. On the related issue of predestination, see Halverson, *Peter Aureol on Predestination*, pp. 143–57, building on Vignaux, *Justification*, ch. 4.

gents. For example, special emphasis on the problems posed by revelation, an issue pursued at great length in Oxford in the 1330s, was absent at Paris until John of Mirecourt, who read 1344–45. Rimini thought there was unfinished business with Auriol, and that only some of the Oxford debate was applicable to the specific, and real, threat that Auriol's stance posed.

Rimini attacked Auriol on Auriol's terms. As in the case of Auriol's own distinction 38, article three, Rimini's distinction 38, question one, where he asks "whether any singular categorical statement about the future, concerning what inheres in reality, in matters contingent *ad utrumlibet*, is true," is a classic of medieval logic.[27] There are several things to note about the question. One is that Rimini is a very careful thinker and writer. Part of the reason for the length of his treatment is his precision of language, which leads him to draw distinctions continually about the meaning of words or phrases. Unlike some scholastics in the Middle Ages, who seem to have drawn distinctions on occasion merely to side-step an important issue, Rimini is aiming for absolute clarity on the reader's part. Rimini is also exhaustive; he tries to cover all possibilities. For example, his treatment of exactly when propositions can or cannot be or change from being true or false is more extensive even than Auriol's own. A third thing to note is that this question almost entirely omits theological considerations. It is in this way also similar to Auriol's treatment.

Rimini's second question is "whether God is foreknowing of all futures,"[28] and although he is aware of and sometimes uses Auriol's refutations of others in describing God's foreknowledge, after he refuting Auriol's position he deals mostly with the opinions of Aquinas, Scotus, and Giles of Rome. Here Rimini enters the intense Oxford discussion over God's power with respect to the past and future, and it is also here that Rimini joins the debate that developed in Oxford, in the thought of Ockham, Chatton, Wodeham, and others, concerning the precise content of God's knowledge, and involving terms such as *complexe significabile*. Rimini goes on to deal with the latter issue in the short question of distinction 39, "Whether God's knowledge or foreknowledge can increase or decrease."[29] Later this topic will be a primary focus of debate in Paris, but one that involves Auriol only slightly.

Rimini begins in article one of the first question by attempting to show conclusively that Aristotle did in fact deny determinate truth, or any truth, in propositions about future contingents. Rimini does this because, he says, there is some controversy about this matter.[30] This section is rather lengthy, and in it Rimini proves two conclusions according to Aristotle's thinking:

---

[27] Gregorius Ariminensis (Rimini), *I Sent.*, d. 38, q. 1 (vol. 3, eds. Damasus Trapp and Venecio Marcolino [Berlin 1979], p. 237, ll. 3–4): "Utrum aliqua enuntiatio singularis de inesse categorica de futuro in materia contingenti ad utrumlibet sit vera?"
[28] Rimini, *I Sent.*, d. 38, q. 2 (ed. Trapp-Marcolino, p. 271, l. 20): "Utrum Deus sit praescius omnium futurorum?"
[29] Rimini, *I Sent.*, d. 39, q. 1 (ed. Trapp-Marcolino, p. 311, l. 3): "Utrum scientia vel praescientia Dei possit augeri vel minui?"
[30] Rimini, *I Sent.*, d. 38, q. 1, a. 1 (ed. Trapp-Marcolino, p. 238, ll. 13–14).

Not every singular categorical proposition, affirmative or negative, about the future, concerning the inhering of a simple predicate, is true or false;

Although neither of such [propositions] is determinately true, nevertheless a singular negative proposition concerning a predicate united out of the predicates of the two [propositions] is not true; for example although neither this is true: 'The Antichrist will be', nor is this true either: 'The Antichrist will not be', nevertheless this is not true: 'The Antichrist will neither be nor not be', which nevertheless could appear to some people to follow from the first.[31]

Rimini gives an unbiased presentation of Aristotle's position, mentioning that in effect Aristotle is denying Bivalence and the Law of Contradictories for future-tensed sets of contradictory propositions. He concludes by saying that he is amazed that a certain intelligent man thinks that Aristotle held differently, and that some claim that since absurdities follow from this position, Aristotle must be interpreted differently:

[This] is apparently a friendly excuse, but in truth it is more of an accusation, because the ensuing of absurdities does not convince us that he did not think that, but convinces us that he ought not to have thought that... Moreover, some modern theologians, great teachers, said that the conclusion set up before not only was the Philosopher's intention, but also that it is the truest and indeed demonstrated...[32]

So much for the Philosopher as an authority. Rimini was probably refering to Wodeham, and perhaps Scotus, in the first place, for as we have seen most thinkers did not try to salvage Aristotle, but merely gave his opinion.[33] In the

[31] Rimini, *I Sent.*, d. 38, q. 1, a. 1 (ed. Trapp-Marcolino, p. 239, ll. 3–5): "Unde quantum ad hoc ponit ipse duas conclusiones, quarum prima est quod non omnis propositio singularis de futuro categorica et de inesse de simplici praedicato affirmativa vel negativa est vera vel falsa..." and (ll. 21–6) "Secunda conclusio Philosophi est quod, licet neutra talium determinate sit vera, non tamen propositio singularis negativa de praedicato copulato ex praedicatis illarum ambarum est vera; verbi gratia quamvis nec haec sit vera, 'Antichristus erit', nec ista etiam vera sit, 'Antichristus non erit', ista tamen non est vera, 'Antichristus neque erit neque non erit', quod tamen posset aliquibus apparere sequi ex primo."

[32] Rimini, *I Sent.*, d. 38, q. 1, a. 1 (ed. Trapp-Marcolino, p. 243, ll. 16–17): "Et miror multum, quomodo aliquis intelligens putet Philosophum non istud sensisse"; (ll. 20–23): "...apparenter est amicabilis excusatio, sed secundum veritatem potius acusatio, quia sequela inconvenientium non eum illud non sensisse, sed non debuisse sensisse convincit"; (ll. 28–30): "Item moderni aliqui theologi, magni doctores, dixerunt conclusionem praemissam non solum fuisse de intentione Philosophi, sed etiam esse verissimam et utique demonstratam."

[33] The editors of Rimini maintain that it is Ockham whom Rimini means as the "intelligent man," but Boehner and most others, including myself, think that Ockham clearly knew Aristotle's position. In fact, as I have said, Ockham claims Aristotle would have denied foreknowledge. The editors say that Wodeham makes the "friendly excuse," but it could just as easily have been Scotus, whose remarks 'saving' Aristotle on the matter are similar to Wodeham's. In fact, Genest thinks that Rimini means Bradwardine in this instance, in "Le *De futuris contingentibus* de Thomas Bradwardine," (PhD dissertation, l'École Practique des Hautes Études, 5ᵉ section 1975), p. xlvi. It is ironic that the locus the editors cite in Wodeham also includes the statement

second place, the "great teacher" is Peter Auriol, whose position Rimini now presents.

As with Aristotle's position, Rimini's presentation of Auriol's stance shows that he has a good understanding of the author's intent, and that he is able to give a proof of that position which Auriol himself might have approved. Rimini proves two propositions of Auriol's that he rightly takes to represent Auriol's stance, the two propositions on which Gregory's Augustinian predecessor at Paris, Michael of Massa, also focussed. It is probable, in fact, that Massa exerted some influence on Rimini in this regard, if only to draw Rimini's attention to Auriol's stance. Moreover, in the *concluding* arguments for question one, Rimini employs Francis of Marchia's distinction between determination *de inesse* and *de possibili*, which implies that it had become common by then. Recall that Massa had adopted this doctrine in full.[34] These are the propositions given to represent Auriol's theory: (1) If a proposition about a future is true, then it is immutably and inevitably true, since no instant can be found when it could be false; (2) it follows from the first point that the significate of such a proposition will inevitably and necessarily be put into being. Therefore, things happen necessarily if such propositions are true. At this point Rimini gives a quick summary of Auriol's discussion of when a proposition can or cannot go from truth to falsity and vice versa.[35]

Rimini's own position is not unusual in itself, but is notable for the clarity with which he presents it, in a series of eight conclusions. The first conclusion is that "every singular proposition about the future is true or false, such that for any such contradiction it happens that 'this part is true and that false' is said truly, although *we* do not know which is determinately true or which is determinately false."[36] Rimini agrees with both Aristotle and Auriol in adopting a definition of truth from Aristotle's *Metaphysics*, namely that a proposition is true if what it asserts is, was, or will be in reality, depending on the tense of the proposition.[37] This definition of truth in propositions helped Auriol deny that future-tense propositions were either true or false, because their significates' future existence was not yet determined. Plainly following Marchia and/or Massa, however, Rimini argues at great length — for seven pages — against Aristotle and Auriol in defending Bivalence, which he says

discussed above which seems to indicate that Wodeham thought Ockham actually agreed with Aristotle in denying determinate truth to future contingent propositions.

[34] See Rimini, *I Sent.*, d. 38, q. 1, a. 3 (ed. Trapp-Marcolino, p. 268, ll. 29–38; p. 270, ll. 28–34).

[35] Rimini, *I Sent.*, d. 38, q. 1, a. 1 (ed. Trapp-Marcolino, pp. 244–5).

[36] Rimini, *I Sent.*, d. 38, q. 1, a. 2 (ed. Trapp-Marcolino, p. 245, ll. 30–32): "Prima est quod omnis propositio singularis de futuro est vera vel falsa, ita quod cuiuslibet talis contradictionis contingit vere dici 'haec pars est vera et illa falsa', quamvis non quae sit vera determinate aut quae falsa nesciamus."

[37] Rimini, *I Sent.*, d. 38, q. 1, a. 2 (ed. Trapp-Marcolino, p. 247, ll. 23–9): "Et primam probo, sicut ipse Philosophus ubi supra 4 *Metaphysicae* probat antecedens; sumit enim pro principio definitionem veri et falsi dicens: 'Dicere namque ens non esse aut hoc,' scilicet non-ens, 'esse, falsum; ens autem esse et non-ens non esse, verum.' Ex quo patet quod quaelibet propositio enuntians esse quod est, vel fuisse quod fuit, aut futurum esse quod erit, vel non esse quod non est, vel non fuisse quod non fuit, vel non fore quod non erit, est vera; secus autem est falsa."

holds universally, as even Aristotle himself held in places.[38] Turning Auriol's argument on its head, Rimini asserts that since de facto the Antichrist will exist or will not exist, either 'the Antichrist will exist' or 'the Antichrist will not exist' is determinately true, and the other determinately false, although we do not know which is which.

In order to save contingency in the face of this determinate truth in future-contingent propositions, Rimini adopts elements of the *opinio communis*, affirming the contingency of everything in the world, and the ultimate contingency of any proposition about the world.[39] This is the main focus of the next seven conclusions, which are all shorter than the first. They assert that true propositions about the contingent future have always been true and are immutably true, but contingently and never necessarily true, so that they are able never to have been true. He agrees with Auriol concerning the conditions in which propositions can and cannot go from truth to falsity and vice versa, although Rimini is so exhaustive in his discussion that he corrects Auriol on small matters.[40]

In question one, article three, Rimini gives an argument that looks like Auriol's when he says that whatever is possible for God to do, God does.[41] This occurs in the midst of Rimini's essay on the meaning of 'contingent', where he describes the different ways in which something can be other than it is. Here his treatment, as elsewhere, is wonderfully organized and comprehensive. Rimini's main points are that 'determinate' and 'necessary' are not equal; that, contrary to what Auriol implies, a free God must be able to do what He does not in fact do, and not do what He in fact does; and that it is possible absolutely and without qualification for something that exists in an instant not to be in that instant.[42] Rimini means this, however, in the traditional way that relies on the composite and divided senses of propositions, not in any radical sense that seems to admit contradictories simultaneously.

Along with this traditional sense of contingency, however, usually comes necessity *ex suppositione*. It may strike one as odd that Rimini actually accepts Auriol's second proposition about what is entailed by future-contingent propositions being determinately true: their significate will inevitably and nec-

[38] For example, Rimini, *I Sent.*, d. 38, q. 1, a. 2 (ed. Trapp-Marcolino, p. 247, ll. 18–20): "Ex hoc arguo sic: Impossible est esse medium isto modo inter aliqua contradictoria, igitur impossibile est aliquam propositionem esse neque veram neque falsam..." The first conclusion occupies pp. 245–252 of the edition.
[39] This is one point where Rimini has to stop and discuss the content of God's foreknowledge.
[40] An example of such a correction is at Rimini, *I Sent.*, d. 38, q. 1, a. 3 (ed. Trapp-Marcolino, pp. 269, l. 30–270, l. 7).
[41] Rimini, *I Sent.*, d. 38, q. 1, a. 3 (ed. Trapp-Marcolino, p. 262, ll. 5–15).
[42] For example, Rimini, *I Sent.*, d. 38, q. 1, a. 3 (ed. Trapp-Marcolino, p. 265, ll. 22–8): "Ad tertium dico quod absolute et simpliciter loquendo potest poni in esse quod illa volitio non sit in illo instanti, quia possibile est quod eius causa non producat eam in illo instanti. Et, si ita ponatur, tunc oppositum nec ponitur nec positum est, nec ipsa est in illo instanti, sicut nec ipsam producit sua causa. Et sic non sequitur contradictio. Sequeretur autem, si ipsa ponatur in esse et simul cum hoc esset possibile illam non tunc esse, ita quod haec propositio enuntians illam non esse posset esse tunc vera; quod ego non dico."

essarily be put into being.[43] But Rimini has explained that this 'inevitability' or 'necessity' is equivalent to conditional necessity, which does not cause or compel. Rimini often discusses the types of necessity found in Boethius and Anselm. He wants to avoid attaching necessity to God's foreknowledge, and shows repeatedly that conditional necessity, and all its synonyms, are not really necessity.[44] Auriol held the contrary, however, saying that if God knew the future, we could not be free to do other than what is already foreknown. Rimini holds that if one considers this necessity to be strong, as Auriol does, then this is the same conditional necessity that applies to the present. He understands Auriol as holding that the past is necessary, and the future is contingent. What about the present? Rimini says that if a proposition's being determinately true makes the corresponding state of affairs necessary, then Auriol would have to say that everything happens of necessity anyway, since all true propositions about the present would be necessarily true:

> I maintain further that, if it were valid, it would be proven that no proposition about the present is contingent, but that every one is necessary. But this is obviously false even according to everyone. The proof: I take this proposition: 'Peter is sitting', which everyone would concede is not a necessary proposition. And let it be posited that now it is first true. Supposing this, I prove that it is immutably true, because, if it could be changed, either in the instant at which it is true, and then it would be true and not true at the same time, which is impossible; or in some preceding instant, and not this, because it was not true before and it cannot lose truth before it has it; nor in the following instant, because then that truth goes over into the past, etc. Therefore, since the instant is not found in which it could change, it is immutably true. All proofs are his, and nevertheless the conclusion is false.[45]

Rimini denies that Aristotle's "*omne quod est, quando est, necesse est esse*" is true in all senses, so he reduces Auriol's own arguments to an absurdity. Rimini had already spoken again Ockham's doctrine of the necessity of the present at great length. Without going into detail, I suggest that Rimini's general goal is not radical: he wishes to clarify the *opinio communis*, which refuses to accept

[43]   Rimini, *I Sent.*, d. 38, q. 1, a. 3 (ed. Trapp-Marcolino, p. 270, ll. 25–6): "Secunda propositio eius est vera nec contra praedicta, ideo ad eius rationes non oportet respondere."
[44]   For example Rimini, *I Sent.*, d. 38, q. 2, a. 3 (ed. Trapp-Marcolino, pp. 298–300) for a discussion of the types of necessity in Boethius and Anselm.
[45]   Rimini, *I Sent.*, d. 38, q. 1, a. 3 (ed. Trapp-Marcolino, p. 270, ll. 8–19): "Dico ulterius quod, si valeret, probaretur quod nulla propositio de praesenti est contingens, sed quaelibet necessaria; quod tamen est evidenter falsum etiam secundum omnes. Probatio: Sumo istam: 'Petrus sedet', quam quilibet concederet non esse necessariam, et ponatur quod nunc primo sit vera. Probo hoc posito quod sit immutabiliter vera, quia, si posset mutari, aut in instanti in quo est vera, et tunc simul esset vera et non vera, quod est impossibile, aut in instanti aliquo praecedenti, et hoc non, quia ante non fuit vera et non potest perdere veritatem antequam illam habeat, nec in instanti sequente, quia tunc illa veritas transit in praeteritum etc. Igitur, cum non inveniatur instans, in quo possit mutari, ipsa est immutabiliter vera. Probationes omnes sunt suae, et tamen conclusio est falsa."

the equivalence of immutability and necessity and emphasizes the overarching contingency of everything in the world. What Rimini does, and I think success-fully, is to show a way in which Ockham would accept the contingency of the present. This is where Rimini's exhaustive analysis results in great profit. Rimini supports his point by showing where Ockham himself, perhaps be-cause of Walter Chatton's critique, accepted the contingency of the present in his quodlibetal question on whether an angel was able to merit and demerit in the first instant.[46] But this section of text is neither here nor there according to Auriol's way of thinking, since he would not grant the premisses on which Rimini and Ockham agree.

One might also ask whether Rimini supports the *opinio communis* in assert-ing the necessity of the past. Rimini treats this problem in the first question for distinctions 42–44, but he also makes remarks pertinent to this issue in dis-tinction 38. The short answer is that the past is immutable, but not necessary. This is why false future contingent propositions are immutably false, and true future contingent propositions are immutably true, until their significate it put into being. But this suggests that the future is immutable too, so the question is, is there any difference in the modal status of the past and future? Rimini admits that, in contrast to the future, *we* cannot bring it about that the past did not exist, but he is very reluctant to say that *God* cannot make the past not to have been. Still, it is important to stress that he never says God can *change* the past. In fact, Rimini even accepts the *opinio communis*'s analysis of propositions such as 'God foreknew that Peter would sin in A':

One must know that some of the propositions about the past depend on the truth of some propositions about the future in order for them to be true, just as this proposition. For in order for it to be true, it is required that this proposition be true: 'Peter will sin in A', which indeed is about the future... But there are some propositions whose truths do not depend on the truths of any propositions about the future, just as these: 'God created the world', 'God was incarnated', 'Peter was white', and innumerable other propositions. But *whatever the case about these last propositions*, it is agreed concerning the first ones that they are contin-gent, if the propositions about the future, on which they depend, are contingent...[47]

---

[46] Rimini deals with Ockham's position in *I Sent.*, d. 38, q. 1, a. 3 (ed. Trapp-Marcolino, pp. 263, l. 1 – 267, l. 22). Ockham's quodlibetal question is *Quodlibet* II, q. 6.

[47] Rimini, *I Sent.*, d. 38, q. 2, a. 3 (ed. Trapp-Marcolino, pp. 302, l. 30–303, l. 5): "Dico quod etiam de illa de praeterito 'Deus praescivit Petrum peccaturum in A' est simpliciter contin-gens. Unde sciendum quod propositionum de praeterito quaedam sunt quae, ut sint verae, depend-ent a veritate quarundam de futuro, sicut ista, nam ad hoc ut ipsa sit vera, requiritur quod Haec sit vera 'Petrus peccabit in A', quae utique est de futuro... Quaedam vero sunt quarum veritates non dependent a veritatibus aliquarum de futuro, sicut hae 'Deus creavit mundum', 'Deus fuit in-carnatus', 'Petrus fuit albus', et aliae innumerabiles. Quidquid autem sit de ultimis, de primis tamen constat quod illae sunt contingentes, si illae de futuro a quibus dependent sint contingen-tes..."

I thus disagree with Richard Gaskin, "Peter of Ailly and other Fourteenth-Century Thinkers on Divine Power and Necessity of the Past," *Archiv für Geschichte der Philosophie* 79 (1997), pp.

However, when Rimini makes statements that seem to emphasize human power and control over God, for example statements saying that a creature can make it so that something which is foreknown is not future, such propositions are to be understood in the divided sense.[48] John of Mirecourt, however, would find himself in trouble over such remarks, and later John of Ripa will attack them. Clearly Mirecourt was not alone in the way he phrased things, and certainly when Rimini said them he did not mean to take away from divine power.[49]

At any rate, declares Rimini, quoting Augustine, it is insane to deny God's foreknowledge. Without foreknowledge God has little more knowledge than we do.[50] In the end of his defense of the Principle of Bivalence in question one, Rimini gives a few quotations from Scripture to show that future contingent propositions must be determinately true or false. These arguments are exceptional in their force. First, he quotes a passage in Acts about the second coming. If a proposition about the second coming is not determinately true, Rimini says, then it is false, according to Bivalence. Second, he cites a passage in Revelations, chapter 21: "'And God shall wipe away all tears from their eyes, etc.,' which is a singular foretelling about a future contingent, and immediately it is said to John: 'Write. For these words are most faithful and true.'" Henry of Zomeren would eventually use this *auctoritas* against Peter de Rivo, Auriol's late fifteenth-century defender, whom Zomeren charged with heresy. Indeed, without calling Auriol's denial of Bivalence itself heretical, Rimini claims that it follows from this denial that "God would not foreknow certainly and determinately which part of a contingent is future." For Rimini, this is "expressly heretical."[51]

273-91, who considers Rimini to have held that the past and future were equally contingent. One problem in Gaskin's treatment is that he still takes the "*additiones*" in Rimini's text as actual additions, rather than deletions as the Rimini editors argue (vol. 1, pp. xiv–xvii, xciii–xcvii). William Courtenay modified his opinion accordingly in "John of Mirecourt (Part II)," p. 157, in the later reprint in idem, *Covenant and Causality in Medieval Thought. Studies in Philosophy, Theology, and Economic Practice* (London 1984), p. 174a.

[48] For example Rimini, *I Sent.*, d. 38, q. 2, a. 3 (ed. Trapp-Marcolino, p. 303, ll. 30–34): "Si igitur, quamdiu res futura est futura, potest fieri ut non sit futura, et per consequens quod numquam fuerit futura et numquam praescita, ut dicit, sicut in potestate alicuius est facere quod non sit futura, ita in eius potestate est facere quod numquam fuerit praescita, et per consequens quod numquam fuerit verum quod Deus illam fore praescivit."

[49] This is another area in the discussion of future contingents in which Oxford scholars had an impact, particularly Campsall, Holcot, and, most importantly, Wodeham, who routinely made statements at Oxford thought ill-sounding to some in Paris.

[50] Rimini, *I Sent.*, d. 38, q. 2, a. 1 (ed. Trapp-Marcolino, p. 277, ll. 2–4; p. 278, ll. 3–6).

[51] Rimini, *I Sent.*, d. 38, q. 1, a. 2 (ed. Trapp-Marcolino, p. 251, ll. 31–4): "Sumo enim hanc scriptum Actuum 1: 'Hic Iesus, qui assumptus est a vobis in coelum, sic veniet etc': aut haec est vera, et habeo propositum; aut non est vera, et tunc sequitur quod hic Iesus non veniet, quod est expresse haereticum." (P. 251, l. 35–p. 251, l. 4): "Praeterea, in sacra scriptura non solum tales praenuntiationes ponuntur, sed etiam habetur expresse quod ipsae sunt verae; igitur dicere illas non esse veras est haereticum. Assumptum patet ex Apocalypsi 18 capitulo, ibi enim dicitur: 'Et absterget Deus omnem lacrimam ab oculis eorum etc,' quae est praenuntiatio singularis de futuro contingenti, et immediate dicitur Iohanni: 'Scribe, quia haec verba fidelissima sunt et vera.'" (P. 252, ll. 15–18): "Secundo, si nulla enuntiatio singularis etc, sequeretur quod Deus non certe et determinate praesciret quae pars contingentis futura vel non... Sed consequens est haereticum ex-

In question two Rimini proves that God is foreknowing of all futures, before presenting Auriol's view that denies foreknowledge to God.[52] After ridiculing Auriol's opinion, Rimini concludes: "Therefore one must not hold that opinion, and I have wished to dwell only a little on the proofs for the conclusions in question on account of the opinion, since among Catholics these conclusions are not at all brought into doubt."[53] After dealing with Auriol, Rimini devotes the remainder of the question to showing how God can have determinate foreknowledge of what is contingent, and that some propositions, in fact almost all true propositions, are determinately, yet contingently true. Like Ockham, Rimini says that the way in which God knows the future with certainty is incomprehensible and inexplicable to us.[54] This admission did not prevent Rimini, from ridiculing, tongue in cheek, Auriol's notion of God's knowledge of contingents, abstracted from time (in distinction three): "I ask, what do you understand by 'abstractive'? Will you say, just as some say, it is that knowledge by which such contingent truths *cannot* be known?"[55]

Somewhat influenced by Ockham, Rimini adopts a version of Aquinas and Giles of Rome's eternal presence solution to the problem of divine foreknowledge, having rejected divine Ideas and the determination of the divine will. Interestingly, he presents the Ideas theory in Auriol's words, gives Scotus's arguments against it, and finally Auriol's reservations about those arguments. Unlike his later follower Pierre d'Ailly, Rimini understands that Auriol did not in fact accept this solution, which Rimini rejects because it posits a medium for God's knowledge of creatures. Rimini's refutaton of Scotus's divine will theory also relates to Auriol: although instants of nature do not exist, even if they did, no proposition about the future could be neutral for any instant of nature, because it violates Bivalence.[56]

Rimini understood the threat posed by Peter Auriol, although he would not have convinced Auriol to change his mind. Auriol set out to defend human free will and a particular notion of divine perfection based on atemporality, but it is easy to see that Rimini began with a vow to defend God's *fore*knowledge per se, and proceeded from there, for he is most incensed with Auriol's

---

presse, ut patebit in sequenti quaestione."

[52] Rimini, *I Sent.*, d. 38, q. 2, a. 1 (ed. Trapp-Marcolino, p. 277, ll. 6–17). The editors here did not locate the direct quotations from Auriol, even though they are followed by the words "Haec ipse" and the marginalia cited give the correct location. Thus Rimini, ed. Trapp-Marcolino, p. 277, ll. 7–8 "Deus... erit" = Auriol, ed. Schabel, p. 191, l. 932; Trapp-Marcolino, p. 277, ll. 8–9 "Deus... erit" = Schabel, p. 191, ll. 933–5; and Trapp-Marcolino, p. 277, ll. 12–17 "Ista... falsum" = Schabel, p. 195, ll. 1014–1019.

[53] Rimini, *I Sent.*, d. 38, q. 2, a. 1 (ed. Trapp-Marcolino, p. 278, ll. 12–14): "Opinio igitur illa tenenda non est, propter quam tantummodo praedictarum conclusionum probationibus aliquantulum volui insistere; nam apud alios catholicos nullatenus vertuntur in dubium."

[54] Rimini, *I Sent.*, d. 38, q. 2, a. 2 (ed. Trapp-Marcolino, p. 283, ll. 2–5): "Dico ergo quantum ad istum articulum...quod modus ille, quo Dei sapientia cuncta futura certe praenoscit, incomprehensibilis et inexplicabilis nobis est."

[55] Rimini, *I Sent.*, d. 3, q. 1, a. 1 (ed. cit., vol. 1, p. 307): "...quaero, quid per abstractivam intelligis. Vel dices, sicut aliqui dicunt, eam notitiam qua *non* possunt sciri tales veritates contingentes?"

[56] Rimini, *I Sent.*, d. 38, q. 2, a. 2 (ed. Trapp-Marcolino, pp. 278–84).

claim that statements such as 'God knows the Antichrist will be' are simply false. In a sense, Rimini appreciates Auriol as much as anyone else before him did, and agrees with Auriol in many ways. He knew Auriol's text, used its arguments against others, and expended much time and effort to refute him, although in the end Rimini's solution is not really new. In showing in strong terms the theological ramifications of Auriol's view, Rimini hoped to make Auriol's view unacceptable to others, and his treatment would influence later figures such as Pierre d'Ailly, Henry of Langenstein, and Fernando of Cordova. If one were to put both of their works side by side, however, one might despair of any solution. But Rimini did not put the matter to a final rest: the very next year Rimini's fellow Augustinian dealt at length with Auriol again.

Alphonsus Vargas of Toledo

The Augustinian Alphonsus Vargas of Toledo lectured on the *Sentences* at Paris in 1344-45, became master in 1347, and died while serving as archbishop of Seville in 1366.[57] Fortunately for scholars studying the academic year 1344-45 at Paris, Alphonsus Vargas supplements the information we already have from the *Sentences* commentaries of the Carmelite Paul of Perugia and the Cistercian John of Mirecourt by concentrating on a small controversy over future contingents which involved the Dominican Francis of Treviso, and Vargas's *socii* — fellow bachelors lecturing on the the the *Sentences* — the secular theologian John Rathe Scotus and the Franciscan Rudolph de Tornaco, whose commentaries have not been found.[58]

Vargas was, like Rimini, a careful and organized scholar, whose remarks were not expressed vaguely. There has been controversy over the views of many theologians writing in the fourteenth century. Often this controversy is the result of the theologian's own imprecision, as with William of Ockham. This imprecision, however, could result from the state of the question when Ockham wrote. By the 1340s, the problem of future contingents was acute enough at Paris, largely because of Peter Auriol, that precise language and clarity about certain issues were necessary. Nevertheless, this does not mean that these remarks were understood, for the nature of the debate was intellectually demanding.

---

[57] There are frequent references to Vargas on issues related to the present one, in for example Hoenen, *Marsilius of Inghen*, and Courtenay, *Capacity and Volition*, but nothing in depth has been written. See also Trapp, "Augustinian Theology," pp. 213-23.

[58] Treviso lectured the previous year with Rimini. Rathe Scotus and Rudolph incepted fourth and third after Vargas respectively, as Vargas himself says, Alphonsus Vargas Toletanus, *In Primum Sententiarum*, dd. 38-39, aa. 3-4 (ed. Venice 1490; reprint New York 1952, col. 615, ll. 60-61): "Magister Johannes Scotus. Contra secundam conclusionem quidam reverendus doctor qui quartus post me inceptit hoc ordine procedit..." and dd. 42-44 (col. 631, ll. 65-6): "Magister Rodulphus ordinis minorum. Circa rationem istam quidam reverendus doctor ordinis minorum qui tertius post me incepit sic precedit..." A *socius* is a fellow bachelor at the same stage of lecturing on the *Sentences* or the Bible. In both cases, and in others, Vargas gives us much important information that we would not otherwise have.

Vargas cites only a couple of figures who lived after 1200 in his discussion in distinction 38–39: Giles of Rome (*'doctor noster'*) and Peter of Tarantasia (Pope Innocent V) in passing, Francis of Treviso, John Rathe Scotus, and Peter Auriol. Unlike Rimini, and perhaps because of Rimini's defense of Bivalence, Vargas refutes Auriol's position only as far as it denies foreknowledge. Vargas's first article deals with certain suppositions, to which we shall return. He gives conclusions in his second article, and the first one is that "God is foreknowing of all futures." Like Rimini, Vargas says that this "ought not be doubtful to catholics," and the only reason he discusses it is on account of Auriol, who denies it.[59] Vargas gives some of the authoritative quotations that Rimini does, then infers a corollary against Auriol's position denying that such propositions as "God knows the Antichrist will be" are false, defending his corollary with "the saints and Scripture."[60]

In articles three and four Vargas presents and refutes doubts about his position. The first doubt is again that of Auriol, whose opinion hardly deserves mentioning, according to Vargas. Here he criticizes Auriol's position as to his conclusion and deduction. The conclusion is obviously false, for it goes against the saints and Scripture, as was said. According to Vargas, Auriol's *basis* for denying foreknowledge was that no proposition about the future is true or false, which suggests that Vargas has limited or indirect knowledge of Auriol's theory. Vargas retorts that this is not "catholically said" and denies the truth of prophecy. Vargas himself deduces the opposite conclusion by taking the opposite of Auriol's premisses.[61] Thus, propositions about the future are true or false, and God knows them.

Vargas 'defends' his own position with citations from Augustine and, more importantly, Anselm, though he may have been aware of some of Thomas of Strasbourg's statements. In article one he makes four suppositions, repeated almost verbatim from Anselm's *De concordia*, which Vargas cites explicitly: (1) "It is necessary for whatever God foreknows to be future in the way that it is

---

[59] Vargas, *I Sent*, dd. 38–39, a. 1 (ed. Venice, col. 612, ll. 44–9): "Prima conclusio est quod Deus est prescius omnium futurorum, et licet ista conclusio non debeat catholicis esse dubia, et aliqualiter sit nota ex suppositionibus premissis, confirmo tamen eam propter quandam opinionem minus tutam iudicio meo expressa determinatione Beati Augustini..."

[60] Vargas, *I Sent.*, dd. 38–39, a. 2 (ed. Venice, col. 612, l. 66–613, l. 4): "Ex ista conclusione infero correlarie quod illa opinio non est vera nec consona dictis sanctorum nec scripture sacre que ponit quod ista propositio est falsa — Auriolus, I, distinctione 39, questione 1, articulo 1, propositione 1, et articulo 3, propositione secunda — Deus scit Antechristum venturum vel quod erit, et consimiles omnes..."

[61] Vargas, *I Sent.*, dd. 38–39, aa. 3–4 (ed. Venice, col. 615, ll. 13–36): "Contra primam conclusionem et propositionem deductam ex ipsa est quedam opinio sicut tangebatur ibidem que ponit — opinio Aurioli ubi supra — quod ista propositio: 'Deus scivit hoc vel illud esse futurum'... Ratio fundamentalis illius opinionis, si opinio meretur dici, quod non credo, est quia illa propositio que nec est vera nec falsa non est scibilis... Contra Auriolum: Sed ad veritatem ista positio non videtur mihi catholica, nec quantum ad conclusionem nec quantum ad motivum sive deductionem. Non quidam quantum ad conclusionem, quia non consonat dictis sactorum nec sacre scripture... Nec quantum ad motivum sive deductionem. Motivum enim ipsius est quod nulla propositio de futuro est vera vel falsa, quod non videtur catholice dictum, quia ad hoc sequitur quod nulla prophecia de futuro sit vera..." Hoenen, *Marsilius of Inghen*, pp. 197–8, makes this point as well.

foreknown by God"; (2) "God foreknows that something is future without any necessity"; (3) "It is necessary for something to be future without any necessity"; and (4) "God's foreknowledge, which necessity follows, and the contingency of things, from which necessity is removed, are not inconsistent."[62]

In article two, Vargas presents and proves four conclusions. The first was against Auriol. The others are as follows: (2) "The future is future by as much necessity as it is necessary for every future to be future"; (3) "Every proposition about the future foreknown by God — supposing this — has necessary and infallible truth in the way that it is foreknown," and this has the corollary "Every proposition about the future revealed by God — this having been supposed — has necessary and infallible truth in the way that it was revealed"; (4) "Necessary and infallible truth of this type not withstanding, God, from His absolute power, can make the opposite of what is foreknown and revealed, as for example [He can make] the Antichrist not come about."[63]

According to Vargas, the Dominican Francis of Treviso held the opposite of the fourth conclusion in his evening lectures, or "vespers," saying: "I deduce this conclusion first thus: If God were not able to make the Antichrist not come about, this then would be because He foreknows that he will come about and His foreknowledge cannot be mistaken."[64] This small quotation makes it appear that Francis held an opinion close to that of John XXII. Vargas refutes it, holding that God can foreknow, for example, that I will sin, and yet I am able not to sin. Vargas points out that Francis's position entails that it would be impossible for anything to happen other than as it does, "which no one of sound mind would assert," and he goes on to give specific examples of things God foreknew He Himself would do, but nevertheless was able to do differently. For example, God foreknew He would redeem the world through His Son's death, but He could have done it in another way. Vargas cites Augustine and Lombard in support.[65]

---

[62] Vargas, *I Sent.*, dd. 38–39, a. 1, supp. 1 (ed. Venice, col. 611, l. 69–612, l. 1): "necesse est quicquid Deus prescit futurum esse sicut prescitur a Deo"; supp. 2 (col. 612, ll. 6–7): "Deus prescit aliquid esse futurum sine omni necessitate"; supp. 3 (col. 612, ll. 14–15): "necesse est aliquid esse futurum sine omni necessitate"; supp. 4 (col. 612, ll. 20–22): "prescientia Dei, quam sequitur necessitas, et contingentia rerum, a qua removetur necessitas, non repugnant." Cf. Anselm, *De concordia*, I.1 (ed. Schmitt, p. 246, ll. 9–13).

[63] Vargas, *I Sent.*, dd. 38–39, a. 2, conc. 2 (ed. Venice, col. 613, ll. 10–11): "tanta necessitate futurum est futurum quod necesse est omne futurum esse futurum"; conc. 3 (col. 613, ll. 43–5): "omnis propositio de futuro a Deo prescita, hoc supposito, habet necessariam et infallibilem veritatem, sicut est prescita"; conc. 3, corr. (col. 613, ll. 67–9): "omnis propositio a Deo revelata, hoc supposito, habet necessariam et infallibilem veritatem, sicut est revelata"; conc. 4 (col. 614, ll. 15–17): "non obstante huiusmodi necessaria et infallibili veritate, Deus potest facere de potentia sui absoluta oppositum presciti et revelati, ut pote Antechristum non fore."

[64] Vargas, *I Sent.*, dd. 38–39, a. 2 (col. 614, ll. 17–23): "..cuius oppositum quidam reverendus doctor ordinis predicatorum ponit in vesperiis suis. Magister Franciscus de Tarvisio: 'Istam conclusionem deduco primo sic: Si Deus non posset facere Antechristum non fore, hoc ideo esset quia prescit ipsum fieri et eius prescientia falli non potest.'" The evening lectures called 'vespers' were sometimes published as independent works, as, for example, John Hiltalingen of Basel's.

[65] Vargas, *I Sent.*, dd. 38–39, a. 2 (ed. Venice, col. 614–15). E.g. col. 614, ll. 41–5: "Tertio, quia sequeretur quod cuiuslibet contradictionis altera pars esset simpliciter impossibilis sic

In articles three and four Vargas again brings up Francis of Treviso's opposition to his fourth conclusion. It is clear that in his vespers Treviso argues directly against Vargas's position, for Vargas declares that Treviso expressly identifies that stance with Vargas. Vargas gives Treviso's argument at length and Treviso basically claims that when God reveals something, supposing this, what is revealed is absolutely and without qualification necessary, because it is in a certain way 'past', both revealed and foreknown by God. Treviso's example is that 'the Antichrist will be' is absolutely necessary, and its opposite is impossible.[66]

Vargas concedes that everything revealed by God, supposing that revelation, has necessary and infallible truth, but only in the way it is foreknown by God. God revealed not simply that the Antichrist would come, but that he would come about freely and contingently. Because it is necessary for what God foreknows to come about, then it is necessary that the Antichrist freely and contingently come about without any necessity. This was also Thomas of Strasbourg's position. Vargas holds that the faith only requires that the Antichrist come about, not that the Antichrist cannot not come about.[67] Like Anselm and Francis of Marchia, Vargas admits that something can be done freely and contingently when de facto there is only one option.

Although this response is also Thomas of Strasbourg's, it is not the popular one, which merely states that God could have willed and thus foreknown differently. Vargas recognizes that "This response is not new, nor was this invented by the *moderni*, but by Hugh of St. Victor, in *De sacramentis*, book I, part two, chapter 18." It is here that Vargas gives his sole citation of other scholars of the university era, maintaining that Giles of Rome and Peter of Tarantasia held this. Vargas relates that some used this argument against Anselm, because Anselm seemed to say that things happened with absolute necessity as God foreknew them.[68] Vargas then shows that Anselm did not mean this, and describes how Anselm drew the distinction between antecedent and subsequent necessity, the latter not being compulsive in any way. Vargas admits this second type of necessity, as many Parisians had, and asserts that it is compatible with the possibility to be otherwise. Hence the Antichrist is able not to come about, and God can make the Antichrist not come about, although the Antichrist necessarily will come about by subsequent necessity. Vargas reminds the reader to be careful to note that the term 'necessity' is used equivocally when he says it is (subsequently) necessary, because God foreknows it, for the Antichrist to come about freely and contingently without any (preceding) necessity. Vargas did say 'absolutely and without qualification'

---

quod per nullam potentiam nec finitam nec infinitam posset poni in esse, quod nullus sane mentis assereret."

[66] Vargas, *I Sent.*, dd. 38–39, aa. 3–4 (ed. Venice, col. 622–3).

[67] Vargas, *I Sent.*, dd. 38–39, aa. 3–4 (ed. Venice, col. 623).

[68] Vargas, *I Sent.*, dd. 38–39, aa. 3–4 (ed. Venice, col. 623, l. 69–624, l. 5): "Ista responsio non est nova nec per modernos doctores inventa, sed Hugo De sacramentis, libro primo, parte secunda, capitulo 18, et ipsam videtur sequi Magister... et ponit eam Petrus de Tarantarum... et doctor noster..."

with respect to revelations, and Treviso picked up on it. Apparently, however, Vargas was merely making a distinction between something that is really (absolutely and without qualification) revealed, and something that is only conditionally or threateningly revealed, as the fall of Ninevah, which was not strictly speaking a revelation.[69]

It is against John Rathe Scotus, however, that Vargas has his primary debate, and this takes up half of Vargas's distinction 38–39.[70] The disagreement revolves around the interpretation of a passage in Augustine in *Against Faustus* that reads: "Future things are not able not to come about just as much as past, done, things are not able not to have been, because it is not in God's will that something be false which is true; wherefore all which truly are future without doubt will come about, just as all which are truly past without doubt went past."[71] John Rathe Scotus, in his vespers, wanted to follow the *opinio communis* in retaining the difference between the past and future, the past being necessary and the future contingent. He interpreted the passage that Vargas had adduced as saying the opposite of what is in fact said in the quotation. Rathe Scotus concluded that the future is not necessary, and Vargas responds that to be consistent he would then have to admit that through some power the past is able not to have been. While repeating that Rathe Scotus had good intentions, Vargas continually ridicules Rathe Scotus's use and interpretation of Augustine's quotation, saying at one point, "And if one is allowed to explain the sayings of the saints and the text of Holy Scripture like this, certainly little could be concluded from what has been said."[72]

In sum, Vargas's position is that by a tautology it is necessary for all futures, assuming they are futures, to be future, just as it is necessary for all pasts to have been past. It is not necessary, however, for any particular thing to be future. God's foreknowledge does entail a subsequent necessity for the future, a necessity which follows the being of a thing, just as the necessity of the past is subsequent to the being of the past thing. The future is contingent, he says against Francis of Treviso, but the future is necessary, he says against John Rathe Scotus, just as is the past.

In this way Vargas, like Bradwardine, *seems* to dissolve the difference between the future and the past.[73] Vargas's position is not radical, however,

---

[69] Vargas, *I Sent.*, dd. 38–39, aa. 3–4 (ed. Venice, col. 624–5).

[70] Vargas, *I Sent.*, dd. 38–39, aa. 2–4 (ed. Venice, col. 615–22).

[71] Vargas, *I Sent.*, dd. 38–39, a. 2 (ed. Venice, col. 613): "Tam non possunt futura non fieri quam non fuisse facta preterita; quoniam non est in Dei voluntate ut eo sit aliquid falsum quo verum est; quapropter omnia que vere futura sunt sine dubio fient, sicut omnia que vere preterita sunt sine dubio preterierunt."

[72] Vargas, *I Sent.*, dd. 38–39, aa. 3–4 (ed. Venice, col. 617, ll. 52–7): "Et ad veritatem, expositio ista est mihi valde mirabilis. Textus 'futura non possunt non fore,' sed glosa dicit 'futura possunt non fore,' et si sic liceret exponere dicta sanctorum et textum sacre scripture, pro certo modicum posset ex dictis concludi."

[73] I do not think Vargas position is "a surprising break with Rimini and most contemporary opinion" accepting "Bradwardine's position that future events, *de potentia ordinata*, can only happen as God ordains and know them" (Courtenay, *Capacity and Volition*, p. 176). Vargas's position is not different from Rimini's or that of many other Parisian scholars. Accepting a subsequent necessity for future events, based on God's foreknowledge, was the common *Parisian*

agreeing as it does with Anselm's stance throughout. In fact Vargas does say, contrary to Bradwardine, that the past is absolutely necessary.[74] In distinction 42-44, Vargas asks "whether every determinately true proposition about a future contingent is able never to have been true through divine power."[75] Against John Rathe Scotus, again, Vargas takes the side of another *socius*, the Franciscan Rudolph de Tornaco, and claims that God cannot make the future not come about, and that God cannot make it so that what has been revealed never was revealed.[76] Then against what Vargas claims to be Rimini's position, Vargas says it entails a contradiction for God to make Adam not to have been, but it cannot be proven that it is a contradiction to say that God can make it so the Antichrist will not be. If one says '*future* Antichrist' however, instead of simply 'Antichrist', then one does run into a contradiction.[77] What exactly does Vargas mean? It is hard to say, but he seems to admit an extra necessity concerning the past beyond that of the necessity of a tautology and subsequent necessity.

On such a touchy issue, then, with precision in writing and reading so important, it is not surprising that Vargas's *socii* had difficulty understanding his position. One could say that Auriol's treatment, passed on by Rimini, required the sort of treatment Vargas gives, whose very precision led to some new controversy on the subject, not necessarily owing much to the new English thought. When Vargas cites, for example, Fitzralph, he does so insultingly, saying that his opinion is better called an error, and stressing that he is a "doctor of another school."[78] Whatever impact English theology had on Paris

---

opinion. Rimini discussed this type of necessity in his own treatment, and probably only avoided using it himself on account of his sensitivity to Auriol's attack on the distinction between necessities. Vargas chose to discuss such necessity explicitly, and his remarks caused a small controversy which led him to focus his treatment in his *Sentences* commentary on this type of necessity. Courtenay himself notes that Vargas sided with Buckingham and not Bradwardine on whether God could change the past (p. 176). Courtenay cites Vargas's distinction 42-44, so he probably means Michael of Massa when he says that Vargas never went beyond distinction 38 (p. 175).

[74] Vargas's strongest statement of this opinion in on column 635, ll. 5-11 (*I Sent.*, dd. 42-44, a. 2), in a *reductio ad absurdum*: "Deus potest facere preteritum non fuisse; igitur potest facere quod pater meus numquam fuerit me remanente, et quod non habuerim patrem, nec fuerim productus ab aliquo, et quia (sic) Christus non fuerit natus de virgine nec passus in cruce, et quod mundus numquam fuerit, vel quod non duravit nisi unum diem, et similia, quod nullus sanus assereret, ut mihi videtur."

[75] Vargas, *I Sent.*, dd. 42-44 (ed. Venice, col. 630, ll. 67-9): "Utrum omnis propositio de futuro contingenti determinate vera per divinam potentiam possit numquam fuisse vera?"

[76] Vargas, *I Sent.*, dd. 42-44, a. 2 (ed. Venice, col. 631-9).

[77] Vargas, *I Sent.*, dd. 42-44, aa. 3-4 (ed. Venice, col. 640, ll. 39-49): "...ad rem preteritam non fuisse sequitur contradictio; et ad probationem, dico quod satis evidenter potest probari quod ad Adam non fuisse sequitur aliqua contradictio... licet non possit evidenter probari quod sequatur ad Antichristum non fore. Nec iste doctor <Rimini> probat oppositum. Concedo tamen quod non plus sequitur contradictio ad Adam sive ad aliam rem preteritam non fuisse quam ad Antichristum futurum non fore; et ideo concedo quod sicut Deus non potest facere Adam vel aliquam rem preteritam non fuisse, ita nec Antichristum non fore futurum, ut patet ex dictis."

[78] Vargas, *I Sent.*, dd. 42-44, aa. 3-4 (ed. Venice, col. 641, ll. 31-5): "Hybernicus in I, questione de revelatione in responsio<ne> ad primum argumentum. Contra tertiam est quedam opinio, vel potius error, ut credo, cuiusdam doctoris alterius scole qui ponit quod Deus non solum potest revelare falsum..." (Hybernicus is FitzRalph).

thought generally, it did not always provide any stimulus for the continuation of the heated disputes native to Paris, and in such an air of hostility and confusion, it is no wonder that some doctors came under suspicion of holding problematic opinions.

Auriol's Threat Fades

The questions of time, necessity, God's power, etc., that did not involve Auriol directly were stimulating enough to push Auriol's particular worries about divine foreknowledge to the background. These sub-issues of the question of foreknowledge provided their own conflicts. The delicate and demanding nature of discussions surrounding God's power made it difficult to predict whether one's remarks would be understood, or taken out of context and misunderstood. The latter appears to have happened to John of Mirecourt, many of whose propositions concerning God's power came under suspicion. The Cistercian Mirecourt, who read the *Sentences* at Paris in the same year as Vargas, was the subject of controversy in the Middle Ages, and of some confusion in the historiographic tradition. By the 1340s theologians were devoting more and more space to questions of future contingents, both concerning God's knowledge and God's power, and Mirecourt even has one involving revelation, thus incorporating the Oxford tradition where Rimini had not. In these expanded discussions, theologians often made statements that seemed to say that God can undo the past, or that humans can make it so that God did not know that something would be future. These assertions were ill-sounding to some of the more conservative theologians, although personal differences probably had a hand in amplifying such cacophony. At any rate, several such propositions were taken from Mirecourt's *Sentences* commentary, although many were later removed from suspicion after Mirecourt wrote two explanations of his positions.[79]

That some modern historians still consider Mirecourt to have held the suspect opinions in the suspect way is therefore not surprising. William Courtenay has shown that Mirecourt was in fact not making any radical claims about God's power to undo the past. I doubt anyone, including Peter Damian, ever held the opinion that 'God could undo the past', in the common-sense meaning of the phrase, but unless one reads carefully entire questions, or perhaps entire *Sentences* commentaries, one might misunderstand passages or take

---

[79] Mirecourt's two "Apologies" are discussed and edited in Frederick Stegmüller, "Die zwei Apologien des Jean de Mirecourt," RTAM 5 (1933), pp. 40–78 and pp. 192–204. On issues of past contingents in the 1340s, and Mirecourt's problems, see Courtenay, "John of Mirecourt." Mirecourt's q. 38 of book I involves revelation: "Utrum futurum revelatum esse futurum possit non esse futurum," Jean-François Genest and Paul Vignaux, "La bibliothèque anglaise de Jean de Mirecourt: 'subtilitas' ou plagiat?" in Olaf Pluta, ed., *Die Philosophie im 14. und 15. Jahrhundert* (Amsterdam 1988) (pp. 275–301), p. 291, note that Mirecourt was occupying a Paris void with the Oxford material Rimini had not touched.

them out of context.[80] Most of the disagreement among historians seems to concern the language in which theologians couched their positions. Not all theologians chose to stress the 'fact' that God's power is not diminished through time. Thus while Gregory of Rimini continually avoids the word 'necessary', Alphonsus Vargas admits that God cannot now make it so that his father never existed, while he himself remains. Thomas of Strasbourg holds both that God's power is not reduced through time and yet that de facto the past cannot be changed. While it is certainly the case that there was some real disagreement on this issue, nevertheless much of the controversy simply revolved around the correct way to *express* the status of our past with respect to God in eternity.

Part of Mirecourt's problem was that a portion of his questions on future contingents was simply borrowed from English theologians: Bradwardine, Buckingham, Richard Kilvington, and the Franciscans Wodeham, Robert Halifax, and Alexander Langeley. In his attempt to display 'his' new knowledge, Mirecourt offended his Parisian audience that was unused to the 'English subtleties'.[81] Moreover, as Courtenay has noted, in the case of John of Mirecourt there was added confusion in that the organization of his *Sentences* commentary, particularly in the questions at issue, was not nearly as straightforward as that of, say, Gregory of Rimini. It was easy for readers to become confused. This is exemplified in Mirecourt's question 35, which has many exchanges back and forth between him and his unnamed adversaries.[82] Thus while Mire-

---

[80] Courtenay himself is not immune to this pitfall. When demonstrating correctly that Mirecourt made no radical claims in the matter, Courtenay states concerning Thomas Bradwardine's views: "Moreover, it does not imply a contradiction for a past event to be *altered*" (italics mine). The passage he quotes in support, Bradwardinus, *De causa Dei* III, c. 52 (ed. London, p. 857B), reads: "Respondebitur forsitan, quod ex praeteritione rei praeteritae oritur quaedam relatio, qua necesse est simpliciter illam fuisse, quare impossibile est simpliciter illam non fuisse. Sed hoc reprobatum est prius, quando monstrabatur A non fuisse, nullam contradictionem formaliter implicare. Illam etiam relationem, non est necesse simpliciter esse vel fuisse; aliquando enim non fuit; quare nec repugnaret formaliter eam nunc non esse; ergo nihil facit necessarium simpliciter. Illa quoque relatio vel est ad Deum seu ad voluntatem divinam, vel rem aliquam naturalem seu res aliquas naturales. Primum erat destructum per 30um huius; secundum stare non potest" (Courtenay, "John of Mirecourt [Part II]," pp. 149–50, n. 99). Two things can be noted. First, Bradwardine continually uses the word '*simpliciter*'; as we have seen, many if not most theologians in the fourteenth century thought that God was the only entity that is necessary *simpliciter*, that is absolutely and without qualification. Everything else, past, present, and future, is ultimately contingent, and certainly not absolutely necessary. Second, nowhere does Bradwardine use the verb 'alter' or 'change' (*mutare*) with respect to the past. Bradwardine merely states that it is not impossible for, say, King Charles not to have been beheaded. Without any other consideration, 'King Charles was not beheaded' does not imply a contradiction. If Bradwardine had said that this is possible: 'King Charles was beheaded and King Charles was never beheaded', then we would have real grounds for drawing the conclusion Courtenay infers.
[81] This is the subject of Genest and Vignaux, "La bibliothèque anglaise," which includes (pp. 293–301) a nice table of Mirecourt's plagiarized passages with their English sources for the pertinent questions 35–38!
[82] For a rough transcription of this question, see my "Quarrel with Aureol," pp. 771–87, and for the parts of the text taken from Bradwardine, see Genest's unpublished dissertation, "Le *De futuris contingentibus*," pp. 129–35. John of Mirecourt's overall treatment of the problem of foreknowledge and future contingents is over 2000 lines long. Because his *Sentences* commentary has not yet been edited (Massimo Parodi is working on it, however) and because I am concerned

court makes all the now common arguments about it being impossible for something to begin or cease to be future, and that propositions about future contingents are determinately true or false, he also makes statements indicating that a creature can make it so that something which was in one way *ab eterno* never was in that way. Nevertheless, Mirecourt immediately says that he is taking 'make' in a loose sense.[83] He, like Rimini before him, does not mean to say that the past can now be changed, a possibility he explicitly denies in distinguishing between the future and the past.[84] Mirecourt also makes frequent use of the traditional distinction between the composite and divided senses. In sum Mirecourt holds like most others that human free will and divine foreknowledge are compatible, although his way of expressing this might have seemed ill-sounding to some.

Although his treatment is not radical for the most part, and he relies heavily on earlier discussions, most notably that of Gregory of Rimini, there is at least one interesting and perhaps novel discussion in Mirecourt. When discussing the causal relationship between God's foreknowledge and future things, Mirecourt states the conclusion that it is not possible for God to know something one way and afterwards know it another way without a change in the object of his knowledge. An objection to Mirecourt's position is that then a thing's being future would be naturally prior to God's knowing the thing to be future. The objection claims this cannot be, because then God could make or will something to be future, and yet not know it to be future. Mirecourt responds by drawing analogies. If the objection holds, God could make Socrates an animal and not a man, since being an animal is prior in nature to being a

---

primarily with Peter Auriol, I have not looked closely at Mirecourt's other questions concerning the future. For a general analysis, see Schwamm, *Das göttliche Vorherwissen*, pp. 321–9; Hoenen, *Marsilius of Inghen*, passim.

    [83] Johannes de Mirecourt, *I Sent.*, q. 35 (ms. Paris, BN lat. 15882, fol. 142va): "Tertia, aliqualiter fuit ab eterno, et creatura potest facere quod numquam sic fuit; et aliqualiter potest semper fuisse et numquam taliter futurum. Et quando arguitur oppositum, 'illud quod est posterius etc', dico quod non debet concedi quod aliquod impediat scientiam vel prescientiam Dei; sed creatura que nunc primo est, potest facere, capiendo large 'facere' sicut dicitur in questione de preteritis, quod A fore futurum non est a Deo prescitum, quia veritas huius dependet ab aliquo quod est futurum et posterius."

    [84] Mirecourt, *I Sent.*, q. 35 (Paris 15882, fol. 142ra–b): "Ad primum, potest dici quod Deus non novit facta tanquam fienda quantum ad certitudinem, sed habeat evidentem notitiam de utrisque; aliter tamen et aliter novit facta quam fienda, quia necessario novit facta esse facta, sed contingenter novit futura esse fienda; sicut iam creatura potest ita certitudinaliter vel evidenter scire quod ipsa sedet, sicut ipsa scit quod si homo est, animal est, et unum tamen est contingens, aliud necessarium, in hoc igitur est differentia quod de quocumque vero de [142rb] presenti et de preterito, quod Deus non scit certe esse vel fuisse, necessarium erit statim post hoc Deum illud cognovisse; sed non sic de vero futuro, et causa est quia Deum scire hoc esse, fore, vel fuisse non est aliud nisi hoc esse, fuisse, vel fore, et hoc notum est Deo. Modo si Antichristus sit futurus, et Deus hoc noscat, adhuc est contingens quod Antichristus sit futurus; et per consequens an Deus sciat Antichristum fore, adhuc est contingens; sed si Adam fuit et Deus hoc noscat, non est possibile quod Adam numquam fuit et Deum hoc nosse; sed est necessarium Adam fuisse et Deum hoc nosse. Vel potest dici quod non aliter novit facta quam fienda quia non per mutationem sui novit preterita esse facta nec futura esse futura."

man. Likewise someone could be building a house without a house being built, because building is prior in nature to being built. These are absurdities.[85] Mirecourt says nothing directly about Auriol, but we see in Mirecourt how Auriol's concerns became absorbed into the overall general debate. Mirecourt focusses on propositions, rules about their truth, Bivalence, etc. He speaks concerning Aristotle's denial of truth and falsity to future contingent proposi-

---

[85] Mirecourt, *I Sent.*, q. 35 (Paris 15882, fol. 145ra): "Quinta conclusio est quod non est possibile quod aliqualiter (?) Deus sciat vel velit esse et postea non taliter sciat vel velit esse, et nulla mutatio actualis vel possibilis facta sit in aliquo alio a Deo. Probatur sic: Quia impossibile est fieri transitum de contradictorio in contradictorium sine aliqua mutatione actuali vel possibili; sed ibi est transitus, igitur mutatio; sed non in Deo; ergo in alio a Deo, et sic sequitur propositio.

(A) Contra conclusionem arguitur sic: Si non est possibile quod Deus sciens aliquid esse futurum non sciat illud esse futurum, sed sciat illud esse sine mutatione prius naturaliter facta in alio quam Deus sciat illud esse, tunc mutatio facta in re foret cum scire Dei [145rb]. Consequens falsum, et contra Beatum Augustinum, 5 *De trinitate*, capitulo 13, et allegat Magister, libro primo, distinctione 40, capitulo secundo.

(B) Secundo, sciat Deus Antichristum fore futurum, quia posito per ymaginationem quod numquam postea fiat mutatio realis aliqua, tunc foret hoc verum quod Deus non scit Antichristum fore futurum, quia sequitur: 'Nichil mutabitur et Antichristus non est, et [antecedens] <Antichristus> non erit'. Antecedens potest esse verum sine mutatione; ergo et consequens.

Confirmatur, quia ad hoc quod Deus sciat Antichristum esse futurum requiritur aliqua mutatio futura ad productionem Antichristi; ergo ad hoc quod Deus nesciat Antichristum esse futurum, non requiritur aliqua mutatio, sed sufficit non mutatio alterius rei.

(C) Tertio, si sic, tunc prius naturaliter foret rem esse futuram quam Deum scire rem esse futuram. Probatur consequentia, quia non est possibile quod Deus, nescirens rem esse futuram, sciat rem esse futuram, nisi per mutationem factam prius naturaliter in alio vel in illo quam Deus sciat ipsam esse futuram. Consequens falsum, quia tunc cum illud quod est prius alio naturaliter possit per divinam potentiam esse sine posteriori, sequitur quod Deus possit facere quod res erit futura, et quod Deus non sciret rem esse futuram vel quod esset futura.

(D) Quarto, si sic, tunc Deus sciret rem fore quia res erit, et cum [illud] <idem> sit [Deum esse] Deum esse et Deum scire, ergo Deus esset quia res erit, et ita Creator dependeret in esse a creatura. Et consequentia patet per argumentum Augustini quo probat quod Pater non sapit sapientia qua genuit, quia cum idem sit sapere et esse, si Pater saperet sapientia qua genuit, Pater esset sapientia quam genuit.

Pro istis potest dici, sicut dictum est in solutione secundi argumenti contra secundam conclusionem, quod non ideo scit Deus res esse futuras quia res sunt future. Aliter potest dici cum Magistro, libro primo, distinctione 35, capitulo quarto, quod capiendo causam pro illo sine quo non, posset dici quod rem esse est causa quare Deus sciat rem esse: nisi quia res aliqua esset, Deus nesciret rem esse, et similiter, nisi res esset futura, non Deus sciret rem esse futuram.

Si dicatur quod tunc nec econverso res non esset futura nisi Deus sciret eam esse futuram, quare ergo [145va] dicit quod non quia sunt res ideo novit, sed ideo sunt quia novit, responsio: quod etiam capiendo causam modo predicto, concederem non solum illam: 'Quia res sunt future, novit Deus esse futuras', sed etiam aliam: 'Quia Deus novit eas esse futuras, res sunt future'. Dico tamen quod illa non est vera: 'Quia res sunt, ideo Deus novit eas', quia esto quod non essent, <sed> adhuc cognoscit eas, nec ista: 'Quia Deus novit res, ideo res sunt', propter eandem causam. Dico etiam illam condicionalem esse veram: 'Si res sunt, Deus novit eas', non tamen: 'Si res novit, res ipse sunt'.

(~A) Ad Augustinum, dico quod sub nomine 'notitie', secundum Magistrum, comprehenditur 'beneplacitum Dei', quod est causa quare sit.

(~B) Ad secundum et eius confirmationem, dico quod probat sexta conclusio.

(~C) Ad tertium, quidquid sit de formis, aliter nego consequentiam istam: 'Res prius natura est [res] futura [quod]<quam> Deus sciat quod res sit futura; ergo Deus potest facere quod res sit futura et quod non sciat ipsam esse futuram'. Verbi gratia: 'Sortes prius naturaliter est animal [quod] <quam> sit homo; ergo Deus potest facere quod Sortes sit animal et quod Sortes non sit homo'."

tions, for example, without mentioning Auriol. Of course, Mirecourt does not mention any *modernus* at all. Mirecourt does not spend much energy responding to Aristotle (and Auriol), however, simply concluding "nevertheless, it stands that one is determinately true and the other determinately false."[86] Aristotle and Auriol were not Mirecourt's direct concern. Perhaps Rimini had done his job successfully after all.

Unlike Mirecourt, who devoted more than one long question to the future, the only question concerning future contingents of his Carmelite *socius*, Paul of Perugia, "whether God has certain knowledge concerning future contingents," is fairly short. Part of this Paul devotes to the growing debate at Paris over the content of God's foreknowledge. He has a discussion with a certain Franciscus, perhaps Franciscus of Treviso, over whether God can know different types of infinites, a question which involves such things as ratios between infinites. A certain Gerard also plays a part in this debate.[87] Most of Paul's treatment, however, again reflects the absorption of Auriolist foci into the discussion, and involves the consequence 'God knows X will be; therefore X will be', and the problems of necessity and contingency relating to the consequence. Paul's solution is basically the common one, and he stresses the necessity of the past, distinguishes between the the the necessities of the consequence and consequent, makes use of the difference between the composite and divided senses, follows the path associated with Ockham about propositions only vocally about the past, etc. He cites Alexander of Hales, and, interestingly, defends some of Thomas Aquinas's ideas which had not seen supporters for many years, at least outside the ranks of the Dominican order.[88] Like

---

[86] Mirecourt, *I Sent.*, q. 35 (Paris 15882, fol. 141rb): "Unde dicendum est de facto, si per impossibile Deus non plus sciret que pars eveniet quam nos sciamus, nichilominus tamen adhuc una pars contradictionis esset in talibus vera et reliqua falsa, si formetur."

[87] Paul cites a "Magister Gherardus, in *Summa*," almost certainly the Carmelite Gerard of Bologna (†1317), but possibly the "Gerardus Novariensis, in *Summa*" cited by Hugolinus de Urbe Veteri (Orvieto), *Commentarius in quattuor libros Sententiarum* I, d. 40, q. 4, a. 2 (vol. 2, ed. Willigis Eckermann [Würzburg 1984], p. 357, l. 61), since the contexts are similar. A transcription of Paul's q. 37, from ms. Praha, Narodni Museum XIII. D. 5, is in my "Quarrel with Aureol," pp. 789–96.

[88] See for example Paulus de Perugia, *I Sent.*, q. 37 (Praha, XIII, D. 5, fol. 117va): "Respondetur. Ad primam dico quod minor de inesse est duplex, quia quedam est de inesse simpliciter, scilicet quando predicatum habet necessariam habitudinem ad subiectum, sicud dicendo: 'Homo est animal, vel rationale'; alia est de inesse ut nunc, scilicet quando predicatum conditionatam habitudinem ad subiectum, sicud dicendo: 'Homo currit', quia non est vera nisi dum movetur modo. Dico quod ex maiori de necessario secundo modo, non; et sic est in proposito, quia: 'Antichristum fore est prescitum', ista est de inesse ut nunc.

Ad secundum nego assumptum. Ad probationem, dico quod omne de preterito verum quod est prescientie de preterito est necessarium; sed dictum de preterito includens in suo intellectu futurum non est necessarium. Sic est hic cum dico: 'Deus prescivit hoc fore futurum'.

Ad tertium, dico quod duplex est necessitas, scilicet consequentis et consequentie. Concedo ergo quod est necessaria necessitate consequentie, sed non consequentis, et sic hic dicit Anselmus. Sed hoc nihil est contra conclusionem, quia talis necessitas non solum compatitur secum consequentis contingentia, quin vero falsitatem, sicud in hac consequentia: 'Apparet si asinus volat, habet alas'.

Ad quartum dico quod distinguendus est intellectus (?) assumpto, quia potest intelligi in sensu composito vel diviso. Si primo modo, est verum quod inquantum scitum a Deo est impossibile non

Mirecourt, Paul makes no mention of Peter Auriol, and he cites Aristotle's *Peri Hermeneias* only briefly and largely through Boethius. The debate over the content of God's foreknowledge, accompanied by a more or less traditional Parisian account of contingency and necessity, perhaps interspersed with apparently shocking statements about the ultimate contingency of the past, continued in the period after the Black Death. The refutation of Peter Auriol's views, which dominated Parisian discussions of the problem from Auriol's own time to the mid-1340s with the Augustinian Hermits Gregory of Rimini and Alphonsus Vargas, faded for a quarter of a century in the face of this new excitement.

---

esse, et sic non intendo negare; sed in sensu diviso est possibile non esse, et sic si ponatur in esse, non fallitur sapientia vel scientia Dei, quia non accipitur sic ut infertur ad scientiam Dei. Et in isto modo dictum Sancti Doctoris potest intelligi sane, qui concedit quod quidquid scit necessario scit, et ideo concedit hoc consequens esse necessarium, scilicet: 'Hoc erit'. Nec infert de antecedente hec: 'Deus scit hoc fore, sed non absolute, sed inquamtum scitum a Deo'. Nec intendo negare quod hoc consequens sic modifi<ca>tum non sit necessarium absolute, ut ponit Sanctus Doctor talem regulam: 'Ut quando ponitur in antecedente quod pertinet ad actum anime, in consequente oportet accipere idem dictum, ut verbi gratia, si arguatur sic: «Omne quod intelligitur est immateriale; ergo lapis est immateriale», non sequitur absolute sed sic lapis est immateriale inquantum intelligitur.'"

Chapter 12

Auriol's Theory in the Late Middle Ages

One of the most spectacular episodes in medieval intellectual history was what is now generally known as the quarrel over future contingents at the University of Louvain in the late fifteenth century. Starting with his quodlibetal debates in late 1465, Peter de Rivo, a master of arts who had once lectured on the *Sentences*, began a systematic and high-profile defense of Peter Auriol's doctrine of divine foreknowledge and future contingents. Rivo no doubt had access to Auriol's own *Scriptum*,[1] but there were other conduits for the passing of Auriol's ideas to Rivo. In his *Sentences* commentary of 1378, Peter of Candia, later Pope Alexander V, expounded in great detail Auriol's defense of Aristotle's position denying that future-contingent propositions were true or false, and his unique theory of foreknowledge. Candia's discussion of Auriol was, besides the works of Auriol himself, the most important vehicle for the transmission of Auriol's treatment of the subject to Peter de Rivo. What else between Rimini's and Rivo's activities kept Auriol's ideas on the subject current, or at least current enough, for Rivo to adopt them as his own? What else stimulated Rivo to resort to such an unpopular position? Rivo himself provides us with clues, but despite the fact that over 700 pages of published Latin texts survive from the quarrel, we do not yet know about the general status of Auriol's doctrine in 1465.

General Trends 1348–1370

This era is largely unexplored, but I have looked at the treatments of over three dozen thinkers active between the Black Death and the Quarrel.[2] One thing we can say is that although Auriol's position was the focus of the problem of foreknowledge and future contingents at Paris in the quarter century af-

---

[1] See Schabel, "Peter de Rivo (Part I)," p. 381.
[2] For a recent general survey of the period after 1345, see Zénon Kaluza, "Late Medieval Philosophy, 1350–1500," in Marenbon, ed., *Medieval Philosophy*, pp. 426–51. For notes on the pertinent views of Andrew of Novocastro OFM; Henry of Cervo OP; the Augustinians John Klenkok, Bonsemblans, John Hiltalingen of Basel, and Facinus de Ast; the Carmelites Michael Aiguani and Francis Bacon; the Cistercian Conrad of Ebrach; and Richard Barbe, all active from 1350 to 1370, see my "The Quarrel with Aureol," pp. 299–327 (an edition of Hiltalingen's question for dd. 38–39, which cites the opinions of eight scholastics writing after 1340, is on pp. 798–807). For future contingents in this era and the sub-issues mentioned below, see especially Hoenen, *Marsilius of Inghen*, ch. 7; and also Hubert Elie, *Le complexe significabile* (Paris 1936); Courtenay, "John of Mirecourt"; and Friedman, "Andreas de Novo Castro."

ter his own lectures on the *Sentences*, it did *not* dominate either Parisian or Latin theology generally after the mid 1340s. Instead, there was a proliferation of sub-issues, some coming from Oxford and some already apparent in the works of Rimini and Alphonsus Vargas: the content of God's knowledge, revelation, and the modal status of the past. Indeed, in these decades, I have found in this context explicit citations of numerous Oxford scholars active in the first half of the century: Campsall, Ockham, Wodeham, Rodington, Kilvington, Buckingham, Bradwardine, William Heytesbury, Nicholas Aston, and the Carmelite Osbert Pickingham. As a result, while in the course of the fourteenth century the average size of *Sentences* commentaries was gradually reduced, the space devoted the questions involving future contingents actually increased, not only relative to the diminished length of the commentaries, but also in absolute terms.

The new foci of attention are reflected in the *Sentences* commentary of the Augustinian Hugolino of Orvieto, who read at Paris in 1348–49. Hugolino's treatment is large and he concentrates on the treatments of Rimini and Vargas, yet he does not discuss Auriol. At one point Hugolino does use some 'Auriolist' language, saying that "Any future whatever is eternally equally present to God through an *indistance* of duration."[3] Still, aside from the word 'indistant', there is little to indicate a concern with Peter Auriol. Moreover, the Cistercian Pierre Ceffons, who was a *socius* of Hugolino's, merely states on the basis of authorities that those theologians who say that God has no knowledge of the future except under a disjunction are in error, for even "I know the future in that way, because I know that this will exist or it will not exist."[4] There is no reason to think Ceffons was overly concerned with Auriol either.

Yet Hugolino's extensive discussion deals with revelation, the complex and incomplex content of God's foreknowledge, and the contingency and necessity of the past. He does not like Vargas's statements that equate the necessity of the future with the necessity of the past, although he does not mention that Vargas himself elsewhere held the past to be necessary in a stronger sense.[5] For Hugolino, the ontological status of God's foreknowledge, an issue intimately connected with the discussion of the *complexe* and *incomplexe significabile*, has particular prominence. It was to remain an important element of the Augustinian debate with, for example, John Klenkok (Oxford 1354–55), Bonsemblans Badoar (Paris 1358–59), and John Hiltalingen of Basel (Paris 1365–66), but members of other orders participated, for example the Dominican Henry of Cervo (Cologne ca. 1362), Bonsemblans's *socius* the Franciscan

---

[3]   Orvieto, *I Sent.*, d. 40, q. 1 (ed. Eckermann, p. 322): "Quodlibet futurum est Deo per indistantiam durationis aeternaliter aeque praesens."

[4]   Petrus de Ceffona, *In libros Sententiarum* I, d. 39 (Troyes, Bibliothèque municipale 62, fol. 59ra): "Et ex hoc patet quod manifeste errant illi theologi qui astruunt quod Deus nihil scit de futuro nisi sub disiunctione quia dicunt quod futura non sunt scibilia nisi sub disiunctione, quia ita ego scio futurum, quia ego scio quod hoc erit aut hoc non erit," reading 'aut hoc' instead of 'hoc aut.'

[5]   See Orvieto, *I Sent.*, d. 40, q. 3, a. 1 (ed. Eckermann, pp. 335–8) for Hugolino's discussion of Vargas, in which he also treats John Rathe Scotus and Rimini.

Andrew of Novocastro (Paris 1358–59), and the Cistercian Conrad of Ebrach (Paris 1370–71).

The Franciscan John of Ripa, who lectured on the *Sentences* around 1350, demonstrates that Parisian Franciscans had not abandoned Scotus over the years.[6] Thus Ripa follows Scotus in holding that the intellect knows the future via the determinations of the divine will, and Peter of Candia would later say that "Master John of Ripa's position is nothing but the Subtle Doctor's position explained at greater length."[7] Andrew of Novocastro would also adopt and clarify the Scotist position. Ripa adds remarks regarding the freedom and contingency of God's intrinsic will *ad extra*, perhaps indirectly against Auriol, for Ripa wants to avoid holding that God's intrinsic will is indifferent to being and non-being outside Himself.[8] That this is only indirectly related to Auriol is suggested by Schwamm's study of Ripa's ideas on foreknowledge, which is almost a primary source for Ripa's *Sentences* commentary: Schwamm mentions Auriol only in regard to the fact that Peter of Candia later treats him.[9]

But Ripa does not confine himself to the Franciscan debate. With Bradwardine, he does not want to go so far as to assert that God's will necessitates created wills,[10] but he does maintain that the created will is not absolutely free:[11] the necessity of the consequence and the determination of the divine will do not endanger human free will, but it is on a lower grade of freedom. On the other hand, without naming his adversary, Ripa attacks Wode-

---

[6] For Ripa's ideas on future contingents, see Hermann Schwamm, *Magistri Ioannis de Ripa O.F.M. Doctrina de Praescientia Divina.*

[7] For example Johannes de Ripa, *I Sent.*, d. 39, a. 1, conclusion 7 states: "Intellectus divinus respectu cuiuslibet veri contingentis de creatura habet evidentem noticiam ex sola predeterminacione intrinseca voluntatis" (Schwamm, *Magistri*, p. 52). Cf. Petrus de Candia, *I Sent.*, q. 6, a. 2 (ms. Vat. lat. 1081, fol. 128rb): "Undi si quis bene advertit, positio magistri Iohannis de Ripa nil aliud est quam positio Doctoris Subtilis diffusius declarata."

[8] Ripa, *I Sent.*, d. 39, a. 1, conclusion 4: "Voluntas divina respectu cuiuslibet effectus producibilis ad extra est intrinsece predeterminabilis per actum volendi vel nolendi, seu velle vel nolle...Nam si non, igitur quidquid est intrinsecum voluntati divine, est ex se indifferens ad esse vel non esse cuiuscumque effectus contingentis, et per consequens Deum velle A esse vel non-esse non est intrinsecum ipsi Deo, sed solum denominatio extrinseca relativa" (Schwamm, *Magistri*, pp. 48–9). I have checked Ripa's commentary on book I in Vat. lat. 1083, but I could not find any direct citation of Auriol, or indeed Aristotle's *Peri Hermeneias*, in Ripa's treatment of foreknowledge and future contingency.

[9] Schwamm's work on John of Ripa was an important second step (Ehrle's book on Peter of Candia being the first) to an understanding of the important discussion concerning future contingents in the late fourteenth century. When Schwamm wrote the book (1930), however, he was not fully conversant with Scotus's position, and it appears not at all with Mirecourt's, partially relying on later figures such as Hiltalingen to tell him that Ripa's position is 'Scotist' in many ways. Though of course Schwamm later (by 1934) became an expert in the thought of Scotus in the matter, it is important for someone to write a new and comprehensive history of the problem in the late fourteenth century based on what has come to light in the past 60 plus years. Hoenen has made an important contribution in this regard.

[10] For example Ripa, *I Sent.*, d. 39, a. 1: "Dico ergo quod talis necessitas non est necessitas antecedens ad voluntatem creatam agere... Sed talis necessitas est precise consequentie..." To which Schwamm concludes: "Interim sufficit notare posita determinacione voluntatis divinae infrustrabiliter et necessario sequi actum liberum creaturae. Stat tamen libertas, quia haec necessitas non est necessitas antecedens, sed necessitas consequentiae" (Schwamm, *Magistri*, p. 59).

[11] For example Ripa, *I Sent.*, d. 39, a. 4, conclusion 5: "Sola voluntas divina est simpliciter libera libetate contradiccionis..." (Schwamm, *Magistri*, p. 88).

ham, Rimini, and John of Mirecourt's statements indicating that a creature can make it so that God has never known what He knows, calling such remarks "childish and laughable."[12] As we have seen, Rimini and Mirecourt did not intend anything radical by such remarks, and Hiltalingen would assert that Ripa, "not Gregory, spoke in ignorance." But Ripa, leaning as he did to the side of determinism, even objected to the *apparent* subordination of the divine will to the created will, and thought those statements more than 'ill-sounding'. This argument over the modal status of and humans' power over the past, often stimulated by Bradwardine's treatment of antecedent necessity in *De causa Dei*, occupied scholars from every *studium* and every order in these decades, for example Facinus de Ast OESA (Paris 1361–63), Henry of Cervo, and the Carmelite Francis Bacon (Paris 1364–65).

With all of these exciting new developments, which for the most part presupposed that Auriol had been proven wrong about future contingents, Auriol was largely relegated to the background for the quarter century between Vargas and the Paris lectures of the Cistercian James of Eltville in 1369–70, with one notable exception: the anonymous Franciscan author of the first *Sentences* commentary in Vat. lat. 986 (fol. 1–31), a particularly rich source of citations, which help date it to about 1359.[13] I shall discuss him later. From 1370 on Auriol is again a factor, but not *the* factor, and the half-dozen or so important scholastics who treat him in the next four decades do so in apparent isolation from each other, so that there does not appear to be any intellectual conversation about his stance. Thus it would appear that Rivo did not pick up on Auriol's position because it was in vogue in the fifteenth century, or because everyone else was attacking it. We must look for other explanations, and there are several possibilities.

John Wyclif

The Hussite revolt in Bohemia was the Church's nightmare for decades until it was apparent that a larger Reformation was underway in the early sixteenth century. The participants at the Council of Constance had the theologian Jan Hus burned at the stake in 1415, but this did not end the Hussite threat. Hus had been heavily influenced by John Wyclif, who himself had helped to create

---

[12] For example Ripa, *I Sent.*, d. 39, a. 1: "Et ex hoc concludunt isti quod ego possum facere quod Deus ab eterno sciverit A fore, si A sit actus in potestate mea. Concludunt... multa consimilia, que satis sunt puerilia et digna derisu," and slightly later: "Non oportet multum laborare in respondendo, quoniam nedum apud theologum, sed apud omnem probabilem philosophum est danda contemptui et deresui" (Schwamm, pp. 60–61).

[13] For dating of the commentary see Katherine H. Tachau, "French Theology in the Mid-Fourteenth Century: Vatican Latin 986 and Wroclaw, Milich F.64," AHDLMA 51 (1984) (pp. 41–80), pp. 42–6. The author cites many Franciscans, whom Tachau lists together with his other citations on pp. 44–5. To her list could be added the following citations: Peter Auriol, 3ra, 28vb; 29ra, and 30rb; Nicolas of Autrecourt, 16rb; Geraldus Odonis, 24va; Monachus, 27vb; Alexander de Ianna (?), 28ra; Scotus, 28rb; Nicolas Bonet, 28rb and 28va; Osbertus Pickingham, 30ra; Kimmeton (?), 30ra; Astensius, 31vb; Bradwardine, 31vb.

a heterodox movement in England, the Lollards.[14] Wyclif later became known and condemned both for his determinism and for his posthumous role in the Hussite rebellion. As we shall see, in defending Auriol's position Rivo would hold that his adversary, Henry of Zomeren, was in danger of falling into the heresy of Wyclif, who, according to Rivo, held that all things came about of absolute necessity. Rivo expressly linked Wyclif's determinism with the Hussite problems of the Kingdom of Bohemia. Moreover, in a statute of the University of Louvain that Rivo had helped draw up in 1446, arts masters were warned generally not to explain Aristotle's text according to Wyclif. The statute, aimed against Zomeren among others, also included what appears to be a defense of Aristotle's position on future contingent propositions, and Rivo would use this statute for support years later.[15]

If opposition to Wycliffism was a factor in Rivo's decision to take up Auriol's position, however, it was not based on Wyclif's *writings*. Although Wyclif became master of theology at Oxford in 1372, his *Sentences* commentary is not extant, but we do have some logical treatises where he treats the problem of future contingents, mostly written in the 1360s. His *De universalibus* contains a substantial discussion of necessity and contingency.[16] Anthony Kenny has analyzed Wyclif's treatment in *De universalibus* and his supposed determinism, and rightly concludes that Wyclif was not a radical determinist, but rather orthodox by fourteenth-century standards.[17]

In addition to being orthodox, however, Wyclif was also, for the most part, unoriginal. In *De universalibus*, chapter 14, Wyclif puts forth his solution to the problem of foreknowledge and contingency, a solution heavily influenced by Aquinas, Scotus, and later developments. First, Wyclif draws the common distinction between absolute necessity and conditioned, or *ex suppositione*, necessity. Wyclif holds, along with Aquinas, that true contingents are necessary with respect to God's knowledge, but contingent in relation to secondary

---

[14] On Wyclif, Lollards, and Hussites, see the collection of essays edited by Margaret Aston, *Lollards and Reformers: Images and Literacy in Late Medieval Religion* (London 1984), another collection of articles by Anne Hudson, *Lollards and Their Books* (London 1985), and the second half of Anne Hudson and Michael Wilks, eds., *From Ockham to Wyclif* (Oxford 1987). For the intellectual climate surrounding Wyclif in the period between the Black Death and the Louvain controversy, see Jeremy I. Catto, "Wyclif and Wycliffism at Oxford 1356–1430," in idem and R. Evans, eds., *The History of the University of Oxford II: Late Medieval Oxford* (Oxford 1992), pp. 175–261.
[15] For Rivo's references to the Wyclif danger, see Baudry, *Querelle*, pp. 85–7, 403, and 455, and Schabel, "Peter de Rivo (Part I)," p. 442, ll. 38–41, and Part II, pp. 391, ll. 80–83; pp. 392–3, ll. 137–49; p. 409, ll. 1–4; p. 411, ll. 67–9; p. 415, ll. 221–3; and p. 435, ll. 141–7. The statute's warning against following Wyclif is in Baudry, *Querelle*, p. 68.
[16] Johannes Wyclif, *Tractatus de universalibus*, ed. Ivan J. Mueller (Oxford 1985), and John Wyclif, *On Universals (Tractatus de universalibus)*, trans. Anthony Kenny (Oxford 1985).
[17] Kenny's remarks about Wyclif and the Louvain controversy are in his "The Accursed Memory: The Counter-Reformation Reputation of John Wyclif," (pp. 147–68), pp. 156–9, in idem, ed., *Wyclif in His Times* (Oxford 1986), which is another rich collection of essays on Wyclif and his influence. A more lengthy discussion of Wyclif's orthodoxy in *De universalibus*, with regard to matters of necessity and contingency, is chapter 3, "Freedom and Necessity" in Kenny's *Wyclif* (Oxford 1985), pp. 31–41. See also Kenny's article "Realism and Determinism in the Early Wyclif" in Hudson and Wilks, eds., *From Ockham to Wyclif*, pp. 165–78.

causes. Thus, in the consequence 'God knows X; X will exist', the antecedent is eternal and necessary *ex suppositione*. Wyclif follows Scotus, however, in stressing that contingency is ultimately grounded in God, and that the consequence's antecedent is an eternal contingent truth. This truth is not absolutely necessary, and can be false, although God's willing cannot by any means change, begin, or cease.[18]

This is neither unorthodox nor innovative, nor particularly sophisticated. Wyclif even makes a point of arguing against Thomas Bradwardine's determinism, or at least against what some interpret to be his determinism.[19] If anything, on a superficial reading Wyclif leans toward an emphasis on human free will, rather than divine preordination. Thus Wyclif admits what John of Ripa thought ill sounding: that we can make the past not to have been. Of course, Wyclif explains that it is impossible to change the past, or to make a deflowered woman a virgin again, but the fact remains for Wyclif that the past could have been otherwise.[20] In this respect, again, Wyclif is in good company.

At the heart of Wyclif's solution is his reliance on the presence of things to God in eternity. Wyclif recognizes that the difficulty is in showing that God can will us to do something, yet we will freely. He admits we are not free to the same, ultimate degree God is, but stresses that some freedom must remain to save merit and demerit. To reconcile foreknowledge and freedom, Wyclif shows that conditioned necessity and contingent liberty are compatible, because in eternity the causal connection between the two goes both ways:

---

[18] Wyclif, *De universalibus*, ch. 14 (ed. Mueller, p. 332): "Hic oportet distinguere de necessitate: quod quaedam est absoluta quae non potest non esse, alia autem est necessitas ex suppositione quam oportet esse ex antecedente aeterno... Alia etiam est necessitas naturalis extra necessitationem creati liberi arbitrii et alia dependet a tali arbitrio. Alia etiam est necessitas coactionis... et alia est necessitas libera sive libertate contradictionis sive libertate a coactione"; p. 333: "Et sic omne verum contingens est necessarium secundum dispositionem divinae notionis, licet sint multa contingentia ad utrumlibet secundum causas secundas, nam sequitur: Deus vult vel scit hoc fore, ergo hoc est pro tempore suo. Antecedens est aeternaliter verum respectu cuiuscumque effectus praeteriti vel futuri. Ideo quoad praescientiam Dei omnem effectum est necessarium evenire"; p. 334: "Et patet, detecta aequivocatione necessitatis, quomodo cum summa contingentia stat conditionata necessitas"; p. 335: "Et patet ulterius quod fons primae necessitatis et primae contingentiae est in Deo... unde notandum quod, quamvis Deus potest contingentissime velle et non velle datum volubile, non tamen potest incipere vel desinere ipsum velle et sic non potest mutari de volutione in non-volutionem vel econtra." On the basis of this last quotation, I do not agree with Kenny that Wyclif "departs from his colleagues... in assigning unusual contingency to divine volitions" (*Wyclif*, p. 38), for Wyclif's remarks are not unusual at all in the fourteenth century.

[19] Wyclif, *De universalibus*, ch. 14 (ed. Mueller, p. 342): "Hic videtur Doctorem Profundum dicere quod in omni vero contingenti est par necessitas quoad Deum necessitantem et par impotentia impendiendi quemquam effectum quoad singulas creaturas. Sed, cum hoc stat summa contingentia quoad Deum! Sed videtur ex hoc tolli libertas arbitrii cum nemo foret sic dominus suorum actuum..."

[20] Wyclif, *De universalibus*, ch. 14 (ed. Mueller, pp. 346–7): "Sed facile est respondere ad ista, concedendo quod omnia futura necessario — necessitate ex suppositione — sunt futura, quae tamen contingentissime sunt futura. Et sic veritates sic necessitantes necessario fuerunt et tamen potest esse quod non fuerunt. Immo, tu potes facere quod non fuerunt et tamen non potest facere illa desinere fuisse vel commutare genitum in ingenitum. Et sic potes facere quod haec non fuit corrupta sed quod perpetuo fuit virgo, et tamen non potes mutare eam a corrupta in virginem."

On this it is to be noted that the volition of God, with respect to the existence of a creature, can be understood as a relationship: a mental entity with its basis in God's willing the thing to be according to its mental being — which is something absolutely necessary — and with its
terminus in the existence of the creature in its own kind. And such a relationship depends on each of the terms, since if God is to will that Peter or some other creature should be it is requisite that it should in fact
be. And thus the existence of the creature, even though it is temporal,
causes in God an eternal mental relationship, which is always in [the]
process of being caused and yet is always already completely caused.[21]

It is not my intention to analyze fully Wyclif's position, but only to show that
it is neither determinist nor unusual. Wyclif believed in the same, over-arching
contingency that many of his Oxford predecessors did. It is also true, however, that Wyclif annoyed many important people with his positions on subjects unrelated to the present one. By the time of the Council of Constance, his
notorious relationship with the Lollard and Hussite problems affected how
the participants in the council looked at all of his ideas. As Kenny notes, Wyclif himself warned that "no one should casually speak simply of contingent
and necessity,"[22] but this is exactly what they did at the council. The statement 'all things happen by absolute necessity', "truncated and taken out of
context," was condemned at the council, and forever afterwards Wyclif and
the Hussite heresy were linked with determinism, incorrectly it seems.[23]

As evidence that their interpretation of Wyclif's determinism was erroneous is the fact that Jan Hus himself, the most visible follower of Wyclif, had
nothing of note to say in distinctions 38 and 39 of book I of his *Sentences*
commentary, based on lectures at University of Prague in 1409.[24] Nevertheless, Wyclif's name, linked with determinism at Constance, would provide a
valuable weapon for Rivo years later in his fight with Zomeren. It is doubtful,
however, that one condemned proposition among many could have been
Rivo's prime motivation.

---

[21]   Kenny, *Wyclif*, p. 37, translating from *De universalibus*, ch. 14 (p. 343).
[22]   Kenny, *Wyclif*, p. 41, translating from *De universalibus*, ch. 8 (p. 166).
[23]   Kenny, "The Accursed Memory," p. 157.
[24]   Johannes Hus, *I Sent.*, d. 38, in *Joannis Hus opera omnia* II, ed. W. Flajshans and M. Kominkova (Osnabrück 1905; reprint 1966), p. 160: "Utrum prescientia Dei imponit necessitatem futuris contingentibus?" and p. 162: "Tunc ad questionem dicitur, quod in uno sensu est vera, puta
in isto: prescientia Dei imponit necessitatem, sc. condicionatam futuris contingentibus. Unde dicit
Bonaventura, ubi supra: 'In prescito non est necessitas absoluta, sed necessitas consequencie,
quia necessario sequitur «Deus prescit hoc, ergo hoc erit».' Hec ille. In alio autem sensu questio
est falsa, sc. in isto 'prescientia Dei imponit necessitatem, sc. absolutam vel coaccionis futuris
contingentibus', quia ex illo sensu sequeretur, quod nullum esset contingens ad utrumlibet, quod
est contra liberum arbitrium..."

Humanist Discussions

Anyone active in higher education in the latter half of the fifteenth century cannot have been completely unaware of the humanist currents of his day, which were a continuation of a movement that had been going on for a century. Even the proceedings of a 'conference' at Cardinal Bessarion's house in 1471 concerning Rivo and his adversary Henry of Zomeren is recorded in dialogue form, a humanist genre, certainly not the scholasticism of the universities. Rivo himself was professor of rhetoric, and his writings reflect an interest in polemics (against Zomeren) and history not found in *Sentences* commentaries with their predominant syllogisms and consequences. Moreover, as we shall see, in his first major writing Rivo emphasizes the ancient origin of the problem, not just with Aristotle, but with Chrysippus and Epicurus. In Rivo's next treatise he sets out to describe the "root of the dissension of theologians concerning Aristotle's opinion," framing his entire discussion in terms of the Chrysippus-Epicurus disagreement as reported in Cicero's *De fato*,[25] which is not treated by Augustine when he attacks Cicero in *City of God*.[26]

If we ask what is new and exciting about humanist discussions of foreknowledge and free will up to the time of the Louvain quarrel, however, the answer appears to be, 'not much', and it is likely Rivo's information about Chrysippus and Epicurus comes directly from Cicero, whose *De fato* was certainly available in Rivo's time.[27] The two most important humanist treatments of the problem in the late fourteenth and early fifteenth centuries are those of Coluccio Salutati and Lorenzo Valla. Salutati dealt with the issue at length in his recently edited *De fato et fortuna*, mostly completed by 1397.[28] Viewed in light of the historiographical tradition as it stood in 1970, Salutati appeared as something of an original contributor to the scholastic philosophical discussion in the eyes of Charles Trinkaus.[29] More familiar with recent scholarship, however, Ronald Witt, wishing to take nothing away from Salutati's faith, states: "The work [*De fato et fortuna*], while important as an indication of Salutati's intellectual life from this period, had nothing new to say on the problem of the relationship of an all-powerful God to man's moral responsibility."[30] Witt goes on to point correctly to the many possible sources of Salutati's ideas, above all Scotus, concluding: "Salutati borrowed his conceptions

[25]   For Rivo's discussion of Chrysippus and Epicurus, see the texts in Baudry, *Querelle*, pp. 71–2, 79, 367, and 372, and *Questio quodlibetica disputata Lovanii per Petrum de Rivo, anno LXIX*, in Schabel, "Peter de Rivo (Part I)," pp. 416–45, and mentions in Part II, e.g. pp. 389, ll. 8–22 and 404, ll. 12–13. Cicero treats Epicurus and Chrysippus in *De fato*, ch. 9 and 10.

[26]   That is, *De civitate Dei* V, ch. 9.

[27]   On the availability of *De fato* in the Late Middle Ages, see L.D. Reynolds, ed., *Texts and Transmission. A Survey of the Latin Classics* (Oxford 1983), pp. 76, 80, and 124–8.

[28]   Coluccio Salutati, *De fato et fortuna*, ed. C. Bianca (Florence 1985).

[29]   See Charles Trinkaus, *In Our Image and Likeness. Humanity and Divinity in Italian Humanist Thought*, vol. 1 (London 1970), pp. 76–102.

[30]   Ronald Witt, *Hercules at the Crossroads. The Life, Works, and Thought of Coluccio Salutati* (Durham, NC 1983), 316. Witt treats *De fato et fortuna* on pp. 315–30; see his notes for more of the secondary literature.

of evil and predestination almost *en bloc* from previous writers, yet his having nothing original to say did not indicate a lack of intensity in his convictions."[31]

Although Salutati is not the source of Rivo's interest in Auriol or the problem, nor of Rivo's references to Chrysippus and Epicurus, it is curious that the only 'nominalist' theologian with whom Salutati has been linked personally is Peter of Candia, who most certainly was both well-versed in Auriol's doctrine and a positive influence on Rivo, as we shall see. In addition, Candia's *Sentences* commentary was widely available in Salutati's Florence.[32] There are still no grounds for linking Rivo with Salutati, however.

Lorenzo Valla's *De libero arbitrio*, written in 1439, is less scholastic and more humanist than Salutati's *De fato et fortuna*. Perhaps for this reason, Trinkaus was able to find and present (and criticize somewhat) in the introduction to his translation such odd statements as these:[33]

> The Renaissance concept of individuality, rooted in the idea of the greatness and the uniqueness of man, naturally implies his liberty. It was therefore one of the primary interests of Renaissance thinkers to prove that divine foreknowledge does not circumscribe human liberty of action or invalidate man's creative role in history.

> [F]or the first time since the days of the ancients the problem of freedom was cited before a worldly forum, before the judgement chair of 'natural reason'... And still one traces above all in [Valla's] work the power of the new critical-modern spirit which begins to become conscious of its might and its intellectual tools.

This critical spirit was already at least a century old by Valla's day, of course, and Auriol's solution was driven by natural reason. Moreover, preserving human freedom was one of Auriol's prime goals all along, although in the humanistic climate of the fifteenth century his solution may have been more attractive to Rivo and his general audience.

At any rate, Valla has nothing philosophical in his discussion to stimulate a scholar like Rivo, so steeped in the deep scholastic discussion, nor does Valla introduce Cicero, Chrysippus, or Epicurus, but instead concentrates on Boethius. In fact, a recent overview of the humanist discussion agrees with this analysis, finding "little new" in Valla's admittedly influential treatise, and concluding: "Valla's undeniable fideism and his passionate condemnation of philosophical rationalism in theological debate account for the slenderness of his contribution to the controversy about freedom."[34] There were general wor-

---

[31]   Witt, *Hercules*, 329.
[32]   On Salutati's links with Candia and the availability of the latter's commentary, see Witt, *Hercules*, 319, n. 26
[33]   See Charles Trinkaus, "Lorenzo Valla," in E. Cassirer, P.O. Kristeller, and J.H. Randall, eds., *The Renaissance Philosophy of Man* (Chicago 1948), introduction pp. 147–54, translation pp. 155–82. The quotations are on p. 152, the first from R. Niebuhr, the second from Cassirer.
[34]   Antonino Poppi, "Fate, Fortune, Providence and Human Freedom," in C.B. Schmitt and Q. Skinner, eds., *The Cambridge History of Renaissance Philosophy* (Cambridge 1988) (pp.

ries in the mid-fifteenth century about Epicurean determinism, but we must conclude that when Rivo was led to a reevaluation of the entire problem, there was little new stimulus from Renaissance humanism, other than a general emphasis on human free will.

Secundum Rimini

Wycliffism and humanism were not primary motives for Peter de Rivo, but although Auriol's doctrine did not dominate the discussion after 1345, it did remain a factor, and there are many positive paths that Auriol's treatment could have taken to reach Rivo. One path is Gregory of Rimini. Rimini's lengthy attack on Aristotle and Auriol was known to Peter de Rivo and used as a source for older positions, although Rivo claimed, perhaps correctly, that Rimini did not read the whole of Auriol's treatment of the subject, and thus failed to understand it. Rimini was also followed closely by one of Rivo's main adversaries, Fernando of Cordova.[35] And not only was Rimini's own *Sentences* commentary available in many manuscripts in the fifteenth century, many late fourteenth-century theologians mimicked Rimini on the subject of future contingents, either explicitly or implicitly.

There is evidence that via Rimini Auriol's name had become linked with Aristotle's in stock arguments *ad oppositum* in the beginning of questions. Thus Rimini's fellow Augustinian Hiltalingen writes:

> There is no true future contingent; therefore the question is false. The consequence is noted, and one argues for the antecedent first: It follows that some proposition about a future contingent would be determinately true or determinately false, the opposite of which Aristotle proves in the book *Peri Hermeneias*, and some theologians agree with him, like Auriol.[36]

The author of a commentary in Vat. lat. 986 mentioned above also shows Rimini's influence. In the question for "distinction 33 and those following"[37]

641–67), p. 650. For Valla's later scholastic influence, one might mention that at the end of the 15th century John Major cites him in the context of future contingents. Cf. Johannes Maior, *In Primum Sententiarum*, d. 38, q. unica (ed. Paris 1510; 1519, fol. 95va)

[35]   For Rivo's citations of Rimini, see Schabel, "Peter de Rivo (Part I)," pp. 417, ll. 5–7 – 418, ll. 16–19; p. 429, ll. 152–4; and Baudry, *Querelle*, p. 228 and also p. 109, where Rivo complains of Rimini's and Franciscus's insufficient understanding of Auriol. The Franciscus in question was probably Meyronnes, for Marchia had extensive knowledge of Auriol's stance. Giovanni Gatti also cites Rimini, in Baudry, *Querelle*, 206. On Fernando and Rimini, see below, Epilogue.

[36]   Johannes Hiltalingen de Basilea, *In I Sententiarum*, dd. 38–39 (ed. Schabel, "The Quarrel with Aureol," p. 799, ll. 28–32): "Nullum est verum futurum contingens; igitur questio falsa. Consequentia nota; antecedens arguitur, tum primo: Sequitur quod aliqua propositio de futuro contingenti foret determinate vera vel determinate falsa, cuius oppositum probat Aristoteles in libro *Peryarmenias*, et concordant cum eo aliqui theologi, sicut Aureolus."

[37]   Anonymous, *In I librum Sententiarum*, d. 33 et sequentes (Vat. lat. 986, fol. 27rb): "Circa distinctionem 33 et sequentes, ubi Magister agit de predestinatione, quero utrum cum Dei

the discussion quickly turns to the necessity or contingency of the present. If true present-tensed propositions are contingently true, says our author, then the present is contingent and all things occur contingently. If, however, a true present-tensed proposition is necessarily true, then its corresponding future-tensed proposition was necessarily true in the past, and all things happen necessarily, or so suggests our author. The argument surrounds Aristotle's claim that *omne quod est, quando est, necesse est esse*, and the author puts a Master Jacob and Ockham on one side, defending the necessity of the present, and the Monachus Niger and Gregory of Rimini arguing the opposite. He cites Rimini's defense of the idea of God's simultaneous capacity for opposites, as put forth by Scotus. Our author sides with Rimini here, who was arguing against Auriol that God acts contingently in an instant.[38] Perhaps most of his discussion comes from Rimini.

Article two concerns whether this consequence is necessary: 'God foreknew the Antichrist would be; therefore the Antichrist will be'. The author denies that it is a necessary consequence, but, as we have seen in chapter seven, he cites Auriol, Nicolas Bonet, and Poncius as holding the opposite.[39] Here our author stresses the same point that Rimini had. The discussion of the antecedent is deferred to article three, which asks "whether, supposing contingency, foreknowledge exists concerning these [contingent things]?" The author immediately states a conclusion: "God determinately knows contingent futures and also present ones, and not only incomplex future things, but also propositions about future contingents."[40]

In defense of this claim the author gives scriptural backing, including, the famous quotation from Revelations 21.5: "Write. For these words are most

---

prescientia et eterna scientia stet vel stare possit rerum contingentia?"

[38]   These arguments are given in a. 1 (fol. 27rb–vb), e.g.: "Tertio et nostri difficilius: Aliqua propositio est contingenter vera, et aliquando verum est quod res est indifferens ad esse et non esse, aliter non esset contingenter vera; igitur res, quando est, contingenter est, et propositio, quando est vera, contingenter est vera; maior et communiter concessum, et Magister Jacobus et alii adversarii huius opinionis dicunt quod illud est possibile quod est indifferens ad esse et non esse... Quarto arguitur... si ista propositio nunc est vera, 'Sortes currit in ista mensura', fuisset propositio vera; igitur si ista est nunc vera necessaria quando Sortes currit, illa ab eterno fuisset necessaria, vel necessario vera, et sic fuit impossibile quin Sortes curreret... Sexto sic: Omne quod est, quando est, necesse est esse; sed omne ens est, quando est; igitur omne ens necesse est esse. Conclusio falsa... [fol. 27va] Septimo arguitur per argumenta Gregorii Hermite [tenens?] <tenentis> oppositum in primo suo: Deus, cum voluntate, potest actum voluntatis producere et non producere per B; et determinate in B est productus vel in B non est productus; igitur actus ille, quando est, contingenter est, et quando non est, contingenter non est... Contra conclusionem arguit Magister Jacobus, tenens oppositum... quarto arguitur per argumenta Ockham tenentis oppositum: Res, quando est, non est in potentia ad non esse... Pro solutione istorum pono distinctionem quam ponit Gregorius... res, quando est, potest non esse simpliciter et absolute, non per motum et mutationem, ut postea dicetur... [27vb]... ad tertium dico cum Monacho quod contradictoria possunt simul esse vera, ut ly 'simul' determinant ly '*potentiarum*', unde est ibi simultas *potentie*, et non potentia simultatis."

[39]   Anon., *I Sent.*, d. 33 et sequentes (Vat. lat. 986, fol. 28rb). See above, chapter 7.

[40]   Anon., *I Sent.*, d. 33 et sequentes (Vat. lat. 986, fol. 28va): "Tertius articulus est utrum, supposita contingentia etc., stet de illis divina prescientia? Pono hanc conclusionem, quod Deus scit determinate futura contingentia et etiam presentia, et non solum res futuras incomplexas, verum etiam propositiones de futuris contingentibus."

faithful and true." Then, interestingly, he explicitly cites John Rodington's citation of Richard Campsall's rules in his *Notabilia* about contingent propositions, e.g., "Some proposition about a future contingent is contingently true and cannot go from truth over to falsity, because if it is false now it was false *ab eterno.*" He gives ten of these rules.[41] Summarizing his position the author says he maintains along with Rimini the following: (1) God determinately knows all complex knowables; (2) He determinately knows all incomplex knowable things also; and (3) propositions about future contingents are determinately true now.

In opposition, however, he cites Auriol, giving the two 'Auriolist' propositions perhaps first cited in Michael of Massa, but made famous by Rimini: "If propositions about a future contingent were true, they would be inevitably and immutably true," and "If they were immutably true, all things would come about of necessity."[42] The author summarizes Auriol's arguments in defense of his propositions, and his accompanying conclusions that God does not know future complexes or incomplexes.[43] He does not, however, present Auriol's opinion comprehensively, for like Rimini he has no discussion of God's indistant knowledge, for example. Still, the question has been laid out in such a way that the reader sees the difficulty of the problem by the third article.

One could respond as Poncius does, says our author, by accepting the mutability of such propositions as 'so-and-so is predestined' and, therefore, the mutability of God's knowledge.[44] This has obvious difficulties, and our author merely answers by giving the traditional distinction between the composite and divided senses, relying on the contingency of God's willing in His eternal present, as he had shown via Rimini in article one. He goes on to say, as others had, that propositions such as 'Socrates will be' *will* be true, because:

> truth is not any thing... but it is a connotative term. Therefore we ought to say that it will be true rather than that it is true, such that the truth of this, 'Socrates will be', should be explained in this way: 'I announce that Socrates will be, and thus it will be as I say'; and so the truth of

---

[41] Anon., *I Sent.*, d. 33 et sequentes (Vat. lat. 986, fol. 28va–b): "dicit Apocalypsus Johanni: 'Scribe hec, quia verba fidelissima sunt et vera.' ...pono aliquas propositiones quas ponit Rodinton in primo suo — sint a Ricardo Compsaley. Prima est quod aliqua propositio de futuro contingenti est contingenter vera et non potest transire de veritate in falsitatem, quia si nunc est falsa, ab eterno fuit falsa." Tachau notes this passage as well when discussing Rodington's connections with Campsall. See *Vision and Certitude*, p. 217, n. 32.

[42] Anon., *I Sent.*, d. 33 et sequentes (Vat. lat. 986, fol. 28vb): "Contra tamen conclusionem principalem, que ponit quam tria, primum quod Deus determinate scit omnia scibilia complexa, et etiam res scibiles incomplexas, et quod propositiones de futuris contingentibus nunc sunt determinate vera: primum (*mg*: rationes Petri Aurioli) arguam contra ultimum a quo cetera dependent, et primo quod rationes Petri Aurioli, qui primo supponit quod si propositiones de futuro contingenti essent determinate vere, essent [se] inevitabiliter et immutabiliter vere. Secundo, si ille essent immutabiliter vere, omnia evenirent de necessitate."

[43] See Anon., *I Sent.*, d. 33 et sequentes (Vat. lat. 986, fol. 28vb–29ra) for the explanation of Auriol's stance.

[44] Anon., *I Sent.*, d. 33 et sequentes (Vat. lat. 986, fol. 29ra): "Ad prima argumenta (*mg*: ad argumenta Petri Aurioli) potest responderi per propositiones <Poncii> prius positas, nam illa argumenta supponunt quod propositiones de futuro possunt mutari de veritate etc."

this, 'Socrates will be' is future in the same way as the thing is to be put in reality, for the future, because the truth of the proposition exists only in the ordering of the proposition to the thing. And therefore the truth is now in the future (*futuro modo*)...[45]

The author of the commentary in Vat. lat. 986, while showing Rimini's influence, showed some independence in his knowledge of Bonet, Poncius, Campsall, and Rodington. In his emphasis on Auriol, however, he seems to be an isolated case between 1345 and 1370. After 1370 Auriol again plays a prominent role in the discussion, but, again, often via Rimini. In general the period is noted for reading *secundum alium* or 'according to another', what we might call plagiarism. More often than not, Rimini is the victim, and any of these 'Riminists' may have been available to Rivo.

One such thinker is the Cistercian James of Eltville, who lectured on the *Sentences* at Paris 1369–70. Damasus Trapp found that James read *secundum* Hiltalingen and that he found that James had taken "very many and copious passages" verbatim from Hiltalingen's work.[46] If James read *secundum* Hiltalingen in the many places of books I-II that Trapp inspected, he did not do so in his question on distinctions 38 and 39. He does, however, copy rather copious passages from the Augustinian Alphonsus Vargas of Toledo, and to a lesser extent Rimini, and probably others, without citing them. Therefore, in the cases where I have not identified his source, it is not possible to tell whether James is being original or not. At least he had the originality to use several sources, even if the resulting doctrine is a curious mix indeed.

Vargas had himself followed Rimini is his attack on Auriol, so not surprisingly, James too is very much aware of Auriol's position, although unexpectedly he considers it quite comprehensively. In fact he rejects most of what Auriol says, but important elements of Auriol's language find their way into James's own position: "From this conclusion I infer first that God has no memorative knowledge of the past nor expectative knowledge of the future. This is clear from the third proof of the conclusion, because God is *indistant* from every past and future, and presently and simultaneously exists with all." In this James follows Hugolino of Orvieto and was followed by the Augustinian Angelus de Dobelin (Paris 1374–75).[47] One would expect then that James would agree with Auriol's position, but he does not adopt it.

[45]   Anon., *I Sent.*, d. 33 et sequentes (Vat. lat. 986, fol. 29ra): "dico quod veritas non est aliqua res...sed est terminus connotativus. Ideo potius debemus [dici]<dicere> quod erit vera quam quod est vera, ita quod veritas huius 'Sortes erit' debet sic resolvi: 'enuncio quod Sortes erit, et ita erit sicut dico'; et sic veritas huius 'Sortes erit' est ita de futuro sicud res ponenda est, pro futuro, quia veritas propositionis non est nisi in ordine propositionis ad rem. Et ideo veritas est futuro modo..." Tachau, *Vision and Certitude*, p. 223, n. 56, finds our author using "terminus connotativus," via Rodington, to disarm Auriol's arguments claiming one could have intuitive cognition *de facto* without the object being present, since 'intuitive' connotes the presence of the object.
[46]   Trapp, "Augustinian Theology," p. 252.
[47]   Jacobus de Altavilla (Eltville), *I Sent.*, dd. 38–39 (Besançon, Bibliothèque de la ville 198, fol. 110rb; Cambrai, Bibliothèque de la ville 570, fol. 106rb): "Ex ista conclusione infero primo quod Deus nullam habet notitiam memorativam de preterito nec expectativam de futuro. Pa-

James cites Auriol at length in two ways, both in relation to James's first conclusion: "From eternity God distinctly and determinately has known every future infallibly to be future."[48] First he cites Auriol's opposition to divine foreknowledge involving his denial of truth in future contingent propositions. Here James paraphrases Gregory of Rimini. He summarizes Auriol's position in the two propositions from Auriol mentioned above that Michael of Massa and Rimini had used, i.e. that if a proposition about a future contingent is true, it is immutably and inevitably true, and if it is inevitably true now, its significate will necessarily be put in being. James paraphrases Rimini's own paraphrase of Auriol's defense, giving Auriol's conclusion that no such propositions are true or false, or known by God.[49]

James responds by first giving and defending two propositions, the first about how future-tensed propositions can go from truth to falsity and vice versa. This too is based on Rimini. The second states that "in an absolute sense it must be conceded that a true proposition about the future was able never to have been true," and James explains this by turning to the composite and divided senses of the proposition. Then to Auriol's position he simply denies that absolute necessity is involved, allowing only the necessity of the consequence.[50] This is the common position.

The second place James cites Auriol follows immediately upon the first, when James investigates how God could know the future. After quickly presenting and rejecting the stance based on divine Ideas of both complexes and incomplexes, he presents Auriol's position by quoting verbatim four propositions Auriol defended in his own distinction 38, article one. These propositions together hold that Deity and only Deity can be and is the eminent similitude and exemplar representing the actuality of all future contingents, existing

---

tet ex probatione conclusionis tertia, quia Deus est *indistans* a quolibet preterito et futuro, et presentialiter et simultanee adest omnibus." There is an indication that the notion of 'indistance' had many adherents toward to the end of the century. Angelus wrote, "Secundo, quia non quasi distanter Deus preteritis vel futuris est presens, sed eque presens sicud eternitas a qualibet parte temporis est indistans" (Angelus de Dobelin, *In I Sententiarum*, d. 38, a. 1 [Jena, Univ. El., fol. 54ra]). On Angelus and future contingents, see Schabel, "The Quarrel with Aureol," pp. 327–30.

[48] Eltville, *I Sent.*, dd. 38–39 (Besançon 198, fol. 109vb; Cambrai 570, fol. 106ra): "Quodlibet futurum Deus distincte et determinate ab eterno scivit et novit esse infallibiliter futurum."

[49] Eltville, *I Sent.*, dd. 38–39 (Besançon 198, fol. 111ra; Cambrai 570, fol. 107ra): "Contra conclusionem arguo primo sic per rationes Aurioli, qui tenet oppositum, quamvis bene suum argumentum potest reduci ad duas propositiones. Prima est ista, quod si propositio de futuro contingenti est vera, ipsa immutabiliter et inevitabiliter est vera. Secunda est hec: Si inevitabiliter est ipsa nunc vera, nunc ponetur sic necessario in esse." Auriol's position continues for almost a column. It might be noted that James gives Aristotle's position in *Peri Hermeneias* as the first principal argument against his own position on the question "Utrum divine scientie respectu quorumlibet futurorum infallibilis certitudo ipsorum que non necessaria sed contingentia sint ad aliquam contradictionem antecedentia?" (Besançon 198, fol. 109rb; Cambrai 570, fol. 105va).

[50] Eltville, *I Sent.*, dd. 38–39 (Besançon 198, fol. 111rb–va; Cambrai 570, fol. 107rb–va): "Secunda propositio, quod ante mensuram pro qua ponitur propositio de futuro verificari, licet absolute sit concedendum quod propositio vera de futuro potuit numquam fuisse vera, sed semper falsa, et econtra falsa numquam falsa sed semper vera, nullo modo tamen est concedendum quod quecumque earum posset mutari de veritate in falsitatem. Et ratio huius, quia prima istarum facit sensum divisum, qui est verus; secunda sensum compositum, qui est falsus..."

indistantly from them according to the line of succession.[51] While admitting that Auriol's position "could have some sense of truth," and incorporating portions of it, James still claims that it is not sufficient. He gives the argument Auriol himself leveled at the Ideas solution, and others had aimed at Auriol, that the position does not explain how God, as the exemplar, can distinguish between possible futures that will come about and those that will not. James wants to know what the basis of God's distinguishing between possibles and futures is, but Auriol, he says, does not give it.[52]

Considering James's procedure elsewhere, one cannot even conclude that he knew Auriol directly. Still, although part of James' information comes from Rimini, he seems to have known more about Auriol's position than the Augustinian had. James's portrayal of Auriol's opinion is docile, and James's description of Auriol is doubly important for our present purposes. James commentary on book I is extant in a half dozen or so manuscripts, no small number, but because of the fact that Henry of Langenstein in turn read James's commentary while visiting Abbot James's abbey at Eberbach, Auriol's ideas were copied and passed through that channel to the fifteenth century in a t least an additional four or five witnesses. James's question could also be one of the stimuli for Pierre d'Ailly's attack on Auriol's views, or Peter of Candia's much longer presentation of it.

In turn, Langenstein's own Sentences commentary, from his Paris lectures in the late 1370s, became a conduit for Auriol's ideas. Langenstein was enticed along with Henry Totting of Oyta to the new University of Vienna, one of the beneficiaries of the Great Schism with the exodus of German scholars. Book I of Langenstein's commentary is extant in only one manuscript: Alençon 144.[53] Michalski cites a quotation from Langenstein demonstrating that Auriol's position was known to Langenstein, for in his commentary he recognized that Auriol had claimed this proposition was false: "God knows that something is future or that something will be." Of course Langenstein says Auriol's own position is false.[54] An examination of Langenstein's book I, question six — one

---

[51]   See Eltville, I Sent., dd. 38–39 (Besançon 198, fol. 111vb; Cambrai 570, fol. 107va), for the citation.

[52]   See Eltville, I Sent., dd. 38–39 (Besançon 198, fol. 111vb; Cambrai 570, fol. 107vb): "Sed licet hoc posset habere aliqualem sensum veritatis, tamen non sufficit, quia ita Deitas est exemplar possibilium que non erunt sicut que erunt, et tamen equaliter sit exemplar quomodo distincte cognoscit et sic hec futura et illa non futura. Forte dicetur quod hoc est per hoc quia futura de facto ymitabuntur illud exemplar et non sic non futura. Sed hoc non valet, quia quero per quid Ipse hoc scit rebus non existentibus, quod hec ymitabuntur et hec non. Et sic stabit difficultas principalis."

[53]   For Langenstein see Michael Shank, "Unless You Believe You Shall Not Understand": Logic, University, and Society in Late Medieval Vienna (Princeton 1988). Langenstein's authorship of the Eberbach commentary is discussed and refuted on pp. 215–17. I have access to this commentary in manuscript Erfurt, Wissenschaftliche Bibliothek C.A. 2° 118, and the question for distinctions 38 and 39 (fol. 77ra–84ra) does match with Eltville's. Incidentally, Oyta, who sometimes follows Rimini in his Quaestiones, also treated Auriol on future contingents in Oyta's 'middle' version of his Sentences commentary contained in ÖNB 4690. See Schabel, "The Quarrel with Aureol," 364–5.

[54]   Michalski, "Le problème de la volonté," p. 85 (reprint, p. 365), quotes Langenstein from Alençon, Bibliothèque de la ville 144, though he wrongly cites fol. 77v, instead of the cor-

quarter of which, again, comes from Rimini — shows that he cites Auriol in several places, and not only with respect to Auriol's agreement with Aristotle's stance in *Peri Hermeneias*.[55]

Langenstein's legacy vis-à-vis Auriol, as with Eltville's, does not end with his own commentary, however. In the 1400s a new generation of theologians at Vienna (the 'Vienna group', I shall call them), heavily influenced by Oyta and Langenstein, lectured on the *Sentences*: Nicholas of Dinkelsbühl, Peter of Pulkau, Arnold of Seehausen, and John Berwart of Villingen. The relationship between these scholars, Oyta and Langenstein, and later theologians at Vienna such as John Wuel de Pruck and Thomas Ebendorfer de Haselbach (both around 1421–22), is extremely confusing. Let us begin by stating a few facts with respect to their questions on future contingents: (1) The questions on future contingents of Dinkelsbühl, Villingen, Pulkau, and Haselbach are virtually *identical* (I have not seen Seehausen's commentary).[56] (2) The title of Langenstein's book I, question six is the same as that of the Vienna group: "Whether every future contingent is eternally foreknown by God and determined toward coming about,"[57] and the texts of the Vienna group are identical to the first folio and a half of Langenstein, consisting of his principal arguments.[58] Immediately following their principal arguments, the texts of the Vienna group match the first folio of Langenstein's article two, which is also the same as Rimini's treatment of the possible ways God could know the future (which partly paraphrases Auriol in the first place). However, some of the members of the Vienna group (at least based on the manuscripts I have seen) omit Auriol's position as found in Rimini. (3) The quotation mentioned by Michalski actually comes from Rimini, though it is also in Pierre d'Ailly.[59] Langen-

rect 78r (78rb): "Ex his propositionibus manifestum est quod non est vera opinio Aurioli nec consona dictis Sanctorum et Scripturae quae dicit quod ista est falsa: 'Deus scit quod aliquid est futurum vel aliquid erit'."

[55] For example Alençon, fol. 73va, 73vb, and 76ra. On 73va, Langenstein discusses Auriol's opinion on how God knows things other than Himself.

[56] I have made a rough folio by folio table of Villingen, Dinkelsbühl, and Haselbach. In general, Haselbach and Dinkelsbühl agree. In several instances, however, Villingen adds, subtracts, or rearranges small sections, though otherwise he stays very close to the others.

[57] For example Thomas Ebendorfer de Haselbach, *I Sent.*, d. 38 (ÖNB lat. 4369, fol. 126r): "Utrum omne futurum contingens a Deo eternaliter sit prescitum et ad fore determinatum." Ebendorfer's question is in ÖNB 4369, fol. 126r-138r. I have access to question in Pulkau in ÖNB 4668, from fol. 200v on; to Dinkelsbühl in ÖNB 4820, fol. 102v–114r; to Villingen in Klosterneuberg, Augustinerchorherrenstift 41, fol. 86va–95va; to Pruck in ÖNB 5067, fol. 216r–240r; and to the anonymous author in Innsbruck, Universitätsbibliothek 677, fol. 161r–163v.

[58] Langenstein has two articles for his question. The Vienna group copies his preliminary remarks and principal arguments (in Alençon, fol. 71va–72ra), then almost immediately copies the first folio of his second article, "videndum est qualiter et quomodo huiusmodi futura contingentia certitudinaliter cognoscuntur a Deo" (Alençon, fol. 80ra–81va). After this, however, the texts diverge.

[59] Rimini, *I Sent.*, d. 38, q. 2, a. 1 (ed. Trapp-Marcolino, p. 277, ll. 6–8): "Ex praedictis patet manifeste quod nec vera nec consona dictis sanctorum et scripturae est opinio illius doctoris, qui dicit quod ista est falsa 'Deus scit quod aliquod est futurum vel quod aliquid erit'." Petrus de Alliaco, *In libros Sententiarum* I, q. 11 (ed. Paris s.a., fol. 165ra): "Ex his patet manifeste quod periculosa est et fidei contraria opinio Aurioli que dicit quod hec est falsa: 'Deus scit quod aliquid est futurum'."

stein's wording is closer to Rimini's, but Langenstein does not use the quotation in the context of a larger Rimini citation. Thus the Vienna group, whose collective *Sentences* commentary is probably almost entirely a cut-and-paste work of sections of Langenstein and Oyta,[60] included Langenstein's paraphrase of Rimini's description of Auriol's position, so that their audience and readers came into contact with Auriol.

Yet another figure who is known to have 'borrowed' what would now be considered the intellectual property of others was the secular theologian and polymath Pierre d'Ailly, who read the *Sentences* at Paris around 1375–76. Unlike others, however, d'Ailly cites his sources occasionally in his *Sentences* commentary, and more often than not, in the context of divine foreknowledge the font is Gregory of Rimini, whom d'Ailly follows and even copies throughout his future contingents treatment. Indeed, Peter de Rivo himself knew d'Ailly's work, and recognized his heavy dependence on Rimini and, therefore, opposition to Auriol.[61] Answering the question, "whether the contingency of things exists along with God's knowledge," which is to cover distinctions 35 through 39, d'Ailly first gives Aristotle's position, and Rimini's presentation and refutation of Aristotle, noting that William of Ockham was also aware of Aristotle's stance in *Peri Hermeneias*. He does not mention Auriol by name in this section, merely noting that "a certain catholic doctor asserts the aforesaid conclusion of the Philosopher to be true," and giving the summary of Auriol's position that Rimini and James of Eltville gave. D'Ailly continues with his summary of Rimini, occasionally throwing in something he picked up somewhere else, but never citing anyone who lectured during the thirty years between Rimini and himself.[62]

More clues as to the precise relationship between d'Ailly and Rimini surface when D'Ailly returns again to Auriol in asking "whether God is the foreknowledge of all future contingents." This time he cites Auriol by name, and gives his opinion denying such foreknowledge, an opinion that d'Ailly calls

---

[60]　For example most of Oyta, Graz, fol. 172rb is in Dinkelsbühl, ÖNB 4820, fol. 109v; Oyta 187ra equals Dinkelsbühl 113v; Oyta 181va is Dinkelsbühl 112r, etc.

[61]　See Rivo, *Questio quodlibetica*, in Schabel, "Peter de Rivo (Part I)," p. 417, ll. 5–11. For d'Ailly on issues related to future contingents, see various citations in Courtenay, *Covenant and Causality*; Normore, "Future Contingents," pp. 377–8; and Courtenay, *Capacity and Volition*, pp. 178–81. There is also Leonard Kennedy's *Peter of Ailly and the Harvest of Fourteenth-Century Philosophy* (Lewiston, NY 1986), which concerns God's powers and modality. This work, however, is suspect. For example, although Kennedy covers material of present concern, he makes no mention of d'Ailly's wholesale copying from Rimini. In fact, Kennedy only mentions Gregory of Rimini twice, in lists of important names. For d'Ailly's paraphrasing Rimini and, to a lesser extent, Ockham, in the later questions of book I, see Paul Bakker and my "*Sentences* Commentaries of the Later Fourteenth Century," in Evans ed., *Commentaries on Peter Lombard's Sentences*, forthcoming.

[62]　D'Ailly, *I Sent.*, q. 11 (ed. Paris, fol 156vb): "Utrum cum Dei scientia stet rei contingentia." Aristotle's position is given briefly in the same place, then at greater length at fol. 157rbA–157vaC, and Auriol's position is discussed at fol. 157vaD: "Tamen etiam quidam doctor catholicus predictam conclusionem Philosophi asserit esse veram, et ostendit inconvenientia sequi ad oppositum. Ad cuius declarationem probat duas conclusiones..." The summary of Rimini continues for several folios, with some interjections.

blasphemous and dangerous.[63] Paraphrasing Rimini, D'Ailly devotes one half of a column to him, then cites him again almost immediately concerning divine Ideas as a basis for knowing futures.[64] Recall that Auriol himself rejected the Ideas solution, although he found Scotus's rejection of that same solution inconclusive. The marginal comment in the Paris edition of d'Ailly says that "Auriol seems to hold this [Ideas] position," and in the next column, after citing Scotus's opposition to this solution, d'Ailly states, "It is true that Auriol said these arguments [of Scotus] were not efficacious against that opinion." The question is, did d'Ailly have Auriol's text in front of him or Rimini's? When Rimini discusses the Ideas position, he cites it via Auriol, as the editors of Rimini note. Rimini does not name Auriol, because he knows it is not Auriol's position. Thus when Rimini relates, "Another man says these arguments are not efficacious, etc.," he means Auriol, but Rimini is also aware that Auriol did not actually hold the position, because he knows that Auriol rejects it just afterwards. If d'Ailly were reading Auriol, he would not take the Ideas position to be Auriol's, especially given the fact that Auriol goes on to devote an entire article to his own very different solution. According to the marginal comment in his own commentary (in the Paris edition, at least), d'Ailly was unaware that Auriol's rejection of Scotus did not entail that Auriol himself held the divine Ideas position. Thus, because of this error, d'Ailly sounds a bit silly in his response to Auriol's comment about Scotus's arguments: "I don't care about [what Auriol said], because whether it is thus or not, this opinion is false anyway..." Rimini himself added almost the same words, without the "I don't care," and *with* over fifty lines of detailed argument that d'Ailly did not wish to copy.[65]

D'Ailly knew Rimini's text well enough to jump around, and he did not simply read him word for word, start to finish, as some scholastics did. It is still the case, however, that in this question it is most likely that d'Ailly had only Rimini's text in front of him, and did not read anyone else. Nevertheless, d'Ailly is another way in which Auriol's ideas may have been passed to Rivo: d'Ailly's commentary exists in four printed editions and eight manuscripts. By

---

[63] Michalski noted this in his quest to find the man who defended a three-valued logic. Michalski chased him through Rimini and d'Ailly, and finally found Auriol's name in Henry of Langenstein (see Michalski, "Le problème de la volonté," pp. 82–5 [reprint, pp. 362–5]). Hoenen also mentions d'Ailly's remarks (*Marsilius of Inghen*, p. 198).

[64] The question in a. 2 (fol. 164vbF): "Quantum ad secundum punctum in quo videndum est utrum Deus sit prescientia omnium futurorum contingentium, sciendum est..." Auriol's position is on fol. 165ra–b, B. Compare Rimini, *I Sent.*, d. 38, q. 2, a. 1 (ed. Trapp-Marcolino, pp. 274–7).

[65] D'Ailly's marginal comment is found on fol. 165rbC: "Prima opinio, quam videtur tenere Auriolus." His comments on Auriol's reaction to Scotus's rejection of divine ideas are on fol. 165va, C: "Verum est quod Auriolus dicit has rationes non esse efficaces contra opinionem illam. Sed de hoc non curo, quia sive sic sit sive non, tamen ista opinio falsa est..." For Rimini's remarks, see Rimini, *I Sent.*, d. 38, q. 2, a. 2 (ed. Trapp-Marcolino, pp. 278, l. 24–279, l. 10). Rimini's arguments against ideas are from p. 279, l. 16 to p. 280, l. 39, where he concludes: "Sive tamen rationes illae simpliciter sint efficaces contra opinionem sive non, ipsa opinio in se stare non potest..." For d'Ailly's strict reliance on Rimini throughout this question, see the chart of corresponding passages in my "The Quarrel with Aureol," p. 334.

1469, Rivo's knew d'Ailly's opinion on the matter, and that he followed Rimini.

Return to Past Masters

Another figure whom Rivo cited, this time in support, was Peter of Nugent. Nugent was part of the conservative movement to return to the old masters, that is Aquinas and Scotus, in the turmoil of the Great Schism and the frustration of the failure of fourteenth-century scholastic theology. These conservative theologians often saw Peter Auriol as their champions' most dangerous foe. In the case of Nugent, it is fairly clear he was a Scotist, at least in the matter of future contingents. Nugent read the *Sentences* at Paris in 1403–04, and continued to teach at the university for several years. Doucet found that the Carmelite William of Domqueur read *secundum* Peter of Nugent at the *studium* in Angers in 1466. Doucet discovered a manuscripts of Domqueur, Vat. lat. 1090, to go with Nugent's Pamplona, Biblioteca de la Catedral 36.[66] I have examined them, and they both contain the same question on future contingents. Fortunately, Peter de Rivo quotes Nugent much later in the controversy at Louvain. Rivo's citations are contained virtually verbatim in both manuscripts, and we can now be certain that Domqueur, at least in his discussion of future contingents, was literally reading Nugent's *Sentences* commentary.

It has been claimed that Nugent actually was one of Auriol's supporters. Reading Rivo's text, however, we merely find that Nugent is a Scotist, and like all strict Scotists on this matter, he held that in the first instant of nature in the divine mind, the divine intellect knows propositions about the future as neutral, and not determinately true or false. Of course in the second instant of nature the divine will makes these propositions determinately true or false, and in the third or fourth instant the divine intellect knows them as such. If one thinks on that basis that Nugent supported Auriol's position, one would have to say the same for just about any Scotist. Nugent was not a follower of Auriol, and I have found no one between Auriol and Rivo who really was. Peter de Rivo had to elicit any kind of support he could, however, and besides Nugent he also called upon Peter of Candia. Taken out of context, Peter of Candia could give strong support also, but, as we shall see, he was not a supporter of Auriol's 'three-valued logic' either.[67]

What Baudry did not have was Nugent's text to see whether he was an Auriolist. As Rivo says, Nugent was "treating the matter of future contin-

---

[66] For Nugent's dates, see the *Chartularium Univeritatis Parisiensis* IV, eds. Heinrich Denifle and E. Châtelain (Paris 1897; reprint Brussels 1964), p. 98, which lists Nugent as "actu legenti *Sententias*" on 21 October 1403, on p. 161, "Licentiatus in Facultate Theologiae" in 1408, and on p. 180, "Magister in Theologia." V. Doucet read vol. III of the *Chartularium* (Paris 1894; reprint 1964), p. 457, incorrectly and obtained the date 1350. For Doucet's discussion, see *Commentaires sur les Sentences*, pp. 69–70. Doucet's source actually says that Nugent was a regent master in arts and a student in theology on 31 July 1387.

[67] For Rivo's citations of Nugent, see Schabel, "Peter de Rivo (Part I)," pp. 387–8, n. 52.

gents," and Nugent asks "on the matter of future contingents whether God has certain and infallible knowledge of future contingents?" In the long question Nugent follows Scotus closely, in article one explaining then refuting through Scotus various Thomist solutions, based on divine Ideas, the presence of things to God in eternity, and the distinction between things being necessary with respect to God but contingent in themselves.[68] In article two Nugent asks how contingency is in things, where it is, and how certitude and contingency are compatible. When he gives the argument that contingency is a *per se notum*, he says "these two great doctors, Auriol and Scotus," prove it best.[69] He goes on to discuss Auriol's position at length in a full eight columns of the Pamplona manuscript. Significantly, none of this material is from Auriol's distinctions 38 and 39; it is a quotation of most of distinction 47, article one, of Auriol's *Scriptum*, where, against Aquinas and Scotus, Auriol presents his theory of the divine will.[70] Nugent presents Auriol in a more favorable light on this issue than just about anyone else, but as Rivo knew, Nugent did not actually follow Auriol, and he immediately went on to refute Auriol's argument, for seven columns.[71] Although a dubious ally, Nugent was nevertheless a possible source of Auriol's ideas on the will for Rivo, and perhaps it is no coincidence that Domqueur read *secundum* Nugent in 1466, just after the quarrel had begun, and that only in December 1466 does Rivo show familiarity with Auriol's will distinction.

While Nugent championed Scotus, the Parisian Dominican John Capreolus was the Thomist defender par excellence. Capreolus's first part of his *Defensiones theologiae Thomae Aquinatis*, as his *Sentences* commentary is called, includes the distinctions on future contingents and was written after 1408, and probably ca. 1422. Capreolus's principal adversary on most topics dealing with God (book I) was Peter Auriol, and sometimes when Capreolus has to defend Aquinas against Scotus or others, his source for the ideas of Aquinas's attackers is still Auriol. In the problems of divine foreknowledge, future contingency, and predestination, Auriol is again the main opponent.[72] Capreolus

---

[68]   Petrus de Nongento, *In primum, secundum, et tertium Sententiarum* I, q. circa materiam de futuris contingentibus (Vat. lat. 1090, fol. 83va; Pamplona 36, fol. 89ra): "Circa materiam de futuris contingentibus quero utrum Deus habeat notitiam certam et infallibilem de futuris contingentibus. Videtur quod non, quia secundum Philosophum in libro *Peryarmenias*, de futuris contingentibus non est determinata veritas." The solutions and their refutations are given in a. 1, Vat. lat. 1090, fol. 83va–85ra.

[69]   Nongento, *I Sent.*, q. circa materiam f.c., a. 2 (Vat. lat. 1090, fol. 85rb–vb; Pamplona 36, fol. 91vb): "Quantum ad secundum videndum est utrum contingentia sit in rebus, ubi sit, et si sit, quomodo certitudo stare potest cum tali contingentia," and (Vat. lat. 1090, fol. 85rb): "Isti duo magni doctores Aurioli et Scotus..."

[70]   Nongento, *I Sent.*, q. circa materiam f.c., a. 2 (Pamplona 36, ff. 93vb–95vb) = Auriol, *Scriptum* I, d. 47, a. 1 (ed. Halverson, ll. 168–248, 279–91, 303–313, 313–43 [skimmed], 344–65, 384–402, 406–80, 494–508, 531–603, 611–92).

[71]   The refutation begins (Vat. lat. 1090, fol. 89va; Pamplona 36, fol. 95vb–97va): "In precedenti lectione posita est opinio Petri Aurioli de futuris contingentibus. Nunc restat eam improbare et respondere ad rationes suas."

[72]   Thus Halverson, *Peter Aureol on Predestination*, p. 158, states that "Aquinas's most influential late Medieval apologist, John Capreolus, saw Auriol's version of GE as the only significant threat to Aquinas's understanding of predestination." Unlike Capreolus, the Oxford

devotes even more of his distinction 38 to Auriol than did Peter of Candia, more than 1400 lines. 600 lines are quoted verbatim from Auriol, 500 to give Auriol's position, and 100 to give the positions of others, including Scotus. Thus Capreolus used Auriol's text as a source that summarized the positions opposed to that of Aquinas that were developed between the time of Aquinas' death and Auriol's *Scriptum*.

It must be said that Capreolus does an excellent job of defending Aquinas on this issue. His main thrust, against both Auriol and Scotus, is to point out that they were too selective in what they sifted out of Aquinas' doctrine. Of course Aquinas was too prolific for everybody to search through his entire œuvre for the most favorable reading, and only a diligent apologist would do so. Capreolus knows Aquinas, and if anyone were certain that he understood Aquinas' position after reading Scotus and Auriol, he would feel confused after looking through Capreolus. Scotus and Auriol's attack was directed at a few points: the presentiality of future things to God's eternity; the contingency of things deriving from secondary, proximate causes; the solution based on divine Ideas; the same things being considered necessary with respect to God, but contingent in themselves, etc. Auriol also attacked the necessity *ex suppositione* connected with Aquinas' notion of divine foreknowledge. In all cases, either Capreolus shows that Aquinas' position is more complex than Scotus and Auriol gave it credit for being, or he shows how they were incorrect in their criticism.

The relationship between Capreolus and Auriol is certainly a subject worthy of continued study. I will merely pose two questions. First, what are the main differences between Capreolus and Auriol? They have vastly differing notions of what is intrinsic to the divine will. Auriol says that intrinsically God is necessary, and therefore if there is to be contingency in the world, God must be content with either side of each and every contradiction indifferently. If God intrinsically wills to create the world, then it was impossible for Him not to have willed the world, since what is possible for God intrinsically, is actualized in God. Intrinsically willing X and intrinsically willing not-X are not the same, and a God who does one is not the same as the God who does the other.[73] Sometimes God does 'choose' intrinsically, as in Auriol's doctrine of general election, where God says He will accept certain people based on certain conditions being met. In this case, these conditions are absolutely necessary, since they are set up by God's intrinsic will.

Capreolus denies that God is intrinsically indifferent in the way Auriol describes. God's intrinsic will is in fact necessary, but its relationship with things outside God is contingent. This relationship is a mere 'respect of reason', and

---

Dominican Thomas Claxton (ca. 1400), otherwise considered a Thomist (see Courtenay, *Schools and Scholars*, p. 360), appears to have held a somewhat Scotistic view on this issue (see my "Quarrel with Aureol," pp. 353–5).

[73] Capreolus's quotation of Auriol's position is in Johannes Capreolus, *Defensiones theologiae Thomae Aquinatis* I (henceforth as *I Sent.*) d. 38, a. 1, in *Defensiones theologiae Thomae Aquinatis* II, eds. Ceslaus Paban and Thomas Pègues (Tours 1900; reprint Frankfurt 1967), pp. 442a–443a.

not real, and thus, according to Capreolus, Auriol confuses God Himself with the relation God has to the world. The God who wills the creation of the world is not different from the God who wills the non-creation of the world, because the 'disposition (*habitudo*) toward a secondary object' (in this case the world) is not part of God. God can either will or not will the world's creation, but this does not admit possibility into God, and God is the same in either case.[74] Thus God actually wills things by His intrinsic will, and can will otherwise, but this has no bearing on God's necessity, and that He wills one or the other adds nothing to God intrinsically.[75]

When Auriol argues that the necessity *ex suppositione* which accompanies God's willing, if it is intrinsic, is equivalent to absolute necessity, Capreolus denies it:

> I say that there is no contingency in God, but only necessity, although an act of the divine will has contingent dispositions with respect to secondary objects. For it only has a necessary disposition with respect to what is willed principally, namely His goodness; but with respect to other things, it does not have a necessary ordering absolutely, but [only] *ex suppositione*; for supposing that God wills or willed something, it is impossible for Him not to will or to have willed, so that His will is immutable; whence necessity of this kind is known among theologians as the 'necessity of immutability'.[76]

Of course Capreolus in turn ignores Auriol's position on the external 'will of operation', with which God does actively will things, like create the world. This would seem to be a vulnerable part of Auriol's stance, but Capreolus is

---

[74] Capreolus, *I Sent.*, d. 38, q. 1 (ed. Paban-Pègues, p. 444a–b): "Dico quod argumentum peccat per fallaciam dictionis; mutatur enim quid in ad aliquid. Nam, cum dicitur 'velle non entitatem mundi potuit in Deo esse ab eterno,' in hoc quod dico, 'velle non entitatem mundi', non solum includitur actus divinae voluntatis, sed etiam habitudo ad objectum secundarium, scilicet non entitatem mundi...; et ideo, cum illud sumitur sub ista majore, quidquid est possibile, etc., mutatur quid in ad aliquid... Sed determinatio ad actum vel objectum contradictorium, non fuit aeternaliter in Deo, et fuit possibilis esse in Deo. Sed cum arguit, 'quidquid fuit possibile poni in Deo, est actu in Deo; sed determinatio ad mundi non entitatem,' etc.; — dico, sicut prius, quod committitur fallacia figurae dictionis. Cum enim dicitur in minori, quod determinatio ad hoc, etc., ibi includitur relatio ad objectum. Ad secundam, eodem modo. Falsum enim est quod omnis determinatio intrinseca Deo possibilis, insit Deo actualiter. Determinatio enim dicit unum actum absolutum, et respectum ejus ad unam partem contradictionis; modo, licet ille actus absolutus necessario sit in Deo, non tamen illi respectus..."

[75] Capreolus, *I Sent.*, d. 38, a. 1 (ed. Paban-Pègues, p. 445a): "Idem actus divinae voluntatis potest indifferenter cadere super utrumque istorum contradictoriorum: Petrus currit, Petrus non currit; et dum cadit super alterum tantum, ita quod non super aliud, non sibi aliquid additur intrinsece, sed solum respectus rationis ad tale vel tale objectum."

[76] Capreolus, *I Sent.*, d. 38, a. 1 (ed. Paban-Pègues, p. 444b): "Ad tertiam dico quod in Deo nulla est contingentia, sed mera necessitas, licet actus divinae voluntatis contingentes habitudines habeat ad objecta secundaria. Solum enim habet necessariam habitudinem respectu principalis voliti, scilicet suae bonitatis; sed respectu aliorum, non habet necessarium ordinem absolute, sed ex suppositione; supposito enim quod Deus aliquid velit vel voluerit, impossibile est eum non voluisse vel non velle, eo quod ejus voluntas est immutabilis; unde hujusmodi necessitas, apud Theologos vocatur necessitas immutabilitatis..."

mostly interested in defending Aquinas, not in attacking Auriol's position for its own sake.

Capreolus admits a strong sort of necessity *ex suppositione* here, one that Auriol would not have accepted. To avoid this type of necessity, Auriol said that God knows future contingents indistantly, not as future. Although Auriol had argued against Aquinas's notion of things being present to God in eternity, Auriol's theory was still rather close to Aquinas's. Capreolus is not willing to move to Auriol's 'indistant' solution, and instead wholly embraces necessity *ex suppositione* in article two, where he gives his position in a series of eight conclusions. For our purposes, the gist of this second article is the same as before: Auriol rejects necessity *ex suppositione*, Capreolus does not; Auriol says 'God knowing X' is not the same as 'God knowing not-X', Capreolus denies this difference. One is tempted to say that Auriol is here a realist, holding that God with a certain positive intrinsic disposition, or respect of reason, toward a secondary object in the world object, is ontologically different from a God without the disposition, or with a different disposition. Capreolus is less of a realist, holding that God's disposition to secondary objects is unimportant. Thus for Capreolus, if God knows X, then He necessarily knows X, by necessity *ex suppositione*; but God is able not to know X, in the divided sense, because the God not knowing X is not a different God from the God knowing X. Both agree, of course, that God must be as He is. The question is, what *is* God?[77]

The second question we must ask is, what role did Capreolus's treatment of Auriol here (and elsewhere) play in passing Auriol's position on to Rivo? At this stage of research, it is not possible to tell. Perhaps Rivo knew, or even learned from Capreolus's work, but did not cite him because of the latter's vehement opposition to Auriol.

Peter of Candia

What is certain is that Peter de Rivo drew significant support from the Greek Franciscan Peter of Candia, who may even have introduced Rivo to Auriol's theory. Nevertheless, Candia did not adopt Auriol's stance, contrary to a common historiographical opinion based on misleading remarks from Rivo. Still, Candia's text provides a good picture of the common attitude toward Auriol's opinion on the matter toward the end of the fourteenth century, and illuminates the overriding theological, rather than strictly logical, basis of Auriol's entire discussion.

---

[77] Halverson, *Peter Aureol on Predestination*, pp. 166-8, sees a related problem in soteriology, except that he thinks Capreolus both failed to understand Auriol and thought Auriol had not understood Aquinas. In future contingents, I think they understood each other's position, but disagreed.

Peter of Candia was born to Greek parents around 1340 in Crete, then a Venetian territory.[78] Orphaned at a young age, Candia was raised by a community of Franciscans, whose order he joined in 1357. He studied at the Franciscan *studium generale* in Norwich, was a bachelor of theology at Oxford, and finally he lectured on the *Sentences* at Paris in 1378–80. The following year he became a master of theology, and from that point Candia rose in the ecclesiastical ranks, becoming cardinal priest of the Church of the Twelve Apostles in 1405. Meanwhile Candia held various secular offices for the Duke of Milan, Giangaleazzo, and Candia came into direct contact with humanism and the leading humanists of the day, including Salutati. In 1409 the Council of Pisa elected Candia pope in an attempt to end the Great Schism. Although the two other popes were deposed at Pisa, they refused to step down, and Candia, now Alexander V, died in the following year as one of three popes.

Peter of Candia's *Sentences* commentary was one of the most popular of the Late Middle Ages, and over three dozen witnesses of major portions survive. Candia's treatment of foreknowledge, question six, article two, of book I, at about 3000 lines, ranks among the largest single medieval treatments of the problem.[79] Candia begins the discussion by presenting Aristotle's position with Averroes's comments. Unlike most theologians, however, Candia does not emphasize Aristotle's treatment in *Peri Hermeneias*, but instead concentrates on other *loci* in the Philosopher's *opera* that, by showing that God cannot know singulars, cannot know corruptibles, and so forth, taken together deny divine knowledge of future contingents. Second, Candia refutes Aristotle's position, calling it an "error."[80] Third, Candia presents the solutions "of doctors of the theological faculty" at Paris, all Candia's fellow Franciscans from the fourteenth century: Auriol, John of Ripa, and John Duns Scotus. Indeed, Candia seems most interested in presenting the opinions of others, to such a degree that he is more a historian of theology than a theologian. In expounding these opinions, Candia devotes more space to Auriol than to the others. Thus Candia appears at his most sophisticated, treating a theologian who, as Brown has shown, exercised a strong, if mixed, influence on his own thought.[81]

---

[78]   Citations of Candia's text will refer to paragraphs in Chris Schabel, "Peter of Candia and the Prelude to the Quarrel at Louvain," *Epetirida of the Cyprus Research Centre* 24 (1998), pp. 87–124. The standard work on Peter of Candia is Ehrle, *Der Sentenzenkommentar Peters von Candia*. See recently Stephen F. Brown, "Peter of Candia on Believing and Knowing," FcS 54 (1994–97), pp. 251–76; idem, "Peter of Candia's Hundred-Year 'History' of the Theologian's Role," *Medieval Philosophy and Theology* 1 (1991), pp. 156–90; and idem, "Peter of Candia's Sermons in Praise of Peter Lombard," in Romano S. Almagno and Conrad L. Harkins eds., *Studies Honoring Ignatius Charles Brady, Friar Minor* (St. Bonaventure, NY 1976), pp. 141–76.

[79]   Petrus de Candia, *In primum librum Sententiarum*, q. 6, a. 2 (ms. Vat. lat. 1081, fol. 116ra): "Secundus articulus erat iste: utrum intellectiva divine substantie habeat distinctam et infallibilem noticiam contingentium futurorum. Pro cuius declaratione sic procedam: primo recitabo motum Philosophi et sui Commentatoris cum suis motivis. Secundo contra ipsum obiciam et suis rationibus respondebo. Tercio <procedam> [procedetum] ad articulum secundum vias doctorum theologice facultatis. Et quarto sub certis conclusionibus modus dicendi securior eligetur."

[80]   Candia, *I Sent.*, q. 6, a. 2 (Vat. lat. 1081, fol. 116vb): "Contra tamen istum errorem diversi doctores diversimode arguunt...."

[81]   On the influences on Candia and his role as historian, see Brown, "Peter of Candia's Hundred-Year 'History'," pp. 156–74. See also Brown's "Peter of Candia's Sermons," pp. 142–5,

Candia's lengthy explanation of Auriol's position, based on the latter's *Scriptum*, was the most comprehensive exposition of Auriol's views on future contingents since Auriol's own, to such a degree that Rivo would later claim that Candia gave a clearer description of Auriol's position than Auriol himself had.[82] First Candia presents Auriol's position in a series of thirteen propositions, all of which are found in Auriol's own distinction 38, little of which is omitted in Candia's treatment. After having paraphrased Auriol's attacks on Aquinas and Scotus, his defense of Aristotle, and his solution to the problem, Candia summarizes Auriol's position succinctly in one paragraph:

> Therefore this doctor's view, as I see it, consists in this: Because God is eternity, and consequently excludes every temporal characteristic (*ratio*), while every creature is temporal and consequently formally excludes every characteristic of a being of eternity, therefore strictly speaking there is no priority, posteriority, or simultaneity between God and creature. Thus He can neither be said to be distant from [that creature] by duration (*durative*) nor be at the same time with it, because this would either be on the basis (*per rationem*) of eternity or on the basis of temporality. But [it cannot be] by either of these, since neither is common to the other. And so truly and strictly speaking, God's knowledge attains the 'actuality' of a contingently future creature via some sort of negative *in*distance. From this it appears that His knowledge of the actuality of a future contingent does not make a proposition about the future true or false, but leaves it neutral, since with respect to [that future contingent] He does not have 'expecting' knowledge. This is because He would then be distant from such a future, which is not true, unless the line of [temporal] succession were applied to Him. But that [is] false, because [such a line] is repugnant to the nature of eternity. And thus what this doctor thinks is apparent.[83]

Thus Candia correctly held that the "foundation" (*fundamentum*) of Auriol's theory was his view of divine eternity, that is, God's simple, necessary, and

---

in which Brown links John of Ripa and Auriol to their fellow Franciscan with respect to their praise of Lombard.

[82]   See Peter de Rivo, *Tractatus responsalis ad oppugnationes cuiusdam qui postea deprehensus est fuisse dominus Wilhelmus Boudini*, c. 5, in Schabel, "Peter de Rivo" (Part II), p. 405, ll. 36–7.

[83]   Candia, *I Sent.*, q. 6, a. 2 (ed. Schabel, par. 28): "Ymaginatio ergo istius doctoris consistit in hoc, ut possum perpendere: Quia enim Deus est eternitas, et per consequens excludens omnem rationem temporalem, creatura vero quelibet est temporalis, et per consequens excludens formaliter rationem entis eternitatis, ideo proprie nec est prioritas nec posteritas nec simultas inter Deum et creaturam. Ideo nec dicitur ab ea durative distare nec simul esse, quia aut hoc esset per rationem eternitatis aut per rationem temporalitatis; non per aliquam illarum, cum neutra sit communis alteri. Et ideo vere et proprie cognitio Dei attingit actualitatem creature contingenter future per quandam indistantiam negativam. Et ex hoc apparet quod eius cognitio de actualitate futuri contingentis non facit ut propositio de futuro sit vera vel falsa, sed ipsam reliquit neutram, cum respectu illius non habeat cognitionem expectativam, quia tunc distaret a tali futuro. Quod non est verum, nisi sibi competeret ratio linee successive, quod falsum est, quia rationi eternitatis repugnat. Et sic apparet quid doctor iste ymaginatur." Candia's presentation of Auriol's position is in par. 2–27.

immutable atemporality.[84] Candia recognized that Auriol defended Aristotle's position on future contingent propositions because he thought that it logically followed from his own position on God's relationship to time and creation.

The two most controversial aspects of Auriol's stance, of course, were the notion of indistance and the defense of Aristotle's opinion on the neutrality of propositions about future contingents. As we have seen, these two points had drawn the most fire from Auriol's earlier opponents. Aware of this, Candia proceeds to argue against Auriol's position on neutrality and indistance at great length. This lengthy attack and defense might be taken to betray Candia's own position, but in truth Candia simply expands on Auriol's objections against his own solution, and then clarifies Auriol's responses to those objections.[85]

While Candia takes more care with Auriol's theory for the sake of clarity, there is no reason to maintain that Candia actually agreed with Auriol with respect to any part of his position. Thus, Candia often says "according to him" [par. 37, 50, 51, 67] and "for the sake of argument" [par. 33, 35, 57], or uses the conditional mood [par. 50, 52, 54, 64], when he 'defends' Auriol. The following sections on John of Ripa and Scotus similarly reflect this technique, and Candia remarks at one point:

> Next we must explain God's cognition with respect to future contingents according to John of Ripa's imagination, and to explain this according to his way of thinking I posit some conclusions. I don't much care whether they are true of false; I only want to show what he thinks.[86]

Candia ends by 'defending' Ripa as he does Auriol and Scotus. Reinforcing the neutral nature of his presentation of Auriol, Candia concludes the section by deferring judgment, saying: "Thus it is apparent what must be said according to their way [of solving the problem], the truth or falsity of which *will be seen later (consequenter).*"[87]

What, then, is Candia's position? The way that Candia ends the article does not clarify matters: "Now, lastly, to round out this article the most common position of all will be brought together, for the exposition of which I will lay down four conclusions," which he had earlier called "the safer way of speaking," although not necessarily his own. The first of these conclusions argues against Auriol: "No positive or negative condition of indistance is for God the formal basis of knowing future contingents." The second and third

---

[84]   See Candia, *I Sent.*, q. 6, a. 2 (ed. Schabel, par. 29 and 31).

[85]   See Candia, *I Sent.*, q. 6, q. 2 (ed. Schabel, par. 29–69).

[86]   Candia, *I Sent.*, q. 6, a. 2 (Vat. lat. 1081, fol. 122vb): "Nunc consequenter est declaranda Dei cognitio respectu contingentium futurorum secundum ymaginationem magistri Iohannis de Ripa. Pro cuius declaratione iuxta mentem suam aliquas pono conclusiones, que sive sint vere sive false non multum curo, nisi solum ostendere mentem suam."

[87]   Candia, *I Sent.*, q. 6, a. 2 (ed. Schabel, par. 69): "Et sic apparet quid esset dicendum secundum viam istorum, cuius veritas vel falsitas videbitur consequenter."

conclusions are aimed at Ripa and Scotus respectively.[88] If we are to trust Candia, then the common, safer, opinion of the time went against Auriol, Ripa, and even Scotus.

This common position argues against Auriol's notion of indistance, the most distinctive element of his description of the relationship between God's knowledge and temporality. Although certain theologians from the later fourteenth century, i.e. Hugolino of Orvieto, James of Eltville, and Angelus de Dobelin, were attracted to this concept, the three arguments against indistance that Candia provides were already popular among Auriol's Franciscan successors, such as Meyronnes and Caracciolo. The arguments even resemble those Auriol gave against his own position, before he refuted them. The first is based on the claim that "No merely negative basis (ratio) is formally the basis of knowing anything positive." The second states that the position based on indistance does not include the means by which God can distinguish between possible futures that can come about but will not, and real futures that will in fact come about. The third claims that if one tries to avoid the first objection and maintain positive indistance, then one merely posits that future contingents are eternally present in eternity, as Aquinas held. In that case, they would exist eternally.

This is not to say that Auriol had no impact on the common opinion, for Candia's fourth conclusion shows that in his time many theologians shared some of Auriol's notions about divine simplicity and necessity: "For God, supersimple Deity is the only basis for evident adhesive knowledge with respect to future contingents." The conclusion asserts that God's knowledge of future contingents is intuitive, via 'similitudes', although they are used interchangeably with 'Ideas'. This language is characteristically Auriol's, and the long explanation of this conclusion involves a discussion of modality with regard to what is intrinsic and extrinsic to God, and a denial that true future-tensed propositions are *necessary*, both 'Auriolist' concerns.[89] Indeed, the common position as described in Candia's overall conclusion to article two is even more Auriolist: "Deity itself is eminently the similitude of all, and the intuitive knowledge of them":

> Recapitulating, on the basis of all of these things, it is apparent that we can understand God's knowing future contingents in six ways: (1) Ei-

[88]   Candia, *I Sent.*, q. 6, a. 2 (ed. Schabel, par. 70, 73, and 74): "Nunc ultimo pro complemento istius articuli est colligenda positio communior inter omnes. Pro cuius declaratione quatuor pono conclusiones, quarum prima sit ista: Nulla indistantie positiva vel negativa conditio est Deo formalis ratio cognoscendi futura contingentia. Ista conclusio ponitur contra primam opinionem, videlicet domini fratris Petri Aureoli... Secunda conclusio est hec: Nulla ratio quovismodo contingens est Deo formalis noticia certitudinaliter futura contingentia cognoscendi. Hec conclusio ponitur contra magistrum Iohannem de Ripa... Tertia conclusio est hec: Nulla causalitatis effective conditio est Deo respectu futurorum contingentium ratio formaliter cognitiva. Ista conclusio infert oppositum opinionis Doctoris Subtilis..."
[89]   See Candia, *I Sent.*, q. 6, a. 1 (ed. Schabel [par. 75–91], esp. 75): "Quarta conclusio est hec: Sola ratio supersimplicis deitatis est Deo respectu futurorum contingentium evidens cognitio adhesiva."

ther through distinct Ideal characteristics (*rationes*) of them; (2) or through the fact that by reason of His immensity God is present to the entire imaginary flow of time; (3) or through the fact that He is negatively indistant from the actualities of futures; (4) or through various contingent characteristics of things; (5) or through the fact that God sees clearly the determination of His own will; (6) or at least through the fact that Deity itself is eminently the similitude of all, and the intuitive knowledge of them.

And every one of these ways contains some element of imperfection, for the first declares only that God has cognitions of incomplexa; the second posits that in some way [things] have been eternally; the third does not assign a basis a difference between what is possible and what is future; the fourth, according to the common evaluation, attributes some imperfection to God, namely contingency; and the fifth posits, by interpretation, a discourse in God; and the sixth fundamentally declares nothing, but only responds to arguments. All things considered, the fifth way, namely the Subtle Doctor's, is more satisfying to the intellect than any other. The sixth, however, because it is easy, is the one commonly held, but Master John of Ripa ridicules it more than the rest.

I, like a little dog, have started the hare for you. Capture it through whatever path of the aforesaid ways you wish. And thus the second article ends.[90]

One could not really say that Candia has 'determined' the question. Although the scribe of the Melk manuscript attributes the fourth conclusion giving the common position to Candia in the marginalia no less than three times, even this does not seem to be Candia's opinion, because he suggests that the difficulty with the solution presented in his fourth conclusion (number 6) is that it basically "declares nothing" positive and concrete. After using Auriol, Ripa, and Scotus to display the main solutions (Aquinas's eternity position is also presented via Auriol), Candia confirms our suspicion that he is merely describing the options when he leaves the matter to the reader. As for indistance, the third position listed, Candia gives once more the popular objection that it

---

[90]   Candia, *I Sent.*, q. 6, q. 2 (ed. Schabel, par. 92–4): "Ex quibus omnibus recapitulando, apparet quod sex modis possumus intelligere Deum cognoscere futura contingentia: (1) Vel per distinctas ipsorum rationes ydeales; (2) vel per hoc quod Deus ratione sue immensitatis est presens toti fluxui ymaginario temporis; (3) vel per hoc quod indistat negative ab actualitatibus futurorum; (4) vel per rationes rerum varias contingentes; (5) vel per hoc quod Deus conspicit limpide determinationem proprie voluntatis; (6) aut certe per hoc quod ipsa deitas est eminenter similitudo omnium et ipsorum noticia intuitiva.

Et quilibet istorum modorum aliquid imperfectionis dicit, nam (~1) primus non declarat nisi quod Deus habet noticias incomplexorum; (~2) secundus ponit eternaliter quodammodo fuisse; (~3) tercius non assignat differentiam inter possibile et futurum; (~4) quartus iuxta communem extimationem Deo attribuit aliquam imperfectionem, videlicet contingentiam; (~5) quintus ponit interpretative in Deo discursum; (~6) et sextus fundamentaliter nichil declarat, sed solum ad argumenta respondet. Unde omnibus computatis, magis satisfacit intellectui modus quintus, videlicet Doctoris Subtilis, quam aliquis. Sextus vero, quia facilis est, communiter tenetur, quem tamen pre ceteris deridet magister Iohannes de Ripa.

Sicut parvus canis, excitavi vobis leporem. Capiatis eum per quamcumque predictarum viarum semitam vultis. Et sic secundus articulus terminatur."

does not explain how God can distinguish between true futures and merely possible futures. It seems, then, that Peter of Candia found Auriol's position to have many points of merit, and little that was dangerous; at least Candia presented Auriol's solution in a harmless light. This is a very different approach from that of many of Candia's predecessors, such as Rimini, or Pierre d'Ailly.

Of the texts from the quarrel over future contingents at Louvain, we have hundreds of pages from Rivo himself, and in many of these writings, Rivo refers to Peter of Candia's discussion of Auriol. Rivo drew support from the fact that Candia had treated Auriol at such length, had not come out in open opposition to Auriol's teachings, and had become Pope Alexander V. Occasionally Rivo even claimed that Candia had agreed with Auriol, and hence Aristotle, insofar as future-tensed propositions were concerned.[91] Of course, since Rivo's quotations in support were taken out of the general context of Candia's neutral explanation of Auriol's ideas, they did not constitute a true defense.[92] Rivo himself is honest enough to suggest this, saying that Candia "seems to adhere to [Auriol's] opinion" since he "faithfully recited Lord Peter Auriol's opinion... and did not attack it, although he speaks against Lord Peter Auriol in many other places."[93] In one instance Rivo admits that Candia's attitude toward Auriol in this context is simply neutral:

> And consequently [Auriol] investigates the way in which it seems to him that God has certain and infallible knowledge of future contingents, which [way] Peter of Candia recited along with many other [methods], in the end leaving it up to the reader's judgment to choose the most pleasing one.[94]

Moreover, in an interesting dialogue written during the quarrel, the participants show their awareness of the connection between the 'Peters', i.e. Auriol and Candia, the latter referred to as "Peter the Cretan" (*Petrus Cretensis*).[95] With such publicity, perhaps it was just a matter of time before someone defended Auriol and started a quarrel over future contingents.

[91] See instances in Baudry, *Querelle*, pp. 79, 223, 224, 227, 392–3, and 409–10.
[92] This is contrary to Baudry's assertion that Candia actually supported Auriol in *Querelle*, pp. 17–18. Baudry's opinion is cited by Normore, "Future Contingents," p. 370, n. 30. Brown also mentions Candia's supposed Auriolism in his philosophical introduction to Etkorn's edition of Salviati, *De arcanis Dei*, e.g. pp. 24 and 30.
[93] Rivo, *Questio quodlibetica... anno LXIX*, c. 1 (ed. Schabel, "Peter de Rivo" [Part I], p. 418, ll. 20–27).
[94] Rivo, *Questio quodlibetica... anno LXIX*, c. 5 (ed. Schabel, p. 428, ll. 120–23).
[95] Cf. Georgius Benignus Salviati, *De arcanis Dei* I, c. 18 (Girard Etkorn, ed., *Cardinal Bessarion, De arcanis Dei* [Rome 1997], p. 101, ll. 1066–74): "Bessarion: ...Id tamen dixi propter illud commune dictum quo aiunt 'in futuris contingentibus non esse veritatem determinatam', quamvis non sic Aristoteles dixerat.—Gattus: Illa itaque neutralis novus auctores forsan sui, sicut Aureolus et Petrus Cretensis, prima determinatione propositiones futuras neutras posuere.—Iohannes: Neque id ego dubito et Petris quamquam de isto neutrali moderno ambigem propter Henricum nostrum."

Epilogue

The Quarrel at Louvain

No one adopted all of Peter Auriol's theory in the fourteenth century. Perhaps Walter Chatton came the closest, but only after ostensibly rejecting it and making a point of disowning anything he said. Still, although many theologians called Auriol's opinion erroneous or even dangerous, only Gregory of Rimini and Pierre d'Ailly hinted that it was heretical. In the fifteenth century, however, Auriol found a true sympathizer in Peter de Rivo (ca. 1420–1500), master of arts at the University of Louvain. But Rivo's defense of Auriol provoked an angry reaction from a member of the Faculty of Theology, Henry of Zomeren (ca. 1417–72), who labeled Auriol and Rivo's position heresy. In 1474, as a result of this clash over Auriol's doctrine, Rivo was condemned by Pope Sixtus IV, and Zomeren's supporters at the University of Paris, the nominalist faction, were condemned by the King Louis IX of France.

The University of Louvain, 1446–1470

In November 1446[1] the Faculty of Arts of the University of Louvain passed a statute declaring that eleven propositions must not be taught, the fifth of which was "that determinately one part of a contradiction in future contingents is true and the other false, just as in present and past contingents, and furthermore [that] the opposite of this conclusion is inconsistent with the faith."[2] In addition, no one was to defend propositions that opposed the traditional understanding of Aristotle, where it was not contrary to the faith, unless he followed the interpretation of Averroes, Albert the Great, Aquinas, or Giles of Rome. Wyclif's and Ockham's interpretations were forbidden. Eight of the eleven propositions *could* be sustained under very restricted circumstances, but the other three propositions, the third being the one about future contingents, "and similar ones, that is, equally offensive or more properly dangerous, must be totally suppressed."[3]

---

[1]   I am writing an intellectual biography of Rivo, but see my "Peter de Rivo (Part I)," pp. 363–415, which I follow here unless otherwise noted. For day to day documents surrounding the quarrel, see Frédericq, "L'hérésie à Louvain vers 1470"; Laminne, "La controverse sur les futurs contingents à l'Université de Louvain au XVe siècle"; and Gilbert Tournoy, "Een onbekende autograaf van Petrus de Rivo (Leuven, ca 1470)," in Edmund J.M. van Eijl ed., *Facultas S. Theologiæ Lovaniensis 1432–1797: Bijdragen tot haar geschiedenis* (Louvain 1977), pp. 293–7. For philosophical texts, see Baudry, *Querelle* (translated by Guerlac, *The Quarrel*; henceforth as Baudry and Guerlac, respectively); my "Peter de Rivo"; and Etzkorn's edition of *De arcanis Dei*. Since all of these texts are readily available, I will not give the Latin in the notes.

[2]   Guerlac, pp. 33–4; Baudry, pp. 67–8.

[3]   Guerlac, p. 34; Baudry, p. 68.

At first glance, the statute seems to say not only that Peter Auriol's position is consistent with the faith, but also that the opposite conclusion is not, and should be suppressed. The evidence, however, does not support this: we have found no one who explicitly defended Auriol, and only one or two theologians who did not simply attack Auriol when mentioning him. It is more likely that statute merely meant to draw a distinction between the kind of determinacy in true past propositions and true future contingent propositions as, for example, Scotus had.[4] Unfortunately, although both of the major figures in the later quarrel over future contingents at Louvain, Henry of Zomeren and Peter de Rivo, were members of the Arts Faculty at the time of the statute, their pertinent early writings have not survived.[5] Whatever the statute's intent, when the quarrel erupted two decades later, only a few of those directly involved with the statute were still alive and active at the university. By then Rivo may have radicalized the original aim of the statute to suit his own purposes.

Peter de Rivo lectured on the *Sentences* at Louvain in 1448-49, but he was still bachelor *formatus* in theology, not yet master, when the quarrel began in 1465. Zomeren went to Paris to study theology, read the *Sentences* there in 1451-52, and became master of theology in 1462. In a Parisian *Quaestio disputata* of 1462, which may have some connection with his inception, Zomeren focusses on the absolute trustworthiness of prophecy and revelation, including those about future contingents.[6] It is not unlikely that Rivo heard about this

---

[4]   Astrik Gabriel, "Intellectual Relations between the University of Louvain and the University of Paris in the 15th Century," in Jozef Ijsewijn and Jacques Paquet, eds., *The Universities in the Late Middle Ages* (Louvain 1978), pp. 82–132, destroys both the context of the statute and of *Peri Hermeneias* when he says (p. 121), "It was forbidden to teach 'quod in futuris contingentibus determinate altera pars contradictionis est vera et altera falsa'. This was in direct opposition with the teaching of Aristotle, who said: 'In the case of that which is or which has taken place, propositions, whether positive or negative, must be true or false'." Gabriel's article is generally quite good, but he twice declares that Rivo was "a Cologne-trained professor" (pp. 119 and 131), when he correctly states elsewhere (p. 121) that "Rivo was a product of the University of Louvain."

[5]   Only book IV of Zomeren's *Sentences* commentary is extant, and Rivo's *Sentences* lectures do not survive at all. Rivo's works fall into three main categories: future contingents, calendar reform, and Aristotelian commentaries. Baudry published some 40 percent of his writings on future contingents in 1950, and I published most of the rest just recently. Some of the calendar reform treatises were printed in Rivo's own lifetime. Potentially the bulk of Rivo's œuvre lies in his thirteen Aristotelian commentaries, which were contained in three manuscripts of the library of Magdeburg's Dom Gymnasium. Sadly ms. 165 was lost in the 1939–45 war. It consisted of some 180 folios on the *Metaphysics* and six logical works, including *Peri Hermeneias*, of interest to the present study. The remaining two mss., now in Berlin, preserve 190 folios of commentaries on six works of natural philosophy. For an inventory of Zomeren's and Rivo's works, see Luc Burie, "Proeve tot inventarisatie van de in handschrift of in druk bewaarde werken van de Leuvense Theologieprofessoren," in Edmund J.M. van Eijl ed., *Facultas S. Theologiæ Lovaniensis 1432-1797: Bijdragen tot haar geschiedenis* (Louvain 1977), pp. 249–51 and 252–60.

[6]   See Henricus de Zomeren, *Quaestio solemniter disputata anno Domini XIIII LXII° in Universitate Parisiensi* (ms. Brussel, Koninklijke Bibliotheek, 708–719 [ff. 186v–190r], fol. 186v): "Hos autem prophetas credendum est spiritu Dei fuisse inspiratos, cum constet eos futurorum contingentium veracem et certam notitiam habuisse, quos in omnibus que predixerunt, tam etsi sine numero erunt eventu rerum, constat fuisse veracissimos. Contingentium autem futurorum certam noticiam non habet homo nisi ex divina revelatione... Quod si quis calumpniosus

disputation, and perhaps he took time to prepare a rebuttal, which would serve as a defense of the statute of 1446.

During the quodlibetal disputations at Louvain in December 1465, Rivo was asked to answer the common question "Was it in Peter's power to deny Christ after Christ had said to him, 'Thou wilt deny me thrice'?" An audience of five hundred was present to hear his response, which is recorded as part one of the *Five-Part Treatise* Rivo gathered together a few years later.[7] Rivo's answer was unusual: without explicitly saying so, he adopted Auriol's position. Rivo declared that propositions about future contingents are neither true nor false, but neutral, and further asserted that God's knowledge does not antecede the coming about of future things. As Zomeren attests, Rivo's main thrust was that nothing precedes the coming about of the future, using Auriol's words, "in an intervening line of succession," that would determine that future, not even divine knowledge, otherwise the future would come about necessarily. To explain this, Rivo plays to the neo-Platonists in the audience by drawing an analogy using Plato's opinion about Ideas: Ideas are indistant from their singulars just as God's knowledge is indistant from particulars in the world. Although not yet a master of theology, Rivo had ventured into theological territory. Following Auriol, Rivo claims that God's knowledge of future contingents cannot be expressed properly by any proposition, so denying truth to future contingent propositions does not affect His knowledge. As for prophetic propositions, Rivo agrees with Auriol that they signify divine knowledge by the intention of the prophets, and that although they are not true in Aristotle's sense, by the rigor of logic and with the truth inhering in them, they are true by the "Uncreated Truth" that the prophet makes them signify. The notion of Uncreated Truth was a development of Auriol's opinion that such propositions express some truth in the divine mind, where there is no time, and Rivo shows he is further following Auriol by saying that prophets therefore often expressed prophecies in the past tense. Moreover, such prophecies are also true by the created truth in the soul of the one who faithfully expects them to be fulfilled.[8]

Rivo is most at home defending Auriol's theory of future-contingent propositions, however. Rivo explains how others usually solve the problem of the

---

contradictor asserere audeat libros prophetarum aput Latinos mendosos esse aut falsatos, ex manifesta omni tam inter se quam cum nostris ac Grecis exemplaribus Hebreorum voluminum consonancia evidentissime refelitur."

[7]   See Petrus de Rivo, *Questio quodlibetica disputata anno LXV° Lovanii per Petrum de Rivo* (Guerlac, pp. 36–45; Baudry, pp. 70–78). Gabriel ("Intellectual Relations," p. 121), states that the treatise was composed in 1470, but later (p. 122) remarks that it was attacked in February 1469, citing Laminne, "La controverse," pp. 395–7. Laminne, however, doubts the "attack" was ever public, and implies that the date is uncertain.

[8]   Therefore Gabriel's remark ("Intellectual Relations," p. 122) that Zomeren "adhered to the *theologically-correct opinion* that propositions concerning future contingents must be either true or false" whereas "Rivo [was] more a philosopher than a theologian" must be qualified. Rivo, a bachelor *formatus* of theology and future master, was defending a master of theology, Peter Auriol. But Gabriel never mentions Auriol, and although he cites Baudry's introduction, he prefers to use the edition of the one text of Rivo published by Du Plessis d'Argentré from the early eighteenth century, that of the 1465 *Quodlibet*, which fails to mention Rivo.

consequence 'God foreknows X; therefore X will happen necessarily', using the composite and divides senses of the proposition, and the distinction between absolute and conditional necessity. After showing these to be inadequate, he concludes sarcastically: "And so I have been astonished at some people who explored the greatest causes with the utmost subtlety, so that they scarcely left a particle undiscussed, and yet they are satisfied with these solutions."

In all of Rivo's writings, one admires not only his philosophical acumen, but also his abilities as a rhetorician, which were sometimes employed less effectively in *ad hominem* diatribes. Holding the chair of rhetoric at Louvain since 1460, Rivo never misses the opportunity to try to win over each potential segment of his audience. Thus, speaking to the humanists and theologians, Rivo cleverly divides the opposite sides of the debate into that of Epicurus, who agrees with Aristotle, and that of the determinists Chrysippus and Cicero. Rivo's audience would not have forgotten that Augustine attacked Cicero on this very issue. Moreover, Rivo shows himself willing to abandon Aristotle where his ideas are contrary to the faith, maintaining that even causation among the celestial bodies, which Aristotle himself held to be necessary, was actually contingent, since God could and has, according to the Bible, impeded celestial causes.

Rivo had adopted Auriol's position en masse, but not yet explicitly. Rivo was not a yet a master of theology, but his opponent, Henry of Zomeren, was — at Paris no less — and had already shown a particular zeal for the truth of prophecy. During the quodlibetal debates in the Faculty of Arts the following year, probably December 1466, a bachelor of theology and student of Zomeren responded to Rivo's remarks of the previous year. The bachelor, who may have been sent by the Faculty of Theology, presented several *auctoritates* from Scripture and (Pseudo) Augustine against the possibility that neutral propositions were compatible the faith.[9] Rivo's replies to this 1466 attack do not survive, but a "Record (*Cedula*) of the Time of Events" reports the propositions defended by Rivo in 1466.[10] These propositions show that Rivo was following Auriol's distinctions on the divine will in this matter, as the *Cedula* itself mentions. Rivo maintained that God is intrinsically indifferent to producing or not producing something outside Himself, and that He is pleased with every creature that is in fact produced, though this will of good pleasure is not actively productive. As was mentioned, there may be a connection with William of Domqueur, who had just re-read Peter of Nugent's *Sentences* commentary, in which Auriol's theory of the divine will is recited in the context of future contingents. By the 1466 quodlibetal debates Rivo was directly acquainted with and supported all of Peter Auriol's main points on the issue.

After the 1466 quodlibetal disputations, in Zomeren's words:

---

[9]   See Henricus de Zomeren, *Heinrici de Zoemeren tractatus adversus sententiam Petri de Rivo de futuris contingentibus* (Guerlac, p. 251; Baudry, pp. 294–5).
[10]   *Cedula designationis temporum* (Guerlac, pp. 75–6; Baudry, pp. 108–9).

... the matter more or less quieted down until the 13th of November in the year '69. On that day, when two students of mine were to be made licentiates in theology, and I, according to custom, was to dispute in the College of Theology, I thought the opportune time had come in which, because of the great number and solemnity of the hearers, I could opportunely follow up what I had always had in mind, in order to contradict, in the open, to the best of my powers, such pestiferous teachings; when I was describing the nature of the chair of theology to which they were called, I said, among other things: 'This is the chair of catholic faith and truth, this chair abominates the presumption of those who dare assert that these propositions are not now true: The dead will rise again, there will be a judgement...; this [chair] determines the assertion of these things to be heresy, indeed of the most glaring.'[11]

The game had changed now that Zomeren accused Rivo of heresy. On the defensive, Rivo replied in quodlibetal debate just five weeks later, on 18 December, and the text of the quodlibetal question is the second part of his *Five-Part Treatise*.[12] The procedure was obviously engineered by Rivo and his arts students. Rivo quickly turns the question "Did the philosophers posit the three theological virtues, faith, hope, and charity, in the number of virtues?" into the problem "Whether Aristotle's opinion concerning future contingents can be defended along with the firm faith in the said articles?" This treatise is Rivo's first comprehensive work on the problem. Although Rivo organizes most of his discussion in terms of a debate between Epicurus and Chrysippus, his first chapter attempts to persuade his audience that the great scholastics had not come to a consensus. On the one side, Rivo cites Gregory of Rimini and his follower, Pierre d'Ailly, who calls the opinion heretical; the audience would have known that both Rimini and d'Ailly were considered followers of Ockham, whose interpretation of Aristotle was outlawed at Louvain. Nevertheless, Rivo reminds his listeners, Henry of Zomeren agreed with them, and Rivo quotes him as asserting the Apostle's statement publicly: "If an angel from heaven were to say that it should be believed, he would be believing an anathema." On the other side there is the *"Doctor Facundus, Dominus Petrus Aureoli,"* Rivo's first citation of "Lord" Peter Auriol. For good measure, Rivo adds that "Lord Peter of Candia, who afterwards, when elevated to the pinnacle of apostolic rank, was called Alexander V, appears to agree with his opinion." Not only do a famous doctor and a pope support Aristotle, but Albert the Great, Aquinas, and Durand of St. Pourçain, in their commentaries on *Peri Hermeneias*, do not claim that Aristotle's opinion is contrary to the faith, and even tried to reconcile it with the faith. Finally, Giles of Rome does not list Aristotle's opinion in his treatise on the errors of the philosophers.[13] Rivo is of course aware that the Louvain arts statute required that Aristotle's doctrines

[11] Zomeren, *Heinrici de Zoemeren tractatus* (Guerlac, pp. 251–2; Baudry, p. 295).
[12] Rivo, *Questio quodlibetica... anno LXIX* (ed. Schabel, pp. 416–45).
[13] Rivo, *Questio quodlibetica... anno LXIX*, c. 1 (ed. Schabel, p. 417–18, ll. 4–36).

be defended according to the interpretation of Albert, Aquinas, or Giles. Clearly, by 1469, Peter de Rivo had researched the history of the problem.

Obviously, philosophers in antiquity and the great scholastics were not of one mind on the issue, and so the root of the present dispute must lie elsewhere. Rivo declares that it began when (in 1446) Henry of Zomeren, in the Faculty of Arts, defended the position that there was determinate truth in future contingents, just as in present and past contingents:

> ... the same faculty, thrown into confusion by the novelty of the position, consulted the Faculty of Theology, in which our masters Heymeric de Campo, Peter Welle, and John Warenacher reigned at that time; very famous men in sacred theology, who along with other professors of the same faculty unanimously judged that the said position be completely silenced, and whose judgement, approved with agreement by the university, the said Faculty of Arts inscribed in perpetual memory in their book of statutes.[14]

This is probably skillful propaganda: it is doubtful (a) that Zomeren defended the position as stated, although it is the opinion in the statute, for it makes no distinction at all between the future and past; (b) that Zomeren's defense of this position was the pretext for the entire statute, since the statute covers eleven propositions, three absolutely forbidden; (c) that Rivo thought such a position was new; and (d) that it threw the Faculty of Arts into such confusion. Clearly Rivo hoped to gain the Arts Faculty's alliance, and Rivo's subtle half-truths about a statute made a quarter-century in the past probably went undetected by the members of the Arts Faculty who were listening. Moreover, Zomeren had recently taken over the late Heymeric de Campo's position in the faculty of theology, and it was clever of Rivo to remind the theologians of the roles of de Campo, Welle, and Warenacher, who was still alive and active in the Faculty of Theology in 1469.

Rivo again preaches to his fellow *artistae* in chapter six, an interesting discussion of the authority of Aristotle in the medieval university. Rivo accuses his opponents, among them Zomeren, of perjury, right in the title of the chapter, for not upholding their oath to defend Aristotle's doctrines when they are demonstrated and do not contradict the faith. And so Rivo defends Aristotle's *demonstration* in *Peri Hermeneias* against logical arguments opposed to neutral propositions, arguments often based on Aristotle himself in many other places of his œuvre. Leaving no potentially helpful stone unturned, Rivo states that those who follow the logic of a "certain William of Ockham," instead of Aristotle's, might disagree, but he explicitly reminds his readers that the same statute that opposed determinate truth in future contingent propositions, opposed solving problems in Ockham's way.

Rivo realizes that the issue is also theological, and he has to counter the accusation of heresy. Therefore he claims for the first time that the position op-

---

[14]   Rivo, *Questio quodlibetica... anno LXIX*, c. 1 (ed. Schabel, pp. 418–19, ll. 40–46).

posed to Aristotle's on the issue of the truth of future contingent propositions leads to the "abominable articles of John Wyclif, which were condemned at the Council of Constance..." This served as yet another reminder of the terms of the Louvain arts statute, and not only neutralized Zomeren's charge, but put him on the defensive. Of course Rivo cannot simply ignore Zomeren's biblical quotations, so he tries to explain how some sort of truth can be in future contingent propositions, and how God's knowledge does not precede the coming about of future things, since all things are indistant to God. Although future contingent propositions are not true in the Aristotelian sense, they are true in other senses. One sense, already mentioned in the 1465 *Quodlibet*, is the created truth faithfully expected. Rivo draw an analogy here. If Plato, whom Aristotle trusts, says to Aristotle, "I will have breakfast with you tomorrow," Aristotle will believe it faithfully, and say that it is true. He will not, however, say that the truth inheres in Plato's assertion, but that does not really affect Aristotle's faith in the truth of the proposition. If Aristotle can believe Plato, without maintaining his promise to be true with logical rigor, then we can believe in God's foreknowledge, or in divine prophecies, so much more, without maintaining that truth actually inheres in the proposition. Rivo goes on to defend Auriol against his attackers, saying that Auriol in no way denied God's knowledge of future contingents, and adding that Peter of Candia recited Auriol's solution while leaving it up to the reader to decide as he pleased which way to understand God's knowledge.

Rivo also cleverly and skillfully gathers support for Aristotle's position from various unlikely sources. He cites Scotus and Peter of Nugent for admitting the possibility of neutral propositions, at least in the first instant of nature, or sign. Next he cites Aquinas that according to their 'real' existence, all future contingent states of affairs are present to God's view, although they do not yet exist in time; for this reason they are still in the power of their causes, and are not determined by the fact that God 'sees' them. Finally, Rivo even draws support from Anselm, whose notion of subsequent necessity, following the positing of the thing in being, seems to agree with Rivo's position. In sum, for Rivo there are only three choices in the matter: (a) Hold that all things come about from necessity; (b) admit that there is power with respect to the past, just as with the future; or (c) follow Aristotle. Rivo shows the first option to be heretical for seven reasons. As for the second option, Rivo says, "all agree that there is no power with respect to the past." In support he cites Aristotle, Jerome, Augustine, Anselm, and Hugh of St. Victor, and adds that the distinction between God's absolute and ordained powers will not help matters. The only choice, then, is to follow Aristotle. These options are a recurring theme in Rivo's works, and his discussions about the past are interesting because we see Rivo explaining how the past is necessary in greater detail than Auriol did in this context. In this he defends Auriol's doctrine against developments that came later, at Oxford and Paris in the 1330s and 1340s, in the works of such figures as Bradwardine, Wodeham, Rimini, and Mirecourt.

322   THEOLOGY AT PARIS 1316–1345

Since Aristotle's stance is the only option, Rivo concludes the treatise by showing that there is nothing disturbing about following Aristotle's position. A possible objection to Rivo's opinion is that it is the position of Epicurus, who contradicted the faith in many other ways. Rivo refutes this by using an interesting analogy, based on Gregory the Great. Just as Israelites were able to make captive virgins of foreign races their wives, after their hair had been cut, Gregory says we can accept doctrines of the gentiles, after "we cut away their superfluities, that is errors contrary to healthy doctrine." And if someone should say that Rivo's position could seem offensive and promote scandal in the common people, Rivo says that his adversaries defend positions that would seem just as scandalous to the people:

> For example, among the adversaries of the said opinion of Aristotle, one is said to have maintained as doctrine that it is not to be conceded without qualification that the son of God was made man; another is asserted to have said that God could damn someone existing in grace, even a *beatus*, and send him down into hell; and further that if a viator's damnation were divinely revealed to him, he would not have to pray to God for his salvation. And if these propositions were made public to the people, they would cause great scandal, first because the people hear the Church singing about the Son of God, in public and without qualification, 'and he was made man'...[15]

Later Rivo will mention Henry de Zomeren's name explicitly in connection with these teachings.[16]

Rivo's response, and his remarks about perjury and the heresies of Wyclif, led Zomeren to answer in turn two days later, on 20 December, when Zomeren responded to a quodlibetal question in the Arts College. He essentially declared that all propositions of the faith about the future are absolutely true, and all their contradictories are absolutely false. Zomeren also claimed that Aristotle contradicted himself, and that he would prove it, adding that Rivo's way of discussing the truth of such propositions of the faith was erroneous.[17]

During his response Zomeren had remarked that he was speaking about truth in the popular sense. Thus Rivo, on the next day, 21 December, replied that Zomeren spoke of truth in the popular sense, but Aristotle used the term in a philosophical and logically rigorous way. In the philosophical sense, the truth inheres in the propositions, and thus is unimpedible by any power. In the popular sense, truth is not so rigorous. For example, people call someone rich who does not yet have riches, but expects riches via a rich father. The brief third part of Rivo's *Five-Part Treatise* must have been written about this time. Its arguments are also found in other treatises, but, notably, Rivo explicitly as-

---

Rivo, *Questio quodlibetica... anno LXIX*, c. 10 (ed. Schabel, pp. 444–5, ll. 79–86)
Petrus de Rivo, *Tractatus Petri de Rivo responsalis ad opusculum quoddam magistri Heynrici de Zoemeren*, c. 14 (Guerlac, p. 345; Baudry, p. 384).
See Zomeren, *Heinrici de Zoemeren tractatus* (Guerlac, pp. 254–5; Baudry, pp. 296–7), and Baudry's introduction (Guerlac, p. 18; Baudry, pp. 31–2).

serts that Pope Alexander V agreed with "Master Peter Auriol, the *Cardinal*," that Aristotle's theory was a demonstrated conclusion.[18] Rivo convinced the Faculty of Arts, for on the same day as his response to Zomeren, 21 December, it asked the university to order Zomeren to obey the 1446 statute. The university replied on 30 December, pleading with everyone to cease discussion, but Zomeren did not comply. Instead he gave a series of four magisterial lectures to the Faculty of Theology, between 8 and 13 January 1470, criticizing Rivo's explanation of the truth of such propositions of the faith, and complaining that Rivo held Aristotle in higher esteem than Scripture, glossing Scripture with Aristotle. Since Zomeren thought that Rivo was using the 1446 statute to his own advantage, Zomeren further remarked that the statute was really intended to keep the discussion out of the Arts College, as it was a theological matter. It was a useful enough statute for that purpose, but if Rivo was going to use it to defend his arguments, it would be better to destroy the statute, as it was necessary to destroy the bronze serpent placed in the ark by Moses to commemorate a miracle, because the people began to worship the serpent as an idol.[19]

This final point explains why Rivo thought it necessary to defend his ability as a member of the Faculty of Arts to debate the topic. He did so in the fourth part of the *Five-Part Treatise*, based on the reply he gave on Sunday, 14 January, explaining the statute of 1446 at the instruction of the Faculty of Arts.[20] Directed solely at the arts masters, it has no reference to Auriol, but there is a defense of the ability of a master of arts to stray into what might seem to be theological territory. The treatise is of considerable interest philosophically and theologically, in that it focuses on how Rivo thinks propositions of the faith about future contingents can (and cannot) be said to be true, and how those types of truth affect the contingency and necessity of future things. Aside from a detailed defense of Aristotle's and Auriol's position, it is also a more extensive description of the ways in which things can be true than Rivo had heretofore given. Peter de Rivo's originality lies in the articulation of these types of truth. We have already discussed how Rivo thinks such propositions are true in the sense that the faithful expect them to be verified, as in the Plato-breakfast analogy. There are also other ways they can be true:

> ... because the One speaking through propositions reveals both the knowledge that He has of the thing and the thing itself insofar as it is governed by His knowledge, therefore through 'said' or 'revealed' we can understand three things: first, the knowledge of the One who speaks which is revealed; second, the thing itself, which is revealed

---

[18]   Petrus de Rivo, *Petri de Rivo alius tractatus* (#1) (Guerlac, pp. 46–52; Baudry, pp. 79–84).

[19]   Zomeren, *Heinrici de Zoemeren tractatus* (Guerlac, pp. 255–6; Baudry, pp. 297–9).

[20]   This is Rivo's *Defensio statuti per Petrum de Rivo* (ed. Schabel, "Petrus de Rivo [Part I]," pp. 446–73). It is clear that Rivo personally instigated the defense of the statute, and he was not merely "the spokesman for the arts faculty," as Anthony Kenny has claimed ("The Accursed Memory," p. 157).

insofar as it is governed by the knowledge of the One speaking; and third, the proposition itself through which there is a revelation. Thus after God thought us worthy to reveal something of future things, then the first thing revealed, i.e. His knowledge of future things, is true by the truth said in the first way. Again, the second thing revealed, i.e. the future thing insofar as it is governed by divine knowledge, is determinately true, because a thing of this sort is eternally indistant to the divine view according to the thing's actuality; wherefore the truth of the thing taken thus is eternally indistant to God, although in the course of time it is awaited as future. Therefore in these two ways the said propositions are true, not only by the truth of the One saying or revealing, but also by the truth of what is said or revealed. But truth does not inhere in the proposition through which the revelation was made, for if truth did inhere in it, it could not be impeded by any power...[21]

Rivo was rudely interrupted by John Beyaert, a student, who was taken before the university tribunal three days later, on 17 January. The quarrel threatened to become physically violent, and the university turned the matter over to the theologians and again called upon everyone to refrain from discussing the matter. The theologians were asked to respond quickly, and the Faculty of Arts was told to show respect to Zomeren.

The brief fifth part of the *Five-Part Treatise* probably dates from just after these events. It records an argument that Rivo made in front of a high local prelate, William Fillastre, Bishop of Tournai. Directing his remarks at Zomeren, who was present, Rivo began by stating that "those who claim there is determinate truth in propositions about a future contingent seem to fall into a certain abominable heresy of John Wyclif, condemned by Pope Martin at the Council of Constance, namely, that all things come about from absolute necessity." He also said that the 1446 statute was written expressly to avoid such heresy.[22]

The Bessarion Circle and the Nominalist-Realist Debate

Rivo had brought the quarrel outside the University, virtually charging Zomeren with heresy before the Bishop of Tournai. Immediately after Rivo's public accusation, Zomeren appealed to the powerful Cardinal Bessarion, describing Rivo's stance and asking Bessarion's judgment.[23] While Bessarion was papal legate to Germany in 1459–60, Zomeren acted as his secretary and

---

[21] Rivo, *Defensio statuti*, c. 4 (ed. Schabel, p. 457, ll. 38–53).
[22] Petrus de Rivo, *Petri de Rivo alius tractatus* (#2) (Guerlac, pp. 53–5; Baudry, pp. 85–8).
[23] On Bessarion, see for example Henri Vast, *Le Cardinal Bessarion (1403–1472): Étude sur la Chrétienté et la Renaissance* (Paris 1878); Ludwig Mohler, *Kardinal Bessarion als Theologe, Humanist und Staatsmann*, 3 vols. (Paderborn 1923–42); the collection of articles in *Miscellanea Marciana di studi Bessarionei* (=*Medioevo e Umanesimo* 24) (Padua 1976); and John Monfasani's studies collected in *Byzantine Scholars in Renaissance Italy: Cardinal Bessarion and Other Émigrés* (Aldershot 1995).

chaplain and, at Bessarion's request, composed a summary of one of William of Ockham's works, the *Epytome Dialogorum Ocham de Haereticis*.[24] Zomeren correctly believed that Bessarion would be his ally, but he did not simply report his version of Rivo's views; he also wanted to know if Rivo was a heretic. If so, he said that because Rivo was intelligent enough to know what he was doing, he should not be allowed to recant, for if he did so it would only be to avoid punishment. Was he calling for Rivo's execution?

Cardinal Bessarion had a circle of close intellectual acquaintances. On this occasion he sought the advice of several people whose written responses survive: Francesco della Rovere OFM, Giovanni Gatti OP, Fernando of Cordova, and Guillaume Baudin, whose treatises Baudry edited; John Foxal OFM, who probably wrote one that is no longer extant; and Giorgio Benigno Salviati OFM, who composed the dialogue purporting to record a conference of all of the above, except Baudin, taking place at Bessarion's house in Rome in 1471.

Bessarion had supported the career of Francesco della Rovere (1414–84), later Pope Sixtus IV, who had been a theologian at the University of Padua.[25] Francesco's work on future contingents was not the only one he wrote at the cardinal's request. In Bessarion's capacity as Protector of the Greyfriars from 1458 until his death, he helped the Franciscan Francesco become minister general of the order in 1464 and cardinal in 1467. In his somewhat brief treatise on future contingents of early 1470, Francesco focuses explicitly on the main points of Zomeren's letter, probably since he did not know Rivo's works at first hand.[26] Rivo gathered together his *Five-Part Treatise* and sent it to Rome, probably in March or April, and it perhaps arrived too late for Francesco to take it into account.[27]

Francesco agrees with Zomeren that it is heretical to maintain that propositions of the faith about the future are not determinately true and that God does not know the future before it arrives, but tries to calm Zomeren and stresses that Rivo should be allowed to recant. Francesco showed not a little acquaintance with Peter Auriol's ideas, but he follows Francis of Marchia's defense of Bivalence and, more vaguely, his distinction between determinate *de inesse* and determinate *de possibili*. Francesco had a general interest in showing the compatibility between Aquinas and Scotus, the topic of his main,

---

[24] Lotte Labowsky, *Bessarion's Library and the Biblioteca Marciana: Six Early Inventories* (Rome 1979), p. 120. I have found another manuscript: Vaticano, Chigi. B. IV 45 (239 folios). See "Peter de Rivo (Part I)," pp. 394–5, n. 64.

[25] On Sixtus IV see Egmont Lee, *Sixtus IV and Men of Letters* (Rome 1978); Lorenzo Di Fonzo, "Sisto IV. Carriera scolastica e integrazioni biografiche (1414–1484)," *Miscellanea Francescana* 86, fasc. II-IV (1986), pp. 1–491; and Lucio Pusci, "Gli scritti e il pensiero di Francesco della Rovere dei Frati Minori Conventuali," ibidem, pp. 493–502.

[26] The text, *Francisci cardinalis sancti Petri ad vincula tractatus*, is in Guerlac, pp. 80–90; Baudry, pp. 113–25. Francesco's treatise on future contingents is also in Vat. lat. 1050 (not 1056) and was even printed in Rome in 1473. On the treatise, see Pusci, "Scritti e pensiero," pp. 499–502, and Di Fonzo, "Sisto IV", pp. 380–84, who also treats the Lignami edition (Rome 1473).

[27] Pusci ("Scritti e pensiero," p. 499) mistakenly says Francesco's treatise is "frutto della disputa accademica tenuta il 1 giugno 1471 nella residenza del. Card. Della Rovere."

but incomplete, opus. Thus in his treatise on future contingents Francesco tries to harmonize their views, adopting a solution to the problem of future contingents based on eternal presence. He realizes that Auriol's answer to the dilemma resembles Aquinas's, and that it still allows for God's knowledge of the future. Thus Francesco says Auriol and Aristotle do not agree entirely, and adds that Auriol himself, like Scotus, posited some sort of instants of nature account, in which such propositions could be said to be determinately true. This suggests that rather than the *Scriptum*, Francesco knew the Borghese 123 *Reportatio* of Auriol's commentary, the sole surviving manuscript of which had been in the papal collection since the fourteenth century.[28] Francesco's attitude later led Rivo, when his position had weakened, to believe that Sixtus IV in some way supported his ideas.

The author of the second treatise, who does not mention Auriol at all, is certainly Giovanni Gatti. It cannot be the Franciscan John Foxal, the only other candidate from Salviati's dialogue besides Giovanni himself. Foxal was a bachelor of theology at Oxford in 1451,[29] who composed a commentary on book I of Scotus's *Ordinatio*. Later he taught in Bologna and perhaps Padua. Foxal was so learned about Scotus that he distinguished between three schools of Scotist thought in the fifteenth century: Bonetists, Meyronnists, "pure" Scotists, and in the dialogue, he displays his knowledge of Bonet and Meyronnes, and defends the Scotist cause for the Franciscans against Giovanni Gatti, the token Dominican and Thomist in Bessarion's circle.[30] In the second treatise, however, the author never shows the kind of familiarity the others do with the opinions of illustrious Franciscan writers. Most of the work comprises a typical Dominican discussion of contingency, e.g. *"ut in pluribus"* and *"ad utrumlibet,"* together with a Thomist denial of the possibility of obtaining certain knowledge of future contingents via their causes. In the conclusion the author follows Aquinas implicitly: he uses the argument that because things future to us are present to God's eternity, future-tensed propositions of the faith, communicated by God to humans, are determinately true, but this does not make the future necessary. Thus Giovanni Gatti must be the author, and since he does not attempt to refute any of Auriol's or Rivo's specific arguments against the Thomist position, and the treatise is even shorter than Francesco's, Giovanni probably wrote around the same time as Francesco, before any of Rivo's texts were available in Rome.

The theologian and polymath Fernando of Cordova, the author of the third extant treatise, was more familiar with both Rivo's and Auriol's views than

---

[28] See Brown, "Petrus Aureoli," p. 207, citing catalogues of 1369 and 1375 published by Ehrle.

[29] On John Foxal, see Girard Etzkorn, "John Foxal, O.F.M.: His Life and Writings," FcS 49 (1989), pp. 17–24.

[30] Giovanni's text, *Anonymi tractatus de futuris contingentibus*, is in Guerlac, pp. 91–8; Baudry, pp. 126–33. On Giovanni, see recently John Monfasani, "Giovanni Gatti of Messina: A Profile and an Unedited Text," in Vincenzo Fera and Giacomo Ferraú, eds., *Filologia umanistica per Gianvito Resta* II (Padua 1997), pp. 1315–38. In a personal communication, Monfasani agrees with my attribution of this text to Giovanni.

was Francesco, so we can date the treatise later in 1470, after the arrival of Rivo's works in Rome.[31] Like Francesco, Fernando had close relations with Cardinal Bessarion, and wrote other works for him. He was not so favorable to Auriol's views as Francesco had been, but he knew them well enough to see that Rivo followed Auriol very closely. Fernando, however, may have had most of his knowledge of Auriol from Gregory of Rimini. His basic refutation of Rivo generally follows the lines of Rimini's response to Auriol, with some phrases taken verbatim from the fourteenth-century Augustinian. Indeed, Fernando's eight rules about propositions are simply Rimini's eight conclusions, except that Fernando's second and third rules both come from Rimini's second conclusion, and Rimini's eighth conclusion is omitted. Fernando augments his anti-Rivo arsenal by paraphrasing Francis of Marchia's defense of Bivalence against Auriol and, more explicitly than had Francesco della Rovere, by appealing to Marchia's distinction between determination *de inesse* and determination *de possibili* to diffuse Rivo's arguments that determinacy prior to an event entailed that the event came about necessarily. Rimini had mentioned Marchia's distinction more than once, but the long paraphrases make it clear that Fernando has Marchia's text before his eyes. For good measure, Fernando borrows a few paragraphs verbatim from Francis of Meyronnes, and one cannot rule out other loans from Auriol's Parisian successors. In the tradition of the mid-fourteenth century, Fernando relies on an over-arching contingency in the world, and emphasizes that since everything except God is contingent, all propositions are contingent, although they are determinately true or false. Almost nothing of Fernando's original, except his probably correct rejection of Rivo's appeal to Scotus, Aquinas, and Anselm for support. Fernando at least lives up to his reputation for broad learning, if not originality. He ends by suggesting that Rivo's way is heretical, leaving little hope for Rivo to claim that he was misunderstood.[32]

Thus it appears that when Rivo's *Five-Part Treatise* arrived in Rome, Bessarion's group did the sensible thing: they went back to see how Auriol's successors at Paris had responded to his radical theory, in order to learn how they themselves should reply to Rivo. Perhaps unwittingly, Rivo gave them clues by pointing to Rimini and d'Ailly. The books the Bessarion Circle gath-

---

[31] Fernando's treatise, *Tractatus M. Fernandi de Corduba*, is in Guerlac, pp. 99–134; Baudry, pp. 134–70. On Fernando, see John Monfasani, *Fernando of Cordova. A Biographical and Intellectual Profile* (Philadelphia 1992), discussing Fernando's role in the controversy on pp. 35–7.

[32] Compare Fernando's *rationes* 1–11 (Guerlac, pp. 108–116; Baudry, pp. 144–52) with Rimini, *I Sent.*, d. 38, q. 1, a.2 (ed. Trapp-Marcolino, pp. 245–56), and Fernando's eight rules (Guerlac, pp. 122–3; Baudry, pp. 158–9) with the headings of Rimini's first seven conclusions on the same pages (ed. Trapp-Marcolino, pp. 245–56). Fernando's *rationes* 12–13 (Guerlac, pp. 116–19; Baudry, pp. 152–5) are paraphrased from Marchia's response to Auriol and *opinio propria* in *I Sent.*, d. 35 (ed. Schabel, pp. 73–80, ll. 78–226). Finally, Fernando's *rationes* 17–19 (Guerlac, pp. 120–21; Baudry, pp. 156–7) are in Meyronnes, *I Sent.*, dd. 38–39, q. 4, a. 2 and a. 4 (ed. Venice 1520, fol. 114vbP–Q and 115rbE–F). Monfasani, *Fernando of Cordova*, p. 37, claims that Fernando did not adopt the *opinio communis*, but aside from the necessity of the past, which he simply does not address here, Fernando does defend the common opinion.

ered in this effort probably make up many of the codices in the Vatican Library between Vat. lat. 1050 and 1110, which includes pertinent works of not only Rimini, Marchia, Meyronnes, Candia, Peter of Aquila (Scotellus), Henry of Ghent, d'Ailly, and Capreolus, which were popular, but also Salviati's dialogue, Francesco della Rovere's treatise, and William of Domqueur's reading of Peter of Nugent. Indeed, Sixtus IV's secretary, Bishop John Andreae of Aleria, was the head of the Vatican Library, and became good friends with Henry of Zomeren when the latter eventually came to Rome.[33]

The author of the fourth treatise, from which Rivo later quotes passages verbatim, was Guillaume Baudin. Giovanni Gatti no doubt speaks of the absent Baudin in Salviati's dialogue when he replies to Fernando: "The erudite man and our *familiaris* Henry [of Zomeren] reported this to be the most powerful argument for a neutral proposition, but Guillaume the Frenchman, a man indeed of keen ability, entirely demolished the little traps of this argument, as have many others of those who are present."[34] In his treatise, composed at some time before 12 November 1470, Baudin calls the University of Paris "our university."[35] This Baudin appears to have been a *familiaris* of Bessarion at the university, who played the important role of introducing the Paris theologian, humanist, and printer Guillaume Fichet to the cardinal.[36] Rivo assumes, perhaps correctly, that based on what was said in Baudin's treatise the author was a disciple of Zomeren's. Not surprisingly, then, Baudin attacks Rivo's views as vehemently as had Zomeren himself. Baudin spent considerable time preparing his text, because he displays deep knowledge of Auriol's *Scriptum*, and cites the opinions of a number of scholastics on the subject of Aristotle's opinion in *Peri Hermeneias*. He not only thinks that Aristotle and Auriol were contrary to the faith concerning future-contingent propositions, but he chas-

---

[33] Cf. Francesco (Vat. lat. 1050), Salviati (1056), Aquila (1077, 1078, 1080), Meyronnes (1079), Candia (1081), Nugent (Domqueur, 1090), Henry of Ghent (1095), Marchia (1096), Capreolus and d'Ailly (1097), Rimini (1104, 1105), and others.

[34] Salviati, *De arcanis Dei* I, c. 18 (ed. Etzkorn, p. 97, ll. 942–50). One manuscript has John Foxal as the speaker, the other Giovanni Gatti. Etzkorn chose Foxal, perhaps because his guess for the identity of Guillaume, Guillaume Vaurouillon, was a Scotist (cf. text cited in n. 55, and the introduction, p. 9). We now know he was Baudin, however.

[35] Guillelmus Baudinus, *Anonymi tractatus de veritatibus futurorum contingentium adversus Petrum de Rivo* (Guerlac [pp. 135–70], p. 141; Baudry [pp. 171–208], p. 178). Baudin does not mention an important pertinent decision of the Faculty of Theology at Paris, dated 12 November 1470, so that is the likely *terminus ante quem*.

[36] See a letter from Bessarion to Fichet, dated 13 December 1470, in Mohler, *Kardinal Bessarion*, vol. 3, p. 554: "Bessarion Cardinalis Guillelmo Ficheti: 'Reverende et doctissime pater, amice noster carissime, Guillermus Baudinus, vir doctissimus ac magna nobiscum familiaritate coniunctus, de ingenio et doctrina vestra excellenti multa nobis narravit.'" On Fichet's relationship with Bessarion, see Jules Philippe, *Guillaume Fichet, sa vie, ses œuvres. Introduction de l'imprimerie à Paris* (Annecy 1892), pp. 55–66 and 99–151. Interestingly, another Fichet-Bessarion go-between, Peter Montanus, was thought a candidate as the author, but Zénon Kaluza, "La crise des années 1474–1482: l'interdiction du nominalisme par Louis XI," in Maarten J.F.M. Hoenen, J.H. Josef Schneider, and Georg Wieland, eds., *Philosophy and Learning. Universities in the Middles Ages* (Leiden 1995) (pp. 293–327), p. 314, n. 54, considered this unlikely because Fichet was a member of the realist faction that supported Rivo and the author was a nominalist who copied from Pierre d'Ailly's nominalist treatise against Monzon. Obviously, however, Baudin was both nominalist and go-between.

tises Rivo for misrepresenting Auriol in appealing to Aquinas and others in order to evade objections. In effect, Baudin has checked up on Rivo, and he devotes all his energies to proving him heretical.

The four treatises demonstrate that Zomeren's appeal to Bessarion was paying off. Having learned of this appeal, Rivo requested a university investigation of the suspect propositions that Henry of Zomeren claimed Rivo taught. Around September of 1470, Rivo's faction grew impatient waiting for the Faculty of Theology's decision, and sent Rivo's *Five-Part Treatise* to the Faculty of Theology of Cologne for analysis. Zomeren turned to the Faculty of Theology at his Alma Mater, the University of Paris, which exonerated Zomeren of charges of the Wyclif heresy. When Cologne came out in official support of Rivo, the University of Louvain moved against Zomeren. Rivo decided to have his own try in Paris, and he sent his *Five-Part Treatise* to the theologians. In 1471 individual theologians at the University of Louvain expressed their support of Rivo, as did twenty-four theologians at Paris.[37]

But the Paris Faculty of Theology did not officially support Rivo. Fifteenth-century scholasticism was an era of schools of thought, factions variously labeled. The broadest labels were the *via antiqua* and the *via moderna*, or the 'realists' and 'nominalists', but within those groups their were sub-factions, like the Ockhamists, Albertists, Thomists, and Scotists. Most new universities, especially in the Empire, chose an official position. One result was that increasingly the charge of heresy was hurled at philosophers, who therefore had to exercise censorship, and appeals were made to the secular authorities[38] — Zomeren himself not only made use of his Bessarion and Paris connections, but he wrote the Duke of Burgundy. As early as 1427 Louvain opted for the *via antiqua*, the 'realists', against Buridan, Marsilius of Inghen, and Ockham; throughout the fifteenth century, as witnessed by the 1446 statute, complaints are heard about the 'illegal' views expressed in the way of Ockham and others. Now, the quarrel between Zomeren and Rivo had little to do with these factions at Louvain or, directly, with the problem of universals. It was a more specific dispute about a philosophical and theological problem, and to the extent that it expanded within Louvain it became an argument between the Faculties of Arts and Theology.[39]

Paris, however, had never chosen an official side, and so it was home to and source of both realists and nominalists. Relations between the two groups were far from harmonious, and Rivo's appeal to the Paris theologians acted as a catalyst, "revealing the division in the bosom of the Faculty of Theology at Paris." Although an argument could be made that nominalists would support

[37]   The texts of Rivo's petition for an investigation, the suspect propositions, Rivo's responses, the sentence against Zomeren, and the decisions of the various theologians and theological faculties are in Guerlac, pp. 61–73 and 171–212; Baudry, pp. 93–106 and 209–258.
[38]   Cf. Zénon Kaluza, "La crise des années 1474–1482." On the 'realist' sub-factions at Cologne (Thomists and Albertists), see M.J.F.M. Hoenen, "Late Medieval Schools of Thought in the Mirror of University Textbooks. The *Promptuarium argumentorum* (Cologne 1492)," in idem et al., eds., *Philosophy and Learning. Universities in the Middles Ages* (Leiden 1995), pp. 329–69.
[39]   Gabriel, "Intellectual Relations," pp. 117–28, makes these points.

the determinacy of future-contingent propositions and realists would be more likely to oppose it, it is more likely that the nominalists made it a partisan issue, championing Zomeren who was in truth more Scotist than nominalist, despite his abbreviation of Ockham's *Dialogue*. Guillaume Baudin probably played the key role. He had shown his nominalist leanings when, as a printer like Fichet, he published Ockham's *Summa logicae* twice, in 1455 and 1463. In support of his colleague Zomeren, who was also a Paris theologian and familiaris of Bessarion, Baudin may have prevented the Parisian nominalists from signing the document in support of Rivo: all twenty-four signers were realists.[40] Indeed, Baudin in his treatise silently quoted a nominalist tract by Pierre d'Ailly. Baudin's work against Rivo was the most antagonistic of the four that were written at Bessarion's request, and as Salviati's dialogue suggests, Baudin's accusation of heresy influenced the participants. Thus Baudin had a hand in causing the momentous condemnations of 1474.

While the Parisian theologians were rallying around their favorites, the Bosnian Juraj Dragisic, a Franciscan who called himself a Macedonian and eventually took the name Giorgio Benigno Salviati, wrote the dialogue that claims to be a report of a conversation which took place on 1 June 1471.[41] Probably a meeting at Bessarion's house in Rome at least inspired the composition. No doubt Salviati had before him the four earlier treatises written for Bessarion, and perhaps Foxal's as well, in addition to Rivo's. A comparison between the statements of the participants and their treatises shows that they are portrayed accurately. Additional research may have been required, however, for Salviati to familiarize himself with the opinions on the issue of Aristotle, Avicenna, Averroes, Aquinas, Henry of Ghent, Scotus, Auriol, Antonius Andreas, Bonet, Meyronnes, Rimini, and Candia. We have seen, however, that their works were at hand.

Interestingly, Francesco della Rovere, who had taken a somewhat conciliatory attitude toward Auriol in his treatise, changed his mind by June 1471. He nevertheless admits that he once supported Auriol's argument based on indistance, although now he has a neutral stance. It appears that in the year between Francesco's writing on future contingents and the dialogue, he investi-

---

[40] The quote is from Kaluza, "La crise des années 1474–1482," p. 314. Kaluza mentions (p. 312) Baudin's nominalist printing activities, suggests (p. 314) that the nominalists were "prévenus peut-être par un théologian actif à Rome" from signing the pro-Rivo document, and cites (n. 54) the anonymous treatise that we know was written by Baudin, who copied from d'Ailly. It fits Kaluza's scenario even better that the author was back in Paris in 1471.

[41] The text is Salviati, *De arcanis Dei* (ed. Etzkorn). On Salviati, see the works of Cesare Vasoli, e.g. "Notizie su Giorgio Benigno Salviati (Juraj Dragisic)," in *Studi storici in orone di Gabriele Pepe* (Bari 1969), pp. 429–97 (dialogue discussed on pp. 437–42), and "Giorgio Benigno Salviati (Dragisic)," in Marjorie Reeves, ed., *Prophetic Rome in the High Renaissance Period* (Oxford 1992), pp. 121–56. Several of the works cited in the above notes make passing mention of the dialogue. Originally it was dedicated to Cardinal Bessarion, but this was later changed to Francesco della Rovere. When the dedication was changed, almost all of Bessarion's quotations were reassigned to Francesco, and vice versa, and other modifications were effected. Labowsky, *Bessarion's Library*, pp. 119–20, n. 228, suggests that the names were switched after Bessarion's death, which was on 18 November 1472, but it could also be the case that they were switched after Francesco was elected Pope Sixtus IV, on 9 August 1471.

gated the thoughts of his fellow Franciscans Nicolas Bonet and Francis of Meyronnes concerning foreknowledge, and specifically their rejection of indistance.[42] In the dialogue it is Bessarion himself who decides the matter, however, going against Auriol's idea of indistance, saying that the truth of a proposition does not remove contingency from things, but the neutrality of propositions destroys the knowledge of the future.[43] Francesco was persuaded in the end.

However, almost the whole University of Louvain was against Zomeren, who perhaps began to hear the disturbing reports from Paris. It is probably around this time that Zomeren wrote his own treatise, against Rivo's *Five-Part Treatise*, including in it a brief history of the entire affair up until 1470. In his treatise, Zomeren refers to the date as "the year 1470." Zomeren himself departed for Rome and probably arrived around the time of Francesco's elevation to the papacy on 9 August 1471. He is not present in the dialogue, so his appearance in Rome should be dated after 1 June. Sixtus received him warmly, and quickly bestowed on him two benefices of Antwerp cathedral and took him into his service. Zomeren persuaded the pope to summon Peter de Rivo to Rome, on 24 April 1472, but Zomeren did not live to see his temporal victory. He died on 14 August of that year. The "entire papal household grieved," and his good friend John Andreae, Bishop of Aleria, the pope's secretary and the head of the Vatican library, composed an epitaph.[44]

[42] Salviati, *De arcanis Dei* III, c. 19 (ed. Etzkorn, p. 174, ll. 482–8).

[43] Salviati, *De arcanis Dei* I, c. 18 (ed. Etzkorn, pp. 97–8, ll. 958–68).

[44] In a later note attached to Zomeren's *Quaestio disputata* — not a separate disputatio as Burie ("Werken," p. 249) suggests — we are told (ms. Brussel 708–791, fol. 189r): "Nota quod dictus magister Henricus, existens Lovanii in theologia regens, venit in magnam disceptationem contra magistrum Petrum de Rivo, tunc in artibus magistrum et in theologia bacchalarium formatum, propter propositiones de futuris contingentibus, et adeo invaluit altricatio, quia dixit Zomeren dictum de Rivo defendere propositiones hereticas, quod quasi tota universitas et specialiter facultas artium coniu‹n›cta fuit contra eum, inherens dicto Rivo sustinenti dictum Aristotilis quod de futuris contingentibus non est determinata veritas. Proficiscebatur propterea dictus Zoemeren ad curiam Romanam anno primo coronationis Sixti pape, cui ab ante erat familiarissimus, qui sibi post paucos dies dedit decanatum et canonicatum Antwerpienses, et eum [s.l.] assumpsit in cubicularium, etc. Sed pius Deus, nolens tantum virum beneficiis temporalibus sed pocius eternis munerare, assumpsit eum illo anno [s.l.] de medio. Unde doluit tota domus pape et specialiter consocius suus carissimus, dominus Aleriensis episcopus, pape secretarius, qui composuit dicti Henrici empithaphium in modum subsequentem :
'Dic, Cythera, Henrico carmen miserabile Zoemren;
  Elogium extincto, tibia nostra, refer.
Nobilis Henrici revolavit ad ethera Zoemren
  Spiritus; exequias, pulla Minerva, cole.
Meror et attonitis comitatus luctibus horror
  Perstrepit in Sixti domate pontificis.
Profuit hoc illi divinis artibus apto,
  Profuit, in terris facta fuisse (*pro* sciisse?) Dei.
Sed neque lugendis contrivit in artibus evum
  Nec defecturas accumulavit opes;
Ergo igitur vivit; nostrum est iactura gemenda,
  Ditabat studiis quos pater Ipse piis.
Heu nimium servata fides! vir maximus idem
  Suetus inaccessi luminis ore loqui,

Rivo had to have been disappointed upon learning of Sixtus's change of attitude. In all this time the dispute continued at Louvain, even after Henry of Zomeren's death. In September, Rivo set off for Rome. He had probably already composed his responses to the works written at the request of Cardinal Bessarion, but he made some modifications and copied or dictated them into one manuscript containing all of his related works, describing it as "A Defense of the doctrine of Lord Peter Auriol on the matter of future contingents."[45] Rivo had previously thought that Sixtus IV's treatise was not overly unfavorable to him. In his paragraph by paragraph response, Rivo agrees that to deny truth to propositions of the faith about the future, and to deny flat out that God knows the future before it comes about, would be heretical, but he makes it plain that Zomeren had misrepresented him in the letters to Bessarion. Indeed, Rivo repeats many of the points made in earlier writings, including that to disagree with Rivo is to fall into the heresy of John Wyclif. Rivo again relates Zomeren's obstinate remark, building on Saint Paul, that if an angel from heaven were to say that it should be believed, he would not. This time, however, Rivo says Zomeren would not believe it if a bishop, *pope*, or angel from heaven said it. This must have stung Sixtus at least briefly. Rivo gently explains to the pope that although Peter Auriol and Aristotle did not agree fully, Auriol said Aristotle's position was demonstrated, and since Rivo follows Auriol, if Sixtus wants to defend Auriol, then he must also defend Rivo. Of course, Rivo asserts that he never did maintain the heretical propositions that Zomeren claimed he did. Zomeren's claims are based on erroneous syllogisms, Rivo declares, explaining and giving examples:

> He thought he could deduce the first of the said heretical propositions by virtue of this syllogism: No proposition about the contingent future is true, according to Aristotle, whom I said could be upheld with the faith; but propositions of the faith about the future are about the contingent future; therefore propositions of the faith about the future are

---

Pro vero certans, veri certissimus autor,
   Mutavit vita pro meliore locum;
Nos anime (*pro* autem?), terris et rebus inanibus orti,
   Reddamus merito funera iusta viri (*pro* viro?).
Terra viri corpus vacuataque sensibus ossa,
   Doctrinam et nomen pectora nostra colant,
Qui si sint ut sunt, numquam peritura beatis
   Premia cum divis regna superna tenet.'"

[45] That is Vat. lat. 4865, which may be an autograph. In the treatise *Petri de Rivo annotationes marginales tractatui Francisci* (ed. Schabel, "Peter de Rivo (Part II)," pp. 369–82), Rivo refers in the text to "Sixtus quartus," who became pope on 9 August 1471 (p. 369, l. 6) and he uses the past tense in describing Bessarion, who died on 18 November 1472 ("Iste fuit Bissarion," p. 379, l. 319). Still, the Bessarion remark is probably a last minute change: Vat. lat. 4865 appears to be in chronological order, and the next work, against Zomeren (*Tractatus Petri de Rivo responsalis* [Guerlac, pp. 290–350; Baudry, pp. 332–89]), implies throughout that he is still alive. The title of the last treatise, *Tractatus responsalis ad oppugnationes cuiusdam qui postea deprehensus est fuisse dominus Wilhelmus Boudini* (ed. Schabel, Part II, pp. 383–435) shows that Rivo did not know Baudin's name while writing. Rivo returned to Louvain following his first condemnation in March 1473, and he was in no position to attack Zomeren or Baudin afterwards.

not true... I admit also that I said similarly that the knowledge God has of futures is not expectative nor is it properly called foreknowledge. In this I imitated Anselm, who says in *De casu Diaboli* that God's foreknowledge is not properly called foreknowledge. For this reason lord Henry thought he could deduce the second of the said propositions by virtue of this syllogism: He whose knowledge of futures is not expectative nor is properly called foreknowledge, does not know futures before they come about; but according to me God's knowledge of futures is not expectative nor is it properly called foreknowledge; therefore God does not know futures before they come about.[46]

Rivo shows that the first syllogism needs to say that he agrees with Aristotle that future-tensed propositions of the faith are not true *at all*. The second needs to use 'knowledge' univocally, for there is our knowledge, within time and God's knowledge, outside of time. Thus Rivo gives two syllogisms of his own:

Whatever proposition is true by unimpedible truth, it true *simpliciter*; but as I maintained as dogma, propositions of the faith are true by an unimpedible truth, namely the truth of divine knowledge; therefore, propositions of this sort are true *simpliciter*... He, to whose perspective future contingents are eternally indistant, knows futures before they come about; but according to my dogma future contingents are eternally indistant to God's perspective; therefore God knows them before they come about.[47]

Although Rivo was overstating his case in his use of the adjective 'unimpedible' here and elsewhere, and in his suggestion that one could construe his position as affirming foreknowledge per se, nevertheless he does show Zomeren to have oversimplified his position. So Rivo concludes by comparing himself with those in the Bible who were falsely and cruelly accused, and gravely injured and punished.

The most violent attacks on Rivo had come from Zomeren himself and from Guillaume Baudin. The treatise against Zomeren is Rivo's most comprehensive and topically organized. In general he reiterates the main elements of his position, but there are a few items of note, the most interesting being his long rejection of power over the past and of the claim that 'God knew the Antichrist was future' are really about the future, and thus free from the necessity of the past. Rivo's last work on the problem, against Baudin, is also splendid reading, and in it Rivo expresses all he had expressed before, but with more emotion. He is frustrated in his efforts to discover the name of the author of the work he is refuting (as we have seen, he finds out later that it is Guillaume Baudin). He is completely annoyed by Baudin and Zomeren, and he continually mumbles about the heresy of Wyclif "by whose distressingly destructive

---

[46] Rivo, *Petri de Rivo annotationes* (ed. Schabel, pp. 379–80, ll. 332–46).
[47] Rivo, *Petri de Rivo annotationes* (ed. Schabel, p. 381, ll. 402–10).

doctrine the Kingdom of Bohemia was pitiably polluted to the greatest difficulty and detriment of the mother Church." It is not just Baudin and Zomeren who annoy Rivo here, for he even takes time to attack Fernando of Cordova's principal arguments, including Fernando's defense of Francis of Marchia's distinction between determinate *de inesse* and determinate *de possibili*:

> If truth determinate *de inesse* inhered presently in propositions about the contingent future, therefore so would [truth determinate] *de possibili*. This is clear, because the truth that is posited to inhere presently in a proposition of this sort would have inhered in it beforehand; and because there is no power with respect to the past, through no power could it come about that it had not inhered in it; wherefore it would be determinate *de possibili*.[48]

Also of interest is a paragraph in which Rivo defends his case as well as in all his other writings combined:

> If true propositions about future contingents are required to express divine foreknowledge, one asks of my adversary, by what truth must they be true, unimpedible truth or impedible truth? If by unimpedible [truth], it follows that all futures will come about unimpedibly. If by impedible truth, it follows first that God's foreknowledge can be maintained along with the said opinion of Aristotle, by which he only denies unimpedible truth in propositions about future contingents.[49]

Another passage re-connects us with the Parisian dispute between the nominalists and realists. The quarrel between Rivo and Zomeren did not involve the nominalist-realist debate directly, but we have seen that the Parisian nominalists and perhaps the realists as well used the controversy for their own ends. Nevertheless the issue could and did take on realist-nominalist philosophical significance: when Baudin the nominalist objects that "truth does not signify an absolute or respective entity that inheres in a proposition... because [otherwise] through the movement of my finger I could cause *de novo*, in the mind of an angel or in the soul of Christ, a real entity, i.e. the truth of this proposition: 'moved digit'," Rivo responds that Baudin's argument fails:

> It does *not* appear ridiculous that from the motion of my finger some positive entity is caused in the mind of an angel or in the soul of Christ. For if I moved my finger in their view, they would at least acquire a cognition, by which they would know the movement of my finger, which [cognition] they did not have before; but a cognition is an absolute entity; therefore what is the wonder if they also acquire a respective entity?[50]

[48]   Rivo, *Tractatus responsalis... Wilhelmus Boudini*, c. 9 (ed. Schabel, p. 433, ll. 80–84).
[49]   Rivo, *Tractatus responsalis... Wilhelmus Boudini*, c. 1 (ed. Schabel, p. 388, ll. 119–25).
[50]   Rivo, *Tractatus responsalis... Wilhelmus Boudini*, c. 6 (ed. Schabel, p. 415, ll. 171–81 and 215–20).

If Zomeren had been a nominalist, he certainly would have opposed Rivo's notion of truth inhering in propositions, but so might a moderate realist. But
whether or not the Louvain quarrel involved the realist-nominalist debate doctrinally, it became directly involved politically.

Conclusion: the Interventions of Sixtus IV and Louis XI

In Rome, Rivo presented his comprehensive defense of Peter Auriol's position
on future contingents to Pope Sixtus IV. The defense was unsuccessful, and
Rivo signed a retraction on 19 March 1473. After returning to Louvain by 9
May, however, Rivo tried to downplay what had happened in Rome, especially after Sixtus IV's favorable letter of 9 April was read at a university
meeting on 31 May.[51] Sixtus was not pleased when he learned of the new developments. In the bull "Ad Christi vicarii", of 3 January 1474, Sixtus officially damned some of Rivo's statements that denied truth to articles of the
faith about future contingents, one of the condemned positions being "that for
the truth of a proposition it is not sufficient that the thing [signified] will be,
but it is required that it will inevitably be." The bull concludes, "they are
damned as scandalous and deviant from the path of the catholic faith."[52]
    When word reached Paris, the realists, who already feared a resurgence of
nominalism that had begun in the 1460s, reacted by appealing to King Louis
XI. The realist theologian John Bouchard persuaded Louis to condemn the
nominalists, which he did on 1 March 1474. Nominalist theses were not to be
taught in public or private, and nominalist books were to be confiscated. The
nominalists responded on 10 April with a letter accusing the realists of seeking Louis's support in order to cover up their own explicit defense of a condemned heretic. Regardless of whether Zomeren was actually a nominalist, "in
the eyes of the Paris nominalists, Henry became one of their own to dramatize
the scandal of the of the support that the realists had given to a doctrine condemned by Rome." And so the Parisian nominalist theologians hailed
Zomeren's posthumous victory over their twenty-four realist counterparts.[53]
    Before Peter Auriol wrote his *Scriptum*, there were two basic opinions on
divine foreknowledge: one ancient, most notably defended by Thomas Aquinas, the other quite new, developed by John Duns Scotus building on Henry of
Ghent. Auriol provided a third alternative, with elements from Aquinas,
Henry, and perhaps Thomas Wylton. There was a negative reaction to all elements of Auriol's doctrine, but Walter Chatton, Gerard Odonis, and Nicholas

---

[51]   Events in Louvain after 1473 are described in more detail in Laminne, "La controverse," pp. 410–27.
[52]   "Item, quod non sufficit ad veritatem propositionis de futuro, quod res erit, sed requiritur, quod inimpedibiliter erit... Damnatae sunt ut 'scandalosae et a catholicae fidei semita
deviae'; sunt ab ipso Petro scripto revocatae," *Enchiridion symbolorum: definitionum et declarationum de rebus fidei et morum*, ed. Henricus Denzinger (Barcelona 1948), p. 269.
[53]   Kaluza, "La crise des années 1474–1482," p. 315, and generally pp. 313–27; cf.
Gabriel, "Intellectual Relations," pp. 124–7.

Bonet adopted fragments, and Auriol's language of indistance and eminent similitudes in this context found its way into the common solution toward the end of the fourteenth century. But no one actually took his side on the issue of future contingent propositions, the role of the divine will, and the equation of immutability and necessity. Peter de Rivo was the first and only vocal defender of Peter Auriol's opinion on divine foreknowledge and future contingents, but ironically Rivo's defense of Auriol resulted in the official condemnation of Auriol's theory by the pope. It was not until 1477, after John Warenacher's death and after a new, longer investigation, that Rivo was allowed to become a master of theology. Henry of Zomeren was the most vocal opponent of Peter Auriol's stance, but ironically his opposition to Auriol appears to have resulted in the official condemnation of the Parisian nominalists by the king. It was not until 1482 that the anti-nominalist ordinance was finally lifted. But the medieval debate over Auriol's theory, which began in 1316, had been decided in 1474.

Bibliography

Reference Works

Denifle, Heinrich, and E. Châtelain, eds., *Chartularium Universitatis Parisiensis*, vols. III–IV (Paris 1894–97).

Denzinger, Henricus ed., *Enchiridion symbolorum: definitionum et declarationum de rebus fidei et morum* (Barcelona 1948).

Doucet, Victorin, *Commentaires sur les Sentences: supplément au répertoire de M. Frédéric Steg-muller* (Florence 1954).

Du Plessis d'Argentré, Charles, *Collectio Judiciorum de Novis Erroribus*, vol. 1, part 2 (Paris 1728; reprint Brussels 1963).

Friedman, Russell L., "Auriol Web Page"(http://www.igl.ku.dk/~russ/auriol.html).

Glorieux, Paul, *La littérature quodlibétique de 1260 à 1320*, 2 vols. (Kain, Belgium 1925; Paris 1935).

Roest, Bert, and Maarten van der Heijden, "Franciscan Authors, 13th–18th Century" website (http://users.bart.nl/~roestb/franciscan).

Sarton, George, *Introduction to the History of Science, Volume III: Science and Learning in the Fourteenth Century* (Baltimore 1947).

Schönberger, Rolf, and Brigitte Kible, *Repertorium edierter Texte des Mittelalters* (Berlin 1994).

Stegmüller, Fridericus, *Repertorium commentariorum in Sententias Petri Lombardi*, 2 vols. (Würzburg 1947).

Weijers, Olga, ed., *Le travail intellectuel à la faculté des arts de Paris: textes et maîtres (ca. 1200–1500), II, C-F* (Turnhout 1996).

Primary Sources

Manuscripts

Adam Wodeham, OFM, *In libros Sent., Opus Oxoniense*, in Paris, Bibliothèque Mazarine 915.

Angelus de Dobelin, OESA, *In libros Sent.*, in Jena, Universitätsbibliothek El. Fol. 47.

Anonymous, *In I Sent.*, in Innsbruck, Universitätsbibliothek 677, ff. 145–179.

Anonymous, *In I Sent.*, in Vaticano, Biblioteca Ottob. lat. 360; Lyon, Bibliothèque de la ville 653.

Anonymous, *In I Sent.*, in Vaticano, Biblioteca Apostolica Palat. lat. 329, ff. 1–37.

Anonymous, *In I Sent.*, in Vaticano, Biblioteca Apostolica Vat. lat. 829, ff. 149–201.

Anonymous, *In I Sent.*, in Vaticano, Biblioteca Apostolica Vat. lat. 869, ff. 166–189.

Anonymous, *In I Sent.*, in Vaticano, Biblioteca Apostolica Vat. lat. 1112, ff. 3–21.

Anonymous, *In I Sent.*, in Vaticano, Biblioteca Apostolica Vat. lat. 4269, ff. 1–72.

Anonymous, OFM, *In I Sent.*, in Vaticano, Biblioteca Apostolica Vat. lat. 986, ff. 1–31.

Bernardus Lombardi, OP, *In libros Sent.*, in Erfurt, Wissenschaftliche Bibliothek, C.A. 2° 368.

Dionysius de Burgo Sancti Sepulcri, OESA, *In I et II libros Sent.*, in Erfurt, Wissenschaftliche Bibliothek, C.A. 2° 131.

Durandus de Sancto Porciano, OP, *In I Sent. redactio prima*, in Paris, BN lat. 12330 and 14454

Franciscus de Marchia, OFM, *Reportatio in I Sent., versio A*, in Napoli, BN VII. C. 27; Vaticano, Biblioteca Apostolica Ross. lat. 525.

—— *Reportatio in I Sent., versio B*, in Paris, BN lat. 3071.

338 BIBLIOGRAPHY

Franciscus de Mayronis, OFM, *Reportatio in I Sent.*, in Admont, Bibliothek der Benediktinerabtei 91.

Gerardus de Bononia, OCarm, *Summa theologica*, in Vaticano, Biblioteca Apostolica Borghese 27.

Gerardus de Senis, OESA, *In I Sent.*, in Chicago, University Library 22.

Guido de Terrena, OCarm, *Quodlibeta*, in Vaticano, Biblioteca Apostolica Borghese 39.

Guillelmus de Alnwick, OFM, *In I-II libros Sent.*, in Padova, Biblioteca Antoniana 291.

Guillelmus de Brienna, OFM, *Reportatio in libros Sent.*, in Praha, Universitní knihovna [Statní knihovna], VIII. F. 14.

Guillelmus de Dumoquerci, OCarm, *In I-III libros Sent.*, in Vaticano, Biblioteca Apostolica Vat. lat. 1090.

Gualterus de Chatton, OFM, *Quodlibet*, in Paris, BN lat. 15805.

Henricus Heinbuche de Langenstein (de Hassia), *In libros Sent.*, in Alençon, Bibliothèque de la ville 144.

—— *In libros Sent. secundum Jacobum de Altavilla*, in Erfurt, Wissenschaftliche Bibliothek C.A. 2° 118.

Henricus Totting de Oyta, *In libros Sent.*, *lectura textualis*, Wien, ÖNB 4690.

Henricus de Zomeren, *Epytome Dialogorum Ocham de Haereticis*, in Vaticano, Biblioteca Apostolica Chigi B IV 45.

—— *Quaestio solemniter disputata anno Domini XIIII LXII° in Universitate Parisiensi*, in Brussel, Koninklijke Bibliotheek, 708–719.

Himbertus de Garda, OFM, *In I Sent.*, in Vat. lat. 1091; Krakow, Bibl. Jagiellonska 1584.

Jacobus de Altavilla, OCist, *In libros Sent.*, in Besançon, Bibliothèque de la ville 198; Cambrai, Bibliothèque de la ville 570.

Jacobus de Apamiis, OESA, *Quodlibeta*, in Padova, Biblioteca universitaria 2006.

Johannes Baconthorpe, OCarm, *In I-III libros Sent.*, in London, British Library, Royal 11 C. VI.

Johannes Berwardi de Villingen, *In I et II libros Sententiarum*, Klosterneuburg, Augustinerehorherrenstift 41.

Johannes de Mirecourt, OCist, *In libros Sent.*, in Paris, BN lat. 15882.

Johannes de Neapoli, OP, *Quodlibeta*, Tortosa, Archivo Capitular 244.

Johannes de Ripa, OFM, *In I Sent.*, in Vaticano, Biblioteca Apostolica Vat. lat. 1083.

Johannes de Rodington, OFM, *In libros Sent.*, in Brussel, Bibliothèque Royale 11578 (1552).

Johannes Wuel de Pruck, *In I Sent.*, in Wien, ÖNB 5067.

Michaelis de Massa, OESA, *In I Sent.*, in Bologna, Università 2214.

Nicolaus de Dinkelsbühl, *Quaestiones magistrales in libros Sent.*, in Wien, ÖNB 4820.

Pastor de Serrescuderio, OFM, *In I Sent.*, in Saint-Omer, Bibliothèque municipale 239.

Paulus de Perugia, OCarm, *In libros Sent.*, in Praha, Narodni Museum XIII.D.5.

Petrus Aureoli, OFM, *Reportatio Parisiensis in I Sent.*, in Vaticano, Biblioteca Apostolica Borghese 123.

Petrus de Candia, OFM, *In libros Sent.*, in Vaticano, Biblioteca Apostolica Vat. lat. 1081.

Petrus de Ceffona, OCist, *In I, II, et IV libros Sent.*, in Troyes, Bibliothèque municipale 62.

Petrus de Nogento, *In libros Sent.*, in Vaticano, Biblioteca Apostolica Vat. lat. 1090; Pamplona, Biblioteca de la Catedral 36.

Petrus de Pulkau, *In I Sent.*, in Wien, ÖNB 4668.

Petrus Thomae, OFM, *In I Sententiarum*, in Vatican, Biblioteca Apostolica Vat. lat. 1106.

Richardus Fitzralph, *In libros Sent.*, in Oxford, Oriel College 15; Firenze, BN A.III.508.; Paris, BN lat. 15880; Vaticano, Biblioteca Apostolica Ottob. lat. 179; Vaticano, Biblioteca Apostolica Ottob. lat. 869; Worcester Cathedral, Q 71.

—— *Summa de quaestionibus Armenorum*, in Padova, Biblioteca universitaria 1439.

Thomas Bradwardinus, *Summa de causa Dei contra Pelagium et de virtute causarum ad suos Mertonenses*, in Klosterneuburg, Augustinerehorherrinstift 317.

Thomas Ebendorfer de Hasselbach, *In libros Sent.*, in Wien, ÖNB 4369.

Thomas de Sutton, OP, *Contra Robertum de Cowton*, in Vaticano, Biblioteca Apostolica Ross. lat. 431.

Thomas Wylton, *Quaestio de praescientia et de praedestinatione*, in Tortosa, Archivo Capitular 88; Barcelona, Archivo de la Corona de Aragón, Ripoll 95.
—— *Quaestiones super Physicam*, in Cesena, Biblioteca Malatestiana, Plut. VIII sin. 2.

Early Printed Editions

Alphonsus Vargas Toletanus, OESA, *In Primum Sententiarum* (Venice 1490; reprint New York 1952).
Antonius Andreas, OFM, *Scriptum in Arte Veteri et in divisionibus Boetii cum questionibus eiusdem* (Venice 1508).
Durandus de Sancto Porciano, OP, *In Petri Lombardi Sententias theologicas commentariorum libri IIII* (Venice 1571).
Gerardus de Senis, OESA, *Super primum librum Sententiarum* (Padua 1598).
Franciscus de Mayronis, OFM, *In primum Sententiarum foecundissimum scriptum sive conflatus nominatum* (Venice 1504–07); (Venice 1520).
Guillelmus de Rubione, OFM, *Disputata in quatuor libros Magistri Sententiarum*, vol. 1 (Paris 1518)
Henricus de Gandavo, *Quaestiones quodlibetales*, vol. 2 (Venice 1613).
Hervaeus Natalis, OP, *In quatuor libros Sententiarum commentaria* (Paris 1647).
—— *Quodlibeta* (Venice 1513).
Johannes Baconthorp, OCarm, *Super quattuor libros Sententiarum* (Venice 1526; Cremona 1618).
—— *Quaestiones Quodlibetales* (Cremona 1618).
Johannes Maior, *In Primum Sententiarum* (Paris 1510; 1519).
Nicolaus Bonetus, OFM, *Habes Nicholai Bonetti viri perspicacissimi quattuor volumina: Metaphysicam videlicet, naturalem phylosphiam, praedicamenta, necnon theologiam naturalem* (Venice 1505).
Petrus de Alliaco, *In libros Sententiarum* (Paris, s.a.).
Petrus de Aquila, OFM, *In libros Sententiarum* (Speyer 1480).
Petrus Aureoli, OFM, *Commentariorum in Primum Librum Sententiarum* (Rome 1596).
—— *Commentariorum in Secundum, Tertium, Quartum Libros Sententiarum* (Rome 1605).
—— *Tractatus de paupertate et usu paupere*, in *Firmamenta trium ordinum beatissimi Patris nostri Francisci*, part IV (Paris 1511), ff. 116r–129r.
Richardus de Mediavilla, OFM, *Super quatuor libros Sententiarum* (Brescia 1591).
Thomas Anglicus, *Liber propugnatorius* (Modena 1523).
Thomas de Argentina, OESA, *Commentaria in IIII libros Sententiarum* (Venice 1564).
Thomas Bradwardinus, *De causa Dei, contra Pelagium, et de virtute causarum, ad suos Mertonenses, libri tres* (London 1618).

Critical Editions, Single Questions, and Translations

Anonymus, OFM, *In I Sententiarum*, dd. 38–39, q. 2, in Schabel, "Landulphus Caracciolo," pp. 339–43.
Anselmus, *De concordia praescientiae et praedestinationis et gratiae cum libero arbitrio*, in *S. Anselmi Cantuariensis archiepiscopi opera omnia* II, ed. Franciscus Salesius Schmitt, OSB (Edinburgh 1946).
Aristoteles, *The Basic Works of Aristotle*, ed. Richard McKeon (New York 1941).
Arnoldus de Strelley, OP, *Circa praedestinationem et praescientiam*, in Gelber, "Ockham's early influence," 271–89.
Aufredus Gonteri Brito, OFM, *In I Sententiarum*, d. 38, q. 7, and d. 39, q. 2, in Schabel, "Aufredo Gonteri Brito secundum Henry of Harclay," pp. 165–95.
—— *In I Sententiarum*, d. 39, qq. 1, 3, and 4, in Friedman and Schabel, "Hugh of Novo Castro's Questions," forthcoming.
—— *In III Sententiarum*, d. 3, in J. Alfaro, "La Immaculada Concepción en los escritos de un discípolo de Duns Escoto, Aufredo Gontier," *Gregorianum* 36 (1955), pp. 590–617.

Augustinus, *City of God*, trans. Marcus Dods (New York 1950).
—— *Earlier Writings*, trans. J.H.S. Burleigh (Philadelphia 1953).
—— *The Literal Meaning of Genesis*, trans. J. Taylor (New York and Ramsey, N.J. 1982)
—— *The Trinity*, trans. Stephen McKenna (Washington 1963).
Bernardus Lombardi, OP, *In I Sententiarum*, q. 21, in Porebski, "La question de Bernard Lombardi," pp. 169–85.
Boethius, *Boethii Commentarii in librum Aristotelis Peri Hermeneias*, 2 vols., ed. C. Meisner (Leipzig 1877–80).
—— *The Consolation of Philosophy*, trans. Richard Green (Indianapolis 1962).
Bonaventura, OFM, *Commertarius in quattuor libros Sententiarum*, in *Opera Omnia* I (ed. Grottaferrata 1882).
Coluccio Salutati, *De fato et fortuna*, ed. C. Bianca (Florence 1985).
Fernandus de Corduba, *Tractatus M. Fernandi de Corduba*, in Baudry (Guerlac, pp. 99–134; Baudry, pp. 134–70).
Franciscus de Marchia, OFM, *Improbatio contra libellum Domini Johannis qui incipit 'Quia vir reprobus'*, ed. Nazareno Mariani (Grottaferrata 1993).
—— *Quodlibet cum quaestionibus selectis ex commentario in librum Sententiarum*, ed. Nazareno Mariani (Grottaferrata 1997).
—— *Scriptum in I Sententiarum*, dd. 35, 36, et 38, in Schabel, "Il Determinismo (Parte I)," pp. 69–95, and Parte II, 18–55.
——*Sententia et compilatio super libros Physicorum Aristotelis*, ed. Nazareno Mariani (Grottaferrata 1998).
Geoffrey Chaucer, *Canterbury Tales*, trans. Nevil Coghill (Harmondsworth 1951).
Georgius Benignus Salviati, OFM, *De arcanis Dei*, ed. Girard J. Etkorn, *Cardinal Bessarion, De arcanis Dei* (Rome 1997).
Gerardus Odonis, OFM, *Lectura in I Sententiarum*, d. 38 and d. 39, q. 1, in Schabel, "*Non aliter novit facienda quam facta*," forthcoming.
—— *Logica*, in Lambert M. de Rijk, ed. *Giraldus Odonis O.F.M., Opera Philosophica* I (Leiden 1997).
Gregorius Ariminensis, OESA, *Lectura in I et II libros Sententiarum*, eds. A. Damasus Trapp, V. Marcolino, W. Eckermann, M. Santos-Noya, M. Schulze, W. Simon, W. Urban, and V. Vendland (Berlin–New York 1979–84).
—— *Modality, Order, and Transcendence: Gregory of Rimini on God's Knowledge, Power, and Will. An English Translation of His Lectures on the Sentences, Book I, Dist. 35–48*, trans. Russell Friedman and Chris Schabel (New Haven, forthcoming).
Gualterus de Burley, OFM, in Brown, "Walter Burley's Middle Commentary," pp. 42–134.
Gualterus de Chatton, OFM, *Reportatio in primum librum Sententiarum vol. III: distinctiones 10–48*, ed. Girard Etzkorn (Toronto, forthcoming).
Guillelmus de Alnwick, OFM, *Determinationes*, q. 12, in Schmaus, "Guilelmi de Alnwick," pp. 203–225.
Guillelmus Baudinus, *Anonymi tractatus de veritatibus futurorum contingentium adversus Petrum de Rivo*, in Baudry (Guerlac, pp. 135–70; Baudry, pp. 171–208).
Guillelmus Crathorn, OP, *Quästionen zum ersten Sentenzenbuch*, ed. Fritz Hoffman (Münster 1988).
Guillelmus de Ockham, OFM, *Ordinatio in primum librum Sententiarum*, eds. Girard Etzkorn and Francis Kelley, in *Guillelmi de Ockham Opera Theologica* IV (St. Bonaventure, NY 1979).
——*Predestination, God's Foreknowledge, and Future Contingents*, trans. Marilyn McCord Adams and Norman Kretzmann (New York 1969).
—— *Quodlibeta septem*, ed. Joseph Wey, in *Guillelmi de Ockham Opera Theologica* IX (St. Bonaventure, NY 1980).
—— *Quodlibetal Questions Volume I, Quodlibets 1–4*, trans. Alfred J. Freddoso and Francis E. Kelley (New Haven 1991).

—— *Tractatus de praedestinatione et de praescientia Dei et de futuris contingentibus*, ed. Philotheus Boehner and Stephen F. Brown, in *Guillelmi de Ockham Opera Philosophica* II (St. Bonaventure, NY 1978).

Guillelmus de Rubione, OFM, *Quodlibeta*, in Rubert Candau, *Archivo Ibero-Americano* 15 (1928), pp. 5–32; 16 (1929), pp. 145–81; and 17 (1930), pp. 5–42; and L.M. Farré, "La conceptió inmaculada de la Verge segons Fr. G. Rubió," *Analecta Sacra Tarraconensia* 7 (1931), pp. 95–138.

Henricus de Harclay, *In I Sententiarum*, dd. 38–39, in Schabel, "Aufredo Gonteri Brito *secundum* Henry of Harclay," pp. 165–95.

—— *Quaestiones de praescientia divina et de praedestinatione*, in Henninger, "Henry of Harclay's Questions on Divine Prescience and Predestination," pp. 195–243.

Henricus de Zomeren, *Heinrici de Zoemeren tractatus adversus sententiam Petri de Rivo de futuris contingentibus*, in Baudry (Guerlac, pp. 213–80; Baudry, pp. 259–321).

Hugo de Novocastro, OFM, *In I Sententiarum*, dd. 38–41, in Friedman and Schabel, "Hugh of Novocastro's Questions," forthcoming

Hugo de Sancto Victore, *On the Sacraments of the Christian Faith*, trans. Roy. J. Deferrari (Cambridge, Mass 1951).

Hugolinus de Urbe Veteri, OESA, *Commentarius in quattuor libros Sententiarum*, vol. 2, ed. Willigis Eckermann (Würzburg 1984).

Johannes Buridanus, *Questiones longe super librum Perihermeneias*, ed. Rita van der Lecq (Nijmegen 1983).

Johannes Capreolus, *Defensiones theologiae Thomae Aquinatis* II, eds. Ceslaus Paban and Thomas Pègues (Toronto 1900; reprint Frankfurt 1967).

Johannes Duns Scotus, OFM, *Duns Scotus, Philosophical Writings*, trans. Allan B. Wolter (Edinburgh 1962)

—— *Lectura in librum primum Sententiarum*, in *Joannis Duns Scotis Opera Omnia* XVII, ed. Carolus Balic et al. (Vatican City 1973).

—— *Ordinatio in primum librum Sententiarum*, in *Joannis Duns Scoti Opera Omnia* VI, ed. Carolus Balic et al. (Vatican City 1963).

Johannes Gattus, *Anonymi tractatus de futuris contingentibus*, in Baudry (Guerlac, pp. 91–98; Baudry, pp. 126–133).

Johannes Hiltalingen de Basilea, OESA, *In I Sententiarum*, dd. 38–39, in Schabel, "The Quarrel with Aureol," pp. 798–807.

Johannes Hus, *In libros Sententiarum*, in *Joannis Hus opera omnia* II, ed. Wenzel Flajshans and Marie Kominkova (Osnabrück 1905; reprint 1966).

Johannes de Mirecourt, "Die zwei Apologien des Jean de Mirecourt," ed. F. Stegmüller, in RTAM 5 (1933), pp. 40–78 and 192–204.

Johannes Wyclif, *On Universals (Tractatus de universalibus)*, trans. Anthony Kenny (Oxford 1985).

—— *Tractatus de universalibus*, ed. Ivan J. Mueller (Oxford 1985).

Landulphus Caracciolo, OFM, *In I Sententiarum*, dd. 38–40, in Schabel, "Landulphus Caracciolo," pp. 307–338.

Michaelis de Massa, OESA, *Scriptum in I Sententiarum*, dd. 35, 36, and 38, in Schabel, "Questions on Future Contingents," pp. 175–229.

Petrus de Aquila, OFM, *Commentarium in libros Sententiarum*, ed. C. Paolini (books I-III, Recco 1907; book IV, Levanto 1909).

Petrus Aureoli, OFM, *Compendiosa Expositio Evangelii Johannis*, ed. Frederick Stegmüller, FzS 33 (1951), pp. 207–219.

—— *Compendium Sensus Litteralis Totius Divinae Scripturae a Cl. Theologo Fr. Petri Aureoli Ord. Min.*, ed. P. Seeboeck (Florence 1896).

—— *De principiis naturae*, ed. Martin Bauer, forthcoming.

—— *Recommendatio et divisio sacrae Scripturae*, ed. Nancy Spatz, forthcoming.

—— *Repercussorium editum contra adversarium innocentiae matris Dei*, in *Fr. Gulielmi Guarrae, Fr. Ioannis Duns Scoti, Fr. Petri Aureoli Quaestiones Disputatae de Immaculata Conceptione Beatae Mariae Virginis* (Quaracchi 1904), pp. 95–153.

—— *Reportatio in primum librum Sententiarum* (VQ, Berlin-Padua), ed. Lauge Nielsen and Chris Schabel, forthcoming.

——*Reportatio Parisiensis in I Sententiarum*, d. 2, part 1, qq. 1–3 and part 2, qq. 1–2, in Brown, "Petrus Aureoli," pp. 209–248.

—— *Reportatio in II Sententiarum*, d. 2, part 3, q. 1, in Schabel, "Place, Space, and the Physics of Grace," pp. 143–54.

—— *Reportatio in III Sententiarum*, d. 3, qq. 1–2 in Eligius Buytaert, "Aureoli's Unpublished *Reportatio* III, Dist. 3, q. 1–2," in FcS (1955), pp. 159–74.

—— *Scriptum in primum librum Sententiarum*, Prologue and dd. 1–8, in Eligius Buytaert, ed. *Peter Aureoli Scriptum Puper Primum Sententiarum, prooemium-dist. 8*, 2 vols. (St. Bonaventure, NY 1952–56).

—— *Scriptum in I Sententiarum*, d. 9, part 1, and d. 27, in Friedman, "*In principio erat Verbum*," pp. 365–496.

—— *Scriptum in I Sententiarum*, d. 23, a. 2, in Jan Pinborg, "Radulphus Brito on Universals," CIMAGL 35 (1980), pp. 133–7; further excerpts in Perler, "Peter Aureol vs. Hervaeus Natalis," pp. 242–62.

—— *Scriptum in I Sententiarum*, dd. 38–39, in Schabel, "Peter Aureol on Divine Foreknowledge," pp. 87–212.

—— *Scriptum in I Sententiarum*, d. 40, aa. 1 and 4, d. 41, aa. 1 and 3, and 45–47, in Halverson, "Peter Aureol and the Re-emergence," pp. 295–436.

—— *Tractatus de conceptione Beatae Mariae Virginis*, in *Fr. Gulielmi Guarrae, Fr. Ioannis Duns Scoti, Fr. Petri Aureoli Quaestiones Disputatae de Immaculata Conceptione Beatae Mariae Virginis* (Quaracchi 1904), pp. 23–94.

Petrus de Candia, *In I Sententiarum*, q. 6, a. 2, in Schabel, "Peter of Candia," pp. 97–124.

Petrus Damianus, *De divina omnipotentia*, PL vol. 145.

Petrus Lombardus, *Sententiae in IV libris distinctae*, vol. 1, ed. Ignatius Brady (Quaracchi 1916; Grottaferrata 1971).

Petrus de Navarra, OFM, *Doctoris Fundati Petri de Atarrabia sive de Navarra, OFM, In Primum Sententiarum Scriptum*, 2 vols., ed. Pius S. Azcona, OFM (Madrid 1974).

Petrus de Palude, *In I Sententiarum*, d. 38, q. 3, in Schabel-Balkoyiannopoulou-Friedman, "Peter of Palude," forthcoming.

Petrus de Rivo, *Defensio statuti per Petrum de Rivo*, in Schabel, "Petrus de Rivo (Part I)," pp. 446–73.

—— *Petri de Rivo alius tractatus* (#1), in Baudry (Guerlac, pp. 46–52; Baudry, pp. 79–84).

—— *Petri de Rivo alius tractatus* (#2), in Baudry (Guerlac, pp. 53–5; Baudry, pp. 85–8).

—— *Petri de Rivo annotationes marginales tractatui Francisci*, in Schabel, "Petrus de Rivo (Part II)," pp. 369–82.

—— *Questio quodlibetica disputata anno LXV° Lovanii per Petrum de Rivo*, in Baudry (Guerlac, pp. 36–45; Baudry, pp. 70–78).

—— *Questio quodlibetica disputata Lovanii per Petrum de Rivo, anno LXIX°*, in Schabel, "Peter de Rivo (Part I)," pp. 416–45.

—— *Tractatus Petri de Rivo responsalis ad opusculum quoddam magistri Heynrici de Zoemeren*, in Baudry (Guerlac, pp. 290–350; Baudry, pp. 332–89).

—— *Tractatus responsalis ad oppugnationes cuiusdam qui postea deprehensus est fuisse dominus Wilhelmus Boudini*, in Schabel, "Peter de Rivo" (Part II), pp. 383–435.

Petrus Thomae, OFM, *Quodlibet*, eds. M.R. Hooper and E.M. Buytaert (St. Bonaventure, NY 1957).

Richardus Campsall, *The Works of Richard of Campsall*, ed. Edward Synan, 2 vols. (Toronto 1982).

Richardus Fitzralph, *Quaestio biblica*, in Genest, "Contingence et révélation," pp. 215–46.

BIBLIOGRAPHY

343

Robertus Holcot, OP, *Seeing the Future Clearly: Questions on Future Contingents by Robert Holcot*, eds. Paul A. Streveler and Katherine H. Tachau (Toronto 1995).

Thomas Aquinas, OP, *The Basic Writings of Saint Thomas Aquinas*, trans. Anton C. Pegis (New York 1945).

————*Scriptum super libros Sententiarum*, vol. 1, ed. R.P. Mandonnet, OP (Paris 1929).

————*Summa Contra Gentiles* in *Opera Omnia* XIII, ed Leonis (Rome 1918).

————*Summa Contra Gentiles. Book One: God*, trans. Anton C. Pegis (Notre Dame 1975).

Thomas Bradwardinus, *De futuris contingentibus*, in Genest, "Le *De futuris contingentibus* de Thomas Bradwardine," pp. 281–336.

Thomas Buckingham, *De contingentia futurorum et arbitrii libertate*, in de la Torre, *Thomas Buckingham*, pp. 149–379; and in Genest, *Prédétermination et liberté créée*, pp. 185–290.

Secondary Sources

Adams, Marilyn McCord, *William Ockham*, 2 vols. (Notre Dame 1987).

Aertsen, Jan A., and Andreas Speer, eds., *Was ist Philosophie im Mittelalter* (Berlin 1998).

Alliney, Guido, "Fra Scoto e Ockham: Giovanni di Reading e il dibattito sulla libertà a Oxford (1310–1320)," DSTFM 7 (1996), pp. 243–368.

Aston, Margaret, ed., *Lollards and Reformers: Images and Literacy in Late Medieval Religion* (London 1984).

Baier, Walter, "Michael von Massa OESA (†1337) — Autor einer *Vita Christi*. Kritik der Diskussion über ihre Zuordnung zur *Vita Christi* des Kartäusers Ludolf von Sachsen (†1378)," in Adolar Zumkeller and Achim Krümmel, eds., *Traditio Augustiniana. Studien über Augustinus und seine Rezeption* (Würzburg 1994), pp. 495–524.

Bakker, P.J.J.M., *La raison et le miracle: les doctrines eucharistiques (c. 1250–c. 1400)* (Nijmegen 1999).

Bakker, Paul, and Chris Schabel, "*Sentences* Commentaries of the Later Fourteenth Century," in Evans ed., *Commentaries on Peter Lombard's Sentences*, forthcoming.

Baldwin, John W., *The Scholastic Culture of the Middle Ages 1000–1300* (Lexington, Mass. 1971).

Balic, Charles, "The Life and Works of John Duns Scotus," in J.K. Ryan and B.M. Bonasea, eds., *John Duns Scotus 1265–1965* (Washington D.C. 1965), pp. 1–27.

Barbet, Jeanne, ed., *François de Meyronnes — Pierre Roger: Disputatio (1320–1321)* (Paris 1961).

Baudry, Léon, ed., *La querelle des futurs contingents (Louvain 1465–1475)* (Paris 1950).

—— *The Quarrel over Future Contingents. Louvain, 1465–1475*, trans. Rita Guerlac (Dordrecht 1989).

Bianchi, Luca, "1277: A Turning Point in Medieval Philosophy?" in Aersten and Speer, eds., *Was ist Philosophie*, pp. 90–110

Boehner, Philotheus, *The Tractatus de praedestinatione et de praescientia Dei et de futuris contingentibus of William Ockham, Together with a Study of a Three-Valued Logic* (St. Bonaventure, NY 1945).

Boland, Vivian, *Ideas in God According to Saint Thomas Aquinas. Sources and Synthesis* (Leiden 1996).

Bolyard, Charles, "Knowing *Naturaliter*: Auriol's Propositional Foundations," *Vivarium* 38.1 (2000), pp. 163–76.

Borchert, Ernst, *Die Quaestiones speculativae et canonicae des Johannes Baconthorp über den sakramentalen Charakter* (Munich 1974).

Bos, E.P., ed., *John Duns Scotus (1265/6–1308). Renewal of Philosophy* (Amsterdam 1998).

Bosely, Richard N., and Martin Tweedale, trans., *Basic Issues in Medieval Philosophy. Selected Readings Presenting the Interactive Discourses among the Major Figures* (Peterborough, Ontario 1997).

Brown, Stephen F., "Petrus Aureoli: De unitate conceptus entis (*Reportatio Parisiensis in I Sententiarum*, dist. 2, p. 1, qq. 1–3 et p. 2, qq. 1–2)," *Traditio* 50 (1995), pp. 199–248.

—— "Peter of Candia on Believing and Knowing," FcS 54 (1994–7), pp. 251–76.

—— "Peter of Candia's Hundred-Year 'History' of the Theologian's Role," *Medieval Philosophy and Theology* 1 (1991), pp. 156–90.

—— "Peter of Candia's Sermons in Praise of Peter Lombard," in Romano Almagno and Conrad Harkins, eds., *Studies Honoring Ignatius Charles Brady, Friar Minor* (St. Bonaventure, NY 1976), pp. 141–76.

—— "The Treatise: *De arcanis Dei*," *Miscellanea Francescana* 96 (1996), pp. 572–620.

—— "The Unity of the Concept of Being in Peter Aureoli's '*Scriptum*' and '*Commentarium*.' With a Critical Edition of the '*Commentarium*'," 2 vols. (PhD Dissertation, Université catholique de Louvain 1964).

—— "Walter Burley, Peter Aureoli, and Gregory of Rimini," in Marenbon, ed., *Medieval Philosophy*, pp. 368–85.

—— "Walter Burley's Middle Commentary on Aristotle's *Perihermeneias*," FcS 33 (1973), pp. 42–134.

—— "Walter Chatton's *Lectura* and William of Ockham's *Quaestiones in Libros Physicorum Aristotelis*," in William A. Frank and Girard J. Etzkorn, eds., *Essays Honoring Allan B. Wolter* (St. Bonaventure, NY 1985), pp. 81–115.

Brown, Stephen F., and Stephen D. Dumont, "The Univocity of the Concept of Being in the Fourteenth Century: III. An Early Scotist," *Mediaeval Studies* 51 (1989), pp. 19–38.

Bucichowski, Waclaw, "Le principe d'individuation dans la question de Henri de Lubeck 'Utrum materia sit principium individuationis'," MPP 21 (1975), pp. 89–103 (ch. 1–3).

Burie, Luc, "Proeve tot inventarisatie van de in handschrift of in druk bewaarde werken van de Leuvense theologieprofessoren uit de XVe eeuw," in Edmund J.M. van Eijl ed., *Facultas S. Theologiae Lovaniensis 1432–1797: Bijdragen tot haar geschiedenis* (Louvain 1977), pp. 215–72.

Buytaert, Eligius, "The Scholastic Writings of Petrus Thomae," in J. Auer and H. Volk, eds., *Theologie in Geschichte und Gegenwart* (Munich 1957), pp. 927–40.

Candau, Rubert, *La filosofía del siglo XIV a través de G. Rubió* (Madrid 1952).

Cassidy, John, "Logic and Determinism: A History of the Problem of Future Contingent Propositions from Aristotle to Ockham" (PhD Dissertation, Bryn Mawr College 1965).

Catto, Jeremy I., "Wyclif and Wycliffism at Oxford 1356-1430," in J.I. Catto and R. Evans eds., *The History of the University of Oxford II: Late Medieval Oxford* (Oxford 1992), pp. 175–261.

Clagett, Marshall, *The Science of Mechanics in the Middle Ages* (Madison 1959)

Cleary, Gregory, "Pontius Carbonell," *The Catholic Encyclopedia* XII (New York 1911), p. 234.

Colish, Marcia, *Peter Lombard*, 2 vols. (Leiden 1994).

—— "Peter Lombard and Abelard: The *Opinio Nominalium* and Divine Transcendence," *Vivarium* 30.1 (1992), pp. 139–56.

—— "Systematic Theology and Theological Renewal in the Twelfth Century," *Journal of Medieval and Renaissance Studies* 18.2 (Fall, 1988), pp. 135–56.

Conti, Alessandro, "Divine Ideas and Exemplar Causality in Auriol," *Vivarium* 38.1 (2000), pp. 99–116.

Copleston, Frederick, *A History of Philosophy III: Ockham to Suárez* (Westminster, Maryland 1953).

Counet, Jean-Michel, "La cosmologie de François de Marchia. À propos d'un livre récent," *Bulletin de philosophie médiévale* 34 (1992), pp. 215–20.

Courtenay, William J., *Adam Wodeham: An Introduction to His Life and Writings* (Leiden 1978).

—— *Capacity and Volition: A History of the Distinction of Absolute and Ordained Power* (Bergamo 1990).

—— *Covenant and Causality in Medieval Thought. Studies in Philosophy, Theology, and Economic Practice* (London 1984).

—— "Foreign Study in a Time of War: English Scholars at Paris 1325-1345," *History of Universities* 14 (1995–96), pp. 31–41.

—— "John of Mirecourt and Gregory of Rimini on Whether God Can Undo the Past," RTAM 39 (1972), pp. 224–56, and 40 (1973), pp. 147–74.

—— "Ockham, Chatton, and the London *Studium*: Observations on Recent Changes in Ockham's Biography," in Wilhelm Vossenkuhl and Rolf Schönberger, eds., *Die Gegenwart Ockhams* (Weinheim 1990), pp. 327-37.

—— *Parisian Scholars in the Early Fourteenth Century. A Social Portrait* (Cambridge 1999).

—— "Pastor de Serrescuderio (d. 1356) and MS Saint-Omer 239," AHDLMA 63 (1996), pp. 325–56.

—— "The *Quaestiones in Sententias* of Michael de Massa, OESA. A Redating," *Augustiniana* 45 (1995), pp. 191–207.

—— "The Role of English Thought in the Transformation of University Education in the Late Middle Ages," in J.M Kittelson and P.J. Transue eds., *Rebirth, Reform and Resilience, Universities in Transition 1300–1700* (Columbus, Ohio 1984), pp. 103–162.

—— *Schools and Scholars in Fourteenth-Century England* (Princeton 1987).

Craig, William Lane, *Divine Foreknowledge and Human Freedom* (Leiden 1991).

—— *The Problem of Divine Foreknowledge and Future Contingents from Aristotle to Suarez* (Leiden 1988).

Dal Pra, Mario, "Il tempo e la problematizzazione dell'attualità della verità nel pensiero di Pietro De Rivo," in Antonio Banfi, ed., *La Crisi dell'uso dogmatico della Ragione* (Milan 1953), pp. 33–59.

Damiata, Marino, "Ockham e Pietro Aureolo," *Studi Francescani* 92 (1995), pp. 71–106.

Decorte, Jos, "*Sed modum exprimere nescio.* Franciscan Solutions to the Problem of Divine Foreknowledge and Future Contingents," FzS 70 (1988), pp. 123–75.

de Libera, Alain, "Philosophie et censure. Remarques sur la crise universitaire de 1270–1277," in Aersten and Speer, eds., *Was ist Philosophie*, pp. 71–89.

Denery, Dallas G., "The Appearance of Reality: Peter Aureol and the Experience of Perceptual Error," FcS 55 (1998), pp. 27–52.

De Rijk, Lambert M., "Gerardus Odonis O.F.M. on the Principle of Non-Contradiction and the Proper Nature of Demonstration," FcS 54 (1994–97), pp. 51–67.

—— "Guiral Ot (Giraldus Odonis) O.F.M. (1273–1349): His View of Statemental Being in His Commentary on the *Sentences*," in Marmo, ed., *Vestigia, Images, Verba*, pp. 355–69.

—— "Works by Gerald Ot (Gerardus Odonis) on Logic, Metaphysics and Natural Philosophy Rediscovered in Madrid, Bibl. Nac. 4229," AHDLMA 60 (1993), pp. 173–93.

Dettloff, Werner, *Die Entwicklung der Akzeptations-und Verdienstlehre von Duns Scotus bis Luther, mit besonderer Berücksichtigung der Franziskanertheologen* (Münster 1963).

Di Fonzo, Lorenzo, "Sisto IV. Carriera scolastica e integrazioni biografiche (1414–1484)," *Miscellanea Francescana* 86, fasc. II-IV (1986), pp. 1–491.

Dolnikowski, Edith Wilks, *Thomas Bradwardine. A View of Time and a Vision of Eternity in Fourteenth-Century Thought* (Leiden 1995).

Donovan, Steven, "Bonet, Nicholas," *The Catholic Encyclopedia* II (New York 1911), p. 655.

Doucet, Victorin, "Der unbekannte Skotist des Vaticanus Lat. 1113, Fr. Anfredus Gonteri O.F.M. (1325)," FzS 25 (1938), pp. 201–240.

Dreiling, Raymond, OFM, *Der Konzeptualismus in der Universalienlehre des Franziskanererzbischofs Petrus Aureoli (Pierre d'Auriole). Nebst biographisch-bibliographischer Einleitung* (Münster 1913).

Duba, William, "The Afterlife in Medeival Frankish Cyprus," *Epetirida of the Cyprus Research Centre* 26 (2000), pp. 167-94.

—— "Aristotelian Traditions in Franciscan Thought: Matter and Potency According to Scotus and Auriol," in I. Taifacos, ed., *The Origins of European Scholarship*, forthcoming

—— "Auriol, Aristotle, and Averroes," DSTFM 12 (2001), forthcoming.

—— "The Immaculate Conception in the Works of Peter Auriol," *Vivarium* 38.1 (2000), pp. 3–34.

Duhem, Pierre, *Medieval Cosmology. Theories of Infinity, Place, Time, Void, and the Plurality of Worlds*, trans. Roger Ariew (Chicago 1985).

—— *Le système du monde*, 10 vols. (Paris 1913–59).

Dumont, Stephen D., "Henry of Ghent and Duns Scotus,"in Marenbon, ed., *Medieval Philosophy*, pp. 291–328.

—— "New Questions by Thomas Wylton," DSTFM 9 (1998), pp. 341–79.

—— "The Origin of Scotus's Theory of Synchronic Contingency," *The Modern Schoolman* 72 (Jan/March 1995), pp. 149–67.

—— "The Scotist of Vat. lat. 869," *Archivum franciscanum historicum* 81 (1988), pp. 254–83.

—— "Time, Contradiction and Freedom of the Will in the Late Thirteenth Century," DSTFM 3.2 (1992), pp. 561–97.

—— "The Univocity of the Concept of Being in the Fourteenth Century: II, The *De ente* of Peter Thomae," *Mediaeval Studies* 50 (1988), pp. 186–256.

Ehrle, Franz, *Der Sentenzenkommentar Peters von Candia, des Pisaner Papstes Alexanders V* (Münster in Westfallia 1925).

Élie, Hubert, *Le complexe significabile* (Paris 1936).

Etzkorn, Girard, "Franciscus de Mayronis: A Newly Discovered Treatise on Intuitive and Abstractive Cognition," FcS 54 (1994–7), pp. 15–50.

—— "John Foxal, O.F.M.: His Life and Writings," FcS 49 (1989), pp. 17–24.

—— "A Symposium on God's Knowledge of Future Contingents," *Miscellanea Francescana* 96 (1996), pp. 561–71.

Etzwiler, James P., "John Baconthorpe, 'Prince of the Averroists'?" FcS 36 (1976), pp. 148–176.

Evans, Gillian R., ed., *Commentaries on Peter Lombard's Sentences* (Leiden, forthcoming).

Ferguson, R., "Francis of Marchia: the Historical Context of His Understanding of the Nature of Theology" (PhD Dissertation, University of Wisconsin 1973).

Fischer, John Martin, ed., *God, Foreknowledge, and Freedom* (Stanford 1989).

Frakes, Jerome C., *The Fate of Fortune in the Early Middle Ages. The Boethian Tradition* (Leiden 1988).

Frédericq, Paul, "L'hérésie à Louvain vers 1470," *Bulletin de la classe des Lettres et de la classe des Beaux-Arts* (Académie royale de Belgique, Brussels 1905), pp. 11–77.

Friedman, Russell L., "Andreas de Novo Castro (fl. 1358) on Divine Omnipotence and the Nature of the Past: I *Sentences*, Distinction Forty-Five, Question Six," CIMAGL 64 (1994), pp. 101–150.

—— "Conceiving and Modifying Reality: Some Modist Roots of Peter Auriol's Theory of Concept Formation," in Marmo, ed., *Vestigia, Imagines, Verba*, pp. 305–321.

—— "Francis of Marchia and John Duns Scotus on the Psychological Model of the Trinity," *Picenum Seraphicum* 18 n.s. (1999), pp. 11–56.

—— "*In Principio Erat Verbum*. The Incorporation of Philosophical Psychology into Trinitarian Theology, 1250–1325" (PhD Dissertation, University of Iowa 1997).

—— "Peter Auriol on Intellectual Cognition of Singulars," *Vivarium* 38.1 (2000), pp. 177–93.

—— "Peter Auriol on Intentions and Essential Predication," in Sten Ebbesen and idem, eds., *Medieval Analyses in Language and Cognition* (Copenhagen 1999), pp. 415–30.

—— "The *Sentences* Commentary, 1250–1320," in Evans, ed., *Commentaries on Peter Lombard's Sentences*, forthcoming.

Friedman, Russell L., and Chris Schabel, "Hugh of Novocastro's Questions on Divine Foreknowledge and Predestination," forthcoming.

Friedman, Russell L., and Chris Schabel, "The Vitality of Franciscan Theology at Paris in the 1320's: MS Wien, Palatinus 1439," AHDLMA 63 (1996), pp. 357–72.

Friedman, Russell L., and Chris Schabel, "Francis of Marchia's Commentaries on the *Sentences*," forthcoming.

Fumagalli, M.T. Beonio Brocchieri, *Durando di S. Porziano. Elementi filosofici della terza redazione del "Commento alle Sentenze"* (Florence 1969).

Gabriel, Astrik, "Intellectual Relations between the University of Louvain and the University of Paris in the 15th Century," in Jozef Ijsewijn and Jacques Paquet, eds., *The Universities in the Late Middle Ages* (Louvain 1978), pp. 82–132.

Gál, Gedeon, "Geraldus Odonis on the Unity of the Concept of Being," FcS 52 (1992), pp. 23–51.

—— "Petrus Thomae's Proof for the Existence of God," FcS 56 (1998), pp. 115–51.

Gaskin, Richard, "Fatalism, Foreknowledge and the Reality of the Future," *The Modern Schoolman* 71 (Jan. 1994), pp. 83–113.
——— "Peter Damian on Divine Power and the Contingency of the Past," *British Journal of the His-
tory of Philosophy* 5.2 (1997), pp. 229–47.
——— "Peter of Ailly and other Fourteenth-Century Thinkers on Divine Power and Necessity of
the Past," *Archiv für Geschichte der Philosophie* 79 (1997), pp. 273–91.
Gelber, Hester G., *It Could Have Been Otherwise: Modal Theory and Theology among the Domini-
cans at Oxford, 1310–1340* (Princeton, forthcoming).
——— "Ockham's Early Influence: A Question about Predestination and Foreknowledge by
Arnold of Strelley, O.P.," *AHDLMA* 55 (1988), pp. 255–89.
Genest, Jean-François, "Contingence et révélation des futurs, la *Quaestio biblica* de Richard
FitzRalph," in J. Jolivet, Z. Kaluza, and A. de Libera, eds, *Lectionum varietates, Hommage
à Paul Vignaux (1904–1987)* (Paris 1991), pp. 199–246.
——— "Le *De futuris contingentibus* de Thomas Bradwardine," (PhD Dissertation, L'École Prac-
tique des Hautes Études, 5ᵉ Section 1975).
——— "Le *De futuris contingentibus* de Thomas Bradwardine," *Recherches Augustiniennes* 14
(1974), pp. 249–336.
——— *Prédétermination et liberté créée à Oxford au XIVᵉ siécle: Buckingham contre Bradwardine*
(Paris 1992).
Genest, Jean-François, and Katherine H. Tachau, "La lecture de Thomas Bradwardine sur les
Sentences," AHDLMA 57 (1990), pp. 301–306.
Genest, Jean-François, and Paul Vignaux, "La bibliothèque anglaise de Jean de Mirecourt: 'sub-
tilitas' ou plagiat?" in Olaf Pluta, ed., *Die Philosophie im 14. und 15. Jahrhundert* (Am-
sterdam 1988), pp. 275–301.
Gensler, Marek, "Antonius Andreae — the Faithful Pupil? Antonius Andreae's Doctrine of In-
dividuation," MPP 31 (1992), pp. 23–37
Goris, Harm J.M.J., *Free Creatures of an Eternal God: Thomas Aquinas on God's Foreknowledge and
Irresistible Will* (Utrecht 1996).
Grant, Edward, "The Condemnation of 1277, God's Absolute Power and Physical Thought in the
Late Middle Ages," *Viator* 10 (1979), pp. 211–44.
Grassi, Onorato, "Probabilismo teologico e certezza filosofica: Pietro Aureoli e il dibattito sulla
conoscenza nel '300," in Giulio d'Onofrio, ed., *Storia della teologia nel Medioevo III: La te-
ologia delle scuole* (Casale Monferrato 1996), pp. 515–40.
Groblecki, Julianus, *De scientia Dei futurorum contingentium secundum s. Thomam eiusque pri-
mos sequaces* (Krakow 1938).
Halverson, James "Franciscan Theology and Predestinarian Pluralism in Late-Medieval
Thought," *Speculum* 70.1 (January 1995), pp. 1–26.
——— "Peter Aureol and the Re-emergence of Predestinarian Pluralism in Latin Theology,
1317–1344," (PhD Dissertation, University of Iowa 1993).
——— *Peter Aureol on Predestination. A Challenge to Late Medieval Thought* (Leiden 1998).
Henninger, Mark, "Henry of Harclay's Questions on Divine Prescience and Predestination," FcS
40 (1980), pp. 167–243.
Heynck, Valens, "Die Kommentare des Petrus Aureoli zum dritten Sentenzenbuch," FzS 5 1
(1969), pp. 1–77.
——— "Der Skotist Hugo de Novo Castro, OFM," FzS 43 (1961), pp. 244–70.
Hissette, Roland, *Enquête sur les 219 articles condamnés à Paris le 7 mars 1277* (Louvain 1977).
Hoenen, Maarten J.F.M., "Late Medieval Schools of Thought in the Mirror of University Text-
books. The *Promptuarium argumentorum* (Cologne 1492)," in idem, J.H. Josef Schneider,
and Georg Wieland, eds., *Philosophy and Learning. Universities in the Middles Ages*
(Leiden 1995), pp. 329–69.
——— *Marsilius of Inghen: Divine Knowledge in Late Medieval Thought* (Leiden 1993).
——— "Scotus and the Scotist School. The Tradition of Scotist Thought in the Medieval and Early
Modern Period," in Bos, ed., *John Duns Scotus*, pp. 197–210.

Hoenen, Maarten J.F.M., and Lodi Nauta, eds., *Boethius in the Middle Ages. Latin and Vernacular Traditions of the Consolatio Philosophiae* (Leiden 1997).

Holopainen, Toivo, *Dialectic and Theology in the Eleventh Century* (Leiden 1996).

Hudson, Anne, *Lollards and Their Books* (London 1985).

Hudson, Anne, and Michael Wilks, eds., *From Ockham to Wyclif* (Oxford 1987).

Hyman, Arthur, and James J. Walsh, eds., *Philosophy in the Middle Ages. The Christian, Islamic, and Jewish Traditions* (Indianapolis 1973).

Incandela, Joseph M., "Robert Holcot, O.P., on Prophecy, the Contingency of Revelation, and the Freedom of God," *Medieval Philosophy and Theology* 4 (1994), pp. 165–88

Isaac, J., *Le Peri Hermeneias en occident de Boèce à Saint Thomas* (Paris 1953).

Jung-Palczewska, Elzbieta, and Z. Kuksewicz, "The Date of Thomas Wylton's Quodlibet," *Studia Mediewistyczne* 32 (1997), pp. 59–63.

Kaluza, Zenon, "La crise des années 1474–1482: l'interdiction du nominalisme par Louis XI," in Maarten J.F.M. Hoenen, J.H. Josef Schneider, and Georg Wieland, eds., *Philosophy and Learning. Universities in the Middles Ages* (Leiden 1995), pp. 293–327.

—— "Late Medieval Philosphy, 1350–1500," in Marenbon, ed., *Medieval Philosophy*, pp. 426–51.

—— "La prétendue discussion parisienne de Thomas Bradwardine avec Thomas de Buckingham: Témoignage de Thomas de Cracovie," RTAM 43 (1976), pp. 219–236.

—— "*Serbi un sasso il nome*: une inscription de San Gimignano et la rencontre entre Bernard d'Arezzo et Nicolas d'Autrecourt," in Burkhard Mojsisch and Olaf Pluta, eds., *Historia Philosophiae Medii Aevii*, vol 1 (Amsterdam 1991), pp. 437–66.

Kennedy, Leonard, *Peter of Ailly and the Harvest of Fourteenth-Century Philosophy* (Lewiston, NY 1986).

Kenny, Anthony, "The Accursed Memory: The Counter-Reformation Reputation of John Wyclif," in idem. ed., *Wyclif and His Times* (Oxford 1986), pp. 147–68.

—— "Realism and Determinism in the Early Wyclif," in Hudson and Wilks, eds., *From Ockham to Wyclif*, pp. 165–78.

—— *Wyclif* (Oxford 1985).

—— ed.,*Wyclif in His Times* (Oxford 1986).

Knuuttila, Simo, *Modalities in Medieval Philosophy* (London 1993).

—— "Modal Logic," CHLMP, pp. 342–357.

—— "Time and Modality in Scholasticism," in idem ed., *Reforging the Great Chain of Being*, pp. 163–257.

—— *Reforging the Great Chain of Being* (Dordrecht 1981).

Knuuttila, Simo, and Anja Inkeri Lehtinen, "Change and Contradiction: A Fourteenth-Century Controversy," *Synthèse* 40 (1979), pp. 189–207.

Kretzmann, Norman, "*Nos ipsi principia sumus*: Boethius and the Basis of Contingency," in Rudavsky ed., *Divine Omniscience*, pp. 23–50.

—— "*Sensus Compositus, Sensus Divisus*, and Propositional Attitudes," *Medioevo* 7 (1981), pp. 195–229.

Kretzmann, Norman, and Eleanor E. Stump, eds. and trans., *Logic and the Philosophy of Language* (Cambridge 1988).

Krieger, Gerhard, "Studies on Walter Burley 1989–1997," *Vivarium* 37.1 (1999), pp. 94–100

Labowsky, Lotte, *Bessarion's Library and the Biblioteca Marciana: Six Early Inventories* (Rome 1979).

Laminne, Jacques, "La controverse sur les futurs contingents à l'Université de Louvain au XVe siècle," *Bulletin de la classe des Lettres et de la classe des Beaux-Arts* (Académie royale de Belgique, Brussels 1906), pp. 372–438.

Langston, Douglas C., *God's Willing Knowledge. The Influence of Scotus' Analysis of Omniscience* (University Park, Pennsylvania 1986).

Lee, Egmont, *Sixtus IV and Men of Letters* (Rome 1978).

Lee, Richard A., "Peter Aureoli as Critic of Aquinas on the Subalternate Character of the Science of Theology," FcS 55 (1998), pp. 121–36.

Leff, Gordon, *Bradwardine and the Pelagians. A Study of His 'De causa Dei' and Its Opponents* (Cambridge 1957).
—— *Gregory of Rimini. Tradition and Innovation in Fourteenth Century Thought* (Manchester 1961).
MacDonald, Scott, "Synchronic Contingency, Instants of Nature, and Libertarian Freedom: Comments on the 'Background to Scotus's Theory of the Will'," *The Modern Schoolman* 72 (Jan/March 1995), pp. 169–73.
—— "Ultimate Ends in Practical Reasoning: Aquinas's Aristotelian Moral Psychology and Anscombe's Fallacy," *The Philosophical Review* 100.1 (1991), pp. 31–66.
Maier, Anneliese, *An der Grenze von Scholastik und Naturwissenschaft* (Rome 1952).
—— "Die Pariser Disputation des Geraldus Odonis über die Visio beatifica Dei," *Archivio italiano per la storia della pietà* 4 (1965), pp. 213–51.
—— *Die Vorläufer Galileis im 14. Jahrhundert* (Rome 1949).
—— *Metaphysische Hintergründe der spätscholastische Naturphilosophie* (Rome 1955).
—— "Wilhelm von Alnwicks Bologneser Quaestionen gegen den Averroismus (1323)," in eadem, *Ausgehendes Mittelalter* I (Rome 1964), pp. 1-40.
——*Zwei Grundprobleme der scholastischen Naturphilosophie* (Rome 1968³).
—— *Zwischen Philosophie und Mechanik* (Rome 1958).
Maierú, Alfonso, "Logica e teologia trinitaria nel commento alle *Sentenze* attribuito a Petrus Thomae," in J. Jolivet, Z. Kaluza, and A. de Libera, eds., *Lectionum Varitates. Hommage à Paul Vignaux (1904–1987)* (Paris 1991), pp. 177–98.
Marenbon, John, ed., *Medieval Philosophy (=The Routledge History of Philosophy: Volume III)* (London 1998).
—— "Philosophy and its Background in the Early Medieval West," in idem, ed., *Medieval Philosophy*, pp. 108–113.
Marmo, Costantino, ed., *Vestigia, Imagines, Verba. Semiotics and Logic in Medieval Theological Texts (XIIth–XIVth Century)* (Turnhout 1997).
Michalski, Konstanty, "Le problème de la volonté à Oxford et à Paris au XIVe siècle," *Studia Philosophica* 2 (Lemberg 1937), reprinted in idem, *La philosophie au XIVe siècle: six études* (Frankfurt 1969), pp. 279–413.
Miscellanea Marciana di studi Bessarionei (=Medioevo e Umanesimo 24) (Padua 1976).
Mohler, Ludwig, *Kardinal Bessarion als Theologe, Humanist und Staatsmann*, 3 vols. (Paderborn 1923–42).
Monfasani, John, *Byzantine Scholars in Renaissance Italy: Cardinal Bessarion and Other Émigrés* (Aldershot 1995).
—— *Fernando of Cordova. A Biographical and Intellectual Profile* (Philadelphia 1992).
—— "Giovanni Gatii of Messina: A Profile and an Unedited Text," in Vincenzo Fera and Giacomo Ferraú, eds., *Filologia umanistica per Gianvito Resta* II (Padua 1997), pp. 1315–38
Murdoch, John F., "*Mathesis in philosophiam scholasticam introducta*: The Rise and Development of the Application of Mathematics in Fourteenth Century Philosophy and Theology," in *Arts libéraux et philosophie au moyen âge* (Montreal-Paris 1969), pp. 215–54.
—— "1277 and Late Medieval Natural Philosophy," in Aersten and Speer, eds., *Was ist Philosophie*, pp. 111–21
Nielsen, Lauge Olaf, "The Critical Edition of Peter Aureoli's Scholastic Works," in Alvaro Cacciotii and Barbara Faes de Mottoni, eds., *Editori di Quaracchi 100 anni dopo. Bilancio e prospettive* (Rome 1997), pp. 217–25.
—— "The Debate between Peter Auriol and Thomas Wylton on Theology and Virtue," *Vivarium* 38.1 (2000), 35–98.
—— "Dictates of Faith versus Dictates of Reason: Peter Auriole on Divine Power, Creation, and Human Rationality," DSTFM 7 (1996), pp. 213–41.
—— "The Intelligibility of Faith and the Nature of Theology: Peter Auriole's Theological Programme," *Studia Theologica* 53 (1999), pp. 26–39.

—— "Peter Auriol's Way with Words. The Genesis of Peter Auriol's Commentaries on Peter Lombard's First and Fourth Books of the Sentences," in Evans, ed., Commentaries on Peter Lombard's Sentences, forthcoming.

—— "Signification, Likeness, and Causality. The Sacraments as Signs by Divine Imposition in John Duns Scotus, Durand of St. Pourçain, and Peter Auriol," in Marmo, ed., Vestigia, Imagines, Verba, pp. 223–53.

Normore, Calvin, "Divine Omniscience, Omnipotence and Future Contingents: An Overview," in Rudavsky, ed., Divine Omniscience, pp. 3–22.

——"Future Contingents," CHLMP, pp. 358–81.

—— "Peter Aureoli and His Contemporaries on Future Contingents and the Excluded Middle," Synthèse 96 (1993), pp. 83–92.

North, John D., "Astonomy and Mathematics," in J. I. Catto and R. Evans, eds., The History of the University of Oxford. Volume II: Late Medieval Oxford (Oxford 1992), pp. 103–174.

Oakley, Francis, review of William Courtenay's Capacity and Volition, in Speculum 68.3 (1993), pp. 739–42.

Oberman, Heiko, Archbishop Thomas Bradwardine: A Fourteenth-Century Augustinian, A Study of His Theology in Its Historical Context (Utrecht 1958).

—— ed., Gregor von Rimin: Werk und Wirkung bis zur Reformation (Berlin 1981).

—— The Harvest of Medieval Theology: Gabriel Biel and Late Medieval Nominalism (Cambridge, Mass. 1963; reprint Durham, NC 1983).

Osborne, Kenan, ed., The History of Franciscan Theology (St. Bonaventure, NY 1994).

Ozment, Steven, The Age of Reform, 1250–1550: An Intellectual and Religious History of Late Medieval and Reformation Europe (New Haven 1980).

Pasnau, Robert, "Aureol, Peter (c. 1280–1322)," in Routledge Encyclopedia of Philosophy I (London 1998), pp. 565a–567a.

—— Theories of Cognition in the Later Middle Ages (Cambridge 1997).

Pelster, F., "Zur ersten Polemik gegen Aureoli," FcS 15 (1955), pp. 30–47

Perler, Dominik, "Notwendigkeit und Kontingenz. Das Problem der 'futura contingentia' bei Wilhelm von Ockham," in Olaf Pluta, ed., Die Philosophie im 14. und 15. Jahrhundert (Amsterdam 1988), pp. 39–65.

—— "Peter Aureol vs. Hervaeus Natalis on Intentionality. A Text Edition with Introductory Remarks," AHDLMA 61 (1994), pp. 227–62.

—— Prädestination, Zeit und Kontingenz: philosophisch-historische Untersuchungen zu Wilhelm von Ockhams 'Tractatus de praedestinatione et de praescientia Dei respectu futurorum contingentium' (Amsterdam 1988).

—— "What Am I Thinking About? John Duns Scotus and Peter Aureol on Intentional Objects," Vivarium 32.1 (1994), pp. 72–89.

Philippe, Jules, Guillaume Fichet, sa vie, ses œuvres. Introduction de l'imprimerie à Paris (Annecy 1892).

Poppi, Antonino, "Fate, Fortune, Providence and Human Freedom," in C.B. Schmitt and Q. Skinner, eds., The Cambridge History of Renaissance Philosophy (Cambridge 1988), pp. 641–67.

Porebski, Stanislaw A., "La question de Bernard Lombardi concernant la différence réelle entre l'essence et l'existence," MPP 17 (1973), pp. 157–85.

Pusci, Lucio, "Gli scritti e il pensiero di Francesco della Rovere dei Frati Minori Conventuali," Miscellanea Francescana 86, fasc. II-IV (1986), pp. 493–502.

Randi, Eugenio, "Onnipotenza divina e futuri contingenti nel XIV secolo," DSTFM 1.2 (1990), pp. 605–630.

—— Il sovrano e l'orologiaio: Due immagini di Dio nel dibattito sulla 'potentia absoluta' fra XIII e XIV secolo (Florence 1987).

Rashdall, Hastings, The Universities of Europe in the Middle Ages, 3 vols., revised and ed. F. M. Powicke and A. B. Emden (Oxford 1936; 2nd edition).

Resnik, Irven Michael, Divine Power and Possibility in St. Peter Damian's De divina omnipotentia (Leiden 1992).

Reynolds, L.D., ed., Texts and Transmission. A Survey of the Latin Classics (Oxford 1983).

Roest, Bert, *Reading the Book of History. Intellectual Contexts and Educational Functions of Franciscan Historiography 1226–ca. 1350* (Groningen 1996).

Rosato, Leo, *Doctrina de Immaculata B.V.M. Conceptione secundum Petrum Aureoli* (Rome 1959).

Rosier, Irène, and Alain de Libera, handout for their respective papers "Les difficultés logico-grammaticales de la formule 'Hoc est corpus meum'" and "Les enjeux logico-sémantiques de la formule de consécration eucharistique."

Rossini, Marco, "'Quod coexsistit exsistit': Alessandro di Alessandra e i futuri contingenti," in Leonardo Sileo, ed., *Via Scoti. Methodologica ad mentem Joannis Duns Scoti* II (Rome 1995), pp. 1049–1063.

—— "*Scientia Dei conditionata*: Francesco di Meyronnes e i futuri contingenti," *Medioevo* 19 (1993), pp. 287–322.

Rossmann, H., "Die Sentenzenkommentare des Franz von Meyronnes OFM," FzS 53 (1971), pp. 129–227.

Rudavsky, Tamar, ed., *Divine Omniscience and Omnipotence in Medieval Philosophy. Islamic, Jewish, and Christian Perspectives* (Dordrecht 1985).

Scaramuzzi, D., "L'immaculato concepimento di Maria. Questione inedita di Landolfo Caracciolo, O.F.M. (†1351)," *Studi Francescani* 28 (1931), pp. 33–69.

Schabel, Chris, "Archbishop Elias and the *Synodicum Nicosiense*," *Annuarium Historiae Conciliorum* 32 (2000), forthcoming.

—— "Aufredo Gonteri Brito *secundum* Henry of Harclay on Divine Foreknowledge and Future Contingents," in Carol Poster and Richard Utz, eds., *Constructions of Time in the Late Middle Ages* (= *Disputatio* 2) (Evanston, Illinois 1997), pp. 159–95.

—— "*Haec Ille*: Citation, Quotation, and Plagiarism in 14th-Century Scholasticism," in I. Taifacos, ed., *The Origins of European Scholarship*, forthcoming.

—— "Il Determinismo di Francesco di Marchia (Parte I)," *Picenum Seraphicum* 18 n.s. (1999), pp. 57–95, and Parte II, 19 n.s. (2000), pp. 3–55.

—— "Landulphus Caracciolo and a Sequax on Divine Foreknowledge," AHDLMA 66 (1999), pp. 299–343.

—— "*Non aliter novit facienda quam facta*. Gerard Odonis's Questions on Divine Foreknowledge," forthcoming.

—— "Notes on a Recent Edition of Parts of Marchia's *In primum librum Sententiarum*," *Picenum Seraphicum* 19 n.s. (2000), forthcoming.

—— "Oxford Franciscans after Ockham: Walter Chatton and Adam Wodeham," in Evans, ed., *Commentaries on Peter Lombard's Sentences*, forthcoming.

—— "Paris and Oxford between Aureoli and Rimini," in Marenbon, ed., *Medieval Philosophy*, pp. 386–401.

—— "Parisian Commentaries from Peter Auriol to Gregory of Rimini, and the Problem of Predestination," in Evans, ed., *Commentaries on Peter Lombard's Sentences*, forthcoming.

—— "Peter Aureol on Divine Foreknowledge and Future Contingents: *Scriptum in Primum Librum Sententiarum*, distinctions 38–39," CIMAGL 65 (1995), pp. 63–212.

—— "Peter de Rivo and the Quarrel over Future Contingents at Louvain: New Evidence and New Perspectives (Part I)," DSTFM 6 (1995), pp. 363–473, and Part II, 7 (1996), pp. 369–435.

—— "Peter of Candia and the Prelude to the Quarrel at Louvain," *Epetirida of the Cyprus Research Centre* 24 (1998), pp. 87–124.

—— "Place, Space, and the Physics of Grace in Auriol's *Sentences* Commentary," *Vivarium* 38.1 (2000), pp. 117–61.

—— "The Quarrel with Auriol: Peter Auriol's Role in the Late-Medieval Debate over Divine Foreknowledge and Future Contingents, 1315–1475 (PhD Dissertation, University of Iowa 1994).

—— "Questions on Future Contingents by Michael of Massa, OESA," *Augustiniana* 48 (1998), pp. 165–229.

Schabel, Chris, Irene Balcoyiannopoulou, and Russell L. Friedman, "Peter of Palude and the Parisian Reaction to Durand of St. Pourçain on Future Contingents," *Archivum Fratrum Praedicatorum*, forthcoming.

Schmaus, Michael, *Der "Liber propugnatorius" des Thomas Anglicus und die Lehrunterschiede zwischen Thomas von Aquin und Duns Scotus, II Teil: Die Trinitarischen Lehrdifferenzen* (Münster 1930).

—— "Guilelmi de Alnwick O.F.M. doctrina de medio, quo Deus cognoscit futura contingentia," *Bogoslovni Vestnik* 12 (1932), pp. 201–225.

—— "Uno sconosciuto discepolo di Scoto. Intorno alla prescienza di Dio," *Rivista di Filosofia Neoscolstica* 24 (1932), pp. 327–55.

Schmitt, Clément, *Un Pape réformateur et un défenseur de unité de l'Eglise. Benoît XII et l'Ordre des Frères Mineurs (1334–1342)* (Florence 1959).

Schmitt, F., *Die Lehre des hl. Thomas von Aquin vom göttlichen Wissen des Zukünftig Kontingenten bei seinen grossen Kommentatoren* (Nijmegen 1950)

Schmücker, Rainulf, *Propositio per se nota, Gottesbeweis und ihr Verhältnis nach Petrus Aureoli* (Werl in Westfallia 1941).

Schneider, Johannes, *Die Lehre vom dreieinigen Gott in der Schule des Petrus Lombardus* (Munich 1961).

Schneider, Notker, *Die Kosmologie des Franciscus de Marchia: Texte, Quellen, und Untersuchungen zur Naturphilosophie des 14. Jahrhunderts* (Leiden 1991).

——"Franciscus de Marchia über die Wirklichkeit der Materie (Metaph. VII q. 5)," *FzS* 71 (1989), pp. 138–58.

Schoedinger, Andrew B., ed., *Readings in Medieval Philosophy* (Oxford 1996).

Schwamm, Hermann, *Das göttliche Vorherwissen bei Duns Scotus und seinen ersten Anhängern* (Innsbruck 1934).

—— *Magistri Ioannis de Ripa O.F.M. Doctrina de Praescientia Divina* (Rome 1930).

—— *Robert Cowton O.F.M. über das göttliche Vorherwissen* (Innsbruck 1931).

Senko, Wladislaw, "Quelques contributions à l'histoire de la littérature philosophique de XIVᵉ siècle d'après le ms 53/102 de la Bibliothèque du Grand Seminaire de Pelplin," *MPP* 11 (1963), pp. 69–85.

Serene, Eileen F., "Anselm's Modal Conceptions," in Knuuttila ed., *Reforging the Great Chain of Being*, pp. 117–62.

Shank, Michael, *"Unless You Believe You Shall Not Understand": Logic, University, and Society in Late Medieval Vienna* (Princeton 1988).

Sirat, Colette, "Jewish Philosophy," in Marenbon, ed., *Medieval Philosophy*, pp. 65–95.

Söder, Joachim Ronald, *Kontingenz und Wissen: Die Lehre von den futura contingentia bei Johannes Duns Scotus* (Münster 1998).

Sorabji, Richard, *Time, Creation, and the Continuum* (Ithaca, NY 1983).

Spade, Paul Vincent, "Quasi-Aristotelianism," in Norman Kretzmann ed., *Infinity and Continuity in Ancient and Medieval Thought* (Cornell 1982), pp. 297–307.

Spruyt, Joke, "Gerard Odonis on the Universal," *AHDLMA* 63 (1996), pp. 171–208.

Streuer, Severin Rudolf, *Die theologische Einleitungslehre des Petrus Aureoli. Auf Grund seines Scriptum super Primum Sententiarum und ihre theologiegeschichtliche Einordnung* (Werl in Westfallia 1968).

Streveler, Paul, "Anselm on Future Contingencies. A Critical Analysis of the Argument of the De Concordia," *Anselm Studies. An Occasional Journal* 1 (1983), pp. 165–73.

—— "The Problem of Future Contingents: A Medieval Discussion," *The New Scholasticism* 47.2 (1973), pp. 233–47.

—— "The Problem of Future Contingents from Aristotle through the Fifteenth Century, with Particular Emphasis upon Medieval Views," (PhD Dissertation, University of Wisconsin 1970).

Sylwanowicz, Michael, *Contingent Causality and the Foundations of Duns Scotus' Metaphysics* (Leiden 1996).

Tachau, Katherine H., "French Theology in the Mid-Fourteenth Century: Vatican Latin 986 and Wroclaw, Milich F.64," AHDLMA 51 (1984), pp. 41–80.

—— "Logic's God and the Natural Order in Late Medieval Oxford: the Teaching of Robert Holcot," *Annals of Science* 53 (1996), pp. 235–67.

—— "The Preparation of a Critical Edition of Pierre Auriol's *Sentences* Lectures," in Alvaro Cacciotii and Barbara Faes de Mottoni, eds., *Editori di Quaracchi 100 anni dopo. Bilancio e prospettive* (Rome 1997), pp. 205–216.

—— *Vision and Certitude in the Ages of Ockham: Optics, Epistemology, and the Foundations of Semantics, 1250–1345* (Leiden 1988).

Teetaert, A., "Ot Guiral," DTC XI (Paris 1932), cols 1658–63.

—— "Pierre d'Auriole," DTC XII, 2 (Paris 1935), cols. 1810–81.

—— "Pignano (François de)," DTC XII (Paris 1933), cols. 2104–09.

Thijssen, J.M.M.H., *Censure and Heresy at the University of Paris, 1200–1400* (Philadelphia 1998).

Torre, Bartholomew de la, *Thomas Buckingham and the Contingency of Futures: The Possibility of Human Freedom* (South Bend 1987).

Tournoy, Gilbert, "Een onbekende autograf van Petrus de Rivo (Leuven, ca 1470)," in Edmund J.M. van Eijl ed., *Facultas S. Theologiae Lovaniensis 1432–1797: Bijdragen tot haar geschiedenis* (Louvain 1977), pp. 293–7.

Trapp, Damasus, "Augustinian Theology of the 14th Century: Notes on Editions, Marginalia, Opinions, and Book Lore," *Augustiniana* 6 (1956), pp. 146–274.

—— "Hiltalinger's Augustinian Quotations," *Augustiniana* 4 (1954), pp. 412–49.

——"Notes on some Manuscripts of the Augustinian Michael de Massa (†1337)," *Augustinianum* 5 (1965), pp. 58–133.

—— "The *Quaestiones* of Dionysius de Burgo O.S.A.," *Augustinianum* 3 (1963), pp. 63–78.

Travis, Peter W., "Chaucer's *Chronographiae*, the Confounded Reader, and Fourteenth-Century Measurements of Time, " in Carol Poster and Richard Utz, eds., *Constructions of Time in the Late Middle Ages* (= *Disputatio* 2) (Evanston, Illinois 1997), pp. 1–34.

Trinkaus, Charles, *In Our Image and Likeness. Humanity and Divinity in Italian Humanist Thought*, vol. 1 (London 1970).

—— "Lorenzo Valla," in E. Cassirer, P.O. Kristeller, and J.H. Randall, eds., *The Renaissance Philosophy of Man* (Chicago 1948), pp. 147–82.

Trottman, Christian, *La vision béatifique des disputes scolastiques à sa définition par Benoît XII* (Rome 1995).

Tuggy, Dale, "Indeterminism, Faith and Al Gore," forthcoming.

—— "Logic without Bivalence: Taking the Leap," forthcoming.

Työrinoja, Reijo, "Auriol's Critique of Henry of Ghent's *Lumen medium*," in Aersten and Speer, eds., *Was ist Philosophie*, pp. 622–8.

Valois, N., "Pierre Auriol," *Histoire littéraire de la France* XXXIII (Paris 1908), pp. 479–527.

Vasoli, Cesare, "Giorgio Benigno Salviati (Dragisic)," in Marjorie Reeves, ed., *Prophetic Rome in the High Renaissance Period* (Oxford 1992), pp. 121–56.

—— "Notizie su Giorgio Benigno Salviati (Juraj Dragisic)," in *Studi storici in orone di Gabriele Pepe* (Bari 1969), pp. 429–97.

Vast, Henri, *Le Cardinal Bessarion (1403–1472): Étude sur la Chrétienté el la Renaissance* (Paris 1878).

Vignaux, Paul, *Justification et prédestination au XIVe siècle: Duns Scot, Pierre d'Auriole, Guillaume d'Occam, Grégoire de Rimini* (Paris 1934).

Vos, A., et al., eds. and trans., *John Duns Scotus: Contingency and Freedom: Lectura I, 39* (Dordrecht 1994).

Walsh, Katherine, *A Fourteenth-Century Scholar and Primate: Richard FitzRalph in Oxford, Avignon, and Armagh* (Oxford 1981).

Wippel, John F., "The Condemnations of 1270 and 1277 at Paris," *The Journal of Medieval and Renaissance Studies* 7 (1977), pp. 169–201.

—— "Divine Knowledge, Divine Power and Human Freedom in Thomas Aquinas and Henry of Ghent," in Rudavsky ed., *Divine Omniscience*, pp. 213–41.

—— "Quodlibetal Questions Chiefly in Theology Faculties," in B. Bazan, idem, G. Fransen, and D. Jacuart, *Les Questions disputées et les questions quodlibétiques dans les facultés de théologie, de droit, et de médecine* (Turnhout 1985), pp. 151-222.

—— "Thomas of Sutton on Divine Knowledge of Future Contingents (Quodlibet II, qu. 5)," in S. Knuuttila, R. Työrinoja, and S. Ebbesen, eds., *Knowledge and the Sciences in Medieval Philosophy. Proceedings of the Eighth International Congress of Medieval Philosophy*, vol. 2 (Helsinki 1990), pp. 364–72.

Witt, Ronald, *Hercules at the Crossroads. The Life, Works, and Thought of Coluccio Salutati* (Durham, NC 1983).

Wittneben, Eva Luise, and Roberto Lambertini, "Un teologo Francescano alle strette. Osservazioni sul testimone manoscritto del processo a Francesco d'Ascoli," *Picenum Seraphicum* 18 n.s. (1999), pp. 97–122.

Wolter, Allan B., "Scotus' Paris Lectures on God's Knowledge of Future Events," in A.B. Wolter, *The Philosophical Theology of John Duns Scotus*, ed. Marilyn McCord Adams (Ithaca, NY 1990), pp. 285–333.

Xiberta, Bartholomaeus Maria, *De scriptoribus scholasticis saeculi XIV ex ordine Carmelitarum* (Louvain 1931).

Zagzebski, Linda Trinkaus, *The Dilemma of Freedom and Foreknowledge* (New York-Oxford 1991).

Zoubov, Vassili P., "Walter Catton, Gerard d'Odon, et Nicolas Bonet," *Physis. Revista di storia della scienza* 1 (1959), pp. 261–78.

Zumkeller, Adolar, "Die Augustinerschule des Mittelalters: Vertreter und philosophisch-theologische Lehre," *Analecta Augustiniana* 27 (1964), pp. 167–262.

Index of Manuscripts

Index of Medieval Names

Index of Modern Authors

Index of Topics and Places

abstraction: 10, 39, 86–7, 95, 100–2, 104, 115, 119–22, 144–5, 148, 160–2, 167, 169, 186–7, 273

actuality of future contingents: 10, 34, 96–104, 106, 113, 115–7, 120, 122–4, 138, 143, 145, 165, 167–8, 186, 261, 299, 310, 313, 324

Aix-en-Provence: 2, 70

Albertists: 329

Aleria: 331

Amalfi: 138

Ancona: 189, 191

Angers: 304

Antioch: 158

Antwerp: 331

Aquitaine: 70

Aragon: 170, 172–3, 210

Ascoli Piceno: 189

assent: 237–9

attributes, divine: 3, 12, 77, 177, 205

Augustinianism: 96, 137

Augustinian Hermits: 11–2, 32, 51, 75, 92, 172, 175, 180–4, 188, 190, 214–6, 220, 259–60, 264, 268, 274, 285–7, 289, 298, 300, 327

Avignon: 149, 157, 173, 189–90, 225, 240, 252, 254, 256

Barcelona: 170, 172–4, 208

beatific vision: 150, 158–9, 163, 224

Benedictines: 149

Bible: 2, 11, 69–70, 77, 116–7, 120–1, 128, 131, 145, 154, 170–1, 212, 220, 239, 272, 274–5, 278, 296–7, 318–9, 323, 333

Bivalence, Principle of: 18–9, 112–4, 131, 154, 193, 207, 212–3, 220, 241, 246, 267–8, 272–3, 275, 283, 325, 327

Black Death: 11, 158, 285–6

Bohemia: 289–90, 334

Bologna: 2, 28, 49, 52, 69, 74, 264, 326

Burgundy: 329

Cahors: 2, 69

Cambridge: 41

capacity for opposites: 43–5, 58–9, 63, 77, 125, 130, 143, 147, 201, 225. 236, 244, 296

Carmelites: 11, 32, 54, 137, 156, 175–6, 180, 182, 274, 284, 286–7, 289, 304

Castellammare: 138

Catania: 158

causation: 29–30, 32–4, 42–3, 47, 50–2, 61–2, 82, 88–9, 91–3, 99, 113–4, 140, 143 159, 193, 196–204, 209, 211–3, 218, 226, 290–1, 306, 326

Cistercians: 274, 280, 286, 288–9, 298

cognition vs. knowledge: 234–5, 237–40, 242–4

Cologne: 316, 329

complexe significabile: 94, 224, 237–8, 244, 266, 287, 297, 299, 313

composite and divided senses: 28, 30–2, 36, 43, 77–8, 80–1, 85, 153–4, 178, 202, 209, 220, 226, 235–6, 245, 250–1, 254, 258, 269, 272, 282, 284, 297, 299, 308, 318

Condemnations of 1277: 39–40, 81–2

connotation: 77

contingency, types of: 24–5, 43–4, 196–7, 218–20, 326

Council of Constance: 289, 292, 321, 324

Council of Pisa: 309

Creation: 10, 12, 22, 29, 48, 77, 125, 127–9, 141, 146–7, 157, 160–2, 177, 179, 215–6, 307

Crete: 309

Cyprus: 70

damnation: 1, 124–5, 128, 147, 157, 178, 259–60, 322

denominatively: 96, 102, 177, 216

determination, de inesse-de possibili: 11, 146, 198–204, 209–14, 218–9, 220, 223, 268, 325, 327, 334

differentiae of time: 39, 73, 95, 116, 148, 160–2

disjunction: 20, 111–2, 114, 193–5, 216–7, 287

Dominicans: 11, 32, 34, 38–9, 41, 47, 50–2, 67, 92, 131, 175, 180–2, 184, 187–8, 220, 243, 247–8, 258, 274, 284, 286–7, 325–6

DPO/DPA: 10, 78, 81–2, 150, 178, 251–2, 276, 321

Early Modern period: 10, 149, 163, 191

Eberbach: 300

England: 172, 176, 223, 240, 253, 290

55 Wyelton dale